Frommer's®
Washington, D.C. 2013

by Elise Hartman Ford

WILEY
John Wiley & Sons, Inc.

Published by:
JOHN WILEY & SONS, INC.
111 River St.
Hoboken, NJ 07030-5774

ISBN 978-1-118-28855-9 (paper); ISBN 978-1-118-33162-0 (ebk); ISBN 978-1-118-33493-5 (ebk); ISBN 978-1-118-33382-2 (ebk)

Editor: Andrea Kahn
Production Editor: Eric T. Schroeder
Cartographer: Elizabeth Puhl
Photo Editor: Cherie Cincilla
Cover Photo Editor: Richard Fox
Design and Layout by Vertigo Design
Graphics and Prepress by Wiley Indianapolis Composition Services

Front cover photo: Blossoming cherry tree by the Jefferson Memorial. ©Brian Jannsen / Alamy Images.
Back cover photos: *Left:* Gilbert Stuart's painting of George Washington at the National Portrait Gallery. ©Ken Cedeno. *Middle:* Mobile by Alexander Calder at the National Gallery of Art. ©David S. Holloway. *Right:* The Star-Spangled banner at the National Museum of American History. ©Ken Cedeno.

For information on our other products and services or to obtain technical support, please contact our Customer Care Department within the U.S. at 877/762-2974, outside the U.S. at 317/572-3993 or fax 317/572-4002.

Wiley also publishes its books in a variety of electronic formats. Some content that appears in print may not be available in electronic formats.

Manufactured in China

5 4 3 2 1

CONTENTS

LIST OF MAPS

ABOUT THE AUTHOR

Elise Hartman Ford has been a freelance writer in the Washington, D.C. area since 1985. Her writing has appeared in the *Washington Post, Washingtonian* magazine, *Ladies Home Journal, National Parks* magazine, *National Geographic Traveler,* the travel website Home & Abroad, the London-based *Bradman's North America Guide, The Essential Guide to Business Travel,* and other national, regional, and trade publications. She has written several other guidebooks in addition to this one, and she is the author of the travel app Washington, DC ★ A to Z, published by Sutro Media.

HOW TO CONTACT US

In researching this book, we discovered many wonderful places—hotels, restaurants, shops, and more. We're sure you'll find others. Please tell us about them, so we can share the information with your fellow travelers in upcoming editions. If you were disappointed with a recommendation, we'd love to know that, too. Please write to:

Frommer's Washington, D.C. 2013
John Wiley & Sons, Inc. • 111 River St. • Hoboken, NJ 07030-5774
frommersfeedback@wiley.com

ADVISORY & DISCLAIMER

Travel information can change quickly and unexpectedly, and we strongly advise you to confirm important details locally before traveling, including information on visas, health and safety, traffic and transport, accommodations, shopping, and eating out. We also encourage you to stay alert while traveling and to remain aware of your surroundings. Avoid civil disturbances, and keep a close eye on cameras, purses, wallets, and other valuables.

While we have endeavored to ensure that the information contained within this guide is accurate and up-to-date at the time of publication, we make no representations or warranties with respect to the accuracy or completeness of the contents of this work and specifically disclaim all warranties, including without limitation warranties of fitness for a particular purpose. We accept no responsibility or liability for any inaccuracy or errors or omissions, or for any inconvenience, loss, damage, costs, or expenses of any nature whatsoever incurred or suffered by anyone as a result of any advice or information contained in this guide.

The inclusion of a company, organization, or website in this guide as a service provider and/or potential source of further information does not mean that we endorse them or the information they provide. Be aware that information provided through some websites may be unreliable and can change without notice. Neither the publisher nor author shall be liable for any damages arising herefrom.

FROMMER'S STAR RATINGS, ICONS & ABBREVIATIONS

Every hotel, restaurant, and attraction listing in this guide has been ranked for quality, value, service, amenities, and special features using a **star-rating system.** In country, state, and regional guides, we also rate towns and regions to help you narrow down your choices and budget your time accordingly. Hotels and restaurants are rated on a scale of zero (recommended) to three stars (exceptional). Attractions, shopping, nightlife, towns, and regions are rated according to the following scale: zero stars (recommended), one star (highly recommended), two stars (very highly recommended), and three stars (must-see).

In addition to the star-rating system, we also use **seven feature icons** that point you to the great deals, in-the-know advice, and unique experiences that separate travelers from tourists. Throughout the book, look for:

special finds—those places only insiders know about

fun facts—details that make travelers more informed and their trips more fun

kids—best bets for kids and advice for the whole family

special moments—those experiences that memories are made of

overrated—places or experiences not worth your time or money

insider tips—great ways to save time and money

great values—where to get the best deals

The following abbreviations are used for credit cards:

AE American Express	**DISC** Discover	**V** Visa
DC Diners Club	**MC** MasterCard	

TRAVEL RESOURCES AT FROMMERS.COM

Frommer's travel resources don't end with this guide. Frommer's website, **www. frommers.com**, has travel information on more than 4,000 destinations. We update features regularly, giving you access to the most current trip-planning information and the best airfare, lodging, and car-rental bargains. You can also listen to podcasts, connect with other Frommers.com members through our active-reader forums, share your travel photos, read blogs from guidebook editors and fellow travelers, and much more.

THE BEST OF WASHINGTON, D.C.

T he sun has come up, dappling the surface of the Potomac. It warms the front plaza of the Supreme Court Building, where visitors stand in line awaiting their chance to attend an oral argument. Sunlight pours through the south-facing windows of the Oval Office, where the President works away at the problems of the day, even as staff elsewhere in the White House roll back the rugs and otherwise prepare for the flow of 1,600 people expected to tour the house today. Commuters of all sorts, from diplomats to nonprofit wonks to corporate execs, spill from cars and buses and Metro stations onto sunlit downtown streets armed with briefcases, coffee cups, PDAs, and newspapers. They rub elbows from sunup to sundown, in the halls of Congress, in Penn Quarter restaurants, in bars along 14th Street. The city bustles. Bustle with it. It's a beautiful day.

Things to Do   Lively arguments fly in the **Capitol's Senate** and **House** chambers, where resolute legislators hash out U.S. laws. A different perspective awaits atop the steps of the **Lincoln Memorial**—a stunning view from the Reflecting Pool to the **Washington Monument,** to the green-swept **Mall,** and beyond to the **Capitol.** Every spring, **cherry trees** erupt in delicate pink and white blossoms, and the town goes mad. Da Vinci's mysterious *Ginevra de' Benci* outstares you in the **National Gallery of Art,** while Renoir's *Luncheon of the Boating Party* reels you in at the **Phillips Collection.** Glide past stately memorials, stunningly illuminated, on a nighttime **Potomac River** cruise.

ABOVE: **Crowds enjoying cherry trees in bloom.** LEFT: **The Capitol's iconic dome.** PREVIOUS PAGE: **Independence Day fireworks on the Mall.**

John F. Kennedy Center for the Performing Arts from across the Tidal Basin.

Shopping   Georgetown=shopping. Fashionistas traipse through the international outposts and homegrown boutiques lining busy M Street and Wisconsin Avenue. On weekends, join locals at the 140-year-old **Eastern Market** on Capitol Hill for exuberant bartering with area farmers hawking fresh produce; don't miss the market's famous blueberry pancakes. Shoppers head to **U and 14th streets** for vintage clothing and inventive housewares.

Eating & Drinking   Washington's restaurants reflect its population: international and always game. Dine at the Penn Quarter's sexy **Rasika** for imaginative takes on Indian cuisine. Craving Ethiopian? Head to **Ethiopic** in the Atlas District for the city's best spicy stews and meat-and-onion stir-fries. Watch power brokers cut deals at posh **Charlie Palmer Steak** on Capitol Hill, or follow a trendier crowd to savor oysters prepared every which way at the latest "it" spot, the **Pearl Dive Oyster Palace,** on 14th Street.

Nightlife & Entertainment   Theater is huge, the options many, and the standards excellent, whether the production is *Anything Goes* at the splendid **John F. Kennedy Center for the Performing Arts** or *A Midsummer Night's Dream* at the world-renowned **Shakespeare Theatre.** Satisfy a yen for straight-ahead jazz at the suitably divey **Blues Alley,** or for indie sounds at the nationally recognized **9:30 Club.** Young urbanistas rule the bar/lounge scene, roosting at mellow pubs like **ChurchKey** on 14th Street, and hitting the dance floor at Dupont Circle's **Eighteenth Street Lounge.**

THE most unforgettable
WASHINGTON, D.C.
EXPERIENCES

o **Watching the Supreme Court in Action:** Behind the stately marble facade of the Supreme Court Building, the nation's nine black-begowned justices reveal their intellectual brilliance and individual personalities as they listen to and question both sides of an argument. Is the famously silent Justice Thomas really silent? Is the notably aggressive Justice Scalia really so blunt? Only one

The White House by night.

The base of the Washington Monument at dusk.

way to find out: Wait in line for entry and a coveted seat inside the Courtroom. See p. 69.

o **Viewing Washington Landmarks by Moonlight:** There is nothing as spectacular as the Lincoln Memorial illuminated at night, unless it's the sight of the White House, the Capitol, or the Washington Monument lit up after dark. Go by Gray Line bus, by bike via a Bike and Roll excursion, or by boat aboard a Potomac Riverboat Co. cruise; all three operations offer narrated day- and nighttime tours. See p. 89.

o **Visiting Your Senator or House Representative:** If you're a U.S. citizen, take advantage of your constituent status and stop by your senator's and/or representative's office on Capitol Hill to offer your two cents on current issues. Pick up passes to the Capitol's Senate and House chambers and attend a session to observe your elected politicians at work. Make sure you've reserved Capitol tour passes online and tour the Capitol. See p. 58.

o **Bicycling Past the Potomac River and Around the Tidal Basin:** Rent a bike and cycle the paved bike/pedestrian path that extends 11 miles from the Lincoln Memorial to the Maryland border (through Rock Creek Park). Or head the other direction, following the combination of street, sidewalk, and pathway that encircles the Tidal Basin. You'll enjoy a view of the Potomac River, Rock Creek, and spectacular Washington sites on either side of you as you make your way. For a really long ride, follow the pathway past the Lincoln Memorial, cross the Arlington Memorial Bridge to the trail on the other side, and pedal the 19 miles to Mount Vernon. See p. 155 and 322.

THE best FAMILY EXPERIENCES

o **Hanging out at the National Zoo:** Make faces at the cute giant pandas; listen to the mighty lion's roar; laugh at the playful monkeys; watch an elephant exercise. The National Zoo is essentially one big (163 acres!), family-friendly park, offering the chance to observe some 2,400 animals at play (or snoozing or eating). See p. 141.

o **Ice Skating at the National Gallery:** The pool in the National Gallery of Art Sculpture Garden turns into an ice-skating rink in winter. Rent some skates and twirl around on the ice, admiring sculptures as you go. Treat yourself to hot chocolate and sandwiches at the Pavilion Café in the garden. See p. 102.

o **Paddling Your Way Around the Tidal Basin:** Rent a paddle boat for four people and skim the surface of the Tidal Basin for an hour. You'll still be sightseeing as you pedal away, in full view of the Washington Monument on the Mall, the Jefferson and the Martin Luther King, Jr. memorials bordering the Basin, and, should you be here during cherry blossom season, the blooming cherry trees encircling the Tidal Basin. See chapter 4.

o **Riding a Roller Coaster or Piloting a Jet:** Two Smithsonian museums offer amusement-park-like rides in their simulator machines. At the National Air and Space Museum, these machines allow children to experience the feeling of being airborne in a jet or in the pilot's seat of a World War II fighter airplane. At the National Museum of American History, your simulated adventures feel real in race car and roller coaster machines. *Note:* Height requirements and fees apply. See p. 99 and 107.

THE best FOOD & DRINK EXPERIENCES

o **Michel Richard Citronelle,** in the Latham Hotel, 3000 M St. NW, Georgetown (© **202/625-2150**): This hot spot for fine French dining is world renowned, thanks to the irrepressible Richard and his culinary artistry. If

Paddle boats in the Tidal Basin.

Citronelle is booked, try for a table at his other restaurant, **Central,** 1001 Pennsylvania Ave. NW, Penn Quarter (☎ **202/626-0015**). Either way, you're in for a treat. See p. 213 and 188.

○ **Komi,** 1509 17th St. NW, Dupont Circle (☎ **202/332-9200**): A dinner at Komi restores through creative concoctions (try the grilled asparagus with watercress and feta, or squab stuffed with foie gras and figs), polished service, and a remarkably relaxed atmosphere. And then there's the chef, the unassuming Johnny Monis, who somehow had figured this all out by the tender age of 30 (Monis is 33 now). See p. 206.

○ **minibar by José Andrés,** 405 8th St. NW, Penn Quarter (☎ **202/393-0812**): At this world-famous restaurant, chef extraordinaire José Andrés (or one of his stand-ins) concocts whimsical little tastes—like foie gras in a cocoon of cotton candy. (His many enterprises sometimes keep Andrés away from minibar, but customers will taste the thrill of the experience Andrés has created whether or not he's at the counter preparing the taste sensations himself.) Thirty or more of such creations make an unforgettable meal for 12 lucky people, six per seating. Reservations at minibar are tougher to come by than at any other restaurant in town, but it's worth the effort it takes to snag them; if you're determined to go, call at 10am a month in advance. See p. 183.

○ **Sitting at an Outdoor Cafe and Watching the Washington World Go By:** The capital is full of seats offering a front-row view of the bustle of this high-powered city. Among them are Capitol Hill's Johnny's Half Shell, where movers and shakers hurry past you on the sidewalk and peer out from limos on their way to the Capitol; the Penn Quarter's Café du Parc, from which you'll glimpse Pennsylvania Avenue, the Washington Monument, and the grounds of the White House; and Hank's Oyster Bar, whose Dupont Circle perch is the perfect spot for watching a passing parade of live entertainment. See chapter 6.

THE best THINGS TO DO FOR FREE IN WASHINGTON, D.C.

○ **Peruse the Constitution:** Only in Washington and only at the National Archives will you be able to read the original documents that grounded this nation in liberty. Here you'll find the Declaration of Independence, the Constitution of the United States, and the Bill of Rights—all on display behind glass. See p. 101.

○ **People-Watch at Dupont Circle:** This traffic circle is also a park—an all-weather hangout for mondo-bizarre biker-couriers, chess players, street musicians, and lovers. Sit on a bench and watch scenes of Washington life unfold around you. See p. 73.

○ **Attend a Millennium Stage Performance at the Kennedy Center:** Every evening at 6pm, the Kennedy Center presents a free 1-hour concert performed by local, up-and-coming, national, or international musicians. After the performance, head through the glass doors to the terrace for a view of the Potomac River. See p. 76.

○ **Groove to the Sounds of Live Jazz in the Sculpture Garden:** On summery Friday evenings at the National Gallery of Art Sculpture Garden, you can dip your toes in the fountain pool and chill out to live jazz from 5 to 8pm. The jazz

A chess game in Dupont Circle.

Locals and visitors alike love to relax in the National Gallery of Art Sculpture Garden.

is free; the tapas, wine, and beer served in the garden's Pavilion Café are not. See p. 104.

o **Pick a Museum, (Just About) Any Museum:** Because this is the U.S. capital, many of the museums are federal institutions, meaning admission is free. The National Gallery of Art, the U.S. Botanic Garden, and the Smithsonian's 17 Washington museums, from the National Air and Space Museum to the Freer Gallery, are among many excellent choices. See chapter 4.

o **Attend an Event on the Mall:** Think of the National Mall as the nation's public square, where something is always going on. There's the National Book Festival in the fall, the splendid Independence Day celebration every Fourth of July, and soccer, baseball, and even cricket games year-round. See p. 106 for a calendar of annual events.

The National Mall is the setting of frequent free performances.

THE best NEIGHBORHOODS FOR GETTING LOST

- **Georgetown:** The truth is, you *want* to get lost in Georgetown because it's the neighborhood's side streets that hold the history and centuries-old houses of this one-time Colonial tobacco port. And not to worry—Georgetown is so compact that you're never very far from its main thoroughfares, M Street and Wisconsin Avenue. For a back-streets tour of Georgetown, see p. 167.

- **Old Town Alexandria:** Just a short distance from the District (by Metro, car, boat, or bike) is George Washington's Virginia hometown. On and off the beaten track are quaint cobblestone streets, charming boutiques and antiques stores, 18th-century houses and other historic attractions, and fine restaurants. See p. 316.

- **Dupont Circle:** Explore Dupont Circle's lovely side streets extending off Connecticut and Massachusetts avenues. You'll discover picturesque 19th-century town houses serving as homes to small art galleries, historic museums, and actual residences. Stroll Embassy Row (northward on Massachusetts Ave.) to view Beaux Arts mansions, many built by wealthy magnates during the Gilded Age. See p. 38 for information on how to see the interiors of some of these embassies.

- **Foggy Bottom:** Stroll the White House walking tour (p. 159) if you like, then continue westward from the White House to mingle with George Washington University's students on its urban campus and with international employees of the World Bank and the International Monetary Fund, both headquartered here. Foggy Bottom is one of the oldest parts of the city, so you'll come across rows of 19th-century town houses; historic sites, like the building at 2017 I St. NW, where James Monroe briefly lived; and old churches, like St. Mary's Episcopal, at 728 23rd St. NW, designed by James Renwick (see the Renwick Gallery, p. 82).

Georgetown.

Embassy Row.

Produce at Eastern Market on Capitol Hill.

THE best WAYS TO SEE WASHINGTON, D.C. LIKE A LOCAL

o **Shop at Eastern Market:** Capitol Hill is home to more than government buildings; it's a community of old town houses, antiques shops, and the veritable institution of Eastern Market. Here locals shop and barter every Saturday and Sunday for fresh produce, baked goods, and flea-market bargains. Trying the blueberry pancakes at the Market Lunch counter is an absolute must. See p. 228.

o **Pub and Club It in D.C.'s Hot Spots:** Join Washington's footloose and fancy-free any night of the week (but especially Thurs–Sat) along U Street between 9th and 16th streets, in Adams Morgan, and in the Penn Quarter. See chapter 8.

o **Go for a Jog on the National Mall:** Lace up your running shoes and race down the Mall at your own pace, admiring famous sites as you go. Your fellow runners will be buff military staff from the Pentagon, speed-walking members of Congress, and downtown workers doing their best to stave off the telltale pencil pusher's paunch. It's about 2 miles from the foot of the Capitol to the Lincoln Memorial. See p. 106.

o **Attend a Hometown Game:** Depending on the season, you can take yourself out to a Washington Nationals baseball game at Nationals Ballpark, drive to FedEx Field to root for the

Joggers on the National Mall.

Washington Redskins, stay in town to catch a Washington Wizards or Mystics basketball game at the Verizon Center, or take the Metro to RFK Stadium for a D.C. United soccer match. To experience the true soul of the city, attend a Washington Capitals ice hockey match at the Verizon Center; at the moment, there's no more loyal fan than a Caps fan. Wear red. See p. 271.

THE best OFF-BEAT EXPERIENCES

- **Listen to "Help Me Fake It to the Right" and "Desperate Housemembers" tunes:** The Capitol Steps, a musical political satire troupe, performs these and other irreverent original tunes in skits that skewer politicians on both sides of the aisle. You can see them every weekend at the Ronald Reagan Building. See p. 265.

- **Dare to Dine at a Drag Brunch:** Sassy drag queens dressed to the hilt sashay around the room, lip-synching to the DJ's tunes and entertaining all who've turned up for the all-you-can-eat $23.95 buffet at **Perry's Drag Brunch,** 1811 Columbia Rd. NW (www.perrysadamsmorgan.com; © **202/234-6218**), held every Sunday 10am to 3pm. The brunch is a Washington institution: Everyone comes to this Adams Morgan hot spot at some point, so expect to see partiers burning the candle at both ends and straight-laced types likely heading to the office after the show, even though it's Sunday.

- **Explore Washington from an Unconventional Angle:** Yes, it's a graveyard, but Oak Hill Cemetery is also a beautiful wooded and landscaped garden with a grand view of the city from its hillside perch. Here lie monuments and resting places for some of Washington's most illustrious residents, from the city's early days as well as recent years. See p. 173.

- **Play Street Hockey in Front of the White House:** Pennsylvania Avenue in front of the White House is closed to traffic, which makes it a perfect place for street hockey fanatics to show up Saturdays and Sundays at noon for pickup games. All you need are skates and a stick. See p. 157.

LEFT: Perry's Drag Brunch in D.C.'s Adams Morgan neighborhood is a Washington institution. ABOVE: Oak Hill Cemetery.

In our progress towards political happiness my station is new....I walk on untrodden ground.

George Washington to
Catherine Macaulay Graham, January 9, 1790

WASHINGTON, D.C. IN DEPTH

E verybody knows at least a little something about Washington, D.C. It's the nation's capital, after all; what goes on here on a daily basis is top-of-the-news stuff. Images such as the Capitol, the Washington Monument, the Potomac River, the National Mall, the White House, and Pennsylvania Avenue are called immediately to mind by the mention of this city's name.

There are others I'd like to introduce to you: cherry blossoms, Black Broadway, the Smithsonian, the Verizon Center, Eleanor Holmes Norton, the U Street Corridor, Rock Creek Park, Mary McLeod Bethune, Komi Restaurant, Eastern Market, José Andrés, Lafayette Square, Embassy Row, the Folklife Festival, the Shakespeare Theatre Free for All, and Good Stuff Eatery, to illustrate just a fraction of the rich history and diverse cultural experiences this city has to offer.

That's what this book is about. This chapter, specifically, aims to provide you with a context for understanding Washington, D.C.'s story and personality beyond the headlines, as well as practical information that will be useful to you while planning your trip and upon your arrival.

WASHINGTON, D.C. TODAY

Washington, D.C. is both the capital of the United States and a city unto itself—and therein lie its charms, but also a host of complications. Control of the city is the main issue. The District is a free-standing jurisdiction, but because it is a city with a federal rather than a state overseer, it has never been entitled to the same governmental powers as the states. For instance, Congress supervises the District's budget and legislation. Origi-

nally, Congress granted the city the authority to elect its own governance, but it rescinded that right in the late 1800s when the District overspent its budget in its attempts to improve its services and appearance after the Civil War. The White House then appointed three commissioners, who ran D.C.'s affairs for nearly 100 years.

In 1972 the city regained the right to elect its own mayor and city council, but Congress retains control of the budget, and the courts and can veto municipal legislation. District residents can vote in presidential primaries and elections and can elect a delegate to

ABOVE: **Rock Creek Park.** PREVIOUS PAGE: **Gilbert Stuart's painting of George Washington at the National Portrait Gallery.**

Congress who introduces legislation and votes in committees, but this delegate cannot vote on the House floor. This unique situation, in which residents of the District pay federal income taxes but don't have a vote in Congress, is a matter of great local concern. Among the ways that D.C. residents publicly protest the situation is by displaying license plates bearing the inscription TAXATION WITHOUT REPRESENTATION.

Another wrinkle in this uncommon relationship is the fact that Washington's economy relies heavily upon the presence of the federal government, which employs about 21.4% of D.C. residents (according to a 2011 Gallup Poll), making it the city's single largest employer, and upon the tourism business that Washington, as the capital, attracts. Even as the city struggles toward political independence, it recognizes the economic benefits of its position as the seat of the nation's capital.

Will any of this affect you as you tour the city this year? Yes.

You will find Washington, D.C. to be a remarkably vibrant city. The economic hard times that the rest of the country is experiencing are muted here. Income is higher than the national average, unemployment is lower, one-third of the population is between the ages of 20 and 35, residents are better educated than elsewhere, and the people are remarkably diverse: 50.7% African American, 9.1% Latino, 13% foreign-born, and 14.6% speaking a language other than English at home. The presence of embassies and the diplomatic community intensifies the international flavor.

In other words, Washington, D.C. is thriving. Restaurants and bars dominate most neighborhoods. In fact, eating out is a way of life here, whether simply for the pleasure of it or for business—the city's movers and shakers meet over breakfast, lunch, and dinner. Washington's restaurant scene offers an immense variety of international cuisines, from Ethiopian to Peruvian, as well as soul food and regional specialties like Chesapeake Bay crabs served in soft-shell, hard-shell, soup, or cake form.

Theaters, music venues, new hotels, and brand-name stores abound. Because of the relative abundance of jobs thanks to tourism and the presence of the federal government, many Washingtonians can afford to go to the theater, attend cultural events, shop, and dine out. And they do.

But it wasn't always this way. About 20 years ago, Washington wasn't so attractive. Tourists came to visit federal buildings like the Capitol, the White House, and the city's memorials but stayed away from the dingy downtown and other off-the-Mall neighborhoods. The city had the potential for being so much more, and certain people—heroes, in my book—helped inspire action and brought about change themselves: Delegate Eleanor Holmes Norton, who fought steadfastly for states' rights and economic revival for the District; former Mayor Anthony Williams, who rescued the District's budget when his predecessor, the notoriously mismanaging Mayor Marion Barry, brought the city to the brink of financial ruin; and the community-minded developers Abe and Irene Pollin, who used their own funds to finance the $200-million MCI sports center, now the Verizon Center, in the heart of town (today the wildly successful arena anchors the utterly transformed Penn Quarter neighborhood, now one of the liveliest city centers in the country).

The city's resident population has grown by more than 5% in the past 10 years and now stands at approximately 618,000, a size not seen in more than 50 years. The growth spurt is especially significant given that the District's population reached a relative low point in 2002, when the U.S. Census counted 572,000

D.C. residents. Revitalization continues to take root throughout the city—from Southeast D.C., where a grand baseball stadium, Nationals Ballpark, opened in March 2008, to the Columbia Heights enclave in upper northwest D.C., now a mélange of Latino culture, loft condominiums, and ethnic eateries. The city's evergreens—the memorials and monuments, the historic neighborhoods, and the Smithsonian museums—remain unflaggingly popular.

But D.C. has its share of problems, starting with its Metro transportation system, which is in the midst of a much-needed overhaul. (See "Getting Around," in chapter 11, for details.) Other problems relate to the city's gentrification efforts, such as the displacement of residents from homes they can no longer afford in revitalized but increasingly expensive neighborhoods. Such concerns were certainly a factor in the 2010 mayoral election, in which the older, amiable, and unhurried D.C. Council Chair Vincent Gray won the race over the young, brash, and bossy incumbent, Adrian Fenty. Mayor Gray has had his work cut out for him in a municipality that struggles to provide health care, good schools, safe neighborhoods, adequate housing, and basic social services to all citizens.

Diverse in demographics, residents are alike in loving their city, despite the issues it faces. Visitors seem to share this love, as statistics bear out: The latest figures show that D.C. welcomes 17.28 million visitors a year, 1.74 million of whom are international tourists.

THE MAKING OF WASHINGTON, D.C.

As with many cities, Washington, D.C.'s past is written in its landscape. Behold the lustrous Potomac River, whose discovery by Captain John Smith in 1608 led to European settlement of this area. Take note of the city's layout: the 160-foot-wide avenues radiating from squares and circles, the sweeping vistas, the abundant parkland, all very much as Pierre Charles L'Enfant intended when he envisioned the "Federal District" in 1791. Look around and you will see the Washington Monument, the U.S. Capitol, the Lincoln Memorial, the White House, and other landmarks, their very prominence in the flat, central cityscape attesting to their significance in the formation of the nation's capital.

But Washington's history is very much a tale of two cities. Beyond the National Mall, the memorials, and the federal government buildings lies "D.C.," the municipality. Righteous politicians and others speak critically of "Washington"—shorthand, we understand, for all that is wrong with government. They should be more precise. With that snide dismissal, critics dismiss, as well, the particular locale in which the capital resides. It is a place of vibrant neighborhoods and vivid personalities, a vaunted arts-and-culture scene, international diversity, rich African-American heritage, uniquely Washingtonian attractions

The original Declaration of Independence and Constitution are on view at the National Archives.

and people—the very citizens who built the capital in the first place and have kept it running ever since.

Early Days

The settlers who arrived in 1608 weren't the region's first inhabitants, of course. Captain John Smith may have been the first European to discover this waterfront property of lush greenery and woodlands, but the Nacotchtank and Piscataway tribes were way ahead of him. As Smith and company settled the area, they disrupted the Indians' way of life and introduced European diseases. The Indians gradually were driven away.

By 1751, Irish and Scottish immigrants had founded "George Town," named for the king of England and soon established as an important tobacco-shipping port. Several houses from those days still exist in modern-day Georgetown: The Old Stone House (on M St. NW), a woodworker's home built around the 1760s, now operated by the National Park Service and open to the public, and a few magnificent ship merchants' mansions still stand on N and Prospect streets, though these are privately owned and not open to the public. (Their properties once directly overlooked the Potomac River, but no longer: The Potomac River has receded quite a bit, as you'll see.) For a walking tour of Georgetown, see p. 167.

Birth of the Capital

After colonists in George Town and elsewhere in America rebelled against British rule, defeating the British in the American Revolution (1775–83), Congress, in quick succession, unanimously elected General George Washington as the first president of the United States, ratified a U.S. Constitution, and proposed that a city be designed and built to house the seat of government for the new nation and to function fully in commercial and cultural capacities. Much squabbling ensued. The North wanted the capital; the South wanted the capital. President Washington huddled with his Secretary of State, Thomas Jefferson, and devised a solution that Congress approved in 1790: The nation's capital would be "a site not exceeding 10 miles square" located on the Potomac. The South was happy, for this area was nominally in their region; Northern states were appeased by the stipulation that the South pay off the North's Revolutionary War debt, and by the city's location on the North–South border. Washington, District of Columbia, made her debut.

The only problem was that she was not exactly presentable. The brave new country's capital proved to be a tract of undeveloped wilderness, where pigs, goats, and cows roamed free, and habitable houses were few and far between. Thankfully, the city was granted the masterful 1791 plan of the gifted but temperamental French-born engineer, Pierre Charles L'Enfant. Slaves, free blacks, and immigrants from Ireland, Scotland, and other countries worked to fulfill L'Enfant's remarkable vision, erecting first the White House (the city's oldest federal structure), then the Capitol and other buildings. (Read *The Great Decision: Jefferson, Adams, Marshall and the Battle for the Supreme Court*, by Cliff Sloan and David McKean, for excellent descriptions of the early days of the capital, its institutions, and the strong personalities that helped forge them.) Gradually, the nation's capital began to take shape, though too slowly perhaps for some.

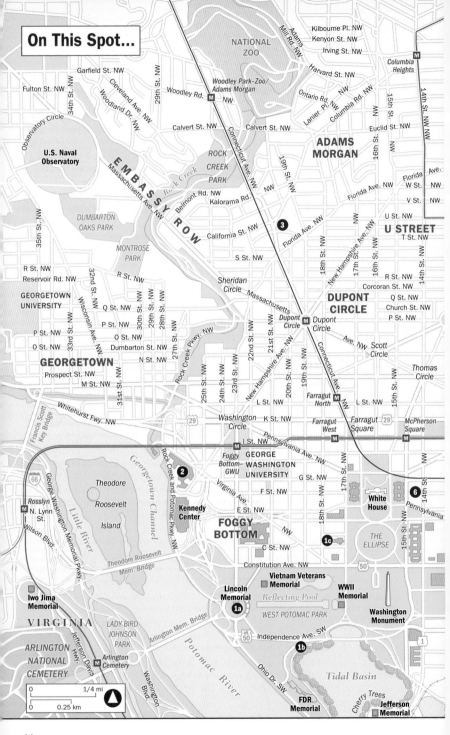

Kilbourne Pl. NW

Kenyon St. NW

Irving St. NW

NATIONAL ZOO

Garfield St. NW

Harvard St. NW

Columbia Heights

Fulton St. NW

Cleveland Ave. NW

Woodland Dr. NW

Woodley Rd. NW

Woodley Park-Zoo/ Adams Morgan

Ontario Rd. NW

Lanier Pl. NW

Columbia Rd. NW

Euclid St. NW

Observatory Circle

Calvert St. NW

Calvert St. NW

ADAMS MORGAN

U.S. Naval Observatory

ROCK CREEK PARK

Florida Ave.

W St. NW

V St. NW

EMBASSY ROW

Belmont Rd. NW

Kalorama Rd. NW

Florida Ave. NW

Rock Creek

DUMBARTON OAKS PARK

California St. NW

❸

U St. NW

T St. NW

U STREET

MONTROSE PARK

S St. NW

Florida Ave. NW

R St. NW

Reservoir Rd. NW

R St. NW

Sheridan Circle

Corcoran St. NW

Q St. NW

GEORGETOWN UNIVERSITY

Massachusetts

DUPONT CIRCLE

Church St. NW

P St. NW

Q St. NW

P St. NW

O St. NW

Dumbarton St. NW

Dupont Circle

Dupont Circle

Ave. NW Scott Circle

GEORGETOWN

N St. NW

Thomas Circle

Prospect St. NW

M St. NW

L St. NW

L St. NW

Farragut North

Farragut West

Farragut Square

McPherson Square

Whitehurst Fwy. NW

Washington Circle

K St. NW

Pennsylvania Ave. NW

Francis Scott Key Bridge

I St. NW

GEORGE WASHINGTON UNIVERSITY

Foggy Bottom-GWU

❷

Theodore Roosevelt Island

Georgetown Channel

Rock Creek and Potomac Pkwy. NW

Virginia Ave.

G St. NW

F St. NW

White House

❻

Pennsylvania

Rosslyn N. Lynn St.

Kennedy Center

E St. NW

FOGGY BOTTOM

THE ELLIPSE

Wilson Blvd.

Little River

C St. NW

❶c

Theodore Roosevelt Mem. Bridge

Constitution Ave. NW

Iwo Jima Memorial

Vietnam Veterans Memorial

WWII Memorial

Washington Monument

VIRGINIA

LADY BIRD JOHNSON PARK

Lincoln Memorial

Reflecting Pool

WEST POTOMAC PARK

Arlington Mem. Bridge

❶a

ARLINGTON NATIONAL CEMETERY

Arlington Cemetery

Independence Ave. SW

❶b

Tidal Basin

Potomac River

Ohio Dr. SW

Cherry Trees

0   1/4 mi

0   0.25 km

FDR Memorial

Jefferson Memorial

1 Built in 1912, directly two miles west of the Capitol, the **Lincoln Memorial** **1a** honors our most inspiring president. Among the inspired was the Rev. Dr. Martin Luther King. Find the marked spot, 18 steps down from the chamber, and you will be standing exactly where King stood on Aug. 28, 1963, when he delivered his remarkable "I Have a Dream" speech to the crowd of 200,000 people who had gathered here after "Marching on Washington" with King to pressure Congress to pass the Civil Rights Act. Forty-eight years later, on October 16, 2011, the country honored King with his own memorial; the **Washington, D.C. Martin Luther King Jr. National Memorial** **1b** lies across Independence Ave., on the lip of the Tidal Basin.

The Lincoln Memorial was the site of another significant moment in civil rights history, on Easter Sunday, 1939, when contralto Marian Anderson sang to a crowd of 75,000 people on the memorial steps, after the Daughters of the American Revolution refused to allow the African American to perform at their **Constitution Hall** **1c**. First Lady Eleanor Roosevelt resigned her DAR membership over the incident. Eventually, Anderson did sing at Constitution Hall (in 1943 and again in 1952), and at the Lincoln Memorial a second time, in 1952.

2 **The Watergate Building** looks harmless enough these days, despite the fact that the very word "Watergate" calls up its scandalous history. In June 1972, members of President Nixon's re-election staff broke into the Democratic National Committee's offices here, an act that eventually forced Nixon to resign. Two decades later, Pres. Clinton carried on an affair at the White House with a 20-something intern, who just happened to live at the Watergate.

3 **The Washington Hilton** was the scene of the attempted assassination of President Reagan on March 30, 1981, when John Hinckley, Jr. shot Pres. Reagan, his press secretary James Brady, a DC police officer, and a Secret Service agent. All survived.

4 President Lincoln was not so lucky. On April 14, 1865, John Wilkes Booth fatally shot Abraham Lincoln as the president sat in the Presidential Box in **Ford's Theatre** watching a performance of "Our American Cousin." Visitors can view Lincoln's seat, but not sit there.

5 In the early to mid-20th century, U Street was known as Black Broadway, and the general area between 7th and 15th streets was the epicenter of a black cultural renaissance. At places like the **Howard Theatre** **5a** and the **Club Caverns** **5b** (now Bohemian Caverns), African Americans came to hear the music of Ella Fitzgerald, Cab Calloway, and most of all, DC native son Duke Ellington. Visit the reborn neighborhood today and you can follow in their footsteps, as you walk by the houses at **1805 and 1816 13th St. NW** **5c**, where the Duke grew up, or take in a show at the restored Howard Theatre or at smaller venues, like Twins Jazz, always ending the night with a half-smoke at the decades-old Ben's Chili Bowl.

6 Since its beginnings in 1850, and continuing on through its current incarnation (built on the site of the original in 1901), **The Willard Hotel** has always played a special role in the life of the capital. At least six presidents, from Zachary Taylor to Abraham Lincoln, lived at the Willard for a while. Julia Ward Howe composed "The Battle Hymn of the Republic" in it in 1861, and the Rev. Dr. Martin Luther King composed his "I Have a Dream" speech here in 1963. Stop in at the hotel to admire the ornate lobby and exquisite architecture, but don't leave without visiting the bar, the city's historic center of activity. Sip a mint julep, introduced here by statesman Henry Clay in 1850, and consider the tradition you're upholding: It was here that Washington Irving brought Charles Dickens for a brandy, Samuel Clemens (Mark Twain) imbibed bourbon with his pal, Nevada Sen. William Stewart, and Nathaniel Hawthorne set up his base for covering the Civil War for the Atlantic Monthly magazine, writing "…for the conviviality of Washington sets in at an early hour, and, so far as I have had the opportunity to observe, never terminates at any hour."

The writer Anthony Trollope, visiting in 1860, declared Washington "as melancholy and miserable a town as the mind of man can conceive."

The Civil War and Reconstruction

During the Civil War, the capital became an armed camp and headquarters for the Union Army, overflowing with thousands of followers. Parks became campgrounds; churches, schools, and federal buildings, including the Capitol and the Patent Office (now the National Portrait Gallery), became hospitals; and forts ringed the town. The population grew from 60,000 to 200,000, as soldiers, former slaves, merchants, and laborers converged on the scene. The streets were filled with the wounded, nursed by the likes of Walt Whitman, one of many making the rounds to aid ailing soldiers. In spite of everything, President Lincoln insisted that work on the Capitol continue. "If people see the Capitol going on, it is a sign we intend the Union shall go on," he said.

Lincoln himself kept on, sustained perhaps by his visits to St. John's Church (p. 162), across Lafayette Square from the White House. Lincoln attended evening services when he could, arriving alone after other churchgoers had entered and slipping out before the service was over. And then on the night of April 14, 1865, just as the days of war were dwindling down and Lincoln's vision for unity was being realized, the president was fatally shot at Ford's Theatre (p. 127) while attending a play.

In the wake of the Civil War and President Lincoln's assassination, Congress took stock of the capital and saw a town worn out by years of war—awash with people but still lacking the most fundamental facilities. Indeed, the city was a mess. There was talk of moving the capital city elsewhere, perhaps to St. Louis or some other more centrally located city. A rescue of sorts arrived in the person of public works leader Alexander "Boss" Shepherd, who initiated a "comprehensive plan of improvement" that at last incorporated the infrastructure so necessary to a functioning metropolis, including

Civil War–era soldiers.

a streetcar system that allowed the District's overflowing population to move beyond city limits. Shepherd also established parks, constructed streets and bridges, and installed water and sewer systems and gas lighting, gradually nudging the nation's capital closer to showplace design. Notable accomplishments included the completion of the Washington Monument in 1884 (after 36 years) and the opening of the first Smithsonian museum, in 1881.

Washington Blossoms

With the streets paved and illuminated, the water running, streetcars and rail transportation operating, and other practical matters well in place, Washington, D.C. was ready to address its appearance. In 1900, as if on cue, a senator from

President Lincoln's box at Ford's Theatre, where he was assassinated by John Wilkes Booth.

Michigan, James McMillan, persuaded his colleagues to appoint an advisory committee to develop designs for a more beautiful and graceful city. This retired railroad mogul was determined to use his architectural and engineering knowledge to complete the job that L'Enfant had started a century earlier. With his own money, McMillan sent a committee that included landscapist Frederick Law Olmsted (designer of New York's Central Park), sculptor Augustus Saint-Gaudens, and noted architects Daniel Burnham and Charles McKim to Europe for 7 weeks to study the landscaping and architecture of that continent's great capitals.

"Make no little plans," Burnham counseled fellow members. "They have no magic to stir men's blood, and probably themselves will not be realized. Make big plans, aim high in hope and work, remembering that a noble and logical diagram once recorded will never die, but long after we are gone will be a living thing, asserting itself with ever growing insistency."

The committee implemented a beautification program that continued well into the 20th century. Other projects added further enhancements: A presidential Commission of Fine Arts, established in 1910, positioned monuments and fountains throughout the city; FDR's Works Progress Administration erected public buildings embellished by artists. The legacy of these programs is on view today, in the cherry trees along the Tidal Basin, the Lincoln Memorial at the west end of the Mall, the Arlington Memorial Bridge, the Library of Congress, Union Station, the Corcoran Gallery, and many other sights, each situated in its perfect spot in the city.

The American capital was coming into its own on the world stage, as well,

WPA workers in 1935.

Presidential Quotes

I greatly fear that my countrymen will expect too much from me.
—George Washington

I have an irrepressible desire to live till I can be assured that the world is a little better for my having lived in it.
—Abraham Lincoln

I'm asking you to believe. Not just in my ability to bring about real change in Washington . . . I'm asking you to believe in yours.
—Barack Obama

emerging from the Great Depression, two world wars, and technological advancements in air and automobile travel as a strong, respected, global power. More and more countries established embassies here, and the city's international population increased exponentially.

Black Broadway Sets the Stage

As the capital city blossomed, so did African-American culture. The many blacks who had arrived in the city as slaves to help build the Capitol, the White House, and other fundamental structures of America's capital stayed on, later joined by those who came to fight during the Civil War, or to begin new lives after the war. (See p. 140 for a description of the African American Civil War Memorial and Museum, which commemorates the lives of the 209,145 black Civil War soldiers.)

From 1900 to 1960, Washington, D.C. became known as a hub of black culture, education, and identity, centered on a stretch of U Street NW, called "Black Broadway," where Cab Calloway, Duke Ellington, and Pearl Bailey often performed in speakeasies and theaters. Many of these stars performed at the Howard Theatre (p. 261), which was the first full-size theater devoted to black audiences and entertainers when it opened in 1910. Nearby Howard University, created in 1867, distinguished itself as the nation's most comprehensive center for higher education for blacks. (The reincarnated "U Street Corridor," or "New U," is now a diverse neighborhood of blacks, whites, Asians, and Latinos, and a major restaurant and nightlife destination.)

The Civil Rights Era Ushers in a New Age

By 1950 blacks made up 60% of Washington's total population of 802,000, a record number that would then steadily decrease throughout the rest of the 20th century. Nearly a century after the passage of the 13th Amendment (abolishing slavery) and the 15th Amendment (outlawing the denial of voting rights based on race or color), blacks generally remained unequal members of society. Despite the best efforts and contributions of individuals—from abolitionist Frederick Douglass (p. 121), a major force in the human rights movement in the 19th century, to educator and civil rights leader Mary McLeod Bethune (p. 140), who served as an advisor to President Franklin Delano Roosevelt in the 1930s—the country, and this city, had a long way to go in terms of equal rights. (Consider reading works by Edward P. Jones, the Pulitzer Prize–winning author whose short-story collections, *Lost in the City* and *All Aunt Hagar's Children,* will take you beyond D.C.'s political and tourist attractions into the neighborhoods and everyday lives of African Americans during the mid-20th century.)

LITTLE-KNOWN facts

- Many people—including Washington, District of Columbia residents themselves—wonder how the city wound up with such an unwieldy name. Here's how: President Washington referred to the newly created capital as "the Federal City." City commissioners then chose the names "Washington" to honor the president and "Territory of Columbia" to designate the federal nature of the area. Columbia was the feminine form of Columbus, synonymous in those days with "America" and all she stood for—namely, liberty. The capital was incorporated in 1871, when it officially became known as Washington, District of Columbia.

- The distance between the base of the Capitol, at one end of the National Mall, and the Lincoln Memorial, at the other, is nearly 2 miles. The circumference of the White House property, from Pennsylvania Avenue to Constitution Avenue and 15th Street to 17th Street, is about 1½ miles.

- More than 27 percent of Washington, D.C. is national parkland, which makes the capital one of the "greenest" cities in the country. The biggest chunk is the 2,000-acre Rock Creek Park, the National Park Service's oldest natural urban park, founded in 1890.

- Every country that maintains diplomatic relations with the United States has an embassy in the nation's capital. Currently, the number of embassies comes to 187, mostly located along Massachusetts Avenue, known as Embassy Row, and other streets in the Dupont Circle neighborhood.

The tipping point may have come in 1954, when Thurgood Marshall (appointed the country's first black Supreme Court justice in 1967) argued and won the Supreme Court case *Brown v. Board of Education of Topeka*, which denied the legality of segregation in America. This decision, amid a groundswell of frustration and anger over racial discrimination, helped spark the civil rights movement of the 1960s. On August 28, 1963, black and white Washingtonians were among the 200,000 who marched on Washington and listened to an impassioned Rev. Dr. Martin Luther King, Jr. deliver his stirring "I Have a Dream" speech on the steps of the Lincoln Memorial, where 41 years earlier, during the memorial's dedication ceremony, black officials were required to stand and watch from across the road.

The assassination of President John F. Kennedy on November 22, 1963, added to a general sense of despair and tumult. On the day before his funeral, hundreds of thousands of mourners stood in line for blocks outside the Capitol all day and night to pay their respects to the president, who lay in state inside the Rotunda of the Capitol.

Then Martin Luther King, Jr. was assassinated on April 4, 1968, and all hell broke loose. The corner of 14th and U streets served as the flashpoint for the riots that followed. Ben's Chili Bowl (p. 204) was ground zero and remained open throughout the riots to provide food and shelter to activists, firefighters, and public servants.

As the 20th century progressed, civil rights demonstrations led to Vietnam War protests and to revelations about scandals, from President Nixon's Watergate political debacle (ever seen *All the President's Men*? You have to), to D.C. Mayor Marion Barry's drug and corruption problems, to President Clinton's sexual shenanigans. It was an era of speaking out to expose corruption and scandal.

A president who authorizes illegal activity? Not acceptable. A mayor with a drug problem? Not acceptable. A president who dallies with a White House intern his daughter's age, then lies about it? Nope, not acceptable.

And still the city flourished. A world-class subway system opened, the Verizon Center debuted and transformed its aged downtown neighborhood into the immensely popular Penn Quarter, and the city's Kennedy Center, Shakespeare theaters, and other arts-and-culture venues came to world attention, receiving much acclaim.

Twenty-First Century Times

Having begun the 20th century a backwater town, Washington finished the century a sophisticated city, profoundly shaken but not paralyzed by the September 11, 2001, terrorist attacks. The first decade of the 21st century was marked by the Afghanistan and Iraq wars and by a precipitous economic

The scandal-ridden Watergate building.

decline. Here in Washington, these situations continue to foment rancorous relations in Congress and between Capitol Hill and the White House, as Democrats and Republicans disagree over how best to resolve these issues. Barack Obama's

President Barack Obama at the Symposium on Global Agriculture and Food Security in May 2012.

A protest on the National Mall.

landmark win as the first African-American president, in 2008, temporarily restored some hope and an "all things are possible" perspective. Four years later, however, even as the U.S. is slowly extricating itself from Iraq and Afghanistan, and even as the economy seems to be showing signs of a steady improvement, the outlook is not entirely certain. Peace and prosperity? One can hope. And who will be sworn in as president on January 20, 2013? (At press time, all signs pointed to a second term for President Obama.) In the District, Congresswoman Eleanor Holmes Norton seemed poised to win her 12th term in office. D.C. Mayor Vincent Gray, meanwhile, now in his second year of office, still has time to make his mark before the next mayoral election year approaches, in 2014.

History informs one's outlook, but so does the present. Look again at the Potomac River and think of Captain John Smith, but observe the Georgetown University crew teams rowing in unison across the surface of the water, and tour boats traveling between Georgetown and Old Town Alexandria. As you traverse the city, admire L'Enfant's inspired design, but also enjoy the sight of the tourists and office workers, artists and students, and people of every possible ethnic and national background making their way around town. Tour the impressive landmarks and remember their namesakes, but make time for D.C.'s homegrown attractions, whether a meal at a sidewalk cafe in Dupont Circle, jazz along U Street, a walking tour past Capitol Hill's old town houses, or a visit to an old church where slaves or those original immigrants once worshiped.

WHEN TO GO

The city's peak seasons generally coincide with two activities: the sessions of Congress, and springtime—beginning with the appearance of the cherry blossoms along the Potomac.

Specifically, from about the second week in September until Thanksgiving, and again from about mid-January to June (when Congress is "in"), hotels are full of guests whose business takes them to Capitol Hill or to conferences. Mid-March through June traditionally is the most frenzied season, when families and

WHAT WAS THAT? AN ABRIDGED
dictionary OF POLITICAL LINGO

Washington politicos have their own vernacular, mostly words relating to Capitol Hill business. Here are choice examples, and their definitions, for you to recognize while you're in town and to bandy about in conversation when you return home.

- **Boondoggle:** Also known as a junket: a trip by congressional members and/or staff in which leisure is more of a focus than business.

- **Call up a bill:** To bring up a bill on the floor for immediate consideration.

- **Cloture:** A vote taken, requiring three-fifths of the full Senate (normally 60 votes), to put a time limit on consideration of a bill, typically done to overcome a filibuster.

- **Filibuster:** A tactic used to extend the debate on a proposal in order to block its vote in the Senate.

- **Gerrymander:** To manipulate the geographic shape of a congressional district for political gain.

- **Log rolling:** The process in which two dissimilar interests join to help pass pieces of legislation that, on their own, neither interest could pass.

- **Mark-up:** The meeting of a congressional committee to review and amend the text of a bill before submitting it for review by the full House or Senate.

- **PAC:** The name for special interest groups that are legally permitted to give money to candidates running for political office.

- **Platform:** A formal, written statement of the principles, objectives, and policies of a political party.

- **Whip:** As a verb, whip means to gather votes. As a noun, whip refers to the officers, one Republican and one Democrat in the House, and one Republican and one Democrat in the Senate, responsible for counting potential votes and for promoting party unity in voting. There is a majority whip and a minority whip in both the House and the Senate, corresponding with the number of seats held by each party.

school groups descend upon the city to see the cherry blossoms and enjoy Washington's sensational spring. Hotel rooms are at a premium, and airfares tend to be higher. This is also a popular season for protest marches.

If crowds turn you off, consider visiting Washington at the end of August or in early September, when Congress is still "out" and families have returned home to get their children back to school, or between Thanksgiving and mid-January, when Congress leaves again and many people are busy with their own at-home holiday celebrations. Hotel rates are cheapest at this time, too, and many hotels offer attractive packages.

If you're thinking of visiting in July and August, be forewarned: The weather is very hot and humid. Despite the heat, Independence Day (July 4th) in the capital is a spectacular celebration. Summer is also the season for outdoor concerts, festivals, parades, and other events (see chapter 8 for details about performing arts schedules). If you can deal with the weather, this is a good time to visit: Locals often go elsewhere on vacation, so the streets and attractions are somewhat less crowded. In addition, hotels tend to offer their best rates in July and August.

Weather

Season by season, here's what you can expect of the weather in Washington:

Fall: This is my favorite season. The weather is often warm during the day—in fact, if you're here in early fall, it may seem entirely *too* warm. But it cools off, and even gets a bit crisp, at night. By late October, Washington has traded its famous greenery for the brilliant colors of fall foliage.

Winter: People like to say that Washington winters are mild—and sure, if you're from Minnesota, you'll find Washington warmer, no doubt. But D.C. winters can be unpredictable: bitter cold one day, an ice storm the next, followed by a couple of days of sun and higher temperatures. The winters of 2010 and 2011 were especially severe, bringing record snows, but 2012 was very mild. Pack with all possibilities in mind.

Spring: Early spring weather tends to be colder than most people expect. Cherry blossom season, late March to early April, can be iffy—and very often rainy and windy. As April slips into May, the weather usually mellows, and people's moods with it. Late spring is especially lovely, with mild temperatures and intermittent days of sunshine, flowers, and trees colorfully erupting in gardens and parks all over town. Washingtonians, restless after having been cooped up inside for months, sweep outdoors to stroll the National Mall, relax on park benches, or laze away the afternoon at outdoor cafes.

Summer: Anyone who has ever spent July and August in D.C. will tell you how hot and steamy it can be. Though the buildings are air-conditioned, many of Washington's attractions, like the memorials and organized tours, are outdoors and unshaded, and the heat can quickly get to you. Make sure you stop frequently for drinks (vendors are plentiful), and wear a hat, sunglasses, and sunscreen.

Average Temperatures & Rainfall in Washington, D.C.

	JAN	FEB	MAR	APR	MAY	JUNE	JULY	AUG	SEPT	OCT	NOV	DEC
Temp (°F)	44/29	47/31	56/38	67/47	76/57	84/66	86/71	87/70	80/62	69/51	58/41	47/33
Temp (°C)	7/-2	8/-1	13/3	19/8	24/14	29/19	30/22	31/21	27/17	21/11	14/5	8/1
Rainfall (in.)	2.8	2.6	3.5	3	4	3.8	3.7	3	3.7	3.4	3.1	2.3

Holidays

Banks, government offices, post offices, and many stores, restaurants, and museums are closed on the following legal national holidays: January 1 (New Year's Day), the third Monday in January (Martin Luther King, Jr. Day), the third Monday in February (Presidents' Day), the last Monday in May (Memorial Day), July 4 (Independence Day), the first Monday in September (Labor Day), the second Monday in October (Columbus Day), November 11 (Veterans Day/Armistice Day), the fourth Thursday in November (Thanksgiving Day), and December 25 (Christmas).

Inauguration Day, January 20, is a legal public holiday for employees who work in the District and in nearby Maryland and Virginia suburbs. In 2013, January 20 falls on a Sunday, which means that the government may have decided to push the inauguration ceremony to Monday, January 21, which is, in fact, the federal holiday celebrating Martin Luther King, Jr.'s birthday, and thus will not result in an additional public holiday.

Washington, D.C. Calendar of Events

Washington's 2013 will start off with a bang, with the presidential inauguration in January. Otherwise the city's most popular events are the annual Cherry Blossom Festival in spring, the Fourth of July celebration in summer, and the lighting of the National Christmas Tree in winter. But some sort of special event occurs almost daily. For the latest schedules, check **www.washington.org**, **www.nps.gov/ncro** (click on "Calendar of Events"), **www.cultural tourismdc.org**, **www.dc.gov**, and **www.washingtonpost.com**.

The phone numbers in the calendar below were accurate at press time, but these numbers change often. If the number you try doesn't get you the details you need, call **Destination D.C.** at ✆ **202/789-7000.**

When you're in town, grab a copy of the **Washington Post** (or read it online), especially the Friday "Weekend" section, or a copy of the monthly magazine **Washingtonian,** whose "Where and When" section features a daily calendar as well as that month's recommended goings-on around town.

For annual events in Alexandria, see p. 320. For an exhaustive list of events beyond those listed here, check http://events.frommers.com, where you'll find a searchable, up-to-the-minute roster of what's happening in cities all over the world.

JANUARY

Martin Luther King, Jr.'s Birthday. Events include speeches by prominent leaders and politicians, readings, dance, theater, concerts and choral performances, and prayer vigils at the Martin Luther King, Jr. National Memorial, on the national holiday (third Mon in Jan). Call the National Park Service at ✆ **202/619-7222.**

FEBRUARY

Black History Month. Numerous events, museum exhibits, and cultural programs celebrate the contributions of African Americans to American life, including a celebration of abolitionist Frederick Douglass's birthday. For details check the Washington Post or call the National Park Service at ✆ **202/619-7222.**

Chinese New Year Celebration. A Friendship Archway, topped by 300 painted dragons and lighted at night, marks the entrance to Chinatown at 7th and H streets NW. The celebration begins the day of the Chinese New Year and continues for 10 or more days, with traditional firecrackers, dragon dancers, and colorful street parades. Some area restaurants offer special menus. For details call

Destination D.C. at ✆ **202/789-7000.** Early February.

Abraham Lincoln's Birthday. Expect great fanfare at Ford's Theatre and its Lincoln Center for Education and Leadership, an exploration of Lincoln's legacy in the time since his assassination (p. 129). As always, a wreath-laying and reading of the Gettysburg Address will take place at noon at the Lincoln Memorial. Call Ford's Theatre at ✆ **202/426-6924,** or the National Park Service at ✆ **202/619-7222.** February 12.

George Washington's Birthday/ Presidents' Day. The city celebrates Washington's birthday in two ways: on the actual day, February 22, with a ceremony that takes place at the Washington Monument; and on the federal holiday, the third Monday in February, when schools and federal offices have the day off. Call the National Park Service at ✆ **202/619-7222** for details. The occasion also brings with it great sales at stores citywide. (See chapter 10, "Side Trips from Washington, D.C.," for information about the bigger celebrations held at Mount Vernon and in Old Town Alexandria on the third Mon in Feb.)

International Food & Wine Festival. Now in its 14th year, this annual event, held at the Ronald Reagan Building and International Trade Center, is the largest indoor wine festival in the Mid-Atlantic, with at least 100 international wineries participating, as well as food vendors and other merchants. The 2-day Grand Tasting is the main event. Ticket prices vary by event, but admission to the Grand Tasting will cost you about $95 at the door. Call ✆ **202/505-4933** or visit www.wineandfooddc.com. Mid-February.

D.C. Fashion Week. This biannual event features designers from around the world. The weeklong extravaganza stages parties, runway shows, and trunk shows at citywide venues, always culminating in an international couture fashion show at the French Embassy. Most events are open to the public but may require a ticket. Call ✆ **202/600-9274** or visit www.dcfashionweek.org. Mid-February and mid-September.

MARCH

Women's History Month. Count on the Smithsonian to cover the subject to a fare-thee-well. For a schedule of Smithsonian events, call ✆ **202/633-1000** or visit www.si.edu; for other events, check the websites listed in the intro to this section.

St. Patrick's Day Parade. This big parade on Constitution Avenue NW, from 7th to 17th streets, is complete with floats, bagpipes, marching bands, and the wearin' o' the green. For parade information, call Destination D.C. at ✆ **202/789-7000** or visit www.dcstpatsparade.com. The Sunday before March 17.

APRIL

National Cherry Blossom Festival. Strike up the band! Last year marked the 100th anniversary of the city of Tokyo's gift of cherry trees to the city of Washington. This event is celebrated annually; if all goes well, the festival coincides with the

blossoming of the more than 3,700 Japanese cherry trees by the Tidal Basin, on Hains Point, and on the grounds of the Washington Monument. Events take place all over town and include the Blossom Kite Festival on the grounds of the Washington Monument, fireworks, concerts, special art exhibits, park-ranger-guided talks and tours past the trees, and sports competitions. A Japanese Street Festival takes place on one of the final days of the celebration, and a grand parade caps the festival, complete with floats, marching bands, dancers, celebrity guests, and more. All events are free except for the Japanese Street Fair, which costs $5, and grandstand seating at the parade, which costs $17 (otherwise the parade is free). For information call ✆ **877/44BLOOM** (442-5666) or go to www.nationalcherryblossomfestival.org. March 30 to April 14, 2013.

White House Easter Egg Roll. A biggie for kids 12 and under, the annual White House Easter Egg Roll continues a practice begun in 1878. Entertainment on the White House South Lawn and the Ellipse traditionally includes appearances by costumed cartoon characters, clowns, musical groups (Fergie and the Jonas Brothers are among those who have performed in the past), egg-decorating exhibitions, puppet and magic shows, an Easter egg hunt, and an egg-rolling contest. To obtain tickets, you must use the online lottery system, up and running about 6 weeks before Easter Monday. For details all ✆ **202/208-1631** or visit www.whitehouse.gov/eastereggroll. Easter Monday between 8am and 5pm.

African-American Family Day at the National Zoo. This tradition extends back to 1889, when the zoo opened. The National Zoo, 3001 Connecticut Ave. NW, celebrates African-American families on the day after Easter with music, dance, Easter egg rolls, and other activities. Free. Call ✆ **202/633-1000** for details. Easter Monday.

Thomas Jefferson's Birthday. This date is celebrated at the Jefferson Memorial with wreaths, speeches, and a military ceremony. Call the National Park Service at ☎ **202/619-7222** for time and details. April 13.

Earth Day. This year marks the 43rd anniversary of Earth Day. Official Earth Day is April 22; D.C. often marks the event on a Sunday close to that date. The National Mall is ground zero for green-themed volunteer activities, campaigning, and live music performed by big names—Los Lobos and the Flaming Lips have played in the past. Call ☎ **202/518-0044** or visit www.earthday.org. April 22.

Filmfest D.C. This annual film festival, now in its 27th year, presents more than 100 works by filmmakers from around the globe. Screenings take place in movie theaters, embassies, and museums citywide. Tickets are usually $10 per movie and go fast; some events are free. Call ☎ **202/234-3456** or visit www.film festdc.org. Eleven days in April.

Smithsonian Craft Show. Held in the National Building Museum, 401 F St. NW, this juried show features one-of-a-kind limited-edition crafts by more than 120 noted artists from all over the country. There's an entrance fee of about $15 per adult each day; it's free for children 12 and under. No strollers. For details call ☎ **888/832-9554** or 202/633-5006, or visit www.smithsoniancraftshow.org. Four days in mid- to late April.

MAY

Washington National Cathedral Annual Flower Mart. Now in its 74th year, the flower mart takes place on cathedral grounds, featuring displays of flowering plants and herbs, decorating demonstrations, ethnic food booths, children's rides and activities (including an antique carousel), costumed characters, puppet shows, and other entertainment. Admission is free. For details call ☎ **202/387-2979** or visit www.allhallowsguild.org. First Friday and Saturday in May, rain or shine.

Georgetown Garden Tour. View remarkable private gardens in one of the city's loveliest neighborhoods on this annual tour. Admission ($30–$35) includes light refreshments. Some years there are related events such as a flower show at a historic home. For details visit www. georgetowngardentour.com. Early to mid-May.

Memorial Day. Ceremonies take place at the Tomb of the Unknowns in Arlington National Cemetery (☎ **703/607-8000**), at the National World War II and Vietnam Veterans memorials (☎ **202/619-7222**), and at the U.S. Navy Memorial (☎ **202/737-2300**). A National Memorial Day Parade marches down Constitution Avenue from the Capitol to the White House. On the Sunday before Memorial Day, the National Symphony Orchestra performs a free concert at 8pm on the West Lawn of the Capitol to honor the sacrifices of American servicemen and servicewomen (☎ **202/619-7222**). And one other thing: Hundreds of thousands of bikers from around the country roll into town in an annual event called "Rolling Thunder," to pay tribute to America's war veterans, prisoners of war, and those missing in action (www.rollingthunder1.com).

JUNE

Dupont-Kalorama Museum Walk Day. This 30th annual celebration welcomes visitors to 10 museums and historic houses located in several charming, off-the-Mall neighborhoods. The event includes free food, music, tours, and crafts demonstrations. Shuttle buses travel to each location. Visit www.dkmuseums.com. First full weekend in June.

Smithsonian Folklife Festival. A major event celebrating both national and international traditions in music, crafts, foods, games, concerts, and exhibits, staged the length of the National Mall. Each Folklife Festival showcases three or four cultures or themes; 2012's festival explored the themes of "campus and community" and "creativity and crisis," as well as the country of Wales. All events are free; most take place outdoors. For details call ✆ **202/633-6440,** visit www.festival. si.edu, or check the listings in the *Washington Post.* Ten days in late June and early July, always including July 4.

Independence Day. There's no better place to be on the Fourth of July than in Washington, D.C. The all-day festivities include a massive National Independence Day Parade down Constitution Avenue, complete with lavish floats, princesses, marching groups, and military bands. A morning program in front of the National Archives includes military demonstrations, period music, and a reading of the Declaration of Independence. In the evening, the National Symphony Orchestra plays on the west steps of the Capitol with guest artists. And big-name entertainment precedes the fabulous fireworks display behind the Washington Monument. For details or call the National Park Service at ✆ **202/619-7222** or visit www. nps.gov/mall. July 4.

Capital Fringe Festival. This event debuted in 2005 and celebrates experimental theater in the tradition of the original fringe festival, held annually in Edinburgh, Scotland. More than 130 separate productions take place at some 14 venues daily for 18 days, and it all adds up to about 700-plus individual performances. Local and visiting artists perform in theater, dance, music, and other disciplines. The action centers on the Penn Quarter. All tickets are $15; purchase them on www.capitalfringe.org, call ✆ **866/811-4111,** or visit the Fort Fringe Box Office, 607 New York Ave. NW. For details call ✆ **202/737-7230**. Eighteen days starting around the second week of July.

AUGUST

Shakespeare Theatre Free for All. This free theater festival presents a different Shakespeare play every year for a 2-week run at the Sidney Harmon Hall, across from the Verizon Center, in the Penn

Quarter. Tickets are required, but they're free. Call ✆ **202/547-1122** or visit www. shakespearetheatre.org. Evenings late August through mid-September.

SEPTEMBER

Labor Day Concert. The National Symphony Orchestra closes its summer season with a free performance at 8pm on the West Lawn of the Capitol. For details call the National Park Service at ✆ **202/619-7222**. Sunday before Labor Day. (Rain date: Same day and time at Constitution Hall or the Kennedy Center.)

Black Family Reunion. Performances, food, and fun are part of this 2-day celebration of the African-American family and culture, held on the Mall. Free. Visit www.ncnw.org/events/reunion.htm. Early to mid-September.

Adams Morgan Day. Thousands turn out along 18th Street NW, Columbia Road NW, and other streets in this small multicultural neighborhood to revel in the music, art, dance, and cuisines of its residents. Second Sunday in September.

Library of Congress National Book Festival. The Library of Congress sponsors this festival, welcoming at least 80 established authors and their many fans to the National Mall for readings, author signings, and general hoopla surrounding the love of books.For details call ✆ **888/714-4696** or visit www.loc.gov/ bookfest. A weekend in late September.

OCTOBER

Marine Corps Marathon. Thirty thousand runners compete in this 26.2-mile race (the fifth-largest marathon in the United States). The 2013 running marks its 38th year. It begins at the Marine Corps Memorial (the Iwo Jima statue) and passes many major monuments. For details call ✆ **800/RUN-USMC** (786-8762). Participants must be 14 or older; register online at www.marinemarathon. com. Last Sunday in October.

Halloween. There's no official celebration, but costumed shenanigans seem to get bigger every year. Grown-ups trick or treat at embassies or participate in costumed pub crawls throughout the city. Giant block parties take place in the Dupont Circle neighborhood (including a Drag Queen High Heel race, held the Tues before Halloween at 17th and Q sts.) and in Georgetown. Check the *Washington Post* for special parties and activities. October 31.

NOVEMBER

Veterans Day. The nation's war dead are honored with a wreath-laying ceremony at 11am at the Tomb of the Unknowns in Arlington National Cemetery, followed by a memorial service. The president of the United States or his stand-in officiates, as a military band performs. Wreath-laying ceremonies also take place at other war memorials in the city. Call © **703/607-8000** for details about Arlington Cemetery events and **202/619-7222** for details about war memorial events. November 11.

DECEMBER

Christmas Pageant of Peace/National Tree Lighting. At the northern end of the Ellipse, the president lights the national Christmas tree to the accompaniment of orchestral and choral music. The lighting inaugurates the 4-week Pageant of Peace, a tremendous holiday celebration full of free activities, including musical performances, mostly of local school and church choruses, nightly on the Ellipse. (Brrrr!) For details call © **202/208-1631,** and visit www.thenationaltree.org to enter the lottery for tickets, which are free but required to attend the tree-lighting ceremony. (No tickets are required to attend all other Pageant of Peace activities throughout Dec.) The tree-lighting ceremony takes place at 5pm on a day in early December, and the Pageant of Peace continues every night throughout the month.

RESPONSIBLE TOURISM IN WASHINGTON, D.C.

In some respects, Washington, D.C. has always been ahead of the curve when it comes to green-friendly endeavors. It was Pierre L'Enfant, in 1791, after all, whose vision for the city included a network of parks, an expansive "public walk," beautiful gardens, and sweeping vistas. The capital today stays true to L'Enfant's plan, as anyone can see who has strolled the 2-mile-long National Mall, biked through the 2,000-acre Rock Creek Park (the nation's oldest natural urban park), or picnicked on a verdant spot overlooking the Potomac River. National Park Service spokesman Bill Line says that "the National Park Service maintains, conserves, and preserves 27% of the land space of Washington, D.C.," which means that the nation's capital has to be one of the greenest cities, if not *the* greenest, in the country, especially since that percentage does not include parkland maintained by the D.C. Department of Parks and Recreation.

The capital continues to build upon its green foundation. Consider these facts:

Not only is D.C. the nation's most walkable city, but it also has the greatest number of walkable urban places per capita, according to the Brookings Institution. Biking, always popular here as recreation, is increasingly a commuter transportation choice. The District has more than 50 miles of bike lanes and hopes to add 30 more miles to city streets, and has partnered with **Capital BikeShare** (www.capitalbikeshare.com), a self-service bike rental program, to avail subscribers (membership fees range from $7 for 24 hr. to $75 for a year) of bikes, kept at stations throughout the city. As of this writing, CaBi provides 1,200 bikes at 140 locations throughout the District. Look for bike lanes along stretches of Pennsylvania Avenue and other major downtown streets. Many sightseeing spots are accessible by bike paths along Rock Creek Park and the National Mall.

By the time you read this, you may actually be able to rent and/or return a bike at five different stations on the National Mall. This is a major decision by the National Park Service, which maintains the Mall. If all goes as planned, Capital BikeShare will have locations at Jefferson Drive in front of the Smithsonian Metro Station; at Daniel French Drive, south of the Lincoln Memorial; on East Basin Drive, south of the Jefferson Memorial; on Jefferson Drive east of the Washington Monument; and next to the FDR and Martin Luther King, Jr. Memorials at West Basin and Ohio drives. See p. 155 for even more information about biking and bike rentals in D.C.

D.C.'s excellent public transportation system (see "Getting Around," in chapter 11) provides another inducement for drivers to leave their cars behind—though if you do opt to drive, the following D.C. car rental agencies offer hybrid cars: Zipcar (p. 348), and Enterprise Car Rental at Washington National and Dulles International airports (p. 336).

According to the Washington Metropolitan Area Transit Authority, of Metro's 1,500-Metrobus fleet, 439 buses run on compressed natural gas (CNG), 117 run on advanced technology diesel, and 250 are diesel/electric hybrid.

The list goes on, whether we're talking about construction, hotel trends, or dining options. Washington, D.C. was the first major city to require developers to adhere to guidelines established by the U.S. Green Building Council. Most D.C. hotels are incorporating ecofriendly practices into their daily operations, and many go even further, like the **Willard InterContinental,** which has adopted a nearby park and helps maintain it (p. 283). And the restaurant **Equinox** (p. 196) is known not only as Michelle Obama's choice for celebrating her birthday, but also for its commitment to using ingredients grown within 100 miles of the restaurant.

If participating in the environmental movement is important to you, why not make like a green-leaning local and leave the car behind, instead traveling around the city on foot, by bike, or by Metro? Dine at ecofriendly restaurants? Go paperless by booking restaurant and ticket reservations online, and by jotting down confirmation numbers, rather than printing the confirmation?

To make it easy for you to lean green, I've included specific information about the ecofriendly practices of hotels, restaurants, and attractions in their descriptions within corresponding chapters. For even more in-depth information about Washington, D.C.'s environmental movement, check out the District government's website devoted to the subject, www.green.dc.gov.

3

SUGGESTED WASHINGTON, D.C. ITINERARIES

W hat does a perfect day in the capital mean to you? My daughter Lucy likes to tour the National Mall and memorials by bike, then head to Matchbox (p. 192) in Chinatown for pizza. In winter an alternative activity is ice-skating at the National Sculpture Garden (p. 104), followed by hot chocolate across the street at the French bakery PAUL (p. 195). Her older sister, Caitlin, loves to stroll the pedestrians-only stretch of Pennsylvania Avenue to view the White House (p. 83) and to see what's up in Lafayette Square, the "protest park" across the street; tour exhibits at the National Geographic Museum (p. 73); attend After Five events at the Phillips Collection (p. 74); and eat brunch at Founding Farmers (p. 213).

Ask 10 Washingtonians for their sightseeing hit lists and you'll get 10 different itineraries. There's so much to see here, and everyone has their own way of seeing it—but we can make some suggestions. This chapter lays out a key itinerary for touring the capital's iconic sites, plus two themed itineraries: one devoted to family activities, the other to exploring women's history. Follow them to the letter or adapt them for your own purposes—it's up to you.

If you're the type of traveler who doesn't like surprises, call ahead and make sure all of the attractions on your desired itinerary are open. Be calm and flexible: Lines to enter public buildings are longer than ever, thanks to security clearance procedures and the capital's continuing popularity as a tourist destination. Reserve spots on tours to avoid some of those waits, and book advance reservations at recommended restaurants to make sure you get a table. Most importantly, don't be afraid to ask questions. The police on Capitol Hill, the National Park Service rangers on duty at the memorials, and the staff at all the museums know an awful lot; take advantage of their expertise.

I begin with an overview of D.C.'s neighborhoods as I refer to them throughout this book. Among the most enjoyable activities in D.C. is exploring its neighborhoods on foot, so if you tire of crowded museums and of following a structured itinerary, choose a neighborhood that appeals to you and simply stroll. See chapter 5 for walking tours of a few standout neighborhoods.

THE NEIGHBORHOODS IN BRIEF

ADAMS MORGAN Though this ever-trendy, multiethnic neighborhood is about the size of a postage stamp, it's crammed with boutiques, bars, clubs, and restaurants. Everything is located on either 18th Street NW or Columbia Road NW. In 2013, Adams Morgan expects to welcome the first hotel to be located within its actual boundaries; up until now, the nearest hotel options have been in the nearby Dupont Circle and Woodley Park neighborhoods (see below).

PREVIOUS PAGE: **The Madam's Organ mural in Adams Morgan.**

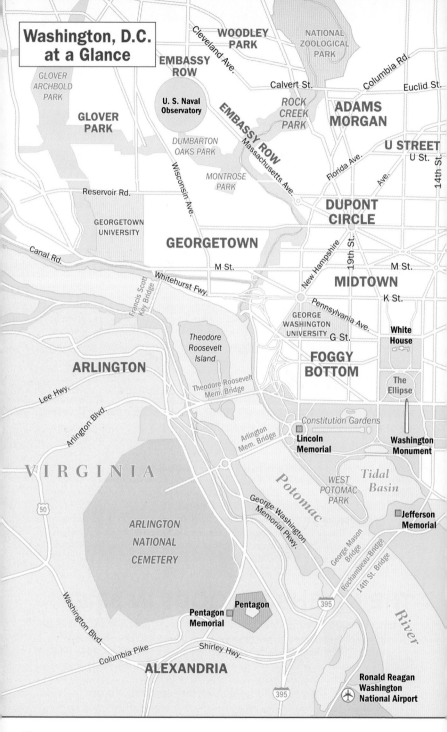

Washington, D.C. at a Glance

GLOVER ARCHBOLD PARK

GLOVER PARK

WOODLEY PARK

EMBASSY ROW

Cleveland Ave.

NATIONAL ZOOLOGICAL PARK

U. S. Naval Observatory

Calvert St.

Columbia Rd.

Euclid St.

ROCK CREEK PARK

ADAMS MORGAN

EMBASSY ROW

Massachusetts Ave.

DUMBARTON OAKS PARK

Florida Ave.

U STREET

U St.

14th St.

Reservoir Rd.

Wisconsin Ave.

MONTROSE PARK

DUPONT CIRCLE

GEORGETOWN UNIVERSITY

GEORGETOWN

New Hampshire

19th St.

M St.

Canal Rd.

M St.

MIDTOWN

Whitehurst Fwy.

Francis Scott Key Bridge

K St.

Pennsylvania Ave.

GEORGE WASHINGTON UNIVERSITY

G St.

White House

Theodore Roosevelt Island

FOGGY BOTTOM

ARLINGTON

Lee Hwy.

Theodore Roosevelt Mem. Bridge

The Ellipse

Arlington Blvd.

Arlington Mem. Bridge

Constitution Gardens

Lincoln Memorial

Washington Monument

VIRGINIA

50

ARLINGTON NATIONAL CEMETERY

Potomac

WEST POTOMAC PARK

Tidal Basin

George Washington Memorial Pkwy.

Jefferson Memorial

George Mason Bridge

Rochambeau Bridge

14th St. Bridge

Washington Blvd.

395

Pentagon Memorial

Pentagon

River

Columbia Pike

Shirley Hwy.

ALEXANDRIA

395

Ronald Reagan Washington National Airport

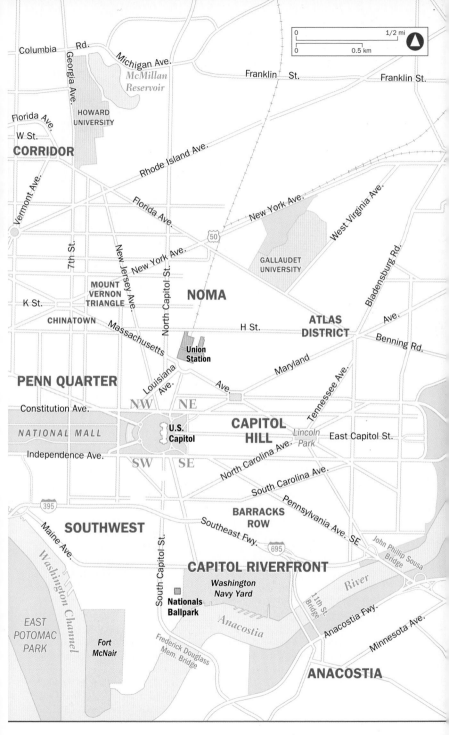

Parking is manageable during the day but difficult at night, especially on weekends (a parking garage on Champlain St., just off 18th St., helps a little). Luckily, you can easily walk to Adams Morgan from the Dupont Circle or Woodley Park Metro stops, or take the bus or a taxi there. (Be alert in Adams Morgan at night and try to stick to the main streets, 18th St. and Columbia Rd.) The weekend begins Thursday nights in the nightlife-centric world of Adams Morgan.

Nightlife in Adams Morgan.

ANACOSTIA   When people talk about the Washington, D.C. that tourists never see, they're talking about neighborhoods like this; in fact, they're usually talking about Anacostia, specifically. Named for the river that separates it from "mainland" D.C., it's an old part of town, with little commercial development and mostly modest, often low-income housing. Anacostia does have two major attractions: the Smithsonian's **Anacostia Community Museum** and the **Frederick Douglass National Historic Site** (see "Museums in Anacostia," p. 121). Of the two, Frederick Douglass's House is the one I most recommend. The city and entrepreneurs are starting to show some interest in Anacostia, so there's a good chance that tourists eventually will have other reasons to visit. In the meantime, one excellent development for residents and tourists alike is the fact that the D.C. Circulator bus now travels to Anacostia, with a stop not far from the Douglass House, in fact. Metrorail and Metrobus also travel here, of course, but the D.C. Circulator is a welcome supplement.

ATLAS DISTRICT   The Atlas District, no more than a section of H Street NE to the northeast of Union Station, stretches between 4th and 14th streets, but centers on the 12th to 14th streets segment. The Atlas District is increasingly known as a nightlife and live music destination, with a couple of recommendable restaurants thrown in. A hardscrabble part of town by day, the Atlas District turns into a playground at night, especially Thursday through Saturday, as the city's thirsty scenemakers hit the street. There are no hotels, for now. A much-talked-about streetcar should be opening here in 2013, finally providing the neighborhood with easier access to and from other parts of town and the nearest Metro stop (Union Station).

BARRACKS ROW   Barracks Row refers mainly to a single stretch of 8th Street SE, south of Pennsylvania Avenue SE, but also to side streets occupied by Marine Corps barracks since 1801 (hence the name). This southeastern subsection of Capitol Hill is known for its lineup of shops, casual bistros, and pubs. Its attractions continue to grow as a result of the 2008 opening of the Nationals baseball team's stadium, Nationals Park, half a mile away. In fact, the ballpark has spawned its own neighborhood, dubbed the Capitol Riverfront (see below). The closest hotels are the Capitol Hill Suites (6 blocks away, at C and 2nd St. SE, close to the Capitol) and those in Capitol Riverfront.

CAPITOL HILL Everyone's heard of "the Hill," the area crowned by the Capitol building. The term, in fact, refers to a large section of town, extending from the western side of the Capitol to the D.C. Armory going east, bounded by H Street to the north and the Southwest Freeway to the south. It contains not only this chief symbol of the nation's capital, but also the Supreme Court Building, the Library of Congress, the Folger Shakespeare Library, Union Station, and Eastern Market. Much of it is a quiet residential neighborhood of tree-lined streets, rows of Federal and Victorian town houses, and old churches. Restaurants keep increasing their numbers, with most located along Pennsylvania Avenue SE on the south side of the Capitol and near North Capitol Street NW on the north side of the Capitol—the north side, near Union Station, is where most of the hotels are, too. Keep to the well-lit, well-traveled streets at night, and don't walk alone—crime occurs more frequently in this neighborhood than in some other parts of town.

CAPITOL RIVERFRONT The opening of Nationals Park in 2008 has led the way in the development of this old and worn part of town. The revitalized 500-acre neighborhood abuts 1½ miles of the Anacostia River and, besides the ballpark, has a relatively new Courtyard by Marriott hotel (other hotels are due to open in 2013 and beyond), several restaurants, and public parks, trails, and docks. More to come.

CLEVELAND PARK Cleveland Park, just north of Woodley Park, is an enclave of beautiful old houses with wraparound porches, found on picturesque streets extending off the main artery, Connecticut Avenue. With its own stop on the Red Line Metro system and a respectable number of excellent restaurants, Cleveland Park is worth visiting when you're near the zoo (just up the street) or in the mood for some fine cuisine and a sense of affluent D.C. neighborliness. Most hotels lie a short walk away in Woodley Park, and farther south in the city.

DOWNTOWN The area bounded roughly by 6th and 21st streets NW to the east and west, and M Street and Pennsylvania Avenue to the north and south, is a

Historic houses on Capitol Hill.

mix of the Federal Triangle's government office buildings; K Street, ground zero for the city's countless law and lobbying firms; Connecticut Avenue restaurants and shopping; historic hotels; the city's poshest small hotels; **Chinatown;** the huge Walter E. Washington Convention Center; and the White House. You'll also find the historic **Penn Quarter,** D.C.'s hottest locale, which has continued to flourish since the 1997 opening of the Verizon Center (the venue for Wizards and Mystics basketball games, Capitals hockey games, and rock concerts). A number of off-the-Mall museums, like the mammoth Newseum, the International Spy Museum, and the Smithsonian's National Portrait Gallery and American Art Museum, are here. This is also where you'll find hip restaurants, boutique hotels, and nightclubs. The total downtown area encompasses so many blocks and attractions that I've divided discussions of attractions, restaurants, and hotels in this area into two sections: "**Midtown,**" referring to the area roughly from 15th Street west to 21st Street, and from Pennsylvania Avenue north to M Street; and "**Penn Quarter,**" roughly from 15th Street east to 6th Street, and Pennsylvania Avenue north to New York Avenue.

DUPONT CIRCLE   One of my favorite parts of town, Dupont Circle is easy fun day or night. It takes its name from the traffic circle minipark, where Massachusetts, New Hampshire, and Connecticut avenues converge. Washington's famous **Embassy Row** centers on Dupont Circle and refers to the parade of grand embassy mansions lining Massachusetts Avenue and its side streets. The streets extending out from the circle are lively, with all-night bookstores, good restaurants, wonderful art galleries and art museums, nightspots, and Washingtonians at their loosest. It is also the hub of D.C.'s gay community. There are plenty of hotel choices in this neighborhood.

FOGGY BOTTOM/WEST END   The area west of the White House, south of Dupont Circle, and east of Georgetown encompasses both Foggy Bottom and the West End. Foggy Bottom, located below, or south, of Pennsylvania Avenue, was Washington's early industrial center. Its name comes from the foul fumes emitted in those days by a coal depot and gasworks, but its original

Chinatown.

LEFT: **The Woodrow Wilson House in Dupont Circle.** RIGHT: **Swing dancers in Dupont Circle.**

name, Funkstown (for owner Jacob Funk), is perhaps even worse. There's nothing foul (and not much funky) about the area today. The West End edges north of Pennsylvania Avenue, booming with the latest big-name restaurants and new office buildings. Together the overlapping Foggy Bottom and West End neighborhoods present a mix of town-house residences, George Washington University campus buildings, offices for the World Bank and the International Monetary Fund, State Department headquarters, small- and medium-size hotels, student bars, several fine eateries, and the Kennedy Center, lining either side of Pennsylvania Avenue and its side streets.

GEORGETOWN This historic community dates from Colonial times. It was a thriving tobacco port long before the District of Columbia was formed, and one of its attractions, the Old Stone House, dates from pre-Revolutionary days. Georgetown action centers on M Street and Wisconsin Avenue NW, where you'll find the luxury Four Seasons hotel (and less expensive digs; see chapter 9), numerous boutiques (see chapter 7), chic restaurants, and popular pubs. Expect lots of nightlife here. Detour from the main drags to relish the quiet, tree-lined streets of restored Colonial row houses, stroll the beautiful gardens of Dumbarton Oaks, and check out the C&O Canal. Georgetown is also home to Georgetown University. (See chapter 5 for a walking tour of Georgetown.) **Note:** Not surprisingly, the neighborhood gets pretty raucous on weekends.

GLOVER PARK Mostly a residential neighborhood, this section of town just above Georgetown and just south of the Washington National Cathedral is worth mentioning because of several good restaurants and bars located along its main stretch, Wisconsin Avenue NW. Glover Park sits between the campuses of Georgetown and American universities, so there's a large student presence here. Its only lodging option is the Savoy Suites Hotel (p. 306).

THE NATIONAL MALL This lovely, tree-lined stretch of open space between Constitution and Independence avenues, extending for nearly 2 miles from the foot of the Capitol to the steps of the Lincoln Memorial, is the hub of tourist attractions. It includes most of the Smithsonian Institution museums and several other notable sites. Tourists as well as natives—joggers, food vendors, kite flyers, and picnickers among them—traipse the 700-acre Mall. Most hotels and restaurants are located beyond the Mall to the north, with a few located south of the Mall, across Independence Avenue. The proper name for the entire parkland area that encompasses the National Mall, as well as the Jefferson, FDR, and Martin Luther King, Jr. memorials, and other sites, is actually **National Mall and Memorial Parks,** which is how I refer to it in chapter 4.

MIDTOWN   This refers roughly to the part of downtown from 15th Street west to 21st Street, and from Pennsylvania Avenue north to M Street. See "Downtown," above.

MOUNT VERNON TRIANGLE   Yet another old neighborhood experiencing renewal, Mount Vernon lies east of the convention center, its boundary streets of New Jersey, Massachusetts, and New York avenues defining a perfectly shaped triangle. Within that triangle, attractions, like the hot restaurant Kushi, are starting to multiply. A luxury hotel is expected to open here in 2013.

NOMA   This fast-developing quarter due north of Union Station, the Capitol, and Massachusetts Avenue (hence the name) seems determined to turn itself into a destination in its own right. Local restaurateurs, like Todd Gray of **Equinox** (p. 196), are branching out here, as are hotels. Gray's **Watershed** restaurant is located inside the new **Hilton Garden Inn** (p. 286).

NORTHERN VIRGINIA   Across the Potomac River from the capital lies Northern Virginia and its close-in city/towns of Arlington and Old Town Alexandria. The Arlington Memorial Bridge leads directly from the Lincoln Memorial to Arlington National Cemetery, and beyond to Arlington and Old Town (see chapter 10, "Side Trips from Washington, D.C."). Commuters travel back and forth between the District and Virginia all day using the Arlington Memorial Bridge and others, including the Key Bridge, which leads to and from Georgetown; the Theodore Roosevelt Memorial Bridge, whose roadways connect Rte. 50 and I-66; and the 14th Street Bridge, whose I-395 roadway connects downtown D.C. and Northern Virginia's access to I-95 and points south.

PENN QUARTER   This refers roughly to the part of downtown from 15th Street east to 6th Street, and Pennsylvania Avenue north to New York Avenue. See "Downtown," above.

SOUTHWEST/WATERFRONT   This stretch of waterfront is a working marina, with fishing boats docked the length of the Washington Channel and vendors selling fresh crabs and fish from stalls up and down the promenade. This is where locals and restaurateurs come to buy fresh seafood. The neighborhood is also home to Arena Stage (p. 247), whose October 2010 reopening after a massive expansion and renovation is bringing more people back to this out-of-the-way part of town. Southwest does have its own Metro station (Southwest-Waterfront, on the Green Line), and change is in the air.

U STREET CORRIDOR   U Street NW and 14th Street NW form the crux of D.C.'s most diverse neighborhood, where people of varied race, color, nationality, and age mix more comfortably than anywhere else in the city. The quarter continues to rise from the ashes of the nightclubs and theaters located here decades ago, when the performances of jazz and blues legends Duke Ellington, Louis Armstrong, and Cab Calloway gave the area the name "Black Broadway." Today clubs like the renovated Howard Theatre and the smaller Twins Jazz honor that legacy, drawing jazz lovers, while the corridor's many bar hangouts fill nightly with the city's young and restless. New restaurants (see chapter 6) and little shops (see chapter 7) are proliferating. The Penn Quarter may be hot and high energy, but the U Street Corridor is hip and laid-back. Go here to party, not to sleep—there are no hotels along this stretch.

WOODLEY PARK   Home to Washington's largest hotel (the Washington Marriott Wardman Park, p. 305), Woodley Park boasts the National Zoo, many good restaurants, and some antiques stores. Washingtonians are used to seeing conventioneers wandering the neighborhood's pretty residential streets with their name tags still on.

ICONIC WASHINGTON, D.C.

If you have limited time in Washington, D.C. and want to sample the city's main attractions, then this is the itinerary for you, taking you to, if not thoroughly through, 20 sites. It's doable in one day, as long as you don't linger long in any one place. (*Tip:* Why not rent a bike to tour the sites? See p. 155 for a list of bike rental places. Alternatively, take the National Park Service's narrated, on/off tour bus, which stops at most of these sites. See p. 89 for more info.) If you have more than one day—fabulous! You might follow this itinerary the first day and return on succeeding days to fill in the blanks at the sites you liked most. Three attractions—the Capitol, the White House, and the Washington Monument—require tickets/reservations to tour, so keep that in mind as well. (The Capitol Visitor Center and the White House Visitor Center require no tickets and are worth touring, too.) **Start:** *Metro on the Blue Line to Capitol South, or on the Red Line to Union Station.*

---

1 Capitol

This is Congress's "House," whose cornerstone was laid in 1793 by President George Washington. Seventy years later, the Capitol was completed when the 19-foot, 6-inch *Statue of Freedom* was placed atop the dome in

Inside the Library of Congress.

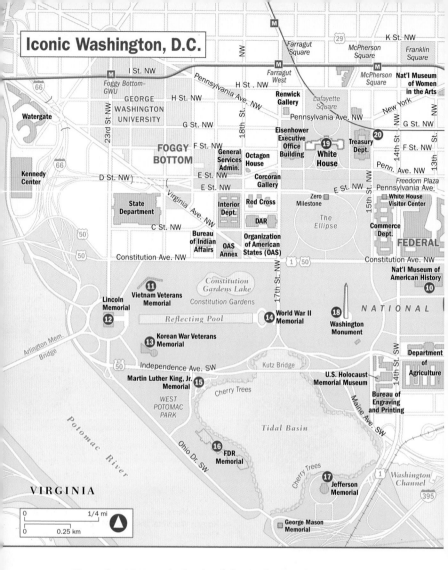

Iconic Washington, D.C.

December 1863, at the height of the Civil War—the same year that Abraham Lincoln issued his Emancipation Proclamation. Tilt your head all the way back to see it. See p. 58.

Not everyone knows it, but there's a tunnel that runs between the Capitol Visitor Center and the Library of Congress. If you're inside the Capitol Visitor Center, find it and follow it to the:

2   Library of Congress

The world's largest library is not only a keeper of books: Ongoing exhibits show off other precious objects, such as an "original Rough Draught" of Thomas Jefferson's much marked-up Declaration of Independence and a

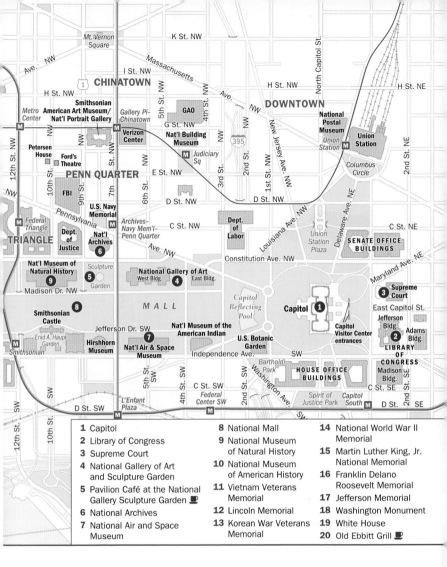

1 Capitol

2 Library of Congress

3 Supreme Court

4 National Gallery of Art and Sculpture Garden

5 Pavilion Café at the National Gallery Sculpture Garden ☕

6 National Archives

7 National Air and Space Museum

8 National Mall

9 National Museum of Natural History

10 National Museum of American History

11 Vietnam Veterans Memorial

12 Lincoln Memorial

13 Korean War Veterans Memorial

14 National World War II Memorial

15 Martin Luther King, Jr. National Memorial

16 Franklin Delano Roosevelt Memorial

17 Jefferson Memorial

18 Washington Monument

19 White House

20 Old Ebbitt Grill ☕

1797 manuscript in George Washington's hand, outlining a plan of government for Virginia. See p. 65.

Exit and cross East Capitol Street to find the:

3   Supreme Court

You may be shocked to know that the U.S. Constitution specifies neither an age nor an education level nor even a citizenship requirement for a person to become a Supreme Court justice. No, all that is required is that the president nominates the person and that the Senate confirms the nomination. Attend a docent lecture or a Supreme Court argument and be further amazed! See p. 69.

Continue north to the end of the block to find Constitution Avenue. Turn left and follow the street to the:

4 National Gallery of Art and Sculpture Garden

You'll come to the East Wing first, whose exterior is under restoration; the museum remains open. The East Wing connects by underground passage to the West Wing, really the best way to go, so follow that route to view galleries of paintings and sculptures spanning the 13th to 19th centuries. Exit and cross 7th Street to enter the Sculpture Garden; look for the newest arrival, *Graft*, by Roxy Paine, a treelike sculpture and the first contemporary work to be installed in 10 years. See p. 102. Ready for a break? You're in the right place:

5 Pavilion Café at the National Gallery Sculpture Garden ☕

Order a sandwich and maybe some sangria (the cafe turns out excellent versions of both), and try to snag a seat at one of the outside tables so you can take in the view. ✆ **202/289-3360.** See p. 105.

See that building directly across Constitution Avenue from the Sculpture Garden? That's your next destination. Cross the street to the:

6 National Archives

Always on view are the original Charters of Freedom. You know that, right? But also look for documents displayed on a rotating basis from the Archives collection, like the original *Marbury v. Madison* Supreme Court decision, which established the role and authority of the judiciary branch of government. See p. 101.

The Supreme Court's formidable columns.

Re-cross Constitution Avenue and proceed across the National Mall to the:

7 National Air and Space Museum

This testament to human ingenuity houses a vast display of the machines we've created to fly through air and space. And yet one of this museum's enduring attractions is something that puts those human accomplishments in perspective: the Albert Einstein Planetarium, which coaxes you to wonder about the dimensions of the universe. (You'll need a ticket to enter.) See p. 99.

The Air and Space Museum.

The African Bush Elephant greets visitors in the lobby of the National Museum of Natural History.

Return to the:

8 National Mall

Walk toward the Washington Monument and take in the magnificent view, from the Capitol to the Lincoln Memorial, but also keep your eyes peeled for your senator or representative trotting past you on the path. A number of congressional members are known to take their daily constitutional along this stretch. See p. 106.

When you reach the Smithsonian Castle, cross back over the Mall to the:

9 National Museum of Natural History

This is a so-much-to-see, so-little-time venue, especially given the fact that this is the largest natural-history museum in the world. In a hurry? Do a straight walk-through: from the Mall into the Rotunda, past the African Bush Elephant, through Ocean Hall, down the stairs to the ground floor and out to Constitution Avenue, turning your head left and right as you go. You'll see a lot this way—just try it! See p. 110.

From here you can go next door (in a manner of speaking) to the:

10 National Museum of American History

This is another of D.C.'s ponderous museums. The Star-Spangled Banner is its most illustrious exhibit, but not its most popular—that would be the First Ladies exhibit of inaugural gowns and biographical information. Second most popular? The American Presidency. See p. 107.

Return to Constitution Avenue and follow the avenue past the Ellipse (count this as your White House stop, too, if you like, or follow this entire route, which ends at the White House), past the Washington Monument, all the way to the monument on Constitution Avenue between 21st and 22nd streets, the:

11 Vietnam Veterans Memorial

If you approach the memorial from this direction, the sculpture kind of sneaks up on you. Also, when you finish here and walk toward the Lincoln Memorial, be sure not to miss two other sculptures: a life-size work of three male soldiers and, nearby, the Vietnam Veterans Women's Memorial, depicting three service-women tending a wounded soldier.

Follow the path that leads to the:

12 Lincoln Memorial

There is joy to be had not just in visiting this memorial, but also in reading aloud the words inscribed on its walls. On a more practical note: Beneath the memorial is a vault with a small museum and . . . restrooms!

Follow the path that leads between the Reflecting Pool and Independence Avenue to the:

13 Korean War Veterans Memorial

The 19 life-size and lifelike stone figures depict soldiers who fought in Korea, but you may notice that they do not all wear the same uni-form. The National Park Service explains that the statues repre-sent all of the American services and are dressed accordingly.

Follow the path back toward the Washington Monument that parallels the Reflecting Pool until you reach the:

The Korean War Memorial.

14 National World War II Memorial

Here's a fact to ponder: 16 million men and women served in the military dur-ing World War II. Each of the 4,048 gold stars you see represents 100 Ameri-can military deaths, so more than 400,000 service people died during the war.

Turn toward Independence Avenue and follow the road until you reach the traffic light that allows you to cross over to the:

15 Martin Luther King, Jr. National Memorial

Since this memorial provides only snippets of Dr. King's speeches engraved on the white stone walls, you won't learn a lot about the man on your own. To get the most out of this memorial, talk to the National Park Service ranger, who is on duty daily 9:30am to 11:30am and conducts interpretive tours throughout the day.

Follow the path that leads south from the MLK Memorial to the:

16 FDR Memorial

This memorial to our 32nd president presents a number of excellent photo ops, thanks to the abundance of accessible life-size statues. Put yourself in the picture with FDR, Eleanor, figures standing in a bread line, or even FDR's doggie, Fala.

Walk through the memorial to the Tidal Basin pathway and follow it to the:

17 Jefferson Memorial

Stand inside this templelike memorial and look straight out for a marvelous view of the cherry-tree-ringed Tidal Basin (most magnificent in springtime, if you don't mind the crowds), the Washington Monument, and the White House just beyond.

From here it's a long walk—about a mile—to circle around the Tidal Basin and up to 15th Street, where you'll cross Independence Avenue to reach the:

18 Washington Monument

People often ask: Which is taller, the Washington Monument or the Capitol? The answer is the Washington Monument. But rising higher still in the landscape than both of those buildings is the Washington National Cathedral, because of its placement on a hill above the city.

Do you have the time and energy for one more site? For a better view of the White House than the one available as you walked by the Ellipse earlier, continue up 15th Street to the Pennsylvania Avenue pedestrian promenade and turn left. Too tired? Go to stop 20.

19 White House

The press seldom remarks upon it, but once you're here, you can't fail to notice that the White House park complex from the Ellipse to Lafayette Square is essentially a fortified blockade, with police and Secret Service agents everywhere: on bikes, on foot, in parked cars, on the roof of the White House, in little huts guarding driveways and garage entrances, and clustered at corners. Gotta do what's necessary. Unfortunately, such safety measures are necessary.

Ta-da, you did it! Reward yourself with a grand meal in one of the many nearby restaurants. Minutes away, at 675 15th St., is one that's always open:

20 Old Ebbitt Grill 🍽

Check out the clientele, which is usually a grab bag of local and national movers and shakers, and their staffs. The place itself is unassuming; oysters, crab cakes, and cocktails are its mainstays. ℂ **202/347-4800.** See p. 193.

WASHINGTON, D.C. FOR FAMILIES

The good thing about the capital, parents, is that history is in plain view. The National Mall, with its green sweep of landmarks from the Capitol to the Lincoln Memorial, offers plenty of opportunities for educational moments. This itinerary leans more toward fun, though as you'll see, there's a lot of learning going on, too. **Start:** *The National Aquarium.*

The Star-Spangled Banner at the National Museum of American History.

The Carousel opposite the Arts and Industries Building is popular among families.

1 National Aquarium

Ever heard of a chain catshark? How about a boneytail chub? You'll find them here, along with some 1,500 sea animals, in the "oldest aquarium in America." Fun fact: The aquarium once was located where the Washington Monument sits now. See p. 131.

Exit the aquarium, turn right on 14th Street, and head south (away from Pennsylvania Ave.) to Constitution Avenue. Cross the street and enter that enormous building right in front of you, the:

2 National Museum of American History

Like all of the Smithsonians, this one has tons of kid-friendly activities and exhibits. Check out the new exhibit on snowboarding; "interactive carts" of objects that children can pick up and experiment with, like a stereoscope; artifacts on display such as Kermit the Frog; sightings of historical figures in your midst (is that Mary Pickersgill? Yes); and the simulator rides that make you feel like you're on a roller coaster or driving a race car. See p. 107.

Exit to the National Mall and walk diagonally across it to reach the part of the Mall between the Smithsonian Castle and the Arts and Industries Building, where you'll find the:

3 Carousel

For little and not-so-little children, the carousel is a treat, operating year-round, weather permitting. It's not free, though: $3.50 per child per ride. See p. 88.

Continue down the Mall toward the Capitol until you reach the:

4 National Museum of the American Indian

Inside the museum's imagiNATIONS Activity Center, children can traipse through Amazonian stilt houses, test their balance while learning about kayaks, weave a giant basket, and learn to make beautiful music using traditional instruments. Follow up that experience with a traditional Indian meal right inside the museum at:

5 Mitsitam 💭

It's easy to learn about Native American culture when learning involves delicious bites of it: fry bread with cinnamon and honey, huckleberry fritters, "totopos," and more. 📞 **202/633-7039.** See p. 109.

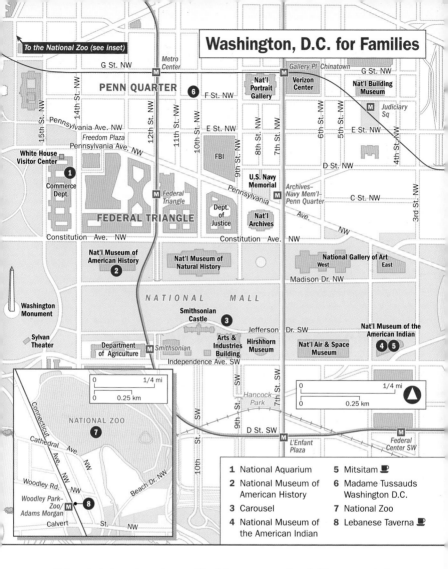

Washington, D.C. for Families

To the National Zoo (see inset)

PENN QUARTER

Metro Center

G St. NW

Gallery Pl–Chinatown

G St. NW

Nat'l Portrait Gallery

Verizon Center

Nat'l Building Museum

F St. NW

6

Judiciary Sq

E St. NW

E St. NW

Pennsylvania Ave. NW

Freedom Plaza

Pennsylvania Ave. NW

White House Visitor Center

1

Commerce Dept.

FBI

D St. NW

U.S. Navy Memorial

Pennsylvania

Federal Triangle

Archives–Navy Mem'l–Penn Quarter

C St. NW

FEDERAL TRIANGLE

Dept. of Justice

Nat'l Archives

Ave.

NW

Constitution Ave. NW

Constitution Ave. NW

Nat'l Museum of American History

2

Nat'l Museum of Natural History

National Gallery of Art

West   East

Madison Dr. NW

Washington Monument

N A T I O N A L   M A L L

Smithsonian Castle

3

Jefferson Dr. SW

Nat'l Museum of the American Indian

Sylvan Theater

Department of Agriculture

Smithsonian

Arts & Industries Building

Hirshhorn Museum

Nat'l Air & Space Museum

4 **5**

Independence Ave. SW

Hancock Park

L'Enfant Plaza

Federal Center SW

NATIONAL ZOO

7

0   1/4 mi

0   0.25 km

Connecticut Ave. NW

Cathedral Ave. NW

Woodley Rd. NW

Woodley Park–Zoo/Adams Morgan

8

Beach Dr. NW

Calvert St. NW

0   1/4 mi

0   0.25 km

1 National Aquarium	**5** Mitsitam
2 National Museum of American History	**6** Madame Tussauds Washington D.C.
3 Carousel	**7** National Zoo
4 National Museum of the American Indian	**8** Lebanese Taverna

Exit to the Independence Avenue side of the museum, walk to 3rd Street, cross Independence Avenue, and follow 3rd Street to the Federal Center SW Metro station, where you should board either a Blue or Orange line train headed in the direction of Franconia/Springfield. Debark at Metro Center, through the 11th and G streets exit, and find your next destination, at 11th and F streets:

6   Madame Tussauds Washington D.C.

Most of D.C.'s attractions are free, so this museum's full ticket price ($21 for ages 13 and over) might come as quite a shock. Purchase your tickets online and you may be able to save as much as 50%. Once inside let your kids get as goofy as they want with all 44 presidents, Beyoncé, and everyone else. See p. 130.

Still going? Return to the Metro Center station and, this time, board a Red Line train in the direction of either Shady Grove or Grosvenor. Debark at the Woodley Park–Zoo station and walk up Connecticut Avenue to reach the:

7   National Zoo

Certain children's exhibits (the Kids Farm, the pizza sculpture) lie at the very bottom of this large zoo, situated on a hill. Keep that part in mind as you explore the zoo, since it'll be all uphill—and quite a long hill it is—back to Connecticut Avenue. But you need not go all the way to the bottom of the hill, as pandas, a new elephant exhibit, and nearly 2,000 other animals that young ones will love to see are on view elsewhere in the zoo. See p. 141.

8   Lebanese Taverna ☕

If you're longing for a pick-me-up, head down Connecticut Avenue to the family-friendly establishment. The menu has something for everyone, including a gluten-free kid's meal, if your child has that allergy. On weekends the restaurant stays open straight through from noon until closing, otherwise the restaurant closes at 2:30pm and reopens at 5pm. ☏ **202/265-8681.** See p. 221.

A WOMEN'S HISTORY TOUR OF WASHINGTON, D.C.

"Remember the ladies," Abigail Adams famously advised her husband, John Adams, in 1776, when he was attending the Continental Congress and busy formulating his ideas about the new government. John Adams, who went on to become the second president of the United States in 1797, did his best. But that was a long time ago, and women have long acted as their own advocates. Perhaps one day a First Man will be compelled to urge Madame President to "remember the men." In the meantime, let us now celebrate the achievements of women in many realms. ***Start:*** *The Sewall-Belmont House on Capitol Hill.*

1   Sewall-Belmont House

The Equal Rights Amendment is just three states' votes short of ratification in Congress. Here is the proposition in its entirety: "Equality of rights under the law shall not be denied or abridged in the United States because of sex." Nineteen words. Is it so controversial? Alice Paul, founder of the National Woman's Party, headquartered here, penned the amendment in 1923. See p. 68.

From the house, head up to 1st Street and turn left. Give a nod to the Supreme Court, where three of the nine justices are women, then cross the street to reach the:

2   Capitol

The 112th Congress had 78 women representatives out of a total of 435, and 17 women senators out of a total of 50. (At press time, the November 2012 election had yet to establish the 113th Congress.) Montana Rep. Jeannette Rankin, in 1917, was the first woman elected to Congress. Look for her statue in the Capitol Visitor Center. And for in-depth information

about women in Congress, consult the excellent website http://womenin
congress.house.gov. See p. 58.

Return to Constitution Avenue and either flag a taxi (easy to do in this part of town) or
make your way on foot (about 1.5 miles) to the:

3 National Museum of American History

As has been noted, the First Ladies exhibit is the most popular one in the
museum and gives First Ladies their due as strong and interesting people in
their own right. But don't miss Julia Child's Kitchen, a tribute to a different
kind of icon. And the Star-Spangled Banner? The handiwork of a woman, or
rather, several women: Mary Pickersgill and daughter, nieces, and a maid.
See p. 107.

You could walk it, but you'll have to navigate a terrifying traffic circle; it will be safer to
hop on one of the National Park Service shuttles that goes to Arlington Cemetery
(p. 123). Hop off and walk to the memorial:

4 Women in Military Service for America Memorial

This is the only major national memorial honoring all servicewomen, from
the American Revolution onward. Its archives include information about
two nurses aboard Commodore Stephen Decatur's ship *United States* during the War of 1812, and the more recent development in 2008 when, for
the first time in military history, a woman was promoted to the rank of four-
star general in the U.S. Army. See p. 124.

**The Women in Military Service for America
Memorial.**

**A sculpture at the National Museum of
Women in the Arts.**

3

SUGGESTED ITINERARIES | A Women's History Tour of Washington, D.C.

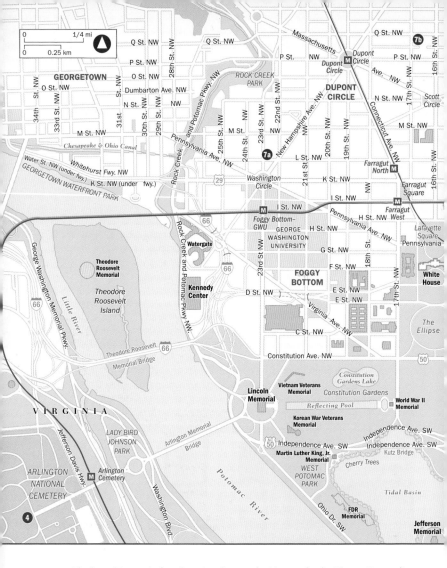

The best thing to do from here is to hop on the Metro, take the Blue or Orange line headed into D.C., and get off at Metro Center, exiting at 13th and G streets and walking a block north to the:

5 National Museum of Women in the Arts

From Renaissance paintings to contemporary sculptures to silver pieces created by 18th- and 19th-century Irish and British female silversmiths, this museum is full of masterpieces by women. See p. 133.

If it's a nice day, considering walking to your last stop, just about half a mile away. Walk to 14th Street and head north, going around Scott Circle at Massachusetts Avenue to pick up Vermont Avenue on the other side. Proceed about a block to the:

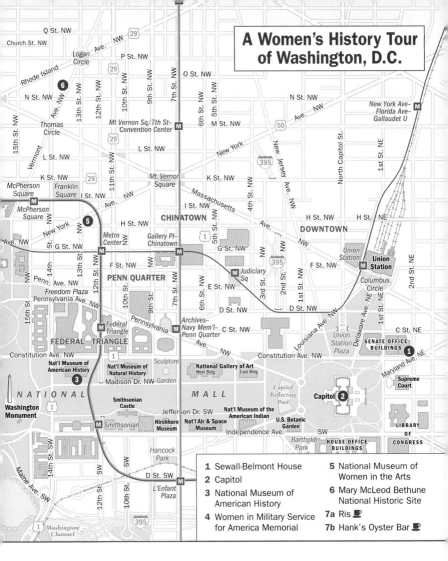

A Women's History Tour of Washington, D.C.

1 Sewall-Belmont House
2 Capitol
3 National Museum of American History
4 Women in Military Service for America Memorial
5 National Museum of Women in the Arts
6 Mary McLeod Bethune National Historic Site
7a Ris
7b Hank's Oyster Bar

6 Mary McLeod Bethune National Historic Site

Mary McLeod Bethune bought this house not as a residence, but to serve as headquarters for the National Council for Negro Women. So while she did live here from 1943 to 1949, it is the sense of her professional rather than personal life that you absorb from the exhibits. They speak volumes. Look for a black-and-white photo of FDR's cabinet in the 1930s, and there you will see a panel of white men and, in their midst, this black woman. When you consider that Bethune was born poor, the 15th of 17 children of former slaves, you start to truly appreciate her accomplishments. See p. 140.

Cap off the itinerary by dining at a restaurant where there's a woman in charge in the kitchen. Ris (p. 212) and Hank's Oyster Bar (p. 208) are among those to recommend.

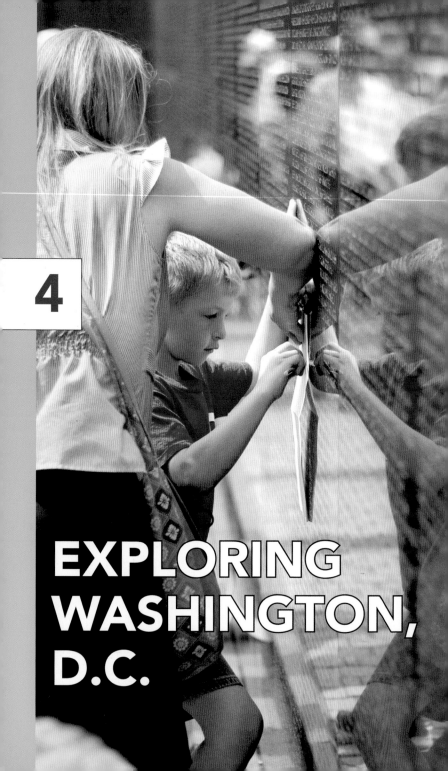

4

EXPLORING WASHINGTON, D.C.

f you've never been to Washington, D.C., your mission is clear: Get thee to the National Mall and Capitol Hill. Within this roughly 2.5-by-.3-mile rectangular plot lie the lion's share of the capital's iconic attractions (see "Iconic Washington, D.C.," in chapter 3), including presidential memorials, the U.S. Capitol, the U.S. Supreme Court, the Library of Congress, most of the Smithsonian museums, the National Gallery of Art, and the National Archives. In fact, even if you have traveled here before, you're likely to find yourself returning to this part of town, to pick up where you left off on that long list of sites worth seeing and to visit new ones, like the Martin Luther King, Jr. National Memorial, which debuted October 16, 2011.

And that's just a taste of all there is to absorb in this living, breathing exploratorium of a city: neighborhoods, standalone museums, historic houses, beautiful gardens. Tour national landmarks and you'll gain a great sense of what this country is about, politically and culturally. Tour off-the-Mall attractions and neighborhoods and you'll get a taste of the vibrant, multicultural local scene that is the real D.C. This chapter will help you do both.

WASHINGTON, D.C.'S TOP 25 SIGHTS & ATTRACTIONS

4

EXPLORING WASHINGTON, D.C.

Washington, D.C.'s Top 25 Sights & Attractions

PREVIOUS PAGE: **Visitors making a rubbing at the Vietnam Veterans Memorial.**

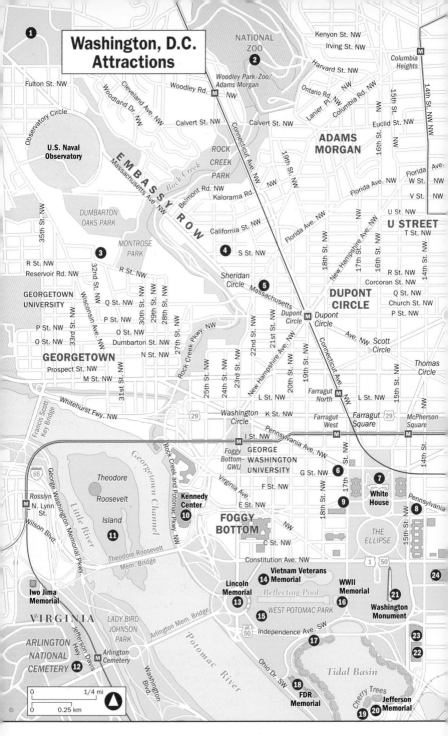

Washington, D.C. Attractions

❶

NATIONAL ZOO **❷**

Kenyon St. NW

Irving St. NW

Harvard St. NW

Columbia Heights **Ⓜ**

Fulton St. NW

Woodley Park-Zoo/ Adams Morgan **Ⓜ**

Woodley Rd. NW

Cleveland Ave. NW

Woodland Dr. NW

Ontario Rd. NW

Lanier Pl. NW

Columbia Rd. NW

Euclid St. NW

15th St.

14th St. NW NW

Observatory Circle

Calvert St. NW

Calvert St. NW

ADAMS MORGAN

16th St.

Florida Ave.

W St. NW

V St. NW

U.S. Naval Observatory

E M B A S S Y   R O W

Massachusetts Ave. NW

Rock Creek

ROCK CREEK PARK

Connecticut Ave. NW

Belmont Rd. NW

Kalorama Rd.

NW

19th St. NW

Florida Ave. NW

Florida Ave. NW

U St. NW

T St. NW

U STREET

35th St. NW

DUMBARTON OAKS PARK

California St. NW

18th St.

17th St. NW

16th St. NW

15th St.

14th St. NW

MONTROSE PARK

❹ S St. NW

Sheridan Circle

New Hampshire Ave. NW

R St. NW

Corcoran St. NW

R St. NW

Reservoir Rd. NW

❸

Massachusetts

❺

Dupont Circle

DUPONT CIRCLE

Q St. NW

Church St. NW

P St. NW

GEORGETOWN UNIVERSITY

32nd St. NW

Q St. NW

31st St. NW

30th St. NW

29th St. NW

28th St. NW

Dupont Circle **Ⓜ**

Wisconsin Ave. NW

P St. NW

O St. NW

Ave. NW

Scott Circle

GEORGETOWN

Prospect St. NW

33rd St. NW

Dumbarton St. NW

N St. NW

Rock Creek Pkwy. NW

25th St. NW

24th St. NW

23rd St. NW

22nd St. NW

21st St. NW

20th St. NW

19th St. NW

Thomas Circle

M St. NW

Farragut North **Ⓜ**

L St. NW

18th St. NW

17th St. NW

16th St.

15th St.

Whitehurst Fwy. NW

31st St. NW

Washington Circle

L St. NW

K St. NW

Farragut West

Ⓜ

Farragut Square

29

McPherson Square

Ⓜ

Francis Scott Key Bridge

66

Pennsylvania Ave. NW

I St. NW

Foggy Bottom-GWU **Ⓜ**

GEORGE WASHINGTON UNIVERSITY

G St. NW

❻

17th St. NW

14th St.

Georgetown Channel

Rock Creek and Potomac Pkwy. NW

Virginia Ave. NW

F St. NW

❼

White House

Pennsylvania

❽

Theodore Roosevelt

Kennedy Center

❿

FOGGY BOTTOM

E St. NW

18th St. NW

❾

15th St. NW

Rosslyn **Ⓜ**

N. Lynn St.

George Washington Memorial Pkwy.

Wilson Blvd.

Island

NW

C St. NW

THE ELLIPSE

Little River

❶❶

Constitution Ave. NW

1 **50**

24

VIRGINIA

Theodore Roosevelt Mem. Bridge

Vietnam Veterans Memorial

❶❹

Reflecting Pool

WWII Memorial

❶❻

❷❶

Iwo Jima Memorial

LADY BIRD JOHNSON PARK

Lincoln Memorial

❶❸

WEST POTOMAC PARK

Washington Monument

Arlington Mem. Bridge

❶❺

❷❸

ARLINGTON NATIONAL CEMETERY

Jefferson Davis Hwy.

Arlington Cemetery

alt **50**

Independence Ave. SW

❶❼

❷❷

❶❷

Washington Blvd.

Potomac River

Ohio Dr. SW

Tidal Basin

Cherry Trees

❶❽

FDR Memorial

Jefferson Memorial

❶❾

❷⓿

0   1/4 mi

0   0.25 km

Anacostia Community
    Museum **53**
Arlington National Cemetery **12**
Arts and Industries Building **30**
Bureau of Engraving
    and Printing **22**
Capitol **47**
Corcoran Gallery of Art **9**
Dumbarton Oaks **3**
Enid A. Haupt Garden **29**
Franklin Delano Roosevelt
    Memorial **18**
Folger Shakespeare Library **50**
Ford's Theatre National
    Historic Site **39**
Frederick Douglass National
    Historic Site **53**
Freer Gallery of Art **27**
George Mason Memorial **19**
Hirshhorn Museum and
    Sculpture Garden **31**
International Spy Museum **43**
Jefferson Memorial **20**
John F. Kennedy Center
    for the Performing Arts **10**
Korean War Veterans
    Memorial **15**
Library of Congress **49**
Lincoln Memorial **13**
Madame Tussauds
    Washington D.C. **40**
Marian Koshland
    Science Museum **44**
Martin Luther King, Jr.
    National Memorial **17**
National Air and Space
    Museum **32**
National Archives **36**
National Gallery of Art **34**

National Gallery
    Sculpture Garden **35**
National Museum of African Art **29**
National Museum of
    American History **24**
National Museum of
    the American Indian **33**
National Museum of
    Crime and Punishment **38**
National Museum of
    Natural History **25**
National Museum of
    Women in the Arts **41**
National Postal Museum **45**
National World War II Memorial **16**
National Zoological Park **2**
Newseum **37**
Phillips Collection **5**
Renwick Gallery of the Smithsonian
    American Art Museum **6**
Ripley Center **26**
Sackler Gallery **28**
Sewall-Belmont House **52**
Smithsonian American Art Museum
    and National Portrait Gallery **42**
Smithsonian Information Center **26**
Supreme Court **51**
Textile Museum **4**
Theodore Roosevelt Island **11**
Union Station **46**
U.S. Botanic Garden **48**
U.S. Holocaust Memorial
    Museum **23**
Vietnam Veterans Memorial **14**
Washington Monument **21**
Washington National Cathedral **1**
White House **7**
White House Visitor Center **8**
Woodrow Wilson House Museum **4**

Heads Up

Security precautions and procedures are a post-9/11 fact of life everywhere in America, but especially in the nation's capital, thanks to the preponderance of federal structures and attractions that are open to the public. What that means for you as a visitor is that you may have to stand in line to enter a national museum (like one of the Smithsonians) or a government building (like the Library of Congress). At many tourist sites, you can expect staff to search handbags, briefcases, and backpacks, either by hand or by X-ray machine. Some sites, including the National Air and Space Museum, require you to walk past metal detectors. During the busy spring and summer seasons, you may be queuing outside as you wait your turn to pass through security. So pack your patience, but otherwise carry as little as possible, and certainly no sharp objects. Museums and public buildings rarely offer lockers for use by visitors.

The Statue of Freedom atop the Capitol dome.

CAPITOL HILL

The U.S. Capitol and its campus of Senate and House office buildings dominate this residential neighborhood of tree-lined streets, 19th-century town houses, and pubs and casual eateries. Across the street from the Capitol lie the U.S. Supreme Court and the Library of Congress; close by are the smaller but fascinating **Folger Shakespeare Library,** the **Sewall-Belmont House,** and **Eastern Market** (pages 64/68/228). A bit farther away is **Union Station,** doing triple duty as historical attraction, shopping mall, and transportation hub. But the neighborhood itself is a pleasure. Explore.

The Capitol ★★★ GOVERN-MENT BUILDING   The U.S. Capitol Building centers a 450-acre campus that includes House and Senate office buildings, the U.S. Botanic Garden (located at the foot of the Capitol, so look for its listing in the National Mall section), the Library of Congress, and the Supreme Court. Immediately surrounding the Capitol are 59 acres of beautifully kept grounds, originally landscaped in 1892 by Frederick Law Olmsted, who also planned New York City's Central Park. Stroll these winding paths and admire the flower plantings and memorial trees. Before you get too close to the Capitol, stand back to take a look at the "Statue of Freedom," the 19-foot, 6-inch bronze female figure crowning the Capitol's dome. (You'll get to see the plaster model for the statue on display in the Capitol Visitor Center's Emancipation

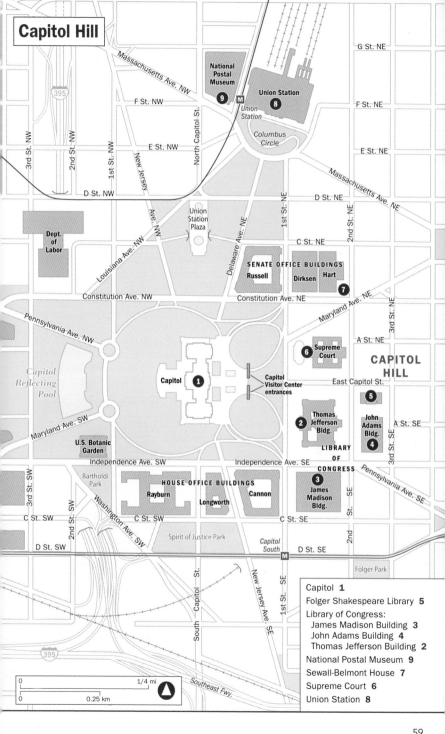

Capitol Hill

National Postal Museum **9**

M Union Station

Union Station **8**

Columbus Circle

G St. NE

F St. NE

E St. NE

Massachusetts Ave. NW

F St. NW

E St. NW

D St. NW

D St. NE

D St. NE

C St. NE

395

3rd St. NW

2nd St. NW

1st St. NW

North Capitol St.

New Jersey Ave. NW

Union Station Plaza

Delaware Ave. NE

1st St. NE

2nd St. NE

Dept. of Labor

Louisiana Ave. NW

SENATE OFFICE BUILDINGS
Russell

Dirksen Hart

7

Constitution Ave. NW

Constitution Ave. NE

Maryland Ave. NE

3rd St. NE

Pennsylvania Ave. NW

A St. NE

Supreme Court **6**

CAPITOL HILL

Capitol Reflecting Pool

Capitol **1**

Capitol Visitor Center entrances

East Capitol St.

Maryland Ave. SW

5

A St. SE

Thomas Jefferson Bldg. **2**

John Adams Bldg. **4**

3rd St. SE

U.S. Botanic Garden

Independence Ave. SW

LIBRARY OF CONGRESS

Independence Ave. SE

Bartholdi Park

HOUSE OFFICE BUILDINGS
Rayburn   Longworth   Cannon

James Madison Bldg. **3**

Pennsylvania Ave. SE

3rd St. SW

2nd St. SW

Washington Ave. SW

C St. SW

C St. SW

C St. SE

2nd St. SE

D St. SW

Spirit of Justice Park

Capitol South **M**

D St. SE

Folger Park

South Capitol St.

1st St. SE

New Jersey Ave. SE

395

Southeast Fwy.

| 0 | | 1/4 mi |
| 0 | 0.25 km | |

Capitol **1**
Folger Shakespeare Library **5**
Library of Congress:
  James Madison Building **3**
  John Adams Building **4**
  Thomas Jefferson Building **2**
National Postal Museum **9**
Sewall-Belmont House **7**
Supreme Court **6**
Union Station **8**

Call Ahead

Here's a crucial piece of advice: **Call the places you plan to tour each day before you set out.** Many of Washington's government buildings, museums, memorials, and monuments are open to the general public nearly all the time—except when they're not.

Because buildings like the Capitol, the Supreme Court, and the White House are offices as well as tourist destinations, the business of the day always poses the potential for closing one of those sites, or at least sections, to sightseers. There's also the matter of maintenance. The steady stream of visitors to Washington's attractions necessitates ongoing caretaking, which may require closing an entire landmark, or part of it, to the public, or changing the hours of operation or procedures for visiting. Finally, Washington's famous museums, grand halls, and public gardens double as settings for press conferences, galas, special exhibits, festivals, and even movie sets. You might arrive at, say, the National Air and Space Museum on a Sunday afternoon, only to find some or all of its galleries off-limits because a movie shoot is underway. (Have you seen *Night at the Museum: Battle of the Smithsonian*, by the way?) To avoid frustration and disappointment, call ahead.

Hall.) December 2, 2013, marks the 150th anniversary of the placement of the statue upon the top of the dome.

The Capitol is as majestic up close as it is from afar. For 135 years it sheltered not only both houses of Congress, but also the Supreme Court and, for 97 years, the Library of Congress. As you tour the Capitol, you'll learn about America's history as you admire the place in which it unfolded. Classical architecture, interior embellishments, and hundreds of paintings, sculptures, and other artworks are integral elements of the Capitol. The hourlong guided tour (for procedures, see below) starts in the Capitol Visitor Center, where you'll watch a 13-minute orientation film, then takes you to the Rotunda, National Statuary Hall, down to the Crypt, and back to the Visitor Center. (Get a jumpstart learning about the history and art of the Capitol by going to www.visitthecapitol.gov and clicking on "About the Capitol," then the link "Evolution of the Capitol." The Architect of the Capitol's website, www.aoc.gov, is even more informative.)

The **Rotunda**—a huge 96-foot-wide circular hall capped by a 180-foot-high dome—is the hub of the Capitol. The dome was completed, at Lincoln's direction, while the Civil War was being fought: "If people see the Capitol going on, it is a sign we intend the Union shall

Bust of Martin Luther King, Jr. in the Capitol's Rotunda.

go on," said Lincoln. Eleven presidents have lain in state here, with former President Gerald Ford, in 2006, being the most recent; when President Kennedy's casket was displayed, the line of mourners stretched 40 blocks. On rare occasions, someone other than a president, military hero, or member of Congress receives this posthumous recognition. In October 2005, Congress paid tribute to Rosa Parks by allowing her body to lie in state here, the first woman to be so honored. (Parks was the black woman who in 1955 refused to relinquish her seat to a white man on a bus in Montgomery, Alabama, thereby helping to spark the civil rights movement.)

Embracing the Rotunda walls are eight immense oil paintings commemorating great moments in American history, such as the presentation of the Declaration of Independence and the surrender of Cornwallis at Yorktown. Inside the eye, or inner dome, of the Rotunda is an allegorical fresco masterpiece by Constantino Brumidi, *The Apotheosis of Washington*, a symbolic portrayal of George Washington surrounded by Roman gods and goddesses watching over the progress of the nation. Brumidi was known as the "Michelangelo of the Capitol" for the many works he created throughout the building. (Take another look at the fresco and find the woman directly below Washington; the triumphant *Armed Freedom* figure is said to be modeled after Lola Germon, a beautiful young actress with whom the 60-year-old Brumidi conceived a child.) Beneath those painted figures is a *trompe l'oeil* frieze depicting major developments in the life of America, from Columbus's landing in 1492 to the birth of the aviation age in 1903. Don't miss the sculptures in the Rotunda, including: a pensive Abraham Lincoln; a dignified Rev. Dr. Martin Luther King, Jr.; a ponderous trinity of suffragists Elizabeth Cady Stanton, Susan B. Anthony, and Lucretia Mott; a bronze statue of President Ronald Reagan, looking characteristically genial and confident; and the newest arrival, a likeness in granite of President Gerald Ford.

The **National Statuary Hall** was originally the chamber of the House of Representatives; in 1864 it became Statuary Hall, and the states were invited to send two statues each of native sons and daughters to the hall. There are 100 statues in all, New Mexico completing the original collection with its contribution in 2005 of Po'Pay, a Pueblo Indian, who in 1680 led a revolt against the Spanish that helped to save Pueblo culture. (Stay tuned: Some believe that Puerto Rico may soon become the country's 51st state.) States do have the prerogative to replace statues with new choices, which is what Michigan did in 2011, swapping out the 1913 choice of Detroit mayor and U.S. Senator Zachariah Chandler for President Ford. Because of space constraints, only 38 statues or so reside in the Hall, with the figures of presidents displayed in the Rotunda, 24 statues placed in the Visitor Center, and the remaining scattered throughout the corridors of the Capitol. Statues include Ethan Allen, the Revolutionary War hero who founded the state of Vermont, and Missouri's Thomas Hart Benton—not the 20th-century artist famous for his rambunctious murals, but his namesake and uncle, who was one of the first two senators from Missouri and whose antislavery stance in 1850 cost him his Senate seat. Nine women are represented, including Alabama-born Helen Keller and Montana's Jeannette Rankin, the first woman to serve in Congress.

The **Crypt** of the Capitol lies directly below the Rotunda and is used mainly as an exhibit space.

In slow seasons, usually fall and winter, your public tour may include a visit to the **Old Supreme Court Chamber,** which has been restored to its mid-19th-century appearance. The Supreme Court met here from 1810 to 1860. Busts of the

THE CAPITOL visitor center

Until the Capitol Visitor Center opened in November 2008 (after 7 years of construction), visitors to the Capitol had to wait outside in long lines in all kinds of weather, first to obtain tour passes and then to actually enter the Capitol. It was miserable. The simultaneous opening of the center and inauguration of an online tour reservation system makes a visit to the Capitol a joy, by comparison.

The enormous, 4,000-person-capacity Capitol Visitor Center is underground, which means that as you approach the East Front of the Capitol, you won't actually see it. But look for signs and the sloping sets of steps on either side of the Capitol's central section, leading down to the center's entrances. Once inside you'll pass through security screening and then enter the two-level chamber. If you have time before or after your tour, you'll find plenty to do here. (Most visitors find it works better to explore the center after touring the Capitol.) You can admire the 24 Statuary Hall statues scattered throughout and tour Exhibition Hall, which is a minimuseum of historic document displays; check out interactive kiosks that take you on virtual tours of the Capitol, filling you in on history, art, and architecture; and marvel at exhibits that explain the legislative process. Emancipation Hall is the large central chamber where you line up for tours; this is also where you'll find the 26 restrooms and 530-seat restaurant. The visitor center is open Monday through Saturday year-round from 8:30am to 4:30pm, but closed on Thanksgiving, Christmas, New Year's Day, and Inauguration Day.

first four chief justices are on display—John Marshall, John Rutledge, John Jay, and Oliver Ellsworth—and so are some of their desks, believed to have been purchased in the 1830s. The justices handed down a number of noteworthy decisions here, including that of *Dred Scott v. Sandford,* which denied the citizenship of blacks, whether slaves or free, and in so doing precipitated the nation's Civil War.

You will not see them on your tour, but the **south and north wings** of the Capitol hold the House and Senate chambers, respectively. The House of Representatives chamber is the setting for the president's annual State of the Union addresses. (See the information below about watching Senate and House activity.)

Procedures for Touring the Capitol: Tours of the Capitol are free and take place year-round, Monday through Saturday between 8:50am and 3:20pm. Capitol Guide Service guides lead the hourlong, general public tours, which can include as few as one or two people or as many as 40 or 50, depending on the season. Here I must sing the praises of these guides, who are often historians in their own right, repositories of American lore, traditions, anecdotes, and, of course, actual fact. Got a question? Ask away. These guides know their stuff.

You and everyone in your party must have a **timed pass,** which you can order online at www.visitthecapitol.gov. During peak spring and summer sessions, you should order tickets at least 2 weeks in advance. But same-day passes are also available daily from the tour kiosks on the east and west fronts of the Capitol and at the information desks on the lower level of the visitor center—in limited supply during peak times, but plentiful at off-peak times, particularly in January (but not around the time of the inauguration!) and February. You can also contact your representative or senator in Congress and request passes for constituent tours, which are usually limited to groups of 15 and conducted by

Brumidi's fresco in the "eye" of the inner dome of the Capitol Building.

congressional staff, who may take you to notable places in the Capitol beyond those seen on the general public tour. No matter what, call ☏ **202/225-6827** in advance of your visit; that way you'll know for sure whether the Capitol is open.

The Capitol has quite a list of items it prohibits; you can read the list online at www.visitthecapitol.gov or listen to a recitation by calling the phone number above. Items ranging from large bags of any kind to food and drink are prohibited; leave everything you can back at the hotel.

The Capitol Guide Service also offers other special tours and talks on an ongoing basis, though the specific topics might change. Recent offerings included tours of the Brumidi Corridors and tours that focused on the Capitol and Congress during the Civil War. Look online or ask at the visitor center information desk for details about these presentations.

Procedures for Visiting the House Gallery or Senate Gallery: Both the Senate and House galleries are open to visitors whenever either body is **in session ★–★★★**, so do try to sit in. (The experience receives a range of star ratings because a visit can prove fascinating or deathly boring, depending on whether a debate is underway and how lively it is.) Otherwise the Senate Gallery is open to visitors during scheduled recesses, Monday to Friday 9am to 4:15pm, and the House Gallery is open to visitors year-round Monday to Friday 9am to 4:15pm. Children 5 and under are not allowed in the Senate gallery. You can obtain visitor passes at the offices of your representative and senator, or in the case of District of Columbia and Puerto Rico residents, from the office of your delegate to Congress. To find out your member's office location, go online at www.house.gov or www.senate.gov and follow the links to your state representative's or your senators' information, or call ☏ **202/225-3121** to speak to a Capitol operator. *Note:* You must have a separate pass for each gallery. Once obtained, the passes are good through the remainder of the Congress.

Contrary to popular belief, members of Congress do not have their main offices inside the Capitol building itself, though many of the senior ranking members do have Capitol "hideaways," which are exactly what they sound like: places away from the fray where they can take care of business without interruption. The main, staffed offices of congressional representatives and delegates are in House buildings on the south (Independence Avenue) side of the Capitol; senators' main, staffed offices are located in Senate buildings on the north (Constitution Avenue) side of the Capitol. If you need help or directions, just ask one of the many Capitol Hill police officers in the area. You should be able to pick up passes to both the Senate and House galleries in one place, at either your representative's office or one of your senators' offices. (*Note:* International visitors can obtain both House and Senate gallery passes by presenting a passport or a valid driver's license with photo ID to staff at the House and Senate Appointments desks on the upper level of the visitor center, near the main entrance.) Visit the Architect of the Capitol's website, **www.aoc.gov**, the Visitor Center website, **www.visitthecapitol.gov**, or call your senator or congressperson's office for more exact information about obtaining passes to the House and Senate galleries.

You'll know that the House and/or the Senate is in session if you see flags flying over their respective wings of the Capitol (**Remember:** House, south side; Senate, north side), or you can visit their websites, **www.house.gov** and **www. senate.gov,** for an in-depth education on the legislative process; schedules of bill debates in the House and Senate, committee markups, and meetings; and links to your Senate or House representative's page.

Capitol and Capitol Visitor Center: E. Capitol St. (at 1st St. NW). www.visitthecapitol.gov, www. aoc.gov, www.house.gov, www.senate.gov. 𝄐 **202/225-6827** (recording), 202/593-1768 (Capitol Guide Service Office), or 202/225-3121 (Capitol operator). Free admission. Year-round Mon–Sat 8:30am–4:30pm (first tour at 8:50am, last tour at 3:20pm). Closed for tours Sun and Jan 1, Thanksgiving, Dec 25, and Inauguration Day. Parking at Union Station or on neighborhood streets. Metro: Union Station (Massachusetts Ave. exit) or Capitol South, then walk to the Capitol Visitor Center, located on the East Front of the Capitol.

Folger Shakespeare Library ★ 🎁 LIBRARY   "Shakespeare taught us that the little world of the heart is vaster, deeper, and richer than the spaces of astronomy," wrote Ralph Waldo Emerson in 1864. A decade later, Amherst student Henry Clay Folger was profoundly affected by a lecture Emerson gave similarly extolling the Bard. Folger purchased an inexpensive set of Shakespeare's plays and went on to amass the world's largest (by far) collection of the Bard's works, today housed in the Folger Shakespeare Library. By 1930, when Folger and his wife, Emily, laid the cornerstone of a building to house the collection, it comprised 93,000 books, 50,000 prints and engravings, and thousands of manuscripts. The Folgers gave it all as a gift to the American people. The library opened in 1932.

John Gregory's 1932 sculpture at the Folger Shakespeare Library depicts Shakespeare's *A Midsummer Night's Dream.*

The Folger Shakespeare Library's Great Hall.

The building itself has a marble facade decorated with nine bas-relief scenes from Shakespeare's plays; it is a striking example of Art Deco classicism. A statue of Puck stands in the west garden. An **Elizabethan garden** on the east side of the building is planted with flowers and herbs of the period. Most remarkable here are eight sculptures, each depicting figures from a particular scene in a Shakespeare play. Each work is welded onto the top of a pedestal, on which are inscribed the play's lines that inspired the sculptor, Greg Wyatt. These statues are half the size of those that Wyatt created for the Great Garden at New Place in Stratford-upon-Avon, England. Inquire about **guided tours** scheduled at 10 and 11am on every first and third Saturday from April to October. The garden is also a nice, quiet place to have a picnic.

The facility, which houses some 256,000 books, 116,000 of which are rare (pre-1801), is an important research center not only for Shakespearean scholars, but also for those studying any aspect of the English and continental Renaissance. Other features entertain the general public: A multimedia computer exhibition called "The Shakespeare Gallery" offers users a close-up look at some of the Folgers' treasures, as well as Shakespeare's life and works. The white-oak-paneled, Tudor-ish **Great Hall** rotates exhibits of items from the permanent collection—Renaissance musical instruments to centuries-old playbills—to highlight a particular theme. In 2012, for instance, Shakespeare's Sisters: Voices of English and European Women Writers, 1500–1700 presented historical documents, manuscripts, and artwork related to the works of more than 50 16th- and 17th-century female writers. Plan on spending at least 30 minutes here.

At the end of the Great Hall is a theater designed to suggest the yard of an Elizabethan inn, where plays, concerts, readings, and Shakespeare-related events take place (see chapter 8 for details).

201 E. Capitol St. SE. www.folger.edu. ✆ **202/544-4600.** Free admission. Mon–Sat 10am–5pm; Sun noon–5pm. Free walk-in tours Mon–Fri 11am and 3pm; Sat 11am and 1pm; Sun 1pm. Closed federal holidays. Metro: Capitol South or Union Station.

Library of Congress ★★ LIBRARY   You're inside the main public building of the Library of Congress—the magnificent, ornate, Italian Renaissance–style **Thomas Jefferson Building.** Maybe you've arrived via the tunnel that connects the Capitol and the Library of Congress, or maybe you've entered through the 1st Street doors. In any case, you may be startled to find yourself suddenly inside a government structure whose every surface is covered in detailed embellishment. Before you stop in the **Orientation Galleries,** line up for that tour, or enmesh yourself in the library's literature, first take time to stroll around the building, from the ground floor to the **Great Hall** to the **Main Reading Room Overlook,** and just gape. Look up to admire the stained-glass skylights overhead; glance down to notice the Italian marble floors inlaid with brass and concentric medallions; gaze right, left, and all around to try to take in the gorgeous murals, allegorical paintings, stenciling, sculptures, and intricately carved architectural elements that make this building a visual treasure.

Now for the history lesson: Established in 1800 by an act of Congress, "for the purchase of such books as may be necessary for the use of Congress," the library today also serves the nation, with holdings for the visually impaired (for whom books are recorded on cassette and/or translated into Braille), scholars in every field, college students, journalists, teachers, and researchers of all kinds. Its first collection of books was destroyed in 1814 when the British burned the Capitol (where the library was then housed) during the War of 1812. Thomas Jefferson then sold the institution his personal library of 6,487 books as a replacement, and this became the foundation of what would grow to become the world's largest library.

The Jefferson Building was erected between 1888 and 1897 to hold the burgeoning collection and to establish America as a cultured nation with magnificent institutions equal to anything in Europe. Originally intended to hold the fruits of at least 150 years of collecting, the Jefferson Building was, in fact, filled up in a mere 13 years. It is now supplemented by the **James Madison Memorial Building** and the **John Adams Building.**

Today the collection contains a mind-boggling 151.8 million items. Its buildings house more than 34.5 million cataloged books; 63 million manuscripts; millions and millions of prints and photographs, audio holdings (discs, tapes, talking books, and so on), movies, and videotapes; musical instruments from the 1700s; and the letters and papers of everyone from George Washington to Groucho Marx. Its archives also include the letters, oral histories, photographs, and other documents of war veterans from World War I to the present, all part of its **Veterans History Project;** go to www.loc.gov/vets to listen to or read some of these stories, especially if you plan on visiting the National World War II Memorial (p. 112).

In addition to its art and architecture, the Library displays ongoing exhibits of objects taken from its permanent collections; Exploring

Visitors at the Library of Congress's Main Reading Room Overlook.

The Library of Congress's Main Reading Room.

the Early Americas and Thomas Jefferson's Library were two shows going on at press time. Be sure to check the LOC website before you come. The concerts that take place in the Jefferson Building's elegant **Coolidge Auditorium** are free but require tickets, which you can obtain through Ticketmaster (www.ticket master.com). Across Independence Avenue from the Jefferson Building is the **Madison Building,** which houses the Copyright Office and the **Mary Pickford Theater,** a venue for classic film screenings.

Anyone 16 and over may use the library's collections, but first you must obtain a user card with your photo on it. You can get the process started by pre-registering online at https://wwws.loc.gov/readerreg/remote. Whether pre-registered or not, you must go to Reader Registration in Room LM 140 (street level of the Madison Building) and present your driver's license or passport. Staff will verify your identity, take a photo, and present you with your user card. Then head to the Information Desk in either the Jefferson or the Madison building to find out about the research resources available to you and how to use them. Most likely, you will be directed to the Main Reading Room. All books must be used on-site.

Jefferson Building: 1st St. SE, between Independence Ave. and E. Capitol St. Madison Building: 101 Independence Ave. SE (at 1st St. SE). www.loc.gov. ✆ **202/707-8000.** Free admission. Madison Building Mon–Fri 8:30am–9:30pm; Sat 8:30am–5pm. Jefferson Building Mon–Sat 8:30am–4:30pm. Closed federal holidays. Stop at an information desk on the 1st floor of the Jefferson Building. Docent-led tours of the Jefferson Building are free, require no reservations or tickets, and take place Mon–Fri 10:30 and 11:30am, and 1:30, 2:30, and 3:30pm; Sat 10:30 and 11:30am, and 1:30 and 2:30pm. Contact your congressional representatives to obtain tickets for congressional, or "VIP," tours (slightly more personalized tours). Metro: Capitol South.

National Postal Museum ★ MUSEUM   By the time you read this, in 2013, the Postal Museum should have expanded to add a 12,000-square-foot gallery at street level (the main section is one level down), with room for a welcome center and more exhibit and public program areas. But whether or not the new **William H. Gross Stamp Gallery** has debuted in time for your visit, you'll still want to stop by.

This museum remains a hit, especially for families, but anyone might spend a pleasant hour here. Bring your address book, and you can send postcards to the folks back home through an interactive exhibit that issues a cool postcard and stamps it. That's just one feature that makes this museum visitor-friendly. Many of its exhibits involve easy-to-understand activities, like postal-themed video games. The museum documents America's postal history from 1673 (about 170 years before the advent of stamps, envelopes, and mailboxes) to the present. (Did you know that a dog sled was used to carry mail in Alaska until 1963, when it was replaced by an airplane?) In the central gallery, suspended from the 90-foot-high atrium ceiling, are three planes that carried mail in the early decades of the 20th century. These, along with a re-created railway mail car, an 1851 mail/passenger coach, a replica of an airmail beacon tower, and city mail vehicles such as the 1931 Ford Model A mail truck,

The National Postal Museum documents America's postal history, from 1673 to the present.

are all part of the **Moving the Mail** exhibit. **Customers and Communities** traces the evolution of mail delivery as it expanded to reach growing populations in both rural areas and the cities. In **Binding the Nation,** historic correspondence illustrates how mail kept families together in the developing nation. Several exhibits deal with the famed **Pony Express,** a service that lasted less than 2 years but was romanticized to legendary proportions by Buffalo Bill and others. In the Civil War section, you'll learn about Henry "Box" Brown, a slave who had himself "mailed" from Richmond to a Pennsylvania abolitionist in 1856. The museum launched two new permanent exhibits in 2012: **Systems at Work,** which re-creates the journey of a single piece of mail from sender to recipient, as it might have occurred at different times in the past 200 years; and **Mail Call,** which tells the story of the military's postal system. In addition, the museum houses a vast research library for philatelic researchers and scholars, a stamp store, and a museum shop. Inquire about free walk-in tours at the information desk.

Opened in 1993, this off-the-Mall Smithsonian museum occupies the lower and street levels of the palatial Beaux Arts quarters of the Old City Post Office Building, which was designed by architect Daniel Burnham and is situated next to Union Station.

2 Massachusetts Ave. NE (at 1st St.). www.postalmuseum.si.edu. ⓒ **202/633-5555.** Free admission. Daily 10am–5:30pm. Closed Dec 25. Metro: Union Station.

Sewall-Belmont House MUSEUM   A must for those interested in women's history, this historic house has served as headquarters for the National Woman's Party since 1929, acting solely as an education and advocacy organization since 1997. Displays of memorabilia from the women's suffrage movement help tell the stories of Alice Paul, founder of the National Woman's Party, and of other leaders in the women's movement, as well as the events that have helped bring about equal rights for women. The house holds the largest collection of suffragist artifacts in the country, including banners, sashes, costumes, and political buttons worn by demonstrators during women's equality campaigns during the 20th century. Only about 250 out of the 2,600-piece collection are on view at any given time.

144 Constitution Ave. NE (at 2nd St.). www.sewallbelmont.org. © **202/546-1210.** Free admission. Mar–Dec Wed–Sun noon–5pm; by appointment only Jan–Feb. Closed Thanksgiving, Dec 25, and New Year's Day. Metro: Union Station or Capitol South.

Supreme Court ★★★ GOVERNMENT BUILDING   The highest tribunal in the nation, the Supreme Court is charged with the power of "judicial review": deciding whether actions of Congress, the president, the states, and lower courts (in other words, of all branches of government and government officials) are in accordance with the Constitution, and applying the Constitution's enduring principles to novel situations and a changing country. Arguably the most powerful people in the nation, the Court's chief justice and eight associate justices hear only about 100 of the most vital of the 10,000 or so petitions filed with the Court every year. The Court's rulings are final, reversible only by an Act of Congress.

Hard to believe, but the Supreme Court—in existence since 1789—did not have its own building until 1935. The justices met in New York, Philadelphia, and assorted nooks of the Capitol (see above) until they finally got their own place. Architect Cass Gilbert, best known for his skyscrapers (like New York's 761-foot-high Woolworth building), designed the stately Corinthian marble palace that houses the Court today.

You'll have plenty of time to admire the exterior of this magnificent structure if you're in town when the Court is in session and decide to try **to see a case being argued ★★★** because—yup, you guessed it—you have to wait in line (sometimes for hours) on the front plaza of the building. But do try! Only in Washington does a wait in line grant one the privilege of watching and listening to the country's nine foremost legal experts nimbly and intensely dissect the merits of both sides of an argument, the outcome of which could profoundly affect the nation.

Starting the first Monday in October and continuing through late April, the Court "sits" for 2 weeks out of every month to hear two to four arguments each day Monday through Wednesday, from 10am to noon and from 1 to 2 or 3pm. You

Protesters on the Supreme Court Plaza.

can find out the specific dates and names of arguments in advance by calling the Supreme Court (☏ **202/479-3211**) or by going to the website, **www.supreme court.gov**, where the argument calendar and the "Merits Briefs" (case descriptions) are posted.

Plan on arriving at the Supreme Court at least 90 minutes in advance of a scheduled argument during the fall and winter, and as early as 3 hours ahead in March and April, when schools are often on spring break and students lengthen the line. (Dress warmly; the stone plaza is exposed and can be witheringly cold.) Controversial cases also attract crowds; if you're not sure whether a particular case has created a stir, call the Court information line to reach someone who can tell you. The Court allots only about 150 first-come, first-served seats to the general public, but that number fluctuates from case to case, depending on the number of seats that have been reserved by the lawyers arguing the case and by the press. The Court police officers direct you into one line initially; when the doors finally open, you form a second line if you want to attend only 3 to 5 minutes of the argument: As of May 2010, for security reasons, visitors now enter the Supreme Court Building at plaza level, through either the northwest or the southwest doors flanking the central marble staircase; in the past, visitors climbed those massive stone steps to venture through the opened 6.5-ton bronze doors securing the Court's west entrance. You'll still have a chance to look at the doors, though, since visitors are allowed to exit the building through that central portal.

Meanwhile, the justices are always at work on their opinions following Court arguments, and release these completed opinions in the courtroom throughout the argument term, October through April, and into May and June. If you attend an oral argument, you may find yourself present as well for the release of a Supreme Court opinion, since the justices precede the hearing of new oral arguments with the announcement of their opinions on previously heard arguments, if any opinions are ready. What this means is, if you're visiting the Court on a Monday in May or June, you won't be able to attend an argument, but you might still see the justices in action, delivering an opinion, during a 10am, 15-minute session in the courtroom. To attend one of these sessions, you must wait in line on the plaza, following the same procedure outlined above.

Leave your cameras, recording devices, and notebooks at your hotel— they're not allowed in the courtroom. ***Note:*** *Do* bring quarters. Security procedures require you to leave all your belongings, including outerwear, purses, books, sunglasses, and so on, in a cloak room where there are coin-operated lockers that accept only quarters.

Once inside pay close attention to the many rituals. At 10am the marshal announces the entrance of the justices, and all present rise and remain standing while the justices take their seats (in high-backed, cushioned swivel chairs) following the announcement: "The Honorable, the Chief Justice and Associate Justices of the Supreme Court of the United States. Oyez! Oyez! Oyez! All persons having business before the Honorable, the Supreme Court of the United States, are admonished to draw near and give their attention, for the Court is now sitting. God save the United States and this Honorable Court!" Unseen by the gallery is the "conference handshake"; following a 19th-century tradition symbolizing a "harmony of aims if not views," each justice shakes hands with each of the other eight when they assemble to go to the bench. The Court has a record of prior proceedings and relevant briefs, so each side is allowed only a 30-minute argument. (***Note:*** Every Friday in an argument week, the Supreme Court posts on its website the audio recordings of all arguments heard that week; to listen, go to the Court's home page, click on "Oral Arguments" and then "Argument Audio," find the argument you want from those listed, and click on the link to get started.)

Not interested in or able to attend an argument or opinion delivery? No worries. At times when the Court is finished with arguments for the day, and on days when the Court is not in session at all, docents offer 30-minute lectures inside the Supreme Court chamber, to introduce visitors of all ages to the Court's judicial functions, the building's history, and the architecture of the courtroom. Lectures take place every hour on the half-hour, beginning at 9:30am on days when the Court is not sitting and at a later time on Court days. You can also tour the building on your own (first stop by the ground-floor Information Desk to pick up a helpful flyer), view exhibits, and watch a film on the workings of the Court. In fact, that short film is a good preliminary to the docent lecture, so you may want to time your visit accordingly.

A gift shop and a public cafeteria are open to the public.

1 1st St. NE (btw. E. Capitol St. and Maryland Ave. NE). www.supremecourt.gov. ⓒ **202/479-3000.** Free admission. Mon–Fri 9am–4:30pm. Closed all federal holidays. Metro: Capitol South or Union Station.

Union Station ★ MARKET   When you visit Union Station, you're stepping into the heart (or at least into a major artery) of everyday Washington life. Located within walking distance and full view of the Capitol, the station is a vital crossroads for locals. You'll see Hill staffers who debark the Metro's Red Line at its stop here ("Union Station" is the station name, naturally); commuters who ride MARC and Amtrak trains from outlying cities such as Baltimore; residents who walk or Metro here to shop, work, dine, or dawdle; and travelers from all over who arrive and depart by train all day long.

When it opened in 1907, this was the largest train station in the world. It was designed by noted architect Daniel H. Burnham, who modeled it after the Baths of Diocletian and the Arch of Constantine in Rome. Its facade includes Ionic colonnades fashioned from white granite, and 100 sculptured eagles. Graceful 50-foot Constantine arches mark the entryways, above which are

The Metro's Red Line stops at Union Station, which is a major crossroads for commuters.

LEFT: Union Station's massive Main Hall has a 96-foot barrel-vaulted ceiling. ABOVE: Old Town Trolley on the Mall.

poised six carved fixtures representing Fire, Electricity, Freedom, Imagination, Agriculture, and Mechanics. Inside is the **Main Hall,** a massive rectangular room with a 96-foot barrel-vaulted ceiling, an expanse of white-marble flooring, and a balcony adorned with 36 Augustus Saint-Gaudens sculptures of Roman legionnaires. Off the Main Hall is the **East Hall,** shimmering with scagliola marble walls and columns, a gorgeous hand-stenciled skylight ceiling, and stunning murals of classical scenes inspired by ancient Pompeian art. (Today this is the station's most pleasant shopping venue: less crowded and noisy, with small vendors selling pretty jewelry and other accessories.)

In its time, this "temple of transport" has witnessed many important events. President Wilson welcomed General Pershing here in 1918 on his return from France. South Pole explorer Rear Admiral Richard Byrd was also feted at Union Station on his homecoming. And Franklin D. Roosevelt's funeral train, bearing his casket, was met here in 1945 by thousands of mourners.

But after the 1960s, with the decline of rail travel, the station fell on hard times. Rain caused parts of the roof to cave in, and the entire building—with floors buckling, rats running about, and mushrooms sprouting in damp rooms—was sealed in 1981. That same year, Congress enacted legislation to preserve and restore this national treasure, to the tune of $160 million. The remarkable restoration involved hundreds of European and American artisans who were meticulous in returning the station to its original design.

At least 32 million people come through Union Station's doors yearly. About 120 retail and food shops on three levels offer a wide array of merchandise and dining options. The sky-lit **Main Concourse,** which extends the entire length of the station, is the primary shopping area, as well as a ticketing and baggage facility. You could spend half a day here shopping or about 20 minutes touring. Several tour companies use the station as a point of arrival and departure; at least two, **Double Decker Tours** and **Old Town Trolley,** operate ticket booths inside the front hall of the main concourse. (See p. 351 for more information about tours.) See chapter 7 for more specific information about Union Station **shops.**

40 Massachusetts Ave. NE. www.unionstationdc.com. ℂ **202/289-1908.** Free admission. Station daily 24 hr. Shops Mon–Sat 10am–9pm; Sun noon–6pm. Machines located inside the station near the exit/entrance to the parking garage will validate your ticket for $1 for 2 hr. of parking; after that fees are as follows: $7 for 1 hr. or less, up to $22 for 24 hr. Metro: Union Station.

DUPONT CIRCLE

In a city of national this-and-that attractions, Dupont Circle provides a charmingly personal counterpoint. Within this lively residential neighborhood of old town houses, trendy boutiques, and bistros, are mostly historic houses (like the Christian Heurich House), embassy buildings, beloved art galleries (like the Phillips Collection), and one-of-a-kind museums (like the Textile Museum).

Anderson House HISTORIC HOME   This limestone-veneered Italianate mansion, fronted by twin arches and a Corinthian-columned portico, was built between 1902 and 1905. Its original owners were career diplomat Larz Anderson III, who served as ambassador to Japan in 1912 and 1913, and his heiress wife, Isabel. The couple traveled a lot and filled their home with beautiful purchases from those journeys. Larz and Isabel were popular hosts in the capital and counted presidents and foreign dignitaries among their guests. Since Larz's death in 1937, the house has served as headquarters for the Society of the Cincinnati, an organization founded in 1783 for descendants of army officers who fought in the Revolutionary War. Anderson's great-grandfather was a founder and George Washington the society's first president-general. A visit to Anderson House is about marveling over the palatial architecture and interior design (love the ballroom), the display of artwork—from Flemish tapestries to Asian and European paintings and antiquities—and Revolutionary War artifacts. Anderson House hosts exhibits, concerts, and lectures throughout the year; all are free and open to the public.

2118 Massachusetts Ave. NW (at Q St.). http://societyofthecincinnati.org. ℂ **202/785-2040.** Free admission. Tues–Sat 1–4pm; highlights tours Tues–Sat 11:15am, 2:15pm, and 3:15pm. Closed Thanksgiving, Dec 25, and Jan 1. Metro: Dupont Circle (Q St. exit).

Heurich House Museum HISTORIC HOME   Wealthy German businessman and brewer Christian Heurich built this turreted, four-story brownstone and brick Victorian castle in 1894, and lived here with his family until he died in 1945. Old Heurich was a character, as a tour of the 31-room mansion-museum reveals. Allegorical paintings cover the ceilings, silvered plaster medallions festoon the stucco walls, and there's a bierstube (tavern room) in the basement sporting the brewer's favorite drinking mottos—written in German, but here's one translation: "There is room in the smallest chamber for the biggest hangover." The Victorian Garden is a good place to pause for a picnic or to page through your guidebook.

1307 New Hampshire Ave. NW (at 20th St.) www.heurichhouse.org. ℂ **202/429-1894.** Garden free admission; house tours $5. Walk-in tours Thurs–Fri 11:30am and 1pm, Sat 1pm. Garden weekdays spring–fall 10am–4pm. Metro: Dupont Circle (19th St. exit).

National Geographic Museum MUSEUM   Inside the headquarters of the National Geographic Society is a museum whose exhibits relate to adventure, exploration, and earth sciences. Sometimes the Society mounts a really big show—like the 2009–10 exhibit of 2,000-plus-year-old terra cotta warriors from the tomb of China's first emperor. More often exhibits are on a smaller scale, like the display of photographs of lions, tigers, cheetahs, leopards, jaguars, and clouded leopards in last year's Big Cats: Vanishing Icons. Whatever the focus or size, exhibits here are always compelling.

1145 17th St. NW (at M St.). www.nationalgeographic.com/museum. ℭ **202/857-7588**. Free admission to ongoing and other exhibits; admission to special exhibits usually $8 per adult and up. Daily 10am–6pm. Closed Dec 25. Metro: Farragut North (Connecticut Ave. and L St. exit).

Phillips Collection ★★ ART MUSEUM   The centerpiece of this charming museum is its elegant 1897 Georgian Revival mansion, the gallery's anchor since the Phillips opened in 1921, making it America's first museum of modern art. Best known for its Renoir masterpiece *Luncheon of the Boating Party,* the Phillips boasts a permanent collection of nearly 3,000 works by artists whose names you'll surely know: Europeans Daumier, Bonnard, Vuillard, van Gogh, Cézanne, Picasso, Degas, Klee, Matisse, Ingres, Delacroix, Manet; American notables Dove, Hopper, Marin, Eakins, Homer, Lawrence, and O'Keeffe; and living artists like Howard Hodgkin, Sean Scully, and Elizabeth Murray.

Initially, the building was, in fact, the lovely family home of founder Duncan Phillips, who lived here as a boy and then with his wife and fellow art collector, Marjorie Phillips, and their two children, until their move in 1930 to a new abode. After 90 years, two expansions (1960, 2006), and a restoration or two (including one in 2010, following a fire), the Phillips remains true to Phillips's vision, of being "an intimate museum combined with an experiment station." Pieces from the permanent collection are on display in the 1897 building, which retains the feel of a gracious home, with its leaded- and stained-glass windows, oak-paneled Music Room, gracefully elliptical stairway, and individually designed fireplaces. The additions, which doubled the original space, house the main entrance, as well as special exhibit galleries, a cafe, a courtyard sculpture garden,

Renoir's *Luncheon of the Boating Party* at the Phillips Collection.

and the Rothko Room, which holds four large, vividly colorful paintings by abstract expressionist Mark Rothko.

You'll enjoy viewing the collection for an hour or so.

A full schedule of events includes temporary shows with loans from other museums and private collections, gallery talks, and concerts in the ornate Music Room. Concerts take place Sundays from October to May at 4pm (arrive early); admission is $20. On the first Thursday of each month, the museum hosts **Phillips After Five,** an evening of live jazz, a cash bar, modern art, and gallery talks. These are immensely popular, so reserve a spot online and expect to pay $12 admission.

Note: You may tour the permanent collection free of charge on weekdays, though a donation is welcome. Those 18 and under receive free admission, always. Weekends when there is no special exhibit, admission is $10 per adult, $8 for seniors 62 and over and students 18 and over. When the museum is staging a special exhibit, you pay the special-exhibit admission price (usually $12 per adult, $10 per student or senior), which covers entry to both the permanent and special collections. You may order tickets in advance online or in person at the Phillips.

1600 21st St. NW (at Q St.). www.phillipscollection.org. © **202/387-2151.** Admission free on weekdays; weekends $10 adults; $8 seniors 62 and older and students 18 and older; free ages 17 and under. Call ahead for a schedule and admission for special exhibits. Tues–Sat 10am–5pm (Thurs until 8:30pm); Sun 11am–6pm. Closed Mon and federal holidays. Metro: Dupont Circle (Q St. exit).

Textile Museum ★ MUSEUM   This lovely museum shows off historic and contemporary handmade textile arts from around the world, and from every imaginable civilization, from ancient India to modern Japan. Special exhibits are always worth a look, as are the gift shop and the garden. The building is notable, too: John Russell Pope, architect of the National Gallery of Art and the Jefferson Memorial, designed it. The Textile Museum is partnering with the George Washington University and plans to open in a new and larger location on GWU's Foggy Bottom campus, sometime in 2014.

2320 S St. NW (at Massachusetts Ave.). www. textilemuseum.org. © **202/667-0441.** Suggested donation $8. Tues–Sat 10am–5pm; Sun 1–5pm. Closed federal holidays and Dec 24. Metro: Dupont Circle (Q St. exit).

Historic and contemporary handmade textiles at the Textile Museum.

Woodrow Wilson House Museum ★ HISTORIC HOME   Located right next door to the Textile Museum is the capital's only presidential house museum. Docents take you on an hourlong tour of this 1915 mansion, home to our 28th president, Woodrow Wilson, who lived here, post–White House, with his second wife, Edith, from 1921 until his death in 1924. The house is decorated as it was when Wilson lived here, and docents both enlighten and entertain you with charming anecdotes and information about the man and his times.

2340 S St. NW (at Massachusetts Ave.). www.woodrowwilsonhouse.org. © **202/387-4062.** Admission $10 adults, $8 seniors, $5 students, free for ages 11 and under. Tues–Sun 10am–4pm. Closed federal holidays. Metro: Dupont Circle (Q St. exit).

FOGGY BOTTOM

Known primarily as the locale for the George Washington University campus, the State Department, the International Monetary Fund, and the World Bank, Foggy Bottom has two main sightseeing attractions: the John F. Kennedy Center for the Performing Arts and the State Department's Diplomatic Reception Rooms. Two new sites are slated to debut in the coming years, both affiliated with GWU: A new location of the **Textile Museum** (see above) opens in 2014, and a brand-new museum devoted to all things Winston Churchill, the **Churchill Centre,** will arrive in 2015.

John F. Kennedy Center for the Performing Arts ★★ PERFORMING ARTS VENUE   Opened in 1971, the Kennedy Center is both the national performing arts center and a memorial to John F. Kennedy. Designed by noted architect Edward Durell Stone and set on 17 acres overlooking the Potomac River, the striking facility encompasses an opera house, a concert hall, two stage theaters, a theater lab, and a theater devoted exclusively to family productions.

The best way to experience the Kennedy Center is to attend a performance, and you can count on grand possibilities in 2013. See chapter 8 for specifics about theater, concert, and dance highlights of the 2012–13 season.

Aside from performances, the center is worth visiting for one of its free 50-minute guided tours, which include some restricted areas.

Tours depart every 10 minutes from the lower level, Level A, in the **Hall of States.** You tour the **Hall of Nations,** which displays the flags of all nations diplomatically recognized by the United States. Throughout the center, you'll see gifts from more than 60 nations, including 3,700 tons' worth of marble donated by Italy and used to line the walls of the Hall of Nations. First stop is the **Grand Foyer,** scene of many free concerts and programs, and the reception area for all three theaters on the main level; the 18 crystal chandeliers are a gift from Sweden. You'll also visit the **Israeli Lounge** (where 40 painted and gilded panels depict musical scenes from the Old Testament); the **Concert Hall,** home of the National Symphony Orchestra; the **Opera House;** the **African Lounge** (decorated with beautiful tapestries and other artwork from African nations); the **Eisenhower Theater;** the **Hall of States,** where flags of the 50 states and four territories are hung in the order in which they joined the Union; the **Performing Arts Library;** and the **Terrace Theater,** a bicentennial gift from Japan. If there's a rehearsal going on, the tour skips the visits to the theaters. Tours conclude on the rooftop terrace, where you'll love the fine view of the Potomac River and the city.

Tours are offered in many languages, including French, German, Spanish, and Japanese, but you should contact the center in advance to arrange for a tour in a particular language other than English. Call ② **202/416-8340** for details, or go to the "Tours" information page on the website to complete and submit a form online.

2700 F St. NW (at New Hampshire Ave. NW and Rock Creek Pkwy.). www.kennedy-center.org. ② **800/444-1324** or 202/467-4600 for information or tickets, or 202/416-8340 for tour info. Daily 10am–midnight. Free guided tours Mon–Fri 10am–5pm; Sat–Sun 10am–1pm. Metro: Foggy Bottom (free shuttle service btw. the station and the center, running every 15 min. weekdays 9:45am–midnight, Sat 10am–midnight, and Sun noon–midnight). Bus: 80 from Metro Center. Parking $20.

Albert Einstein Memorial, 22nd Street & Constitution Avenue NW

In a grove of holly and elm trees at the southwest corner of the National Academy of Science grounds, you'll find this dear memorial displaying the slouching figure of brilliant scientist, great thinker, and peace activist Albert Einstein. He sits slightly bent and sideways, upon a granite bench, leaning on one hand and holding in the other a bronze sheet of paper on which are written mathematical equations for which he is famous. At his feet is a celestial map. His gaze looks worn and warm. The statue measures 12 feet in height and weighs 4 tons, yet children cannot resist crawling upon it and leaning up against this man.

State Department Diplomatic Reception Rooms GOVERNMENT BUILDING   This is a fine-arts tour of rooms that serve as our country's stage for international diplomacy and official entertaining. The rooms house a collection of Early American paintings, furniture, and decorative arts dating from 1740 to 1850. The tour is not recommended for children 11 and under. You must bring a valid picture ID, such as a driver's license, to enter the building.

2201 C St. NW (entrance on 23rd St. NW). https://diplomaticrooms.state.gov. (📞 **202/647-3241.** Free admission. Guided tours only: Mon–Fri 9:30am, 10:30am, and 2:45pm. Advance reservations required. Metro: Foggy Bottom.

GEORGETOWN

One of the oldest parts of the city has long been best known for its major shopping opportunities. Historic Georgetown still exists, however, and a walking tour in chapter 5 will lead you to centuries-old estates and dwellings, including **Tudor Place,** the **Old Stone House,** and **Dumbarton House.** Whether or not you take this tour, you might want to seek out the other two places included in this chapter: Dumbarton Oaks, a historic mansion, museum, and formal gardens; and the Kreeger Museum, located slightly northwest of Georgetown proper and most easily accessible by car or taxi. But very cool.

Dumbarton House HISTORIC HOME Built between 1799 and 1805, Dumbarton House is the headquarters for the National Society of Colonial Dames of America. Stop here to admire gorgeous architecture and antique decorative arts, and to glean a bit of early American history. Self-guide your way or call to arrange in advance for a docent-guided tour.

2715 Q St. NW (at 27th St.). www.dumbarton house.org. © **202/337-2288.** Admission $5; free for students. Tues–Sun 11am–3pm. Closed federal holidays. Metro: Dupont Circle (Q St. exit, with a 20-min. walk).

Dumbarton Oaks ★ 🏛 MUSEUM Located on a side street in upper Georgetown, Dumbarton Oaks is an estate that encompasses an early-19th-century mansion-museum-research center, an art gallery-pavilion, a library, and nearly 16 acres of gorgeous gar-

The formal gardens at Dumbarton Oaks.

dens. Though velvet ropes prevent you from entering the Renaissance-style Music Room, you must stand as close as you can to admire the Flemish tapestries, the painting *The Visitation* by El Greco, and the entrance archway murals that were painted by Allyn Cox (known for his murals in the U.S. Capitol). The museum's Byzantine art galleries display such treasures as a rearing horse from Yemen that dates from the 2nd century, floor mosaics, and religious icons and adornments. Follow the passageway to the glass and travertine pavilion designed by Philip Johnson to view pre-Columbian art, such as centuries-old Inka gold ornaments, Olmec heads, and beautiful Mayan artifacts. But in lovely weather you may never make it inside.

These **formal gardens** include an orangery, a rose garden, wisteria-covered arbors, groves of weeping cherry trees, magnolias, hedge-shielded walkways, stone walls, fountain terraces, and always something blooming, whether it's winter jasmine in January or black-eyed Susans in June. You're likely to spend as much as an hour here in spring, summer, and fall, but expect to share the winding paths with like-minded wanderers. You can't picnic here; instead exit at R Street, turn left, cross an honest-to-goodness Lovers' Lane, and proceed next door to Montrose Park to have your picnic.

Docents lead brief tours of the gardens at 2:15pm and of museum special exhibits at 3pm Tuesday through Thursday and Saturday year-round, except in August.

1703 32nd St. NW (garden entrance at 31st and R sts.). www.doaks.org. © **202/339-6401.** Gardens admission Mar 15–Oct 31 $8 adults, $5 children 12 and under and seniors; free Nov–Mar 14. Museum free admission. Gardens Tues–Sun year-round (weather permitting): Mar 15 to Oct 31 2–6pm; Nov 1 to Mar 14 2–5pm. Museum Tues–Sun 2–5pm. Closed national holidays and Dec 24. Metrobus nos. 31, 32, 36, D1, D2, D3, D6, and G2, plus the D.C. Circulator bus all have stops close to the site.

Kreeger Museum ★ 🎁 ART MUSEUM   If you're a fan of Impressionist and post-Impressionist artists Chagall, Monet, Picasso, Renoir, Cezanne, and Miró, you might want to make the effort to visit the Kreeger, whose collection of some 300 works spans the years 1850 to the present. Once the home of art and music lovers David and Carmen Kreeger, this Philip Johnson–designed structure is located 2 miles from the center of Georgetown, on a hill that surveys the city, including the far-off Washington Monument. You'll notice that view when you tour the outdoor sculpture garden. Indoors lie more sculpture and those awesome paintings, among them very early and very late pieces by Picasso; two by my personal favorite, Bonnard; examples from the Washington colorist school, including a few by Gene Davis; and—surprise!—a modest display of traditional African and Asian art on the lower level.

2401 Foxhall Rd. NW (off Reservoir Rd.). www.kreegermuseum.org. © **202/337-3050.** Admission $10 adults, $7 seniors and students, free for children 12 and under. Fri–Sat 10am–4pm; Tues–Thurs by reservation only, for guided tours at 10:30am and 1:30pm. Closed federal holidays and Aug. About 2 miles from Reservoir Rd. and Wisconsin Ave. in Georgetown (a pleasant walk on a nice day); otherwise drive or take a taxi.

Old Stone House HISTORIC HOME   This 1765 structure is said to be the oldest in Washington. The National Park Service owns and operates the house, and National Park Service rangers provide information and sometimes demonstrations related to the site's pre-Revolutionary history.

3051 M St. NW (at 30th St.). www.nps.gov/olst. © **202/895-6070.** Free admission. Daily noon–5pm. Garden open during daylight hours. Closed Dec 25. Metro: Foggy Bottom with a 15-min. walk, or take the D.C. Circulator.

Tudor Place HISTORIC HOME   Designed by Dr. William Thornton, architect of the Capitol, Tudor Place was constructed between 1796 and 1816 for Martha Parke Custis, who was George Washington's step-granddaughter. Family descendants lived here until 1983. Tour the garden on your own; house tours are docent-led only.

1644 31st St. NW (at R St.). www.tudorplace.org. © **202/965-0400.** House admission $8 adults, $6 seniors, $3 students. Garden admission $3. House Tues–Sat 10am–4pm; Sun noon–4pm. Garden Mon–Sat 10am–4pm; Sun noon–4pm. Closed Dec 25. Metro: Dupont Circle (Q St. exit, with a 20-min. walk).

MIDTOWN

The **White House** is Midtown's main attraction and offers reason enough to visit this part of town. But there are many other great reasons. Midtown is where you'll find Washington's oldest art museum, the **Corcoran Gallery of Art;** an off-the-Mall Smithsonian museum, the **Renwick Gallery;** smaller and more specialized art collections; and several historic houses. Pick and choose from the offerings below, or follow the walking tour of the neighborhood outlined in chapter 5.

Art Museum of the Americas ★ ART MUSEUM   The Organization of American States owns this museum, whose exhibits draw from the museum's permanent collection of 2,000-plus works of contemporary Latin American and Caribbean art. The OAS established the museum in 1976 in gratitude to the United States, its host country, and in recognition of the U.S.'s 200th anniversary of independence. In addition to the art within, you might want to admire the building's exterior architecture; the white-painted, Spanish colonial-style building with a red-tiled roof was designed in 1912 by noted architect Paul Cret.

201 18th St. NW (at Virginia Ave.). http://museum.oas.org. © **202/458-6016.** Free admission. Tues–Sun 10am–5pm. Closed federal holidays and Good Friday. Metro: Farragut West (18th St. exit) or Farragut North (K St. exit).

Corcoran Gallery of Art ★★ ART MUSEUM   This elegant museum, a stone's throw from the White House, opened in 1874 as Washington's first art museum. Its original location was the red-brick and brownstone building that now houses the Renwick Gallery (see below). The collection outgrew its quarters and moved in 1897 to its present Beaux Arts building, designed by Ernest Flagg.

The collection, shown in rotating exhibits, focuses chiefly on American art. Founder William Wilson Corcoran, a prominent Washington banker, was among the first wealthy American collectors to realize the importance of encouraging and supporting this country's artists. Enhanced by further gifts and bequests, the collection comprehensively spans American art from 18th-century portraiture to works by modern artists since 1945, including Louise Nevelson, Andy Warhol, Mark Rothko, and Bruce Nauman. Nineteenth-century works include Albert Bierstadt's and Frederick Remington's imagery of the American West; Hudson River School artists; expatriates like J. M. Whistler, John Singer Sargent, and Mary Cassatt; and two giants of the late 19th century, Winslow Homer and Thomas Eakins. The Corcoran is also a committed exhibitor of Washington artists, especially those associated with the renowned "Washington Color School," including Gene Davis and Kenneth Noland.

The Corcoran is not exclusively an American art museum. On the first floor is the collection from the estate of Senator William Andrews Clark: an eclectic grouping of Dutch and Flemish masters, European painters, French Impressionists, Barbizon landscapes, Delft porcelains, a Louis XVI *salon doré* (an extravagant room with gilded ornaments and paneling) transported in toto from Paris, and more. Clark's will stated that his diverse collection, which any curator would undoubtedly want to disperse among various museum departments, must be shown as a unit. He left money for a wing to house it, and the new building opened in 1928.

The Corcoran Gallery of Art.

Acclaimed chef Todd Gray, of **Equinox** (p. 196), designs the menu and runs the Corcoran's in-house cafe, Todd Gray's Muse, which is open Wednesday to Saturday 10am to 3pm and Sunday 10am to 1pm; every first and third Sunday, the Corcoran hosts brunch from 11am to 2pm, featuring live music. Call ✆ **202/639-1786** for more information. The Corcoran also has a nice gift shop. Gallery tickets can be purchased in person or order in advance from Ticketmaster online at www.ticketmaster.com or by phone at ✆ **800/745-3000.**

500 17th St. NW (btw. E St. and New York Ave.). www.corcoran.org. ✆ **202/639-1700.** Admission $10 adults; $8 seniors, military, and students; always free for children 12 and under. May be higher for special exhibits. Wed and Fri–Sun 10am–5pm; Thurs 10am–9pm. Free highlights tours daily noon, additional tours Thurs 7pm and Sat–Sun 3pm. Closed Mon, Tues, Dec 25, and Jan 1. Metro: Farragut West (17th St. exit) or Farragut North (K St. exit).

Daughters of the American Revolution (DAR) Museum

MUSEUM   DAR occupies three joined buildings; its museum lies in the middle one, where rotating exhibits of artwork, artifacts, and memorabilia reveal a bit about what

TOP: **The Daughters of the American Revolution Museum.** BOTTOM: **The Octagon House.**

life was like in America before 1840. In addition to its extensive collection of decorative arts, the DAR Museum has an Americana Collection of manuscripts, diaries, household inventories, letters, and other papers from Colonial times, the Revolutionary War period, and early days of the newly formed United States. The museum also mounts fine special exhibits, like its recent By, For, and Of the People: Folk Art and Americana in the DAR Museum.

1776 D St. NW (at 17th St.) www.dar.org/museum. **202/628-1776.** Free admission. Museum Mon–Fri 9:30am–4pm; Sat 9am–5pm. Period Rooms Mon–Fri 10am–2:30pm; Sat 9am–4:30pm. Americana Collection Mon–Fri 8:30am–4pm. Closed on federal holidays. Metro: Farragut West (17th St. exit) or Farragut North (K St. exit).

Octagon House HISTORIC HOME   This is the country's oldest museum dedicated to architecture and design. Dr. William Thornton, first architect of the Capitol, designed the house in 1801. As its name suggests, the structure is an architectural marvel. Eight sides, though? Nope, try six. Thornton designed the house for Colonel John Tayloe III, a Virginia planter, a breeder of racehorses, and a friend of George Washington, who would come by to inspect the construction site from time to time. Upon its completion (which Washington did not live to see), the Octagon became a favorite social scene, the Tayloes welcoming John Adams, Thomas Jefferson, James Madison, James Monroe, Daniel Webster, Henry Clay, and their ilk.

1799 New York Ave. NW (at 18th St.). www.theoctagon.org. ✆ **202/626-7439.** Free admission for self-guided tours or $5 for guided tours. Thurs–Fri 1–4pm. Metro: Farragut West (17th St. exit).

Renwick Gallery of the Smithsonian American Art Museum ★ 🎁 ART

MUSEUM A department of the Smithsonian American Art Museum (see "Penn Quarter," later in this chapter), the Renwick Gallery is a showcase for American creativity in crafts and decorative arts, housed in a historic mid-1800s landmark building of the French Second Empire style. It's located on the same block as the White House, just across Pennsylvania Avenue. The original home of the Corcoran Gallery (see above), it was saved from demolition by First Lady Jacqueline Kennedy in 1963, when she recommended that it be renovated as part of the Lafayette Square restoration. In 1965 it became part of the Smithsonian and was renamed for its architect, James W. Renwick, Jr., who also designed the Smithsonian Castle.

On view on the first floor are temporary exhibits of American crafts and decorative arts. On the second floor, the museum's rich and diverse displays boast changing crafts exhibits and contemporary works from the museum's permanent collection, such as Larry Fuente's *Game Fish* or Wendell Castle's *Ghost Clock.* Also on the second floor is the **Victorian Grand Salon,** styled in 19th-century opulence and worth a visit for its own merits: Its 40-foot-high laylight (a skylight unexposed to the outside) and its wainscoted rose walls covered in framed paintings evoke a 19th-century picture gallery. On display indefinitely are 70 paintings by 51 American artists, from between 1840 and 1930. Tour the entire gallery for about an hour, rest for a minute, and then go on to your next destination.

Inside the Renwick Gallery.

The Renwick offers a comprehensive schedule of crafts demonstrations, lectures, and musical performances. Also check out the museum shop near the entrance for books on crafts, design, and decorative arts, as well as craft items, many of them for children.

1661 Pennsylvania Ave. NW (at 17th St.). www.americanart.si.edu/renwick. ✆ **202/633-7970.** Free admission. Daily 10am–5:30pm. Closed Dec 25. Metro: Farragut West or Farragut North.

The White House ★★★ GOVERNMENT BUILDING It's amazing when you think about it: This house has served as residence, office, reception site, and world embassy for every U.S. president since John Adams. The White House is the only private residence of a head of state that has opened its doors to the public for tours, free of charge, and it's been doing this ever since Thomas Jefferson inaugurated the practice. On a typical day, you'll be one of some 1,600 people touring the White House, knowing that meanwhile, somewhere in this very building, the president and his staff are meeting with foreign dignitaries, congressional members, and business leaders, and hashing out the most urgent of national and global decisions. For tour information, see "How to Arrange a White House Tour," below.

An Act of Congress in 1790 established the city now known as Washington, District of Columbia as the seat of the federal government. George Washington and city planner Pierre L'Enfant chose the site for the president's house and staged a contest to find a builder. Although Washington picked the winner—Irishman James Hoban—he was the only president never to live in the White House. The structure took 8 years to build, starting in 1792, when its cornerstone was laid. Its facade is made of the same stone used to construct the Capitol. The mansion quickly became known as the "White House," thanks to the limestone whitewashing applied to the walls to protect them, later replaced by white lead paint in 1818. In 1814, during the War of 1812, the British set fire to the White House and gutted the interior; the exterior managed to endure only because a rainstorm extinguished the fire. What you see today is Hoban's basic creation: a building modeled after an Irish country house (in fact, Hoban had in mind the house of the Duke of Leinster in Dublin).

Note: Tours of the White House exit from the North Portico. Before you descend the front steps, look to your left to find the window whose sandstone still remains unpainted as a reminder both of the 1814 fire and of the White House's survival.

Additions over the years have included the South Portico in 1824, the North Portico in 1829, and electricity in 1891, during Benjamin Harrison's presidency. In 1902 repairs and refurnishing of the White House cost nearly $500,000. No other great change took place until Harry Truman's presidency, when the interior was completely renovated after the leg of Margaret Truman's piano cut through the dining room ceiling. The Trumans lived at Blair House across the street for nearly 4 years while the White House interior was shored up with steel girders and concrete.

In 1961, First Lady Jacqueline Kennedy spearheaded the founding of the White House Historical Association and formed a Fine Arts Committee to help restore the famous rooms to their original grandeur, ensuring treatment of the White House as a museum of American history and decorative arts. "It just seemed to me such a shame when we came here to find hardly anything of the past in the house, hardly anything before 1902," Mrs. Kennedy observed.

The White House.

Every president and first family put their own stamp on the White House. The Obamas installed in their private residence artworks on loan from the Hirshhorn Museum and from the National Gallery of Art, and chose works to hang in the public rooms of the White House. (Changing the art in the public rooms requires approval from the White House curator and the Committee for the Preservation of the White House.) Michelle Obama planted a vegetable garden on the White House grounds, and President Obama altered the outdoor tennis court so that it can be used for both basketball and tennis games.

Highlights of the public tour include the gold and white **East Room,** the scene of presidential receptions, weddings, major presidential addresses, and other dazzling events. This is where the president entertains visiting heads of state and the place where seven of the eight presidents who died in office (all but Garfield) laid in state. It's also where Nixon resigned. The room's early-18th-century style was adopted during the Theodore Roosevelt renovation of 1902; it has parquet Fontainebleau oak floors and white-painted wood walls with fluted pilasters and classical relief inserts. Note the famous Gilbert Stuart portrait of George Washington that Dolley Madison saved from the British torch during the War of 1812; the portrait is the only object to have remained continuously in the White House since 1800 (except during times of reconstruction).

You'll visit the **Green Room,** which was Thomas Jefferson's dining room but today is used as a sitting room. Mrs. Kennedy chose the green watered-silk-fabric wall covering. In the **Oval Blue Room,** decorated in the French Empire style chosen by James Monroe in 1817, presidents and first ladies have officially received guests since the Jefferson administration. It was, however, Martin Van Buren's decor that began the "blue room" tradition. The walls, on which hang portraits of five presidents (including Rembrandt Peale's portrait of Thomas Jefferson and G. P. A. Healy's of John Tyler), are covered in reproductions of early-19th-century French and American wallpaper. Grover Cleveland, the only

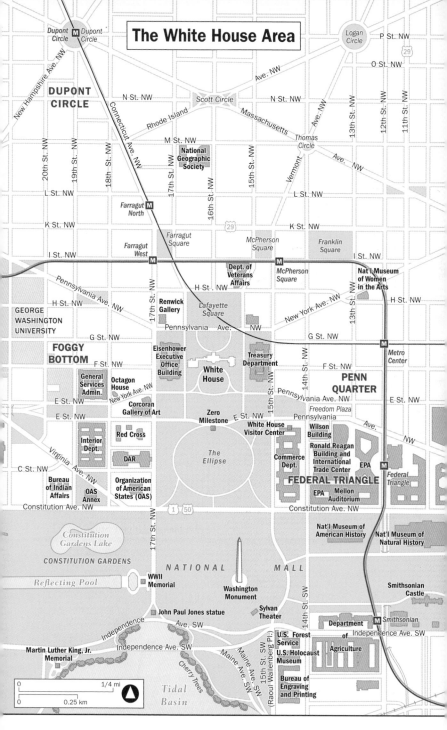

The White House Area

HOW TO ARRANGE A WHITE HOUSE tour

White House tours are available to the general public year-round from 7:30 to 11am Tuesday through Thursday, 7:30am to noon Friday, 7:30am to 1pm Saturday, and at other times as well, depending on the president's schedule. If the president is out of town, it's possible that more tours will be allowed past the usual cutoff time. Tours are self-guided, and most people take no more than an hour to go through. You must have a reservation to tour the White House. At least 21 days and as far as 6 months in advance of your trip, call one of your senators' or your representative's office with the names of the people in your group and ask for a specific tour date. The tour coordinator consults with the White House on availability and, if your date is available, contacts you to obtain the names, birth dates, Social Security numbers (for those 14 and over), and other information for each of the people in your party. The Secret Service reviews the information and clears you for the tour, putting the names of the people in your group on a confirmed reservation list; you'll receive a confirmation number and the date and time of your tour well in advance of your trip. (**Note:** International visitors should contact their embassy for help in submitting a tour request.)

On the day of your tour, call ☏ **202/456-7041** to make sure the White House is still open to the public that day. Then off you go, to the south side of East Executive Avenue, near the Southeast Gate of the White House, with valid, government-issued photo IDs whose information exactly matches that which you provided to your congressional member's office. Everyone in your party who is 18 or older must have an ID. Be sure to arrive about 15 minutes before your scheduled tour time.

Do not bring the following prohibited items: backpacks, book bags, handbags, or purses; food and beverages; strollers; cameras; videorecorders or any type of recording device; tobacco products; personal grooming items, from cosmetics to hairbrushes; any pointed objects, whether a pen or a knitting needle; aerosol containers; guns; ammunition; fireworks; electric stun guns; maces; martial arts weapons/devices; or knives of any kind. Cellphones are okay, but not the kind that are also cameras. The White House does not have a coat-check facility, so there is no place for you to leave your belongings while you go on the tour. There are no public restrooms or telephones in the White House, and photos and videotaping are prohibited. **Best advice:** Leave everything but your wallet back at the hotel.

president to wed in the White House, was married in the Blue Room. This room was also where the Reagans greeted the 52 Americans liberated after being held hostage in Iran for 444 days, and every year it's the setting for the White House Christmas tree.

The **Red Room,** with its red-satin-covered walls and Empire furnishings, is used as a reception room, primarily for afternoon teas. Several portraits of past presidents and a Gilbert Stuart portrait of Dolley Madison hang here. Dolley Madison used the Red Room for her famous Wednesday-night receptions.

From the Red Room, you'll enter the **State Dining Room.** Modeled after late-18th-century neoclassical English houses, this room is a superb setting for state dinners and luncheons. Below G. P. A. Healy's portrait of Lincoln is a quote taken from a letter written by John Adams on his second night in the White House (FDR had it carved into the mantel): i pray heaven to bestow the best of blessings on this house and on all that shall here-after inhabit it. may none but honest and wise men ever rule under this roof.

Note: Even if you have successfully reserved a White House tour for your group, you should still call ✆ **202/456-7041** before setting out in the morning, in case the White House is closed on short notice because of unforeseen events. If this should happen to you, consider following the "Stroll Around the White House" walking tour outlined in chapter 5.

1600 Pennsylvania Ave. NW (visitor entrance gate at E St. and E. Executive Ave.). www.white house.gov. ✆ **202/456-7041** or 202/208-1631. Free admission. Tours for groups of 10 or more who have arranged the tour through their congressional offices. Closed federal holidays. Metro: Federal Triangle.

Gilbert Stuart's famous portrait of George Washington that Dolley Madison saved from the British torch during the War of 1812.

The White House Visitor Center The Visitor Center opened in 1995 to provide extensive interpretive data about the White House (and to serve as a ticket-distribution center, though that function has been suspended). It is run under the auspices of the National Park Service, and the staff is well informed. A 30-minute video about the White House provides interior views of the presidential precincts (it runs continuously throughout the day). Pick up a copy of the National Park Service's brochure on the White House, which tells you a little about what you'll see in the eight or so rooms you tour and a bit about the history of the White House. The White House Historical Association runs a small shop here. Before you leave the visitor center, take a look at the exhibits, which include information about the architectural history of the White House; portrayals by photographers, artists, journalists, and political cartoonists; anecdotes about first families (such as the time prankster Tad Lincoln stood in a window above his father and waved a Confederate flag at a military review); details about what goes on behind the scenes, focusing on the vast staff of servants, chefs, gardeners, Secret Service people, and others who maintain this institution; highlights of notable White House ceremonies and celebrations, from a Wright Brothers aviation demonstration in 1911 to a ballet performance by Baryshnikov during the Carter administration; and photographs of the ever-changing Oval Office as decorated by administrations from Taft to Obama. There are restrooms here and at the Ellipse Visitor Pavilion, at 15th and E streets, south of the White House.

1450 Pennsylvania Ave. NW (in the Department of Commerce Building, btw. 14th and 15th sts.). ✆ **202/208-1631.** Free admission. Daily 7:30am–4pm. Closed Jan 1, Thanksgiving, and Dec 25. Metro: Federal Triangle.

THE NATIONAL MALL & MEMORIAL PARKS

This one's the biggie, folks. More than one-third of the capital's major attractions lie within this complex of parkland that the National Park Service calls **National Mall and Memorial Parks.** The National Mall (see below) is the centerpiece of this larger plot that extends from the Capitol to the Potomac River, and from Constitution Avenue to down and around the cherry-tree-ringed Tidal Basin. Presidential and war memorials, the Washington Monument, the Martin Luther King, Jr. National Memorial, 10 Smithsonian museums, the National Gallery of Art, the National Archives, and the U.S. Botanic Garden are here waiting for you. So let's get started. FYI: The National Mall and Memorial Parks has its own telephone number, ℂ **202/485-9880,** and website, www.nps.gov/nama.

Arts and Industries Building ARCHITECTURE   The building is closed for an extensive renovation, as you'll no doubt guess if the dramatic scaffolding is still in place by the time you visit. Scheduled to reopen in 2014, the structure has a long way to go. Completed in 1881 as the first U.S. National Museum, this red-brick and sandstone structure was the first Smithsonian museum on the Mall. President Garfield's Inaugural Ball took place here. From 1976 to the mid-1990s, it housed exhibits from the 1876 U.S. International Exposition in Philadelphia—a celebration of America's centennial that featured the latest advances in technology.

Weather permitting, and regardless of the construction underway, a 19th-century **carousel** operates across the street on the Mall.

900 Jefferson Dr. SW (on the south side of the Mall). www.si.edu.

D.C. War Memorial MONUMENT/ MEMORIAL   This long-neglected and often overlooked memorial commemorates the lives of the 499 citizens of Washington, D.C. who died in the First World War. Newly restored in 2011, the memorial is surely worth a stop on your way to grander, more famous edifices. President Herbert Hoover dedicated the memorial in 1931; John Phillip Sousa conducted the Marine band at the event. The structure is a graceful design of 12 Doric columns supporting a classical circular dome. The names of the 499 dead are inscribed in the stone base.

On the north side of Independence Ave. SW, between the National World War II and Lincoln memorials. www.wwimemorial.org.

TOP: **A segway tour on the National Mall.**
BOTTOM: **Baseball on the Mall.**

EXPLORING WASHINGTON, D.C. | The National Mall & Memorial Parks

GETTING AROUND THE NATIONAL MALL AND MEMORIAL PARKS by bus

It's easy to access the National Mall and Memorial Parks on foot or by bike, but be aware that bus transportation is also available. In spring 2012, the National Park Service partnered with the Martz Gray Line Company of Washington, D.C. to offer two options for travelers wishing to see the Mall and memorials by bus. **Open Top Sightseeing Buses** (www.opentopsightseeingbus.com; ☏ **202/488-1012**) provides a hop-on hop-off tour with 27 stops, including the museums along the National Mall and the Lincoln, Jefferson, and FDR memorials as well as attractions outside of the Mall and Memorial Parks area such as the White House, Arlington Cemetery, and Ford's Theatre. The air-conditioned double-decker buses feature open-top seating and a recorded narration. They operate daily, year-round, the first bus departing Union Station at 9am, the last at 5pm. You can board at Union Station or at any of the stops along the way; pay when you board or purchase a ticket online ahead of time. Buses arrive at each stop every 15 to 30 minutes. Tickets are $32 per adult and $20 per child (ages 5 to 15); children 4 and under ride free; online tickets are discounted. The bus company offers three routes throughout the city, but it's the Red Loop route that takes you around the National Mall and Memorial Parks. Look for an open-top, bright red bus splattered with stars and stripes and the name of the bus company.

Alternatively, the **Mall Express** trams (www.anctours.com; ☏ **202/488-1012**) provide a faster, unnarrated shuttle service. These open-air trams travel between Union Station and Arlington Cemetery, stopping at the National World War II and the Lincoln memorials in one direction and at the Franklin Delano Roosevelt and Martin Luther King, Jr. memorials on the return trip. The trams are blue and white and display the name "Mall Express." These trams do not provide a hop-on hop-off service; you'll pay $5 each time you board or $9 for a round-trip journey. Buy your ticket in person when you board or online. The trams operate daily, 9am to 6:30pm March through September, 9am to 4:30pm October to February. They depart Union Station every 30 to 45 minutes.

Enid A. Haupt Garden GARDEN   Named for its donor, a noted supporter of horticultural projects, this pretty 4-acre garden presents elaborate flower beds and borders, plant-filled turn-of-the-20th-century urns, 1870s cast-iron furnishings, and lush baskets hung from reproduction 19th-century lampposts. The garden is planted on the rooftops of the subterranean Ripley Center and Sackler and African Art museums. The tranquil **Moongate Garden** near the Sackler Gallery employs water and granite in a landscape design inspired by a 15th-century Chinese temple. Two 9-foot-tall pink-granite moon gates frame a pool paved with half-rounds of granite. Benches backed by English boxwoods sit under the canopy of weeping cherry trees.

A **"Fountain Garden"** outside the African Art Museum provides granite seating with walls overhung by hawthorn trees. Three small terraces, shaded by black sour-gum trees, are located near the Arts and Industries Building. And five majestic linden trees shade a seating area around the **Downing Urn,** a memorial to American landscapist Andrew Jackson Downing, who designed the National Mall. Elaborate cast-iron carriage gates made according to a 19th-century design

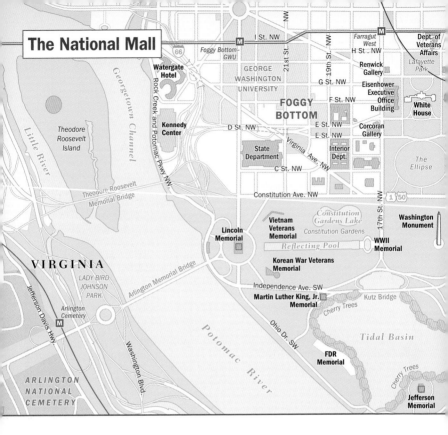

The National Mall

by James Renwick, flanked by four red sandstone pillars, salute the Independence Avenue entrance to the garden.

10th St. and Independence Ave. SW. © **202/633-1000.** Free admission. Daily dawn–dusk. Free tours May–Sept Wed 1pm. Closed Dec 25. Metro: Smithsonian (12th St. and Independence Ave. exit).

Franklin Delano Roosevelt Memorial ★★ MONUMENT/MEMORIAL

The FDR Memorial has proven to be one of the most popular of the presidential memorials since it opened in 1997. Its popularity has to do as much with its design as the man it honors. This 7½-acre outdoor memorial stretches out, rather than rising up, across the stone-paved floor. Granite walls define the four "galleries," each representing a different term in FDR's presidency, from 1933 to 1945. Architect Lawrence Halprin's design includes waterfalls, sculptures (by Leonard Baskin, John Benson, Neil Estern, Robert Graham, Thomas Hardy, and George Segal), and Roosevelt's own words carved into the stone.

The Enid A. Haupt Garden.

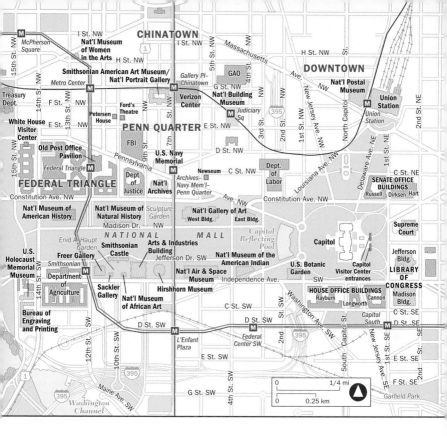

The many displays of cascading water can sound thunderous, as the fountains recycle an astonishing 100,000 gallons of water every minute. The presence of gushing fountains and waterfalls reflects FDR's appreciation for the importance of H_2O. As someone afflicted by polio, he understood the rehabilitative powers of water exercises and established the Warm Springs Institute in Georgia to help others with polio. As president, FDR supported several water projects, including the creation of the Tennessee Valley Authority.

When the memorial first opened, adults and children alike arrived in bathing suits and splashed around on warm days. Park rangers don't allow that anymore, but they do allow you to dip your feet in the various pools. A favorite time to visit is at night, when dramatic lighting reveals the waterfalls and statues against the dark parkland.

Conceived in 1946, the FDR Memorial had been in the works for 50 years. Part of the delay in its construction can be attributed to the president himself: FDR had told his friend Supreme Court Justice Felix Frankfurter, "If they are to put up any memorial to me, I should like it to be placed in the center of that green plot in front of the Archives Building. I should like it to consist of a block about the size [of this desk]." In fact, such a plaque sits in front of the National Archives. Friends and relatives struggled to honor Roosevelt's request to leave it at that, but Congress and national sentiment overrode them.

CAPITAL views

Here are some of the best of the capital's many marvelous views:

- For a bird's-eye view of monumental Washington, take the elevator to the top of the **Washington Monument** (p. 118).

- From the **Capitol Reflecting Pool,** between the Mall and the Capitol (p. 58/106), you can get a great look at the Capitol itself.

- Half the height of the Washington Monument, the **Old Post Office Pavilion's Clock Tower** (p. 136) offers something the monument cannot: a grand look up and down Pennsylvania Avenue, from the Capitol to the White House, and beyond.

- One of the most gorgeous views of the city any time of year, but especially in spring at cherry blossom time, comes from a stroll or bike ride along the **paved pathways that run along the Potomac River** (p. 145). They wind around the memorials and the Tidal Basin and cross Arlington Memorial Bridge to continue from the Virginia side of the Potomac River for the grand finale of vistas: the city's landmark-dotted landscape on full display.

- The **Lincoln Memorial** (p. 97) offers a spectacular view of the entire Mall, all the way to the Capitol in the distance.

- For the highest view of D.C., take the elevator to the Washington National Cathedral's **Pilgrim Observation Gallery** (p. 144).

As with other presidential memorials, this one opened to some controversy. Advocates for people with disabilities were incensed that the memorial sculptures did not show the president in a wheelchair, which he used after he contracted polio. President Clinton asked Congress to allocate funding for an additional statue portraying a wheelchair-bound FDR. You will now see a small statue of FDR in a wheelchair, placed at the very front of the memorial, to the right as you approach the first gallery. Step inside the gift shop to view a replica of Roosevelt's wheelchair, as well as one of the rare photographs of the president sitting in a wheelchair. The memorial is probably the most accessible tourist attraction in the city; as at most of the National Park Service locations, wheelchairs are available for free use on-site. Rangers conduct interpretive tours every hour on the hour. Thirty minutes is sufficient time for a visit.

On West Basin Dr., alongside the Tidal Basin in West Potomac Park (across Independence Ave. SW from the Mall). www.nps.gov/frde. ☎ **202/426-6841.** Free admission. Ranger on duty daily 9:30am–11:30pm, except for Dec 25. Limited parking. Metro: Smithsonian (12th St./Independence Ave. exit), with a 20-min. walk, or take the Open Top Sightseeing Bus or Mall Express shuttle.

Freer Gallery of Art ★★ MUSEUM Charles Lang Freer, a collector of

Visitors at the Franklin Delano Roosevelt Memorial.

The Freer Gallery's central courtyard.

Asian and American art from the 19th and early 20th centuries, gave 7,500 of these works to the Smithsonian in 1906 but did not live to see the opening of his namesake gallery, in 1923. Freer's original interest was American art, but his good friend James McNeill Whistler encouraged him to collect Asian works as well. Eventually the latter became predominant. Freer's gift included funds to construct a museum and an endowment to add to the Asian collection, which now numbers about 25,000 objects and spans 6,000 years. It includes Chinese and Japanese sculpture, lacquer, metalwork, and ceramics; early Christian illuminated manuscripts; Iranian manuscripts, metalwork, and miniatures; ancient Near Eastern metalware; and South Asian sculpture and paintings.

The Freer is mostly about Asian art, but it also displays some of its more than 1,200 American works (the world's largest collection) by Whistler. Most remarkable and always on view is the famous **Harmony in Blue and Gold, the Peacock Room.** Originally a dining room designed for the London mansion of F. R. Leyland, the Peacock Room displayed a Whistler painting called *The Princess from the Land of Porcelain.* But after his painting was installed, Whistler was dissatisfied with the room as a setting for his work. When Leyland was away from home, Whistler painted over the very expensive leather interior and embellished it with paintings of golden peacock feathers. Not surprisingly, a rift ensued between Whistler and Leyland. After Leyland's death, Freer purchased the room, painting and all, and had it shipped to his home in Detroit. It is now permanently installed here. Other American painters represented in the collections are Thomas Wilmer Dewing, Dwight William Tryon, Abbott Handerson Thayer, John Singer Sargent, and Childe Hassam. You could spend a happy 1 to 2 hours here.

The Freer Gallery is an oasis on the Mall, especially if you arrive here after visiting its voluminous and crowded sisters, the Natural History, American History, and Air and Space museums. Housed in a grand granite-and-marble building that evokes the Italian Renaissance, the pristine Freer has lovely sky-lit galleries. The main exhibit floor galleries encircle a beautiful landscaped courtyard, complete with loggia and central fountain. If the weather is right, it's a pleasure to sit out here and take a break from touring. An underground exhibit space connects the Freer to the neighboring Sackler Gallery, and both museums share the **Meyer Auditorium,** which is used for free chamber-music concerts, dance performances, Asian feature films, and other programs. Inquire about these, as well as children's activities, at the information desk. The Freer leads highlights tours daily at 1pm, as well as at 11am Tuesday and Friday, and 2pm Thursday.

The George Mason Memorial.

Jefferson Dr. SW at 12th St. SW (on the south side of the Mall). www.asia.si.edu. ℂ **202/633-1000.** Free admission. Daily 10am–5:30pm. Closed Dec 25. Metro: Smithsonian (Mall/Jefferson Dr. exit).

George Mason Memorial MONUMENT/MEMORIAL This memorial honors George Mason, author of the Virginia Declaration of Rights, which had much to do with the establishment of the United States Bill of Rights. Dedicated on April 9, 2002, the memorial consists of a bronze statue of Mason, set back in a landscaped grove of trees and flower beds (lots and lots of pansies), arranged in concentric circles around a pool and fountain. Mason appears in 18th-century garb, from buckled shoes to tricorner hat, seated on a marble bench but leaning backward on one arm and gazing off in the general direction of the Washington Monument. Two stone slabs are inscribed with some of Mason's words, like these, referring to Mason's rejection of slavery: THAT SLOW POISON, WHICH IS DAILY CONTAMINATING THE MINDS & MORALS OF OUR PEOPLE. Wooden benches at the site present a pleasant opportunity to learn about Mason and take a break before moving on. **Note:** The memorial is easy to miss, since it does not lie on the Tidal Basin path. As you approach the Jefferson Memorial from the direction of the FDR Memorial, or as you approach the FDR Memorial from the direction of the Jefferson, you'll come to the bridge that arches over the inlet leading from the Tidal Basin to the Potomac River; look straight across from the bridge, and there you'll see it.

E. Basin and Ohio drives SW (btw. the Jefferson and FDR memorials). www.nps.gov/gemm. ℂ **202/426-6841.** Free admission. Open daily, though rangers generally are not posted here. To find out more about George Mason, visit the Jefferson Memorial, a 5-min. walk away, on the Tidal Basin, where a park ranger is on duty 9:30am–11:30pm. Limited parking. Metro: Smithsonian (12th St./Independence Ave. exit), with a 25-min. walk, or take the Open Top Sightseeing Bus or Mall Express shuttle.

Hirshhorn Museum and Sculpture Garden ★★ ART MUSEUM This museum of modern and contemporary art is named after Latvian-born Joseph H. Hirshhorn, who, in 1966, donated his vast collection—more than 4,000 drawings and paintings, and 2,000 pieces of sculpture—to the United States "as a small repayment for what this nation has done for me and others like me who arrived here as immigrants." The Hirshhorn opened in 1974 to display these works, adding 5,500 more bequeathed by Hirshhorn in 1981, upon his death. The Hirshhorn's current inventory numbers about 11,500.

Constructed 14 feet aboveground on sculptured supports, the doughnut-shaped concrete-and-granite building stands 82 feet high and measures 231 feet in diameter. The cylindrically shaped building encloses a hollow core, where a fountain spouts water five stories high. The building's light and airy interior holds three levels of galleries, each following a circular route that makes it easy to see every exhibit without getting lost in a honeycomb of galleries. Natural light from floor-to-ceiling windows makes the inner galleries the perfect venue for regarding sculpture—second only to the beautiful tree-shaded sunken **Sculpture Garden ★** across the street (don't miss it). Make your way to the third-floor oculus and you'll be rewarded with a dramatic view of the National Mall.

A rotating show of about 600 pieces is on view at all times. The collection features just about every well-known 20th-century artist and touches on most of the major trends in Western art since the late 19th century, with particular emphasis on our contemporary period. Among the best-known pieces are Rodin's *Monument to the Burghers of Calais* (in the Sculpture Garden), Hopper's *First Row Orchestra,* de Kooning's *Two Women in the Country,* and Warhol's *Marilyn Monroe's Lips.*

Pick up a calendar when you enter to find out about free films, lectures, concerts, and temporary exhibits. Some of these events are quite popular; for instance, the Hirshhorn hosts **Hirshhorn After Hours** three or four times a year, and it's always a sellout. Twenty-somethings especially love to attend the function, which takes place from 8pm to midnight and combines socializing with art, music, or other performance, and cocktails. The $18 tickets are available in advance online at www.hirshhorn.tumblr.com.

The Hirshhorn hopes to debut an exciting new space, created by a temporary, inflatable, blue "bubblelike" structure that sits in the museum's inner courtyard and balloons above it to a height of 145 feet. The balloon emerges from the middle of the museum's doughnut shape and is visible from various points along the Mall. It plans to inflate the balloon twice a year, in May and October, and use it as a seasonal auditorium, cafe, and cultural hub. Be on the lookout!

Meanwhile docents continue to give impromptu, free, 30-minute tours to anyone who stops by the information desk, noon to 4pm daily.

Independence Ave. at 7th St. SW (on the south side of the Mall). www.hirshhorn.si.edu. ✆ **202/633-4674.** Free admission. Museum daily 10am–5:30pm. Sculpture Garden daily 7:30am–dusk. Closed Dec 25. Metro: L'Enfant Plaza (Smithsonian Museums/Maryland Ave. or Smithsonian exit).

Jefferson Memorial ★★ MONU-MENT/MEMORIAL President John F. Kennedy, at a 1962 dinner honoring 29 Nobel Prize winners, told his guests that they were "the most extraordinary collection of talent, of human knowledge, that has ever been gathered together at the White House, with the possible exception of when Thomas Jefferson dined alone." Jefferson penned the Declaration of Independence and served as George Washington's secretary of state, John Adams's vice president, and America's third president. He

The Hirshhorn Museum's cylindrical shape encloses a hollow core.

The Jefferson Memorial, a columned rotunda in the style of the Pantheon in Rome.

spoke out against slavery—although, like many of his countrymen, he kept slaves himself. He also established the University of Virginia and pursued wide-ranging interests, including architecture, astronomy, anthropology, music, and farming.

Franklin Delano Roosevelt, a great admirer of Jefferson, spearheaded the effort to build him a memorial, although the site choice was problematic. The Capitol, the White House, and the Mall were already located in accordance with architect Pierre L'Enfant's master plan for the city, and there was no spot for such a project that would maintain L'Enfant's symmetry. So the memorial was built on land reclaimed from the Potomac River, perched upon the lip of the manmade reservoir now known as the Tidal Basin. Roosevelt laid the memorial cornerstone in 1939 and had all the trees between the Jefferson Memorial and the White House cut down so that he could see the memorial every morning.

The memorial is a columned rotunda in the style of the Pantheon in Rome, whose classical architecture Jefferson himself introduced to this country (he designed his home, Monticello, and the earliest University of Virginia buildings in Charlottesville). On the Tidal Basin side, the sculptural group above the entrance depicts Jefferson with Benjamin Franklin, John Adams, Roger Sherman, and Robert Livingston, all of whom worked on drafting the Declaration of Independence. The domed interior of the memorial contains the 19-foot bronze statue of Jefferson standing on a 6-foot pedestal of black Minnesota granite. The sculpture is the work of Rudolph Evans, chosen from among more than 100 artists in a nationwide competition. Jefferson is depicted wearing a fur-collared coat given to him by his close friend, the Polish General Tadeusz Kosciuszko. If you follow Jefferson's gaze, you see that, sure enough, the Jefferson Memorial and the White House have an unimpeded view of each other.

Rangers present 20- to 30-minute programs throughout the day as time permits. Twenty to 30 minutes is sufficient time to spend here.

Ohio Dr. SW, at the south shore of the Tidal Basin (in West Potomac Park). www.nps.gov/thje. ☎ **202/426-6841.** Free admission. Ranger on duty daily 9:30am–11:30pm, except Dec 25. Limited parking. Metro: Smithsonian (12th St./Independence Ave. exit), with a 20- to 30-min. walk, or take the Open Top Sightseeing Bus or Mall Express shuttle.

Korean War Veterans Memorial ★ MONUMENT/MEMORIAL This
privately funded memorial, founded in 1995, honors those who served in the Korean War, a 3-year conflict (1950–53) that produced almost as many casualties

as Vietnam. It consists of a circular "Pool of Remembrance" in a grove of trees and a triangular "Field of Service," highlighted by lifelike statues of 19 infantrymen who appear to be trudging across fields. A 164-foot-long black granite wall depicts the array of combat and support troops that served in Korea (nurses, chaplains, airmen, gunners, mechanics, cooks, and others); a raised granite curb lists the 22 nations that contributed to the UN's effort there; and a commemorative area honors KIAs, MIAs, and POWs. Plan to spend 15 minutes here.

Southeast of the Lincoln Memorial, on the Independence Ave. SW side of the Mall. www.nps.gov/kowa. © **202/426-6841.** Free admission. Ranger on duty daily 9:30am–11:30pm, except Dec 25. Limited parking. Metro: Foggy Bottom, with 30-min. walk, or take the Open Top Sightseeing Bus or Mall Express shuttle.

Lincoln Memorial ★★★ ☺ MONUMENT/MEMORIAL   This beautiful and moving tribute to the nation's 16th president attracts millions of visitors annually. Like its fellow presidential memorials, the Lincoln was a long time in the making. Although it was planned as early as 1867—2 years after Lincoln's death—Henry Bacon's design was not completed until 1912, and the memorial was dedicated in 1922.

The neoclassical templelike structure, similar in architectural design to the Parthenon in Greece, has 36 fluted Doric columns representing the states of the Union at the time of Lincoln's death, plus two at the entrance. On the attic parapet are 48 festoons symbolizing the number of states in 1922, when the monument was erected. (Hawaii and Alaska are noted in an inscription on the terrace.) Due east is the Reflecting Pool, lined with American elms and stretching 2,000 feet toward the Washington Monument and the Capitol beyond.

The memorial chamber has limestone walls inscribed with the Gettysburg Address and Lincoln's second inaugural address. Two 60-foot-high murals by Jules Guerin on the north and south walls depict, allegorically, Lincoln's principles and achievements. On the south wall, an Angel of Truth freeing a slave is flanked by groups of figures representing Justice and Immortality. The north-wall mural portrays the unity of North and South, and is flanked by groups of figures symbolizing Fraternity and Charity. Most powerful, however, is Daniel Chester French's 19-foot-high seated statue of Lincoln, which disappears from

The Lincoln Memorial illuminated at night.

An inscription on the steps of the Lincoln Memorial commemorates the spot on which Martin Luther King, Jr. delivered his famous "I Have a Dream" speech.

your sightline as you get close to the base of the memorial, then emerges slowly into view as you ascend the stairs.

Lincoln's legacy has made his memorial the site of numerous demonstrations by those seeking justice. Most notable was a peaceful demonstration of 200,000 people on August 28, 1963, at which Martin Luther King, Jr. proclaimed, "I have a dream." Look for the words I HAVE A DREAM. MARTIN LUTHER KING, JR., THE MARCH ON WASHINGTON FOR JOBS AND FREEDOM, AUGUST 28, 1963, inscribed and centered on the 18th step down from the chamber. The inscription, which the National Park Service added in July 2003, marks the precise spot where King stood to deliver his famous speech.

Rangers present 20- to 30-minute programs as time permits throughout the day. Thirty minutes is sufficient time for viewing this memorial.

On the western end of the Mall, at 23rd St. NW (btw. Constitution and Independence aves.). www.nps.gov/linc. ✆ **202/426-6841.** Free admission. Ranger on duty daily 9:30am–11:30pm, except Dec 25. Limited parking. Metro: Foggy Bottom, then a 30-min. walk, or take the Open Top Sightseeing Bus or Mall Express shuttle.

Martin Luther King, Jr. National Memorial ★★ MONUMENT/ MEMORIAL   Authorized by Congress in 1996, this memorial pays tribute to the Baptist minister who was committed to nonviolence and direct action to force social change, and whose efforts and compelling speeches profoundly moved the country toward that achievement. The memorial debuted on Oct. 16, 2011. Hurricane Irene prevented it from opening on its originally planned date, August 28, exactly 48 years after the Rev. Dr. Martin Luther King, Jr. delivered his momentous "I Have a Dream" speech on the steps of the nearby Lincoln Memorial, to the 200,000 people who had gathered on the Mall during the "March on Washington" to pressure Congress to pass the Civil Rights Act. King was assassinated on April 4, 1968, at the age of 39.

The memorial's site along the northwest lip of the Tidal Basin is significant for the "visual line of leadership" it creates between the Lincoln Memorial, representing the principles of equality and civil rights as embodied in the personage of Abraham Lincoln and carried forward in King, and the Jefferson Memorial, which symbolizes the democratic ideals of the founding fathers. Set on a crescent-shaped, 4-acre parcel of land surrounded by the capital's famous cherry trees, the mammoth sculpture rests on 300 concrete piles driven into the muddy basin terrain. A 28-foot, 6-inch statue of Dr. King in a business suit, arms folded, stands front and center, representing the "Stone of Hope"; he is flanked by two enormous background pieces, representing the "Mountain of Despair." A curving boundary wall enclosing the grounds perhaps commemorates the slain civil rights leader best, with inscriptions of excerpts from his remarkable sermons and speeches.

I must confess my disappointment in the memorial, which provides no context for King's life in those tumultuous times. I would have preferred a memorial more like the one for FDR, whose panels illustrate scenes from FDR's presidency; or like Lincoln's or Jefferson's, whose remarkable words are rendered more fully in the stone walls. The memorial includes a bookstore, a ranger station, and restrooms. By the time you read this, audio guides may be available for rent that will allow you to listen to King's speeches and/or life story as you tour the memorial. That, at least, will be an improvement.

Adjacent to the FDR Memorial, along the northwest side of the Tidal Basin, at Independence Ave. SW, in West Potomac Park. www.nps.gov/mlkm. (✆ **202/426-6841.** Free admission. Ranger on duty daily 9:30am–11:30pm, except Dec 25. Limited parking. Metro: Smithsonian (12th St./Independence Ave. exit), with a 25-min. walk, or take the Open Top Sightseeing Bus or Mall Express shuttle.

National Air and Space Museum ★★ ☺ MUSEUM   The National Air and Space Museum has two locations: its flagship museum on the National Mall and a second facility, the **Steven F. Udvar-Hazy Center,** located on the grounds of Washington-Dulles International Airport.

Let's start with the original, ever-popular Air and Space Museum on the Mall. The museum, now in its 36th year, chronicles the story of the mastery of flight, from Kitty Hawk to outer space. It holds the largest collection of historic aircraft and spacecraft in the world, about 50,000—so many, in fact, that the museum is able to display only about 10% of its artifacts at any one time, hence the opening of the Udvar-Hazy Center in 2003.

During the tourist season and on holidays, arrive before 10am to make a beeline for the film ticket line when the doors open. The not-to-be-missed **IMAX films ★** shown here are immensely popular, and tickets to most shows sell out quickly. You can purchase same-day tickets by phone or in person at the Lockheed Martin IMAX Theater box office on the first floor, or in advance online up to 24 hours before showtime. Surcharges apply to phone and online orders. Two or more films play each day, most with aeronautical or space-exploration themes; *To Fly!* and *Legends of Flight 3D* are two that were running in 2012. Ticket prices range based on the film and the age of the audience member, from $7.50 for youth (ages 2–12) for admission to a 60-minute-or-less presentation, to $15 for an adult (ages 13–59) for admission to a feature presentation (defined as "longer than 60 minutes"; this category includes commercial blockbusters like *Toy Story 3* or *Night at the Museum: Battle of the Smithsonian*). Admission is free for children 1 and under. IMAX films play throughout the day and also most evenings after the museum's closing; call for details (✆ **866/868-7774**).

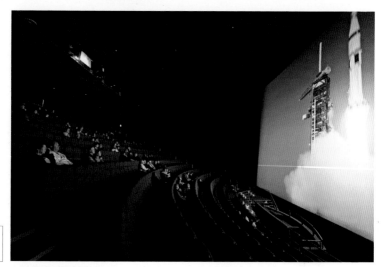

Two or more IMAX films play daily at the National Air and Space Museum.

You'll also need tickets to attend a show at the **Albert Einstein Planetarium ★**, which creates "an astronomical adventure." Projectors display space imagery upon a 70-foot-diameter dome, making you feel as if you're traveling in 3-D through the cosmos. In 2012 the planetarium's features included *Journey to the Stars* and *Cosmic Collisions,* each about 25 minutes long. Ticket prices correspond to those for the IMAX films (see above), but the planetarium also offers a couple of free presentations as well.

Among the more than 22 exhibitions on display throughout the museum is one that children especially love: **How Things Fly,** which includes wind and smoke tunnels, a boardable Cessna 150 airplane, and dozens of interactive exhibits that demonstrate principles of flight, aerodynamics, and propulsion. All the aircraft are originals. Kids also flock to the walk-through **Skylab orbital workshop,** part of the **Space Race** exhibition on the first floor. Both children and adults stand in line to take their turn on the museum's **flight simulators.** (The Udvar-Hazy Center has several, too.) You'll have a choice of experiencing a simulated ride or an interactive simulated piloting. For the interactive simulation, you are strapped in and given a joystick, and for about 5 minutes you'll truly feel as if you are in the cockpit and airborne, maneuvering your craft up, down, and upside-down on a wild adventure, thanks to virtual-reality images and high-tech sounds. The ride simulator costs $7; the interactive simulator costs $8. To board the ride simulators, children must be 42 inches tall unless accompanied by an adult; they must be 48 inches tall to ride the interactive simulators.

Other galleries highlight the solar system, U.S. manned spaceflights, sea-air operations, and aviation during both world wars. **Explore the Universe** presents the major discoveries that have shaped the current scientific view of the universe; it illustrates how the universe is taking shape and probes the mysteries that remain. Hundreds of space and aircraft artifacts dangle before your eyes everywhere you look, but don't miss the **1903 Flyer,** hanging in the exhibit called **The Wright Brothers and the Invention of the Aerial Age. Moving Beyond Earth** immerses visitors in the space flight experience through interactive kiosks, displays of space shuttle artifacts, and views of Earth from the International Space Station. One of the museum's newest exhibits is an updated version of the longtime and popular **Pioneers of Flight,** which highlights air and space developments during the first half of the 20th century.

The museum's cafeteria, the Wright Place, offers food from three popular American chains: McDonald's, Boston Market, and Donatos Pizzeria. Its three-level, 12,000-square-foot shop is the largest Smithsonian store.

At the Udvar-Hazy Center, you'll find two hangars—one for aviation artifacts, the other for space artifacts—and a 164-foot-tall observation tower for watching planes leave and arrive at Dulles Airport. The center's James S. McDonnell Space Hangar stretches the length of three football fields and stands 10 stories high, the better to house the enormous *Enterprise,* NASA's first space shuttle; the tiny "Anita," a spider carried on Skylab inside a bottle for web formation experiments; the manned maneuvering unit used for the first untethered spacewalk; a full-scale prototype of the Mars Pathfinder Lander; and Pegasus, the first aircraft-launched rocket booster to carry satellites into space. Currently, the gallery displays 163 aircraft and 154 spacecraft. This location also shows IMAX films. *Note:* The National Air and Space Museum used to run a shuttle between its two locations, but no longer. Virginia Regional Transit buses provide direct bus service between Dulles Airport and the Udvar-Hazy Center. Visit the Ground Transportation section of the Dulles Airport website, www.mwaa.com/dulles, for fare and schedule details.

Mall museum: Independence Ave. SW, btw. 4th and 7th sts. (on the south side of the Mall, with 2 entrances, one on Jefferson Dr. and the other on Independence Ave.). Udvar-Hazy Center: 14390 Air and Space Museum Pkwy., Chantilly, VA. www.nasm.si.edu. ✆ **202/633-1000** (for both locations), or 877/932-4629 for IMAX ticket information. Free admission. Both locations daily 10am–5:30pm (Mall museum often until 7:30pm in summer, but call to confirm). Free 1½-hr. highlight tours daily 10:30am and 1pm. Closed Dec 25. Metro: L'Enfant Plaza (Smithsonian Museums/Maryland Ave. exit) or Smithsonian (Mall/Jefferson Dr. exit).

National Archives ★★ GOVERNMENT BUILDING The Rotunda of the National Archives displays the country's most important original documents: the Declaration of Independence, the Constitution of the United States, and the Bill of Rights (collectively known as the Charters of Freedom), as part of its exhibit **The National Archives Experience.** Fourteen document cases trace the story of the creation of the Charters and the ongoing influence of these fundamental documents on the nation and the world. A restoration of Barry Faulkner's two larger-than-life murals brings the scenes to vivid life. One mural, titled *The Declaration of Independence,* shows Thomas Jefferson presenting a draft to John Hancock, the presiding officer of the Continental Congress; the other, titled *The Constitution,* shows James Madison submitting the Constitution to George Washington and the Constitutional Convention. Be sure not to miss viewing the original 1297 Magna Carta, on display as you enter the Rotunda; the document is one of only a few known to exist, and the only original version residing permanently in the United States.

Public Vaults is an exhibit that features interactive technology and displays of documents and artifacts. You can listen to recorded voices of past presidents as they deliberated over pressing issues of the time, and you can scour newly declassified documents. During the day, the **William C. McGowan Theater** continually runs dramatic films illustrating the relationship between records and democracy in the lives of real people, and at night it serves as a premier documentary film venue for the city. The **Lawrence F. O'Brien Gallery** rotates exhibitions of Archives documents.

As a federal institution, the National Archives is charged with sifting through the accumulated papers of a nation's official life—billions of pieces a year—and determining what to save and what to destroy. The Archives' vast accumulation of census figures, military records, naturalization papers, immigrant passenger lists, federal documents, passport applications, ship manifests, maps, charts, photographs, and motion picture film (and that's not the half of it) spans 2 centuries. Anyone 16 and over is welcome to use the National Archives center for genealogical research. Call for details.

The National Archives' building itself is worth an admiring glance. The neoclassical structure, designed by John Russell Pope (also the architect of the National Gallery of Art and the Jefferson Memorial) in the 1930s, is an impressive example of the Beaux Arts style. Seventy-two columns create a Corinthian colonnade on each of the four facades. Great bronze doors mark the Constitution Avenue entrance, and four large sculptures representing the Future, the Past, Heritage, and Guardianship sit on pedestals near the entrances. Huge pediments crown both the Pennsylvania Avenue and Constitution Avenue entrances to the building.

In peak season, you may want to reserve a spot on a guided tour (Mon–Fri 9:45am) or simply a timed visit entry, to help avoid a long wait in line. Admission is always free, but you'll pay a $1.50 convenience fee when you place your order online.

Allow about 90 minutes to view everything.

700 Constitution Ave. NW (btw. 7th and 9th sts. NW; tourists enter on Constitution Ave., researchers on Pennsylvania Ave.). www.archives.gov/nae. (𝒞 **202/357-5000.** Free admission. Mar 15 to Labor Day daily 10am–7pm; day after Labor Day to Mar 14 daily 10am–5:30pm. Call for research hours. Closed Dec 25. Metro: Archives–Navy Memorial.

National Gallery of Art ★★★ ART MUSEUM   This museum is a treasure. Housing one of the world's foremost collections of Western paintings,

Leonardo da Vinci's *Ginevra de' Benci* in the National Gallery of Art.

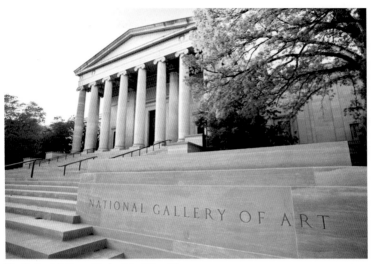
The National Gallery of Art's original West Wing.

sculpture, and graphic arts, from the Middle Ages into the 21st century, the National Gallery has a dual personality. The original West Building, designed by John Russell Pope (architect of the Jefferson Memorial and the National Archives), is a neoclassical marble masterpiece with a domed rotunda over a colonnaded fountain and high-ceilinged corridors leading to delightful garden courts. At its completion in 1941, the building was the largest marble structure in the world. It was a gift to the nation from financier/philanthropist Andrew W. Mellon, who also contributed the nucleus of the collection, including 21 masterpieces from the Hermitage, two Raphaels among them. The modern East Building, designed by I. M. Pei and opened in 1978, is composed of two adjoining triangles with glass walls and lofty tetrahedron skylights. The pink Tennessee marble from which both buildings were constructed was taken from the same quarry; it forms an architectural link between the two structures.

Only a small percentage of the National Gallery's collection of 116,000 works is on display at one time. The Gallery's permanent collection offers reason enough to visit, but its mounted exhibitions make this museum a further must; they're always fantastic.

The West Building: From the Mall entrance, you can stop first at the **Art Information Room** to design your own tour on a computer, if you like. But don't spend too much time here. Step into the gorgeous Rotunda, which leads right and left to light-filled halls punctuated with sculpture; off these long corridors stem intimate **painting galleries** organized by age and nationality. To your left, as you face away from the Mall, are works by the older masters, from 13th-century Italians to 17th-century Dutch. To your right are their younger counterparts, from 18th- and 19th-century French and Spanish artists to later works by British and American artists. These are creations by El Greco, Bruegel, Poussin, Vermeer, Van Dyck, Rubens, Fra Angelico, Gilbert Stuart, Winslow Homer, Constable, Turner, Mary Cassatt—you name it. The Western Hemisphere's only Leonardo da Vinci

LEFT: **The National Gallery Sculpture Garden.** RIGHT: **The National Gallery's East Building showcases 20th-century art.**

painting, *Ginevra de' Benci,* hangs here—just another masterpiece among this bevy of masterpieces.

Descend the grand marble staircase to the ground floor, where the museum's **sculpture galleries** are columned, vaulted, and filled with light. Highlights among the 900 works on display range from Chinese porcelain, to Renaissance decorative arts, to 46 wax statuettes by Degas, to Honoré Daumier's entire series of bronze sculptures, including all 36 of his caricatured portrait busts of French government officials.

The **National Gallery Sculpture Garden ★**, just across 7th Street from the West Wing, takes up 2 city blocks and features open lawns; a central pool with a spouting fountain (the pool turns into an ice rink in winter); an exquisite glassed-in pavilion housing an excellent cafe; 18 sculptures by renowned artists like Roy Lichtenstein and Ellsworth Kelly, and a Paris Metro sign; and informally landscaped shrubs, trees, and plants. It continues to be a hit, especially in warm weather, when people sit on the wide rim of the pool and dangle their feet in the water while they eat their lunch. Friday evenings in summer, the gallery stages immensely popular live jazz performances here.

The East Building: *Note:* Work underway to remove, restore, and replace the East Wing's exterior of pink marble panels requires that sidewalks along the Mall and Pennsylvania Avenue sides of the building be closed until Spring 2014; use 3rd Street or the tunnel that connects the two wings to enter/exit the East Building.

This wing is a showcase for the museum's collection of 20th-century art, including works by Picasso, Miró, Matisse, Pollock, and Rothko; for an exhibit called Small French Paintings, which I love; and for the gallery's special exhibitions. But chances are, the first thing you'll notice in this wing is the famous, massive aluminum **Alexander Calder mobile** dangling in the

Alexander Calder's mobile in the National Gallery Atrium.

seven-story, sky-lit atrium. And here's a tip that lots of people don't know: If you make your way to the tippy-top of the East Wing, whether by elevator or stairs, you reach a level that's actually named the "Tower," the tiny setting for the gallery's ongoing series of shows highlighting artistic developments since 1970. In 2012 the Tower featured 40 works by conceptual artist Mel Bochner. (For anyone who remembers that the Tower was the longtime home for four Matisse cutouts, no worries; you will now find the cutouts displayed on the Concourse level of the East Wing, Mon–Sat 10am–3pm and Sun 11am–3pm.)

All together you should allow at least 2 hours to tour the gallery, but you won't see everything here.

Pick up a floor plan and a calendar of events at an information desk to find out about National Gallery exhibits, films, tours, lectures, and concerts. Immensely popular is the gallery's Sunday concert series, now in its 71st year, with concerts performed most Sunday evenings October through June, at 6:30pm in the beautiful garden court of the West Building. Admission is free, and seating is on a first-come, first-served basis; my suggestion is to tour the gallery in late afternoon, lingering until 6pm, when the galleries close and the queuing begins in the Rotunda. The concerts feature chamber music, string quartets, pianists, and other forms of classical music performances. Call ℂ **202/842-6941.**

The gallery conducts school tours, wide-ranging introductory tours, and tours in several languages. The gift shop is a favorite. You'll also find several pleasing dining options, among them the Concourse-level Cascade Café, which has multiple food stations; the Garden Café, on the ground floor of the West Building; and the Sculpture Garden's Pavilion Café.

Constitution Ave. NW, btw. 3rd and 7th sts. NW (on the north side of the Mall). www.nga.gov. ℂ **202/737-4215.** Free admission. Gallery: Mon–Sat 10am–5pm; Sun 11am–6pm. Sculpture Garden: Memorial Day to Labor Day Mon–Thurs and Sat 10am–7pm, Fri 10am–9:30pm, Sun 11am–7pm; Labor Day to Memorial Day Mon–Sat 10am–5pm, Sun 11am–6pm. Ice Rink: Mid-Nov to mid-Mar Mon–Thurs 10am–9pm, Fri–Sat 10am–11pm, Sun 10am–9pm. Closed Dec 25 and Jan 1. Metro: Archives–Navy Memorial, or Gallery Place/Verizon Center (Arena/7th and F sts. exit).

 ## The Mall Gets a Makeover

The beauteous National Mall is showing its age. But help is on the way! You may notice construction areas and fencing in different locations around the Mall, in some cases obstructing the way to a landmark you'd hoped to visit. Just know it's all for a good cause. Improvements that will be underway or completed by the time you visit in 2013 include updated signage and maps on the National Mall; a new, permanent screening facility to replace the makeshift temporary structure at the Washington Monument (lots of arguments about this one, with some wanting the center to go underground); repair of the Washington Monument's masonry that was damaged by the August 2011 earthquake; permanent, more attractive security barriers at the Lincoln Memorial; and repairs to the Lincoln Memorial's Reflecting Pool and walkways. One other upgrade you may be interested in: Parts of the Mall, near the Smithsonian museums and the National Gallery of Art, will offer free Wi-Fi service.

National Mall ★★★ ICON   As part of his vision for Washington, Pierre L'Enfant conceived of the National Mall as a bustling ceremonial avenue of embassies and other distinguished buildings. Today's 2-mile, 700-acre stretch of land extending westward from the base of the Capitol to the Potomac River, just behind the Lincoln Memorial, fulfills that dream to some extent. Ten Smithsonian buildings, plus the National Gallery of Art and its Sculpture Garden, and a stray government building (Department of Agriculture), stake out the Mall's northern border along Constitution Avenue and southern border along Independence Avenue. More than 2,000 American elm trees shade the pebbled walkways paralleling Jefferson and Madison drives. In a single year, more than 25 million tourists and locals crisscross the Mall as they visit the Smithsonian museums; hustle to work; pursue exercise; participate in whatever festival, event, or demonstration is taking place on the Mall that day; or simply go for a stroll—just as L'Enfant envisioned, perhaps.

What L'Enfant did not foresee was the toll that all of this activity might take on this piece of parkland. In recent years, visitors to the Mall often have been dismayed to see an expanse of browned rather than green grass, crumbling walkways, and an overall worn appearance. The National Park Service maintains the land but struggles to keep up with needed repairs and preservation work, mostly due to lack of sufficient funds, despite monies from Congress and from the Trust for the National Mall (**www.nationalmall.org**), the Park Service's official fundraising partner. A third organization called the National Coalition to Save Our Mall (**www.savethemall.org**), made up of professional and civic groups as well as assorted concerned artists, historians, and residents, advocates for a public voice in Mall enhancement decisions, and for more support from Congress. These organizations don't necessarily agree on their visions for the Mall.

From the foot of the Capitol to the Lincoln Memorial. www.nps.gov/mall. (C) **202/426-6841.** Public space, open 365/24/7. Metro: Smithsonian.

National Museum of African Art ★ MUSEUM   Founded in 1964, and part of the Smithsonian since 1979, the National Museum of African Art moved to the Mall in 1987 to share a subterranean space with the **Sackler Gallery** (see above) and the **Ripley Center** (p. 114). Its aboveground domed pavilions reflect the arch motif of the neighboring Freer Gallery of Art (see above).

The museum collects and exhibits ancient and contemporary art from the entire African continent and rotates displays of its 9,100-piece permanent collection. The museum's contemporary African art collection comprises the largest public holding in the United States. Among the museum's holdings are the **Eliot Elisofon Photographic Archives,** encompassing 80,000 photographic prints and transparencies, and 120,000 feet of film on African arts and culture. A small, ongoing permanent exhibit of ceramic arts displays 14 traditional and contemporary pieces from the museum's 140-works collection. Always on view are items from the Walt Disney–Tishman African Art collection, which the Walt Disney World Company donated to the museum in 2005. Its Tishman collection of 525 objects represents every area of Africa, dating from ancient to contemporary times and spanning art forms from textiles to jewelry. A rotating selection of at least 60 works is permanently on display in the museum.

Inquire at the desk about special exhibits, workshops (including excellent children's programs), storytelling, lectures, docent-led tours, films, and demonstrations. A comprehensive events schedule provides a unique opportunity to

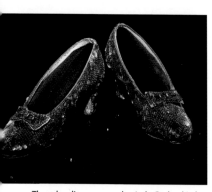

The ruby slippers worn by Judy Garland in her portrayal of Dorothy in the classic 1939 film "The Wizard of Oz."

learn about the diverse cultures and visual traditions of Africa. Plan on spending a minimum of 30 minutes here.

950 Independence Ave. SW. www.nmafa. si.edu. ⓒ **202/633-4600.** Free admission. Daily 10am–5:30pm. Closed Dec 25. Metro: Smithsonian.

National Museum of American History ★★★ ☺ MUSEUM As a bastion of U.S. culture and history, this museum tells America's story in terms of everyday life. Its objects can evoke feelings of awe (the desk on which Thomas Jefferson wrote the Declaration of Independence), affection (Dorothy's ruby slippers), or connection (Julia Child's kitchen). And some things here—the museum's ultimate possession, the huge **original Star-Spangled Banner ★★★**, for example—evoke all three emotions at once.

A grand renovation completed in November 2008 has much improved the museum. A skylight lightens up the place, and a redesign creates better flow; both rid the building of its old sense of clutter. Better yet the museum brings American history to full-blooded life by staging entertainment in different locations throughout the day, whether a performance of American standards sung in the atrium or a historic re-creation of the 1960 Greensboro student lunch-counter sit-ins, which takes place at the actual lunch counter, located on the second floor of the east wing.

Meanwhile renovations continue in the west wing. In 2013 you may find certain exhibits closed, as the museum is creating brand-new exhibit areas and features, including a first-floor panoramic window revealing sweeping views of the Washington Monument and National Mall, and, up on the third floor, a state-of-the-art Hall of Music to host live performances of the Smithsonian's Chamber Music Society and the Jazz Masterworks Orchestra. When the west wing reopens in winter 2014, timed to coincide with the museum's 50th anniversary, you'll find improved exhibits from the past, including Spark!Lab, dedicated to the stories behind inventions, and new exhibits altogether, like the one on American business history and innovation.

The piece de resistance of the museum always has been the original 30×34-foot wool and cotton Star-Spangled Banner, which Francis Scott Key observed the morning of September 14, 1814, waving above Fort McHenry in Baltimore's harbor, at the height of the War of 1812. Key's emotion at the sight moved him to pen the poem that, when put to music, eventually became the National Anthem. The carefully preserved flag now rests in its own dimly lit—no, make that almost completely dark—multistory gallery, on view through an enormous window. The gallery lies on the second floor behind the atrium wall, whose abstract depiction of the flag is meant to lead you to the exhibit entrance. (If you are like me, you might not catch on; just look for the straightforward signs showing you where to enter.) Take the time to examine the artifacts on display, like the piece of burned timber from the torched White House, and to read about the flag's seamstress, professional flagmaker Mary Pickersgill, who sewed the flag in 6 weeks with the help of her daughter, nieces, and a maid.

On the third floor lies the exhibit **The American Presidency: A Glorious Burden,** which explores the power and meaning of the presidency by studying those who have held the position. Continue on this floor to the exhibit **The Price of Freedom: Americans at War,** which examines major American military events and explores the idea that America's armed forces reflect American society. Among the items on display here are George Washington's commission from Congress as commander-in-chief of the Continental Army and the uniform jacket that Andrew Jackson wore during the Battle of New Orleans in the War of 1812.

Adjacent to the American Presidency is the museum's most popular exhibit, **The First Ladies,** which displays 26 first ladies' gowns, including the fabulous Jason Wu–designed, white chiffon, one-shoulder inaugural-ball gown worn by Michelle Obama in 2009; 14 watercolor paintings of the dresses; 160 objects; and information about the role of the first lady as seen from the points of view of fashion, nation's hostess, inauguration and opportunities, and changing times.

Following that, find the second-floor exhibit called **Within These Walls . . . ,** which interprets the rich history of America by tracing the lives of the people who lived in a 200-year-old house transplanted from Ipswich, Massachusetts. Then explore the temporary home for the National Museum of African American History and Culture (see "Preview the Next Smithsonian," below).

First-floor exhibits include one that focuses on food and wine in America, its centerpiece the much-visited ***Bon Appétit!* Julia Child's Kitchen at the Smithsonian,** which is, in fact, the famous chef's actual kitchen from her home in Cambridge, Massachusetts. When she moved to California in late 2001, Child donated her kitchen and all that it contained (1,200 items in all) to the museum. Most of these are on display, from a vegetable peeler to the kitchen sink. Also look here for **America on the Move,** which details the story of transportation in America since 1876: 300 artifacts displayed within period settings.

Best to start your tour at the second-floor Welcome Center, near the Mall entrance, to figure out how you'd like to proceed. Inquire about highlight tours (daily 10:15am and 1pm), spotlight tours (a docent's 15-min. focused talk on a particular object or exhibit, given between 10am and 3pm most days), and daily performances, as well as films, lectures, concerts, and hands-on activities for children and adults. Be sure to visit the museum's gift shops and dining options, also revamped during the remodeling.

The American History Museum has gotten into simulators, only these are different than the popular rides at the Air and Space Museum (p. 99). Located on the lower level and across from the Stars and Stripes Café are four rides that

Preview the Next Smithsonian

The **National Museum of African American History and Culture** won't open until 2015 (across 14th St. from the American History Museum, at Constitution Ave., northeast of the Washington Monument). In the meantime, tour the American History Museum's gallery dedicated to exhibits that eventually will be on display in the completed museum. On view in 2012, for example, was Slavery at Jefferson's Monticello: Paradox of Liberty, which featured artifacts, documents, and artworks that told the individual stories of the slaves who lived at Monticello.

The National Museum of the American Indian's striking exterior.

simulate roller coaster and race car adventures. The cost is $7 per ride; each simulator accommodates eight people, and children unaccompanied by an adult must be at least 42 inches tall.

Constitution Ave. NW, btw. 12th and 14th sts. NW (on the north side of the Mall, with entrances on Constitution Ave. and Madison Dr.). www.americanhistory.si.edu. *Ⓒ* **202/633-1000.** Free admission. Daily 10am–5:30pm. Closed Dec 25. Metro: Smithsonian or Federal Triangle.

National Museum of the American Indian ★ ☺ MUSEUM

The National Museum of the American Indian officially opened on September 21, 2004, having taken 5 years and $219 million to construct. Outside and in, this museum is strikingly handsome. Its burnt-sand-colored exterior of Kasota limestone wraps around the undulating walls of the museum, making the five-story building a standout among the many white-stone structures on the National Mall. Its interior design incorporates themes of nature and astronomy. For instance, the Potomac (a Piscataway word meaning "where the goods are brought in") is a rotunda that serves as the museum's main gathering place; it is also "the heart of the museum, the sun of its universe" (as noted in the museum's literature). Measuring 120 feet in diameter, with an atrium rising 120 feet to the top of the dome overhead, the Potomac is the central entryway into the museum, a venue for performances, and a hall filled with celestial references, from the equinoxes and solstices mapped on the floor beneath your feet to the sights of sky visible through the oculus in the dome above your head.

A gift shop, a theater, and the museum's excellent restaurant, Mitsitam, occupy most of the remaining space on the first floor. A second shop and the museum's main galleries lie upstairs on the second and third levels. Three permanent exhibits—Our Universes: Traditional Knowledge Shapes Our World, Our Peoples: Giving Voice to Our Histories, and Our Lives: Contemporary Life and Identities—use videos, interactive technology, and displays of artifacts to help you learn about cosmologies, history, and contemporary cultural identity, both of Native Americans as a group and of certain individual tribes. Throughout the museum are glass displays and pullout drawers wherein lie some 3,500 objects from an exhibit called Window on the Collections: Many Hands, Many Voices. A computer kiosk in front of each case allows museumgoers to zoom in and learn more about a particular item on view. These precious wood and stone carvings, masks, pottery, feather bonnets, and so on are a fraction of the 825,000 objets d'art amassed by a wealthy New Yorker named George Gustav Heye (1874–1957). Heye founded the New York Museum of the American Indian, this museum's predecessor.

The Butterfly Garden at the Natural History Museum.

New as of 2012 is the imagiNATIONS Activity Center, where visitors of all ages can weave a basket, learn how to build an igloo, wander through an Amazonian stilt house, test their knowledge of Indian culture by participating in a game show, and so on.

The National Museum of the American Indian does not provide much direction to self-guided touring, which tends to leave visitors at a loss as to how to proceed through the museum. (Families, you might want to head straight up to the third-floor Activity Center.) Faced with the vast display of objects and galleries that have no obvious beginning or end, tourists wander around, adopting a scattershot approach to the information, emerging eventually with more of an impression than with a coherent understanding of the Indian experience, and overwhelmed by the variety and number of artifacts and details. Perhaps that's intentional. Best advice? Stop at the Welcome Desk when you enter to sign up for a highlights tour.

4th St. and Independence Ave. SW. www.nmai.si.edu. ℂ **202/633-1000.** Free admission. Daily 10am–5:30pm. Closed Dec 25. Metro: Federal Center Southwest or L'Enfant Plaza (Smithsonian Museums/Maryland Ave. exit).

National Museum of Natural History ★★★ ☺ MUSEUM   Children often refer to this Smithsonian showcase as "the dinosaur museum," because of the **dinosaur hall,** or as "the elephant museum," since a huge **African bush elephant** is the first thing you see in the Rotunda when you enter from the Mall. Whatever you call it, the National Museum of Natural History is the largest of its kind in the world and one of the most visited museums in Washington. It contains more than 127.3 million artifacts and specimens, everything from Ice Age mammoths to the legendary Hope Diamond.

This old gal turned 100 in 2010 and celebrated in the most suitable way possible, by debuting a grand new exhibit, the 15,000-foot **Hall of Human Origins,** showcasing 285 early human fossils and artifacts. "What does it mean to be human?" is the theme explored here, through exhibits that probe evolution and the ecological and genetic, physical and cultural connections that humans have had with the natural world. Among the most popular of the 23 interactive exhibits is the morphing station that allows you to see what you would have looked like as an early human.

Also on the first floor is the **Sant Ocean Hall,** the largest, most diverse exhibit of its kind in the world. The hall's interactive devices and state-of-the-art technology illustrate our oceans' essential role in life on earth. Look for a model of a 45-foot-long North Atlantic right whale, 274 living specimens including a live giant squid, and a 1,500-gallon coral reef aquarium.

Meanwhile the museum's older, permanent exhibits still appeal, starting with the one that lies just outside the building. Before you enter the museum, stop first on the 9th Street side to visit the **butterfly garden.** Four habitats—wetland, meadow, wood's edge, and urban garden—are on view, designed to beckon butterflies and visitors alike. The garden is at its best in warm weather, but it's open year-round. (And if you like that, you're going to love the museum's Butterflies and Plants exhibit, which includes a Butterfly Pavilion—keep reading!)

Now go inside and admire the African bush elephant. If you have children, you might want to head next to the first-floor **Discovery Room,** filled with creative hands-on exhibits "for children of all ages." Call ahead or inquire at the information desk about hours. Also on this floor is the **Kenneth E. Behring Hall of Mammals.** Set in the restored west wing and boasting up-to-date lighting and sound, the Hall of Mammals features interactive dioramas that explain how mammals evolved and adapted to changes in habitat and climate over the course of millions of years. At least 274 taxidermied mammals, from polar bear to tiger, are on display, along with a dozen mammal fossils. From time to time, the hall erupts with animal sounds, all part of exhibit wizardry that helps make this a lifelike experience.

Other Rotunda-level displays include the **fossil collection,** which traces evolution back billions of years and includes a 3.5-billion-year-old stromatolite (blue-green algae clump) fossil—one of the earliest signs of life on earth—and a 70-million-year-old dinosaur egg. **Ancient Seas** features a 100-foot-long mural depicting primitive whales, a life-size walk-around diorama of a 230-million-year-old coral reef, and more than 2,000 fossils that chronicle the evolution of marine life. The **Dinosaur Hall** displays giant skeletons of creatures that dominated the earth for 140 million years before their extinction about 65 million years ago. Mounted throughout the Dinosaur Hall are replicas of ancient birds, including a life-size model of *Quetzalcoatlus northropi,* which lived 70 million years ago, had a 40-foot wingspan, and was the largest flying animal ever. Also residing above this hall is the jaw of an ancient shark, *Carcharodon megalodon,* which lived in the oceans 5 million years ago. A monstrous 40-foot-long predator with teeth 5 to 6 inches long, it could have consumed a Volkswagen Bug in one gulp. Elsewhere on this floor is **African Voices,** which presents the people, cultures, and lives of Africa through photos, videos, and more than 400 objects.

Upstairs lies another exhibit popular among the under-10 crowd: the **O. Orkin Insect Zoo ★**, where kids enjoy looking at tarantulas, centipedes, and the like, and crawling through a model of an African termite mound. Right next door is **Butterflies and Plants: Partners in Evolution ★**, a 4,000-square-foot exhibit that illustrates the evolving relationship between butterflies and plants over millions of years. The exhibit includes a walk-through, 1,400-square-foot, tropical **Butterfly Pavilion ★**, where hundreds of live colorful butterflies and giant moths alight upon the plants, the ceiling, the walls, the floor—upon you, in fact. (When you exit, you're politely patted down to make sure you're not inadvertently transporting an exotic creature out the door.)

Note: The museum charges a $6 fee for admission (but free admission on Tues) to the pavilion portion of the exhibit. Honestly? Not sure it's worth it. The space is tiny, you don't spend a lot of time there, and, from my observations, some visitors, especially children and teenagers, are not all that thrilled to have butterflies perch upon their heads.

The Hall of Gems in the Natural History Museum.

Ever a big draw is the **Janet Annenberg Hooker Hall of Geology, Gems, and Minerals ★**, which showcases the Hope Diamond; the 23.1-carat Burmese Carmen Lucia ruby, one of the largest and finest rubies in the world; and other treasures of the National Gem Collection. Besides staring spellbound at priceless jewelry, you can learn all you want about earth science, from volcanology to the importance of mining. Interactive computers, animated graphics, and a multimedia presentation of the "big picture" story of the earth are some of the things that have moved the exhibit and the museum a bit further into the 21st century.

Don't miss the Samuel C. Johnson **IMAX Theater,** with a six-story-high screen for 2-D and 3-D movies (*Dinosaurs 3D* and *Tornado Alley* were among those shown in 2012), a six-story Atrium Cafe with a food court, and expanded museum shops. The museum also offers the small **Fossil Café,** located within the Fossil Plants Hall on the first floor. In this 50-seat cafe, the tables' clear plastic tops are actually fossil cases that present fossilized plants and insects for your inspection as you munch away on smoked-turkey sandwiches, goat-cheese quiche, and the like.

The theater box office is on the first floor of the museum; you can purchase tickets by phone (ⓒ **202/633-4629** or 866/868-7774), online, or at the box office at least 30 minutes before the screening. The box office is open daily from 10am to the last show. Films are shown continuously throughout the day. Ticket prices range based on the film and the age of the audience member, from $7.50 for ages 2 to 12 for admission to a 60-minute-or-less presentation, to $15 for ages 13 to 59 for admission to a feature presentation, defined as "longer than 60 minutes." Admission is free for children 1 and under. IMAX films play throughout the day and also most evenings after the museum's closing.

Constitution Ave. NW, btw. 9th and 12th sts. (on the north side of the Mall, with entrances on Madison Dr. and Constitution Ave.). www.mnh.si.edu. ⓒ **202/633-1000,** or 633-4629 for information about IMAX films. Free admission. Daily 10am–5:30pm (in summer often until 7:30pm, but call to confirm). Closed Dec 25. Free highlight tours Feb–July Tues–Fri 10:30am and 1:30pm. Metro: Smithsonian (Mall/Jefferson Dr. exit) or Federal Triangle.

National World War II Memorial ★★ MONUMENT/MEMORIAL
When this memorial was dedicated on May 29, 2004, 150,000 people attended:

President Bush; members of Congress; Marine Corps General (retired) P. X. Kelley, who chaired the group that spearheaded construction of the memorial; actor Tom Hanks and now-retired news anchor Tom Brokaw, both of whom had been active in soliciting support for the memorial; and last, but most important, thousands of World War II veterans and their families. These legions of veterans—some dressed in uniform, many wearing a cap identifying the name of his division—turned out with pride, happy to receive the nation's gratitude, 60 years in the making, expressed profoundly in this memorial.

Designed by Friedrich St. Florian and funded mostly by private donations, the memorial fits nicely into the landscape between the Washington Monument grounds to the east and the Lincoln Memorial and its Reflecting Pool to the west. St. Florian purposely situated the 7½-acre memorial so as not to obstruct this long view down the Mall. Fifty-six 17-foot-high granite pillars representing each state and territory stand to either side of a central plaza and the Rainbow Pool. Likewise 24 bas-relief panels divide down the middle so that 12 line each side of the walkway leading from the entrance at 17th Street. The panels to the left, as you walk toward the center of the memorial, illustrate seminal scenes from the war years as they relate to the Pacific front: Pearl Harbor, amphibious landing, jungle warfare, a field burial, and so on. The panels to the right are sculptured scenes of war moments related to the Atlantic front: Rosie the Riveter, Normandy Beach landing, the Battle of the Bulge, the Russians meeting the Americans at the Elbe River. Architect and sculptor Raymond Kaskey sculpted these panels based on archival photographs.

Large open pavilions stake out the north and south axes of the memorial, and semicircular fountains create waterfalls on either side. Inscriptions at the base of each pavilion fountain mark key battles. Beyond the center Rainbow Pool is a wall of 4,000 gold stars, one star for every 100 American soldiers who died in World War II. People often leave photos and mementos around the memorial, which the National Park Service gathers up daily for an archive. For compelling, firsthand accounts of World War II experiences, combine your tour here with an online visit to the **Library of Congress's Veterans History Project,** at www.loc.gov/vets; see the Library of Congress entry (p. 65) for more information.

The National World War II Memorial, dedicated in 2004.

From the 17th Street entrance, walk south around the perimeter of the memorial to reach a ranger station, where there are brochures as well as registry kiosks for looking up names of veterans. Better information and faster service is available online at **www.wwiimemorial.com**.

17th St., near Constitution Ave. NW. www.nps.gov/nwwm. ℰ **800/639-4992** or 202/426-6841. Free admission. Ranger on duty daily 9:30am–11:30pm, except Dec 25. Limited parking. Metro: Farragut West, Federal Triangle, or Smithsonian, with a 20- to 25-min. walk, or take the Open Top Sightseeing Bus or Mall Express shuttle.

Boy Viewing Mount Fuji by Katsushika Hokusai, displayed at the Sackler Gallery.

Ripley Center CULTURAL INSTITUTION   Part of the Smithsonian complex but not officially counted as a museum, the S. Dillon Ripley Center is notable for housing **Discovery Theater** (p. 153), which stages children's plays and entertainment, and the International Gallery, which hosts rotating exhibits of works from various Smithsonian collections (like the 2012 photography exhibit Pushing Boundaries: Portraits by Robert Weingarten). Look for the copper-domed hutlike structure next to the Smithsonian Castle. Galleries and the Discovery Theater are actually subterranean and connect underground to the Freer, Sackler, and African Art museums.

1100 Jefferson Dr. SW. www.si.edu/museums/ripley-center. (€) **202/633-1000.** Free admission. Daily 10am–5:30pm. Closed Dec 25. Metro: Smithsonian (Mall exit).

Sackler Gallery ★ MUSEUM   Asian art is the focus of this museum and the neighboring Freer (together they form the National Museum of Asian Art in the United States). The Sackler opened in 1987, thanks to Arthur M. Sackler's gift of 1,000 priceless works. Since then the museum has received 11th- to 19th-century Persian and Indian paintings, manuscripts, calligraphies, miniatures, and bookbindings (from the collection of Henri Vever), and art collector Robert O. Muller's entire collection of 4,000 Japanese prints and archival materials.

Your visit begins in the entrance pavilion, where a series of rotating installations, collectively titled Perspectives, showcases the works of contemporary artists from Asia and the Asian Diaspora. The Sackler is preparing you to appreciate the less familiar aspects of Asian art and culture.

The Sackler's permanent collection displays Khmer ceramics; ancient Chinese jades, bronzes, paintings, and lacquerware; 20th-century Japanese ceramics and works on paper; ancient Near Eastern works in silver, gold, bronze, and clay; stone and bronze sculptures from South and Southeast Asia; and a sumptuous graphic arts inventory covering a century of work by Japanese master printmakers. Supplementing the permanent collection are traveling exhibitions from major cultural institutions in Asia, Europe, and the United States. In the past, these have included such wide-ranging areas as 15th-century Persian art and culture, photographs of Asia, and art highlighting personal devotion in India. A visit here is an education in not just Asian decorative arts, but also in antiquities.

To learn more, arrive in time for a highlights tour, offered at noon daily, with other times added on other days. Allow an hour to tour the Sackler on your own.

Also enlightening, in a different way, are the public programs that both the Sackler and the Freer Gallery frequently stage, such as performances of contemporary Asian music, tea ceremony demonstrations, and Iranian film screenings. Most are free, but you might need tickets; for details call the main information number or check out the website. In 2009 the Freer and Sackler galleries inaugurated a program called Asia After Dark, which copies the one hosted by the Hirshhorn Museum (see above) and is aimed at the 20- and 30-something hipster crowd. Staged twice or more a year, the nightlife programs charge $18 admission ($20 at the door) and include tours of both the Freer and the Sackler, cocktails, and DJ-spun music. For information visit www.asia.si.edu/asiaafterdark.

The Sackler is part of a museum complex that houses the National Museum of African Art and the S. Dillon Ripley Center. It shares its staff and research facilities with the adjacent Freer Gallery, to which it is connected via an underground exhibition space.

1050 Independence Ave. SW. www.asia.si.edu. (C) **202/633-4880.** Free admission. Daily 10am–5:30pm. Closed Dec 25. Metro: Smithsonian (Mall/Jefferson Dr. exit).

Smithsonian Information Center ("The Castle") MUSEUM   Make this your first stop, and enter through the **Enid A. Haupt Garden** (see above) for a pleasurable experience. Built in 1855, this Norman-style red sandstone building, popularly known as "the Castle," is the oldest building on the Mall.

The main information area here is the Great Hall, where a 10-minute video overview of the institution runs throughout the day in two theaters. There are two large schematic models of the Mall (as well as a third in Braille), which allow visitors to locate nearly 100 popular attractions and Metro stops.

The entire facility is accessible to persons with disabilities, and information is available in a number of foreign languages. The information desk's volunteer staff can answer questions and help you plan a Smithsonian sightseeing itinerary. Most of the museums are within easy walking distance of the facility.

The Smithsonian "Castle."

While you're here, notice the charming vestibule, which has been restored to its turn-of-the-20th-century appearance. It was originally designed to display exhibits at a child's eye level. The gold-trimmed ceiling is decorated to represent a grape arbor with brightly plumed birds and blue sky peeking through the trellis. This is also where the Castle Cafe is located; though the items are awfully pricey, you can't beat the convenience and the fact that it's open at 8:30am. So why not grab a cup of joe and a muffin, then settle yourself outside on a bench in the Enid A. Haupt Garden with your guidebook and maps to plan your day? Ask about castle and garden tours. As in most Smithsonian cafes, free Wi-Fi is available here.

1000 Jefferson Dr. SW. www.si.edu. ℂ **202/ 633-1000.** Daily 8:30am–5:30pm (info desk 9am–4pm). Closed Dec 25. Metro: Smithsonian (Mall exit).

The United States Botanic Garden holds 4,000 living species.

United States Botanic Garden ★ GARDEN   For the feel of summer in the middle of winter, and for the sight of lush, breathtakingly beautiful greenery and flowers year-round, stop in at the Botanic Garden, located at the foot of the Capitol and next door to the National Museum of the American Indian. The grand conservatory devotes half of its space to exhibits that focus on the importance of plants to people, and half to exhibits that focus on ecology and the evolutionary biology of plants. But those finer points may escape you as you wander through the various chambers, outdoors and indoors, upstairs and down, gazing in stupefaction at so much flora. The conservatory holds 4,000 living species (about 26,000 plants); a high-walled enclosure, called "the Jungle," of palms, ferns, and vines; an Orchid Room; a meditation garden; a primeval garden; and gardens created especially with children in mind. Stairs and an elevator in the Jungle take you to the top of this windowed tower, where you can admire the sea of greenery 24 feet below and, if condensation on the glass windows doesn't prevent it, a view of the Capitol Building rising up on Capitol Hill. And there are sounds—I swear I heard a frog or two. Just outside the conservatory is the National Garden, which includes the First Ladies Water Garden, a formal rose garden, a butterfly garden, and a lawn terrace. Tables and benches make this a lovely spot for a picnic anytime but in winter, though you should keep in mind that the entire garden is unshaded.

Ask at the front desk about tours. The USBG sometimes offers entertainment and special programs.

Also visit the garden annex across the street, **Bartholdi Park.** The park is about the size of a city block, with a stunning cast-iron classical fountain created by Frédéric Auguste Bartholdi, designer of the Statue of Liberty. Charming flower gardens bloom amid tall ornamental grasses, benches are sheltered by vine-covered bowers, and a touch and fragrance garden contains such herbs as pineapple-scented sage.

100 Maryland Ave. SW (btw. 1st and 3rd sts. SW, at the foot of the Capitol, bordering the National Mall). www.usbg.gov. ℂ **202/225-8333.** Free admission. Conservatory and National Garden daily 10am–5pm. Bartholdi Park dawn–dusk. Metro: Federal Center SW (Smithsonian Museums/Maryland Ave. exit).

Vietnam Veterans Memorial ★★

MONUMENT/MEMORIAL The Vietnam Veterans Memorial is possibly the most poignant sight in Washington: two long, black-granite walls in the shape of a V, each inscribed with the

The walls of the Vietnam Veterans Memorial list close to 60,000 names.

names of the men and women who gave their lives, or remain missing, in the longest war in American history. Even if no one close to you died in Vietnam, it's heartwrenching to watch visitors grimly studying the directories to find out where their loved ones are listed, or rubbing pencil on paper held against a name etched into the wall. The walls list close to 60,000 people, most of whom died very young.

Because of the raging conflict over U.S. involvement in the war, Vietnam veterans had received almost no recognition of their service before the memorial was conceived by Vietnam veteran Jan Scruggs. The nonprofit Vietnam Veterans Memorial Fund raised $7 million and secured a 2-acre site in tranquil Constitution Gardens to erect a memorial that would make no political statement about the war and would harmonize with neighboring memorials. By separating the issue of the wartime service of individuals from the issue of U.S. policy in Vietnam, the VVMF hoped to begin a process of national reconciliation.

Yale senior Maya Lin's design was chosen in a national competition open to all citizens ages 18 and over. Erected in 1982, the memorial's two walls are angled

🖉 Washington Monument Visitors: Read This First

Where were you on August 23, 2011? That's when a 5.8-magnitude earthquake struck the East Coast. Here in Washington, D.C., the earthquake's rumbling damaged several buildings, most notably the Washington Monument and the Washington National Cathedral, which were forced to close to the public. The cathedral was deemed structurally sound and reopened November 12, 2011, although repairs of pinnacles, flying buttresses, and gargoyles will continue for years.

The Washington Monument's interior and exterior masonry has taken a bit longer to pass the safety test; repairs are still ongoing. The monument is expected to reopen to the public in late 2013, although the exact date was not known at the time of this writing. Furthermore, even if the monument reopens, procedures for visiting may have changed. Call the National Park Service at ℂ **202/426-6841** for the latest information. The information below was accurate at press time.

A view of the Washington Monument and the Lincoln Memorial Reflecting Pool.

at 125 degrees to point to the Washington Monument and the Lincoln Memorial. The walls' mirror-like surfaces reflect surrounding trees, lawns, and monuments. The names are inscribed in chronological order, documenting an epoch in American history as a series of individual sacrifices from the date of the first casualty in 1959. The National Park Service continues to add names as Vietnam veterans die eventually of injuries sustained during the war. A movement is underway to create a visitor center for the Vietnam Veterans Memorial on the plot of land across Henry Bacon Drive from the memorial.

You should allow about 20 to 30 minutes here.

Northeast of the Lincoln Memorial, east of Henry Bacon Dr. (btw. 21st and 22nd sts. NW, on the Constitution Ave. NW side of the Mall). www.nps.gov/vive. ✆ **202/426-6841.** Free admission. Ranger on duty daily 9:30am–11:30pm, except Dec 25. Limited parking. Metro: Foggy Bottom, with 25-min. walk, or take the Open Top Sightseeing Bus or Mall Express shuttle.

Washington Monument ★★★ ☺
MONUMENT/MEMORIAL The idea of a tribute to George Washington first arose 16 years before his death, at the Continental Congress of 1783. But the new nation had more pressing problems and funds were not readily available. It wasn't until the early 1830s, with the 100th anniversary of Washington's birth approaching, that any action was taken.

Celebrating spring at the Tidal Basin near the Washington Monument.

JAMES SMITHSON AND THE smithsonians

You must be wondering by now: How did the Smithsonian Institution come to be? It's rather an unlikely story. It's all because of the largesse of a wealthy English scientist named James Smithson (1765–1829), the illegitimate son of the duke of Northumberland. Smithson willed his vast fortune to the United States, to found "at Washington, under the name of the Smithsonian Institution, an establishment for the increase and diffusion of knowledge." Smithson never explained why he left this handsome bequest to the United States, a country he had never visited. Speculation is that he felt the new nation, lacking established cultural institutions, most needed his funds.

Smithson died in Genoa, Italy, in 1829. Congress accepted his gift in 1836; 2 years later, half a million dollars' worth of gold sovereigns (a considerable sum in the 19th c.) arrived at the U.S. Mint in Philadelphia. For the next 8 years, Congress debated the best possible use for these funds. Finally, in 1846, James Polk signed an act into law establishing the Smithsonian Institution and authorizing a board to receive "all objects of art and of foreign and curious research, and all objects of natural history, plants, and geological and mineralogical specimens . . . for research and museum purposes." In 1855 the first Smithsonian building opened on the Mall, not as a museum, but as the home of the Smithsonian Institution. The red sandstone structure, suffered a fire and several reconstructions over the years, to serve today as the Smithsonian Information Center, known by all as "the Castle."

Today the Smithsonian Institution's 19 museums (D.C. has 17, soon to be 18, when the National Museum of African American History and Culture opens in 2015), nine research centers, and the National Zoological Park comprise the world's largest museum complex. Millions of people visit the Smithsonians annually—about 30 million toured the museums in 2011. The Smithsonian's collection of nearly 137 million objects spans the entire world and all of its history, its peoples and animals (past and present), and our attempts to probe into the future.

So vast is the collection that Smithsonian museums display only about 1% or 2% of the collection's holdings at any given time. Artifacts range from a 3.5-billion-year-old fossil to inaugural gowns worn by the first ladies. Thousands of scientific expeditions sponsored by the Smithsonian have pushed into remote frontiers in the deserts, mountains, polar regions, and jungles.

Individually, each museum is a powerhouse in its own field. The National Museum of Natural History and the National Air and Space Museum are the most visited of the Smithsonians, each welcoming about seven million people in 2011. The National Air and Space Museum maintains the world's largest collection of historic aircraft and spacecraft. The Smithsonian American Art Museum is the nation's first collection of American art and one of the largest in the world. And so on.

To find out information about any of the Smithsonian museums, call © **202/ 633-1000** or 633-5285. The Smithsonian museums also share a website, **www. si.edu**, which helps you get to their individual home pages.

Then there were several fiascoes. A mausoleum under the Capitol Rotunda was provided for Washington's remains, but a grandnephew, citing Washington's will, refused to allow the body to be moved from Mount Vernon. In

1830, Horatio Greenough was commissioned to create a memorial statue for the Rotunda. He came up with a bare-chested Washington, draped in classical Greek garb. A shocked public claimed he looked as if he were "entering or leaving a bath," and so the statue was relegated to the Smithsonian. Finally, in 1833, prominent citizens organized the Washington National Monument Society. Treasury Building architect Robert Mills's design was accepted.

The cornerstone was laid on July 4, 1848, and construction continued for 6 years, until declining contributions and the Civil War brought work to a halt at an awkward 153 feet (you can still see a change in the color of the stone about one-third of the way up). It took until 1876 for sufficient funds to become available, thanks to President Grant's authorization for use of federal moneys to complete the project, and another 4 years after that for work to resume on the unsightly stump. The Washington Monument's dedication ceremony took place in 1885, and the monument finally opened to the public in 1888.

Assuming the Washington Monument has reopened since the earthquake (see "Washington Monument Visitors: Read This First" above), here's what you need to know:

Visiting the Washington Monument: A series of security walls encircles the Washington Monument grounds, a barrier to vehicles but not to people; the National Park Service has gone to a good bit of trouble to incorporate these 33-inch-high walls into a pleasing landscape design. Please be aware that large backpacks and open containers of food or drink are not allowed inside the monument. You'll need a ticket (see below), and then you'll pass through a small screening facility before entering the monument's large elevator, which whisks you upward for 70 seconds. By the time you read this, the National Park Service may have replaced that temporary screening structure with a more permanent visitor center, possibly moving it underground.

When you reach the top of this 555.5-foot-tall obelisk, you'll be standing in the tip of the world's tallest free-standing work of masonry. The Washington Monument lies at the very heart of Washington, D.C. landmarks, and its 360-degree views are spectacular. Due east are the Capitol and Smithsonian buildings; due north is the White House; due west are the World War II and Lincoln memorials (with Arlington National Cemetery beyond); due south is the Martin Luther King, Jr. and Jefferson memorials, overlooking the Tidal Basin and the Potomac River. "On a clear day, you can see west probably 60 miles, as far as the Shenandoah Mountains," says National Park Service spokesperson Bill Line.

The glass-walled elevator slows down in its descent, to allow passengers a view of some of the 192 carved stones inserted into the interior walls that are gifts from foreign countries, all 50 states, organizations, and individuals. One stone you usually get to see is the one given by the state of Alaska in 1982—it's pure jade and worth millions. There are stones from Siam (now Thailand), the Cherokee Nation, the Vatican, and the Sons of Temperance, to name just a few.

Allow half an hour here, plus time spent waiting in line. A concession stand is open at the corner of 15th Street and Madison Drive NW.

MUSEUMS IN anacostia

This historic, largely African-American residential neighborhood located east of the Capitol and away from the center of the city is not a tourist destination, but two attractions do reside here. The Frederick Douglass home is by far the more compelling and merits a visit. The Anacostia Community Museum's narrow focus and bare-bones exhibits don't necessarily make it worth the effort for an out-of-towner, but if you're in Anacostia already, it's worth checking out.

Frederick Douglass National Historic Site ★ HISTORIC HOME

Crowning one of the highest hills in Washington is Cedar Hill, abolitionist Frederick Douglass's home for the last 18 years of his life. Your tour will begin at ground level in the visitor center, where you'll watch a 20-minute film about Douglass's life, from his birth on a Maryland slave plantation in 1818 to his death here at Cedar Hill in 1895. Then it's a climb of 85 steps to the top of the hill to enter the house for the 30-minute tour, after first taking in the amazing view that sweeps from the Washington Monument and the Capitol to neighborhood landmarks. A National Park Service ranger takes you upstairs and down, and fills you in on the life of the brilliant, brave, and charismatic abolitionist here at this house, but with detours to Douglass's life story: his love of reading, his escape from slavery, his married life, and his embrace of emancipation for all oppressed people. Wallcoverings and woodwork have been reproduced, but just about everything else is original to the house and belonged to Douglass.

All tours are guided, and it's a good idea to make a reservation online. The visitor center and first floor of the house are wheelchair accessible; those unable to climb the 85 steps can drive up the driveway to the entrance. 1411 W St. SE (at 14th St.). www.nps.gov/frdo. ℂ 202/426-5961. Free admission. Spring–summer 9am–5pm; fall–winter 9am–4pm. Closed Thanksgiving, Dec 25, and Jan. 1.

Metro: Anacostia; from the station take the B-2 bus to the park, or you can catch the D.C. Circulator, get off at Good Hope Rd. and 14th St. SE, and walk up 14th St. to the site.

Anacostia Community Museum

MUSEUM   Unique among the Smithsonians, the Anacostia Community Museum was created in 1967 as a neighborhood museum and continues to function as such by offering free educational programs and community workshops to the neighborhood at large. The museum's mission has expanded over the years to include an examination of the impact of social and cultural issues on the local black community from a historical and contemporary perspective. Black Baseball in the District of Columbia, a small, ongoing exhibit mostly consisting of old photos, gives you an idea of the kinds of themes showcased here. The permanent collection includes about 6,000 artifacts, ranging from videotapes of African-American church services to art, sheet music, historical documents, textiles, glassware, and anthropological objects, dating from the early 1800s. The trouble is, only a small portion of these items is on display; you can see most of them in 30 minutes. 1901 Fort Place SE (off Martin Luther King, Jr. Ave.). www.anacostia.si.edu. ℂ 202/633-4820. Free admission. Daily 10am–5pm. Closed Dec 25. Metro: Anacostia (Local exit); turn left after exiting, then take a W2 or W3 bus on Howard Rd. directly to the museum.

Ticket Information: Admission to the Washington Monument is free, but you still have to get a ticket. The ticket booth is located in the Monument Lodge, at the bottom of the hill from the monument, on 15th Street NW between Madison and Jefferson drives; it opens daily at 8:30am. Tickets are often gone by 9am, so plan to get there by 7:30 or 8am, especially in peak season. The tickets grant admission at half-hour intervals between the stated hours on the day you visit. If you want to get tickets in advance, call the **National Park Reservation Service** (*C* **877/444-6777**) or go to www.recreation.gov and type "Washington Monument" into the "Search for Places" field on the left-hand side of the page. The tickets themselves are free, but you'll pay $1.50 per ticket if you order in advance, plus $2.85 for shipping and handling if you order 10 or more days in advance and want the tickets mailed to you; otherwise you can pick up the tickets at the "will call" window at the ticket kiosk. To make sure that you get tickets for your desired date, reserve these tickets at least 2 weeks in advance. You can order up to six tickets.

15th St. NW, directly south of the White House (btw. Madison Dr. and Constitution Ave. NW). www. nps.gov/wamo. *C* **202/426-6841.** Free admission. Labor Day to Memorial Day 9am–4:45pm; Memorial Day to Labor Day 9am–10pm (until noon July 4). Last elevators depart 15 min. before closing (arrive earlier). Closed Dec 25. Limited parking. Metro: Smithsonian (Mall/Jefferson Dr. exit), with a 10-min. walk, or take the Open Top Sightseeing Bus or Mall Express shuttle.

NORTHERN VIRGINIA

The land that today comprises Arlington County, Virginia, was included in the original parcel of land demarcated as the nation's capital. In 1847 the state of Virginia took its territory back, referring to it as "Alexandria County" until 1920, when Arlington at last became Arlington, a name change made to avoid confusion with the city of Alexandria.

And where did the county pick up the name "Arlington"? From its famous estate, Arlington House, built by a descendant of Martha Washington, George Washington Parke Custis, whose daughter married Robert E. Lee. The Lees lived in Arlington House on and off until the onset of the Civil War in 1861. After the

A 24-hour honor guard watches over the Tomb of the Unknowns.

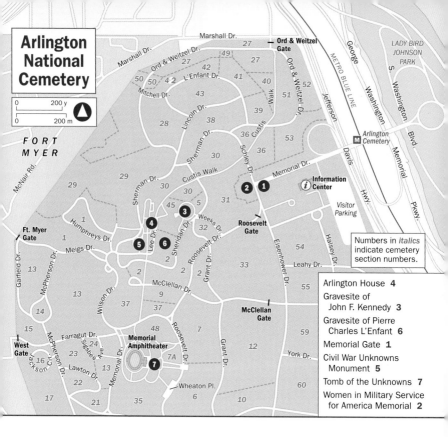

Arlington National Cemetery

FORT MYER

Numbers in *italics* indicate cemetery section numbers.

Arlington House **4**
Gravesite of
  John F. Kennedy **3**
Gravesite of Pierre
  Charles L'Enfant **6**
Memorial Gate **1**
Civil War Unknowns
  Monument **5**
Tomb of the Unknowns **7**
Women in Military Service
  for America Memorial **2**

First Battle of Bull Run, at Manassas, several Union soldiers were buried here; the beginnings of Arlington National Cemetery date from that time.

The Arlington Memorial Bridge leads directly from the Lincoln Memorial to the Robert E. Lee Memorial at Arlington House, symbolically joining these two figures into one Union after the Civil War.

Beyond Arlington the cemetery, is Arlington, a residential community from which most residents commute into Washington to work and play. In recent years, however, the suburb has come into its own, booming with businesses, restaurants, and nightlife, giving residents reasons to stay put and tourists more incentive to visit. Here are some sites worth seeing:

Arlington National Cemetery ★ CEMETERY   Upon arrival head over to the visitor center, where you can view exhibits, pick up a detailed map, use the restrooms (there are no others until you get to Arlington House), and purchase an **ANC Tours by Martz Gray Line ticket** ($8 adults, $7 seniors, $4.50 children 3–11), which stops at the Kennedy gravesites, the Tomb of the Unknowns, and Arlington House. You can also purchase tickets online at www.graylinedc.com. Service is continuous, and the narrated commentary is informative; this is the only guided tour of the cemetery. If you've got plenty of stamina, consider doing part or all of the tour on foot. Remember as you go that this is a memorial frequented not just by tourists but also by those attending burial services or visiting the graves of beloved relatives and friends who are buried here.

This shrine occupies approximately 624 acres on the high hills overlooking the capital from the west side of Memorial Bridge. More than 300,000 people are buried here, including veterans of all national wars, from the American Revolution to the Iraq and Afghanistan conflicts; Supreme Court justices; literary figures; slaves; presidents; astronauts; and assorted other national heroes. Many graves of the famous at Arlington bear nothing more than simple markers.

Cemetery highlights include the **Tomb of the Unknowns,** which contains the unidentified remains of service

Arlington National Cemetery.

members from both world wars and the Korean War—but no longer the from the Vietnam War. In 1998 the entombed remains of the unknown soldier from Vietnam were disinterred and identified as those of Air Force 1st Lt. Michael Blassie, whose A-37 was shot down in South Vietnam in 1962. The Blassie family buried Michael in his hometown of St. Louis. The crypt honoring the dead but unidentified Vietnam War soldiers remains empty. A 24-hour honor guard watches over the massive, white marble sarcophagus, with the changing of the guard taking place every half-hour April to September, every hour on the hour October to March, and every hour at night year-round.

Within a 20-minute walk, all uphill, from the visitor center is **Arlington House** (www.nps.gov/arho; ✆ **703/235-1530**), whose structure was begun in 1802, by Martha and George Washington's adopted grandson, George Washington Parke Custis. Custis's daughter, Mary Anna Randolph, inherited the estate, and she and her husband, Robert E. Lee, lived here between 1831 and 1861. When Lee headed up Virginia's army, Mary fled, and federal troops confiscated the property. An ongoing restoration, as well as repairs to areas damaged by the August 2011 earthquake, may limit access to some parts of the house, which nevertheless remains open. Slave quarters and a small museum adjoin. You tour the house on your own; park rangers are on-site to answer your questions. Admission is free. It's open daily from 9:30am to 4:30pm (closed Dec 25 and Jan 1).

Pierre Charles L'Enfant's grave was placed near Arlington House at a spot that is believed to offer the best view of Washington, the city he designed.

Below Arlington House is the **gravesite of John Fitzgerald Kennedy.** John Carl Warnecke designed a low crescent wall embracing a marble terrace, inscribed with the 35th president's most famous utterance: "And so, my fellow Americans, ask not what your country can do for you; ask what you can do for your country." Jacqueline Kennedy Onassis rests next to her husband, and President Kennedy's two brothers, Senators Robert Kennedy and Edward Kennedy, are buried close by. The Kennedy graves attract streams of visitors. Arrive close to 8am to contemplate the site quietly; otherwise it's often crowded. Looking north, there's a spectacular view of Washington.

In 1997 the **Women in Military Service for America Memorial** (www.womensmemorial.org; ✆ **800/222-2294** or 703/533-1155) was added to Arlington Cemetery to honor the more than two million women who have served in the armed forces from the American Revolution to the present. The impressive memorial lies just beyond the gated entrance to the cemetery, a 3-minute walk from the visitor center. As you approach, you see a large, circular reflecting pool, perfectly placed within the curve of the granite wall rising behind it. Arched passages within the 226-foot-long wall lead to an upper terrace and dramatic views of Arlington National Cemetery and the monuments of Washington; an arc of large glass panels (which form the roof of the memorial hall) contains etched quotations from famous people about contributions made by servicewomen. Behind the wall and completely underground is the **Education Center,** housing a **Hall of Honor,** a gallery of exhibits tracing the history of women in the military, a theater, and a computer register of servicewomen, which visitors may access for the stories and information about 250,000 individual military women, past and present. Hours are 8am to 5pm (until 7pm Apr–Sept). Stop at the reception desk for a brochure that details a self-guided tour through the memorial. The memorial is open every day but Christmas.

Plan to spend half a day at Arlington Cemetery and the Women in Military Service Memorial.

Just across the Memorial Bridge from the base of the Lincoln Memorial. www.arlingtoncemetery. mil. ✆ **877/907-8585.** Free admission. Apr–Sept daily 8am–7pm; Oct–Mar daily 8am–5pm. Metro: Arlington National Cemetery. If you come by car, parking is $1.75/hr. for the 1st 3 hr., $2.50/ hr. thereafter. The cemetery is also accessible via the ANC Tours by Martz Gray Line Express bus.

The Pentagon GOVERNMENT BUILDING   On September 11, 2001, terrorists hijacked American Airlines Flight 77 and crashed it into the northwest side of the Pentagon, killing 125 people working at the Pentagon and 59 people aboard the plane. The Pentagon has since been completely restored, and tours are once again available, in accordance with certain procedures (see below).

You'll be touring the headquarters for the American military establishment, which is one of the world's largest office buildings—it houses about 23,000 employees. The free, 60-minute tour covers 1½ miles as it takes you along corridors commemorating the history, people, and culture of the Air Force, Navy, Army, and Marine Corps.

The tour also includes a visit to the **Pentagon Memorial,** better known as the **9/11 Memorial.** The memorial, which is located on the northwest side of the

The 9/11 Memorial at the Pentagon is open to the public 24 hours a day, every day.

building, near where the plane crashed, opened to the public on the seventh anniversary of the 9/11 attacks, September 11, 2008. On view are 184 granite-covered benches, each engraved with a victim's name, and arranged in order of birth date. The names are written in such a way on each bench that you must face the Pentagon to be able to read the names of those killed there and face away from the Pentagon, toward the western sky, to read the names of those who perished on the plane. To me, at least, the benches resemble birds about to take flight.

Pentagon tours are available Monday to Friday 9am to 3pm; if you are a friend or family member related to personnel assigned to the Pentagon, an active-duty military person, or a school, church, or other group, you can request the tour online, at **http://pentagon.osd.mil**. Individuals and families must contact one of their senator's or their representative's office and ask a staff person in charge of constituent tours to arrange for the tour. ***Please note:*** You do not need to sign up for a Pentagon tour to visit the 9/11 Memorial, which is outside and open to the public 24 hours a day, every day. The best way to reach the memorial is to take the Metro to the Pentagon station and follow the signs that lead from the station to the northwest side of the Pentagon. Memorial staff are on hand to answer questions daily between 10am and 8pm.

Department of Defense, 1155 Defense Pentagon. http://pentagon.osd.mil or www.whs.mil/memorial. *✆* **703/697-1776.** Free admission, but reservations required; guided tours only. Pentagon Mon–Fri 9am–3pm. Pentagon Memorial Daily 24 hr. Metro: Pentagon.

PENN QUARTER

Most of this bustling downtown neighborhood's attractions congregate near the Verizon Center, on or just off 7th Street, the main artery. The ones that aren't there, like Ford's Theatre and the National Museum of Women in the Arts, are just a short walk away. If you enjoy layering your touring experience with stops for

Ford's Theatre.

Lincoln Center on 10th Street

The 500 block of 10th Street NW, between E and F streets, is Washington's very own Lincoln Center. The reference has nothing to do with the New York entity, but everything to do with all things Lincoln. Straddling this short section of 10th Street are Ford's Theatre, where Lincoln was shot in 1865; its basement museum of interactive exhibits and artifacts that reveal Washington life in the 1860s; Petersen House, where Lincoln died hours after he'd been shot; and, now, the grand two-level Center for Education and Leadership, devoted to exploring the aftermath of Lincoln's assassination and his continuing legacy. The Center debuted on Lincoln's birthday, February 12, 2012, opening to the public on February 21. The center's exact address is 514 10th St. NW. Check the Ford's Theatre website, www.fords.org, for more information.

delicious meals or snacks, this is your neighborhood. The Penn Quarter is loaded with great restaurants, bars, and bakeries.

Ford's Theatre National Historic Site ☺ HISTORIC SITE   On April 14, 1865, President Abraham Lincoln was in the audience at Ford's Theatre, one of the most popular playhouses in Washington. Everyone was laughing at a funny line from Tom Taylor's celebrated comedy, *Our American Cousin,* when John Wilkes Booth crept into the president's box, shot the president, and leapt to the stage, shouting, *"Sic semper tyrannis!"* ("Thus ever to tyrants!"). With his left leg broken from the vault, Booth mounted his horse in the alley and galloped off. Doctors carried Lincoln across the street to the house of William Petersen, where the president died the next morning.

The theater was closed after Lincoln's assassination and used as an office by the War Department. In 1893, 22 clerks were killed when three floors of the building collapsed. It remained in disuse until the 1960s, when the NPS remodeled and restored Ford's to its appearance on the night of the tragedy. Grand renovations and developments completed in phases between 2009 and 2012 have since brought about a wholly new experience for visitors.

Ford's Theatre today stands as the centerpiece of the **Ford's Theatre National Historic Site**, a campus of three buildings straddling a short section of 10th St. and including the **Ford's Theatre** and its **Ford's Theatre Museum**; **Petersen House**, where Lincoln died; and the **Center for Education and Leadership,** which debuted in 2012 and is dedicated to exploring Lincoln's legacy and promoting leadership.

I recommend visiting all four attractions if you have the time. You'll need a timed ticket to tour any part of the campus. Tickets are free and tours take place daily. Visit the website, www.fords.org, for a list of "brief visit" and "full experience" offerings, which range from a simple museum and theater walk-through (25 minutes) to a full tour encompassing the museum; the theater, including either a National Park Service ranger's interpretive program or a miniplay, each of which brings to life the Civil War in Washington and the events of April 14, 1865 (highly recommended); Petersen House; and the Center for Education and Leadership (for a total of about 2 hours and 15 minutes).

A single ticket admits you to all parts of the campus, so don't lose it! Ford's really wants you to order tickets in advance online—only 20% of the daily

The room where President Lincoln died.

allotment of tickets are available for same-day pickup. And even though Ford's says tours are free, the fact is that tickets are free only to those 20% lucky enough to get same-day passes. Online tickets cost $3.50 each to cover processing fees. You order the tickets online and can print them yourself or pick them up at the theater's will-call booth. Good to know: The Ford's Theatre website shows same-day tickets as unavailable, but that just means they are unavailable to order online; go in person to the box office and you may score one of those same-day passes.

Briefly, here's what you'll see at the Ford's Theatre National Historic Site:

The Ford's Theatre: The President's Box is still on view, and no, you are not allowed to enter it and sit where Lincoln sat. A portrait of George Washington hangs beneath the President's Box, as it did the night Lincoln was shot. Again, the National Park Service presentations vividly recreate the events of that night, so try for a tour that includes one of these. Ford's remains a working theater, so consider returning in the evening to attend a play. Ford's productions lean toward historical dramas and classic American musicals; the 2012-2013 season includes *Fly*, which relates the experiences of four African American pilots, known as the "Tuskegee Airmen," during World War II, and the musical *Hello Dolly!*. The production schedule means that the theater and sometimes the museum may be closed to sightseers on some days; check the online schedule before you visit.

The **Ford's Theatre Museum**, on the lower level of the theater, displays artifacts that tell the story of Lincoln's presidency, his assassination, and what life was like in Washington and in the United States during that time. Unfortunately, when the museum is crowded, as it often is, it can be hard to get close enough and have enough time at each of the exhibits to properly absorb the information. An exhibit about life in the White House shines a little light on Mary Todd Lincoln; a display of artifacts that includes the Dellinger gun used by John Wilkes Booth connects the dots between the assassin and those who aided him.

Across 10th St. from the theater and museum is **Petersen House**. The doctor attending to Lincoln and other theatergoers carried Lincoln into the street, where boarder Henry Safford, standing in the open doorway of his rooming house, gestured for them to bring the president inside. So Lincoln died in the home of William Petersen, a German-born tailor. Now furnished with period pieces, the dark, narrow town house looks much as it did on that fateful April night. You'll see the front parlor where an anguished Mary Todd Lincoln spent the night with her son, Robert. In the back parlor, Secretary of War Edwin M. Stanton held a cabinet meeting and questioned witnesses. From this room, Stanton announced at 7:22am on April 15, 1865, "Now he belongs to the ages." Lincoln died, lying diagonally because he was so tall, on a bed the size of the one in the room. (The Chicago Historical Society owns the actual bed and other items from the room.) The exit from Petersen House leads to an elevator that transports you to the fourth floor of the:

Center for Education and Leadership, where your tour begins with the sights and sounds in the capital in the days following the assassination of Lincoln. You hear church bells tolling and horseshoes clopping and view exhibits of mourning ribbons and coffin handles and newspaper broadsheets announcing the tragic news. Details convey the sense of piercing sorrow that prevailed: 25,000 people attended Lincoln's funeral on April 21, 1865, though not Mary Todd Lincoln, who was too overcome with grief. A staircase that winds around a sculptured tower of some 6,800 books all to do with Lincoln leads down to the center's third floor. Here, a short film, videos, and exhibits explore Lincoln's influence and legacy: Lincoln's name and image pop up on all sorts of commercial products, from the children's building game of Lincoln Logs to jewelry. Lincoln's words and life have inspired leaders around the world including, we learn, the founder of modern Chinese government, Sun-Yat Sen, who hung a portrait of Lincoln in his home. Following the staircase another level down takes you to a gallery whose displays use real-life examples of brave individuals, like Rosa Parks, to pose the question "What Would You Do?" in their circumstances.

Spring through early fall, Ford's also sells tickets ($15 each, available online) to its popular "History on Foot" 2-hour walking tours. A costumed actor brings Civil War Washington to life, leading tourists on a 1½-mile traipse to about eight historically significant locations.

511 10th St. NW (btw. E and F sts.). **www.fords.org.** ℂ **202/426-6925.** Daily 9am–5pm. Closed Thanksgiving, Christmas and other days subject to the theater's schedule. Timed tickets required for the free tours offered throughout the day. See above for details. Metro: Metro Center (11th and G sts. exit).

International Spy Museum ★★ ☺ MUSEUM   A visit here begins with a 5-minute briefing film, followed by a fun indoctrination into "tricks of the trade." Interactive monitors test one's powers of observation and teach you what to look for when it comes to suspicious activity. In addition to surveillance games, this first section displays trick equipment (such as a shoe transmitter used by Soviets as a listening device and a single-shot pistol disguised as a lipstick tube) and runs film in which spies talk about bugging devices and locks and picks. You can watch a video that shows individuals being made up for disguise, and you can crawl on your belly through ductwork in the ceiling overhead. (The conversations you hear are taped, not floating up from the room of tourists below.)

Try to pace yourself, though, because there's still so much to see, and you can easily reach your limit before you get through the 68,000-square-foot museum. The next section covers the history of spying (the second-oldest profession) and tells about famous spy masters over time, from Moses; to Sun Tzu, the Chinese general, who wrote *The Art of War* in 400 b.c.; to George Washington, whose Revolutionary War letter of 1777 setting up a network of spies in New York is on view. Learn about the use of codes and code-breaking in spying, with one room of the museum devoted to the Enigma cipher machine used by the Germans (whose "unbreakable" codes the Allied cryptanalysts succeeded in deciphering) in World War II.

An interactive exhibit at the International Spy Museum.

Much more follows: artifacts from all over (this is the largest collection of international espionage artifacts ever put on public display); a re-created tunnel beneath the divided city of Berlin during the Cold War; the intelligence-gathering stories of those behind enemy lines and of those involved in planning D-Day in World War II; and the tales of spies of recent times, told by the CIA and FBI agents involved in identifying them.

The museum is constantly adding new features, like **Operation Spy,** a 1-hour interactive immersion into espionage activities. Participants pretend to be intelligence officers and work in small teams as they conduct video surveillance of clandestine meetings, decrypt secret audio conversations, conduct polygraph tests, and so on, all in a day's work for a real-life spy. Check out information about the GPS-guided **Spy in the City** tour and other excellent adventures, on the museum's website.

You exit the museum directly to its gift shop, which leads to the Spy City Café.

While you may look with suspicion on everyone around you when you leave the museum, you can trust that what you've just learned at the museum is authoritative. The Spy Museum's executive director was with the CIA for 36 years, and his advisory board includes two former CIA directors, two former CIA disguise chiefs, and a retired KGB general.

Consider ordering advance tickets for next-day or future-date tours on the Spy Museum's website, which offers you the choice of printing your tickets at home or picking them up at the will-call desk inside the museum. The convenience comes at a price, though: an additional $2 per ticket purchased online. You can also purchase advance tickets, including those for tours later in the day, at the box office. *Note:* Neither the main museum nor its special features are recommended for children 11 and under.

800 F St. NW (at 8th St. NW). www.spymuseum.org. © **866/779-6873** or 202/393-7798. Admission $19.95 plus tax ages 18–64, $14.95 plus tax seniors (65 and over), $13.95 plus tax ages 7–17. Operation Spy $14.95 plus tax ages 12 and over (combined admission fee $27.95 plus tax). Open daily 9 or 10am to 6pm, sometimes later, rarely earlier; check website for details. Closed Jan 1, Thanksgiving, and Dec 25. Metro: Gallery Place–Chinatown (9th and G sts. exit) or Archives–Navy Memorial.

Madame Tussauds Washington D.C. ☺ MUSEUM   Twelve other Madame Tussauds exist, but only three others are located in the U.S., and only one allows you the pleasure of sizing up George Washington, mingling with Beyoncé, helping

Tiger Woods line up his putt, or discussing the state of the world up close and personal with President Barack Obama and Michelle Obama. Madame Tussauds is a wax museum whose more than 120 life-size wax replicas of famous Americans and historic icons appear in various themed galleries, music to sports to politics. The museum is always adding to its collection. In February 2011, the museum launched its **3D Presidential Gallery,** which takes visitors on a walk-through of American history, from the days of King George, the American Revolution,

President Bill Clinton's wax figure at Madame Tussauds.

the birth of the nation, and the election of the first U.S. president, George Washington, to the present-day presidency of Barack Obama. All 43 figures of the country's 44 presidents (remember, Grover Cleveland served two nonconsecutive terms) are on display, along with interactive devices that allow visitors to step into the picture and, for instance, attend George Washington's inauguration. In 2012 the museum welcomed the figure of abolitionist Harriet Tubman. You'll know you've found the museum when you spot Whoopi Goldberg's figure waiting to welcome you, just outside the building. (She heads inside in cold weather, though.)

1001 F St. NW (btw. 10th and 11th sts.). www.madametussaudsdc.com. © **866/823-9565** or 202/942-7300. Walk-up admission $21 plus tax ages 13 and pver, $16 plus tax ages 3–12, children 2 and under free. Purchase advance tickets online and receive a 15% discount. Open daily, but hours fluctuate; call or check the website for exact hours on the day you wish to visit. Metro: Metro Center (11th and G sts. exit).

Marian Koshland Science Museum MUSEUM   The National Academy of Sciences operates this small museum, which was conceived by molecular biologist Daniel Koshland, in memory of his wife, the immunologist and molecular biologist Marian Koshland, who died in 1997. The museum opened in April 2004 in the heart of downtown D.C. Recommended for children 14 and over, and especially for those with a scientific bent, the museum presents state-of-the-art exhibits that explore the complexities of science. (Do pay attention to the museum's age recommendation; I had a hard time wrapping my brain around the various exhibits, interesting though they were, and I'm a little bit older than 13.) Exhibits currently on show are the **Wonders of Science,** which includes animations of groundbreaking research and an introductory film about the nature of science; **Global Warming Facts and Our Future; Infectious Disease,** which covers the challenges to human health; and **Lights at Night,** which allows satellite views that zoom in on places nearby and around the world.

525 E St. NW. www.koshlandsciencemuseum.org. © **202/334-1201.** Admission $7, $4 students and military (with ID). Wed–Mon 10am–6pm. Closed Jan 1, Thanksgiving, and Dec 25. Metro: Gallery Place–Chinatown or Judiciary Sq.

National Aquarium ☺ AQUARIUM   Not to be confused with Baltimore's stellar National Aquarium, this much, much smaller one is the nation's first aquarium and rather cute, with 1,500 specimens of 250 different species on display in illuminated fish tanks. Sharks, alligators, eels, and piranha are among those on view. Feedings take place daily at 2pm. Kids love it.

1401 Constitution Ave. NW (on the lower level of the Dept. of Commerce Building). www.national aquarium.org. ✆ **202/482-2825.** Admission $9.95 adults, $8.95 seniors 60 and over and military, $4.95 children 3–11. Daily 9am–5pm, with extended hours in summer. Closed Thanksgiving and Dec 25. Metro: Federal Triangle.

National Building Museum MUSEUM As is appropriate for a museum devoted to "building," the museum's own structure is perhaps the most notable exhibit here. The building takes up an entire block, stretching the length of a football field. This fact is most impressive when you stand inside the Italian Renaissance–style courtyard, which consumes the entire first floor. The ceiling is 159 feet overhead, with the upper floors arranged around the central atrium. Built between 1882 and 1887 to house the Pension Bureau, the building now functions as a museum devoted to exhibits on design, architecture, and urban development, including an ongoing exhibit titled Washington: Symbol and City. Because of its size, the National Building Museum hosts many galas, including inaugural balls. Firehook Bakery, one of my favorites, runs the cafe here; the gift shop is an especially good one (p. 241).

401 F St. NW (btw. 4th and 5th sts.). www.nbm.org. ✆ **202/272-2448.** Free admission to view the inside of the building; exhibit tour $8 adults, $5 students (with ID), children 3–17, and seniors 65 and over. Mon–Sat 10am–5pm; Sun 11am–5pm. Closed Thanksgiving and Dec 25. Metro: Gallery Place (7th and F sts. exit) or Judiciary Sq. (F St. exit).

National Museum of Crime and Punishment ☺ MUSEUM No kidding—this museum has the feel of a haunted house, complete with dark passages, faux stone walls, a crawl space, and scary figures (mannequins dressed up as dangerous characters) placed here and there. Personally, I find it a bit lame, but I am definitely in the minority, as you'll likely observe if you visit on a Saturday when the single-file line to get in extends out the door. Located in the heart of the Penn Quarter, the museum occupies three floors of a renovated town house, which limits the numbers of people who can shuffle through its five main chambers at any one time. Most of the museum offers a history of crime and punishment, along with tales of famous criminals, from the Middle Ages to the present.

Interactive exhibits allow visitors to place head and hands through a pillory, crack a safe, compare shooting skills to those of Old West outlaws, take a lie detector test, and simulate a police motorcycle chase. Exhibits display a hodgepodge of weapons, including hand irons and spiked chairs used to torture baddies during the Middle Ages. A replica of Wild Bill Hickock's revolver joins other sundry objects such as sample prison garb, a re-creation of Al Capone's jail cell, John Dillinger's brilliant red 1933 Essex Terraplane car, and the getaway car used in the 1964 film *Bonnie and Clyde.*

The National Museum of Crime and Punishment.

The last section of the museum explores crime fighting and solving, encouraging one to channel his or her inner detective to solve a case using interactive kiosks within a replica crime-scene lab. On the lower level of the museum is the *America's Most Wanted* TV studio, from which John Walsh occasionally broadcasts the show. (Walsh is a partner in the privately owned museum.) The museum operates a gift shop, the Cop Shop.

575 7th St. NW (at E St.). www.crimemuseum.org. ✆ **202/621-5550.** Admission online tickets $18.95 adults (ages 12–59), $14.95 children 5–11, $15.95 all others; tickets by phone may be slightly higher. Sept to May 20 Sun–Thurs 10am–7pm, Fri–Sat 10am–8pm; May 21 to Sept 4 Mon–Thurs 9am–7pm, Fri–Sat 9am–8pm, Sun 10am–7pm. Metro: Gallery Place/Verizon Center (7th and F sts./Arena exit) or Archives–Navy Memorial.

National Museum of Women in the Arts ★ ART MUSEUM   Now in its 26th year, this museum remains the world's foremost collection dedicated to celebrating "the contribution of women to the history of art." Founders Wilhelmina and Wallace Holladay, who donated the core of the permanent collection—more than 250 works by women from the 16th to the 20th century—became interested in women's art in the 1960s. After discovering that no women were included in H. W. Janson's *History of Art*, a standard text (which did not address this oversight until 1986!), the Holladays began collecting art by women, and the concept of a women's art museum soon evolved.

Since its opening, the collection has grown to more than 3,000 works by more than 800 artists, including Rosa Bonheur, Frida Kahlo, Helen Frankenthaler, Barbara Hepworth, Georgia O'Keeffe, Camille Claudel, Lila Cabot Perry, Mary Cassatt, Elaine de Kooning, Käthe Kollwitz, and many other lesser-known artists from earlier centuries. You will discover here, for instance, that the famed Peale family of 19th-century portrait painters included a talented sister, Sarah Miriam Peale. Complementing the collection is an ongoing series of changing exhibits. You should allow an hour for touring.

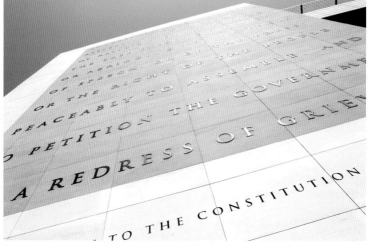

The Newseum's 75-foot-high tablet inscribed with the First Amendment.

The Journalists Memorial, commemorating those who have died in pursuit of news.

The museum is housed in a magnificent Renaissance Revival landmark building designed in 1907 as a Masonic temple by noted architect Waddy Wood. The museum's sweeping marble staircase and splendid interior make it a popular choice for wedding receptions. Lunch (weekdays only) in the Mezzanine Café (✆ **202/628-1068**), and you'll be surrounded by works from the museum's permanent collection.

Don't miss the wonderful outdoor sculpture displayed along a portion of New York Avenue near the museum. On view through March 9, 2014, are large-scale creations by artist Chakai Booker, who works almost exclusively with recycled tires to explore themes of racial and economic differences, globalization, and gender.

1250 New York Ave. NW (at 13th St.). www.nmwa.org. ✆ **800/222-7270** or 202/783-5000. Admission $10 adults, $8 students 18 and over (with ID) and seniors 65 and over, free for youths 18 and under (general admission rates; special exhibition prices may be higher). Mon–Sat 10am–5pm; Sun noon–5pm. Closed Jan 1, Thanksgiving, and Dec 25. Metro: Metro Center (13th St. exit).

Newseum ★★ ☺ MUSEUM Opened in April 2008, the Newseum is as much a fun house of participatory experiences and special-effects exhibits as it is a museum. Its tag line, "World's Most Interactive Museum," conveys its desire to allow the visitor to play the reporter, TV journalist, researcher, or editor. The museum boasts 125 interactive game stations, two state-of-the-art broadcast studios, 15 galleries, and 15 theaters. At this particular time in history, with the business of journalism undergoing a world of change, the six-story Newseum manages to capture the magic of past, current, and future methods of news coverage. In April 2012, the Newseum opened its 15th gallery,

Visitors at the Newseum.

whose interactive and 3-dimensional exhibits explore the development and role of social media in covering the news.

First take a look at the exterior, best viewed from across Pennsylvania Avenue. Covering the left side of the facade is a 75-foot-high tablet inscribed with words from the First Amendment (congress shall make no law . . . abridging the freedom of speech or of the press . . .). Through its glass front, one can see (though much better at night) the huge high-definition screen hanging inside the atrium, spinning news images. Once inside staff direct you first to the orientation film on the lower level (personally, I'd skip this), then to the glass elevators that shoot you to the sixth floor. The outdoor promenade on its own is worth the price of admission, since it offers a breathtaking view of Pennsylvania Avenue and the Capitol. Also take time to read the fascinating history of Pennsylvania Avenue and of the city, presented in an exhibit that runs the length of the terrace.

Fifth-floor exhibits cover history. A display of "Great Books" presents 20 books and documents (originals, not copies) that are widely considered our cornerstones of freedom. These include the 1475 printing of Thomas Aquinas's *Summa Theologica* and a 1542 edition of the Magna Carta. Nearby the **History Gallery** showcases the Newseum's extensive collection of historic newspapers and magazines, tracing 500 years of news. Several theaters on this floor continuously play short documentaries in which esteemed journalists talk about ethics, sources, "getting it right," and other topics.

On the fourth floor, the **First Amendment Gallery** explores the historical contexts of the five freedoms. The 9/11 Gallery displays items recovered at the World Trade Center, images and reporting from that day, and an 11-minute film featuring personal stories by journalists who covered the attacks. While at first glance it appears to be a modern sculpture, one artifact on display here in fact a 360-foot piece of the antenna that had stood on top of the North Tower.

On the third floor, check out the display of *New Yorker* cartoons joshing the news. In the **World News Gallery,** you can tune in to a current news broadcast from one of many countries. The Dateline: Danger exhibit displays artifacts from hazardous missions that journalists have undertaken—including the laptop computer used by *Wall Street Journal* reporter Daniel Pearl before he was killed and the bloodstained notebook of *Time* reporter Michael Weisskopf, who lost his hand in an explosion in Iraq. Following that exhibit is the **Journalists Memorial,** a sobering display of more than 2,084 names written in a glass tablet to mark the deaths of those journalists who have died in pursuit of the news since 1837; the museum rededicates the memorial each year to add the names of journalists who died on the job the previous year. Elsewhere on this floor are several studios actually used by news organizations—including NPR and ABC—to broadcast programs. Visitors can sit in the audience during broadcasts or take behind-the-scenes tours when the studios are not in use.

A veritable playground for news junkies of all ages awaits on the second floor. An interactive newsroom with 48 kiosks allows you to test your skills as a photojournalist, editor, reporter, or anchor. An ethics center tests your sense of ethics. And you can take a turn as news anchor, reading from a teleprompter as a staff person tapes you, then watching your performance on screen. The experience is free, but it'll cost you $5 to buy a photo and the taped video of your performance.

The first floor's gallery of Pulitzer Prize photographs leaves one speechless. The gallery's database of interviews with some of the photographers, a documentary, and vignettes accompanying the photos offer fascinating context to the craft and to the stories behind the photographs.

EXPLORING WASHINGTON, D.C.

Penn Quarter

Last but not least, return to the concourse level to view *I-Witness,* a 4-D film feature that makes you feel as if you're on the scene with legends Isaiah Thomas (radical printer, not basketball legend), Nellie Bly, and Edward R. Murrow. I'm not saying another word, except: Don't miss it.

The Newseum has a casual food court, called The Food Section, whose menu has been designed by Wolfgang Puck, as well as Puck's fancier the **Source** (p. 186), a favorite of Washingtonians. The museum has several gift shops.

555 Pennsylvania Ave. NW (at 6th St.). www.newseum.org. © **888/639-7386.** Admission $22 plus tax ages 19–64, $18 plus tax seniors (65 and over), $13 plus tax ages 7–18, free for children 6 and under. Purchase tickets online for 10% discount. Daily 9am–5pm. Closed Jan 1, Thanksgiving, and Dec 25. Metro: Judiciary Sq. (4th St. exit), Gallery Place/Verizon Center (7th and F sts./Arena exit), or Archives–Navy Memorial.

Old Post Office Clock Tower ☺ HISTORIC SITE

You may have heard that Donald Trump has bought the historic Old Post Office Pavilion and plans to turn the building into a hotel. This is true. However, the National Park Service, which operates and maintains the pavilion's 1899 Clock Tower, continues to state that the tower is off-limits and will remain open to the public. Hope so. Here's why: The tower offers a fabulous view of Pennsylvania Avenue, from the Capitol to the White House, and all around the town. Though the tower, at 315 feet tall, stands only about half the height of the Washington Monument, the outlook is still panoramic. Plus, inside the tower, you're able to see the clock-work, visible through glass panels. The directions for getting to the top of the tower may change once hotel construction gets underway; for now you should look for signs to the elevator to take you to the ninth floor, where you switch to a second elevator that takes you to the 12th.

1100 Pennsylvania Ave. NW (at 12th St.). www.oldpostofficedc.com or www.nps.gov/opot. © **202/606-8691.** Free admission. Mon-Sat 9am–5pm (until 8pm Memorial Day to Labor Day); Sun 10am–6pm. Metro: Federal Triangle.

Smithsonian American Art Museum and National Portrait Gallery ★★★ ART MUSEUM

This historic landmark building houses two Smithsonian museums, the Smithsonian American Art Museum and the National Portrait Gallery. The structure itself is magnificent. Begun in 1836 and completed in 1868 to serve as the nation's Patent Office, it is the third-oldest federal building in the capital. With immense porticoes and columns on the outside, and colonnades, double staircases, vaulted galleries, and skylights inside, the museum captures your attention, no matter how or where you stand to look at it. The building occupies 2 city blocks, from 7th to 9th streets NW and from F to G streets NW.

As for the art presented throughout these three levels: It

The Robert and Arlene Kogod Courtyard at the American Art Museum.

The Smithsonian American Art Museum and the National Portrait Gallery are in the capital's third-oldest federal building.

does America proud. You will see here the faces of the country's founding fathers and mothers, great American heroes and cultural icons, and scenes from American history and way of life, from the moment this country's story began 400 years ago: here an Edward Hopper, there a Gilbert Stuart, now a portrait of Samuel Clemens (Mark Twain), and on to contemporary art by Sean Scully.

Together the Portrait Gallery and the American Art Museum display nearly 2,000 works from their permanent collections. The galleries flow one into another, so you may not always realize that you have stepped from an American Art wing into the Portrait Gallery wing—nor is it necessary to notice. Just wander and enjoy: folk art, introductory "American Experience" landscapes and photographs, special exhibits, American Origins portraits, and other works on the first floor; portraits of America's presidents, an exhibit on The Presidency and the Cold War, graphic arts, and American art through 1940 on the second floor; and art since 1945 and portraits of 20th-century Americans on the third floor. Expect to be dazzled by the creations of such American masters as Winslow Homer, Georgia O'Keeffe, David Hockney, Robert Rauschenberg, Thomas Cole, Andrew Wyeth, Mary Cassatt, and so many others. In addition, don't miss the top floor's **Luce Foundation Center for American Art,** which stores another 3,300 objects, from walking canes to wonderful paintings, in such a way that they remain on view to the public. This two-level gallery tends to be less crowded than the lower floors, which makes for a great wandering, take-your-time experience. Adjacent to the gallery is the **Lunder Conservation Center,** where on weekdays you'll be able to watch conservators working to preserve art pieces. Finally, check out the museum's supercool, year-round enclosed courtyard cafe, the setting for regular performances, like the monthly free jazz concerts *Take Five!*.

8th and F sts. NW. www.americanart.si.edu or www.npg.si.edu. © **202/633-1000.** Free admission. Daily 11:30am–7pm. Highlights tours are offered; check online or call for exact schedule. Closed Dec 25. Metro: Gallery Place–Chinatown (7th and F sts. Exit, or 9th and G sts. exit).

SOUTHWEST OF THE MALL

Two main attractions are located on 15th Street SW, across Independence Avenue from the National Mall. These sites are not National Park Service properties, so I separate them from other attractions located nearby in the southwest section of the National Mall and Memorial Parks category. See "National Mall and Memorial Parks," earlier in this chapter, for descriptions of the Jefferson and other memorials, and see "Potomac Park," later in this chapter, for information about the Tidal Basin, the cherry trees, and Potomac Park.

Bureau of Engraving and Printing ☺ GOVERNMENT BUILDING   This is where they will literally show you the money: A staff of about 2,000 works round-the-clock Monday through Friday churning it out at the rate of nearly $500 million a day. Everyone's eyes pop as they walk past rooms overflowing with new greenbacks. But the money's not the whole story. The bureau prints security documents for other federal government agencies, including military IDs and passport pages. FYI: The Bureau, which is an agency of the Treasury Department (p. 160), celebrated its 150th anniversary in August 2012.

Many people line up each day to get a peek at all the moolah, so arrive early, especially during the peak tourist season.

To save time and avoid a line, consider securing VIP, also called "congressional," tour tickets from one of your senators or your congressperson; write or call at least 3 months in advance for tickets. These tours take place at 8:15am and 8:45am year-round, with additional tours added in the summer.

Tickets for general public tours are generally not required from September to February; simply find the visitors entrance at 14th and C streets. March through August, however, every person taking the tour must have a ticket. To obtain a ticket, go to the ticket booth on the Raoul Wallenberg (formerly 15th St.) side of the building and show a valid photo ID. You will receive a ticket specifying a tour time for that same day and be directed to the 14th Street entrance of the bureau. You are allowed as many as four tickets per person. The ticket booth opens at 8am and closes when all tickets are dispersed for the day.

The 40-minute guided tour begins with a short introductory film. Large windows allow you to see what goes into making paper money: inking, stacking of bills, cutting, and examining for defects. Most printing here is done from engraved steel plates in a process known as intaglio; it's the hardest to counterfeit, because the slightest alteration will cause a noticeable change in the portrait in use. Additional exhibits display bills no longer in circulation and a $100,000 bill designed for official transactions. (Since 1969 the largest-denomination bill issued for the general public is $100.)

After you finish the tour, allow time to explore the **visitor center,** open from 8:30am to 3:30pm (until 7:30pm in summer), with additional exhibits and a gift shop, where you can buy bags of shredded money, uncut sheets of currency in different denominations, and copies of historic documents, like a hand-engraved replica ($200) of the Declaration of Independence.

14th and C sts. SW. www.moneyfactory.gov. ☎ **866/874-2330.** Free admission. Sept–Mar Mon–Fri 9–10:45am and 12:30–2pm (last tour at 1:40pm); Apr–Aug 9–10:45am, 12:30–3:45pm, and 5–7pm. Closed federal holidays and Dec 25–Jan 1. Metro: Smithsonian (Independence Ave. exit).

United States Holocaust Memorial Museum ★★ MUSEUM   Since its opening 20 years ago, the museum has welcomed more than 33 million people from 132 countries, and it continues to be a top draw. In the busiest months,

Inside the Holocaust Memorial Museum.

March through August, if you arrive without a reserved ticket specifying an admission time, you may have to wait in a lengthy line (see "Holocaust Museum Touring Tips," below).

Before you visit the museum, you might want to visit its website, **www.ushmm.org**, and download copies of the Visitors Guide and the Permanent Exhibition Guide. These are also available at the museum, of course.

From its collection of more than 15,350 artifacts, the museum has organized some 900 items and 70 video monitors to reveal the Jewish experience in three parts: Nazi Assault, Final Solution, and Last Chapter. Before you board the elevator that takes you to the fourth floor, where the tour begins, you'll select the identity card of an actual victim of the Holocaust. At several points in the tour, you can find out the location and status of the person on your card—by 1945, 66% of those whose lives are documented on these cards were dead.

Fourth-floor exhibits portray the events of 1933 to 1939, the years of Hitler's and the Nazi party's seemingly inexorable rise to power. A 14-minute film clarifies the long history of anti-Semitism. Newsreels show Hitler speaking commandingly to huge crowds of rapt listeners. Displays of newspaper clippings, billboard ads, signs, and other artifacts reveal Hitler's insidious use of propaganda to sway Germans into believing that Jews—and homosexuals, and the mentally ill, and the disabled, and gypsies, and other non-Aryans—were inferior and did not deserve to live.

Third-floor exhibits cover the years 1940 to 1944 and illustrate the narrowing choices of people caught up in the Nazi machine. You board a Polish freight car of the type used to transport Jews from the Warsaw ghetto to Treblinka and hear recordings of survivors telling what life in the camps was like.

The second floor recounts a more heartening story: It depicts how non-Jews throughout Europe, by exercising individual action and responsibility, saved Jews at great personal risk. Denmark—led by a king who swore that if any of his subjects wore a yellow star, so would he—managed to hide and save 90% of its Jews.

 ## Holocaust Museum Touring Tips

Because so many people want to visit the museum (it has hosted as many as 10,000 visitors in a single day), tickets specifying a visit time (in 15-min. intervals) are required during the busiest months, March through August. Reserve as many as 40 tickets in advance by ordering online at https://tix.cnptix.com/Online/ushmm, for $1 per pass (you print your own tickets), or by calling ℂ **877/808-7466**, for $4 per pass. If you call well in advance, you can have tickets mailed to you at home. You can also get as many as 20 same-day tickets (if they're available) at the museum beginning daily at 10am (lines form earlier, usually around 8am).

Exhibits follow on the liberation of the camps, life in Displaced Persons camps, emigration to Israel and America, and the Nuremberg trials. At the end of the permanent exhibition is a most compelling and heartbreaking hourlong film called *Testimonies,* in which Holocaust survivors tell their stories. The tour concludes in the hexagonal Hall of Remembrance, where you can meditate and light a candle for the victims. The museum notes that most people take 2 to 3 hours on their first visit; many people take longer.

In addition to its permanent and temporary exhibitions, the museum has a Resource Center for educators, which provides materials and services to Holocaust educators and students; an interactive computer learning center; and a registry of Holocaust survivors, a library, and archives, which researchers may use to retrieve historical documents, photographs, oral histories, films, and videos.

The museum recommends not bringing children 11 and under; for older children, it's advisable to prepare them for what they'll see. You can see some parts of the museum without tickets, including two special areas on the first floor and concourse: **Daniel's Story: Remember the Children** and the **Wall of Remembrance** (Children's Tile Wall), which commemorates the 1.5 million children killed in the Holocaust, and the **Wexner Learning Center.** There's a cafeteria and museum shop on the premises.

100 Raoul Wallenberg Place SW (formerly 15th St. SW; near Independence Ave., just off the Mall). www.ushmm.org. ℂ **202/488-0400.** Free admission. Daily 10am–5:20pm, staying open later in peak seasons. Closed Yom Kippur and Dec 25. Metro: Smithsonian (12th St. and Independence Ave. SW exit).

U STREET CORRIDOR

In these old stomping grounds of Duke Ellington and his fellow Black Broadway jazz greats, the main attractions are of the nightlife and dining variety—jazz clubs, like Twins Jazz, that carry Duke's legacy forward, and many restaurants and bars that cater to a range of appetites and interests. See the U Street Corridor listings in chapters 6 and 8 for more information. The two museums located here reflect the neighborhood's identity as a stronghold of African-American history and heroes. *Note:* These two museums are located about half a mile from each other.

African American Civil War Memorial and Museum MUSEUM Newly expanded in 2011, this museum reveals the history of slavery and the African-American experience during the Civil War. Across the street from the museum is the memorial that bears the names of the 209,145 African Americans mustered into military service during that war.

1925 Vermont Ave. NW (at 10th St.; in the Grimke Building). www.afroamcivilwar.org. ℂ **202/667-2667.** Free admission. Tues–Fri 10am–6:30pm; Sat 10am–4pm; Sun noon–4pm. Metro: U St./Cardozo (10th St. exit).

Mary McLeod Bethune Council House National Historic Site HISTORIC HOME This town house is the last D.C. residence of African-American activist/educator Bethune, who was a leading champion of black and women's rights during FDR's administration. Born in South Carolina in 1875, the 15th of 17 children of former slaves, Mary McLeod grew up in poverty but learned the value of education through her schooling by missionaries. It was a lesson she passed forward. By the time she died in 1955 at the age of 79, McLeod—now Bethune, from her marriage in 1898 to Albert Bethune—had founded a school for "Negro girls" in

Daytona Beach, Florida that would later become the Bethune-Cookman College, today Bethune-Cookman University; received 11 honorary degrees; served on numerous government advisory commissions, including the National Child Welfare Commission (appointed by presidents Calvin Coolidge and Herbert Hoover); and acted as Special Advisor on Minority Affairs to President Franklin Delano Roosevelt from 1935 to 1944. Bethune also established this headquarters of the National Council of Negro Women to advance the interests of African-American women and the black community. Maintained by the National Park Service, the Bethune House exhibits focus on the professional achievements of this remarkable woman.

1318 Vermont Ave. NW (at O St.). www.nps.gov/mamc. © **202/673-2402.** Free admission. Daily 9am–5pm. Metro: U St./Cardozo (13th St. exit).

UPPER NORTHWEST D.C.: GLOVER PARK, WOODLEY PARK & CLEVELAND PARK

Follow each of D.C.'s major boulevards northwest of the city and you reach less urban, more residential neighborhoods: Wisconsin Avenue leads out of Georgetown to Glover Park; Connecticut Avenue leads to Woodley Park and Cleveland Park; Massachusetts Avenue leads to American University Park. A handful of attractions lie in these just-beyond-downtown enclaves.

Hillwood Museum and Gardens HISTORIC HOME   This magnificent estate of Post cereal heiress, businesswoman, and socialite Marjorie Merriweather Post includes the beautiful mansion, where she lived from 1955 until her death in 1973, and 13 acres of gardens. The Georgian-style manse is filled with Post's collections of art and artifacts from 18th-century France and 18th- and 19th-century Russia, from Fabergé eggs to tapestries. The gardens include a Russian dacha, a French parterre, and a pet cemetery.

4155 Linnean Ave. NW (at Connecticut Ave.). www.hillwoodmuseum.org. © **202/686-5807.** Admission $15 adults, $12 seniors, $10 college students, $5 students 18 and under. Tues-Sat 10am–5pm; select Sun 1–5pm. Metro: Van Ness/UDC (east side of Connecticut Ave. exit), with a 20-minute walk.

National Zoological Park ★★ ☺ ZOO   The eagle has landed! Sorry, couldn't resist: As of July 2012, the zoo once again has on view its bald eagles, as well as ravens, seals, sea lions, Mexican wolves, beavers, and river otters in a brand-new Seals and Sea Lions exhibit and another nearby rebuilt area, located at the bottom of the hill, where the zoo abuts Rock Creek Park. The animals lived at other zoos and sanctuaries for a couple of years while the new exhibit was being built. An artificial tidal pool is now part of the display, and visitors are welcome to dip their toes in and touch model sea creatures.

Also located at the bottom of the hill is the **Kids' Farm.** Ducks, chickens, goats, cows, and miniature donkeys are among the animals that kids can observe up close. A vegetable garden and pizza sculpture are also popular among the age-3-to-8 crowd.

In all the park, established in 1889, is home to about 400 species—some 2,000 animals, many of them rare and/or endangered. A leader in the care, breeding, and exhibition of animals, it occupies 163 beautifully landscaped and wooded acres and is one of the country's most delightful zoos. You'll see cheetahs, zebras, camels, elephants, tapirs, antelopes, brown pelicans, kangaroos, hippos, rhinos, giraffes, apes, and, of course, lions, tigers, and bears. But the zoo's biggest draws continue to be two **giant pandas,** Mei Xiang and Tian Tian.

Elephant Trails, a new permanent exhibit that provides an improved elephant habitat, including exercise trails, is nearly complete; all that remains is the construction of an "Elephant Community Center" (no lie!), which is expected to wrap up in 2013.

Enter the zoo at the Connecticut Avenue entrance; you'll be right by the Education Building, where you can pick up a map and find out about feeding times and any special activities. *Note:* From this main entrance, you're headed downhill; the return uphill walk can prove trying if you have young children and/or it's a hot day. But the zoo rents strollers, and snack bars and ice-cream kiosks are scattered throughout the park.

The zoo animals live in large, open enclosures—simulations of their natural habitats—along easy-to-follow paths. The **Olmsted Walk** winds from the zoo's Connecticut Avenue entrance all the way to the zoo's end, at Rock Creek Park. Stemming off the central Olmsted Walk is the **Asia Trail,** which takes you past sloth bears, frolicking giant pandas, fishing cats, clouded leopards, and Japanese salamanders. You can't get lost, and it's hard to miss a thing. Be sure to catch **Amazonia,** where you can hang out for an hour peering up into the trees and still not spy the sloth. (Do yourself a favor and ask the attendant where it is.)

Keep on the lookout for a newly installed carousel, just outside the Great Cats habitat.

The zoo offers several dining options, including the Mane Restaurant, the Panda Café, and a number of snack stands. Other facilities include stroller rental stations, a handful of gift shops, a bookstore, and several paid-parking lots. The lots fill up quickly, especially on weekends, so arrive early or take the Metro.

Giant pandas at the National Zoo.

Early Risers?

Zoo grounds open daily at 6am, which might be too early for a lot of tourists, but not for families whose young children like to rise at the crack of dawn. You know who you are. If you find yourselves trapped and restless in the hotel room, hop on the Red Line Metro, which opens at 5am weekdays, 7am Saturday and Sunday (or drive—the zoo parking lot opens at 6am, too), get off at the Woodley Park–Zoo station, and walk up the hill to the zoo. Lots of animals are outdoors and on view. A Starbucks, which opens at 6am Monday to Saturday and 6:30am Sunday, is directly across from the zoo's entrance on Connecticut Avenue. Good morning.

3001 Connecticut Ave. NW (adjacent to Rock Creek Park). www.nationalzoo.si.edu. © **202/ 633-4888.** Free admission. Apr–Oct (weather permitting) grounds daily 6am–8pm, animal buildings daily 10am–6pm; Nov–Mar grounds daily 6am–6pm, animal buildings daily 10am–4:30pm. Closed Dec 25. Metro: Woodley Park–Zoo or Cleveland Park.

Washington National Cathedral ★ CATHEDRAL Pierre L'Enfant's 1791 plan for the capital city included "a great church for national purposes." Possibly because of early America's fear of mingling church and state, more than a century elapsed before the foundation for Washington National Cathedral was laid. Its actual name is the Cathedral Church of St. Peter and St. Paul. The church is Episcopal, but it has no local congregation and seeks to serve the entire nation as a house of prayer for all people. It has been the setting for every kind of religious observance, from Jewish to Serbian Orthodox.

A church of this magnitude—it's the sixth-largest cathedral in the world, and the second largest in the U.S.—took a long time to build. Its principal (but not original) architect, Philip Hubert Frohman, worked on the project from 1921 until his death in 1972. The foundation stone was laid in 1907 using the mallet with which George Washington set the Capitol cornerstone. Construction was interrupted by both world wars and by periods of financial difficulty. The cathedral was completed with the placement of the final stone on the west front towers on September 29, 1990, 83 years (to the day) after it was begun.

English Gothic in style (with several distinctly 20th-c. innovations, such as a stained-glass window commemorating the flight of *Apollo 11* and containing a piece of moon rock), the cathedral is built in the shape of a cross, complete with flying buttresses and 110 gargoyles. Along with the Capitol and the

The English Gothic–style Washington National Cathedral.

LEFT: Tea at the Washington National Cathedral.
RIGHT: The interior of the Washington National Cathedral, the second largest in the U.S.

Washington Monument, it is one of the dominant structures on the Washington skyline. Its 59-acre landscaped grounds have two lovely gardens (the lawn is ideal for picnicking), three schools, and two gift shops.

Among the many historic services and events that have taken place at the cathedral are: celebrations at the end of World Wars I and II; the burial of President Wilson; funerals for Presidents Eisenhower, Reagan, and Ford; the burials of Helen Keller and her companion, Anne Sullivan, inside the cathedral; the Rev. Dr. Martin Luther King, Jr.'s final sermon; a round-the-clock prayer vigil in the Holy Spirit Chapel when the Iranians held American hostages captive, and a service attended by the hostages upon their release; and President Bush's National Prayer and Remembrance service on September 14, 2001, following the cataclysm of September 11.

The best way to explore the cathedral is to take a 30-minute **guided highlights tour;** the tours leave continually from the west end of the nave. You can also walk through on your own, using a self-guiding brochure available in several languages. Visit the website to find out about group and special interest tours, which require reservations and fees. Allow additional time to tour the grounds and to visit the **Pilgrim Observation Gallery** ★, where 70 windows provide panoramic views of Washington and its surroundings. Among the most popular special interest tours are the Tuesday and Wednesday afternoon **Tour and Tea** events, which start at 1:30pm with an in-depth look at the cathedral and conclude in the Observation Gallery with a lovely "high tea," in both the British and literal sense—you're sitting in the cradle of one of the highest points in Washington, gazing out at the cathedral and the city below, while noshing on scones and Devon cream. The cost is $25 per person, and reservations are required. Call ✆ **202/537-8993** or book online at https://commerce.cathedral.org/exec/cathedral/tourtea.

The cathedral hosts numerous events: organ recitals; choir performances; an annual flower mart; calligraphy workshops; jazz, folk, and classical concerts; and the playing of the 53-bell carillon. Check the cathedral's website for schedules.

Massachusetts and Wisconsin aves. NW (entrance on Wisconsin Ave.). www.nationalcathedral. org. ✆ **202/537-6200.** Requested donation $10 per adult, $5 per child and senior. Cathedral Mon–Fri 10am–5:30pm (nave level until 8pm May to Labor Day); Sat 10am–4:30pm; Sun 1–4pm. Gardens daily until dusk. Regular tours Mon–Fri 10–11:30am and 12:45–3:30pm; Sat 10–11:30am and 12:45–3pm; Sun 1–2:30pm. No tours on Palm Sunday, Easter, Thanksgiving, Dec 25, or during services. Services vary throughout the year, but you can count on a Mon–Thurs Evensong service at 5:30pm, a daily noon service, and an 11:15am service every Sun; call for other service times. Metro: Tenleytown, with a 20-min. walk. Bus: Any N bus up Massachusetts Ave. from Dupont Circle, or any 30-series bus along Wisconsin Ave. This is also a stop on the Old Town Trolley Tour. Parking garage $6 per hr./$16 maximum weekdays until 4pm and a flat rate of $7 after 4pm; flat rate of $9 on Sat; free on Sun.

PARKS

More than 27% of Washington's land space is national parkland, reports Bill Line, spokesman for the National Park Service. When you add in the parks and gardens maintained by the D.C. Department of Parks and Recreation, as well as private estates that are open to the public, you're talking thousands and thousands of green acres!

POTOMAC PARK

The National Mall and Memorial Parks' individual spaces known as West and East Potomac parks are 720 riverside acres divided by the Tidal Basin. The parkland is most famous for its display of **cherry trees,** which bloom for a mere 2 weeks, tops, every spring, as they have since the city of Tokyo first gave the U.S. capital the gift of the original 3,000 trees in 1912. Today there are more than 3,750 cherry trees planted along the Tidal Basin in West Potomac Park, East Potomac Park, the Washington Monument grounds, and other pockets of the city.

The sight of the delicate cherry blossoms is so special and the window of viewing time so brief that the whole city joins in cherry-blossom-related

hoopla, throwing the **National Cherry Blossom Festival** and slinging back cherry-flavored cocktails, or whatever is required or desired. The 2012 festival lasted 5 weeks to commemorate the centennial of Japan's gift to the nation's capital. But it's back to normal in 2013, with a two-week festival that, if all goes well, should coincide with the blossoming of the thousands of Japanese cherry trees. The National Park Service devotes a home page to the subject, **www. nps.gov/cherry**, and the National Cherry Blossom Festival officials

Cherry blossoms in Potomac Park.

A cherry blossom lantern tour around the Tidal Basin.

another: **www.nationalcherryblossom festival.org**. Check those websites for the exact dates of the 2013 festival. The trees usually begin blooming sometime between March 20 and April 17; April 4 is the average date.

To get to the Tidal Basin by car (*not* recommended in cherry-blossom season—actually, let me be clear: *impossible* in cherry-blossom season), you want to get on Independence Avenue and follow the signs posted near the Lincoln Memorial that show you where to turn to find parking and the FDR Memorial. If you're walking, you'll want to cross Independence Avenue where it intersects with West Basin Drive and follow the path to the Tidal Basin. There is no convenient Metro stop near here. If you don't want to walk or ride a bike, your best bet is the National Park Service's newly authorized express shuttles and tour buses. (See p. 89, "Getting Around the National Mall and Memorial Parks by Bus.")

West Potomac Park encompasses Constitution Gardens; the Vietnam, Korean, Lincoln, Jefferson, World War II, and FDR memorials; the D.C. World War I Memorial; the Reflecting Pool; the Tidal Basin and its paddle boats; and countless flower beds, ball fields, and trees. It has 1,678 cherry trees bordering the Tidal Basin, some of them Akebonos with delicate pink blossoms, but most are Yoshinos with white, cloudlike flower clusters.

East Potomac Park has 1,681 cherry trees in 10 varieties. The park also has picnic grounds, tennis courts, three golf courses, a large swimming pool, and biking and hiking paths by the water. East Potomac Park's **Hains Point** is located

West Potomac Park.

on a peninsula extending into the Potomac River; locals love to ride their bikes out to the point; golfers love to tee up in view of the Washington Monument. See "Outdoor Activities," below, for further information.

Part of National Mall and Memorial Parks, bordering the Potomac River along the west and southwest ends. www.nps.gov/nama. © 202/426-6841. Free admission. Daily 24 hr. Metro: Smithsonian (12th St./Independence Ave. exit), or take the Open Top Sightseeing Bus or Mall Express shuttle.

ROCK CREEK PARK ★

Created in 1890, **Rock Creek Park** was purchased by Congress for its "pleasant valleys and ravines, primeval forests and open fields, its running waters, its rocks clothed with rich ferns and mosses, its repose and tranquility, its light and shade, its ever-varying shrubbery, its beautiful and extensive views," according to a Corps of Engineers officer quoted in the National Park Service's administrative history. A 1,750-acre valley within the District of Columbia, extending 12 miles from the Potomac River to the Maryland border, it's one of the biggest and finest city parks in the nation. Parts of it are still wild; coyotes have been sighted here, joining the red and gray foxes, raccoons, and beavers already resident. Most tourists encounter its southern tip, the section from the Kennedy Center to the National Zoo, but the park widens and travels much farther from there.

The park's offerings include D.C.'s oldest standing structure, the 1765 **Old Stone House** (see p. 79) in Georgetown (located on a busy street in Georgetown, outside the park but considered a park property, nonetheless); playgrounds; an extensive system of beautiful hiking and biking trails; sports facilities; remains of Civil War fortifications; and acres and acres of wooded parklands. In upper Georgetown, Rock Creek Park includes the family-friendly Montrose Park, a favorite place for picnicking and playing tennis, and Dumbarton Oaks Park, a 27-acre rustic preserve. Both Montrose and Dumbarton Oaks parks adjoin each other and the Dumbarton Oaks estate and formal gardens (p. 78).

For full information on the wide range of park programs and activities, visit the **Rock Creek Nature Center and Planetarium,** 5200 Glover Rd. NW (© 202/895-6070), Wednesday through Sunday from 9am to 5pm. To get to the center by public transportation, take the Metro to Friendship Heights and transfer to bus no. E2 to Military Road and Oregon Avenue/Glover Road, then walk up the hill about 100 yards. Call © 202/895-6070 to request a brochure that provides details on picnic locations.

The Nature Center and Planetarium is the scene of numerous activities, including weekend planetarium shows for kids (minimum age 4) and adults, nature films, crafts demonstrations, live animal demonstrations, guided nature walks, plus a daily mix of lectures, films, and other events. Self-guided nature trails begin here. All activities are free, but for planetarium shows you need to pick up tickets a half-hour in advance.

There is excellent hiking in Rock Creek Park.

Picnicking in Montrose Park, adjacent to Dumbarton Oaks.

There are also nature exhibits on the premises. The Nature Center is closed on federal holidays.

At Tilden Street and Beach Drive, you can see a water-powered 19th-century gristmill, used until not so long ago to grind corn and wheat into flour. It's called **Peirce Mill** (a man named Isaac Peirce built it), and though the mill isn't currently operating, it is open for tours.

You'll find convenient free **parking** throughout the park.

From the Potomac River near the Kennedy Center northwest through the city into Maryland. www.nps.gov/rocr. *C* **202/895-6070.** Free admission. Daily during daylight hours. Metro: Access points near the stations at Dupont Circle, Foggy Bottom, Woodley Park–Zoo, and Cleveland Park.

THEODORE ROOSEVELT ISLAND PARK ★

A serene, 91-acre wilderness preserve, Theodore Roosevelt Island is a memorial to the nation's 26th president in recognition of his contributions to conservation. During his administration, Roosevelt, an outdoor enthusiast and expert field naturalist, set aside a total of 234 million acres of public lands for forests, national parks, wildlife and bird refuges, and monuments.

Native American tribes were here first, inhabiting the island for centuries until the arrival of English explorers in the 1600s. Over the years, the island passed through many owners before becoming what it is today—an island preserve of swamp, marsh, and upland forest that's a haven for rabbits, chipmunks, great owls, foxes, muskrats, turtles, and groundhogs. It's a complex ecosystem in which cattails, arrow arum, and pickerel-weed grow in the marshes, and willow, ash, and maple trees root on the mud flats. You can observe these flora and fauna in their natural environs on 2.5 miles of foot trails.

In the northern center of the island, overlooking a terrace encircled by a water-filled moat, stands a

Relaxing in the shadow of Theodore Roosevelt's statue at Theodore Roosevelt Island Park.

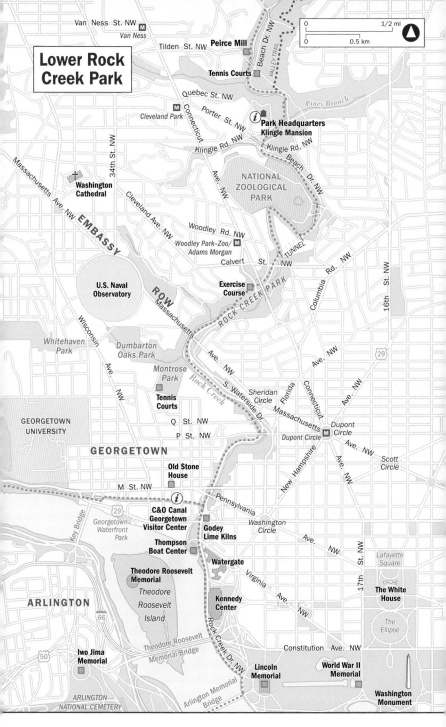

Lower Rock Creek Park

Van Ness St. NW
Van Ness

Tilden St. NW
Peirce Mill

Tennis Courts

Quebec St. NW

Cleveland Park

Porter St. NW

Park Headquarters
Klingle Mansion

Klingle Rd. NW

Klingle Beach Dr. NW

34th St. NW

Connecticut Ave. NW

Washington
Cathedral

EMBASSY

NATIONAL
ZOOLOGICAL
PARK

Cleveland Ave. NW

Woodley Rd. NW

Woodley Park-Zoo/
Adams Morgan

Calvert St. NW

TUNNEL

Massachusetts Ave. NW

U.S. Naval
Observatory

ROW

Massachusetts

ROCK CREEK PARK

Exercise
Course

Columbia Rd. NW

16th St. NW

Wisconsin Ave. NW

Whitehaven
Park

Dumbarton
Oaks Park

Rock Creek

Montrose
Park

Tennis
Courts

Ave. NW

S. Waterside Dr.

Sheridan
Circle

Florida

Massachusetts

Ave. NW

29

Ave. NW

Connecticut

Ave. NW

Dupont
Circle

Scott
Circle

GEORGETOWN
UNIVERSITY

GEORGETOWN

Q St. NW

P St. NW

Dupont Circle

Old Stone
House

M St. NW

C&O Canal
Georgetown
Visitor Center

Pennsylvania

New Hampshire Ave. NW

Ave. NW

Key Bridge

29

Georgetown
Waterfront
Park

Thompson
Boat Center

Godey
Lime Kilns

Washington
Circle

Ave. NW

17th St. NW

Lafayette
Square

ARLINGTON

Theodore Roosevelt
Memorial

Theodore
Roosevelt
Island

Watergate

Virginia

Kennedy
Center

Ave. NW

The White
House

66

Rock Creek Dr. NW

The
Ellipse

Iwo Jima
Memorial

50

Theodore Roosevelt
Memorial Bridge

Constitution Ave. NW

Lincoln
Memorial

World War II
Memorial

Washington
Monument

ARLINGTON
NATIONAL CEMETERY

Arlington Memorial
Bridge

0   1/2 mi
0   0.5 km

Piney Branch

Beach Dr. NW

VALLEY TRAIL

17-foot bronze statue of Roosevelt. Four 21-foot granite tablets are inscribed with tenets of his conservation philosophy.

To drive to the island, take the George Washington Memorial Parkway exit north from the Theodore Roosevelt Bridge. The parking area is accessible only from the northbound lane; park there and cross the pedestrian bridge that connects the lot to the island. You can also rent a canoe at Thompson Boat Center (p. 155) and paddle over, or take the pedestrian bridge at Rosslyn Circle, 2 blocks from the Rosslyn Metro station. You can picnic on the grounds near the memorial; if you do, allow about an hour here. Expect bugs in summer and muddy trails after a rain.

In the Potomac River, btw. Washington and Rosslyn, VA (see above for access information). www.nps.gov/this. (☏ **703/289-2500.** Free admission. Daily 6am–10pm. Metro: Rosslyn, then walk 2 blocks to Rosslyn Circle and cross the pedestrian bridge to the island.

CHESAPEAKE & OHIO CANAL NATIONAL HISTORICAL PARK

One of the great joys of living in Washington is the **C&O Canal** and its unspoiled 185-mile towpath. You leave urban cares and stresses behind while hiking, strolling, jogging, cycling, or boating in this lush, natural setting of ancient oaks and red maples, giant sycamores, willows, and wildflowers. But the canal wasn't always just a leisure spot for city people. It was built in the 1800s, when water routes were considered vital to transportation. Even before it was completed, though, the canal was being rendered obsolete by the B&O Railroad, which was constructed at about the same time and along the same route. Today its role as an oasis from unrelenting urbanity is even more important.

A good source of information about the canal is the National Park Service office at **Great Falls Tavern Visitor Center,** 11710 MacArthur Blvd., Potomac, Maryland (☏ **301/767-3714**). At this 1831 tavern, you can see museum exhibits and a film about the canal; there's also a bookstore on the premises. The park charges an entrance fee: $5 per car, $3 per walker or cyclist.

In Georgetown the **Georgetown Information Center,** 1057 Thomas Jefferson St. NW (☏ **202/653-5190**), can also provide maps and information. The center is open mid-April through September.

The park offers many opportunities for outdoor activities (see below), but if you or your family would prefer a less strenuous form of relaxation, consider the park's **mule-drawn 19th-century canalboat trip,** led by Park

TOP: **The C&O Canal in the late 19th century.**
BOTTOM: **The C&O Canal today.**

Great Falls.

Service rangers in period dress. They regale passengers with canal legend and lore, and sing period songs. Georgetown barge rides have been suspended for the foreseeable future, but boats operate at Great Falls April 15 to October 31. Barge rides last about 1 hour and 10 minutes, and cost $8 per adult, $6 for seniors, $5 per child, and free for children 3 and under.

Enter the towpath in Georgetown below M Street via Thomas Jefferson Street. If you hike 14 miles, you'll reach **Great Falls,** a point where the Potomac becomes a stunning waterfall plunging 76 feet.

Enter the towpath in Georgetown below M St. via Thomas Jefferson St. www.nps.gov/choh. ✆ **301/767-3714.** Free admission. Daily during daylight hours. Metro: Foggy Bottom, with a 20-min. walk to the towpath in Georgetown.

ESPECIALLY FOR KIDS

As far as I know, Pierre L'Enfant and his successors were not thinking of children when they incorporated the long, open stretch of the Mall into their design for the city. But they may as well have been. This 2-mile expanse of lawn running from the Lincoln Memorial to the Capitol is a playground, really, and a backyard to the Smithsonian museums and National Gallery of Art, which border it. You can visit any of these sites assured that if one of your little darlings starts to misbehave, you'll be able to head right out the door to the National Mall, where numerous distractions await. The Mall is always busy with walkers, joggers, and bikers. Vendors sell ice cream, soft pretzels, and sodas. Festivals of all sorts take place on a regular basis, whether it's the busy **Smithsonian Folklife Festival** for 10 days at the end of June into July (see "Washington, D.C. Calendar of Events," in chapter 2), or the **Kite Festival** in spring. Weather permitting, a 19th-century carousel operates in front of the Arts and Industries Building, on the south side of the Mall. Right across the Mall from the carousel is the children-friendly National Gallery Sculpture Garden, whose shallow pool is good for splashing one's feet in summer and for ice-skating in winter.

You don't need the excuse of recalcitrant children to enjoy the Mall, of course, though it's always good to have an escape route. The truth is that many of Washington's attractions hold various enchantments for children of all ages. It

Kids love the Kite Festival on the grounds of the Washington Monument.

might be easier to point out which ones are not recommended for your youngest: the Supreme Court, the chambers of Congress, the U.S. Holocaust Memorial Museum, and the Marian Koshland Science Museum; the International Spy Museum is now recommending that its museum is most suitable for children 12 and over. Generally speaking, the bigger and busier the museum, the better it is for kids. On the Mall, these would be the three top draws: the **National Museum of Natural History** (p. 110), the **National Air and Space Museum** (p. 99), and the **National Museum of American History** (p. 107), each of which has special areas and exhibits aimed specifically at children. D.C.'s newest attractions might have the rest

The Smithsonian Folklife Festival.

beat: the **Newseum** (p. 134), **Madame Tussauds Washington D.C.** (p. 130), and the **National Museum of Crime and Punishment** (p. 132).

For more ideas, consult the online or print version of the Friday "Weekend" section of the *Washington Post,* which lists numerous activities (mostly free) for kids: special museum events, children's theater, storytelling programs, puppet shows, video-game competitions, and so forth. Call the Kennedy Center and the National Theatre to find out about children's shows; see chapter 8 for details.

I've noted "Family-Friendly Hotels" in chapter 9; a few, though not many, hotels have pools, and some offer little goodie packages at check-in. Also see

FAVORITE children's ATTRACTIONS

Check for special children's events at museum information desks when you enter. As noted within the listings for individual museums, some children's programs are also great fun for adults. I recommend the programs at the **Folger Shakespeare Library** (p.64), the **Phillips Collection** (p. 74), and the **Sackler Gallery** (p. 114) in particular. (The gift shops in most of these museums have wonderful toys and children's books.) Call ahead to find out what programs are running. Here's a rundown of great kid-pleasers in town:

- **Madame Tussauds Washington D.C.** (p. 130): There are two kinds of people in this world: those who think wax museums are hokey, and children. Yeah, watch your offspring pretend to sing with Beyoncé, box with Evander Holyfield, stand tall next to George Washington, and whoop it up with Whoopi. Maybe you'll find your inner child and start loving these wax figures, too.

- **Discovery Theater, inside the S. Dillon Ripley Center** (p. 114): Right next to the Smithsonian Castle (Information Center) on the National Mall is this underground children's theater that puts on live performing arts entertainment for the kiddies, about 30 productions each season, including puppet shows, storytelling, dances, and plays.

- **National Museum of Crime and Punishment** (p. 132): Your little darlings can pretend to be little Dillingers and test their safecracking skills, or little Elliot Nesses as they learn how to take fingerprints and gather clues.

- **Newseum** (p. 134): Proceed directly to the interactive newsroom on the second floor, where your children will happily, endlessly play computer games while testing their news knowledge and journalism skills, and where they'll have the chance to play an on-camera reporter.

- **Lincoln Memorial** (p. 97): Kids know a lot about Lincoln and enjoy visiting his memorial. A special treat is visiting after dark.

- **National Air and Space Museum** (p. 99): Spectacular IMAX films (don't miss), thrilling flight simulators, planetarium shows, missiles, rockets, and a walk-through orbital workshop.

- **National Museum of American History** (p. 107): Living-history performances and lively musical numbers staged in public areas throughout the museum switch a typical museum visit into something more fun and memorable. And the museum has gotten into simulators, offering rides on machines that make you believe you're driving a race car or riding on a roller coaster.

- **National Museum of Natural History** (p. 110): A Discovery Room just for youngsters, the Butterfly Pavilion and exhibit, as well as the outdoor butterfly garden, an insect zoo, shrunken heads, dinosaurs, and the IMAX theater showing 2-D and 3-D films.

- **National Zoological Park** (p. 141): Pandas! Cheetahs! Kids always love a zoo, and this is an especially good one.

- **Washington Monument** (p. 118): Spectacular 360-degree views from the center of Washington, D.C.— when the monument opens to the public again, which may not be until late 2013.

chapter 3, "Suggested Washington, D.C. Itineraries," for a family-themed list of things to do in D.C., as well as "Guided Tours," in chapter 11—sometimes nothing beats getting off your feet and touring a town by boat or bus.

But first here's a sure-thing list of favorite children's attractions.

OUTDOOR ACTIVITIES

For information about spectator-sports venues, including how to buy tickets and where to go to watch **Wizards** (men's) and **Mystics** (women's) basketball, **Capitals** ice hockey, and **Nationals** baseball games, see chapter 8.

But if you prefer to work up your own honest sweat, Washington offers plenty of pleasant opportunities in many lush surroundings. See "Parks," earlier in this chapter, for complete coverage of the city's loveliest green spaces.

BIKING

Biking is big in D.C., not just as a leisure activity but as an environmentally friendly form of transportation. See p. 30 to read about the Capital BikeShares program. So much of the city is flat, and paths are everywhere, notably around the National Mall and Memorial Parks. Rock Creek Park has an **11-mile paved bike route** ★ from the Lincoln Memorial through the park into Maryland. Or you can follow the bike path from the Lincoln Memorial and go over Memorial Bridge to pedal to Old Town Alexandria and on to Mount Vernon (see chapter 10). On weekends and holidays, a large part of Rock Creek Parkway is closed to vehicular traffic. The C&O Canal park's towpath, described in "Parks," earlier in this chapter, is a popular bike path. The **Capital Crescent Trail** takes you from Georgetown to the suburb of Bethesda, Maryland, following a former railroad track that parallels the Potomac River for part of the way and passes by old trestle bridges and pleasant residential neighborhoods. You can pick up the trail at the **Thompson Boat Center**, in Georgetown near the waterfront, and at

A biker along the Potomac.

A kayaker on the Tidal Basin.

Fletcher's Cove, along the C&O Canal; visit **www.cctrail.org** for maps and more information.

Bike rental locations include:

- The **Boat House at Fletcher's Cove,** 4940 Canal Rd. NW (www.fletchers cove.com; ✆ **202/244-0461**).

- **Bike and Roll/Bike the Sites,** (www.bikethesites.com; ✆ **202/842-2453**), with three locations: 1100 Pennsylvania Ave. NW, at the rear plaza of the Old Post Office Pavilion (Metro: Federal Triangle, on the Blue and Orange lines); Union Station (✆ **202/962-0206**); or Old Town Alexandria, 1 Wales Alley, off of King Street at the waterfront (✆ **703/548-7655**). Rates vary depending on the bike you choose but always include helmet, bike, lock, and pump; there's a 2-hour minimum.

- **Thompson Boat Center,** 2900 Virginia Ave. NW, at Rock Creek Parkway (www.thompsonboatcenter.com; ✆ **202/333-9543**; Metro: Foggy Bottom, with a 10-min. walk). Both Fletcher's and Thompson rent bikes, weather permitting, from about mid-March to mid-October.

- **Big Wheel Bikes,** 1034 33rd St. NW, right near the C&O Canal just below M Street (www.bigwheelbikes.com; ✆ **202/337-0254**). You can rent a bike here year-round Tuesday through Sunday.

BOATING AND FISHING

See "Guided Tours," in chapter 11, for recommended tour boats that cruise the Potomac. Otherwise look to the same places that rent bikes: **Thompson Boat Center** and the **Boat House at Fletcher's Cove** (see above for both), which **rent boats** following the same schedule as their bike rental season, basically March to November. Thompson has canoes, kayaks, and rowing shells (recreational and racing), and is open for boat and bike rentals daily in season from (generally) 7am to 7pm. Fletcher's is right on the C&O Canal, about 3¼ miles from Georgetown. In addition to renting bikes, canoes, rowboats, and kayaks, Fletcher's also sells fishing licenses, bait, and tackle. Open daily 7am to 7pm in season, Fletcher's is accessible by car (west on M St. NW to Canal Rd. NW) and has plenty of free parking.

Jack's Boathouse, 3500 K St. NW (www.jacksboathouse.com; ☎ **202/337-9642**), located along the Georgetown waterfront beneath Key Bridge, is open daily mid-April to October (check website for hours) for canoe and kayak rentals. Foggy Bottom is the closest Metro station.

From mid-March to mid-October, weather permitting, you can rent **paddle boats** ★ on the north end of the Tidal Basin off Independence Avenue (www.tidalbasinpaddleboats.com; ☎ **202/479-2426**). Four-seaters are $19 an hour, two-seaters $12 an hour, from 10am to 6pm daily mid-March to Labor Day, Wednesday to Sunday Labor Day to mid-October.

GOLF

The District's best and most convenient public golf course is the historic **East Potomac Golf Course** on Hains Point (p. 146), 972 Ohio Dr. SW, in East Potomac Park (www.golfdc.com; ☎ **202/554-7660**). Golfers use the Washington Monument to help them line up their shots. The club rents everything but shoes. In addition to its year-round 36-hole green, the park offers a miniature golf course; open since 1930, this is the oldest continually operating miniature golf course in the country.

HIKING AND JOGGING

Joggers can enjoy a run on the Mall or along the path in Rock Creek Park.

Washington has numerous **hiking paths.** The C&O Canal offers 185 miles stretching from D.C. to Cumberland, Maryland; hiking any section of the flat dirt towpath or its more rugged side paths is a pleasure (and it's free). There are picnic tables, some with barbecue grills, about every 5 miles on the way to Cumberland. Theodore Roosevelt Island has more than 88 wilderness acres to explore, and Rock Creek Park boasts 20 miles of hiking trails (visit www.nps.gov/rocr/planyourvisit/brochures.htm for maps).

At the National Gallery Sculpture Garden Ice Rink, you can take in the sculptures while you skate.

White House Street Hockey

When security hysteria closed Pennsylvania Avenue in front of the White House, some enterprising athletes converted the world's most prestigious address, 1600 Pennsylvania Ave. NW, into a street hockey rink. Since no motor vehicles are allowed on the flat, wide roadway, street hockey players commandeer the spot for their sport every Saturday and Sunday at noon. Anybody can show up to play; all you need are skates and a stick. Other protective equipment, like helmets and padding, is optional, although the veteran players recommend wearing at least hockey gloves. Check out the White House Hockey website (www.sites.google.com/site/whitehousehockey) and sign up for the players' Google group to be informed about schedules and weather-related cancellations.

ICE-SKATING

For a truly memorable experience, head to the **National Gallery Sculpture Garden Ice Rink ★**, on the Mall at 7th Street and Constitution Avenue NW (✆ **202/289-3360**), where you can rent skates, twirl in view of the sculptures, and enjoy hot chocolate and a sandwich in the Pavilion Café next to the rink.

SWIMMING

If it's summer and your hotel doesn't have a **pool,** you might consider one of the neighborhood pools, including a large outdoor pool at 25th and N streets NW (✆ **202/727-3285**) and the Georgetown outdoor pool at 34th Street and Volta Place NW (✆ **202/645-5669**). Keep in mind that these are likely to be crowded.

One of the best places open to the public for swimming in summer and for other outdoor sports year-round is East Potomac Park's **Hains Point,** which lies within walking distance of Independence Avenue and has a large outdoor swimming pool (✆ **202/727-6523**).

TENNIS

Hains Point also has 24 tennis courts (10 clay, 9 outdoor hard courts, and 5 indoor hard courts), including three illuminated at night; the park rents rackets as well; contact East Potomac Park Tennis (www.eastpotomactennis.com; ✆ **202/554-5962**). Fees vary with court surface and time of play.

Finally, one other tennis option: **Montrose Park,** right next to Dumbarton Oaks (p. 78), in Georgetown, has several courts available free on a first-come, first-served basis, but they're often in use.

5

STROLLING AROUND WASHINGTON, D.C.

O ne of the greatest pleasures to be had in the nation's capital is walking. You round a corner and spy the Capitol standing proudly at the end of the avenue. You stroll a downtown street and chance to look up and bam, there it is: the tip of the Washington Monument. People brush past you on the sidewalk speaking a pastiche of languages. You decide to walk rather than take the Metro or a taxi back to your hotel and discover a gem of a museum. A limousine pulls up to the curb and discharges—who? A foreign ambassador? The president himself? A famous author or athlete or human rights activist?

Beautiful sights, historic landmarks, unpredictable encounters, and multicultural experiences await you everywhere in Washington. Follow either or both of these walking tours and see for yourself.

WALKING TOUR 1: **STROLLING AROUND THE WHITE HOUSE**

START:	**White House Visitor Center, 1450 Pennsylvania Ave. NW (Metro: Federal Triangle or Metro Center).**
FINISH:	**The Penn Quarter (Metro: Federal Triangle or Metro Center).**
TIME:	**1½ hours to 2 hours (not including stops). It's about a 1.6-mile trek.**
BEST TIME:	**During the day. If you want to hit all of the museums, stroll on a Thursday or a Friday.**
WORST TIME:	**After dark, as some streets can be deserted.**

The White House is the centerpiece of a national park, President's Park, which includes not just the house itself but also its grounds, from the Ellipse to Pennsylvania Avenue to Lafayette Square; the U.S. Treasury Building on 15th Street; and the Eisenhower Executive Office Building on 17th Street. The individual histories of many of the surrounding buildings and sites are entwined with that of the White House. As you wend your way from landmark to landmark, you'll be mingling with White House administration staff, high-powered attorneys, diplomats, and ordinary office workers. But all of you are treading the same ground as early American heroes, like Stephen Decatur, whose house you'll see, and every president since George Washington (though the White House was not finished in time for him to live there). This tour circumnavigates the White House grounds, with stops at historic sites and several noteworthy museums as well. The White House Visitor Center (see "Midtown," in chapter 4) is a good place to begin and end (for one thing, it's got restrooms!). **Note:** Tours of the White House and the U.S. Treasury Building require advance reservations. Go to www.treasury.gov/about/education/pages/tours.aspx to register for a Treasury Building tour; for White House tour info, see the White House listing in chapter 4.

PREVIOUS PAGE: **Statue of Major General Comte Jean de Rochambeau in Lafayette Square.**

LEFT: **The Treasury Building.** RIGHT: **The Alexander Hamilton statue in front of the Treasury Building.**

From the White House Visitor Center, stroll up 15th Street to your first stop, at 15th and F streets NW.

5

Strolling Around the White House

STROLLING AROUND

1 U.S. Treasury Building

Poor Alexander Hamilton. His statue outside the south end of the U.S. Treasury Building stands too close for security comfort to the White House to allow stray tourists a better look, so now you must resign yourself to gazing at him from a distance through the black iron fencing. (Also, poor Alexander Hamilton, killed in a duel with his political enemy, Vice President Aaron Burr.) Hamilton, who devised our modern financial system, was the first Secretary of the Treasury, established by Congress in 1789. So once you've caught a glimpse of Hamilton's statue, have a look inside the Treasury's headquarters, America's oldest office building, constructed between 1836 and 1869. Its most notable architectural feature is the colonnade you see running the length of the building: 30 columns, each 36 feet tall, carved out of a single piece of granite. In its lifetime, the building has served as Civil War barracks, as a temporary home for President Andrew Johnson following the assassination of President Lincoln in 1865, and as the site of President Ulysses S. Grant's inaugural reception. Today the building houses offices for the U.S. Treasurer, the Secretary of the Treasury, its General Counsel, and their staffs.

Continue north on 15th Street and turn left onto the Pennsylvania Avenue promenade, where you'll notice the statue of Albert Gallatin, the fourth Secretary of the Treasury, standing accessible on the north side of the Treasury Building. Continue along:

2 Pennsylvania Avenue

Say hello to the President, who resides in that big white house beyond the black iron fencing. A wave from the Pennsylvania Avenue plaza is as close as you are going to get unless you've signed up for a tour. Security precautions put in place in 1995 keep this two-block section of Pennsylvania Avenue closed to traffic. But that's a good thing. You may have to dodge bicyclists, roller skaters, joggers, and random Frisbees, but not cars. Ninety Princeton American elm trees line the 84-foot-wide promenade, which offers plenty of great photo ops as you stroll past the White House. There

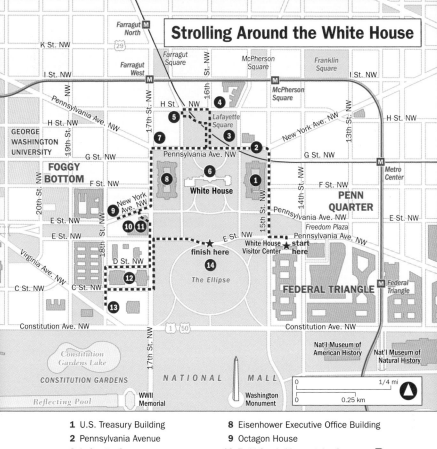

Strolling Around the White House

1. U.S. Treasury Building
2. Pennsylvania Avenue
3. Lafayette Square
4. St. John's Episcopal Church on Lafayette Square
5. Decatur House
6. White House
7. Renwick Gallery
8. Eisenhower Executive Office Building
9. Octagon House
10. Todd Gray's Muse at the Corcoran ☕
11. Corcoran Gallery of Art
12. DAR Museum and Period Rooms
13. Art Museum of the Americas
14. Ellipse

are benches here, too, in case you'd like to sit and people-watch. L'Enfant's original idea for Pennsylvania Avenue was that it would connect the legislative branch (Congress) at one end of the avenue with the executive branch (the president's house) at the other end.

Turn your back on the White House and walk across the plaza to enter:

3 Lafayette Square

This 7-acre public park is known as a gathering spot for protesters. (In pleasant weather, when the White House keeps its doors and windows open, one can actually hear the protesters from inside the White House, as I discovered during a recent White House tour.) In its early days, the park served as an open-air market and as a military encampment. The park is named after the Marquis de Lafayette, a Frenchman who served under George Washington during the Revolutionary War. But it's General Andrew Jackson's statue that centers the park. Erected in 1853, this was America's first equestrian statue. It's said that sculptor Clark Mills trained a horse to maintain a reared-up pose so that Mills could study how the horse balanced its weight. Other park statues are dedicated to foreign soldiers who

Lafayette Square is a scenic, 7-acre public park.

fought in the War for Independence, including Lafayette; Tadeusz Kosciuszko, from Poland; Prussian Baron von Steuben; and Frenchman Comte de Rochambeau.

Walk through the park and cross H Street to reach 1525 H St. NW, the site of:

4 St. John's Episcopal Church on Lafayette Square

St. John's is known as "the Church of the Presidents" because every president since James Madison has attended at least one service here. If you tour the church, look for pew 54, 8 rows from the front, which is the one traditionally reserved for the current president and first family. Other things to notice in this 1816 church, designed by Benjamin Henry Latrobe, are the steeple bell, which was cast by Paul Revere's son and has been in continuous use since its installation in 1822, and the beautiful stained-glass windows. And be careful not to overlook the Lincoln Pew at the very back of the church, where Lincoln would sit alone for evening services during the Civil War, slipping in after other congregants had arrived and slipping out before they left.

Directly across the street from St. John's is the Hay-Adams Hotel, which turns 85 this year (p. 287). Recross H Street to stand in front of 748 Jackson Place NW, the:

5 Decatur House

In addition to St. John's, Latrobe also designed this Federal-style brick town house in 1818 for Commodore Stephen Decatur, a renowned naval hero in the War of 1812. Decatur and his wife, Susan, established themselves as gracious hosts in the 14 short months they lived here. In March

The Decatur House.

STROLLING AROUND | Strolling Around the White House

1820, 2 days after hosting a ball for President James Monroe's daughter, Marie, Decatur was killed in a gentleman's duel by his former mentor, James Barron. Barron blamed Decatur for his 5-year suspension from the Navy, following a court-martial in which Decatur had played an active role. Other distinguished occupants have included Henry Clay and Martin Van Buren, when each was serving as Secretary of State (Clay under Pres. John Quincy Adams, Van Buren under Pres. Andrew Jackson). Decatur House is no longer open for house tours but does host popular jazz concerts in its courtyard throughout the summer. Stop in at the White House Historical Association's gift shop, which is adjacent to Decatur House at 740 Jackson Place NW.

Walk back through Lafayette Square to return to the Pennsylvania Avenue plaza, where you'll have another chance to admire the:

6 White House

As grand as the White House is, it is at least one-fourth the size that Pierre L'Enfant had in mind when he planned a grand palace to house the President. George Washington and his commission had something else in mind, however, and dismissed L'Enfant, though they kept L'Enfant's site proposal. An Irishman named James Hoban designed the building, having entered his architectural draft in a contest held by George Washington, beating out 52 other entries. Though Washington picked the winner, he was the only president never to live in the White House, or "President's Palace," as it was called before whitewashing brought the name "White House" into use. Construction of the White House took 8 years, beginning in 1792, when its cornerstone was laid. Its facade is made of the same stone as that used to construct the Capitol. See p. 83 for in-depth information about the White House and White House tours.

Turn around and head toward the northwest corner of the plaza, at 17th Street, to reach the:

7 Renwick Gallery

Its esteemed neighbors are the White House and, right next door, the Blair-Lee House, where the White House sends overnighting foreign dignitaries. The Renwick (p. 82), nevertheless, holds its own. This distinguished red-brick and brownstone structure was the original location for the Corcoran Gallery of Art. James Renwick designed the building (if it reminds you of the Smithsonian Castle on the Mall, it's because Renwick designed that one, too), which opened in 1874. When the collection outgrew its quarters, the Corcoran moved to its current location in 1897 (see below). Decorative arts and American crafts are the focus of the Renwick, which since 1972 has operated as an annex of the Smithsonian American Art Museum, 8 blocks away in the Penn Quarter. If time allows, step inside for a look at the works in the Grand Salon on the second floor. Return on the second Thursday of the month, between 5:30 and 8pm, for Handi-hour (ages 21 and over; admission $20), where you can enjoy craft beers, crafting activities (knitting, crocheting, clay modeling), and live music.

Turn left on 17th Street, where you'll notice on your left the:

8 Eisenhower Executive Office Building

Old-timers still refer to this ornate building as the "OEOB," for "Old Executive Office Building"; as it sounds, the OEOB houses the offices of people who work in or with the Executive Office of the President. Originally, the structure was called the State, War, and Navy Building; when its construction was completed in 1888, it was the largest office building in

The Executive Office Building.

the world. During the Iran-Contra scandal of the Reagan presidency, the OEOB became famous as the site of document shredding by Colonel Oliver North and his secretary Fawn Hall. Open to the public? Nope.

Cross 17th Street, walk a couple of blocks to New York Avenue, and turn right. Follow it one block to 18th Street, where you'll see the unmistakable:

9 Octagon House

Lot of history in this old house. But first, before you enter, admire its unique shape. Count its sides and you'll discover that the Octagon is, in fact, a hexagon. Designed by Dr. William Thornton, first architect of the U.S. Capitol, this 1801 building apparently earned its name from interior features, though experts disagree about that. Enter the Octagon to view the round rooms; the central, oval-shaped staircase that curves gracefully to the third level; the hidden doors; and the triangular chambers. Built originally for the wealthy Tayloe family, the Octagon served as a temporary president's home for James and Dolley Madison after the British torched the White House in 1814. On February 17, 1815, President Madison sat at the circular table in the upstairs circular room and signed the Treaty of Ghent, establishing peace with Great Britain. The house has served as the national headquarters for the American Institute of Architects since 1899. See p. 81 for more info about tours.

Cross New York Avenue and return to 17th Street, where you should turn right and walk to the Corcoran Gallery of Art. Go ahead and enter, but before you start touring, stop for a delicious break at:

10 Todd Gray's Muse at the Corcoran 💻

How wonderful that one of the city's best chefs, Todd Gray, has designed the menu for the Corcoran's in-house cafe (www.toddgraysmuse.com; ✆ **202/639-1786**). (See p. 196 for a review of his restaurant, Equinox.) The setting itself, behind Doric columns and under a lofty skylight ceiling, is lovely and unusual. The menu includes soups, salads, sandwiches, and select desserts. I've ordered the egg salad sandwich on brioche, which, as it turns out, is layered with a wide, thin slice of crisply peppery organic heirloom watermelon radish. The menu is pricey—sandwiches cost around $8.95 and are unaccompanied by the usual chips or fries—but the food is worth it. See p. 81.

After you've satisfied your hunger, start exploring the:

11 Corcoran Gallery of Art

At the Corcoran, you can view historic American art, like Remington sculptures, Albert Bierstadt landscapes, Edward Hopper iconic scenes, and John Singer Sargent portraits. And you can view astonishing European artwork that ranges from an 18th-century period room (the "Salon Doré," or "gilded drawing room"), transported in toto from Paris, to paintings by Picasso, Corot, and Gainsborough. But this gallery, which was the first art museum in Washington and one of the first in the country, has always had a penchant for playing the wild card. In 1851 gallery founder William Corcoran caused a stir when he displayed artist Hiram Powers's *The Greek Slave,* which was the first publicly exhibited, life-size American sculpture depicting a fully nude female figure. Today provocations might come in the form of a juxtaposition of Civil War photographs and shots of American soldiers in Afghanistan, or of art that engages all of your senses—even smell—as did the recently displayed Mary Early sculpture, which used beeswax and wood to investigate space through the intersection of form, line, light, and shadow.

Exit to 17th Street and turn right, away from the White House. Follow it down to D Street and turn right, following the signs that lead to the entrance to the:

12 DAR Museum and Period Rooms

The National Headquarters of the Daughters of the American Revolution comprises three joined buildings that take up an entire block. The middle building, Memorial Continental Hall, is the one you'll enter. Dedicated to the heroes of the American Revolution, the building's cornerstone was laid in 1902 with the same trowel that George Washington used to lay the cornerstone for the Capitol. At the time, the front of the building faced the White House pasture, where presidential cattle grazed. At any rate, what you're here for is the DAR Museum, which rotates exhibits of items from its 33,000-object collection, and the 31 period rooms, representing decors from the past, as interpreted by different states. The museum's collections veer from folk art to decorative arts and include old rocking chairs, ceramics, needlework samplers, and lots of silver. Quilters from far and wide come to admire a large collection of quilts, many of which are kept in glass sleeves that you can pull out from a case for better viewing. Period rooms are viewable from the doorways, a velvet rope preventing your entry. Highlights include the New Jersey Room, which replicates an English Council chamber of the 17th century, with woodwork and furnishings created from the salvaged oak timbers of the British frigate *Augusta,* which sank during the Revolutionary War; an opulent Victorian Missouri parlor; and New Hampshire's "Children's Attic," filled with 19th-century toys, dolls, and children's furnishings. You can tour the museum and Period Rooms on your own, but you might consider taking a free docent-led tour if you're interested in American decorative arts.

Exit the DAR, turning left and continuing along D Street to 18th Street, where you'll turn left again and follow to 201 18th St. NW, the pretty, Spanish colonial–style building that houses the:

13 Art Museum of the Americas

Off the beaten path, but just slightly—across Constitution Avenue, the World War II Memorial a short walk to the left, the Vietnam Veterans Memorial a short walk to the right—the Art Museum of the Americas (AMA) showcases the works of contemporary Latin American and Caribbean artists. For example, a recent exhibit focused on the theme of mobility and migration, as interpreted by Spanish and Latin

The Art Museum of the Americas.

American artists living in New York City. You'll be on your own; a tour takes 30 minutes, tops. Not to miss: a stunning loggia whose tall beamed ceiling and wall of deep-blue tiles set in patterns modeled after Aztec and Mayan art constitute a work of art on its own. A series of French (and usually locked) doors leads to a terrace and the museum's garden, which separates the museum from the Organization of American States headquarters that owns it. When you leave the museum, you may notice the nearby sculptures of José Artigus, "Father of the Independence of Uruguay," and a large representation of liberator Simón Bolívar on horseback.

From 18th Street, head back in the direction of the White House, turning right on C Street, which takes you past the AMA's garden and the OAS headquarters. Turn left on 17th Street and follow it to E Street. Then cross 17th Street and pick up the section of E Street that takes you between the South Lawn of the White House and the:

14 Ellipse

Sadly, the Ellipse is not the picturesque parkland it once was, thanks to unsightly wire fencing and other barriers that keep you on the circumscribed paths. Should you stray, one of the zillion police officers on duty quickly sets you straight. (I speak from experience.) The Ellipse continues to be the site for the National Christmas Tree Lighting Ceremony and Pageant every December, and a spot near the Zero Milestone monument remains a favored place for shooting photos against

Visitors on the Ellipse.

the backdrop of the White House. Rumor has it that a remodeling of the Ellipse is in the works, so perhaps you will arrive to find a welcoming plaza and picnic area with which to end your tour. If not, keep walking a few more steps to return to 15th Street NW in the Penn Quarter, and its many options for an end-of-stroll repast.

WALKING TOUR 2: STROLLING AROUND GEORGETOWN

START:	**Kafe Leopold's (D.C. Circulator; nearest Metro stop Foggy Bottom).**
FINISH:	**Old Stone House (D.C. Circulator; nearest Metro stop Foggy Bottom).**
TIME:	**2½ to 3 hours (not including stops). The distance is about 3.5 miles.**
BEST TIME:	**Weekday mornings are best to start out. If you want to do the house and museum tours, go Tuesday to Sunday.**
WORST TIME:	**Saturday, when Georgetown's crazy social scene sometimes spills over into the back streets.**

The Georgetown famous for its shops, restaurants, and bars is not the Georgetown you'll see on this walking tour. Instead, the circuit will take you along quiet streets lined with charming houses and stately trees that remind you of the town's age and history. The original George Town, comprising 60 acres and named for the king of England, was officially established in 1751. It assumed new importance in 1790 when President George Washington, with help from his Secretary of State, Thomas Jefferson, determined that America's new capital city would be located on a site nearby, on the Potomac River. Georgetown was incorporated into the District of Columbia in 1871.

Get your stroll off to a good start by stopping first for pastries or something more substantial at 3315 Cady's Alley NW, no. 213, the charming:

1 Kafe Leopold's ☕

Through a passageway and down a flight of stairs from busy M Street NW lies a cluster of chichi shops and **Kafe Leopold's** (www.kafeleopolds.com; (℃ **202/965-6005**), a cute little Austrian coffeehouse that serves breakfast items until 4pm and assorted other delicious dishes all day. Onion tarts, veal schnitzel, tea sandwiches, endive salad, croquet monsieur sandwiches, apple strudel, smoked fish with caperberries, Viennese coffee, and champagne cocktails are all on the menu. Leopold's opens daily at 8am and stays open until at least 10pm. See p. 217.

Return now to M Street, turn left, and continue to 3350 M St. NW, where you'll find the:

2 Forrest-Marbury House

No one notices this nondescript building on the edge of Georgetown near Key Bridge. But the plaque on its pink-painted brick facade hints at reasons for giving the 1788 building a once-over.

Kafe Leopold's.

Most significant is the fact that on March 29, 1791, Revolutionary War hero Uriah Forrest hosted a dinner here for his old friend George Washington and landowners who were being asked to sell their land for the purpose of creating the federal city of Washington, District of Columbia. The meeting was a success, and America's capital was born. Forrest and his wife lived here until Federalist William Marbury bought the building in 1800. Marbury is the man whose landmark case, *Marbury v. Madison*, resulted in the recognition of the Supreme Court's power to rule on the constitutionality of laws passed by Congress and in the institutionalization of the fundamental right of judicial review. The building has served as the Ukrainian Embassy since December 31, 1992. The interior is not open to the public.

Walk to the corner of M and 34th streets, cross M Street, and walk up 34th Street one block to Prospect Street, where you'll cross to the other side of 34th Street to view 3400 Prospect St. NW, the:

3 Halcyon House

Benjamin Stoddert, a Revolutionary War cavalry officer and the first Secretary of the Navy, built the smaller, original version of this house in 1789 and named it for a mythical bird said to be an omen of tranquil seas. (Stoddert was also a shipping merchant.) The Georgian mansion, like neighbor Prospect House, is situated upon elevated land, the Potomac River viewable beyond. The river lapped right up to Stoddert's terraced garden—designed by Pierre Charles L'Enfant, no less—220 years ago.

Sometime after 1900, an eccentric named Albert Clemons, a nephew of Mark Twain, bought the property and proceeded to transform it, creating the four-story Palladian facade and a maze of apartments and hallways between the facade and Stoddert's original structure. Clemons is said to have filled the house with religious paraphernalia, and there are numerous stories about the house involving sightings of shadowy figures and sounds of screams and strange noises in the night. Owners of Halcyon House since Clemons's death in 1938 have included Georgetown University and a noted local sculptor, John Dreyfuss. In 2011, Japanese pharmaceutical moguls Dr. Sachiko Kuno and Dr. Ryugi Ueno purchased Halcyon House and Evermay (see below).

Continue along Prospect Street to no. 3508, the site of:

4 Prospect House

This privately owned house was built in 1788 by James Maccubbin Lingan, a Revolutionary War hero and wealthy tobacco merchant. He is thought to have designed the house himself. Lingan sold the house in the 1790s to a prosperous banker named John Templeman, whose guests included President John Adams and the Marquis de Lafayette. In the late 1940s, James Forrestal, the Secretary of Defense under President Harry Truman, bought the house and offered it to his boss as a place for entertaining visiting heads of state, since the Trumans were living in temporary digs at Blair House while the White House was being renovated. The restored Georgian-style mansion is named for its view of the Potomac River. Note the gabled roof with dormer window and the sun-ray fanlight over the front door; at the rear of the property (i.e., not visible from the street) is an octagonal watchtower used by 18th-century ship owners for sightings of ships returning to port.

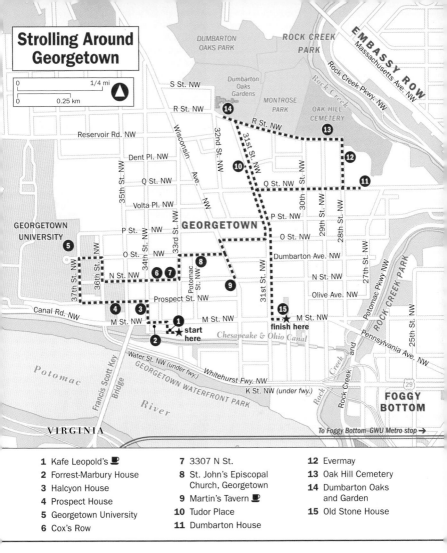

Strolling Around Georgetown

0   1/4 mi
0   0.25 km

1 Kafe Leopold's

2 Forrest-Marbury House

3 Halcyon House

4 Prospect House

5 Georgetown University

6 Cox's Row

7 3307 N St.

8 St. John's Episcopal Church, Georgetown

9 Martin's Tavern

10 Tudor Place

11 Dumbarton House

12 Evermay

13 Oak Hill Cemetery

14 Dumbarton Oaks and Garden

15 Old Stone House

Keep heading west on Prospect Street until you reach 37th Street. Turn right and follow 37th Street to its intersection with O Street, where you'll see:

5   Georgetown University

Founded in 1789, Georgetown is Washington's oldest university and the nation's first Catholic and first Jesuit-run university. Founder John Carroll, the first Catholic bishop in America and a cousin of a Maryland signer of the Declaration of Independence, opened the university to "students of every religious profession." His close friends included Benjamin Franklin and George Washington, who, along with the Marquis de Lafayette, addressed students from "Old North," which is the campus's oldest building. After the Civil War, students chose the school colors blue (the color used for Union uniforms) and gray (the color used for Confederate uniforms) to celebrate the end of the war and to honor slain students. The 104-acre campus is lovely, beginning with the stunning, spired Romanesque-style stone building on display beyond the university's main entrance on 37th Street. That would be Healy Building, which is named for Patrick Healy, president from 1873 to 1882, the first African American to head a major, predominantly white university.

The Georgetown University campus.

Turn right on O Street and walk one block to 36th Street, where you'll turn right again. Stroll past Holy Trinity Church, built in 1829, and continue to N St., where you should turn left to view Holy Trinity's parish chapel (3519 N St.), the city's oldest standing church. Built in 1794, the chapel has been in continuous use ever since. Turn right on 36th Street, then left on N Street, and stroll several blocks until you reach nos. 3327 to 3339, collectively known as:

6 Cox's Row

Built in 1817 and named for their owner and builder, John Cox, these five charming houses exemplify Federal-period architecture, with their dormer windows, decorative facades, and handsome doorways. Besides being a master builder, Cox was also Georgetown's first elected mayor, serving 22 years. He occupied the corner house at no. 3339 and housed the Marquis de Lafayette next door at no. 3337 when he came to town in 1824.

3307 N St. NW, former residence of John and Jacqueline Kennedy.

Follow N Street to the end of the block, where you'll see:

7 3307 N St. NW

John and Jacqueline Kennedy lived in this brick town house while Kennedy served as the U.S. senator from Massachusetts. The Kennedys purchased the house shortly after the birth of their daughter Caroline. Across the street at no. 3302 is a plaque on the side wall of the brick town house inscribed by members of the press in gratitude for kindnesses received there in the days before Kennedy's presidential inauguration. Another plaque honors Stephen Bloomer Balch (1747–1833), a Revolutionary War officer who once lived here.

Turn left on 33rd Street and walk one block north to O Street. Turn right on O Street and proceed to no. 3240, the site of:

8 St. John's Episcopal Church, Georgetown

Partially designed by Dr. William Thornton—first architect of the Capitol, who also designed the Octagon (see above), and Tudor Place (see below)—the church was begun in 1796 and completed in 1809. Its foundation, walls, roof, and bell tower are all original. Its early congregants were the movers and shakers of their times: President Thomas Jefferson (who contributed $50 toward the building fund), Dolley Madison, Tudor Place's Thomas and Martha Peter, and Francis Scott Key. The beautiful stained-glass windows

Martin's Tavern in Georgetown.

include one by Tiffany: the sanctuary window to the right of the altar depicting "Easter Lilies Crowned with the Gifts of God." To tour the church, stop by the office, just around the corner on Potomac Street, weekdays between 10am and 4pm, or attend a service on Sunday at 9am or 11am. Visit www. stjohnsgeorgetown.org or call © **202/ 338-1796** for more info.

Follow O Street to busy Wisconsin Avenue and turn right, walking south to reach this favorite Washington hangout. Too early for a break? Return here or to another choice restaurant later; you're never far from Wisconsin Avenue wherever you are in Georgetown.

9 Martin's Tavern ☕

At 1264 Wisconsin Ave. NW (www.martins-tavern.com; © **202/333-7370**), you'll find this American tavern, run by a string of Billy Martins, the first of whom opened the tavern in 1933. The original Billy's great-grandson is running the show today. So it's a bar, but also very much a restaurant (bring the children, everyone does), with glass-topped white tablecloths, paneled walls, wooden booths, and an all-American menu of burgers, crab cakes, Cobb salad, and pot roast. Martin's is famous as the place where John F. Kennedy proposed to Jacqueline Bouvier in 1953—look for booth no. 3. Open Monday to Thursday 11am to 1:30am, Friday 11am to 2:30am, Saturday 9am to 2:30am, and Sunday 9am to 1:30am.

Back outside, cross Wisconsin Avenue, follow it north to O Street, and turn right. Walk to 31st Street and turn left; follow it until you reach the entrance to the grand estate at 1644 31st St. NW:

10 Tudor Place

Yet another of the architectural gems designed by the first architect of the Capitol, Dr. William Thornton, Tudor Place crowns a hill in Georgetown, set among beautiful gardens first plotted some 200 years ago. The 5.5-acre estate belonged to Martha Washington's granddaughter, Martha Custis Peter, and her husband, Thomas Peter; Martha Custis purchased it in 1805 using an $8,000 legacy left to her by her step-grandfather, George Washington. Custis-Peter descendants lived here until 1983.

Tours of the house ($8) are docent-led only and reveal rooms decorated to reflect various periods of the Peter family tenancy. Exceptional architectural features include a clever floor-to-ceiling windowed wall, whose glass panes appear to curve in the domed portico (an optical illusion: It's the woodwork frame that curves, not the glass itself). On display throughout the first-floor rooms are more than 100 of George Washington's furnishings and other family items from Tudor Place's 8,000-piece collection. Docents reveal the rich history of the estate. From a sitting-room window in this summit location, Martha Peter and Anna Maria Thornton (the architect's wife) watched the Capitol burn in 1814, during the War of 1812. The Peters hosted a reception for the Marquis de Lafayette in the drawing room in 1824. Friend and family relative Robert E. Lee spent his last night in Washington in one of the upstairs bedrooms.

Tours of the gardens ($3) are self-guided, with or without the use of an audio guide; a bowling green and boxwood ellipse are among the plum features. Tudor Place (www.tudorplace.org; ✆ **202/965-0400**) is open Tuesday to Saturday 10am to 4pm and Sunday noon to 4pm, with tours given every hour on the hour. **Note:** Tudor Place is closed for the entire month of January.

From 31st Street, retrace your steps as far back as Q Street, where you'll turn left and walk several blocks to reach 2715 Q St. NW:

11 Dumbarton House

This stately red-brick mansion (www.dumbartonhouse.org; ✆ **202/337-2288**), originally called Bellevue, was built between 1799 and 1805. In 1915 it was moved 100 yards to its current location to accommodate the placement of nearby Dumbarton Bridge over Rock Creek. The house exemplifies Federal-period architecture, which means that its rooms are almost exactly symmetrical on all floors and are centered by a large hall. Federal-period furnishings, decorative arts, and artwork fill the house; admire the dining room's late-18th-century sideboard, silver and ceramic pieces, and paintings by Charles Willson Peale. One of the original owners of Dumbarton House was Joseph Nourse, first Register of the U.S. Treasury, who lived here with his family from 1805 to 1813. Dumbarton House is most famous as the place where Dolley Madison stopped for a cup of tea on August 24, 1814, while escaping the British, who had just set fire to the White House. It is open year-round Tuesday to Sunday from 11am to 3pm. Admission is $5, and tours are self-guided.

Exit Dumbarton House and turn right, retrace your steps along Q Street, and turn right on 28th Street. Climb the hill to reach 1623 28th St. NW, the estate of:

12 Evermay

This is a private residence, purchased in 2011 by Japanese pharmaceutical moguls Dr. Sachiko Kuno and Dr. Ryugi Ueno. And though much of the estate is obscured by brick ramparts and dense foliage, what's on view is impressive. As the plaque on the estate wall tells you, Evermay was built from 1792 to 1794 by Scottish real estate speculator and merchant Samuel Davidson, with the proceeds Davidson made from the sale of lands he owned around the city, including part of the present-day White House and

Lafayette Square properties. By all accounts, Davidson was something of an eccentric misanthrope, guarding his privacy by placing menacing advertisements in the daily papers with such headlines as *evermay proclaims, take care, enter not here, for punishment is near.*

Follow the brick sidewalk and iron fence that run alongside:

13 Oak Hill Cemetery

Founded in 1850 by banker/philanthropist/art collector William Wilson Corcoran (see Corcoran Gallery of Art, p. 80), Oak Hill is the final resting place for many of the people you've been reading about, within this chapter and in other chapters of this book. Corcoran is buried here, in a Doric temple of a mausoleum, along with the Peters of Tudor Place (see above) and the son of William Marbury of the Forrest-Marbury House (see above). Corcoran purchased the property from George Corbin Washington, a great-nephew of President Washington. The cemetery consists of 25 beautifully landscaped acres adjacent to Rock Creek Park, with winding paths shaded by ancient oaks. Look for the Gothic-style stone Renwick Chapel, designed by James Renwick, architect of the Renwick Gallery (p. 82), the Smithsonian Castle (p. 115), and New York's St. Patrick's Cathedral. The Victorian landscaping, in the Romantic tradition of its era, strives for a natural look: Iron benches have a twig motif, and many of the graves are symbolically embellished with inverted torches, draped obelisks, angels, and broken columns. Even the gatehouse is worth noting; designed in 1850 by George de la Roche, it's a beautiful brick-and-sandstone Italianate structure. Want to go for a stroll here? Download a cemetery map from the website, www.oakhillcemeterydc.org, or stop by the gatehouse (© **202/337-2835**) to pick one up. The grounds and gatehouse are open weekdays from 9am to 4:30pm; the grounds are also open on Sunday from 1 to 4pm.

Exit Oak Hill through the main entrance, and continue on the brick pathway to your right, strolling along R Street past Montrose Park until you reach the garden entrance to Dumbarton Oaks, on 31st Street. Or, if you'd prefer to visit the historic house and museum, continue around the corner to enter at 1703 32nd St. NW.

14 Dumbarton Oaks and Garden

In the mood for love? Head straight to the walled gardens, whose tiered park includes masses of roses, a Mexican tile-bordered pebble garden, a wisteria-covered arbor, cherry-tree groves, overlooks, and lots of romantic winding paths. The oldest part of Dumbarton Oaks mansion dates from 1801; since then the house has undergone considerable change, notably at the hands of a couple named Robert and Mildred Bliss, who purchased the property in 1920. As Robert was in the Foreign Service, the Blisses lived a nomadic life, amassing collections of Byzantine and Pre-Columbian art, books relating to these studies, and volumes on the history of landscape architecture. After purchasing Dumbarton Oaks, the Blisses inaugurated a grand re-landscaping of the grounds and remodeling of the mansion to accommodate their collections and the library, which now occupy the entire building. In 1940 the Blisses conveyed the house, gardens, and art collections to Harvard University, Robert's alma mater. In the summer of 1944, at the height of the Second World War, Dumbarton Oaks served as the location for a series of diplomatic meetings that would cement the principles later incorporated

5

STROLLING AROUND

Strolling Around Georgetown

173

into the United Nations charter. The conferences took place in the Music Room, which you should visit to admire the immense 16th-century stone chimney piece, 18th-century parquet floor, and antique Spanish, French, and Italian furniture. (See p. 78 for more information about the museum and gardens.) Dumbarton Oaks Museum (www.doaks.org; ⓒ **202/339-6401**) is open year-round Tuesday to Sunday 2 to 5pm, with free admission. The garden is open Tuesday to Sunday 2 to 6pm from March 15 to October 31, for an admission fee of $8; and Tuesday to Sunday 2 to 5pm from November 1 to March 14, with free admission.

From the intersection of R and 31st streets, follow 31st Street downhill all the way to M Street and turn left to find your final destination at 3051 M St. NW:

15 Old Stone House

Located on one of the busiest streets in Washington, the unobtrusive Old Stone House (www.nps.gov/olst; ⓒ **202/426-6851**) offers a quiet look back at life in early America, starting in 1765, when the Layman family built this home. Originally, the structure was simply one room made of thick stone walls, oak ceiling beams, and packed dirt floors. In 1800 a man named John Suter bought the building and used it as his clock-maker's shop. The grandfather clock you see on the second floor is the only original piece remaining in the house. Acquired by the National Park Service in the 1950s, the Old Stone House today shows small rooms furnished as they would have been in the late 18th century, during the period when

The Old Stone House.

Georgetown was a significant tobacco and shipping port. Park rangers provide information and sometimes demonstrate cooking in an open hearth, spinning, and making pomander balls. Adjacent to and behind the house is a terraced lawn and 18th-century English garden, a spot long frequented by Georgetown shop and office workers seeking a respite. The house is open daily noon to 5pm; the garden is open daily dawn to dusk.

You're in the middle of Georgetown, surrounded by shops, restaurants, and bars. Go crazy! See chapters 6, 7, and 8 for recommendations.

S o many restaurants, so little time. No, seriously: The only thing more astonishing than the number of restaurants in Washington, D.C. (more than 1,000, all told, with at least another 33 slated to open in 2012) is the number of foodies here. Washingtonians dine out like it's their job. Washingtonians dine out like it's their major. Washingtonians dine out like it's a competition as to who can score a table at the hot new place first. In fact, all of these things are true: D.C. is a town full of A-type personalities, expense-account execs and people needing to see and be seen, and college students and 20-somethings with a certain amount of free time and disposable income.

The downside, of course, is that it can be tough to book a reservation (see "Practical Matters: The Restaurant Scene," later in this chapter). But the upside makes it all worth it: D.C. has the most wonderfully delicioius and diverse dining scene, from Hill Country Barbecue Market's barbecue (p. 191) to Komi's salt-baked branzino (p. 206). Our top chefs have made names for themselves in the culinary world at large (among them José Andrés, Michel Richard, Mike Isabella), and big names from other parts of that cosmos happily set up shop here (Wolfgang Puck, Charlie Palmer, Alain Ducasse, to name a few).

Good restaurants are in every neighborhood, although the U Street Corridor is the one attracting the newest and hottest eateries these days. The casual dining trend continues—hardly anyone opens fine dining establishments anymore. But that doesn't mean the food is any less than sensational. Other trends: Restaurateurs increasingly are designing menus that allow you to pick and choose according to your budget. A boisterous bar scene is now a must. And it can get loud.

BEST DINING BETS

- **Best for a Splurge:** You may be in for a surprise, since neither of these top two restaurants stands on formality or requires you to dress up. Another similarity: Instead of a menu of choices, both restaurants serve diners a stream of small bites concocted that day at the whim of the chef. Otherwise the two are as different as night and day. Dupont Circle's **Komi** (p. 206) is a sparely appointed town-house dining room with just 12 tables. The 33-year-old genius chef, Johnny Monis, sends out 15 or so little gastronomic masterpieces that often hint of Greek tastes, like the mascarpone-stuffed dates; the cost is $135 per person. At the circuslike **minibar by José Andrés** (p. 183), you and only five others sit at the bar on the third floor in Andrés's flagship property in the Penn Quarter, where the internationally famous chef, or more likely his stand-ins, have fun whipping up 27 to 30 small taste sensations, like foie gras in cotton candy, for $150 per person.

PREVIOUS PAGE: **D.C. is known for its wealth of excellent Ethiopian restaurants.**

PRICE categories

Keep in mind that the price categories refer to dinner prices, and that some very expensive restaurants offer affordable lunches, early-bird dinners, tapas, or bar meals. The prices within each review refer to the **average cost of individual entrees,** not the entire meal.

Very Expensive	$30-plus	**Moderate**	$10–$19
Expensive	$20–$30	**Inexpensive**	$10 and under

○ **Best for Romance:** At the exquisite **Plume** (p. 207) in the Jefferson Hotel, an impeccable waitstaff serves artful French cuisine, from *amuse-bouche* start to macaroon finale. Only 17 tables fit within its walls of hand-painted silk, including a booth that comes with its own chandelier and drawable curtains. If a trendy, sexy scene and exotic tastes are more your style, consider the Penn Quarter's softly lit **Rasika** (p. 194), whose hot Indian food spices up the night. And then there's **Cashion's Eat Place** (p. 204), a cozy neighborhood joint in Adams Morgan; sit in the intimate, somewhat private bar area and enjoy American comfort food.

○ **Best for Families:** Beyond the usual burger (e.g., Five Guys; p. 195) and pizza (e.g., Pizzeria Paradiso; p. 208) places are assorted options. See "Family-Friendly Restaurants," later in this chapter.

○ **Best for Business: Charlie Palmer Steak** (p. 178), within walking distance from the Capitol, is a favorite spot for expense-account lobbyists and lawyers. On the stretch of Connecticut Avenue NW between the White House and K Street NW are several excellent eateries that get a lot of administration, lawyer, and lobbyist traffic, both at lunch and dinner; among them are the **Oval Room** (p. 199) and **Equinox** (p. 196), both of which serve modern American fare.

○ **Best for Regional Cuisine:** The **Blue Duck Tavern** (p. 210) pays homage to the tastes of various American regional cuisines by stating the provenance of each dish on the menu; seasonal farm vegetables might hail from the Tuscarora Co-op in Pennsylvania, the duck from Crescent Farms in New York. **Johnny's Half Shell** (p. 180), meanwhile, is the place to go for superb Eastern Shore delicacies: crab cakes, crab imperial, and soft-shell crab. While Washington doesn't have its own cuisine per se, its central location within the Mid-Atlantic/Chesapeake Bay region gives it license to lay claim to these local favorite foods. And nobody does 'em better than Johnny's.

○ **Best All-Around for Fun and Food:** Unstoppable José Andrés is behind the always-crowded **Oyamel** (p. 193), where everyone's slurping foam-topped margaritas and savoring small plates of authentic Mexican food. A few blocks away, **Central Michel Richard** (p. 188) makes everybody happy with its convivial atmosphere and chef Richard's take on French bistro and American classics, from mussels in white wine to fried chicken.

○ **Best for Service:** Makes sense that the restaurants where you receive the best service are among the best restaurants, period. For exquisite, upscale French cuisine served with a smile and a flair by a full-court press, consider

Michel Richard's **Citronelle** (p. 213). A quieter but more personal experience is to be had at **Obelisk** (p. 207), where a well-informed, on-its-toes staff serves chef/owner Peter Pastan's elegant Italian-accented modern American fare in this spare and charming room.

o **Best Bang for Your Buck:** It's hard to beat the $13.50 "Maine meal" deal available at **Tackle Box** (p. 218), which gets you an entree of fresh grilled fish plus two sides, from mac and cheese to fried green tomatoes. But you can try, by eating at the bar during happy hour (p. 218) and other times, or for a more sophisticated experience that is not cheap but is still a bargain, consider dining early at one of the many excellent restaurants that serves a pretheater meal.

o **Best for a "Taste of Washington" Experience:** Eat lunch at the **Monocle** (p. 180) and you're bound to see a Supreme Court justice, congressman, or senator dining here, too. For some down-home and delicious Washington fun, sit at the counter at **Ben's Chili Bowl** (p. 204), and chat with the owners and your neighbor over a chili dog or a plate of blueberry pancakes. The place is an institution, and you can stop by anytime—it's open for breakfast, lunch, and dinner.

o **Best for Vegetarians:** Rick, a vegetarian-from-birth friend of mine, especially loves these three establishments: **Ben's Chili Bowl** (p. 204), where options include veggie chili, chili cheese fries, burgers, subs, and hot dogs; **Amsterdam Falafalshop** (p. 206), which draws lovers of its mashed chickpea falafels and 21 possible toppings, plus the twice-cooked Dutch-style fried potatoes; and **Zaytinya** (p. 194), which offers a most diverse selection of sweet and savory veggie tapas, including a Brussels sprouts dish—"Everyone makes a face at the suggestion, but then they try them and fall in love," says Rick.

ATLAS DISTRICT

Inexpensive

Ethiopic ★ ETHIOPIAN In spite of the fact that the U Street Corridor holds the lion's share of D.C.'s Ethiopian restaurants, this is the one you should choose if you want the best. Lentil salad with mustard, spicy long-simmered stews such as the chicken leg braised with red pepper and onion, and the veggie sampler are among the dishes that draw aficionados here. Take your time dining in the airy brick-walled, wooden-floored room and watch the Atlas District's world go by through Ethipic's windowfront.

401 H St. NE (at 4th St.). www.ethiopicrestaurant.com. ✆ **202/675-2066.** Reservations recommended. Main courses $15–$24. AE, DISC, MC, V. Tues–Thurs 5–10pm; Fri–Sat noon–10pm. Drive or take a taxi.

CAPITOL HILL & BARRACKS ROW

Also see "Eating with the Insiders," below.

Very Expensive

Charlie Palmer Steak ★★ STEAK A meal at Charlie Palmer is really about two things—power dining and steak. The glass-fronted restaurant presents a stunning view of the Capitol most of the year (only the grounds and the Capitol dome are visible in summer), should you need reminding that politicking is going on all around you. Although the menu does include an excellent lamb rack and seafood entrees, its best offerings are the beef: hangar steak, rib-eye, petit filet, you name it. Recommended side dishes include Parmesan gnocchi and potato puree and, I kid you not, the roasted Brussels sprouts. Everyone raves about the trio of crème brûlées, so try that for dessert. Oenophiles will happily scroll down the list of 3,500 wines displayed on a handheld eWinebook; in all CP boasts a 10,000-bottle, entirely American inventory. The only steakhouse on Capitol Hill, CP Steak is more elegant, airy, and convivial than one might expect. It's a place to see and be seen, preferably in a big group.

101 Constitution Ave. NW (at Louisiana Ave. and 1st St. NW). www.charliepalmer.com/properties/cpsteak/dc. ℱ 202/547-8100. Reservations recommended. Lunch main courses $14–$45; prix-fixe lunch $25; dinner main courses $23–$64. AE, MC, V. Mon–Fri 11:30am–2:30pm and 5:30–10pm; Sat 5–10:30pm. Metro: Union Station (Massachusetts Ave. exit).

CityZen ★★★ NEW AMERICAN   Make no mistake: CityZen, with its high prices, delicate details, and preciously prepared cuisine, is for foodies. Nonfoodies may find the cooking too subtle, the service too preening. Nevertheless chef Eric Ziebold continues to fill tables nightly and garner AAA five-diamond ratings and local restaurant critics' highest marks annually. Located in the deluxe **Mandarin Oriental Hotel,** CityZen's dining room is templelike: cathedral ceiling, dimly lit, with a coterie of acolytes flitting back and forth between tables and kitchen. The entire menu changes monthly, but you can always expect heavenly tastes, whether from an *amuse-bouche* of fried mushroom with truffle butter, a cream of artichoke soup, or a grilled pork jowl with marinated French green lentils. The restaurant's 700-plus-bottle wine selection concentrates on bordeaux, burgundy, and California cabernet.

Enjoy a drink first on the hotel terrace or in CityZen's handsome bar (with its amazing "wall of fire"). **Note:** You can also dine fabulously and less expensively at the bar (p. 277).

In the Mandarin Oriental Hotel, 1330 Maryland Ave. SW (at 12th St.). www.mandarinoriental.com/Washington/dining/citizen. ℱ 202/787-6148. Reservations required. Sportswear, shorts, and denim discouraged. Prix-fixe 4-course menu $90; 6-course tasting menus $95 (vegetarian) and $110. AE, DC, DISC, MC, V. Tues–Thurs 6–9:30pm; Fri-Sat 5:30–9:30pm. Metro: Smithsonian (12th St./Independence Ave. exit).

Expensive

Belga Café BELGIAN   Belga Café is located on a street called "Barracks Row," named for the Marine Corps barracks bordering the street to the east. This is one of those D.C. neighborhoods that's been here forever—the Marine barracks and the Navy Yard, just blocks away, sprouted 200 years ago—but has been revitalized by merchants and the city, especially with the nearby presence of Nationals Ballpark, the Washington Nationals' baseball stadium.

Enjoy sitting at the outdoor cafe on a fine spring day or inside the bustling, noisy, European-ish dining room. Waffles are the big thing at brunch and lunch, with even some of the sandwiches served on *wafel* (waffled) bread. The menu lists each dish's Flemish name first, followed by the translation: *warme bloemkool soep* (cream of cauliflower soup), or *vlaamse stoverij* (beef stew). My favorites? Belgian fries, beers (several on tap, another 30 or so in bottles), the mussels, and the *eendenborst,* which is duck breast à l'orange with duck confit.

179

514 8th St. SE (at Pennsylvania Ave.). www.belgacafe.com. ☎ **202/544-0100.** Reservations accepted. Main courses brunch and lunch $8.50–$27, dinner $19–$27. AE, DISC, MC, V. Mon–Thurs 11am–10pm; Fri 11am–11pm; Sat 9am–11pm; Sun 9am–9:30pm. Metro: Eastern Market.

Bistro Bis ★★ FRENCH BISTRO   The chic **Hotel George** is the home of this inconsistent, though mostly fine, French restaurant. The chef/owner, Jeff Buben, and his wife, Sallie, also run **Vidalia** (p. 197). You can sit at tables in the always-loud bar area, on the balcony overlooking the bar, at leather banquettes in the main dining room, or, in warm weather, on the sidewalk cafe. The menu covers French classics like bouillabaisse, mussels with cider cream, boeuf bourguignon, and steak frites, each accompanied by a delicious extra, like the butternut squash puree that comes with the pistachio-encrusted sea scallops. Many items, including the sea scallops and the steak frites, appear on both the lunch and dinner menus but are considerably cheaper at lunch. Look around the dining room for nightly news types, since Bis's proximity to the Capitol makes it a must-stop for movers and shakers.

15 E St. NW (at N. Capitol St.). www.bistrobis.com. ☎ **202/661-2700.** Reservations recommended. Main courses breakfast $9–$14, brunch $14–$21, lunch $16–$26, dinner $25–$35. AE, DC, DISC, MC, V. Daily 7–10am, 11:30am–2:30pm, and 5:30–10:30pm. Metro: Union Station.

Johnny's Half Shell ★★ ▮ AMERICAN/SEAFOOD   Good restaurants are sparse in this neighborhood near Union Station and the Senate side of the Capitol, which partly explains why Johnny's, like the nearby Bistro Bis (see above), is always jumping. Mostly, though, it's a matter of a good vibe—there's a healthy bar scene here, with great happy hour specials—and unbeatable regional cuisine. Live jazz combos sometimes play here in the evenings.

If you've heard of Eastern Shore fare but don't know what that means, come here and try farm-raised chicken with old-fashioned slippery dumplings, or the crabmeat imperial with a salad of *haricots verts*, tomatoes, and shallots. If sautéed soft-shell crabs are on the menu, get them. Oysters and Wellfleet clams on the half shell are always available, of course.

400 N. Capitol St. NW (at E St.). www.johnnyshalfshell.net. ☎ **202/737-0400.** Reservations recommended. Main courses breakfast $7.75–$13.75, lunch $8.95–$32.50, dinner $18.25–$32.50. AE, MC, V. Tues–Fri 7–9:30am; Mon–Fri, 11:30am–2:30pm; Mon–Sat 5–10pm. Happy hour Mon–Fri 4:30–7:30pm. Metro: Union Station (Massachusetts Ave. exit).

The Monocle ▮ AMERICAN   A Capitol Hill institution, the Monocle has been around since 1960. At this men-in-suits place, the litter of briefcases resting against the too-close-together tables can make for treacherous navigating. But you might want to take a look at whose briefcase it is you're stumbling over; its proximity to both the Supreme Court and the Capitol guarantees that the Monocle is the haunt of Supreme Court justices and members of Congress. At lunch you'll want to order the hamburger, which is excellent; the tasty "Federal Salad" (field greens and tomatoes tossed with balsamic vinaigrette); or the white-bean soup. At dinner consider the roasted oysters, the pork-rib chop with Pommery mustard sauce, or the "Crab Conrad," a lump crab dish that owner John Valanos created to honor his father, Conrad Valanos, who opened the Monocle. The best deal is the "Luncheon at the Bar" menu served 11:30am to 3pm: from $6.50 for a pair of angus beef sliders topped with cheddar cheese and bacon to $12 for filet mignon.

107 D St. NE. (at 2nd St.). www.themonocle.com. ℰ **202/546-4488.** Reservations recommended. Main courses lunch $12–$28; dinner $17–$38. AE, DC, DISC, MC, V. Mon–Fri 11:30am–midnight. Metro: Union Station (Massachusetts Ave. exit).

Moderate

Montmartre ★ FRENCH   Montmartre's ambience is warmed by its decor—
pale yellow-orange walls, exposed-wood ceiling, cozy bar, and old wooden tables,
all fronted by a sidewalk cafe open in warm weather. It's very much a neighborhood spot. The owners here are French, and Montmartre is their little restaurant
offering big French pleasures: chicory salad tossed with goat cheese and croutons, chestnut soup, pistou, potato gratin, braised rabbit leg with olives, duck leg
confit, lamb stew, seared tuna loin with asparagus, and calves' liver sautéed with
smothered onions. Desserts, like the pear marzipan tart, don't disappoint. Can't
get in? Go next door to Montmartre's sibling, Seventh Hill (ℰ **202/544-1911**),
which opened in 2010 and serves delightful pizza.

327 7th St. SE (at Pennsylvania Ave.). www.montmartredc.com. ℰ **202/544-1244.** Reservations
recommended. Main courses brunch $9.95–$22.95, lunch $16–$22.95, dinner $18.95–$22.95. AE,
DC, DISC, MC, V. Tues–Fri 11:30am–2:30pm; Sat–Sun 10:30am–3pm; Tues–Thurs 5:30–10pm;
Fri–Sat 5:30–10:30pm; Sun 5:30–9pm. Metro: Eastern Market.

Sonoma AMERICAN   Oenophiles and lounge lovers have equal reason to
visit Sonoma, since the restaurant offers 40-plus wines by the glass from its
inventory of 200 Californian wines, as well as a lively lounge scene on the second
floor. (Families with small children should look elsewhere.) Plates of charcuterie,
artisanal cheeses, and pizzas are for sharing, but the menu also includes pastas
(available in half portions) and assorted meat and seafood entrees. Try a small
plate of the charcuterie, follow it up with a house-made risotto with bone mar-
row, and then feast on the roasted Mennonite chicken with lentils. The long,
narrow dining room often fills up with a drinking crowd waiting for a table in the
evening. That's when you'll want to head upstairs and check out the lounge,
which has a fireplace and overlooks Pennsylvania Avenue.

223 Pennsylvania Ave. SE (at 2nd St. SE). ℰ www.sonomadc.com. **202/544-8088.** Reservations
recommended. Main courses $12–$28. AE, DC, DISC, MC, V. Mon–Fri 11:30am–2:30pm; Mon–
Thurs 5–10pm; Fri–Sat 5–11pm; Sun 5–9pm. Metro: Capitol South.

Ted's Bulletin ★ AMERICAN   Retro in appearance (bare wooden floors and
booths, a soda fountain churning out milkshakes) and American comfort food in
tastes (grilled cheese, meatloaf, country fried steak, and breakfast served all day),
Ted's is comfortably hip in vibe. A youngish crowd loves the old-timey coddling,
and they really like the new-fashioned takes on homemade Pop-Tarts and on
milkshakes, which come in flavors ranging from Oreo and Heath almond to
mocha Kahlúa and strawberry daiquiri. And everyone, including parents of small
children, likes the breakfast-served-all-day policy.

505 8th St. SE (at E St.). www.tedsbulletin.com. ℰ **202/544-8337.** Reservations recommended.
Main courses breakfast $8.79–$12.79, lunch $10–$15, dinner $15–$25.79. AE, DC, MC, V. Sun–
Thurs 7am–9:30pm; Fri–Sat 7am–10:30pm. Metro: Eastern Market.

Inexpensive

Good Stuff Eatery AMERICAN   *Top Chef* contestant Spike Mendelsohn is
as much a master of celebrity fanfare as divine burgers. Winner of Rachael Ray's

EATING WITH THE insiders

You just can't beat the atmosphere (political) and value (cheap) of the all-American food served in certain dining spots inside the Capitol, its office buildings, and the Supreme Court. Keep these places in mind while touring the Hill:

You are always welcome (after you've gone through security, of course) in the eateries located in the Capitol office buildings across Constitution Avenue (Senate side) and Independence Avenue (House side) from the Capitol. These are quite affordable—your meal isn't taxed, for one thing. You'll be surrounded by Hill staffers and congressional members who head to places like the House of Representatives' immense, full-service **Rayburn Café** (✆ **202/226-9067**), which is Room B357, in the basement of the Rayburn House Office Building, at 1st Street and Independence Avenue SW. Adjoining the cafeteria is a carryout that sells pizza and sandwiches. In the Long-worth Building's basement-level **Long-worth Café** (Independence Ave. and S. Capitol St. SE; ✆ **202/225-6372**), you can grab a bite from a fairly nice food court. Among the popular Senate dining options are the Dirksen Building's base-ment-level **Southside Buffet** (1st St. and Constitution Ave. NW; ✆ **202/224-4249**), where a carvery station and a dessert station are highlights. All of these eateries are open weekdays only. The carryouts stay open until late afternoon, while the other dining rooms close at 2:30pm. For a complete listing of House of Representatives dining services, go to

http://go.compass-usa.com/house/content/menus.asp, and for Senate din-ing services, go to http://go.compass-usa.com/senate/content/menus.asp.

Across 1st Street from the Capitol is the **Supreme Court** and its **Cafeteria** (✆ **202/479-3246**), where you may spy a famous lawyer or member of the press but not any of the justices, who have their own dining room. The cafeteria is open weekdays 7:30am to 4pm (though it may be closed briefly between noon and 1pm to accommodate Supreme Court employees).

Back in the Capitol, meanwhile, there's the **Capitol Visitor Center's** (✆ **202/593-1785**) mammoth dining hall, which is open 8:30am to 4pm Monday through Saturday, seats 530 people, and serves "meals and snacks that reflect the diverse bounty of America," which trans-lates into the usual hamburgers and hot dogs, croissants and bagels, pizza and pasta, but also specialty sandwiches associated with different pockets of the country, like the New England lobster roll and the Philly cheese steak. You won't see any members of Congress or other political types at the CVC restaurant, but you'll be dining in good company with fellow tourists.

2009 Burger Bash and assorted other kudos, Mendelsohn's burgery is a must for hamburger fans. Most people buy burgers to go, but you can dine in, upstairs, where beers and flatscreen TVs are added distractions. My personal faves are the Big Stuff Bacon Meltdown, made with applewood-smoked bacon, and the toasted marshmallow milkshake. There are also hefty salads and sides. In 2010, Spike opened **We The Pizza** (✆ **202/544-4008**) right next door, and the con-sensus about his pies is the same as that about his burgers: They're excellent. By the time you read this, a Georgetown location of Good Stuff should have opened.

303 Pennsylvania Ave. SE (at 3rd St.). www.goodstuffeatery.com. ✆ **202/543-8222.** Reservations not accepted. Burgers $5.70–$7.90; milkshakes and sundaes $3.75–$5.25. AE, DC, DISC, MC, V. Mon–Sat 11:30am–11pm. Metro: Capitol South.

Le Bon Café 🍴 AMERICAN/CAFE   This tiny cafe is one of my favorite lunchtime eateries on the Hill. Located just off Pennsylvania Avenue, in the shadow of the Capitol, Le Bon Café feeds folks from the mostly residential neighborhood, and lots of young staffers looking for a break from the dive bars, pizza joints, and coffeehouses that have proliferated on this south side ("House side") of the Capitol. The cafe's menu is short but sweet: homemade pumpkin gingerbread and scones, smoked turkey club sandwich on farm bread, grilled salmon Niçoise salad, and the like. And it's cheap: The most expensive single item is that salmon salad for $8.95. Seating inside is minimal; in pleasant weather, you can sit at outdoor tables—or order your food to go and stroll to the nearby Elizabethan Garden at the Folger Shakespeare Library (p. 64) to enjoy your picnic in this little park. *FYI:* Neighbor **Pete's Diner and Carryout** also attracts a loyal Hill following with its low prices and burgers-and-fried-chicken menu, so stop there if you have a greasy-spoon kind of appetite.

210 2nd St. SE (at Pennsylvania Ave. SE). www.leboncafedc.com. ✆ **202/547-7200.** Breakfast items $2.25–$5.25; salads/sandwiches/soups $4.95–$8.95. MC, V. Mon–Fri 7am–3:30pm; Sat 8am–3pm; Sun 9am–2pm. Metro: Capitol South.

DOWNTOWN & PENN QUARTER
Very Expensive

Fiola ★★★ ITALIAN   Fiola became a favorite the moment it opened in April 2011. With its wide swath of bar at the front, white banquettes, and modern art, the dining room has a glamorous, head-turning, New York feel about it, maybe informed by chef Fabio Trabocchi's stint there not so long ago. But it's got a friendly vibe, too, helped along by Trabocchio's charming wife, Maria, who is usually on the scene. The main event is the seasonal Italian cuisine, which might include lobster ravioli in cream sauce, goat cheese fritters, lasagna with morels and truffles, or arugula salad with figs. The main menu changes frequently—and the variety of menus is always changing, too. There's a real sense that Fabio and Maria are having fun as they create the light "Maria's Lunch" menu, the "Bar Bites" menu, a special menu for Valentine's Day, and a menu to celebrate spring.

601 Pennsylvania Ave. NW (entrance on Indiana Ave., between 6th and 7th sts.). www.fioladc. com. ✆ **202/628-2888.** Reservations recommended. Lunch main courses $14–28, $19 prix-fixe light lunch menu, and $32 prix-fixe business lunch menu; dinner main courses $24–$44, 4-course tasting menu $110, 5-course tasting menu $123. AE, MC, V. Mon–Fri 11:30am–2:30pm; Mon–Thurs 5:30–10:30pm; Fri 5:30–11:30pm; Sat 5–11:30pm. Metro: Archives–Navy Memorial or Gallery Place/Verizon Center (7th and F sts. exit).

minibar by José Andrés ★★★ 🍴 SPANISH/PORTUGUESE   Born in Spain in 1969, the award-winning José Andrés, dubbed the "boy wonder of culinary Washington" by the *New York Times,* began his career in D.C. about 2 decades and many kitchens ago. Though his empire now includes restaurants in Los Angeles, Miami, and Las Vegas and three others in Washington (**Jaleo,** p. 191; **Zaytinya,** p. 194; and **Oyamel,** p. 193), minibar may be his star creation.

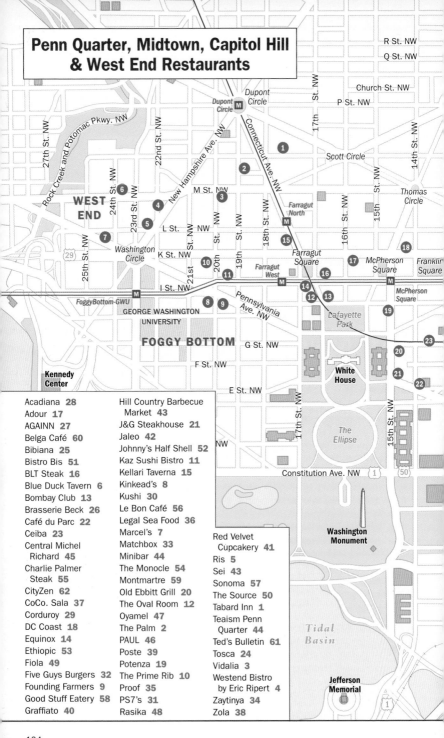

Penn Quarter, Midtown, Capitol Hill & West End Restaurants

Twice a night, at 6 and 8:30pm Tuesday through Saturday and at 5pm and 7:30pm Sunday, Andrés (or his stand-ins) concocts 27 to 30 small creations, from foie gras in a cocoon of cotton candy to pineapple ravioli, for six lucky people per seating. The entire experience is circuslike, as the cooks juggle preparation of each gourmet taste with lively bantering. The adventure costs $150 per person, not including wine, tax, and tip, and requires a reservation that's best obtained by calling at 10am exactly 1 month in advance.

405 8th St. NW (second floor; at D St. NW). www.minibarbyjoseandres.com. ℂ **202/393-0812.** Reservations a must. $150 per person. AE, DC, DISC, MC, V. 2 seatings: Tues–Sat 6 and 8:30pm; Sun 5 and 7:30pm. Metro: Archives–Navy Memorial or Gallery Place/Verizon Center (7th and F sts. exit).

The Source ★★ ASIAN FUSION/AMERICAN   Even if you didn't know the Source was a Wolfgang Puck establishment, you would have to register its L.A.-cool vibe. Like the Newseum, in which the Source resides, the two-level restaurant is glass-fronted, attracting all who happen by. Background music veers from David Bowie to Indian trance. Hostesses look like models in their sexy black dresses and heels. And the place is extremely loud, whether in the downstairs lounge, where a young, hip crowd gathers day and night, or up that long marble staircase to the main dining room, where the lighting is dim and the mood vibrant. The big news here is the food is really, really good—and really, really expensive: My $35 entree of three pan-seared scallops with peanut sauce was tasty, but was each scallop really worth $12? Though Puck himself is not in the kitchen, his inspiration is apparent in every dish. Do try the "tiny dumplings," my favorite item on the menu. Go on from there to lacquered duckling, or the short ribs, and end with the chocolate purse for dessert. Stop by the lounge nightly between 4 and 6pm for happy hour and its less expensive offerings of the same excellent tastes: Items are $8–$15 each, or choose any three items for $20.12.

575 Pennsylvania Ave. NW (in the Newseum). www.wolfgangpuck.com/restaurants. ℂ **202/637-6100.** Reservations recommended. Main courses lounge $8–$15, lunch $14–$29 dinner $32–$49; Sat prix-fixe brunch $35 (5-course) and $40 (8-course). AE, DC, DISC, MC, V. Mon–Fri 11:30am–2pm; Mon–Thurs 5:30–10pm; Fri–Sat 5:30–11pm; Sat brunch 11:30am–3pm. Metro: Judiciary Square (4th St. exit), Gallery Place/Verizon Center (7th and F sts./Arena exit), or Archives–Navy Memorial.

Tosca ★★ NORTHERN ITALIAN   As one of the city's best restaurants, Tosca stands out for its fine Italian dining and gracious service. Tosca's interior of pale pastels, thick carpeting, and heavy drapes creates a hushed atmosphere, a suitable foil to the rich food and an appropriate environment for dealmaking—Tosca is popular with political and legal bigwigs. Even when there's a crowd, Tosca doesn't get too noisy. Recommended dishes include lamb chops encrusted with pistachio nuts, house-made fettucini with baby goat and sunchoke ragu, and a roasted Mediterranean sea bass with balsamic vinegar sabayon and sautéed spinach with pine nuts and raisins. Tosca has something for everyone, including simply grilled fish accompanied by organic vegetables for the health-conscious, and desserts such as tiramisu or warm chocolate cake topped with hazelnut whipped cream. *Tip:* Also read about Tosca's sibling, the casual Italian restaurant **Posto** (p. 203), at 14th and P streets NW.

1112 F St. NW (at 12th St.). www.toscadc.com. ✆ **202/367-1990.** Reservations recommended. Main courses lunch $17–$27, dinner $19–$44; prix-fixe lunch $35; pretheater menu $38; tasting menus $70–$95. AE, DISC, MC, V. Mon–Fri 11:30am–2:30pm; Mon–Thurs 5:30–10:30pm; Fri–Sat 5:30–11pm. Metro: Metro Center (12th and F sts. exit).

Expensive

Acadiana ★ SOUTHERN   This glass-walled, triangle-shaped restaurant lies close to the convention center, so if you're attending an event there, you might be interested to know that Acadiana's bar stays open straight through from lunch to dinner and offers a menu of appetizers, like mini pulled-pork sandwiches on biscuits and crispy catfish, as well as Sazeracs, mint juleps, and other pick-me-ups. The restaurant's high ceilings, ornate chandeliers, and oversize urns fit with the prevailing, over-the-top atmosphere. This is New Orleans central, right here. New Orleanians say the cuisine's the real thing, starting with the biscuits, served with a pepper jelly and cream cheese condiment; continuing on to deviled eggs and charbroiled oysters starters; and even further to gumbo, étouffée, seared red snapper, and barbecue shrimp. Service is excellent.

901 New York Ave. NW (at 9th St.). www.acadianarestaurant.com. ✆ **202/408-8848.** Reservations recommended. Main courses lunch $12–$29, dinner $21–$29; prix-fixe brunch $29; bar items $5–$13. AE, DC, DISC, MC, V. Mon–Fri 11:30am–2:30pm; Mon–Thurs 5:30–10:30pm; Fri–Sat 5:30–11pm; Sun 11am–2:30pm and 5:30–9:30pm. Bar daily 11am–closing. Metro: Mt. Vernon Sq. or Gallery Place/Verizon Center (9th St. exit).

AGAINN ★ GASTROPUB   If the word "gastropub" conjures up dark paneled walls and tarted-up food, think again. This glass-fronted restaurant occupying part of the first floor of a downtown office building has a very modern feel, from white tiled walls to the background music (a staffperson's iPod selections, it turns out: everything from Irish ballads to Johnny Cash). On the plate is pure comfort food using the freshest ingredients of the season: In winter try "Grandmother's braised chicken" surrounded by roasted root vegetables, or pan-seared Loch Duart salmon with pearly barley risotto. Pub grub is on hand as well: delicious versions of shepherd's pie and fish and chips. And naturally, this being a pub, the bar gets down to serious business: single-malt whiskey and beer selections are extensive, which means AGAINN (Gaelic, translated roughly to mean "with us") sees a happy crowd most evenings.

1099 New York Ave. NW (entrance on 11th St., at K St.). www.againndc.com. ✆ **202/639-9830.** Reservations recommended. Main courses lunch $10–$25, dinner $23–$26. AE, DC, DISC, MC, V. Mon–Wed 11:30am–10pm; Thurs–Fri 11:30am–midnight; Sat 5pm–midnight; Sun 11am–4pm. Metro: Metro Center (11th St. exit).

Bibiana ★ ITALIAN   Restaurateur Ashok Bajaj scored another win (see **Bombay Club,** p. 200; **Oval Room,** p. 199; and **Rasika,** p. 194) when he opened Bibiana in 2009. Its great central location, affordable prices, fine-tuned menu, and sleek decor featuring dramatic lighting, black leather, and dark wood pull in business folks for lunch straight through to the evening (Bibiana serves small pizzas in the lounge weekdays 2:30–5:30pm). I have no particular liking for Brussels sprouts, but I found the Brussels sprouts risotto to be clean-the-plate delish. Other menu highlights include mixed grilled seafood, braised veal cheeks, and squid ink spaghetti with crabmeat, with a range of excellent soups, salads, and assorted pastas and crispy-crust pizzas. Eat at the bar during lunch hours to snag the special $15 deal: a pasta dish, a glass of wine or soda, and sorbet.

1100 New York Ave. NW. (entrance on H St., at 12th St.). www.bibianadc.com. © **202/216-9550.** Reservations recommended. Main courses lunch $11–$24, dinner $16–$29. AE, DC, DISC, MC, V. Mon–Wed 11:30am–10:30pm; Thurs–Fri 11:30am–11pm; Sat 5:30–11pm. Metro: Metro Center (11th St. exit).

Café du Parc ★★ FRENCH BRASSERIE   The delightful Café du Parc is the Willard Hotel's main restaurant, now that the famed Willard Room is used only for private events. (The historic Occidental Restaurant, though not included here due to space limitations, is now managed by the Willard and is also worth a visit.) The sunny two-level bistro overlooks Pershing Park and offers terrace seating during clement weather. This is absolutely where you want to be on a beautiful day. Renowned Michelin-starred chef Antoine Westermann oversees the menu and has dispatched his own assistants to staff the cafe; you can watch them at work in the open kitchen on the second floor. The dishes are redolent of Paris—*les tomates farcies aux legumes* (tomatoes stuffed with vegetables), *choucroute alsacienne* (sauerkraut with pork and sausages), and the *pâté en croûte* (pastry-wrapped terrine of veal, pork, and foie gras, cooked with wine and Armagnac). Francophiles find it a must, though most dine here at lunch, when the ambience is decidedly livelier than later in the day. You can carry out certain items daily until 5pm.

1401 Pennsylvania Ave. NW (in the Willard InterContinental Washington Hotel, at 14th St.). www.cafeduparc.com. © **202/942-7000.** Reservations accepted. Main courses breakfast $5.50–$14, lunch $18–$33, dinner $23–$34; Sun brunch $16–$24; prix-fixe pretheater menu $41. AE, DC, DISC, MC, V. Mon–Fri 6:30–10:30am, 11:30am–2pm, and 5:30–10pm; Sat–Sun 7–11am, noon–2:30pm, and 6–10pm; limited menu daily 3–5pm; carryout daily until 5pm. Metro: Metro Center (13th St. exit) or Federal Triangle.

Ceiba ★ CONTEMPORARY LATIN AMERICAN   Ceiba is the creation of Jeff Tunks, the chef maestro behind **DC Coast** (p. 199) and **Acadiana** (p. 187). Here at Ceiba, Tunks works his magic on ceviches, offering four variations—grouper, shrimp, tuna, and striped bass—which you may order individually or as a sampler. Another favorite dish is the Veracruz-style red snapper, topped with tomatoes, capers, olives, and jalapeños. As is true at all Tunks establishments, fulsome drinks are integral to the experience. The ones offered here go down nicely: mojitos, mango margaritas, and pisco sours, as well as fine wines from Argentina and Chile. If you're stopping in for a quick fix, the bar menu complements those cocktails with tastes of pork *pupusas*, conch fritters, ceviches, and assorted others; each item is reasonably priced from $9 to $16. You really want to dine in the main dining room here, to experience the best ambience, but if you've got small children, you're likely to be seated in the nondescript room to your left as you enter. The food will be just as good, but the experience just won't be as fun.

701 14th St. NW (at G St.). www.ceibarestaurant.com. © **202/393-3983.** Reservations recommended. Main courses lunch $12–$17, dinner $15–$28; pretheater menu $29. AE, DC, DISC, MC, V. Mon–Fri 11:30am–2:30pm; Mon–Thurs 5:30–10:30pm; Fri–Sat 5:30–11pm; Sun 5–9pm. Bar weekdays 11:30am–closing; Sat 3pm–closing. Metro: Metro Center (13th and G sts. exit).

Central Michel Richard ★★ FRENCH BISTRO   The same combination of factors that won Central the title "best new restaurant" by the James Beard Foundation in 2008 is still at work. Central makes you feel good as soon as you walk through the door. It's a French-American brasserie with a *joie de vivre* ambience and a menu full of innovatively re-created American and French classics. A lobster burger is layered with scallop mousse, macaroni and cheese is creamy with sour cream as well as cheeses, the fried chicken is an ungreasy version lightly dusted with bread crumbs. On and on it goes, the names of French dishes pingponging with American, hanger steak and onion soup to carrot cake and banana split. The french fries are perfection. Genius Michel Richard, a Frenchman who has lived in the U.S. for nearly 40 years, has a special fondness for his adopted country, and it shows in both the menu and the ambience. *Tip:* If you've called too late to book a table, try walking in and asking to sit in the small lounge or at the bar; I've had good luck dining this way, and it's just as fun as sitting at a table. Richard is best known for his ultraexpensive, wildly innovative **Citronelle** (p. 213), which many consider the city's best restaurant.

1001 Pennsylvania Ave. NW (at 11th St.). www.centralmichelrichard.com. ℂ **202/626-0015.** Reservations recommended. Main courses lunch $14–$30, dinner $16–$34. AE, DISC, MC, V. Mon–Fri 11:30am–2:30pm; Mon–Thurs 5:30–10:30pm; Fri–Sat 5–11pm. Metro: Metro Center (12th and F sts. exit).

J&G Steakhouse ★★ STEAK Washington's powerful people like steakhouses, but this is one that ventures beyond steak to offer succulently prepared peppercorn-crusted yellowfin tuna and slowly cooked salmon; starters of parsnip soup, pear and apple salad, and sweet corn ravioli; and wowful desserts, like the molten chocolate cake. The J&G in the name refers to the renowned chef Jean-Georges Vongerichten; this restaurant is his 27th. The elegant dining room itself is spacious and tall-ceilinged, its tables and booths set well apart for private conversations. On view through tall windows are the Washington Monument and Pennsylvania Avenue, and the views inside can be spectacular as well, especially when hotel guests dining here include the likes of Jennifer Lopez—the restaurant attracts as many stars in the arts and entertainment world as in politics.

515 15th St. NW (at Pennsylvania Ave., in the W Washington, D.C. hotel). www.jgsteakhouse washingtondc.com. ℂ **202/661-2440.** Reservations recommended. Main courses breakfast $13–$28, lunch $12–$54; dinner $25–$56; pretheater menu $39. AE, DC, DISC, MC, V. Mon–Fri 7–10:30am and 11:45am–2:30pm; (wine bar and patio stay open 2:30–5pm and serve limited menu); Sat–Sun 8–11am; Sun–Thurs 5–10pm; Fri–Sat 5–11pm. Metro: Metro Center (13th St. exit).

Poste ★★ NEW AMERICAN/FRENCH This lovely brasserie lies within one of Washington's coolest hotels, the **Monaco** (p. 281). You find its separate entrance via an arched carriageway that leads to a stone-paved courtyard, where the restaurant sets up a bar and tables in warm weather. Inside, past a small bar/lounge, is the sky-lit dining area, which includes an exhibition kitchen, banquettes, and a quieter back room. Poste chef Dennis Marron uses seasonal local ingredients (some, like herbs, raspberries, and tomatoes, are very local, as in straight out of the courtyard garden) to create modern American fare heavily influenced by traditional French cuisine. At dinner your selections may include French onion soup, veal blanquette, coq au vin, steak frites, and boeuf bourguignon. A wine list of 100 California and French bottles offers more than 30 wines by the glass. *FYI:* Poste is especially beloved by the 20-something crowd for its cocktails and bar scene in the evening and for brunch on weekends. Families with young children should ask for the fun and tasty kids' menu of $4 to $12 items.

555 8th St. NW (btw. F and G sts., in the Monaco Hotel). www.postebrasserie.com. ℂ **202/783-6060.** Reservations recommended. Main courses breakfast $5–$17, brunch $11–$32, lunch

$13–$32, dinner $13–$39 (most less than $30); pretheater menu $35. AE, DC, DISC, MC, V. Mon–Fri 7–10am and 11:30am–2:30pm; Sat–Sun 8am–3pm; Mon–Thurs 5–10pm; Fri–Sat 5–10:30pm; Sun 5–9pm. Bar daily 10:30am–closing. Metro: Gallery Place/Verizon Center (7th and F sts. exit).

Proof ★★ NEW AMERICAN   Proof plays up its superb location in the Penn Quarter, directly across the street from the Smithsonian American Art Museum/ National Portrait Gallery. The restaurant's windowed front overlooks the stately building, while inside monitors over the bar flash images of works of art displayed in the museum. Message: Visit the museum, if you haven't already.

Meanwhile you're in for a food-and-drink treat in the wine-centric Proof. Put yourself in your waiter's hands and you will likely end up happy. Start with small plates of charcuterie and cheeses to share. Consider the tuna Niçoise salad, spicy little meatballs with goat cheese agnolotti, a miso glazed Alaskan sablefish, pork confit with jicama slaw, and Mediterranean flatbread with chick-pea garlic purée and baby greens. For dessert try the banana bread topped with crispy banana slices and coconut sorbet. Portions are manageable, the dishes delicious. Sommelier Sebastian Zutant knows his stuff and directs diners to those wines that will suit individual budgets and tastes.

775 G St. NW (at 8th St.). www.proofdc.com. ☎ **202/737-7663.** Reservations recommended. Main courses lunch $13–$24, dinner $25–$29. AE, MC, V. Tues–Fri 11:30am–2pm; Mon–Thurs 5:30–10pm; Fri–Sat 5:30–11pm; Sun 5–9:30pm. Metro: Gallery Place–Chinatown (9th and G sts. exit).

PS7's ★★ NEW AMERICAN   Chef Peter Smith opened PS7's in 2006 after many years working the kitchen at the award-winning **Vidalia** (p. 197). His culi-nary artistry is on excellent display here. We've liked the rockfish stew with shrimp and clams in a fish broth; Sarah's salad, a mix of field greens, almonds, dried cranberries, and mascarpone; braised pork loin; tuna sliders (bites of tuna tartare on sesame-seed buns); and the plate of house-made petite hot dogs (PS7 is kind of famous for these). The dining room is elegantly modern, with floor-to-ceiling windows, lots of dark wood, and hues of charcoal, brown, and blue. The restaurant also has an expansive bar/lounge, whose menu features several items from the main menu—including those tuna sliders and the rockfish stew. But the lounge is often overflowing with urbanistas, and its stylish but impractical seating can make noshing problematic, so stand for a drink and then head to the dining room for a proper tuck-in.

777 I St. NW (at 8th St.). www.ps7restaurant.com. ☎ **202/742-8550.** Reservations accepted. Main courses lunch $9–$16, dinner $22–$34; lounge menu $9–$14. AE, DISC, MC, V. Mon–Fri 11:30am–2:30pm; Mon–Thurs 5:30–9:45pm; Fri–Sat 5:30–10:45pm. Lounge menu Mon–Fri all day; Fri–Sat 5:30pm–closing. Metro: Gallery Place–Chinatown (H and 7th sts. exit).

Zola ★ AMERICAN   Zola is a cleverly designed restaurant, taking inspiration from its location next to the International Spy Museum for a decor that includes red-velvet booths, backlit panels of coded KGB documents, and a center-pivoted swinging wall/door that's like something straight out of the TV show *Get Smart.* Zola keeps changing its menu, but I hope it sticks with this latest version offering entrées like brown butter trout with toasted hazelnuts, celery root raviolis, and sweet onion lamb shanks. Don't they sound good? They are. One favorite dish that stays on the menu no matter what else changes is the lobster mac and cheese, available at lunch and as a side at dinner. Good to know: Zola stays open all day and starts serving dinner—yes, dinner—at 3pm, continuing until 10pm. Also, the "Business Lunch" is a fabulous deal: four courses for $20 served with a promise to get you on your way in 45 minutes. Don't miss **Zola Wine & Kitchen,** just around the corner (p. 244).

800 F St. NW (at 8th St.). www.zoladc.com. ℰ **202/654-0999.** Reservations recommended. Main courses lunch $12–$22, dinner $14–$28; 3-course pretheater menu $40. AE, DC, DISC, MC, V. Daily 11:30am–3pm; Mon–Thurs 3–10pm; Fri–Sat 3–11pm. Metro: Gallery Place–Chinatown (7th and F sts. exit).

Moderate

Graffiato ★ ITALIAN   Step in at 11:30am when it opens, 4:30pm in the afternoon, or 11pm at night, there's a crowd and it's loud. This is Top Chef Mike Isabella's place, and he has a following. (By the time you read this, Isabella will have opened Bandolero, a Mexican small plates restaurant, at 3241 M St. in Georgetown.) The two-floor Graffiato is industrial-chic in look, with weathered wood, exposed piping, and cement floors. The same menu is served upstairs and down, but there's more room upstairs, including at the counter in front of the open kitchen. Downstairs is a large bar area, with back bar set up against the pizza kitchen and its woodburning oven. I've sampled and loved the White House pizza (mozzarella, ricotta, prosciutto, black pepper honey), the lobster risotto, the Caesar salad, and the glazed pork cheek. Graffiato is located just south of the Veriozon Center, so it gets all that traffic, Washington Capitals hockey fans to concertgoers; plan your visit accordingly if you're just dropping by, or else book a reservation for the upstairs.

707 6th St. NW (at G St.). www.graffiatodc.com. ℰ **202/289-3600.** Main courses $7–$19. AE, DISC, MC, V. Mon–Fri 11:30am–5pm; Sat–Sun noon–5pm; Sun–Tues 5–11pm; Wed–Thurs 5–midnight; Fri–Sat 5pm–2am. Metro: Judiciary Square (F St. exit) or Gallery Place–Chinatown (7th and F sts. exit).

Hill Country Barbecue Market ★ BARBECUE   This is Texas barbecue (dry-rubbed, not sauced), and it's delicious. The restaurant is a large two-level joint, with the Boots Bar and tables downstairs, where live music plays nightly, mostly country and honkytonk; and the market part and main dining room upstairs. The so-called market is really the kitchen/cafeteria, where you order your meal, get your meal ticket punched, and carry your tray to your table. Servers take care of your drinks and desserts orders, and you hand them the punched ticket at meal's end to settle up. The whole meal ticket thing is kind of confusing, especially when you're standing in a line of hungry people trying to make a quick decision about what you want to eat. But once you've got your corn bread and your ribs, your barbecued chicken, and your pulled-beef barbecue sandwich, you can just sit back and enjoy.

410 7th St. NW (at D St.). www.hillcountrywdc.com. ℰ **202/556-2050.** Main courses $8.50–$29. AE, MC, V. Daily 11:30am–2am (kitchen closes 10pm Sun–Wed, 11pm Thurs–Sat; late-night menu available to 1am). Metro: Archives–Navy Memorial or Gallery Place–Chinatown (7th and F sts. exit).

Jaleo ★★ 🏛 SPANISH   The celebrated José Andrés started here 20 years ago, and, in anticipation of its grand anniversary, Andrés in 2012 renovated the restaurant with a splash. Spanish designer Juli Capella describes it as a "relaxed environment of bold colors, with a hint of madness and irony, and a touch of Mediterranean surrealism." Spanish artwork is everywhere, from tile flooring to chairs to lamps. Artists Daniel Canogar and Mikel Urmenata have art installations on display.

Andrés added two foosball tables, which he helped design. What remains the same is the tapas-driven menu, which is what catapulted the chef into the firmament to begin with. New dishes appear, but you can always count on mainstays, such as a very simple but not-to-be-missed grilled bread layered with a paste of fresh tomatoes and topped with anchovies, dates, and bacon fritters; a skewer of grilled chorizo sausage atop garlic mashed potatoes; and gazpacho, as well as Spanish wines, sangrias, and sherries.

480 7th St. NW (at E St.). www.jaleo.com. (© **202/628-7949.** Reservations accepted at lunch and on a limited basis for dinner. Main courses $8.50–$19; tapas $5–$15; pretheater menu (Tues–Sat 5–7pm) $25. AE, DISC, MC, V. Sun–Mon 11:30am–10pm; Tues–Thurs 11:30am–11:30pm; Fri–Sat 11:30am–midnight. Metro: Archives–Navy Memorial or Gallery Place–Chinatown (7th and F sts. exit).

Legal Sea Foods ★ ☺ SEAFOOD This location of the famous Boston-based, family-run seafood empire is situated in the very heart of the Penn Quarter, directly across the street from the Verizon Center, where crowds throng for big-name concerts and basketball and hockey games. Before and after those events, you'll often find fans here, drawn to Legal's fresh seafood, comfortable atmosphere, and lively bar scene. Within the window-fronted dining room that wraps around the corner of G and 7th streets NW lies an expansive dining room with a racetrack-shaped bar and a nautical decor.

Legal's buttery-rich clam chowder is a classic; critics praise the fluffy pan-fried Maryland lump crab cakes served with mustard sauce. You can have one of several varieties of fresh fish wood-grilled or opt for one of Legal's specialty dishes, like the baked Boston scrod or the New England fried clams. Other pluses: The restaurant offers a gluten-free menu for the allergic, and an unusual, award-winning kids' menu of steamed lobster, popcorn shrimp, and the like, each served with fresh fruit and vegetable. (Kids can check out their own website, http://kids.legalseafoods.com; moms and dads, you might want to bring your iPads or other electronic device.)

704 7th St. NW (btw. G and H sts.). www.legalseafoods.com/restaurants/washington-dc-7th-street. (© **202/347-0007.** Reservations recommended, especially at lunch. Main courses $10–$39 (most $16–$26). AE, DC, DISC, MC, V. Mon–Thurs 11am–11pm; Fri–Sat 11am–midnight; Sun noon–10pm. Metro: Gallery Place–Chinatown (either exit).

Matchbox PIZZA/AMERICAN This skinny, three-level town house in Chinatown is a grazing ground for 20-somethings, who show up at all hours and for every meal, from happy hour to weekend brunch. Because Matchbox accepts limited reservations (see below), you often have to wait in the rowdy bar until a table frees up, so families, be forewarned. Wood-fired brick ovens bake the thin pizza crust at temperatures as high as 900°F (482°C). My favorite is the "prosciutto white," which is topped with prosciutto, kalamata olives, fresh garlic, ricotta cheese, fresh mozzarella, and extra-virgin olive oil, but you can request your own set of toppings, from smoked bacon to artichoke hearts. Matchbox also serves super salads (the chopped salad is another favorite: diced tomatoes, crispy bacon, hair-thin "pasta ringlets," and greens in a creamy herb vinaigrette), appetizers, sandwiches, and entrees (the seared sea scallops is a keeper). Matchbox has other locations: in the Barracks Row section of Capitol Hill, 521 8th St. SE (© **202/548-0369**), and, by the time you read this, in the U Street Corridor, at 14th and T sts NW. *FYI:* Matchbox serves a killer brunch on Saturdays and Sundays, with pastries and egg dishes to satisfy any palate.

713 H St. NW (btw. 7th and 8th sts.). www.matchboxchinatown.com. ☎ **202/289-4441.** Reservations for parties of 6 or more Sun–Thurs only. Main courses $14–$28; pizzas and sandwiches $12–$22; brunch $6–$15. AE, DC, DISC, MC, V. Sat–Sun 10am–10:30pm or later; Mon–Fri 11am–10:30pm or later. Metro: Gallery Place–Chinatown (H and 7th sts. exit).

Old Ebbitt Grill AMERICAN   You won't find this place listed among the city's best culinary establishments, but it's an institution. The original Old Ebbitt was established in 1856, around the corner at 14th and F streets NW. The Ebbitt moved to this location in 1983, bringing much of the old place with it. Among its artifacts are a walrus head bagged by Teddy Roosevelt, antique gas chandeliers, and antique beer steins. The overall feel is of an early-20th-century saloon.

From breakfast 'til the wee hours, suited-up men and women hustle in to talk business, relax over a drink, and catch up; tourists try to find a seat at lunch and dinner; and flirting singles take over at night. You'll generally have to wait for a table if you don't reserve ahead, and the Ebbitt has four full-service bars to help you pass the time. The waiters are friendly and professional in a programmed sort of way; service could be faster. The Ebbitt's assorted menus always include certain favorites: burgers, trout Parmesan (Virginia trout dipped in egg batter and Parmesan cheese, flash fried), crab cakes, and oysters—Old Ebbitt's raw bar is its saving grace when all else fails. Aside from the fresh oysters, the tastiest dishes are usually the seasonal ones, so be sure to ask about the specials.

675 15th St. NW (btw. F and G sts.). www.ebbitt.com. ☎ **202/347-4800.** Reservations recommended. Main courses breakfast $10.95–$16.95, brunch $6.95–$16.95, lunch and dinner $9.95–$19.95. AE, DC, DISC, MC, V. Mon–Fri 7:30am–1am; Sat–Sun 8:30am–1am. Bar until 2am Sun–Thurs, until 3am Fri–Sat. Metro: Metro Center (13th and F sts. exit).

Oyamel ★★ LATIN AMERICAN/MEXICAN   José Andrés, the 40-ish Spaniard who has wowed us repeatedly as chef at Jaleo, Café Atlantico, Zaytinya, and minibar, does it again at Oyamel. With its limited reservations policy meant to encourage spontaneous walk-ins, open-all-day hours, menu of *antojitos* priced below $12 each (the menu also lists some entrees), hearty cocktails, and exuberant atmosphere, Oyamel serves as the ultimate chill pill for the capital's hungry and stressed-out wonks. Order the Oyamel margarita, which is topped with salt-air foam, and the table-made guacamole (ask for the spiciest version, which is still not that spicy). The menu features items you won't find at other D.C. Mexican cantinas, like the $5 *chapulines* (sautéed grasshoppers served in a taco) and "*cochinita pibil con cebolla en escabeche*" (Yucatán-style pit-barbecued pork with pickled red onion and Mexican sour orange); try the taco version at only $4. With its lively bar scene and prime corner location in the heart of the Penn Quarter, Oyamel is always hopping.

401 7th St. NW (at D St.). www.oyamel.com. ☎ **202/628-1005.** Limited reservations. Main courses lunch and dinner $9–$19, brunch $6–$12; small plates and tacos $3–$12. AE, DC, DISC, MC, V. Sun–Mon 11:30am–10pm; Tues–Thurs 11:30am–11pm; Fri–Sat 11:30am–midnight. Metro: Gallery Place–Chinatown (7th and F sts. exit) or Archives–Navy Memorial.

Potenza ITALIAN   This restaurant, named after the owner's grandmother, has that authentic Southern Italian connection going for it, which is evident in the Tuscan bean soup; the spicy duck sausage pizza; the guinea hen with apples, chestnuts, and figs; and its specialty dishes. Just as authentic but more familiar-sounding items are on the menu, too, like bruschetta and manicotti—all delicious. Potenza has a very easygoing ambience and is perfect, in fact, as a place to duck into when taking a break from touring: The White House is just across the street, and the National Mall is half a mile or so down 15th Street. The restaurant is open all day and includes a bakery and bar, and the bar is quite the social scene in the evening. **FYI:** As reasonably priced as the entrees are, the cost of the drinks may throw you off the budgetary rails—my husband's martini cost $11, my manicotti $12.

1430 H St. NW (at 15th St.). www.potenzadc.com. ☏ **202/638-4444.** Reservations accepted. Main courses $11–$26. AE, DC, DISC, MC, V. Mon–Thurs 11:30am–10pm; Fri 11:30am–11pm; Sat 4–11pm; Sun 3–10pm. Bar stays open later. Metro: Metro Center (13th St. exit) or McPherson Square.

Rasika ★★★ INDIAN   This sexy-cool restaurant is a star attraction, drawing Washington glitterati, diplomats, administration stars current and past, and the city's young sophisticates, who hang out in the lounge sipping fancy drinks like Pimm's Cups and champagne cocktails. Soft lighting, cinnamon-and-spice tones, silk panels, and dangling glass beads create a rich and sensuously attractive atmosphere. As for the food, it's divine. Try the crispy spinach (*palak chaat*), ginger scallops, tandoori salmon, black cod, or chicken masala.

633 D St. NW (btw. 6th and 7th sts.). www.rasikarestaurant.com. ☏ **202/637-1222.** Reservations recommended. Main courses $14–$28; pretheater menu $35. AE, DC, DISC, MC, V. Mon–Fri 11:30am–2:30pm; Mon–Thurs 5:30–10:30pm; Fri 5:30–11pm; Sat 5–11pm. Lounge stays open throughout the day serving light meals. Metro: Archives–Navy Memorial or Gallery Place/Verizon Center (7th and F sts. exit).

Sei ★ JAPANESE   This sleek, rapture-in-white dining room is one of D.C.'s latest hot spots. A long communal table sits just beneath the sushi bar, and couples tend to migrate here, filling up the seats like it's the front row in front of the stage. Well, the sushi chefs *are* fun to watch. Meanwhile, directly across the room from the sushi bar, partly obscured by a partition, is the lounge, where more couples and young singles mingle, drinking *sake* and potent signature drinks, like the Asian Pear Sangria. Sushi lovers and others can find happiness here. I like something called the fish and chips roll, which wraps flounder, malt vinegar, and skinny potato strings together; the wasabi guacamole (as spicy as you want it to be); the pork cheek tacos (see? Not everything is sushi); and the decadent tempura bacon and asparagus salad.

444 7th St. NW (at E St.). www.seirestaurant.com. ☏ **202/783-7007.** Reservations accepted. Small plates and sushi $5–$15; lunch prix fixe $20; dinner prix fixe $35. AE, MC, V. Mon–Fri 11:30am–2:30pm; Mon–Thurs 5–10pm; Fri–Sat 5pm–midnight; Sun 5–9pm. Metro: Gallery Place/Verizon Center (7th and F sts. exit).

Zaytinya ★★ GREEK/TURKISH/MIDDLE EASTERN   How popular is Zaytinya? Well, the restaurant serves, on average, 750 people per night during the week and 1,000 per night on weekends. It's big and it's busy, and it always has been. Executive chef José Andrés is behind it all. (See review of **minibar,** p. 183.)

Its limited reservations policy means that Zaytinya's bar scene is often rollicking, since that's the obvious place to wait for a table. Once you're seated, your waiter will explain that the wine list, like the *mezze* dishes, are a mixture of Greek, Turkish, and Lebanese specialties, and inform you that the word "Zaytinya" is Turkish for "olive oil." Vegetarians worship Zaytinya for its variety of delicious options, but in fact, these little dishes please everyone: zucchini-cheese cakes, which come with a caper and yogurt sauce; the carrot-apricot-pine-nut fritters, served with pistachio sauce; *fattoush,* or salad of tomatoes and cucumbers mixed with pomegranate reduction and crispy pita-bread croutons. A seafood mezze favorite is the shrimp with tomatoes, onions, ouzo, and *kefalograviera* cheese; a meat mezze to recommend is the spice-rubbed lamb kebab. Finish with the seductive Turkish coffee chocolate cake.

701 9th St. NW (at G St.). www.zaytinya.com. (☎ **202/638-0800.** Limited reservations. Mezze items $5.50–$15; brunch items $5.95–$6.95. AE, DISC, MC, V. Sun–Mon 11:30am–10pm; Tues–Thurs 11:30am–11:30pm; Fri–Sat 11:30am–midnight. Metro: Gallery Place–Chinatown (9th St. exit).

Inexpensive

Five Guys Burgers and Fries AMERICAN   This local burger joint got its start in 1986 in Arlington and now has 809 locations in 40 states and four Canadian provinces to its name (maybe double that number by the time you read this). And by the way, the five guys in that name refer to the founding Murrell family's five sons. What can I say? The burgers are just great: hamburgers, cheeseburgers, and bacon cheeseburgers, plus hot dogs, fries (regular and Cajun), and sodas. You get your choice of a variety of free toppings. Eat in or take out. No liquor license. The "little hamburger" choices are actually the normal size, so that's what most people order. That's pretty much it. Try 'em; you'll like 'em. Besides the Penn Quarter location, Five Guys has nine others in D.C., including at Dupont Circle and in Georgetown.

808 H St. NW (at 9th St.). www.fiveguys.com. (☎ **202/393-2900.** Burgers $3.79–$6.99; fries $2.89–$4.99. AE, DISC, MC, V. Daily 11am–10pm. Metro: Gallery Place (H St./Chinatown exit).

PAUL ★ FRENCH BAKERY/CAFE   This family-owned French bakery was started in 1889 in a little town called Croix, near Lille, in northern France. More than a century later, PAUL has more than 450 bakeries in 27 countries. Washington, D.C.'s Penn Quarter PAUL is the U.S. flagship location, anchoring others in the city and four in Florida. Its location in Washington is superb: right on Pennsylvania Avenue NW, halfway between the Capitol and the White House, and within a short walk of the National Mall and Penn Quarter sites—ever so perfect for getting treats to go. But PAUL also offers seated dining. On Tuesday evenings in summer, sit outside at cafe tables and enjoy concerts; views of the Navy Memorial fountains and of quintessential capital scenes are on hand year-round. But let's talk about why you're really here: PAUL's buttery croissants and brioche; breads, like the *fougasse aux olives* (made with olive oil and chunky green and black olives); sandwiches of *jambon* (ham) and brie; smoked salmon and lemon-cream spread; and traditional croque-monsieurs. And the pastries—ooh la la, the pastries, like caramelly canale, cream-layered napoleons, and coconut flan. This PAUL opened in May 2011 and at least two others have opened since, including in Georgetown, at 1078 Wisconsin Ave. NW (☎ **202/524-4630**), and in Midtown, at 1000 Connecticut Ave. NW. At press time, Penn Quarter PAUL was working on obtaining a liquor license.

801 Pennsylvania Ave. NW (at 9th St.). www.paul-usa.com. (☎ **202/524-4500.** Reservations not accepted. Breads and pastries 80¢–$7.80; sandwiches and salads $5.95–$12.95. Mon–Fri 7am–7pm; Sat–Sun 8am–7pm. Metro: Archives–Navy Memorial or Gallery Place–Chinatown (9th and G sts. exit or 7th and F sts. exit).

MIDTOWN
Very Expensive

Adour ★★ FRENCH   This is D.C.'s satellite restaurant in the galaxy of famed French chef/restaurateur Alain Ducasse. As any foodie will expect, the cuisine is top-notch, and ingredients like black truffles, foie gras, Armagnac, and rose blossom feature prominently. For all of its exquisiteness, Adour is comfortable, not fussy. The dining room's modern decor features creamy leather banquettes as well as standalone tables and recessed nooks, high ceilings, and wine vaults that serve as walls. On the menu are dishes that show off the talent in the kitchen: sweetbreads, Maine lobster Newburg, and pressed foie gras with organic chicken and black truffle condiment. No matter what you order for dessert—say, the *baba au rhum* (a rich, rum-saturated cake) or the hazelnut soufflé—your table always receives a send-off plate of dainty raspberry and chocolate macaroon cookies.

923 16th St. NW (at K St., in the St. Regis Hotel). www.adour-washingtondc.com. (*) **202/509-8000.** Reservations recommended. Main courses breakfast $8–$22, dinner $27–$44; tasting menus 4-course $70, 5-course $85 (and $70 vegetarian). AE, DC, DISC, MC, V. Daily 7–11am; Tues–Thurs 5:30–10pm; Fri–Sat 5:30–10:30pm. Metro: Farragut West (17th St. exit) or Farragut North (K St. exit).

BLT Steak ★★ STEAK   BLT Steak is a younger, hipper cut of beeferie than one usually associates with Washington steakhouses. The restaurant, with its expansive bar, suede seats, and soul-music sound system, is a popular stomping ground for young professionals on weeknights and sees a steady stream of power brokers at all times. The BLT stands for Bistro Laurent Tourondel, the chef, whose other BLTs are located in New York; San Juan, Puerto Rico; and assorted other hot spots. A meal begins with a basket of enormous, complimentary Gruyère popovers and a little pot of country pâté. Menu recommendations include the raw bar offerings, the hanger steak, the American *wagyu* rib-eye (if you don't mind paying $92 for your entree!), the burgers (choose from the Political Burger Board, whose choices rotate daily), blue cheese tater tots, onion rings, any of the salads, and the souffléd crepe with ricotta cheese for dessert.

1625 I St. NW (at 17th St.). www.e2hospitality.com. (*) **202/689-8999.** Reservations accepted. Main courses lunch $17–$55, dinner $26–$49 (as high as $92, for wagyu beef). AE, DC, DISC, MC, V. Mon–Fri 11:30am–2:30pm; Mon–Thurs 5:30–10:30pm; Fri–Sat 5:30–11pm. Metro: Farragut West (17th St. exit) or Farragut North (K St. exit).

Equinox ★★ NEW AMERICAN   As a committed follower of the seasonal cooking movement, Equinox is a good advertisement for it (as is Gray's Muse Café at the Corcoran Gallery of Art; p. 81). As much as possible, chef Todd Gray uses community-farmed, organic ingredients grown within 100 miles of his restaurant. Home-run dishes have included pan-roasted fluke with braised artichokes; crab cakes made with lump crab mixed with capers, brioche bread crumbs, mayonnaise, and lemon-butter sauce; and seven-spice-roasted Peking duck with pear tart tatin. Pay attention to the vegetables on your plate, whether celery-root fondue or white-bean ragout, and expect a great taste sensation. Equinox has fans in high places, including in that White House across the way, and from its lawyer/lobbyist-laden neighborhood. With its glassed-in atrium and use of blues, whites, and translucent glass in the decor, Equinox is a lovely place to dine.

818 Connecticut Ave. NW (near I St.). www.equinoxrestaurant.com. (*) **202/331-8118.** Reservations recommended. Main courses lunch $18–$24, dinner $14–$34. AE, DC, DISC, MC, V.

Mon–Fri 11:30am–2pm; Mon–Thurs 5:30–10pm; Fri–Sat 5:30–10:30pm; Sun 5–9pm. Metro: Farragut West (17th St. exit).

The Prime Rib ★★ STEAK/SEAFOOD   The 37-year-old Prime Rib has plenty of competition in D.C., but it makes no difference. Beef lovers of a certain age still consider this The Place. Male beef lovers, anyway: The Prime Rib has a definite men's club feel about it, with brass-trimmed black-paneled walls, leopard-skin carpeting, and comfortable black-leather chairs and banquettes. Waiters are tuxedoed, and a pianist at the baby grand plays show tunes and Irving Berlin classics at dinner Monday to Thursday, with a bass player joining in Fridays and Saturdays.

The meat is from the best grain-fed steers and has been aged for 4 to 5 weeks. Steaks and cuts of roast beef are thick, tender, and juicy. In case you had any doubt, the Prime Rib's prime rib is the best item on the menu—juicy, thick, top-quality meat. For less carnivorous diners, there are about a dozen seafood entrees, including an excellent crab imperial. Mashed potatoes are done right, as are the fried potato skins, but I recommend the hot cottage fries.

2020 K St. NW (btw. 20th and 21st sts.). www.theprimerib.com. ℃ **202/466-8811.** Reservations recommended. Jacket required for men at dinner. Main courses lunch $16–$49, dinner $26–$53. AE, DC, MC, V. Mon–Thurs 11:30am–3pm and 5–10:30pm; Fri 11:30am–3pm and 5–11pm; Sat 5–11pm. Bar stays open throughout the day Mon–Fri. Metro: Farragut West (18th St. exit).

Vidalia ★★★ AMERICAN/SOUTHERN   Vidalia frequently wins prestigious culinary kudos from food critics, usually landing among the top 10 in *Washingtonian* magazine's annual list of the D.C. area's 100 best. You'll understand why when you dine here. Vidalia's cuisine marries tastes of various regions of the South, with an emphasis on the Low Country cuisine of Savannah and the Carolinas. Featured dishes might include a roasted young pig with braised savoy cabbage, or rockfish filet with succotash and turnip greens. A signature entree is scrumptious sautéed shrimp on a mound of creamed grits and caramelized onions with tasso ham in a cilantro butter sauce. Corn bread and biscuits with apple butter are served at every meal. Vidalia is known for its lemon chess pie and pecan pie, but always check out alternatives, which might be an apple napoleon or caramel cake. Vidalia offers an extensive wine list; at least 25 are offered by the glass, in both 3-ounce and 6-ounce pours.

If you're hesitant to dine at a restaurant that's down a flight of steps from the street, your doubts will vanish as soon as you enter Vidalia's tiered dining room. There's a party going on down here.

1990 M St. NW (near 20th St.). www.vidaliadc.com. ℃ **202/659-1990.** Reservations recommended. Main courses lunch $14–$18 ($19.90 3-course prix-fixe menu also available), dinner $30–$36 ($78 5-course tasting menu available for whole table). AE, DC, DISC, MC, V. Mon–Fri 11:30am–2:30pm; Mon–Thurs 5:30–9:30pm; Fri–Sat 5:30–10pm; Sun 5–9pm (closed Sun July–Aug). Metro: Dupont Circle (19th St. exit).

Expensive

Corduroy ★★ AMERICAN   For many years, this restaurant was hidden inside the Four Points Sheraton Hotel. When chef Tom Power moved his operation to a historic town house in the up-and-coming Convention Center neighborhood in 2008, he had no trouble enticing his fan base to follow him. He continues to attract new fans, as well, in this easier-to-find location, where the multiple

DINING green IN D.C.

As the debut of the White House kitchen garden demonstrated in March 2009, the First Family is committed to the "green" movement's emphasis on organic gardening, ecofriendly farming, reliance on locally grown produce, and healthy eating. All the White House chef has to do is walk out to the garden to pluck fresh vegetables and herbs for immediate use in cooking for the First Family. The White House kitchen is in good company throughout the city, where restaurants big and small, inexpensive and superpricey, are totally into earth-wholesome and healthy practices of energy and design, and the greenest of ways to grow, obtain, prepare, and replenish ingredients for their meals. Here are but a few examples:

o **Bourbon Steak** (p. 213): Following in the White House's footsteps, the Four Seasons Hotel's popular restaurant introduced its on-site 500-square-foot herb and vegetable garden in June 2009. An Amish farm provided the 400 plants, which represent 62 varieties of produce, all of which are used in Bourbon Steak's dishes . . . and cocktails! Can't get more local than this. And it's all organically grown; no pesticides used.

o **Equinox** (p. 196): Chef Todd Gray uses community-farmed organic ingredients that are grown within 100 miles of the restaurant whenever possible. Gray does the same at his cafe in the Corcoran Gallery of Art (p. 81).

o **Sweetgreen** (p. 209): This Green Restaurant Association–certified eatery powers its restaurants entirely from wind energy obtained through carbon offsets. Nearly all packaging is biodegradable, including the menu, which has been implanted with seeds, so you can plant it in the ground and sprout a sweet green something or

other yourself. Healthy salads and frozen yogurts are the deal here, and all are made fresh. Sweetgreens have sprouted all over D.C.

o **Founding Farmers Restaurant** (p. 213): Owned by a collective of American farmers, the restaurant is LEED Gold certified for its Leadership in Environmental and Energy Design, and Green Restaurant certified, as well. Ingredients used are sustainably farmed, locally sourced, and organically grown.

Sweetgreen's biodegradable menu is implanted with seeds, so you can sprout your own sweet greens.

dining rooms are cozy and the kitchen is on display. Winning dishes here have included antelope with chestnut puree, breast of capon with cabbage, peppered tuna on sushi rice, red snapper bisque, and duck egg and leg salad; and for dessert, pistachio bread pudding or chocolate tart with caramelized bananas. By the time you read this, Corduroy will have a sister right next door, **Velour,** a less expensive and more casual eaterie, serving soups, sandwiches, and pizzas. *FYI:*

Corduroy offers a three-course, $30 prix-fixe menu in the upstairs bar/lounge, away from the dining rooms, which imparts an intimate party feel to the experience.

1122 9th St. NW (btw. L and M sts.). www.corduroydc.com. ℰ **202/589-0699.** Reservations recommended. Main courses $27–$39. AE, MC, V. Mon–Sat 5:30–10:30pm. Metro: Mt. Vernon Sq.

DC Coast ★ NEW AMERICAN   The dining room is sensational: two stories high, with a glass-walled balcony, immense oval mirrors hanging over the bar, and a full-bodied stone mermaid poised to greet you at the entrance. Gather at the bar first to feel a part of the loud and trendy scene and to nosh on bar-menu treats ($6–$14), perhaps the fried oyster sliders or luscious crispy mushroom dumplings. Chef Jeff Tunks, the chef behind **Ceiba** (p. 188) and **Acadiana** (p. 187), started his dynasty with DC Coast, which opened in 1998. Here his executive chef carries out Tunks's specifications, fusing the coastal cuisines of the mid-Atlantic, the Gulf, and the West Coast. Almost always on the menu are Chinese-style smoked lobster with crispy fried spinach, and pan-roasted fish—could be tilefish, could be grouper. Seafood is a big part of the menu, but there are a handful of meat dishes, too; try the crispy pork confit with glazed baby turnips.

1401 K St. NW (at 14th St.). www.dccoast.com. ℰ **202/216-5988.** Reservations recommended. Main courses lunch $14–$29, dinner $21–$29. AE, DC, DISC, MC, V. Mon–Fri 11:30am–2:30pm; Mon–Thurs 5:30–10:30pm; Fri–Sat 5:30–11pm; Sun 5:30–9:30pm. Bar weekdays 2:30pm–closing; Sat 5:30pm–closing. Metro: McPherson Square (14th St./Franklin Sq. exit).

Kellari Taverna ★★ GREEK   This is my kind of restaurant: It's always lively and full of diners, but never gets so loud that you can't easily converse. The pretty dining room feels inviting, with gleaming red-oak floors, grand displays of fresh fish on ice, and huge bowls of olives and fruit, and the sound of Greek music playing in the background. And the food is just superb. No sooner are you seated than a waiter brings you a plate of hummus, olives, radishes, and a basket of bread, to munch on while you're reviewing the menu. Those who know Greek cuisine are delighted by the authentically prepared *paidakia* (grilled lamb chops with olive oil and oregano), the seafood *youvetsi* (oven-roasted orzo with shrimp, mussels, clams, and scallops), and *baklava* (honey and walnut pastry). Even if you know nothing about Greek cuisine, though, you'll be delighted by the crispy eggplant and zucchini served with *tzatziki* (goat yogurt with cucumber, garlic, and dill) and the *bakalao* (cured cod fritters with garlic almond mousse). Ask for Greek wine recommendations and you'll be doubly happy.

1700 K St. NW (near Connecticut Ave.). www.kellaridc.com. ℰ **202/535-5274.** Reservations recommended. Main courses lunch $13–$38 (most $15–$25), brunch $9.95–$38 ($24.95 prix-fixe menu), dinner $25–$39; pretheater menu $35.95. AE, DC, MC, V. Mon–Sat 11:30am–11pm; Sun 11am–10pm. Metro: Farragut North (K St. exit) or Farragut West (17th St. exit).

The Oval Room ★★ NEW AMERICAN   The Oval Room is a local favorite, another winner for owner Ashok Bajaj, who also owns the **Bombay Club** (see below), right across the street; **Rasika** (p. 194), in the Penn Quarter; and **Bibiana** (p. 187), on the northern edge of the Penn Quarter. Current chef Tony Conti offers reasonably priced modern American cuisine, including caramelized beef tenderloin, spice-crusted Japanese snapper, and the like. The Oval Room is a handsome restaurant, with contemporary art hanging on its pale green walls. Its atmosphere is congenial, not stuffy, no doubt because the bar area separating the restaurant into two distinct rooms sends cheerful sounds in either direction. In case you haven't made the connection, the Oval Room is a short walk from the White House—look for familiar faces.

800 Connecticut Ave. NW (H St.). www.ovalroom.com. ℰ **202/463-8700.** Reservations recommended. Main courses lunch $15–$24, dinner $17–$36; pretheater dinner (5:30–6:30pm) $35. AE, DC, DISC, MC, V. Mon–Fri 11:30am–3pm; Mon–Thurs 5:30–10pm; Fri–Sat 5:30–10:30pm. Metro: Farragut West (17th St. exit).

Moderate

Bombay Club ★★ 🍴 INDIAN   Open for more than 2 decades, the delightful Bombay Club is still going strong. A recent sprucing-up added punches of pink in the decor and surprising new tastes in the menu: A kebab of ground duck is flavored with chilies and ginger; eggplant is roasted in a tandoor oven, then combined with sautéed onions, ginger, and yogurt. Yum.

But Bombay Club favorites remain: the ultrafiery green chili chicken tandoori and the lobster moilee, which is lobster cooked in coconut milk with curry leaves. (Look for these on the menu in the category titled "Unabashedly Indian Curries.") Everyone's must-have appetizer is the crispy spinach *chat* (also served at Rasika). The Bombay Club is known for its vegetarian offerings (try the black lentils cooked overnight on a slow fire) and for its Sunday champagne brunch, which offers a buffet of fresh juices, fresh baked breads, and assorted Indian dishes. Patrons are as fond of the service as the cuisine; waiters seem straight out of *Jewel in the Crown*, attending to your every whim. This is one place where you can linger over a meal as long as you like.

815 Connecticut Ave. NW (H St.). www.bombayclubdc.com. ℰ **202/659-3727.** Reservations recommended. Main courses $16–$32; Sun brunch $20.95. AE, DC, DISC, MC, V. Mon–Fri and Sun brunch 11:30am–2:30pm; Mon–Thurs 5:30–10:30pm; Fri–Sat 5:30–11pm; Sun 5:30–9pm. Metro: Farragut West (17th St. exit).

Brasserie Beck ★★ BELGIAN   This place hasn't stopped rocking since the doors opened in April 2007. Beck, named for chef Robert Wiedmaier's younger son (as Wiedmaier's fine-dining establishment, **Marcel's** [p. 211], is named for his older son), is one of the city's best bistros and hot spots. The bar explains part of Beck's popularity, seating 21 people and handling many more beyond that. Beck features an attractive open kitchen of glass, steel, and cobalt-blue tiles, and the overall feel of a large train station, with large round clocks on display beneath 22-foot-high ceilings. But in the end, it comes down to the food, and here Beck pegs it: Belgian tastes of in-house-cured salmon, beef carbonnade, steamed mussels served three ways, frites, duck confit, lamb sausage—the list goes on. Beerlover's bonus: a large assortment of Belgian beers on tap and by the bottle.

1101 K St. NW (11th St.). www.beckdc.com. ℰ **202/408-1717.** Reservations recommended. Main courses $13–$32; brunch $12–$27. AE, MC, V. Mon–Thurs 11:30am–11pm; Fri 11:30am–11:30pm; Sat 11:30am–4pm and 5–11:30pm; Sun 11:30am–9pm. Metro: Metro Center (11th and G sts. Exit), with a few blocks' walk.

MOUNT VERNON TRIANGLE
Moderate

Kushi Izakaya & Sushi ★ JAPANESE   In this emerging hip pocket of D.C., Kushi attracts people from all over the region. The effortlessly jaunty Kushi is part grill room, sushi bar, *sake* pub, and oyster house. The enormous dining room serves up seared fatty salmon negiri, skewered duck breast, grilled oysters, and the like, as well as performances of sushi chefs and grill masters in their open kitchens. You can sit at counters in front of different work areas and be entertained while you dine on small plates of sushi, as well as grilled meats, vegetables, and seafood. Thoroughly Japanese, from paper lanterns to hachimaki head wraps, Kushi draws Japanese expats and youngish others for this lively taste of cuisine and culture.

465 K St. NW (at 5th St). www.eatkushi.tumblr.com. (?) **202/682-3123.** Reservations recommended. Sushi and small plates $3–$15. AE, DISC, MC, V. Mon–Fri 11:30am–2:30pm; Sat–Sun noon–2:30pm; Sun–Thurs 5:30–11pm; Fri–Sat 5:30–11:30pm. Metro: Mt. Vernon Sq.

U STREET CORRIDOR

Expensive

Birch & Barley ★ AMERICAN   Like other establishments in this general neighborhood, the Birch & Barley property offers two venues in one. Upstairs is the large bar, **ChurchKey** (p. 254); downstairs is this beer-centric restaurant. How beer-centric? Well, the menu names 500 labels, as well as the name of a "beer director," who happily helps you pair your brew with your meal. The list of entrees, pastas, and flatbreads includes several standouts, namely the honey-glazed duck breast and the Brat burger (with beer-braised sauerkraut, no less). The dining room is cozy and draws some diners who will end upstairs in the bar after dinner, but mostly those who are just after a tasty time.

1337 14th St. NW (Rhode Island Ave.). www.birchandbarley.com. (?) **202/567-2576.** Main courses $8–$27; brunch $13–$16. AE, MC, V. Sun 11am–3:30pm and 5–8pm; Tues–Thurs 5:30–10pm; Fri–Sat 5:30–11pm. Metro: U St./Cardozo (13th St. exit), or take the D.C. Circulator.

Moderate

Café Saint-Ex ★ AMERICAN   There goes the neighborhood—only we're talking gentrification here. Café Saint-Ex was an early trendsetter in helping transform this longtime residential area. The precious restaurant/bar wins stars from food critics and attracts legions of hungry Washingtonians, as well as enterprising restaurateurs after the same success. Named for author/aviator Antoine de Saint-Exupéry, the dining room builds on the flight idea with black-and-white photos of pilots and aviation memorabilia. Regulars crow about the charming atmosphere and certain items on the menu, like the roast chicken, the grilled mahimahi, and the beets, grapefruit, and feta cheese salad. Personally, I love the fried green tomato BLT. D.C. hipsters stay or arrive later to get in on Saint's nightlife scene, which features a DJ spinning hip-hop or indie tunes downstairs at Gate 54.

1847 14th St. NW (btw. S and T sts.). www.saint-ex.com. (?) **202/265-7839.** No reservations (this policy may change). Main courses lunch and brunch $10–$15, dinner $11–$28. AE, DISC, MC, V. Sun and Tues–Thurs 11am–1:30am; Mon 5pm–1:30am; Fri–Sat 11am–2:30am. Metro: U St./Cardozo (13th St. exit).

Cork ★ AMERICAN   Cozy Cork wows wine lovers and small-plate munchers from its perch on the increasingly popular 14th Street. The crowd draws from the neighborhood, which means you'll see everyone from 20-somethings to 60-somethings, as well as sundry unclassifiable sorts. Ambience is both cheery and hip. The small plates are meant to be shared, which adds to the overall conviviality.

It's just impossible to be unhappy when sharing yummy bites of "chianti salami"; a pan-crisped brioche sandwich of prosciutto, fontina, and Path Valley egg; or the french fries. Of course, the wine pairings may have something to do with the good vibe, too: Cork is also a wine bar, with 50 wines by the glass and 160 bottles for the choosing. For such a small restaurant, Cork offers a lot of variety, including in seating: You can sit on the patio in fine weather, in the front room at tables or the bar, or in the tiny backroom with views of the kitchen. **Note:** Nearby at 1805 14th St. NW (☎ **202/265-2674**) is sibling **Cork Market and Tasting Room,** open daily for sales and tastes of wine.

1720 14th St. NW (at S St.). www.corkdc.com. ☎ **202/265-2675.** Reservations accepted only for pretheater dining (5:30–6:30pm). Brunch items and dinner small plates $5–$15. AE, MC, V. Sun 11am–3pm and 5pm–midnight; Tues–Wed 5pm–midnight; Thurs–Sat 5pm–1am. Metro: U St./ Cardozo (13th St. exit).

Estadio ★★ SPANISH TAPAS   This is one of my favorite restaurants. The team behind wine-centric winner **Proof** (p. 190) opened Estadio in 2010 and hit all the same high marks. Its handsome interior of 19th-century colorful Spanish tiles and decorative ironwork is easy on the eyes, as is the stylish clientele. Three vantage points offer varyingly interesting views: At the marble counter at the rear, you see the chefs at work in front of you and the crazy crowd behind you; at the large central bar, you see the bartender concocting slushitos (a slushy blend of spirits, like the cranberry, anise, cava, and gin cocktail) and imbibers tossing them back; and at windowfront tables, you watch 14th Street scenes unfold before you. But what's on your plate might engage you totally, including a thickly creamy gazpacho (*salmorjero*), little sandwiches (*bocadillos*) of finely cured meats and Spanish cheeses, and skewered grilled veggies. Expect a noisy and deliciously fun time, but also a wait for a table, since Estadio accepts reservations only until 6pm.

1520 14th St. NW (at P St.). www.estadio-dc.com. ☎ **202/319-1404.** Reservations accepted for up to 6 people until 6pm. Tapas $3–$20. AE, MC, V. Tues-Fri 11:30am–2pm; Sat–Sun 11am–2pm; Mon–Thurs 5–10pm; Fri–Sat 5–11pm; Sun 5–9pm. Bar stays open later. Metro: U St./Cardozo (13th St. exit).

Marvin AMERICAN/BELGIAN   Marvin is two things: a bistro and a bar/ lounge. But the nightclub scene is on the second level (p. 256), so the bistro works on its own as a place to stop for a bit of Belgian fare and/or soul food. Named for Marvin Gaye, who lived in Belgium for a while, Marvin's menu features mussels in wine, ratatouille, big burgers, and fried chicken. Marvin might be the noisiest and liveliest place in town. Its servers are among the friendliest. So take a party here and have fun—just make sure you've made reservations or you'll never get in.

2007 14th St. NW (at U St.). www.marvindc.com. ☎ **202/797-7171.** Reservations accepted. Main courses $15–$28; brunch $8–$15. AE, DC, DISC, MC, V. Sun 10:30am–2:30pm and 5:30–10pm; Mon–Thurs 5:30pm–2am; Fri–Sat 5:30pm–3am. Metro: U St./Cardozo (13th St. exit).

Masa 14 ★ LATIN/ASIAN FUSION   This place is happening whenever you stop by. At weekend brunch, last night's rabble-rousers sit dazedly, making silly conversation and gradually coming awake over sips of lychee bellinis and munches of smoked-salmon omelets. These same sorts might have turned up here the night before to dance to the DJ music that plays until 3am Fridays and Saturdays, and to drink one of the 100 varieties of tequila on offer from the very long bar. And any evening around dinner time, Masa is packed with office wonks to artsy types, everyone savoring the smells from the wood-burning oven and the small-plate tastes of flatbread topped with serrano ham and goat cheese, pork belly tacos, barbecued salmon, and crunchy shrimp. Masa has a good feel about it, and good food has a lot to do with it.

1825 14th St. NW (at Swann St.). www.masa14.com. ✆ **202/328-1414.** Limited reservations accepted to allow for walk-ins. Small plates $6–$14; pretheater menu $32 (Mon–Thurs 5–6:30pm and Sun 5pm–close); brunch $6–$12. AE, DISC, MC, V. Mon–Thurs 5pm–2am; Fri 5pm–3am; Sat 11am–2am; Sun 11am–2am. Bar stays open after kitchen has closed. Metro: U St./Cardozo (13th St. exit).

Next Door AMERICAN/SOUTHERN   As in next door to Ben's Chili Bowl (see below). So popular has Ben's grown in its 50-plus years of feeding barflies at 3am and presidents at noon, that the chili dog place has spawned this more genteel brother, and the best news for some is that this restaurant has a bar. A celebrity chef has already come and gone, but that's okay—the menu of American, and especially Southern, tastes continues to please, no matter who's in the kitchen. Next Door tends to keep its front door open, attracting passersby in to sit at its long bar or at hightop tables just to the left of the bar. A quieter dining room lies at the very back. I can attest to the excellence of the shrimp, biscuits, and gravy, the chili fries, and the brioche French toast. The short ribs and the fried chicken are also getting good reviews. Next Door now hosts live music every Tuesday night (no cover).

1211 U St. NW (at 13th St.). www.bensnextdoor.com. ✆ **202/667-8880.** Reservations accepted. Main courses lunch $10–$19, dinner $10–$33 (most under $20); brunch $9–$16. AE, DC, DISC, MC, V. Sun–Thurs 11am–2am; Fri–Sat 11am–3am. Metro: U St./Cardozo (13th St. exit).

Pearl Dive Oyster Palace ★ AMERICAN/SEAFOOD   "Neither a dive nor a palace," Pearl Dive Oyster Palace appears serene and restrained if you arrive in the early evening, but it livens up quickly. In general, by 7pm the place is filled to the gills. (Note that the restaurant does not take reservations.) On busy nights, the street-facing bar raises its windowfront so that patrons can mingle and imbibe both inside and outside the bar. Look for the fey figurines displayed on a ledge above the oyster bar, and listen for Big Band music playing in the background. But about the food: It's New Orleans–delicious. Oyster lovers will sup up the fresh raw oysters, the oyster po' boy (cornmeal-fried oysters, house pickles, and aioli, i.e., garlicky mayo), and the oyster gumbo. An absolute must, however, is the mariscos de Campechana, which is a tower of oyster, blue crab and shrimp, salsa, and avocado. If you have time after dinner, head upstairs to **Black Jack** (p. 253) for a nightcap.

1612 14th St. NW. www.pearldivedc.com. ✆ **202/986-8778.** Reservations accepted for dinner seatings before 6:30pm. Main courses $11–$26. AE, DC, DISC, MC, V. Sun 11am–3pm and 5–11pm; Mon–Thurs 5–11pm; Fri–Sat noon–3pm and 5–11pm. Metro: U St./Cardozo (13th St. exit).

Posto ★ ITALIAN   Posto is located along a theater-filled stretch of 14th Street (**Studio Theatre** is right next door; p. 251), so it's a popular spot for the theater-bound, especially since Posto has become rather expert at feeding them quickly and sending them off fat and happy. As those patrons exit stage left, new ones quickly fill the room in their place. It's a big room, too, with a lot going on: a couple of long communal tables, an open kitchen, a glass front that opens to sidewalk tables, and eager-to-please waiters dressed in black T-shirts and pants hurrying between tables and kitchen. The aroma of pizzas cooking in the wood-fired oven greets you as you enter—the pizza picante, with spicy salami, sausage, tomato, and mozzarella, is a winner. But don't think Posto is simply a pizzeria; this sibling of **Tosca** (p. 186) serves excellent pastas, like the tortelli prepared with ricotta and mushroom ragu, and nonpasta main courses, like the "guance," which is braised veal cheeks served with sautéed spinach and garlic mashed potatoes.

1515 14th St. NW (at P St.). www.postodc.com. *C* **202/332-8613.** Reservations recommended. Main courses $12–$25. AE, MC, V. Mon–Thurs 5:30–10:30pm; Fri–Sat 5–11:30pm; Sun 5–10pm. Metro: U St./Cardozo (13th St. exit).

Inexpensive

Ben's Chili Bowl ⬛ AMERICAN   If you don't know about Ben's, you don't know nothin', man. Ben's is a veritable institution, a mom-and-pop place where everything looks (Formica counters, red bar stools, and a Motown-playing juke-box), tastes, and probably even costs pretty much the same as when the restaurant opened in 1958. Ben's has won James Beard Foundation recognition as an "American Classic" and praise from President Obama, who ate here with then–D.C. Mayor Adrian Fenty 2 weeks before the 2009 presidential inauguration (catch the video on Ben's website), and again a year later, when he brought then–French President Nicolas Sarkozy and his wife, Carla Bruni, here. Bill Cosby's been coming here so long, Ben's has named a chili half-smoke after him.

The most expensive item on the menu is the veggie-burger sub for $9.40. And while we're on the subject, Ben's is an unexpectedly fine choice for vegetarians, who especially like its chili and chili-cheese fries. Carnivores love the regular meat versions of these items and, of course, the half-smokes and the breakfast items: Try the salmon cakes, grits, scrapple, or blueberry pancakes. Everyone turns up here, from folks in the neighborhood on their way to work, to weekend nightclubbers who stream ravenously out of nearby nightclubs at 2 or 3am.

1213 U St. NW (btw. 12th and 13th sts.). www.benschilibowl.com. *C* **202/667-0909.** Reservations not accepted. Main courses $3.40–$9.40. No credit cards. Mon–Thurs 6am–2am; Fri 6am–4am; Sat 7am–4am; Sun 11am–11pm. Metro: U St./Cardozo (13th St. exit).

ADAMS MORGAN

Expensive

Cashion's Eat Place ★ 🍴 AMERICAN   This is very much a neighborhood restaurant—easy, warm, comfortable—that also just happens to serve out-of-this-world cuisine. Owner/chef John Manalatos likes to incorporate a little hint of his Greek heritage in his dishes, which change daily. A recent menu listed eight entrees, including goat, spit-roasted and pulled, with caramelized onions; and herb-marinated halibut over potato puree. An "after dark" menu of five items, from leek tarte to bison burger, is served Friday and Saturday nights from midnight to 2am. Sunday brunch is popular, too; you can choose from breakfast fare (cornmeal waffles) or heartier items (grilled Alaskan scallops).

The charming dining room curves around the slightly raised bar. In warm weather, the glass-fronted Cashion's opens invitingly to the sidewalk and its tables. Tables at the back offer a view of the small kitchen. In winter ask for a table away from the front door, which lets in a blast of cold air with each new arrival.

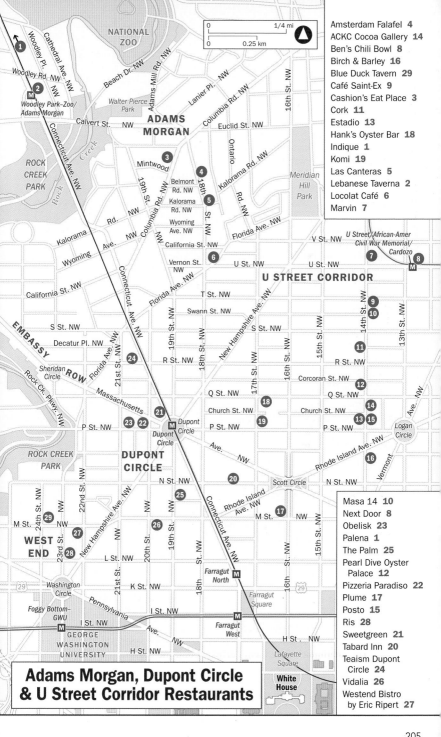

Amsterdam Falafel **4**
ACKC Cocoa Gallery **14**
Ben's Chili Bowl **8**
Birch & Barley **16**
Blue Duck Tavern **29**
Café Saint-Ex **9**
Cashion's Eat Place **3**
Cork **11**
Estadio **13**
Hank's Oyster Bar **18**
Indique **1**
Komi **19**
Las Canteras **5**
Lebanese Taverna **2**
Locolat Café **6**
Marvin **7**

Masa 14 **10**
Next Door **8**
Obelisk **23**
Palena **1**
The Palm **25**
Pearl Dive Oyster
  Palace **12**
Pizzeria Paradiso **22**
Plume **17**
Posto **15**
Ris **28**
Sweetgreen **21**
Tabard Inn **20**
Teaism Dupont
  Circle **24**
Vidalia **26**
Westend Bistro
  by Eric Ripert **27**

Adams Morgan, Dupont Circle
& U Street Corridor Restaurants

1819 Columbia Rd. NW (at 18th St.). www.cashionseatplace.com. ✆ **202/797-1819.** Reservations recommended. Main courses $25–$35; brunch $10.50–$22 (most $13). AE, DC, DISC, MC, V. Tues 5:30–10pm; Wed–Sat 5:30–11pm; Sun 11:30am–2:30pm and 5:30–10pm. Metro: Woodley Park–Zoo, with a walk.

Moderate

Las Canteras ★ LATIN AMERICAN/PERUVIAN   Traditional and contemporary Peruvian dishes are on the menu at this affordable restaurant in the heart of Adams Morgan, including three versions of ceviche, *causa* (a dish made with mashed potatoes stuffed with chicken), and quinoa salad, which tosses the quinoa (grain) with chickpeas, tahini, and lime juice. Las Canteras is a pretty restaurant, decorated with colorful Peruvian fabrics, handcrafted wrought-iron chandeliers, and photographs of Machu Picchu and other Andean landmarks. Arrive any night but Saturday between 5pm and 7pm for the early-bird special, a three-course meal for $24.

2307 18th St. NW (at Kalorama Rd.). www.lascanterasdc.com. ✆ **202/265-1780.** Main courses $11–$18. AE, DC, MC, V. Tues–Thurs 11am–3pm; Tues–Fri and Sun 5–10pm; Fri–Sat 5–11pm; Sat–Sun brunch noon–5pm. Metro: Woodley Park–Zoo, with a walk.

Inexpensive

Amsterdam Falafelshop MIDDLE EASTERN/DUTCH   Vegetarians and late-night barhoppers are crazy about this place, which has become an institution in a mere 6 years; franchises are in the works. The grub is cheap, consisting of delicious falafel sandwiches (warm pita sandwiches filled with fried patties of mashed chickpeas) and double-fried potatoes. Help yourself to any of 21 toppings at the self-serve bar, loading on hummus, peanut sauce, pickled cauliflower, or whatever speaks to you. Regulars recommend Belgian mayo on the fries, with a dash of Old Bay seasoning. The small shop has seating for about 35, but most people get it to go. No alcohol is served.

2425 18th St. NW (at Belmont Rd.). www.falafelshop.com. ✆ **202/234-1969.** Reservations not accepted. Falafel $4–$5.70; Dutch fries $2.75–$3.70. AE, DISC, MC, V. Sun–Mon 11am–midnight; Tues–Wed 11am–2:30am; Thurs 11am–3am; Fri–Sat 11am–4am. Metro: Woodley Park–Zoo, with a walk.

DUPONT CIRCLE

Very Expensive

Komi ★★★ 🍴 NEW AMERICAN/GREEK   For several years in a row now, *Washingtonian* magazine has named Komi the city's best restaurant. Thirty-something chef/owner Johnny Monis looks a bit like Johnny Depp, and he cooks like nobody's business. You may see him at work in the half-exposed kitchen at the back of the house. As young as he is, Monis knows what he wants and continues to fiddle with his menu and dining room to achieve it. In this intimate, comfortably attractive shotgun-length dining room (just 12 tables), Monis serves only that night's particular concoctions, a stream of 15 to 22 small bites that often hint of Greek tastes, like mascarpone-stuffed dates, a ravioli of local beets with feta, Gorgonzola raviolini with pears and almonds, or a slice of slow-roasted local Iberian pig. You don't get to choose (there is no menu); you're here to lap it up. (Komi will accommodate those with allergies or dietary restrictions; just be sure to call ahead.) Servers are some of the most efficient and charming staff in the city. **FYI:** In late 2011, Monis opened **Little Serow,** a stools-only, walk-ins only, family-style restaurant in the basement of the building next door to Komi. The Northern Thai menu is prix fixe, $45 for seven courses and authentic. You'll know you've found Little Serow when you see the line.

1509 17th St. NW (near P St.). www.komirestaurant.com. ℂ **202/332-9200.** Reservations a must (call a month in advance). Prix fixe $135 per person. AE, DC, DISC, MC, V. Tues–Sat 5:30–9:30pm. Metro: Dupont Circle (Q St. exit).

Obelisk ★★★ ITALIAN   Obelisk is one of the city's most consistently excellent restaurants; service and food are simply superb. In this pleasantly spare room that seats only 30, the walls are decorated with 19th-century French botanical prints and Italian lithographs. Obelisk serves sophisticated Italian-accented American cuisine made of the freshest possible ingredients. Every night diners are offered two or three choices for each of five courses. Dinner might begin with an antipasti *misti* of zucchini fritters, deep-fried risotto croquettes, and garbanzo beans with tuna in olive oil; followed by sweetbread and porcini ravioli with sage butter; and then an artfully arranged dish of grilled stuffed quail and duck sausage with spinach, or black bass with peppers, fennel, and green sauce. A cheese course and dessert follow. Breads and desserts are all baked in-house. Chef/owner Peter Pastan's carefully crafted wine list represents varied regions of Italy, as well as California vintages.

2029 P St. NW (at 21st St.). ℂ **202/872-1180.** Reservations required. Fixed-price 5-course dinner $72. MC, V. Tues–Sat 6–10pm. Metro: Dupont Circle.

The Palm ★ 🍴 STEAK   The Palm is one in a chain of 30 locations that started 85 years ago in New York—but here in D.C., it feels like an original. The Washington Palm is 41 years old; though recently renovated and expanded to include a glass-enclosed veranda, its walls are still covered with the caricatures of regulars, the famous and the not-so-famous. If you think you see MSNBC anchor Chris Matthews at a table, you're probably right. You can't go wrong with steak, whether it's the 36-ounce dry-aged New York strip or sliced in a steak salad. Oversize lobsters are a specialty, and certain side dishes are a must: creamed spinach, onion rings, palm fries (something akin to deep-fried potato chips), and hash browns. You can order half portions of these, so you have no excuse not to order at least one. Several of the longtime waiters like to kid with you a bit, but the service is always fast. A good deal is the $22.95 three-course "business lunch."

1225 19th St. NW (btw. M and N sts.). www.thepalm.com/washington-dc. ℂ **202/293-9091.** Reservations recommended. Main courses lunch $13–$49 (most under $25), dinner $17–$55 (most $30–$39). AE, DC, DISC, MC, V. Mon–Fri 11:45am–10pm; Sat 5:30–10pm; Sun 5:30–9:30pm. Metro: Dupont Circle (19th St./South exit).

Plume ★★★ FRENCH   If you're hoping to enjoy one especially wonderful and sophisticated dinner while you're in Washington, try to book a table at Plume, in the dazzling **Jefferson Hotel** (p. 293). Men are encouraged to wear jackets, and women, likewise, should don their stylish best to match the setting and the mood. The 17-table dining room's silk-covered walls are delicately painted with scenes from Monticello; blue velvet chairs have companion footstools for placing a diner's purse or briefcase; a fire crackles in the fireplace; and ravishing tastes, like a truffle-topped vegetable salad, Maryland crab risotto, and cured Atlantic salmon with trio of caviar, arrive on elegant china. Plume honors

Jefferson's passion for wine with a wine list that includes a 1780 Madeira (available by the glass for $225) and at least 50 other vintages that Jefferson enjoyed in his own time. From the *amuse-bouche* welcome of, say, a tiny duo of tuna and avocado, to the complimentary plate of macaroons and house-made chocolates at dinner's end, to the goodie bag farewell (a small package of sweets and a typed list naming the wines you've enjoyed), Plume means to win you over.

1200 16th St. NW (at M St., in the Jefferson Washington, DC hotel). www.plumedc.com. ✆ **202/448-2300.** Reservations recommended. Main courses $30–$52; 7-course tasting menu $110. AE, DC, DISC, MC, V. Tues–Sat 6–10pm. Metro: Dupont Circle (19th St./South exit).

Expensive

Tabard Inn ★ AMERICAN   Nestled inside the funky **Hotel Tabard Inn** (p. 300) is this beloved-by-locals restaurant. Saturday and Sunday brunch is a tradition for bunches of friends and families, weekday lunch pulls in the staff from surrounding embassies and association offices, and dinner seats couples, business partners, and Washingtonians meeting pals in town for meetings. The fetchingly homey main dining room holds wooden tables, hanging plants, a black-and-white tile floor, and windows overlooking a brick-walled garden. The kitchen smokes its own salmon (as it has for 30 years); cures its own pastrami, tasso ham, and prosciutto; and bakes its own bread and pastries, so these items are awfully good. Everything's good, though, and everything's fresh, from the oysters delivered straight from the coast of Maine to the grilled Hereford rib-eye steak, served with Gorgonzola new gold potatoes, broccolini, and bordelaise sauce.

1739 N St. NW (at 17th St., in the Hotel Tabard Inn). www.tabardinn.com. ✆ **202/331-8528.** Reservations recommended. Main courses breakfast $5–$10, lunch and brunch $11–$18, dinner $24–$35. AE, DC, DISC, MC, V. Mon–Fri 7–10am and 11:30am–2:30pm; Sat 8–9:45am; Sun 8–9:15am; Sat brunch 11am–2:30pm; Sun brunch 10:30am–2:30pm; Sun–Thurs 6–9:30pm; Fri–Sat 6–10pm. Metro: Dupont Circle (19th St./South exit).

Moderate

Hank's Oyster Bar ★ SEAFOOD   Deep in the heart of Dupont Circle is this lively, laid-back hangout, fronted by a sidewalk cafe in warm weather. Decor inside is cozy and casual, with exposed brick walls and pipes, and a mix of seating at the bar or tables; an expansion in 2011 kept Hank's character but increased the space. I recommend ordering one of the specials, which on a recent night included a sautéed soft-shell crab in citrus butter and pan-roasted halibut with tomato-lemon relish. Signature dishes feature classics like popcorn shrimp and calamari, and, of course, fresh oysters served on the half shell, fried, or in a po' boy. Hank's easy atmosphere puts you in a good mood and gives you a merry send-off when you've got a fun night on the town planned. Hank's has a second location, in Old Town Alexandria, at 1026 King St. (✆ **703/739-4265**).

1624 Q St. NW (at 17th St.). www.hanksdc.com. ✆ **202/462-4265.** Reservations not accepted. Main courses lunch $9–$18, dinner $12–$32; brunch $10–$23. AE, DC, DISC, MC, V. Mon–Tues 5:30–10pm; Wed–Thurs 5:30–11pm; Fri 11:30am–3pm and 5:30–11pm; Sat–Sun 11am–3pm and 5:30–11pm. Bar stays open later. Metro: Dupont Circle (Q St. exit).

Inexpensive

Pizzeria Paradiso ★ PIZZA/ITALIAN   In spite of awesome competition, this is still one of the best pizza places in the city. An oak-burning oven turns out

Alfresco dining at Hank's Oyster Bar.

exceptionally doughy but light-crusted pizzas, with choices ranging from the plain Paradiso, which offers chunks of tomatoes covered in melted mozzarella, to the robust Siciliana, a blend of 10 ingredients including eggplant and red onion. Or you can choose your own toppings from a list of 30 or so. As popular as the pizza is the panini of homemade focaccia, stuffed with marinated roasted lamb and vegetables, and the salads, such as the *panzanella* (thick crusts of bread with chopped zucchini and peppers tossed with balsamic vinegar and olive oil). Other locations include one in Georgetown, at 3282 M St. NW (📞 **202/337-1245**), and in Old Town Alexandria, at 124 King St. (📞 **703/837-1245**).

2003 P St. NW (btw. 20th and 21st sts.). www.eatyourpizza.com. 📞 **202/223-1245.** Reservations not accepted. Pizzas $10–$19; sandwiches and salads $5.25–$8.95. DC, DISC, MC, V. Mon–Thurs 11:30am–11pm; Fri–Sat 11:30am–midnight; Sun noon–10pm. Metro: Dupont Circle (19th St./South exit).

Sweetgreen LIGHT FARE   Three Georgetown University students tired of searching for "fast-casual and healthy" food options in Georgetown decided to create their own, and thus the first Sweetgreen takeout was born in summer 2007, in the heart of their old neighborhood, at 3333 M St. NW (📞 **202/337-9338**). All five of their current D.C. locations serve a winning, green, healthy, and delicious set of salad and frozen yogurt choices. You can choose a signature salad, like the Santorini (chopped romaine, roasted shrimp, feta cheese, grapes, and chickpeas, with a cucumber, basil, and yogurt dressing), an "old school" salad, like Caesar or Cobb, or make your own. The frozen yogurt is unflavored, but you can add toppings. The restaurant uses biodegradable packaging and sources local ingredients whenever possible.

1512 Connecticut Ave. NW (at Dupont Circle). www.sweetgreen.com. 📞 **202/387-9338.** Reservations not accepted. Salads $7–$12; yogurt $4–$6. AE, DC, DISC, MC, V. Daily 11am–10pm. Metro: Dupont Circle (either exit).

Teaism Dupont Circle 🎁 ASIAN FUSION   Occupying a turn-of-the-20th-century neoclassical building on a tree-lined street, Teaism has a lovely rustic interior. A display kitchen and tandoor oven dominate the sunny downstairs room, which offers counter seating along a wall of French windows that open in warm weather. Upstairs seating is on banquettes and small Asian stools at hand-crafted mahogany tables. The restaurant also sells tea-related gifts.

The tea list's 25 aromatic blends are from India, China, and Japan. On the menu is light Asian fare served on stainless steel plates or in lacquer lunchboxes (one Japanese *bento* box holds teriyaki salmon, cucumber-ginger salad, a scoop of rice with seasoning, and fresh fruit—all for $9.25). Other dishes include Thai chicken curry with sticky rice and a burger with Asian slaw. Baked jasmine crème brûlée and salty oat cookies are favorite desserts. Teaism is also popular at breakfast, when ginger scones and cilantro eggs and sausage are on tap. *Note:* Other locations include **Teaism Lafayette Square,** 800 Connecticut Ave. NW (© **202/835-2233**), near the White House; and **Teaism Penn Quarter ★,** 400 8th St. NW (© **202/638-6010**), which is the only branch that serves beer, wine, and cocktails.

2009 R St. NW (btw. Connecticut and 21st sts.). www.teaism.com. © **202/667-3827.** All items $2–$10. DISC, MC, V. Mon–Thurs 8am–10pm; Fri 8am–11pm; Sat 9am–11pm; Sun 9am–10pm. Metro: Dupont Circle (Q St. exit).

FOGGY BOTTOM/WEST END

Very Expensive

Blue Duck Tavern ★★ CONTEMPORARY AMERICAN   In this light-filled space, where modern American materials like stainless steel and polished glass mesh with classic features like dark oak and blue burlap, the kitchen likewise combines traditional and state-of-the-art cooking methods and equipment to prepare exquisite, one-of-a-kind dishes. The menu identifies the farm or other source of the prime ingredients for each dish. Recent home runs included white asparagus with periwinkles and crispy pancetta, crispy breast of guinea hen leg roulade, jumbo lump crab cakes with rémoulade sauce, and the baked rice with homemade andouille. The house-made steak fries are in a class of their own. Save room for desserts like the chocolate cake flamed in bourbon, accompanied by a scoop of ice cream that you'll see hand-cranked minutes before it's delivered to your table. The wine list features 60 American wines and 300 from around the world.

1201 24th St. NW (at M St., in the Park Hyatt Washington Hotel). www.blueducktavern.com. © **202/419-6755.** Reservations recommended. Main courses breakfast $12–$18, brunch $14–$24, lunch $16–$28, dinner $16–$36 (most around $25). AE, DC, DISC, MC, V. Daily 6:30–10:30am and 5:30–10:30pm; Mon-Fri 11:30am–2:30pm; Sat-Sun 11am–2:30p. Metro: Foggy Bottom or Dupont Circle (19th St./South exit).

Kinkead's ★★ SEAFOOD   Open since 1983, Kinkead's remains a reliable place to go for a festive atmosphere and fresh seafood in the city. Award-winning chef/owner Bob Kinkead orchestrates the action from his second-floor kitchen in this three-tier, 220-seat town house. Best seat: the booth named after the late, incomparable master journalist R. W. Apple, who used to dine here. The worst seat in the house: anywhere in the "atrium," the area that extends outside the doors of the restaurant into an indoor mall.

Kinkead's menu (which changes daily) primarily features seafood but always includes at least one beef and one poultry entree. Among the favorite dishes are the fried Ipswich clams, cod topped with crab imperial, clam chowder, and pepita-crusted salmon with shrimp, crab, and chilies. Chef Kinkead piles on appetizing garnishes—that crab-crowned cod, for instance, comes with sweet potato puree and ham-laced spoon bread. The wine list comprises more than 300 selections. *A plus:* A (mostly jazz) pianist plays Thursdays through Saturdays 7 to 10pm.

2000 Pennsylvania Ave. NW (near 20th St.). www.kinkead.com. ☎ **202/296-7700.** Reservations recommended. Main courses lunch $18–$27, dinner $22–$34; light fare $9–$27. AE, DC, DISC, MC, V. Mon–Fri 11:30am–2:30pm; Sun–Thurs 5:30–10pm; Fri–Sat 5:30–10:30pm (light fare served weekdays 2:30–5:30pm). Metro: Foggy Bottom.

Marcel's ★★★ FRENCH   Chef Robert Wiedmaier's vivid style is firmly on display here, with French dishes that include nods to his Belgian training: duck breast with baby turnips, rose lentils, and Calvados sauce; venison with ragout of winter mushrooms and Madeira sauce; or the *boudin blanc* sausage with chestnut puree. Desserts usually include seasonal tarts, like the spring pear tart with raspberry coulis.

Service and ambience are rather formal in this dining room, whose French country decor includes panels of rough stone framed by rustic shutters and antique hutches displaying Provençal pottery. To the right of the exhibition kitchen is the more casual wine bar, where you also can dine. Marcel's offers seating on the patio—right on Pennsylvania Avenue—in warm weather. See information about Marcel's grand pretheater dinner in "Pretheater Dinners = Great Deals," below.

2401 Pennsylvania Ave. NW (near 24th St.). www.marcelsdc.com. ☎ **202/296-1166.** Reservations recommended. Tasting menus: 4-course $85, 5-course $105, 6-course $125, 7-course $145 (any dish on the menu may be ordered individually); pretheater dinner (5:30–6:30pm; includes round-trip limo to/from Kennedy Center) $65. AE, MC, V. Mon–Thurs 5:30–10pm; Fri–Sat 5:30–11pm; Sun 5:30–9:30pm. Metro: Foggy Bottom.

Expensive

Kaz Sushi Bistro ★ JAPANESE   Amiable chef/owner Kazuhiro ("Kaz") Okochi introduced Washington to sushi long ago, at a restaurant called **Sushiko**

Pretheater Dinners = Great Deals

Some of Washington's finest restaurants make you an offer you shouldn't refuse: a three-course dinner for just a little bit more than the cost of a typical entree. It's the pretheater dinner, available in the early evening on certain nights at certain restaurants, and while your choices may be limited, your meal will undoubtedly be delicious.

At one end of the spectrum is **Marcel's ★★★** (see above), whose $65 fixed-price dinner includes any three courses from the regular menu, perhaps an arugula salad with caramelized shallots to start; an entree, like pan-seared Norwegian salmon; and a dessert, perhaps crème brûlée or chocolate terrine. Marcel's offers this menu nightly from 5:30 to 6:30pm or so and throws in complimentary limo service to and from the Kennedy

Center, returning you to the restaurant after the show for the dessert portion, if you haven't already consumed it.

Rasika's ★★★ (p. 194) pretheater menu allows you three courses for $35: the famous palak chaat among your first course options, tandoori salmon among the second, and carrot pudding on the list for finishing tastes. It's located right next door to the Woolly Mammoth Theater (p. 251) and around the corner from the Shakespeare theaters, so you shouldn't have to rush the meal during the Monday-to-Friday 5:30-to-6:30pm or Saturday 5-to-6:30pm time slots to make your show.

Many other restaurants in this chapter offer a pretheater menu, including **Ceiba ★** (p. 188), **Zola ★** (p. 190), **Masa 14 ★** (p. 202), and **Poste ★★** (p. 189).

(p. 218). Since 1999, Kaz has run his sushi bistro in this handsome town house. Aficionados vie for one of the six chairs at the bar to watch Kaz and his staff do their thing, especially at lunch, when fellow diners are likely to be Japanese men in Washington on business and young Washingtonians. Besides sushi Kaz is known for his seared scallops with lemon salt, his Asian-style tender short ribs, and his *bento* boxes, offering exquisite tastings of pan-seared salmon, spicy broiled mussels, and the like. This is also the place for premium *sakes* and a large selection of teas.

1915 I St. NW (near 19th St.). www.kazsushi.com. © **202/530-5500.** Reservations recommended. Main courses lunch $13–$22, dinner $16–$32; sushi a la carte $4–$10. AE, DC, DISC, MC, V. Mon–Fri 11:30am–2pm; Mon–Sat 6–10pm. Metro: Farragut West.

Ris ★★ AMERICAN   Washingtonians know Ris (short for "Doris" and pronounced accordingly) Lacoste from her chef years at **1789** (p. 214). When she left there in December 2005, fans clamored impatiently for Lacoste to open her own restaurant. She finally obliged in December 2009, and everybody's happy. In her large, glass-fronted dining room on the first floor of the Ritz-Carlton Residences building, diners stream in for lunch, brunch, late lunch, dinner, and happy hour, knowing to ask about Ris classics from her 1789 days, like the fabulous oyster, ham, and champagne stew, and the scallops margarita (lime-marinated scallops served in a margarita glass). Other Ris creations are quickly becoming new favorites: I like the *gnudis* appetizer (ricotta dumplings resting on a mash of eggplant and tomato), the pan-fried sole with citrus butter, and the butterscotch pudding. Lunch and dinner menus offer many of the same entrees at the same prices. Ris is easy to like: delicious comfort food in a comfortable setting, at affordable prices.

2275 L St. NW (at 22nd St.). www.risdc.com. © **202/730-2500.** Reservations recommended. Main courses lunch $11–$28, dinner $18–$40 (most under $30); brunch $6–$27. AE, DISC, MC, V. Mon–Fri 11:30am–11pm; Sat 5–11pm, Sun 10am–9pm. Metro: Foggy Bottom or Dupont Circle (19th St./South exit).

Westend Bistro by Eric Ripert ★ FRENCH/AMERICAN   If you're going to use your name as part of your restaurant's name, you'd better be great. Eric Ripert's name was enough to create a stampede of curious foodies when the bistro opened in November 2007, though the truth is, of course, that Ripert (formerly at the helm of New York City's esteemed Le Bernardin) is not actually in the kitchen. Its success continues. The straight-ahead menu ranges from a classic burger to pan-roasted striped bass with tabbouleh to roasted organic chicken. We were satisfied by the Bibb lettuce salad, the burger, macaroni and cheese, and the crispy duck leg confit. Next time I'd like to try the spoon bread and shrimp and grits, the contributions of Ripert's on-site chef, Joe Palma, who brings a taste for the South with him from his school days spent in Charleston, South Carolina. **FYI:** Check out happy-hour specials at the bar weeknights from 5 to 7pm, when certain drinks and foods (the delicious mac and cheese, the truffled popcorn, and so on) are available for $3 to $7.

1190 22nd St. NW (in the Ritz-Carlton Washington Hotel). www.westendbistrodc.com. © **202/974-4900.** Reservations recommended. Main courses lunch $16–$29, dinner $16–$30; pretheater menu (daily 5:30–6:15pm) $35. AE, DC, DISC, MC, V. Mon–Fri 11:30am–2:30pm; Sun–Thurs 5:30–10pm; Fri–Sat 5:30–11pm. Metro: Foggy Bottom.

Moderate

Founding Farmers AMERICAN   Location, location, location. A voluminous menu that covers every food craving and budget. Artisanal cocktails. Emphasis on organic ingredients and ecofriendly practices. Lots of communal tables. Put it all together and you understand why Founding Farmers is standing-room-only at lunch and dinner. Situated on the first floor of the International Monetary Fund, within walking distance of both the White House and George Washington University, the restaurant fills with international business folks, students, and wonky types all here to loosen up. The first floor, with its central bar surrounded by booths and tables, is always rowdy. You should head to the second floor if you want quiet conversation. The shrimp and grits, the tuna and cabbage entree salad, and the carrot cake dessert are probably the best things on the menu.

1924 Pennsylvania Ave. NW (at 20th St.). www.wearefoundingfarmers.com. ℂ **202/822-8783.** Reservations recommended. Main courses breakfast and brunch $5–$15, lunch and dinner $8–$35 (most under $20). Mon 7am–10pm; Tues–Thurs 7am–11pm; Fri 7am–midnight; Sat 9am–midnight; Sun 9am–10pm. Metro: Foggy Bottom.

GEORGETOWN

The closest Metro stop to Georgetown is the Blue Line's Foggy Bottom station; from there you can walk or catch the D.C. Circulator bus on Pennsylvania Avenue.

Very Expensive

Bourbon Steak ★★ CONTEMPORARY AMERICAN   This is one of D.C.'s hippest dining rooms. The Four Seasons' primary restaurant lies at street level, at the back and center of the property, overlooking the C&O Canal. To reach it, you must first thread your way past the vintage Ferraris and Rolls Royces jamming up the driveway, then enter the hotel and go past the dueling reception desks until you reach the lounge, then the restaurant. Everyone is here: Angelina Jolie, Andrea Mitchell, Oprah, Owen Wilson, Senator Mark Warner. And now you. Pat yourself on the back: You have arrived. So sit down and get to it: the wagyu flat-iron steak, veal schnitzel, oak-fired mahimahi, the lobster pot pie. Delicious. From the staff in the open kitchen, to the tables for two and four and eight, to the partiers out in the lounge, everyone's having a good time. That's really what it's all about here: great food, good stories, and fun. Enjoy.

2800 Pennsylvania Ave. NW (at 28th St., in the Four Seasons Hotel). www.bourbonsteakdc.com. ℂ **202/944-2026.** Reservations recommended. Main courses lunch $13–$29, dinner $25–$68 (most $30–$40); lounge menu $8–$19. AE, DC, DISC, MC, V. Mon–Fri 11:30am–2:30pm; Sun–Thurs 6–10pm; Fri–Sat 5:30–10:30pm. Lounge Sun–Thurs 11am–midnight; Fri–Sat 11am–1am.

Michel Richard Citronelle ★★★ MODERN FRENCH   Food critics continue to name Citronelle among D.C.'s best restaurants, and it's my personal favorite. If you care about creatively delicious French cuisine, do try to book a table there; you're in for a (very expensive) treat. The ebullient Richard produces masterpieces in every form: from appetizers like the fricassee of escargots, an eggshell filled with caviar, sweetbreads, porcinis, and crunchy pistachios; to entrees like the crispy lentil-coated salmon or the squab leg confit with macaroni gratin and black truffles. Each presentation is a work of art. You may want to consider dining at the chef's table in the kitchen, so you can watch Richard at work. This will cost you approximately $350 per person, with a six-person minimum; call for more information. The restaurant's tiered arrangement of tables allows glimpses of the glassed-in kitchen from different vantage points.

Richard's richly layered chocolate "bar" with sauce noisette (hazelnut sauce) is a must for dessert. Citronelle's extensive wine list offers about 20 premium by-the-glass selections, but with all those bottles staring out at you from the wine cellar, you may want to spring for one. Also consider dining at Richard's French/American bistro, **Central Michel Richard** (p. 188), which offers a less expensive, less elaborate, but every bit as delicious a meal.

3000 M St. NW (In the Latham Hotel). www.citronelledc.com. (C) **202/625-2150.** Reservations required. Jacket required, tie optional for men at dinner. Fixed-price 3-course dinner $110; 9-course tasting menu $190 per person, or $280 with wine pairings; bar/lounge main courses $12–$28. AE, DC, DISC, MC, V. Tues–Sat 6–10pm.

1789 ★★ AMERICAN   This 50-plus-year-old restaurant near Georgetown University draws from its upper-crust neighborhood of media types, socialites, politicians, and corporate execs. A new chef is in the kitchen, changing the menu daily to emphasize the use of "sustainable seafood," like the red snapper from Panana City, and cuts of "humanely farmed animals," like the olive-crusted leg of lamb. The menu is consistent in offering savory and rich American fare, accompanied by assorted delicious side dishes, from braised red cabbage to celery root.

The 1789 has a reputation for romance, making it an excellent destination for handholding couples. The five dining rooms, especially those on the first floor, are cozy dens, with a homey decor that includes historical prints on the walls, silk-shaded brass oil lamps on tables, and, come winter, fires crackling in the fireplaces. So put on your best duds and be prepared for a relaxing meal.

1226 36th St. NW (at Prospect St.). www.1789restaurant.com. (C) **202/965-1789.** Reservations recommended. Jacket suggested for men. Main courses $35–$45. AE, DC, DISC, MC, V. Mon–Thurs 6–10pm; Fri 6–11pm; Sat 5:30–11pm; Sun 5:30–10pm.

Expensive

Bistrot Lepic & Wine Bar ★ FRENCH   Bistrot Lepic is the real thing—a charming French restaurant that seems plucked right off a Parisian side street. The atmosphere is bustling and cheery, and you hear a lot of French, spoken not just by the waiters, but also by the customers. This is traditional French cooking, updated. The seasonal menu offers such entrees as grilled rainbow trout with tomatoes, capers, and olives; beef medallions with polenta and shiitake mushroom sauce; and sautéed sea scallops with ginger broccoli mousse. Depending on the season, a special like rare tuna served on fennel with citrus vinaigrette might turn up.

In its 18 years, the restaurant has made some changes to accommodate its popularity, including turning the upstairs into an Asian-accented wine bar and lounge (p. 260). Come here to hang out Wednesday to Monday, sipping a glass of wine and munching on $5 offerings of petite crab cake or homemade pâté from the wine-bar menu (a full menu also available). The wine bar hosts complimentary wine tastings every Tuesday 6 to 8pm and live jazz on Wednesday evenings.

1736 Wisconsin Ave. NW (btw. R and S sts.). www.bistrotlepic.com. (C) **202/333-0111.** Reservations recommended. Main courses lunch $15–$20 (3-course prix fixe Mon–Thurs $18 and $25),

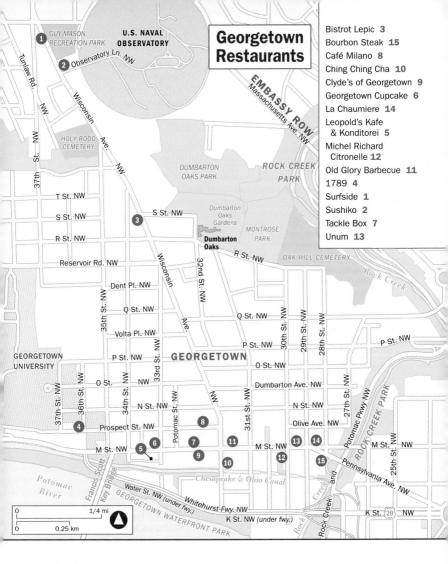

Georgetown
Restaurants

Bistrot Lepic **3**
Bourbon Steak **15**
Café Milano **8**
Ching Ching Cha **10**
Clyde's of Georgetown **9**
Georgetown Cupcake **6**
La Chaumiere **14**
Leopold's Kafe
  & Konditorei **5**
Michel Richard
  Citronelle **12**
Old Glory Barbecue **11**
1789 **4**
Surfside **1**
Sushiko **2**
Tackle Box **7**
Unum **13**

dinner $17–$29. AE, DC, DISC, MC, V. Mon–Fri 11:30am–2:30pm; Sat–Sun 11am-3pm; Sun–Mon 5:30–9:30pm; Tues–Thurs 5:30–10pm; Fri–Sat 5:30–10:30pm. Wine bar daily 5:30pm–midnight.

Cafe Milano ITALIAN   Foodies may head to other hot spots, but Washington's famous, attractive, and powerful—and their visiting Hollywood and international celebrity friends—continue to turn up here, or at least those in the older crowd do. Its food is fine. Salads are big, pasta servings are small, and fish and meat entrees are just the right size. I had the endive, radicchio, and arugula salad topped with thin sheets of Parmesan cheese; a *panzanella* salad of tomatoes, potatoes, red onion, celery, and cucumber basking in basil and olive oil; *cappellacci* (round ravioli) pockets of spinach and ricotta in cream sauce; sautéed sea bass on a bed of vegetables with lemon chive sauce; and the Santa Babila pizza, which has tomatoes, fresh mozzarella, oregano, and basil on a light pizza crust. Cafe Milano opens to a sidewalk cafe during the warm months. A bevy of good-humored waiters takes care of you.

3251 Prospect St. NW (btw. Wisconsin Ave. and Potomac St.). www.cafemilano.com. ℰ **202/333-6183.** Reservations recommended. Main courses $15–$45 (most $20–$35). AE, DC, DISC, MC, V. Mon–Tues 11:30am–1am; Wed–Sat 11:30am–2am; Sun 11:30am–11pm.

Unum ★ AMERICAN   Unum as in "E pluribus unum," meaning "Out of many, one," the Latin phrase that appears on the seal of the United States. Only in the nation's capital. But the name hints at the fact that one of the owners has government credentials—and, in fact, Laura Schiller hasn't quit her day job working for California Senator Barbar Boxer (husband and co-owner Phillip Blane is the chef). Open since February 2012, Unum is ensconced in the space of the former Mendocino Grille and has retained its lovely features: rough-textured walls, painted wooden floors, and the layout with a bar at the front and banquettes lining the walls in back, with a little nook to the side. It's cozy, a good place for couples. Among the standouts on the menu are a rockfish bouillabaisse which tastes fresh from the sea, smoked duck breast with whipped potatoes, and rosemary gnocchi.

2917 M St. NW (btw. 29th and 30th sts.). www.unumdc.com. ℰ **202/621-6959.** Reservations recommended. Main courses $10–$25. AE, MC, V. Sun–Thurs 5:30–10pm; Fri–Sat 5:30–11pm.

Moderate

Clyde's of Georgetown AMERICAN   Clyde's has been a favorite watering hole for an eclectic mix of Washingtonians since 1963. You'll see university students, Capitol Hill types, affluent professionals, Washington Redskins, romantic duos, and ladies out for lunch. Theme park–ish in decor, its dining areas include a cherry-paneled front room with oil paintings of sport scenes, as well as an atrium with vintage model planes dangling from the glass ceiling.

Clyde's is known for its burgers, crab cake sandwiches, and weekend brunch (a tradition); the menu is reassuringly familiar—steak and eggs, omelets, waffles—with an assortment of sandwiches, burgers, and salads thrown in. Among bar selections are about 10 draft beers. Bottles of wine are half price on Sundays until 10:30pm.

Clyde's is part of a family of restaurants that includes the fab new **Hamilton** (restaurant and live music venue; p. 261); **1789** (p. 214); the Penn Quarter **Clyde's of Gallery Place** (p. 254), at 707 7th St. NW (ℰ **202/349-3700**); and Georgetown University student hangout **The Tombs** (p. 258), located right next door to 1789.

3236 M St. NW (btw. Wisconsin Ave. and Potomac St.). www.clydes.com. ℰ **202/333-9180.** Reservations recommended. Main courses lunch and brunch $9.50–$17, dinner $13–$24 (most under $20); burgers and sandwiches (except for crab cake sandwich) $10 or less. AE, DC, DISC, MC, V. Mon–Thurs 11:30am–midnight; Fri 11:30am–1am; Sat 10am–1am; Sun 9am–midnight (Sat–Sun brunch until 4pm).

La Chaumiere ★ FRENCH   After 36 years, La Chaumiere is still a pleasure. This rustically handsome dining room centers on a large hearth, which makes it an especially welcoming place in winter. Year-round the restaurant fills up with locals who know to ask about seasonal specials, like winter's *pot-au-feu* (boiled beef shoulder, oxtails, and winter vegetables in consommé) and daily specials (Tues night's *crabe en chemise*—crabmeat in crepes). La Chaumiere prepares the full range of French classics just right, whether it's cassoulet or a chocolate soufflé. The service is warm but professional. The diners who gather here are a motley bunch, alike at least in their love of this kitchen's authentic French cooking.

2813 M St. NW (at 28th St.). www.lachaumieredc.com. © **202/338-1784.** Reservations accepted. Main courses lunch $17–$21, dinner $19–$37 (most under $30). AE, DC, MC, V. Mon–Fri 11:30am–2:30pm; Mon–Sat 5:30–10:30pm.

Leopold's Kafe & Konditorei ★ 👬 AUSTRIAN   If you find yourself at the western end of Georgetown, caught in the maze of high-end shops collectively known as Cady's Alley, you owe it to yourself to track down Leopold's and treat yourself to a delicious taste of Sacher torte or veal schnitzel. This may be the only place in Washington that serves Austrian food; it is certainly one of the most adorable eateries, with its whimsically modern furniture and bright whites punched up with orange. The customers represent a cross-section of Washington, from chic to bohemian, and offer an intriguing picture to contemplate as you sip your Viennese coffee and enjoy your *apfelstrudel*. At brunch order the lemon soufflé pancakes. The cafe offers a full bar.

3315 Cady's Alley, no. 213 (off of M St. NW; find the passageway at 3318 M St., btw. 33rd and 34th sts., and walk back to Leopold's). www.kafeleopolds.com. © **202/965-6005.** Reservations accepted at dinner only, for parties of more than 6. Main courses breakfast $2–$12, lunch and dinner $7–$25. AE, DISC, MC, V. Sun–Tues 8am–10pm; Wed 8am–11pm; Thurs–Sat 8am–midnight.

Old Glory Barbecue ☺ BARBECUE   Raised wooden booths flank one side of the restaurant; an imposing, old-fashioned dark-wood bar with saddle-seat stools extends down the other. Background music is recorded swing music during the day, more mainstream music into the night. Old Glory boasts the city's "largest selection of single-barrel and boutique bourbons" and a rooftop deck with outdoor seating and views of Georgetown.

After 9pm or so, the two-story restaurant becomes packed with the hard-drinkin' young and restless. In early evening, though, Old Glory is prime for anyone—singles, families, or an older crowd—although it's almost always noisy. Come for the messy, tangy, delicious spareribs; hickory-smoked chicken; tender, smoked beef brisket; or marinated, wood-fired shrimp. Six sauces are on the table, the spiciest being the Southwest Texas (lots of hot peppers!). The complimentary corn muffins and biscuits; side dishes of collard greens, succotash, and potato salad; and desserts like apple crisp and coconut cherry cobbler all hit the spot. See **"Family-Friendly Restaurants,"** p. 223.

3139 M St. NW (btw. 31st St. and Wisconsin Ave.). www.oldglorybbq.com. © **202/337-3406.** Reservations accepted. Main courses $7.95–$22.95. AE, DC, DISC, MC, V. Sun–Thurs 11:30am–2am; Fri–Sat 11:30am–3am.

Inexpensive

Ching Ching Cha 👬 CHINESE   Located just below M Street, this sky-lit tearoom offers a pleasant respite from the crowds. You can sit on pillows at low tables or on chairs set at rosewood tables. Choices are simple: individual items like a tea-and-spice boiled egg, puff pastry stuffed with lotus-seed paste, or five-spice peanuts. Most typical is the $14 "tea meal," which consists of miso soup, your choice of three marinated cold vegetables, rice, and your choice of the featured meal, which might be curry chicken, salmon with mustard-miso sauce, or steamed teriyaki-sauced tofu. Emphasis is really on the tea, of which there are 70 choices, including several different green, black, and oolong teas, plus a Fujian white tea and a ginseng brew.

1063 Wisconsin Ave. NW (near M St.). www.chingchingcha.com. ✆ **202/333-8288.** Reservations not accepted. All food items $4–$12; pot of tea $6–$20. AE, DISC, MC, V. Daily 11am–9pm.

Tackle Box SEAFOOD What a delicious deal: your choice of crisped scallops, shrimp, calamari, clams, or oysters, or wood-grilled fresh fish, from tilapia to rainbow trout, plus two sides (whether fries, grilled asparagus, or assorted other options) for a total of $13.50. Tackle Box is all about ecofriendly practices and top-notch food for a great price. Dine in and you'll sit at picnic tables in a lobster-buoy-bedecked room, in view and smelling range of the wood-grilling kitchen. Tackle Box serves beer and wine; its upstairs bar, Crackle Box, offers a full bar after 4pm (you can also dine there). Tackle Box has a second location in the Cleveland Park neighborhood, at 3407 Connecticut Ave. NW (✆ **202/450-6875**).

3245 M St. NW (btw. Wisconsin Ave. and Potomac St.). www.tackleboxrestaurant.com. ✆ **202/337-TBOX** (8269). Main courses $2–$14. AE, DC, MC, V. Sun–Thurs 11am–11pm; Fri–Sat 11am–1am.

GLOVER PARK

The D.C. Circulator buses travel through Georgetown as far as Whitehaven Street, just a little bit short (south) of Glover Park; you can walk it easily, but it is all uphill. Regular Metro buses (the no. 30 series) travel to Glover Park. Perhaps the easiest thing to do is take a taxi.

Moderate

Surfside AMERICAN/LATIN/SEAFOOD Twenty- and 30-somethings are up on the rooftop deck sipping margaritas and diving into guacamole, while down in the colorful and casual eatery, their married-with-children peers, families in tow, nosh on tacos, quesadillas, burritos, and salads. Surfside is especially known for its fresh grilled fish tacos, but its menu covers assorted options, including a pork carnitas taco served with pineapple jalapeño salsa on corn tortillas that I like. But if the menu combinations don't appeal, you fill out a form indicating your desired ingredients so the cook can custom-prepare your order. Good to know: Surfside does a brisk takeout business, too, and it now operates a food truck—look for its signature ocean-blue van prowling downtown streets.

2444 Wisconsin Ave. NW (near Calvert St.). www.surfsidedc.com. ✆ **202/337-0004.** Reservations accepted. Main courses dinner $7–$14, brunch $7–$10.AE, DC, DISC, MC, V. Sun–Thurs 11am–9pm; Fri–Sat 11am–9:30pm. Bar daily until midnight.

Sushiko ★ JAPANESE Sushiko was Washington's first sushi bar when it opened 37 years ago, and it remains among the best. The sushi chefs are fun to watch, so try to sit at the sushi bar; if you do, ask chef Koji Terano to serve you his choice selections. You can expect superb sushi and sashimi standards, as well as innovations, like a soy- and *sake*-marinated tuna sashimi, salmon and

HUNGRY? MAKE LIKE A LOCAL AND FOLLOW THE food trucks

"Meet you at McPherson Square---lobster rolls!" "Time for a cupcake break---corner of 3rd and D." All day long weekdays and somewhat on weekends, D.C. workers of all trades and echelons text, tweet, e-mail, or phone friends to arrange a food-on-the-move rendezvous. They track the routes of favorite "food trucks," that most unappetizing name for the legion of mobile cook-and-serve vendors, each hawking its own irresistible specialty: gourmet macaroni and cheese, empanadas, Philly cheesesteaks, Maine lobster rolls, all sorts of desserts—you get the idea.

Traditional sidewalk and roadway merchants selling hot dogs and T-shirts still abound in all the usual sightseeing places, including in clusters around the National Mall. These are not them. This next generation of food trucks switches up street fare, tweets its location so hungry patrons know where to go, and still manages to keep prices reasonable (generally ranging from $3 for a Curbside Cupcake to $15 for a Red Hook Lobster Pound lobster roll). These days, about 50 different trucks roll around town, setting up shop at designated spots before driving on to their next location.

For a complete list of DC's food trucks, go to **www.foodtruckfiesta.com**, which also displays a map in real time of food-truck stops and messages. The website includes links to each truck's website, where menus, travel routes, and prices are posted. If you want to sample

the food-truck experience and a little DC social scene, head to the Penn Quarter's **Chinatown Coffee Co.,** 475 H St. NW (www.chinatowncoffee.com; ✆ **202/559-7656**) on Thursday evenings in spring and summer, 6:30 to 8:30pm. That's when the coffeehouse teams up with a food truck—a different one every week—to host happy hour. Customers purchase the food-truck specialty outside, then take it inside Chinatown Coffee, where they can sit and enjoy the meal, as well as $3 beer, wine, or absinthe.

Laws prohibit gourmet food trucks from parking and serving on federal property, so you won't find these trucks parked along the National Mall (though the aforementioned stationary vendors selling hot dogs and T-shirt vendors are allowed, for some reason). They're never far away, though.

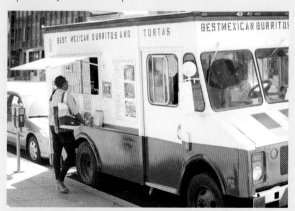

Food trucks are popular among both residents and visitors looking to grab a quick bite.

A SEAT AT THE bar

Dining out in Washington can be many things: a culinary adventure, a happy pastime, a chance to transact business, a romantic interlude . . . and a competitive sport. Most restaurants require reservations, and in this cutthroat town, all the best often seem to be booked. What's a hungry, reservation-less lover of good food to do? Head to the bar, of course. In an effort to please those who haven't managed to reserve a table in their main dining rooms, a number of the city's top restaurants have started serving modified versions of their regular menus at the bar. The experience often proves more intimate and convivial than that in the main dining room, and here's the kicker: It's always less expensive. Consider these:

At **Citronelle** (p. 213), you sit upstairs from the main dining room, so the vibe is different but still a kick. The lounge menu is quite extensive and includes signature Michel Richard dishes, like the lobster burger, tuna napoleon Niçoise, and the chocolate bar with sauce noisette. But the a la carte prices are so much less than you would pay downstairs on the prix-fixe menus.

Ceiba (p. 188), in the Penn Quarter, offers a sweet deal at the bar. Monday to Saturday from 3 to 6pm and again from 9:30pm (10pm Fri–Sat) to close, you can order $5 signature cocktails (the mojitos here may be the best in the city) and items from the bar menu, from guacamole to empanadas, at half their usual ($9–$16) price.

CityZen (p. 179), in the Mandarin Oriental Hotel, offers perhaps the most jaw-dropping bar meal: Chef Eric Ziebold's four-course tasting menu in his main dining room costs $90; at the bar, Ziebold's edited three-course version goes for $50. You can be sure you're dining on the same heavenly fare as those seated at tables: maybe a pickled shad with braised celery and potato crisps, or braised shoat shoulder with English peas. And the service is sublime.

Other bar scenes to recommend: **Bistrot Lepic & Wine Bar** (p. 260), which offers both bar-item menus and specialties of the house at its second-floor wine bar (stop here Tues evenings for complimentary wine tastings); and **Corduroy** (p. 197), whose nightly $30 three-course prix-fixe menu is available only in the intimate bar, a perfect setting and a fabulous deal.

tuna five ways, and the delicately fried soft-shell crab (in season spring and summer). Another option to capture the full range of tastes here: Order a bunch of the "small dishes," like the grilled baby octopus with mango sauce, or asparagus with smoked salmon and mustard *dashi* sauce. The tempuras and teriyakis are also excellent. There's a long list of *sakes*, as well as burgundy wines and Japanese beer. A second location is in Chevy Chase, Maryland, at 5455 Wisconsin Ave. (✆ **301/961-1644**).

2309 Wisconsin Ave. NW. www.sushikorestaurants.com. ✆ **202/333-4187.** Reservations recommended. *Nigiri*, small dishes, individual pieces $6–$15; sushi assortments and main courses $15–$31. AE, MC, V. Tues–Fri noon–2:30pm; Mon–Thurs 6–10:30pm; Fri 6–11pm; Sat 5:30–11pm; Sun 5:30–10pm.

WOODLEY PARK & CLEVELAND PARK

Very Expensive

Palena ★★★ NEW AMERICAN   In this elegant venue, former White House chef Frank Ruta turns out modern American dishes infused with French and Italian influences, such as Portuguese sardines in puff pastry, cod roasted in lavender-infused olive oil, and Dover sole filet stuffed with porcini and pan-roasted with artichokes and endive. Dinner concludes with complimentary caramels to accompany your dessert choice, such as a fresh sorbet, cheesecake, or bread pudding. Because of Palena's enduring success, it's sometimes hard to get a reservation, but it's worth trying. Or dine in the popular, walk-ins-only **Palena Café,** which opened in 2010 in response to the throngs who would descend on Palena's original cafe, the bar area of the main dining room. The cafe area adjoins the main dining room and features comfy banquettes, an open kitchen, and, of course, Ruta's famous Kobe beef cheeseburger layered with *sottocenere* (a creamy Italian cheese with black truffles) and served inside a house-made brioche bun, with a side order of fried lemons (don't knock 'em til you try 'em). Palena Market is now open, selling artisanal and imported products used in the restaurant, and ready-to-eat savories and sweets.

3529 Connecticut Ave. NW. www.palenarestaurant.com. 🕐 **202/537-9250.** Reservations required for the main dining room but not accepted for the cafe. Main courses $12–$27; fixed-price menus about $75 for a 3-course menu, $100 for a 5-course menu; cafe menu brunch and Sun dinner main courses $12–$17. AE, DC, DISC, MC, V. Dining room Tues–Sat 5:30–10pm. Cafe Sat–Sun 11:30am–2:30pm; Mon–Sat 5:30–10pm; Sun 4:30–9pm. Metro: Cleveland Park (exit to the east side of Connecticut Ave.).

Moderate

Indique ★ INDIAN   When it first opened in 2006, Indique was a prime hot spot for hipsters. Things have settled down since then, or more likely, the young and the restless have moved on to another, more of-the-moment restaurant. But Indique still thrives in this upscale residential community of old streets lined with towering trees and Victorian houses, drawing people from the neighborhood: mostly wonks, intellects, journalists, and their families. Pomegranate martinis are ever popular, as are the Cornish hen curry, vegetable samosas, and tandoori shrimp. Its authentic cuisine from different regions in India, from the curries and tandoori specialties of the north to the *appams* and *ishtews* of the southwest, attracts visiting dignitaries from India.

3512–14 Connecticut Ave. NW (btw. Porter and Ordway sts.). www.indique.com. 🕐 **202/244-6600.** Reservations accepted. Main courses $12–$23. AE, DC, DISC, MC, V. Fri–Sun noon–3pm; Sun–Thurs 5:30–10:30pm; Fri–Sat 5:30–11pm. Metro: Cleveland Park (Connecticut Ave. west exit).

Lebanese Taverna ☺ MIDDLE EASTERN   This family-owned restaurant, which opened in 1990, is known for its friendly service and basic but satisfying Lebanese cuisine. The taverna opens onto Connecticut Avenue, making its patio a favorite spot in pleasant weather. The dining room's domed ceiling and soft lighting gives it the feel of an inner courtyard; Lebanese music plays and mouth-watering smells emanate from the wood-burning oven. I recommend the *mezze*

chocolate **LOUNGES & CUPCAKE SHOPS**

Busted! Washingtonians are finally exposed for what we are: all chocoholics and sweet-cake addicts. An explosion of chocolate lounges and cupcake shops has forced us to come clean. If you answer to the same passion for something sweet, join the queue at one of these four personally vouched-for places:

Co Co. Sala, 929 F St. NW (www.coco sala.com; ℂ **202/347-4265**): This chocolate lounge and boutique is a sweet refuge in the heart of the Penn Quarter, dispensing coffees, cocoas, pastries, and small plates of light fare throughout the day. Dessert cocktails and chocolate-spiked liqueurs are on tap into the wee hours. See p. 255.

Georgetown Cupcake, 3301 M St. NW (www.georgetowncupcake.com; ℂ **202/333-8448**): Two sisters, 12 daily flavors, darling designs and packaging, and the best cupcakes. Locals vote the chocolate ganache the best cupcake in the city; I love the lemon cupcake with lemon cream cheese frosting. Georgetown Cupcake is so popular that the TLC network developed a reality TV show featuring the lovely cupcake makers, Sophie LaMontagne and Katherine Kallinis. Georgetown Cupcake now has locations in New York and Boston.

Locolat Café, 1781 Florida Ave. NW (www.belgiumlocolat.com; ℂ **202/518-2570**): The Adams Morgan–based Locolat was already a Belgian chocolate

confiserie when it launched its cafe with sidewalk seating. Chocoholics can sip chocolate-enhanced coffee and hot cocoas, and savor an assortment of cakes, Belgian waffles, pastries, and created-on-the-premises chocolate bonbons.

Red Velvet Cupcakery, 501 7th St. NW (www.redvelvetcupcakery.com; ℂ **202/347-7895**): Located in the heart of the Penn Quarter, Red Velvet stays open until 11pm nightly, happy to accommodate the bar and club crowd when a yen for a sweet something hits. Also serves hot chocolate to go.

dishes: hummus, tabbouleh, baba ghanouj, stuffed grape leaves, and pastry-wrapped spinach pies (*fatayer b' sabanigh*), enough for dinner for two or as hors d'oeuvres for more. Also consider entrees, such as the roasted half chicken wrapped in bread and served with garlic puree. The wealth of meatless dishes will delight vegetarians, while rotisserie items, especially the chargrilled kabobs of chicken and shrimp, will please all others.

2641 Connecticut Ave. NW (near Woodley Rd.). www.lebanesetaverna.com. ℂ **202/265-8681.** Reservations recommended. Main courses $8–$26 (most $15–$17); *mezze* items $6–$11. AE, DC, DISC, MC, V. Mon–Fri 11:30am–2:30pm; Sat noon–11pm; Sun noon–9pm; Mon 5–9pm; Tues–Thurs 5–10pm; Fri 5–11pm. Metro: Woodley Park–Zoo (Connecticut Ave. south exit).

FAMILY-FRIENDLY RESTAURANTS

Nearly every restaurant welcomes families these days, starting, most likely, with the one in your hotel. What you need to know, Mom and Dad, is that many D.C. restaurants are playgrounds for the city's vast population of young professionals. For example, I would love to recommend **Matchbox** (p. 192), which serves an excellent pizza and other items kids love, but its reservations-only-for-six-or-more policy means that you and your little darlings are going to be waiting for your table (and there's almost always a wait) either in the jumping-all-day bar or out on the street in the middle of Chinatown. Consider dining early and getting a table away from the bar scene. Chinese restaurants and museum cafes are always a safe bet, and so are these:

Lebanese Taverna (p. 221)   Its location down the hill from the National Zoo and its lengthy menu (including the $2–$6.50 items marked for "the little ones") make the Taverna attractive to Mom, Dad, and the whole caboodle. Around for nearly 2 decades, the Taverna is a favorite among locals, and the owners keep opening new locations as a result—there are six now.

Legal Sea Foods (p. 192)   Believe it or not, this seafood restaurant has won awards for its kids' menu. It features the usual macaroni and cheese and hot dogs, but it also offers kids' portions of steamed lobster; fried popcorn shrimp; a small fisherman's platter of shrimp, scallops, and clams; and other items, each of which comes with fresh fruit, fresh vegetables, and a choice of rice, mashed potatoes, or french fries. Prices range from $1.95 to $17.

Old Glory Barbecue (p. 217)   A boisterous, laid-back place where the waiters are friendly without being patronizing. Go early; the bar becomes a mob scene as the evening progresses. The children's menu offers a fantastic deal: a flat $5.95 covers an entree, from a barbecue sandwich to a PB&J, plus soda, crispy fries, and an ice cream sundae.

PRACTICAL MATTERS: THE RESTAURANT SCENE

If you have your heart set on eating at a particular restaurant, call ahead for **reservations,** especially for Saturday night. At most restaurants, you can also reserve your table online at www.opentable.com.

If you don't have a reservation, consider eating at the bar, which can be more of a culinary treat than you might imagine; see "A Seat at the Bar," earlier in this chapter.

Few places require men to wear a jacket and tie; I've made a special note in the listings for those places that do. If you're driving, call ahead to inquire about valet parking, complimentary or otherwise—on Washington's crowded streets, this service can be a true bonus.

7

SHOPPING

N o matter how marvelous the shops in your hometown, you don't have a Kramerbooks store, nor an Eastern Market, nor a Tiny Jewel Box, nor a Proper Topper, nor the Folger Shakespeare Library gift shop—to name just a few of the only-in-Washington, D.C. shopping adventures you'll experience here. Perhaps you have some of the chains, say Macy's or J. Crew, but do you have the grand range, from Barneys New York CO-OP to H&M? And if you like specialty boutiques, D.C.'s got them in spades. Wherever you are in the city, shops present a variety of wares, prices, and styles. This chapter leads you to some of the best.

GREAT SHOPPING AREAS

PENN QUARTER   The area bound east and west by 7th and 14th streets NW, and north and south by New York and Pennsylvania avenues NW, continues to develop as a central shopping area, despite the economic crisis. Look for a long list of brand-name stores, including **Urban Outfitters; Bed, Bath & Beyond; Banana Republic; H&M; Forever 21; Zara;** and **Anthropologie.** One-of-a-kind places include museum shops at the National Building Museum, the Smithsonian American Art Museum and Portrait Gallery, and the International Spy Museum, and the delightful jewelry store **Mia Gemma** (p. 235). Macy's (formerly "Hecht's," up until 2006), at 12th and G streets NW, continues as the sole department store downtown.

ADAMS MORGAN   Centered on 18th Street and Columbia Road NW, Adams Morgan is a neighborhood of ethnic eateries and nightclubs interspersed with the odd secondhand bookshop and eclectic collectibles stores. It's a fun area for walking and shopping. Note that parking is possible during the day but impossible at night; take the Metro or the D.C. Circulator bus instead.

CONNECTICUT AVENUE/DUPONT CIRCLE   Running from K Street north to S Street, Connecticut Avenue NW is a main thoroughfare, where you'll find traditional clothing at **Brooks Brothers, Ann Taylor,** and **Burberry;** casual duds at **Gap;** and haute couture at **Rizik's.** Closer to Dupont Circle are coffee bars and neighborhood restaurants, as well as art galleries, funky boutiques, and gift, stationery, and book shops.

U STREET CORRIDOR/14TH STREET   Urbanistas have been promoting this neighborhood for years, but now the number of cool shops, restaurants, and bars has hit critical mass, winning the area widespread notice. If you shun brand names and box stores, you'll love the vintage boutiques and affordable fashion shops along U and 14th streets NW.

GEORGETOWN   Georgetown is the city's ultimate shopping area. Most of the stores sit on the two main, intersecting streets, Wisconsin Avenue and M Street NW. You'll find both chain and one-of-a-kind shops, a handful of art

The shop-lined streets of Georgetown.

galleries, and a bevy of excellent antiques stores. The city's best hair salons and cosmetic stores are also in Georgetown.

UPPER WISCONSIN AVENUE NW   In a residential section of town known as Friendship Heights on the D.C. side and Chevy Chase on the Maryland side (7 miles north of Georgetown, straight up Wisconsin Ave. NW) is a quarter-mile shopping district that extends from **Saks Fifth Avenue** at one end to **Sur La Table** at the other. In between are **Lord & Taylor, Neiman Marcus, Bloomingdale's,** and **Versace** (to name just a few stores), and three malls (the **Mazza Gallerie, Chevy Chase Pavilion,** and the **Shops at Wisconsin Place**). The street is too wide and traffic always too snarled to make this a pleasant place to stroll, although teenagers do love to loiter here. Drive if you want and park in the garages beneath the Mazza Gallerie, Chevy Chase Pavilion, or Bloomingdale's.

OLD TOWN ALEXANDRIA   Old Town, a Virginia neighborhood beyond National Airport, resembles Georgetown in its picturesque location on the Potomac, historic home-lined streets, and plentiful shops and restaurants, as well as in its less desirable aspects: heavy traffic, crowded sidewalks, and difficult parking. Old Town extends from the Potomac River in the east to the King Street Metro station in the west, and from about 1st Street in the north to Green Street in the south, but the best shopping is in the center, where King and Washington streets intersect. Weekdays are a lot tamer than weekends. (For coverage of Alexandria beyond shopping, see chapter 10.)

MALLS & MARKETS

If malls are your thing, the D.C. area, if not D.C. proper, has several for you to choose from. **Chevy Chase Pavilion,** 5335 Wisconsin Ave. NW (www.ccpavilion. com/store-directory; ✆ **202/207-3887;** Metro: Friendship Heights) is a mall in transition (some stores leaving and new, but as yet unknown stores moving in), but expect to find a well-stocked J. Crew and Ann Taylor Loft. A large Bloomingdale's anchors the **Shops at Wisconsin Place,** Wisconsin Avenue at Western Avenue,

Chevy Chase, Maryland (www.shopwisconsinplace.com; ✆ **301/841-4000;** Metro: Friendship Heights), whose other stores include White & Black, Anthropologie, and Sephora. The **Mazza Gallerie,** 5300 Wisconsin Ave. NW (www.mazzagallerie.com; ✆ **202/966-6114;** Metro: Friendship Heights) holds a substantial Neiman Marcus, as well as a Williams-Sonoma, Ann Taylor, and Saks Men. The **Shops at Georgetown Park,** 3222 M St. NW (www.shopsatgeorgetown park.com; ✆ **202/342-8190;** Metro: Foggy Bottom, then take the D.C. Circulator) are less remarkable than those you'll find out on the street, but offerings range from the practical Comfort One Shoes to the seductive Victoria's Secret. **Ronald Reagan Washington National Airport,** Arlington, Virginia (www.shopreagan national.com; ✆ **703/417-0565**), is a 40-store minimall, there to rescue you should you need to purchase a last-minute gift (Smithsonian), a tie to replace the one you stained on the plane (Brooks Brothers), or a book or magazine to read on your flight home (Heritage Booksellers).

Alexandria Farmers' Market   The oldest continuously operating farmers' market in the country (since 1752), it offers locally grown fruits and vegetables, along with delectable baked goods, cut flowers, and plants. Open year-round Saturday mornings from 7am to noon. 301 King St. (at Market Sq. in front of the city hall), Alexandria, VA. www.alexandriava.gov/market. ✆ **703/746-3200.** Metro: King St., then take the free King Street Trolley or the DASH bus (AT2, AT5) eastbound to Market Sq.

Dupont Circle FreshFarm Market ☺   At least 40 local farmers sell their flowers, produce, eggs, and cheeses here. The market also features kids' activities and guest appearances by chefs and owners of some of Washington's best restaurants: Vidalia, Zaytinya, Bis, and 1789. It's held Sundays, rain or shine, from 10am to 1pm January through March and 8:30am to 1pm the rest of the year. The FreshFarm Market organization stages other farmers' markets on other days around town; go to the website for locations, dates, and times. On 20th St. NW (btw. Q St. and Massachusetts Ave.) and in the adjacent PNC Bank parking lot. www.freshfarm markets.org. ✆ **202/362-8889.** Metro: Dupont Circle (Q St. exit).

Chef José Andrés makes a giant paella at the Penn Quarter FreshFarm Market.

Shops at Union Station.

Eastern Market ★ 🍴   Reopened in July 2009 after a devastating fire in April 2007 gutted this Capitol Hill institution, historic Eastern Market can still claim that it has been in continuous operation since 1873. The indoor vendors set up stands across the street in temporary quarters, and the outdoor farmers' market stalls remained open throughout, selling fresh produce and other goods on Saturdays and flea market items on Sundays. Today Eastern Market's restored South Hall is once again a bustling bazaar, where area farmers, greengrocers, bakers, butchers, and others sell their wares Tuesday through Sunday, joined by a second line of farmers outside on the weekend, as well as 100 or so local artisans hawking jewelry, paintings, pottery, woodwork, and other handmade items. For an essential D.C. experience, indulge in the Saturday morning ritual of breakfasting on blueberry pancakes at the Market Lunch counter. The market is open Tuesday to Friday 7am to 7pm, Saturday 7am to 6pm, and Sunday 9am to 5pm. 225 7th St. SE (at North Carolina Ave.). www.easternmarket-dc.org. ℘ **202/698-5253.** Metro: Eastern Market.

Montgomery County Farm Women's Cooperative Market   Vendors set up inside every Wednesday, Friday, and Saturday year-round from 8am to about 4pm to sell preserves, homegrown veggies, cut flowers, slabs of bacon and sausages, and mouthwatering pies, cookies, and breads; there's an abbreviated version on Wednesday. Outside, on Saturday, Sunday, Wednesday, and Friday from 8am to 4pm, you'll find flea market vendors selling everything from rugs to tablecloths to furniture to sunglasses. 7155 Wisconsin Ave., Bethesda, MD. ℘ **301/652-2291.** Metro: Bethesda.

Union Station   It's a railroad station, a historic landmark, an architectural marvel, a Metro stop, and a shopping mall. Yes, the beauteous Union Station offers some fine shopping opportunities, with more than 100 clothing, specialty, and souvenir shops, including **Jos. E. Bank Clothiers** (p. 236) and **Appalachian Spring** (p. 230). Hungry? Grab a bite at one of 40 eateries or at the impressive food court. 40 Massachusetts Ave. NE. www.unionstationdc.com. ℘ **202/371-9441** or 202/289-1908. Metro: Union Station.

emergency SHOPPING

You've just arrived in town, but your luggage hasn't—the airline lost it. Or you're about to depart for home or another destination and you notice that the zipper to your suitcase is broken. Or you've arrived at your hotel all in one piece, only to discover you've forgotten something essential: underwear, allergy medicine, an umbrella. What's a luckless traveler to do? One of these suggestions might prove your salvation.

CVS: This is Washington's main pharmacy and essentials chain. Among the items sold at CVS stores are pantyhose, over-the-counter and prescription medicines, toys, greeting cards, wrapping paper and ribbon, magazines, film and 1-hour photo developing, and batteries. 24-hour branches at 2240 M St. NW (at 23rd St., near the Ritz-Carlton Hotel; www.cvs.com; ℭ 202/296-9877; Metro: Foggy Bottom) and at 6–7 Dupont Circle NW (ℭ 202/785-1466; Metro: Dupont Circle).

Cobbler's Bench Shoe Repair: This shop on the lower (food court) level of Union Station is open daily: Monday to Friday from 7am to 8pm, Saturday 9am to 6pm, and Sunday noon to 6pm, to come to the rescue of travelers whose shoes or luggage need mending. The cobbler also cuts keys and sells repair items. Union Station, lower level (www.cobblersbenchshoerepair.com; ℭ 202/898-9009).

Metro: Union Station. Check the website for the shop's four other D.C. locations.

Macy's: This former Hecht's is the only downtown department store and remains an old reliable. Run here if you need cosmetics, clothes (for men, women, and children), shoes (but not for children), electronics, appliances, lingerie, luggage, raincoats, and countless other need-immediately goods. Open daily: noon to 6pm Sunday, 10am to 8pm Monday through Thursday, 9am to 9pm Friday, and 9am to 10pm Saturday. 1201 G St. NW (www.macys.com; ℭ 202/628-6661). Metro: Metro Center.

Metro Stations: If it starts raining and you're scrambling to find an umbrella, look no further than your closest Metro station, where vendors are at the ready selling umbrellas and other handy items.

SHOPPING A TO Z
Antiques

Brass Knob Architectural Antiques   When old homes and office buildings are demolished in the name of progress, these savvy salvage merchants spirit away salable treasures, from lots and lots of light fixtures and chandelier glass to wrought-iron fencing. 2311 18th St. NW. www.thebrassknob.com. ℭ **202/332-3370.** Metro: Woodley Park–Zoo or Dupont Circle.

Cote Jardin Antiques   This very pretty shop just off busy Wisconsin Avenue specializes in 18th- and 19th-century French formal and country antique home furnishings, and late-19th- and early-20th-century antique French garden ornaments and furniture. 3218 O St. NW. www.cotejardinantiques.com. ℭ **202/333-3067.** Metro: Foggy Bottom, then take the D.C. Circulator.

Galerie L'Enfant   The inventory housed in this mid-19th-century town house changes weekly but always represents a mix of antique early-20th-century vintage and modern French and French-influenced home furnishings. 1442 Wisconsin Ave. NW. www.lenfantmoderne.com. ℂ **202/625-2873.** Metro: Foggy Bottom, then take the D.C. Circulator.

Marston-Luce Stop in here at least to admire, if not to buy, a beautiful 18th- or 19th-century French furnishing or two. The shop is at the upper end of Georgetown. 1651 Wisconsin Ave. NW. www.marstonluce.com. ℂ **202/333-6800.** Metro: Foggy Bottom, then take the D.C. Circulator.

Millennium Decorative Arts This is antiques shopping for the TV generation, where anything made between the 1930s and the 1970s is considered collectible. The shop works with nearly a score or so of dealers; stock changes weekly. Funky wares run from Bakelite to Heywood-Wakefield blond-wood beauties to toasters to used drinking glasses. 1528 U St. NW. www.millenniumdecorativearts. com. ℂ **202/483-1218.** Metro: U St./Cardozo (13th St. exit).

Old Print Gallery ★ Open since 1971, this gallery carries original American and European prints from the 17th to the 19th century, including political cartoons, maps, and historical documents. It's one of the largest antique print and map shops in the United States. In 2010 the Gallery expanded its inventory of works by 20th- and 21st-century printmakers. Prices range from $45 to $10,000. 1220 31st St. NW. www.oldprintgallery.com. ℂ **202/965-1818.** Metro: Foggy Bottom, then take the D.C. Circulator.

Susquehanna Antiques ★ This is Georgetown's largest collection of fine American, English, and European furniture, paintings, and garden items of the late-18th and early-19th centuries. The shop turns 100 in 2013. 3216 O St. NW. www.susquehannaantiques.com. ℂ **202/333-1511.** Metro: Foggy Bottom, then take the D.C. Circulator.

Arts, Crafts & Museum Stores

Addison/Ripley Fine Art This gallery represents internationally, nationally, and regionally recognized artists, from the 19th century to the present; works include paintings, sculpture, photography, and fine arts. 1670 Wisconsin Ave. NW (at Reservoir Rd.). www.addisonripleyfineart.com. ℂ **202/338-5180.** Metro: Foggy Bottom, then take the D.C. Circulator.

A Mano Owner Adam Mahr frequently forages in Europe and returns with the unique handmade French and Italian ceramics, linens, and other decorative accessories for home and garden that you'll covet here. 1677 Wisconsin Ave. NW. www.amano.bz. ℂ **202/298-7200.** Metro: Foggy Bottom, then take the D.C. Circulator.

Appalachian Spring Country comes to Georgetown. This store sells pottery, jewelry, newly made pieced and appliqué quilts, stuffed dolls and animals, candles, rag rugs, handblown glassware, an incredible collection of kaleidoscopes, glorious weavings, and wooden kitchenware. Everything is made by hand in the United States. 1415 Wisconsin Ave. NW (at P St.). www.appalachianspring.com. ℂ **202/337-5780.** Metro: Foggy Bottom, then take the D.C. Circulator. There's another branch in Union Station (ℂ **202/682-0505**).

Burton Marinkovich Fine Art ★ One of the city's leading art galleries, this one showcases fine prints, drawings, and paintings by modern and contemporary international artists, including Jim Dine, Alexander Calder, and Helen Frankenthaler. 1506 21st St. NW (at P St.). www.burtonmarinkovich.com. ℂ **202/296-6563.** Metro: Dupont Circle (19th St. exit).

Museum Shopping

Washington's museum shops hold a treasure-trove of unusual gifts. Right now I'm loving the set of coffee mugs I bought my husband for Christmas at the **Folger Shakespeare Library** (p. 64) gift shop. They're covered in Shakespeare quotes: both for when you're in a foul mood ("Bolting-hutch of beastliness," "Thou art a boil, a plague sore") and for when you're feelin' the love ("Love is a smoke raised with the fume of sighs"). I've always had a weakness for the **Textile Museum's** (p. 75) exquisite one-of-a-kind clothes and accessories, from Japanese silk purses to Turkish tote bags. The shop at the **National Building Museum** (p. 132) is jammed with surprising, useful, and cleverly designed housewares and interesting games, including bookends embossed with a Celtic design, Bauhaus mobiles, and collapsible strainers. And I can never visit the **National Gallery of Art** (p. 102) without lingering a little while in the store to admire captivating catalogue books, note cards, posters, children's games, and a slew of other things. No matter the museum, stop by the store and see whether a particular item or two calls out to you.

Flashpoint Flashpoint is a dance studio, theater lab, office space, and art gallery all in one. Its art gallery is dedicated to nurturing emerging local artists, who tend to use a variety of mediums, including video, sculpture, photography, and drawings, to tell their personal stories. 916 G St. NW (at 9th St.). www.flashpointdc.org. ℂ **202/315-1305.** Metro: Gallery Place (9th and G sts. exit).

Foundry Gallery In business since 1971, this gallery is artist-owned and -operated and features the works of local artists, who work in various media and styles, from abstract painting on silk to mixed-media collages. 1314 18th St. NW (Massachusetts Ave.). www.foundrygallery.org. ℂ **202/463-0203.** Metro: Dupont Circle (19th St. exit).

Hillyer Art Space This hip little two-room gallery lies in an alley behind the Phillips Collection. Its shows of contemporary art fulfill its mission to "increase cross-cultural understanding and exposure to the arts internationally." Hillyer hosts monthly events that draw social 20-somethings. 9 Hillyer Court NW (21st St.). www.artsandartists.org/hillyer.html. ℂ **202/338-0680.** Metro: Dupont Circle (Q St. exit).

Indian Craft Shop ★ 🎒 The Indian Craft Shop has represented authentic Native American artisans since 1938, selling their handwoven rugs and handcrafted baskets, jewelry, figurines, pottery, and other items. Since the shop is situated inside a federal government building, you must pass through security and show a photo ID to enter. Use the C Street entrance, which is the only one open to the public. The shop is open weekdays and the third Saturday of each month. Department of the Interior, 1849 C St. NW, Room 1023. www.indiancraftshop.com. ℂ **202/208-4056.** Metro: Farragut West (17th St. exit), with a bit of a walk from the station.

The Phoenix Around since 1955, the Phoenix sells high-end Mexican folk and fine art; handcrafted sterling silver jewelry from Mexico and all over the world; clothing in natural fibers from Mexican and American designers like Eileen Fisher and Cut Loose; collectors' quality masks; and decorative doodads in tin, brass, copper, and wood. Oaxaca folk and fine art are a specialty. 1514 Wisconsin Ave. NW. www.thephoenixdc.com. ℂ **202/338-4404.** Metro: Foggy Bottom, then take the D.C. Circulator.

A potter at Torpedo Factory Art Center in Alexandria, Virginia.

Studio Gallery This artist-owned gallery—the longest running of its kind in the area—showcases the works of some 30 local and professional artists, fine arts in all mediums. Don't miss the sculpture garden. Open Wednesday through Saturday. 2108 R St. NW. www.studiogallerydc.com. *©* **202/232-8734.** Metro: Dupont Circle (Q St. exit).

Susan Calloway Fine Arts On display are antique European and American oil paintings; contemporary art by local, regional, and international artists; and a carefully chosen selection of 17th- to 19th-century prints. 1643 Wisconsin Ave. NW (Q St.). www.callowayart.com. *©* **202/965-4601.** Metro: Foggy Bottom, then take the D.C. Circulator.

Torpedo Factory Art Center Once a munitions factory, this three-story building from 1918 now houses more than 82 working studios and the works of about 165 artists, who tend to their crafts before your very eyes, pausing to explain their techniques or to sell their pieces. Artworks include paintings, sculpture, ceramics, glasswork, and textiles. 105 N. Union St., Alexandria, VA. www.torpedo factory.org. *©* **703/838-4565.** Metro: King St., then take the free King Street Trolley or the DASH bus (AT2, AT5) eastbound to the waterfront.

Beauty & Cosmetics

Beauty 360 CVS pharmacies are known as drugstores, mainly, where you can buy all your essentials, from candy to cold medicine. With the launching of Beauty 360 (D.C.'s was the first to open), CVS ventures into the high-end cosmetics and skin-treatment market. Trained and licensed professionals provide signature services, including minimanicures and express facials, while trying to interest you in buying, say, Juicy Couture fragrance, Paula Dorf makeup, or Payot skincare items. A regular old CVS lies just around the corner, if you want something not quite so chi-chi. 1350 Connecticut Ave. NW (at Dupont Circle). www.beauty360. com. *©* **202/331-1725.** Metro: Dupont Circle (19th St. exit).

Bluemercury Half "apothecary," half spa, this chain's three D.C. locations offer a smorgasbord of high-end beauty products, from Acqua di Parma fragrances to Kiehl's skincare line, as well as a full selection of facial, massage, waxing, and makeup treatments. If it's the latter that interests you, you might want to call before your trip, as it's very popular. 3059 M St. NW. www.bluemercury.com. ✆ **202/965-1300.** Metro: Foggy Bottom, then take the D.C. Circulator. Other locations at 1619 Connecticut Ave. NW. (✆ **202/462-1300)** and 1145 Connecticut Ave. NW (✆ **202/628-5567).** Metro: Dupont Circle (Q St. exit).

Books, Maps & Stationery

GENERAL

Barnes & Noble This expansive, two-story store in a prime Penn Quarter location is well stocked in all genres and includes sizable travel, children's, software, and music sections. It also hosts frequent author appearances and storytime events for children. There's a cafe on the second floor and free Wi-Fi throughout the store. 555 12th St. NW. www.bn.com. ✆ **202/347-0176.** Other locations in Union Station (✆ **202/289-1724)** and 4801 Bethesda Ave., Bethesda, MD (✆ **301/986-1761).**

Bridge Street Books A small, serious shop specializing in politics, poetry, literature, history, philosophy, and publications you won't find elsewhere. Bestsellers and discounted books are not its specialty, so if you're looking for those categories, head elsewhere. 2814 Pennsylvania Ave. NW (next to the Four Seasons Hotel). ✆ **202/965-5200.** Metro: Foggy Bottom, then take the D.C. Circulator.

Kramerbooks & Afterwords Café ★ Opened in 1976, Kramer's bookstore/cafe has launched countless romances. It's jammed, is often noisy, stages live music Wednesday through Saturday evenings, and is open all night on weekends. Paperback fiction takes up most of its inventory, but the store carries a little of everything. 1517 Connecticut Ave. NW. www.kramers.com. ✆ **202/387-1400** or 387-3825 for cafe reservations. Metro: Dupont Circle (Q St. exit).

Kramerbooks & Afterwords Café is a Dupont Circle favorite.

Politics and Prose Bookstore ★ Located a few miles north of downtown in a residential area, this much-cherished two-story shop may be worth going out of your way for. It has vast offerings in literary fiction and nonfiction alike, and an excellent children's department. The store has expanded again and again over the years to accommodate its clientele's love of books; its most recent enlargement added to the travel and children's sections. The shop hosts author readings nearly every night of the year. A warm, knowledgeable staff will help you find what you need. Downstairs is a cozy coffeehouse. 5015 Connecticut Ave. NW. www.politics-prose.com. ✆ **202/364-1919.** Metro: Van Ness–UDC, and walk, or transfer to an L bus to take you the ¾ mile from there.

OLD & USED BOOKS

Second Story Books If it's old, out of print, custom bound, or a small-press publication, this is where to find it. The store also specializes in used CDs and vinyl, and has an interesting collection of campaign posters. 2000 P St. NW. www.secondstorybooks.com. ✆ **202/659-8884.** Metro: Dupont Circle (South/19th St. exit).

SPECIAL INTEREST BOOKS

Backstage, Inc. Backstage is headquarters for Washington's theatrical community, which buys its books, scripts, trades, and sheet music here. It's also a favorite costume rental shop. 545 8th St. SE. www.backstagecostumes.com. ✆ **202/544-5744.** Metro: Eastern Market.

Reiter's Bookstore Open since 1936, this is D.C.'s oldest independent bookstore. Located in the middle of the George Washington University campus, Reiter's is the go-to place for scientific, technical, medical, and professional books. The store is also known for its intriguing (and often amusing) mathematical and scientific toys in the children's section. 1900 G St. NW. (at 19th St.). www.reiters.com. ✆ **202/223-3327.** Metro: Foggy Bottom.

STATIONERY

Ginza, "for Things Japanese" In business since 1955, Ginza sells everything Japanese, from Hello Kitty merchandise to kimonos to futons to Zen rock gardens. 1721 Connecticut Ave. NW. www.ginzaonline.com. ✆ **202/332-7000.** Metro: Dupont Circle (Q St. exit).

Paper Source If you're a stationery freak like I am, you'll have to stop here to revel in the beautiful writing and wrapping papers, supplies of notebooks, journals, albums, ribbons, folders, containers, and other essentials. I believe it's the best stationery store in D.C. 3019 M St. NW. ✆ www.paper-source.com. ✆ **202/298-5545.** Metro: Foggy Bottom, with a 25-min. walk, or ride the D.C. Circulator.

Clothing & Accessories

CHILDREN

If your youngster has spilled grape juice all over his favorite outfit and you need a replacement, you can always head to the downtown **Macy's** (p. 229) or **H&M** (p. 239). Chic moms undeterred by expense shop at **Gap Kids** in Georgetown (1267 Wisconsin Ave. NW; ✆ **202/333-2411**),while practical moms shop at the midtown **Kid's Closet** (below).

Dawn Price Baby ☺ This store is as much about baby and kid paraphernalia as it is about clothing. Strollers, bedding, carseat covers, toys, games, back packs, cribs, you name it. And it's more about infants and nurseries than older kids, especially when it comes to clothing. 3112 M St. NW (at Wisconsin Ave.). www.dawn pricebaby.com. ✆ **202/333-3939.** Metro: Foggy Bottom, then take the D.C. Circulator. A 2nd location on Capitol Hill at 325 7th St. SE (✆ 202/543-2920).

Kid's Closet ☺   Nearing its 30th year, Kid's Closet has seen numerous children's clothing stores come and go in D.C. The secret to its staying power lies in full view: Its storefront display of affordable and practical kids' clothes, e.g., Osh Kosh and Carter's, are cute enough for you to imagine your child in them, but not so precious as to make you worry in advance about how you're going to remove the inevitable stains. Toys and gifts are also for sale. The store is easy to find, since it stands out among the bank and restaurant facades in this downtown block. 1226 Connecticut Ave. NW. www.kidsclosetdc.com. ✆ **202/429-9247.** Metro: Dupont Circle or Farragut North.

JEWELRY

Beadazzled   The friendly staff demonstrates to you how to assemble your own affordable jewelry from an eye-boggling array of beads and artifacts. The store also sells textiles, woodcarvings, and other crafts from around the world. There are also classes offered to those who prefer a more hands-on experience. 1507 Connecticut Ave. NW. www.beadazzled.net. ✆ **202/265-BEAD (2323).** Metro: Dupont Circle (Q St. exit).

Chas Schwartz & Son   In business since 1888, Chas Schwartz specializes in diamonds and sapphires, rubies and emeralds, and is one of the few distributors of Hidalgo jewelry (enameled rings and bracelets). The professional staff also repairs watches and jewelry. 1400 F St. NW (or enter through the Willard Hotel, 1401 Pennsylvania Ave. NW). www.chasschwartz.com. ✆ **202/737-4757.** Metro: Metro Center (13th St. exit). A 2nd location at the Mazza Gallerie (✆ **202/363-5432**). Metro: Friendship Heights.

Keith Lipert Gallery   This decorative-arts gallery sells Venetian glassware, high-end costume jewelry by designers such as Oscar de la Renta, and cute little things like Art Deco–style handbags. The owner shops in Europe for fashion jewelry and for exquisite gifts suitable for giving to diplomats and international business executives. 2922 M St. NW. www.keithlipertgallery.com. ✆ **202/965-9736.** Metro: Foggy Bottom, then take the D.C. Circulator.

Mia Gemma ★   This pretty boutique sells the original designs of American and European artists, including Judy Bettencourt, Sarah Richardson, and Randi Chervitz. All pieces are handcrafted, either of limited edition or one of a kind. If you'd like a customized design, Mia Gemma can do that, too. 933 F St. NW. www.miagemma.com. ✆ **202/393-4367.** Metro: Gallery Place/Verizon Center (9th St. exit).

Tiffany & Co.   Tiffany is known for exquisite diamonds and other jewelry that can cost hundreds of thousands of dollars. But you may not know that the store carries less expensive items as well, like $35 candlesticks. Tiffany will engrave, too. Other items include tabletop gifts and fancy glitz: china, crystal, flatware, and a bridal registry service. 5481 Wisconsin Ave., Chevy Chase, MD. www.tiffany.com. ✆ **301/657-8777.** Metro: Friendship Heights.

Tiny Jewel Box   The first place Washingtonians go for estate and antique jewelry, this six-story store next to the Mayflower Hotel also sells the pieces of many designers, from Links of London to Christian Tse, as well as crystal and other house gifts. In the month leading up to Mother's Day, Tiny Jewel Box holds its Top-to-Bottom Sale, where you can save anywhere from 10% to 75% on most merchandise, including jewelry, handbags, and home accessories. 1147 Connecticut Ave. NW. www.tinyjewelbox. com. © **202/393-2747.** Metro: Farragut North (L St. exit).

MEN

Local branches of **Banana Republic** are at Wisconsin and M streets NW, in Georgetown (© **202/333-2554**), and F and 13th streets NW (© **202/638-2724**); **Gap** has several locations in Washington, including 1120 Connecticut Ave. NW (© **202/429-0691**) and 1258 Wisconsin Ave. NW (© **202/333-2657**). Also see **J. Crew** and **H&M,** under "Women," as well as "Vintage," below.

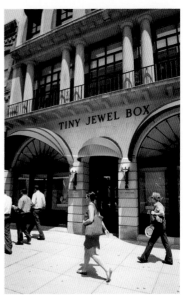

Tiny Jewel Box.

Brooks Brothers   Brooks Brothers sells traditional men's clothes, as well as the fine line of Peal & Company Collection shoes. It also sells an extensive line of women's clothes. 1201 Connecticut Ave. NW. www.brooksbrothers.com. © **202/659-4650.** Metro: Dupont Circle (19th St./ Q St. exit) or Farragut North (L St. exit). Other locations in Georgetown, 3077 M St. NW (© 202/298-8797); National Airport (© **703/417-1071**); and 5504 Wisconsin Ave., Chevy Chase, MD (© **301/654-8202**).

Burberry   Here you'll find those plaid-lined trench coats, of course, along with well-tailored English clothing for men, as well as women. Hot items include cashmere sweaters and camel's hair duffel coats for men. 1155 Connecticut Ave. NW. www.burberry.com. © **202/463-3000.** Metro: Farragut North (L St. exit).

Jos. A. Bank Clothiers   If you admire the Brooks Brothers line but wish it were more affordable, look here. This century-old clothier sells suits, corporate casual, weekend casual, and formal attire at great prices (lots of "buy one, get one free" offers). Union Station. www.josbank.com. © **202/289-9087.** Metro: Union Station. Four other locations: Lincoln Square, 555 11th St. NW (© **202/393-5590**); 1200 19th St. NW (© **202/466-2282**); 1401 I St. NW (© **202/898-0372**); and National Airport (© 703/418-8180).

Sherman Pickey   This store is prep to the max, but also a little fey: Think red corduroys. Both men's and women's clothes are on sale here, including Bill's Khakis and Barbour Outerwear for men, embroidered capris and ribbon belts for women. 1647 Wisconsin Ave. NW. www.shermanpickey.com. © **202/333-4212.** Metro: Foggy Bottom, then take the D.C. Circulator.

Thomas Pink   This boutique-size branch of the London-based high-end establishment is located inside the Mayflower Hotel. Merchandise includes beautifully made, bright-color shirts, along with ties, boxer shorts, women's shirts, cuff links, and other accessories. 1127 Connecticut Ave. NW (inside the Mayflower Hotel). www.thomaspink.com. © **202/223-5390.** Metro: Farragut North (L St. exit).

Urban Outfitters For the latest in casual attire, from fatigue pants to flannel shirts. This is my family's go-to place for funky T-shirts, but be forewarned: They're not cheap. This store has a floor of women's clothes and a floor of men's clothes, as well as apartment wares, travel books, accessories, cards, and candles. 3111 M St. NW. www.urbanoutfitters.com. ⓒ **202/342-1012.** Metro: Foggy Bottom, then take the D.C. Circulator. A 2nd location at Gallery Place, 737 7th St. NW. ⓒ **202/737-0259.** Metro: Gallery Place (7th and H sts. exit).

SHOES & ACCESSORIES

For men's dress shoes, try **Brooks Brothers** (p. 236). For women try the local outlets of **Nine West,** including locations at 1029 Connecticut Ave. NW (www.ninewest.com; ⓒ **202/331-3243**) and in Georgetown at 1227 Wisconsin Ave. NW (ⓒ **202/337-7256**).

Comfort One Shoes This locally owned family business was founded in Old Town Alexandria in 1993. Its six D.C. stores (of more than 20 in the area) sell a great selection of popular styles for both men and women, including Doc Martens, Birkenstocks, and Ecco. You can always find something that looks good and actually feels comfortable. 1630 Connecticut Ave. NW. www.comfortoneshoes.com. ⓒ **202/328-3141.** Metro: Dupont Circle. Other locations at 1625 Connecticut Ave. NW (ⓒ **202/667-5789**), 1329 Wisconsin Ave. NW (ⓒ **202/735-5332**), and many others.

Fleet Feet 📷 Though part of a national chain, this store feels decidedly part of the community, an Adams Morgan neighborhood fixture since 1984. The Fenty family—as in the family that includes former D.C. Mayor Adrian Fenty—owns the shop. You might see the ex-mayor himself, or his brothers, racing next to you during the weekly Sunday morning 5-mile fun run that Fleet Feet launches from its doorstep at 9am. (Just show up if you're interested.) Merchandise-wise the store sells sports and running shoes, apparel, and accessories, and is known for its friendly staff. 1841 Columbia Rd. NW. www.fleetfeetdc.com. ⓒ **202/387-3888.** Metro: U St./Cardozo (13th St. exit) or Woodley Park–Zoo, with a bit of a walk from either station.

Hu's Shoes Fashion models in every D.C. photo shoot wear Hu's shoes, it seems. The Georgetown shop sells designer ready-to-wear footwear, handbags, and accessories. Owner Marlene Hu Aldaba travels to New York, Paris, and Milan in search of elegant specimens to suit her discriminating eye. Across the street, at 2906 M St. NW, is Hu's Wear, a two-level store selling designer outfits to accompany the darling shoes. 3005 M St. NW. www.husonline.com. ⓒ **202/342-0202.** Metro: Foggy Bottom, then walk or take the D.C. Circulator.

VINTAGE

Meeps Vintage Fashionette This pioneer shop opened on U Street but has since moved around the corner to lower Adams Morgan. Its clientele and inventory remain the same: men and women urbanistas attracted to local designerwear and vintage clothes, from 1930s gabardine suits to 1950s cocktail dresses to satiny lingerie. 2104 18th St. NW. www.meepsdc.com. ⓒ **202/265-6546.** Metro: U St./Cardozo (13th St. exit) or Woodley Park–Zoo, with a bit of a walk from either station.

Secondhand Rose 🖋 This small and crowded, but upscale second-floor consignment shop has been around for 36 years, specializing in designer merchandise. Creations by Chanel, Armani, Donna Karan, Calvin Klein, Yves Saint-Laurent, Ungaro, Ralph Lauren, and others are sold at about a third of the original price.

Everything is in style, in season, and in excellent condition. Secondhand Rose is also a great place to shop for gorgeous furs, designer shoes and bags, and costume jewelry. 1516 Wisconsin Ave. NW (btw. P St. and Volta Place). www.secondhandrosedc.com. (℃ **202/337-3378.** Metro: Foggy Bottom, then take the D.C. Circulator.

Secondi Inc. ★ 🖋 On the second floor of a building right above Starbucks is this high-style consignment shop that sells women's clothing and accessories, including designer suits, eveningwear, and more casual items—everything from Kate Spade to Chanel. 1702 Connecticut Ave. NW (btw. R St. and Florida Ave.). www.secondi.com. (℃ **202/667-1122.** Metro: Dupont Circle (Q St. exit).

Secondi Inc. sells high-style secondhand clothing, shoes, and accessories.

WOMEN

Washington women have many more clothing stores to choose from than men. They include the classic designs of **Ann Taylor,** at Union Station (℃ **202/371-8010**), 1140 Connecticut Ave. NW (℃ **202/659-0120**), and 600 13th St. NW (℃ **202/737-0325**); and **J. Crew's** trendier tailored clothes, in Georgetown at 3222 M St. NW (℃ **202/965-4090**), and in Chevy Chase at 5335 Wisconsin Ave. NW (℃ **202/537-3380**). Racy **Victoria's Secret** lingerie stores are located at Union Station (℃ **202/682-0686**) and Georgetown Park (℃ **202/965-5457**), as well as at Connecticut and L streets NW (℃ **202/293-7530**).

See "Men," above, for locations of **Banana Republic, Gap, Sherman Pickey, Brooks Brothers,** and **Urban Outfitters,** all of which also sell women's clothes. Also see "Vintage," above, for bargain shopping.

Anthropologie It's a chain, but the styles seem so individual. Dresses, blouses, sweaters, even accessories are ultrafeminine, their labels bearing names like "Maeve," "Guinevere," and "Left of Center." The Georgetown store also carries whimsical housewares. 950 F St. NW. www.anthropologie.com. (℃ 202/347-2160. Metro: Gallery Place/Verizon Center (9th St. exit). Other locations in Georgetown, 3222 M St. NW (℃ 202/337-1363); and at the Shops at Wisconsin Place, Chevy Chase, MD (℃ 301/652-1056).

Betsey Johnson New York's flamboyant flower-child designer personally decorated the bubble-gum-pink walls in her Georgetown shop. Her sexy, offbeat, play-dress-up styles are great party and club clothes for the young and the still-skinny young at heart. This is the only Betsey Johnson store in D.C. 3029 M St. NW. www.betseyjohnson.com. (℃ **202/338-4090.** Metro: Foggy Bottom, then take the D.C. Circulator.

Betsy Fisher ★ A walk past the store is all it takes to know that this shop is a tad different. Its windows and racks show off whimsically feminine fashions by new American, French, and Italian designers. Visit the website to find out about upcoming events; Betsy Fisher often hosts an evening cocktail hour to introduce a new line or inventory. 1224 Connecticut Ave. NW. www.betsyfisher.com. ✆ **202/785-1975.** Metro: Dupont Circle (South/19th St. exit).

H&M This Swedish-based store sells trendy clothes for men, women, and children at reasonable prices. 1025 F St. NW. www.hm.com/us. ✆ **202/347-3306.** Metro: Metro Center (11th St. exit). A 2nd location, in the Shops at Georgetown Park, 3222 M St. NW (✆ **202/298-6792**), sells only women's and youth lines.

Nana's Owner Jackie Flanagan left the world of advertising and publishing to open this store in 2003, naming it after her fashion-wise grandmother. The shop sells new creations from independent U.S. and Canadian designers, and a small rack of vintage styles of work and play clothes, the idea being to mix old and new for a fresh look. Handbags, gifts, and bath products also on sale. The shop moved in 2011 from its longtime U Street address to a larger location in the Mount Pleasant part of town, north of the old neighborhood. 3068 Mount Pleasant St. NW. www.nanadc.com. ✆ **202/667-6955.** Metro: Columbia Heights, or take the D.C. Circulator.

Proper Topper For the longest time, I thought this store was just a hat boutique. Then my husband came home self-satisfied at Christmas time, having found this "one-stop shop" for stocking stuffers and bigger gifts. I totally approve: lovely designs by Velvet and Nanette Lepore, pretty jewelry, adorable clothes for children, stationery, all sorts of gifty things, and, yes, hats. A new Georgetown location may have opened by the time you read this. 1350 Connecticut Ave. NW. www.propertopper.com. ✆ **202/842-3055.** Metro: Dupont Circle (19th St. exit).

Rizik Brothers The downtown, upscale Rizik's has been around since 1908 selling bridal dresses, couture, and other high-end fashions by European and American designers such as Carolina Herrera, Sylvia Heisel, and Lourdes Chavez. 1100 Connecticut Ave. NW. www.riziks.com. ✆ **202/223-4050.** Metro: Farragut North (L St. exit).

Rue 14 If you like the latest looks in fashion but not the prices that usually go with them, shop here. Owners Andrew Nguyen and Jiwon Paik-Nguyen fill their second-story boutique with the affordable designs of Free People, BB Dakota, Plastic Island, and other trendsetters. 1803A 14th St. NW. www.rue14.com. ✆ **202/462-6200.** Metro: U St./Cardozo (13th St. exit).

Wink Look for Wink beneath the Steve Madden store, and you'll discover Seven jeans and clothes by Diane von Furstenberg, Mystique, and Free People—and happy women of all ages sorting through the mix. 3109 M St. NW (lower level). www.shopwinkdc.com. ✆ **202/338-9465.** Metro: Foggy Bottom, then take the D.C. Circulator.

Zara This cheery store is an outpost of a popular chain started in Spain. Clothes are both dressy and casual, but all trendy. A sprinkling of coats is also found here, when the season calls for it. 1238 Wisconsin Ave. NW. www.zara.com. ✆ **202/944-9797.** Metro: Foggy Bottom, then take the D.C. Circulator. A 2nd location at 1025 F St. NW (✆ 202/393-2810).

Gifts & Souvenirs

See also "Arts, Crafts & Museum Stores," earlier in this chapter. Also check out the **White House Historical Association Gift Shop** at Decatur House, 1610

H St. NW (**www.whitehousehistory.org**) and the **White House Gift Shop,** operated by the U.S. Secret Service Uniformed Division Benefit Fund, at the National Press Building, 529 14th St. NW (**www.whitehousegiftshop.com**). Both shops sell interesting memorabilia, like the White House Christmas tree ornament newly designed each year, and sundry items, from sweatshirts to mugs, stamped with White House or Armed Forces logos.

America! Stop here if you want to pick up a baseball cap with commander in chief printed across its bill, a T-shirt proclaiming i love my country, it's the government i'm afraid of, White House guest towels, Obama coasters, or other impress-the-folks-back-home items. Union Station. www.americastore.com. © **202/842-0540.** Metro: Union Station. Or save your shopping for the airport; America! has at least 4 locations at National, 2 at BWI, and 6 at Dulles.

Chocolate Moose 🎁 Its website welcomes browsers with the words "Serving weirdly sophisticated Washingtonians since 1978, but now attempting to reach out to the rest of you." I guess my family qualifies as weirdly sophisticated, since we're longtime fans. My husband endears himself to me and our daughters when he brings home gifts from this shop: a Wonder Woman daybook; chunky, transparent, red heart-shaped earrings; wacky cards; paperweight snow globes with figurines inside; candies; eccentric clothing; and other funny presents. 1743 L St. NW. www.chocolatemoosedc.com. © **202/463-0992.** Metro: Farragut North (L St. exit).

Pulp Gifts You'll find must-have items here that you never even knew existed: a deck of slang flashcards, dancin' in the streets T-shirts, and crazy greeting cards. 1803 14th St. NW. www.pulpdc.com. © **202/462-7857.** Metro: U St./Cardozo (13th St. exit).

Food & Drink

Demanding jobs and hectic schedules leave Washingtonians less and less time to prepare their own meals. Or so we say. At any rate, when we're not dining out (see chapter 6), we're foraging at the numerous fine-food shops and bakeries that are happy to come to the rescue. Even the busiest bureaucrat can find the time to pop into one of these gourmet shops for a movable feast.

See also "Malls & Markets," above.

BreadLine 🎁 Bread Line attracts the White House crowd for lunch, with favorite sandwiches like the roast pork bun or the muffuletta; tasty soups; and desserts such as bread puddings, pear tarts, and delicious cookies. Seating is available, but most people buy carryout. The shop also sells freshly baked loaves of wheat bread, flatbreads, baguettes, and more. Open weekdays 7:30am to 3:30pm. 1751 Pennsylvania Ave. NW. www.breadline.com. © **202/822-8900.** Metro: Farragut West or Farragut North.

Cowgirl Creamery 🎁 I don't know how D.C. got so lucky as to have the only Cowgirl Creamery outside of California, but we can be grateful. The creamery sells its own seven artisanal cheeses as well as those of the best 60 American and European cheese producers. Taste the brie here and you'll never be happy again with your local grocery store's brand. The creamery also sells freshly made sandwiches, salads, and soups, plus beer and wine. Open Monday through Saturday. 919 F St. NW. www.cowgirlcreamery.com. © **202/393-6880.** Metro: Gallery Place/Verizon Center (9th St. exit).

Dean & Deluca This famed New York emporium operates in a historic Georgetown building that was once an open-air market. Though it is now closed in, this huge space still feels airy, with its high ceiling and windows on all sides. You'll pay top prices, but the quality is impressive—charcuterie, fresh fish, produce, cheeses, prepared sandwiches and cold pasta salads, hot-ticket desserts like crème brûlée and tiramisu, and California wines. Also on sale are housewares; on-site is an espresso bar/cafe. 3276 M St. NW. www.deandeluca.com. (ℂ **202/342-2500.** Metro: Foggy Bottom, then take the D.C. Circulator.

Firehook Bakery Known for its sourdough baguettes, apple-walnut bread, fresh fruit tarts, red-iced elephant and blue-iced donkey cookies, and sandwiches like smoked chicken on sesame semolina bread, Firehook also runs the cafe at the **National Building Museum** (p. 132). In all there are 11 locations, so look for them on Capitol Hill, in Dupont Circle, and in the Penn Quarter, among other places. 1909 Q St. NW. www.firehook.com. (ℂ **202/588-9296.** Metro: Dupont Circle (Q St. exit). Other locations at 912 17th St. NW (ℂ **202/429-2253**), 3411 Connecticut Ave. NW (ℂ **202/362-2253**), 215 Pennsylvania Ave. SE (ℂ **202/544-7003**), 1241 F St. NW (ℂ **202/393-0951**), 441 4th St. NW (ℂ **202/347-1760**), and at 4 locations in VA.

Marvelous Market First there were the breads: sourdough, baguettes, olive, rosemary, croissants, scones. Now there are things to spread on the breads, including smoked salmon mousse and tapenade, as well as pastries to die for, from gingerbread to flourless chocolate cake, and prepared foods, such as soups, empanadas, and pasta salads. The breakfast spread on Sunday mornings is sinful, and individual items, like the croissants, are tastier and less expensive here than at other bakeries. 1511 Connecticut Ave. NW. www.marvelousmarket.com. (ℂ **202/332-3690.** Metro: Dupont Circle (Q St. exit). Other locations include 2424 Pennsylvania Ave. NW (ℂ 202/293-0049), 3217 P St. NW (ℂ **202/333-2591**), 1800 K St. NW (ℂ **202/828-0944**), and 303 7th St. SE (ℂ **202/544-7127**).

Baked goods at Firehook Bakery.

Home Design, Furnishings & Housewares

You may not have come to Washington to shop for housewares or furnishings, but step inside the shops of Cady's Alley or Home Rule and you may change your mind. Also see "Antiques," earlier in this chapter.

Cady's Alley ★   Cady's Alley refers not to a single store, but to the southwest pocket of Georgetown, where about 20 stores reside in and around said alley, which dangles south of M Street. Look for tony, big-name places, like Waterworks, Thos. Moser Cabinetmakers, and Baker Furniture; European outposts, like the hip kitchen furnishings of Bulthaup; and high-concept design stores, like Contemporaria. 3314 M St. NW (btw. 33rd and 34th sts.). www.cadysalley.com. Metro: Foggy Bottom, then take the D.C. Circulator.

GoodWood   This self-described "American Mercantile & Dry Goods Store" could just as easily go in the "Gifts & Souvenirs" and "Clothing & Accessories" categories (see earlier in this chapter). Its inventory of "wonderful objects and curiousities" is just that, ranging from retro women's hats to soaps and scents to antique furnishings to unusual glassware—just about anything that has caught the shopowners' fancy that they think might catch yours. 1428 U St. NW (btw. 14th and 15th sts.). www.goodwooddc.com. ✆ **202/986-3640**. Metro: U St./Cardozo (13th St. exit).

Hill's Kitchen 👕   This gourmet kitchenware store occupies an 1884 town house adjacent to the Eastern Market Metro station on Capitol Hill. Precious take-homes are cookie cutters shaped like the Washington Monument and the Capitol dome, as well as significant shapes for every state in the Union; top-flight stovetop dishes, bakeware, cooking utensils, and tools; colorful aprons and towels; water bottles that filter as you drink; and specialty foods. Cooking classes and demonstrations are also on offer. 713 D St. SE. www.hillskitchen.com. ✆ **202/543-1997.** Metro: Eastern Market.

Home Rule 🗲   Unique housewares, gifts, and bath, kitchen, and office supplies cram this tiny store. You'll see everything from French milled soap to martini glasses. 1807 14th St. NW (at S St.). www.homerule.com. ✆ **202/797-5544.** Metro: U St./Cardozo (13th St. exit; check the website or call for specific directions from the station).

Music

In the age of iTunes and Amazon.com, brick and mortar CD stores are becoming few and far between. But if you still favor browsing music choices in person, or if you love vintage records, head to these independent shops, all of which are located in either Adams Morgan or the U Street Corridor. The Penn Quarter **Barnes & Noble** (p. 233) also has a sizable music section, and **Second Story Books** (p. 234) sells CDs and vinyl.

Crooked Beat Records   Pay no attention to the store's out-of-date website, which makes one wonder whether Crooked Beat still exists. "We're not going anywhere," says the man who answers the phone. This Adams Morgan favorite sells only vinyl records and specializes in the hard-to-find. 2318 18th St. NW. www.crookedbeat.com. ✆ 202/483-2328. Metro: Woodley Park or Dupont Circle.

Red Onion Records & Books   Open since 2006, Red Onion is a relative newcomer in the independent record store category. Red Onion sells, trades, and buys classic vinyls from the 1950s to the present, and receives new merchandise daily. 1901 18th St. NW. www.redonionrecordsandbooks.com. ✆ 202/986-2718. Metro: Dupont Circle.

Smash! Records Located on the second floor of an Adams Morgan townhouse, Smash! is known for its punk and alternative music selections (CDs and LPs) and for its vintage and indie designer fashions. 2314 18th St. NW. www.smashrecords.com. ℰ 202/387-6274. Metro: Woodley Park or Dupont Circle.

Som Records Used, new, imported, and rare vinyl records are on sale at Som, which is located just south of T St. in the U Street Corridor. 1843 14th St. NW. www.somrecordsdc.com. ℰ 202/328-3345. Metro: U St./Cardozo (13th St. exit).

Technology & Cameras

Apple Store Macs, iPads, iPhones, iPods, iTunes, iTouches: All of them are for sale here. Come to hang out and use the floor samples, to check out the merchandise, and to get your questions answered by techy geeks roaming the room. 1229 Wisconsin Ave. NW. www.apple.com/retail/georgetown. ℰ **202/572-1460.** Metro: Foggy Bottom, then take the D.C. Circulator.

Ritz Camera Center Ritz sells camera equipment for the average photographer and offers 1-hour film processing. Call for other locations; there are several in the area. 1750 L St. NW. www.ritzcamera.com. ℰ **202/861-7710.** Metro: Farragut North (L St. exit).

Toys & Games

Toy stores, like children's clothing stores, are hard to find in the District. Your best bets by far are the museum shops, specifically that of the **International Spy Museum** (p. 129) for night-vision goggles, spy listening devices, and assorted other cool gadgetry; the **National Air and Space Museum** (p. 99) for sundry model aircraft and NASA astronaut dolls; and the **National Museum of American History** (p. 107)—how 'bout that Albert Einstein talking bobblehead? Check out the gift shops at every place you tour, because you just never know what you're going to find. Also see the "Children" section under "Clothing & Accessories," above; all of these stores also sell toys and games.

Wine & Spirits

Barmy Wine and Liquor Located near the White House, this store sells it all, but with special emphasis on fine wines and rare cordials. 1912 L St. NW. www.barmywines.com. ℰ **202/833-8730.** Metro: Farragut North (L St. exit).

Central Liquors This store, which opened in 1934, is like a clearinghouse for liquor: Its great volume allows the store to offer the best prices in town on wines and liquor. The store carries more than 250 single-malt Scotches. 625 E St. NW. www.centralliquors.com. ℰ **202/737-2800.** Metro: Gallery Place (9th and F sts. exit).

Central Liquors.

Schneider's of Capitol Hill   Two blocks south of Union Station is this family-run liquor store, in business for more than 60 years. With a knowledgeable and enthusiastic staff, a 12,000-bottle inventory of wine, and a fine selection of spirits and beer, this shop is a find on Capitol Hill. 300 Massachusetts Ave. NE. www.cellar.com. © **202/543-9300.** Metro: Union Station.

Zola Wine & Kitchen ★   Around the corner from Zola the restaurant (p. 190) is its sibling, a wine shop and test kitchen, where you can browse for wines, peer through portholes in the wall to observe chef Robbie Meltzer experiment with recipes in his kitchen, and take an evening class on, say, how to prepare ceviche. Open Monday to Saturday, the shop is a favorite with the noontime crowd because of its $10 weekday lunch specials, every day a different choice (if it's Wed, it might be a choice of miso salmon or roast beef sandwich). You can dine in or take out. The wine shop's inventory includes 400 varieties of international wines. Stop by on Wednesday and Friday evenings 5 to 7pm for wine tastings, paired with artisanal cheeses. 505 9th St. NW. www.zolawinekitchen.com. © **202/639-9463.** Metro: Gallery Place/Verizon Center (9th St. exit).

PRACTICAL MATTERS: THE SHOPPING SCENE

Most Washington, D.C. stores are open from 10am to 5 or 6pm Monday through Saturday; Sunday hours tend to vary, with some stores opting not to open at all and others keeping shortened hours from noon to 5 or 6pm. Two neighborhoods prove the exception to these rules: Many stores in the Penn Quarter and Georgetown keep later hours and are also open on Sunday. One example is the downtown Macy's department store (p. 229), in the heart of Penn Quarter, which is open Sunday noon to 6pm, Monday through Thursday 10am to 8pm, Friday 9am to 9pm, and Saturday 9am to 10pm. Other exceptions include suburban shopping malls, which are open late nightly, and antiques stores and art galleries, which tend to keep their own hours.

Sales tax on merchandise is 6% in the District, 6% in Maryland, and 5% in Virginia.

ENTERTAINMENT & NIGHTLIFE

8

Nightlife in the capital is rollicking and diverse. You can play putt-putt golf in the upstairs bar at the Atlas District's H Street Country Club (p. 268), head to the U Street Corridor to dance your heart out at Marvin (p. 256), take a turn at karaoke at Hill Country (p. 268) in the Penn Quarter, or settle in for top-notch jazz at Blues Alley (p. 259) in Georgetown. Internationally renowned performing-arts venues like the Kennedy Center (p. 248) host performances by top theater and dance companies, while smaller theaters such as Studio Theatre (p. 251) stage bold new productions. Washington's nightlife scene offers something for everyone.

The truth is that D.C. nightlife is not only vigorous but also competitive. One third of the city's population is between 20 and 35; thanks to the capital's strong economy, most have jobs and are ready to party. And then there is everyone else, from Hill staffers to expense-account attorneys, many of whom seek entertainment after a long day at the desk. Whether you're trying to score tickets to *Much Ado About Nothing* at the **Shakespeare Theatre** (p. 250) or nab a seat at the bar at new hot spot **Black Jack** (p. 253), success requires a get-there-first strategy.

The best neighborhoods for nightlife are **Adams Morgan;** the **U and 14th streets NW crossroads** (U St. between 16th and 9th sts., and 14th St. btw. P and V sts.); north and south of **Dupont Circle** along Connecticut Avenue; the **Penn Quarter,** notably 7th and 8th streets NW and from Pennsylvania Avenue north as far as I Street; **Georgetown;** the **Atlas District;** and **Columbia Heights,** an area east of Adams Morgan and north of the U Street district. As a rule, while club-hopping—even in Georgetown—stick to the major thoroughfares and steer clear of deserted side streets. I should add that you should be especially careful in Adams Morgan and Columbia Heights, where criminals sometimes prey upon drunk and otherwise distracted partiers as they leave bars and clubs.

Most of D.C.'s clubs and bars stay open until 1 or 2am Monday through Thursday and until 3am Friday and Saturday; what time they open varies. It's best to call ahead or check the website to make sure the place you're headed is open.

For current concert and club offerings, check the *Washington Post's*

ABOVE: **Dancing at Black Cat.** PREVIOUS PAGE: **A performance by Les Nubians at the Hamilton.**

online "Going Out Guide" (www.washingtonpost.com/gog), which covers all entertainment options, including nightlife, reported minute by minute, venue by venue, by the paper's "Going Out Gurus." If you're here on a weekend, try to pick up a copy of the *Post's* Friday "Weekend" section. **Washington City Paper,** available free at restaurants, bookstores, and other places around town, and online at **www.washington citypaper.com**, is another excellent source. Finally, check out the blog **www.dcist. com** for an irreverent inside look at what's going on around town.

THE PERFORMING ARTS

Washington's performing-arts scene has an international reputation. We have not just one but two Shakespeare theaters. Our **Arena Stage** is renowned for its innovative productions of American masters and new voices. The **Kennedy Center** reigns over all, staging something for everyone in every genre. Don't assume that these three theaters present only classic renditions from a performing-arts hit list; no, they are each wildly creative in their choices and their presentations. On the other hand, for truly avant-garde theater, seek out smaller stages, like **Woolly Mammoth** and **Studio** theaters.

Theater seasons generally span the months of September through May, with the Shakespeare Theatre's calendar often extending into July. The Kennedy Center's season is year-round, though it is certainly less busy in July and August. Performance times at all theaters are usually at 7:30pm or 8pm nightly, with Saturday and Sunday matinee performances at 2pm and occasional Wednesday noon matinee performances on the schedule, especially at Arena Stage and the Shakespeare Theatre.

The bad news is that, as popular as theater-going is in the capital, **ticket prices** have gone through the roof in the past couple of years. A lot of locals subscribe to the big three (Kennedy Center, Shakespeare, Arena), which leaves fewer one-off tickets available. Expect to pay $75 to $100-plus for a ticket—unless you're able to obtain a discounted ticket directly from the theater or from a discounted ticket service; see the "Getting Tickets," below.

Major Theaters and Companies

Arena Stage The Arena Stage is home to one of the oldest acting ensembles in the nation. The theater, whose mission is to celebrate "the rich mosaic of our nation's voices," champions new plays and playwrights, produces works from America's diverse cultures, and reinterprets the works of past masters, all under the leadership of artistic director Molly Smith. Works nurtured here often move on to Broadway; likewise some of the country's top acting talents appear on Arena's stage.

The excellence of Arena productions has brought the theater much success, to the extent that Arena celebrated its 60th anniversary by debuting a grand expansion in late October 2010. The new Mead Center for American Theater at Arena Stage is a 200,000-square-foot, undulating, glass-paned structure housing three theaters and rehearsal and office space.

Among the 2012–13 season highlights are the musical *My Fair Lady* and the world premiere of *Mary T & Lizzie K*, about the relationship between Mary Todd Lincoln and her seamstress. 1101 6th St. SW (at Maine Ave.). www.arenastage.org. ✆ **202/488-3300** for tickets, or 202/554-9066 for general information. Tickets $75–$90; discounts available for students, people with disabilities, groups, and seniors. Metro: Southwest/Waterfront.

GETTING tickets

Most performing-arts and live-music venues mentioned in this chapter require tickets, which you can purchase online at the venue's website, in person at the venue's box office, or through one of the ticket vendors listed below.

The best deals in town might be those posted on the website **www.goldstar.com**. It costs nothing to subscribe, and you'll immediately start receiving e-mail notices of hefty discounts on admission prices to performances and venues, including museums, all over the city.

Washington's discount-ticket outlet, **TICKETPLACE,** 407 7th St. NW, between D and E streets (no phone; Metro: Gallery Place/Verizon Center or Archives–Navy Memorial), displays a chalkboard listing of those performances that still have seats available, including opera, ballet, and events at major Washington-area theaters and concert halls. It's open Wednesday through Friday from 11am to 6pm, Saturday from 10am to 5pm, and Sunday noon to 4pm. Tickets are also available online at **www.ticketplace.org** until 4pm for that day's performances. Whether you purchase tickets online or at the ticket outlet, you pay half price, albeit along with a substantial per-ticket service charge (e.g., a $50 ticket would be sold half price at $25, plus a $4.75 service fee); only American Express, MasterCard, and Visa are accepted. If you've ordered tickets online, you can pick them up at the will-call booth of the performance venue; bring your credit card and purchase confirmation. TICKETPLACE is a program of the Cultural Alliance of Washington. For more information, including performances offered at the TICKETPLACE outlet, visit **www.culturecapital.com**.

Note: **Be careful** when you purchase tickets online at www.ticketplace.org; if you click on the "Browse by Region" section to the left of the screen and use those listings to purchase tickets, you may find yourself taken to the venue's separate online ticket setup, where you'll be paying full price. If you're only interested in half-price tickets, use the "Search by Day" function, which will take you to half-price ticket listings.

Ticket sellers **Live Nation** (www.livenation.com) and **Ticketmaster** (www.ticketmaster.com; ℂ 800/745-3000) merged in January 2010, which means that you can buy full-price tickets for many performances in town from either operation. Expect to pay taxes plus a service charge, an order-processing fee, and a facility fee (if a particular venue tacks on that charge). Or you can visit the Ticketmaster sales booth at the Verizon Center, at 601 F St. NW (Metro: Gallery Place/Verizon Center). For the same kinds of performances, also check out **www.ticketfly.com** (ℂ 877/435-9849).

Finally, check out **www.instantseats.com**, which bills itself as the place to go for "online ticketing for the performing arts." (The site also sells tickets for river cruises on the Potomac, so perhaps the company defines "performing arts" to cover a multitude of entertainment.) This is the site that handles sales of tickets to embassy events (see "The Best of D.C.'s International Scene," later in this chapter, for more information).

John F. Kennedy Center for the Performing Arts Now in its 42nd season, the Kennedy Center stands out as a theater complex that is not just the hub of Washington's cultural and entertainment scene, but a performing-arts theater for the nation. The center lies between the Potomac River and a crisscross of major roadways, just a bit west of the city's main action.

The center stages top-rated performances by the best ballet, opera, jazz, modern dance, musical, and theater companies in the world. Ticket prices vary from $15 for a family concert to $300 for a night at the opera, although most fall in the $45 to $100 range. It is actually made up of six different national theaters: the Opera House, the Concert Hall, the Terrace Theater, the Eisenhower Theater, the Theater Lab, and the Family Theater.

To demonstrate its commitment to being a theater for the peo-

The John F. Kennedy Center's Grand Foyer.

ple, the Kennedy Center continues to stage its **free concert series,** known as "Millennium Stage," which features daily performances by area musicians and, sometimes, national artists each evening at 6pm in the center's Grand Foyer. (You can check out broadcasts of the nightly performances on the Internet at www.kennedy-center.org/millennium.)

Among the Kennedy Center's perennial season highlights are the **National Symphony Orchestra** classical and pops concerts, **ballet** performances by the Suzanne Farrell Ballet Company and other major troupes, **musicals, Kennedy Center jazz** concerts by assorted masters, **festivals** that celebrate a particular theme or heritage, **Washington National Opera Company** productions, **dramatic plays,** and continuing performances of the comedy whodunit *Shear Madness,* now in its 26th year at the Kennedy Center.

2700 F St. NW (at New Hampshire Ave. NW and Rock Creek Pkwy.). www.kennedy-center.org. ✆ **800/444-1324** or 202/467-4600. 50% discounts are offered (for select performances) to students, seniors 65 and over, people with permanent disabilities, enlisted military personnel, and persons with fixed low incomes (✆ **202/416-8340** for details). Garage parking $20. Metro: Foggy Bottom (though it's a fairly short walk, there's a free shuttle btw. the station and the

 Longer Than the Washington Monument Is Tall

Most Kennedy Center performances take place in theaters that lie off the Grand Foyer. But even if the one you're attending is on the Roof Terrace level, one floor up, make sure you visit the foyer anyway. The Grand Foyer is one of the largest rooms in the world. Measuring 630 feet long, 40 feet wide, and 60 feet high, the foyer is longer than the Washington Monument is tall (555⅝ ft.). Millennium Stage hosts free performances here nightly at 6pm, the famous Robert Berks sculpture of President John F. Kennedy is here, and just beyond the foyer's glass doors is the expansive terrace, which runs the length of the building and overlooks the Potomac River.

Kennedy Center, departing every 15 min. 9:45am–midnight Mon–Fri, 10am–midnight Sat, and noon–midnight Sun). Bus: 80 from Metro Center.

National Theatre This splendid Federal-style structure is the oldest continuously operating theater in Washington (since 1835) and the third oldest in the nation. It's exciting just to see the stage on which Sarah Bernhardt, John Barrymore, Helen Hayes, and so many other notables have performed. The 1,672-seat National is the closest thing Washington has to a Broadway-style playhouse. Productions have included the musicals *The*

A performance at the John F. Kennedy Center.

Color Purple and *Mamma Mia!*. Its offerings are modest for a theater of its size, and its schedule is erratic, so there's no guarantee that a show will be on when you're in town; check the website or call. Still, the National is worth knowing about, especially if you have children. The theater offers free public-service programs: Saturday-morning children's theater (puppets, clowns, magicians, dancers, and singers) Monday-night showcases, September through April, of local groups and performers, plus free summer films. 1321 Pennsylvania Ave. NW (at 13th and E sts.). www.nationaltheatre.org. ✆ **202/783-3372** for information, or 800/447-7400 or 202/628-6161 to charge tickets. Tickets $47–$152 (most are in the $70–$90 range); discounts available for students, seniors, military personnel, and people with disabilities. Metro: Metro Center (13th and G sts. exit).

Shakespeare Theatre Company: At the Lansburgh Theatre and Sidney Harman Hall This is top-level Shakespeare, with superb acting. Try your best to get tickets; the productions are reliably outstanding. Season subscriptions claim many of the seats, and the plays often sell out, so if you're interested in attending a play here, buy your tickets now. The popularity of the Shakespeare Theatre Company's productions at the Lansburgh Theatre led in 2008 to the opening of a second location, the 775-seat **Sidney Harman Hall,** at 610 F St. NW, across the street from the Verizon Center and just around the corner from the 451-seat Lansburgh Theatre, on 7th Street NW. The 2012–13 season (its 26th) includes presentations of *A Midsummer Night's Dream* and one by Nicolai Gogol called *The Government Inspector*. Every year, for 2 weeks in late August into mid-September, the company stages a free Shakespeare production, known as the "Free For All," in Harman Hall; *All's Well That Ends Well* was the feature in 2012. The theater's program, **Happenings at the Harman,** also offers a robust schedule of performances by comedy troupes, avant-garde dance companies, and community organizations, mostly aimed at attracting the 20- to 30-something crowd. In the same vein, the theater offers a fantastic deal for those 21 to 35: $15 tickets available after 10am every Tuesday, for performances taking place through the following Sunday. Lansburgh Theatre: 450 7th St. NW (btw. D and E sts.). Sidney Harman Hall: 610 F St. NW. www.shakespearetheatre.org. ✆ **202/547-1122.** Tickets $37–$105; discounts available for students, military, patrons 21–35, seniors, and groups. Metro: Archives–Navy Memorial or Gallery Place/Verizon Center (7th St./Arena exit).

Smaller Theaters

Smaller but no less compelling, these theaters stage productions that are consistently professional and often more contemporary and daring than those you'll find in the better-known theaters. These more intimate theaters have their own strong followings, which means their performances often sell out.

Studio Theatre, 1501 14th St. NW, at P Street (www.studiotheatre. org; ☏ 202/332-3300), since its founding in 1978, has grown in leaps and bounds into a four-theater complex, helping to revitalize this downtown neighborhood in the process. Productions are provocative, from the lively sci-fi story of *Astro Boy and the God of Comics,* bringing to life the action hero of the 1960s animation series *Astro Boy;* to the dramatic rendering of *Time Stands Still,* which follows the story of a globe-trotting photojournalist who returns home after being injured while covering the war in Iraq. Artistic director Joy Zinoman, who retired in 2010, helped to create buzz for Washington's theater scene as well as for the U Street/14th Street neighborhood in which Studio resides. Her legacy lives in Studio's continuing success in showcasing contemporary plays and in nurturing Washington acting talent.

A production of *Henry V* by the Shakespeare Theatre Company.

The **Woolly Mammoth Theatre Company** (www.woollymammoth.net; ☏ 202/393-3939) offers as many as six productions every year, specializing in new, offbeat, and quirky plays, often world premieres. The Woolly resides in a 265-seat, state-of-the-art facility at 641 D St. NW (at 7th St. NW), in the heart of the Penn Quarter.

In addition, I highly recommend productions staged at the **Folger Shakespeare Library,** 201 E. Capitol St. SE, at 2nd Street (www.folger.edu; ☏ 202/544-7077), which celebrated its 80th anniversary in 2012. Plays take place in the library's Elizabethan Theatre, which is styled after the inn-yard theater of Shakespeare's time. The theater is intimate and charming, the theater company is remarkably good, and an evening spent here guarantees an absolutely marvelous experience. The Elizabethan Theatre is also the setting for musical performances, lectures, readings, and other events.

Outdoor Stages

My favorite summer setting for music is the **Wolf Trap National Park for the Performing Arts,** 1551 Trap Rd., Vienna, Virginia (www.wolftrap.org; ☏ 703/255-1868). The country's only national park devoted to the performing arts, Wolf Trap offers performances by the National Symphony Orchestra (it's their summer home) and has hosted Lucinda Williams, Shawn Colvin, Lyle Lovett, Sheryl Crow, Wilco, and many others. Performances take place in the 7,000-seat

Filene Center, about half of which is under the open sky. You can also buy cheaper lawn seats on the hill, which is sometimes the nicest way to go. If you do, arrive early (the lawn opens 90 min. before the performance) and bring a blanket and a picnic dinner—it's a tradition. Wolf Trap also hosts a number of popular festivals, including the Louisiana Swamp Romp Cajun Festival in June. Wolf Trap is about a 30-minute drive from D.C.; the Wolf Trap Express Bus (usually $5 round-trip) runs between the West Falls Church Metro station and the arts center.

The **Carter Barron Amphitheater,** 16th Street and Colorado Avenue NW (𝒞 202/426-0486; www.nps.gov/rocr/planyourvisit/cbarron.htm), is in Rock Creek Park, way out on 16th Street, close to the Maryland border. This is the area's smallest outdoor venue, with 4,250 seats. Summer performances include a range of gospel, blues, and classical entertainment. The shows are usually free, but tickets are required.

Headliner Concert Venues

When Lady Gaga, Bruce Springsteen, or Beyoncé come to town, they play at the 20,600-seat **Verizon Center,** 601 F St. NW, at 7th Street (𝒞 www.verizon center.com; 202/628-3200). Situated in the center of downtown, the Verizon Center hosts plenty of concerts and is also Washington's premier indoor sports arena (see "Spectator Sports," later in this chapter).

In my opinion, a handful of auditoriums in Washington are even better places to catch a performance, though the names aren't always as "big" as those that turn up at the Verizon Center.

DAR Constitution Hall, on 18th Street NW, between C and D streets (www.dar.org; 𝒞 202/628-4780), is housed within a beautiful turn-of-the-20th-century Beaux Arts building and seats 3,746. Its excellent acoustics have supported an eclectic group of performers: Public Enemy, the Count Basie Orchestra, Tori Amos, Anita Baker, Bow Wow, Trisha Yearwood, and the Strokes.

In the heart of happening U Street, the **Lincoln Theatre,** 1215 U St. NW, at 13th Street (www.thelincolntheatre.org; 𝒞 202/328-6000), was once a movie

Wolf Trap National Park for the Performing Arts.

theater, vaudeville house, and nightclub featuring black stars like Louis Armstrong and Cab Calloway. The theater closed in the 1970s and reopened in 1994 after a renovation restored it to its former elegance. Today the theater books jazz, R&B, gospel, and comedy acts, and events like Filmfest DC.

The **Warner Theatre,** 513 13th St. NW, between E and F streets (www. warnertheatredc.com; ℂ **202/783-4000**), opened in 1924 as the Earle Theatre (a movie/vaudeville palace) and was restored to its original, neoclassical-style appearance in 1992. It's worth coming by just to see its ornately detailed interior. The 2,000-seat auditorium offers year-round entertainment, alternating dance performances, like the Washington Ballet's Christmas performance of the *Nutcracker,* with comedy acts, like those of Steven Wright or Damon Wayans, and headliner musical entertainment (PJ Harvey, John Prine, Bob Dylan).

THE BAR SCENE

Washington has a thriving and varied bar scene. But just when you think you know all the hot spots, a spate of new ones pops up. If you're up for a wild time that comes without transportation worries, consider reserving a spot on the **Boomerang Bus** (www.ridetheboomerang.com), which travels to four or five popular bars in different neighborhoods every Friday and Saturday night, picking you up and dropping you off at the same bar location; the current price of $35.50 covers the transportation and any charges for covers or specialty drinks, and allows you to bypass any VIP lines.

Restaurant lounges are ever popular, so be sure to stop in at Sei (p.194), PS7's (p. 190), and Rasika (p. 194) for after-dinner drinks. If you're in the mood for a sophisticated setting, seek out a bar in one of the nicer hotels, like the Willard (p. 283), the Sofitel Lafayette Square (p. 287), the Ritz-Carlton Georgetown (p. 304), the Hay-Adams (p. 287), or the St. Regis (p. 288); also read in this section about Quill, in the Jefferson Hotel, and P.O.V., in the W Washington, D.C. Hotel.

Most bars stay open until 2am Sunday through Thursday and until 3am Friday and Saturday.

Big Hunt   This casual and comfy Dupont Circle hangout for the 20- to 30-something crowd bills itself as a "happy hunting ground for humans" (read: meat market). It has a kind of *Raiders of the Lost Ark* jungle theme. A downstairs room (where music is the loudest) is adorned with exotic travel posters and animal skins; another area has leopard-skin-patterned booths under canvas tenting. Amusing murals grace the balcony level, which adjoins a room with pool tables. The candlelit basement is the spot for quiet conversation. The menu offers typical bar food, and the bar offers close to 30 beers on tap, most of them microbrews. An outdoor patio lies off the back poolroom.

Note: This place and Lucky Bar (see below) might be the perfect antidotes to their exclusive counterparts around town, including the nearby Eighteenth Street Lounge. If you're rejected there, forget about it and come here. 1345 Connecticut Ave. NW (btw. N St. and Dupont Circle). www.thebighunt.net. ℂ **202/785-2333.** Metro: Dupont Circle.

Black Jack   Downstairs is the super popular **Pearl Dive Oyster Palace** (p. 203) restaurant, and upstairs is its super-cool bar. Red velvet curtains part to reveal the fully stocked bar, and old movies project black-and-white images on the brick walls. Other bars may have pool tables and DJs; Black Jack has two full-size bocce courts, with 19 stadium seats for spectators. Lots of comfortable red vinyl seating, crafty cocktails, and "really good house-made pies," as in pizzas, make Black Jack everyone's favorite new hangout. 1612 14th St. NW (at Corcoran St.). www.blackjackdc.com. ✆ **202/986-5225.** Metro: U St./Cardozo (U and 13th sts. exit).

Bourbon    North of Georgetown, in the homey area known as Glover Park, is this neighborhood bar that has a comfortable feel to it. The owners have invited their regulars to bring in black-and-white family photos, which they use to adorn the walls. Downstairs is a narrow room and a long bar; upstairs is a dining room with leather booths. Fifty bourbons are on offer, along with many fine wines and beers, and the usual complement of bar beverages. Bourbon has a second location, in Adams Morgan, at 2321 18th St. NW (at Calvert St.; ✆ **202/332-0800**). 2348 Wisconsin Ave. NW. www.bourbondc.com. ✆ **202/625-7770.** Take a taxi or hop on the D.C. Circulator, which takes you almost all the way.

ChurchKey   The line starts at 4pm daily to enter this delightfully laid-back but totally happening beer bar, where 50 drafts, 500 bottles, and five cask ales are on tap. Downstairs is sibling Birch & Barley (p. 201). 1337 14th St. NW (at Rhode Island Ave.). www.churchkeydc.com. ✆ **202/567-2576.** Metro: McPherson Sq. (14th St. exit) or U St./Cardozo (U and 13th sts. exit).

Clyde's of Gallery Place   This enormous Clyde's, part of the local empire that includes The Hamilton (p. 261) and a Georgetown outpost (p. 216), looks like Las Vegas from the outside. Inside the two-level, 23,000-square-foot salon is filled with eye-catching oil paintings of sailing and equestrian scenes, Tiffany glass, and burnished cherry-wood furnishings. Three bars anchor the place, which is pretty much hopping every night of the week. As big as Clyde's is, it still gets crowded, especially before and after sports events at the Verizon Center, which is on the same block. Late-night prowlers will be happy to know that Clyde's late-night menu is available daily until 1am. 707 7th St. NW (at H St.). www.clydes.com. ✆ **202/349-3700.** Metro: Gallery Place–Chinatown (H St./Chinatown exit).

Fifty types of bourbon are offered at Bourbon in Glover Park.

8

ENTERTAINMENT & NIGHTLIFE | The Bar Scene

Clyde's of Gallery Place.

Co Co. Sala   Chocolate is the watchword at this Penn Quarter lounge, where cocktails are infused with chocolate, and small plates of both savory and sweet treats feature chocolate as an ingredient, too. Consider: malted milk martinis, Co Cojitos (chocolate-infused vodka, fresh mint, and limes, topped with dark-chocolate flakes), crab cakes with chocolate tomato glaze, and hot chocolate soufflés. Attractive waiters and waitresses, a glass-enclosed chocolate room where confections are made, and a sultry clientele make this one of D.C.'s hottest places. 929 F St. NW (at 9th St.). www.cocosala.com. 🕐 **202/347-4265.** Metro: Gallery Place–Chinatown (9th St. exit).

The Dubliner   This is your typical old Irish pub, the port you can blow into in any storm, personal or weather-related. It's got the dark-wood paneling and tables, the etched and stained-glass windows, an Irish-accented staff from time to time, and, most importantly, Auld Dubliner Amber Ale. Most come here to imbibe, but the Dubliner serves food daily from breakfast until very late, so if you're hungry, consider the burgers, grilled-chicken sandwich, or fish and chips. The Dubliner is frequented by Capitol Hill staffers and journalists who cover the Hill. Irish music groups play nightly. In the Phoenix Park Hotel, 520 N. Capitol St. NW (separate entrance on F St. NW). www.dublinerdc.com. 🕐 **202/737-3773.** Metro: Union Station.

Fadó   Another Irish pub, but this one is Ireland as a theme park. The odd thing about it is its location: in the heart of Chinatown. Fadó was designed and built by the Irish Pub Company of Dublin, which shipped everything—the stone for the floors, the etched glass, the milled wood—from Ireland. The pub has separate areas, including an old Irish "bookstore" alcove and a country cottage bar. Authentic Irish food, like potato pancakes, is served with your Guinness. *Fadó,* Gaelic for "long ago," accepts reservations only for large groups. The pub is a hangout for soccer fans, who gather here to watch matches on weekends. Fadó sometimes hosts live music performances, and sometimes charges a cover (about $5), but sometimes not. 808 7th St. NW (at H St.). www.fadoirishpub.com. 🕐 **202/789-0066.** Metro: Gallery Place–Chinatown (H and 7th sts. exit).

The Gibson   Make a reservation for a seat in a bar? Yes, and I must say, it's worth it. The Gibson is a 21st-century speakeasy, hidden inside a nondescript, tenementlike building. You usually have to ring a bell to be admitted. If you haven't made a reservation, you're probably not going to get in. The downstairs is small, with room for only 48 people, and dimly lit; a patio and outdoor bar help out in fine weather. There's an upstairs, too, but the room lacks personality in comparison. A mixologist at the bar concocts swell drinks, like a New Orleans Sazerac or something called the Salad Days Sour (a pisco sour with hints of celery and cinnamon). Patrons sit at booths, tables, or the bar, but when their allotted 2 hours are up, off they must go, so others can take their place. 2009 14th St. NW (at U St.). http://thegibsondc.com. ✆ **202/232-2156.** Metro: U St./Cardozo (13th St. exit).

Lucky Bar   Lucky Bar is a good place to kick back and relax. The bar has a front room overlooking Connecticut Avenue and a back room decorated with good-luck signs, couches, hanging TVs, booths, and a pool table. Lucky Bar is known in the area as a "soccer bar," with its TVs turned to soccer matches going on around the world. Also: Monday through Wednesday and Friday, Lucky Bar's happy hour starts at 3pm and continues until 8pm! There's music most nights, sometimes live, but usually it's courtesy of a DJ. Other times the jukebox plays, but never so loud that you can't carry on a conversation. "Everybody dance now." And they do. 1221 Connecticut Ave. NW (at N St.). www.luckybardc.com. ✆ **202/331-3733.** Metro: Dupont Circle (South/19th St. exit) or Farragut North (L St. exit).

Marvin   Marvin opened in late 2007, and the crowds came. Downstairs is a bistro (p. 202) that serves Belgian specialties, like steak frites and mussels in wine and beer, and American soul-food favorites, such as shrimp-and-grits and fried chicken atop a waffle. The split personality derives from namesake Marvin Gaye, the late soul singer and D.C. native, who lived in Belgium for a while. The split personality applies to Marvin's function, as well, for upstairs from the restaurant is a bar and lounge. Intended as a neighborhood hangout, the club is really more like a scenemaker, especially on weekends. Both bistro and lounge are usually packed, although you can at least make reservations for the dining room. DJs play nightly upstairs, mixing Motown and R&B. Fortunately, an expansive rooftop beer garden extends the space and offers more seating and another bar. 2007 14th St. NW (at U St.). www.marvindc.com. ✆ **202/797-7171.** Metro: U St./Cardozo (13th St. exit).

Park at 14th   This glass-fronted, four-level restaurant/lounge opened in late 2007, unabashedly promoting itself to celebrities, good-lookers, and private parties. Among those seen partying here have been former Washington Wizards star Caron Butler, celebrating his 28th birthday, and comedian Chris Rock, who brought 10 friends with him after he finished his act at Constitution Hall. Luxury pervades the place, from its leather sofas to its arty glass chandeliers. Balconies on the second and fourth floors overlook the interior action. Meanwhile that four-story street-to-roof window front is not intended for those inside to look out, but rather to reveal the celebrating scene to wishful passersby outside. That feature and the velvet rope admission policy emphasize the exclusivity at work. 920 14th St. NW (at K St.). www.park14.com. ✆ **202/737-7275.** Metro: McPherson Sq. (Franklin Sq./14th St. exit).

P.O.V. Roof Terrace and Lounge   This rooftop bar, located on the 11th floor of the trendy W Washington, D.C. Hotel (p. 282), holds only 104 people. The hotel reserves some seats in the lounge for hotel guests and accepts reservations for all others, so if you're not staying here and want to make the P.O.V. scene, you really should call ahead for a spot. Otherwise when the place is full, as it often is, you have to wait your turn down in the lobby (where another bar and party are on hand, by the way). It can be quite chaotic. The procedure and the wait are a turn-off for some, but many find it all worth it, once the elevator delivers them to the terrace and lounge. The big draw here is the unique view of the Washington Monument, the White House, Pennsylvania Avenue, and the Lincoln Memorial—no

CHEAP EATS: happy hours **TO WRITE HOME ABOUT**

Good-value promotions are often available at area bars and nightclubs, like Lucky Bar's half-price burgers every Wednesday night and 50¢ tacos on Mondays. A step above these are certain restaurants around town that set out tasty bites during happy hour, either free or for an astonishingly low price. Here are several you might like:

In the bar and lounge of **Ceiba,** 701 14th St. NW, at the corner of G Street NW (✆ **202/393-3983**), not far from the White House, signature cocktails like margaritas and mojitos are $5 each, Monday to Saturday from 3 to 6pm and again from 9:30pm (Fri–Sat from 10pm) to close. Bar-food items that range from a $12 chicken quesadilla to a $10 ceviche are offered at half those prices.

In Georgetown, **Morton's Steak-house,** 3251 Prospect St. NW, just off Wisconsin Ave. NW (✆ **202/342-6258**), serves up "Power Hour" bar bites in its bar, Sunday to Friday 5 to 6:30pm and 9 to 11pm. Drinks are specially priced—$5 for beer, $6.50 for wine, and $7.50 for certain cocktails—and the bar-bites menu features a variety: cheeseburger trio, four

petite filet mignon sandwiches, blue cheese french fries, and so on, each priced at $6 or $7 per plate.

On Capitol Hill, **Johnny's Half Shell,** 400 N. Capitol St. NW (✆ **202/737-0400**), pulls in young Hill staffers Monday through Friday 4:30 to 7:30pm, not for its deals on drinks—$5.50 drafts, $7 to $9 cocktails—but for its delicious bites of miniburgers, shrimp, grits, and the like, priced from $2.50 to $14.

Finally, in the Penn Quarter's **Oyamel,** at 401 7th St. NW, happy-hour specials 4 to 6pm every weeknight feature $5 margaritas, Dos Equis, or the Mexican *ponche* (tequila, white wine, Cointreau, agave nectar, and fresh fruit), and, for another $5, two of Oyamel's superb tacos.

other place in town serves it up in this kind of setting. Plunk yourself down on a couch, order up a Dark and Stormy (Gosling's rum and house-made ginger soda), and take it all in. In the W Washington, D.C. Hotel, 515 15th St. NW (at F St.). www.point ofviewdc.com. ✆ **202/661-2478.** Metro: Metro Center (13th St. exit).

Pour House This is three separate bars in one. The Pour House, on the first floor, plays on a Pittsburgh theme (honoring the owner's roots), displaying Steelers and Penguins paraphernalia, and drawing Iron City drafts from its tap and pierogi from the kitchen. Downstairs is the game room, with pool tables, Wii, Skee-ball, shuffleboard, a bar, and a lounge area; the street level has booths, a TV wall, 15 flatscreens and two 60-inch plasma screens, and a bar. On the top floor is "Top of the Hill," which is promoted as "hip and upscale," but it's not, really (although you will find leather chairs, art, and chandeliers here). 319 Pennsylvania Ave. SE (at 3rd St.). www.pourhousedc.com. ✆ **202/546-0779.** Metro: Capitol South.

Quill Inside the city's chicest hotel is this ultracool bar/lounge, where you can sip peppered Prosecco, nibble on foie gras bonbons, listen to a jazz pianist, and observe the flirting and hobnobbing ways of visiting and local hipsters. In the Jefferson Hotel, 1200 16th St. NW (at M St.). www.jeffersondc.com. ✆ **202/448-2300.** Metro: Dupont Circle (19th St./South exit) or Farragut North (L St. exit).

The Tombs   Housed in a converted 19th-century Federal-style home, the Tombs, which opened in 1962, is a favorite hangout for students and faculty of nearby Georgetown University. (Bill Clinton came here during his college years.) They tend to congregate at the central bar and surrounding tables, while local residents head for "the Sweeps," the room that lies down a few steps and has red-leather banquettes. Directly below the upscale **1789** restaurant (p. 214), the Tombs has its own chef, who serves up the usual college fare of burgers, sandwiches, and salads, as well as more serious stuff. 1226 36th St. NW (at Prospect St.). www.tombs.com. ✆ **202/337-6668.** Metro: Foggy Bottom, then take the D.C. Circulator to Wisconsin Ave. and walk from there.

Tryst   This is the most relaxed of Washington's lounge bars. The room is surprisingly large for Adams Morgan, and it's jam-packed with worn armchairs and couches, which are usually occupied no matter what time of day. People come here to have coffee or a drink, get a bite to eat, read a book, work on a book, or meet a friend. Free Wi-Fi means laptops are ubiquitous. The place feels almost like a student lounge on a college campus, except alcohol is served. 2459 18th St. NW (at Columbia Rd.). www.trystdc.com. ✆ **202/232-5500.** Metro: U St./Cardozo or Woodley Park–Zoo, then catch the D.C. Circulator.

Tune Inn 🏚   Capitol Hill has a number of bars that qualify as institutions, but the Tune Inn is probably the most popular. So when a serious fire engulfed the place in 2011, the community was devastated. Five months later, the Tune Inn reopened, and now it's business as usual. Capitol Hill staffers and their bosses, apparently at ease in dive surroundings, have been coming here for cheap beer and greasy burgers since it opened in 1955. All longtime Capitol Hillers know that Friday is crab cake day (or, in season, soft-shell crab day) at the Tune Inn, and they all show up. 331½ Pennsylvania Ave. SE (at 4th St.). www.tuneinndc.com. ✆ **202/ 543-2725.** Metro: Capitol South.

THE CLUB & MUSIC SCENE
Live Music

If you're looking for a tuneful night on the town, Washington offers everything from hip jazz clubs to DJ-driven dance halls—both places where you sit back and listen and places where you can get up and rock out. Here are some of the best live-music venues.

JAZZ & BLUES

If you're a jazz fan and are planning a trip to D.C. in early to mid-June, check out **www.dcjazzfest.org** for exact dates of the fabulous, 2-week-long **DC Jazz Festival,** which showcases the talents of at least 100 musicians in various venues around town, including free blowout concerts on the National Mall. And if you're a jazz and blues fan, and you're coming to town at some other time of the year, check out the following venues.

The Birchmere Music Hall and Bandstand   If you're a fan of live music by varied, stellar performers, such as Garth Brooks, Lyle Lovett, Jerry Jeff Walker, Crash Test Dummies, Shawn Colvin, Joe Sample, and John Hiatt, the Birchmere is worth the cab fare (around $12) from downtown. It's unique in the area for providing a comfortable and relatively small (500-seat) setting, where you can sit and listen to the music (there's not a bad seat in the house) and order food and drinks.

ELECTRIC AVENUES FOR live-music LOVERS

Live-music venues are ever more popular in the capital, and one neighborhood is particularly noteworthy for the sheer amount and variety of fabulous music on tap on any given night: **U Street NW,** between 9th and 18th streets, and its side streets. Whether you're a fan of jazz, hip-hop, indie rock, or blues, you're bound to find something to please you just by strolling along the U and 14th street corridors, especially on a Friday or Saturday evening. The fabulous new **Howard Theatre** (p. 261), **Bohemian** **Caverns** (p. 261), **Twins Jazz** (p. 262), **U-Topia** (p. 262), the **9:30 Club** (p. 264), and the **Black Cat** (p. 263) are among many. In another part of town that's come to be known as the **Atlas District,** live-music venues also thrive along H Street NE, between 12th and 14th streets. Three Atlas District music clubs are reviewed in this chapter: the **Red Palace** (p. 264), **HR-57** (p. 261), and the **Rock and Roll Hotel** (p. 264). See "The Club and Music Scene," below.

The Birchmere got started about 38 years ago, when it booked mostly bluegrass and country acts. The place has expanded over the years and so has its repertoire; there are still many bluegrass and country artists, but also folk, jazz, rock, gospel, and alternative musicians. The menu tends toward American favorites, such as nachos, burgers, and pulled-pork barbecue sandwiches. Purchase tickets at the box office or online from www.ticketmaster.com. 3701 Mt. Vernon Ave. (off S. Glebe Rd.), Alexandria, VA. www.birchmere.com. © **703/549-7500.** Tickets $17–$60. Take a taxi or drive.

Blues Alley   Blues Alley, in Georgetown, has been Washington's top jazz club since 1965, featuring such artists as Sonny Rollins, Wynton Marsalis, Rachelle Ferrell, and Ahmad Jamal. There are usually two shows nightly at 8 and 10pm; some

A performance at Blues Alley.

wine bars **WOO THE CAPITAL**

Wine bars have gone from being trendy newcomers to valued old friends. Here are our favorites:

○ **Bistrot Lepic and Wine Bar,** 1736 Wisconsin Ave. NW (www.bistrotlepic.com; *ℂ* **202/333-0111**): This Asian-accented, cozy wine bar and lounge on the second floor of its charming French restaurant offers complimentary tastings every Tuesday 6 to 8pm, as well as wines by the glass at half price Wednesday through Monday 5:30 to 7pm. Open daily 5:30pm to midnight.

○ **Veritas,** 2031 Florida Ave. NW (www.veritasdc.com; *ℂ* **202/265-6270**): Located at the northern end of Dupont Circle, just off Connecticut Avenue, this tiny, exposed-brick-walled place holds no more than 50 people and serves 70 wines by the glass. A few nibbles are on the menu: small plates of cheeses and charcuterie, and some desserts. Open daily 5pm to midnight or later, most nights.

○ **Vinoteca Wine Bar and Bistro,** 1940 11th St. NW (www.vinotecadc.com; *ℂ* **202/332-9463**): Like many of its neighbors in the U Street neighborhood, Vinoteca opens at 5pm (11am Sun) and stays open late. Its town-house setting offers seating at a bar, on banquettes, in the upstairs lounge, or outside at sidewalk tables. Wine lovers can choose from 100 wines by the glass; a full menu of American cuisine is also available.

○ **Cork,** 1720 14th St. NW (www.corkdc.com; *ℂ* **202/265-2675**): Another cozy place, Cork features no American or Australian wines, choosing instead to highlight "Old World" wines. The bar offers 50 wines by the glass and a menu that serves small plates of light fare, meant for sharing (think french fries, charcuterie, sandwiches, roasted vegetables, olives, cheeses, and so on). Wine tastings and classes are also on tap. Open Sunday, Tuesday, and Wednesday 5pm to midnight; Thursday to Saturday 5pm to 1am; and Sunday 11am to 3pm.

Cork offers "Old World" wines and light fare.

performers also do midnight shows on weekends. Reservations are essential; since seating is on a first-come, first-served basis, it's best to arrive as early as possible. Doors open at 6pm for the first show and 9:45pm for the second show. Entrees on the steak-and-Creole seafood menu are in the $19 to $25 range, snacks and sandwiches are $5.25 to $10, and drinks are $5.35 to $9. The decor is "classic dive": exposed-brick walls; beamed ceiling; small, candlelit tables; and a very worn look about it. Sometimes well-known visiting musicians get up and jam with performers. 1073 Wisconsin Ave. NW (in an alley below M St.). www.bluesalley.com. *ℂ* **202/337-4141.** Tickets $16–$75 (most $20–$40), plus a $12-per-person food or drink minimum, plus $4.50 per-person ticket surcharge. Metro: Foggy Bottom, then walk or take the D.C. Circulator.

Bohemian Caverns Rising from the ashes on the very spot where jazz greats such as Duke Ellington, Billie Holiday, and so many others performed decades ago, Bohemian Caverns is starting to come into its own, just as the competition increases. (See **Howard Theatre,** below, for the real thing.) The club's performance schedule seems to fluctuate quite a bit, but when in full swing, it hosts two performances nightly. Items on the Southern-dish menu run $9 to $21. 2001 11th St. NW (at U St.). www.bohemiancaverns.com. ☎ **202/299-0800.** Cover $7–$22. Metro: U St./Cardozo (U and 13th sts. exit).

Habana Village This three-story nightclub has a Cuban bar/restaurant on the first floor and a DJ and dance floor on the second and third floors, where Latin jazz and salsa music set the tone. Salsa and merengue lessons are given Wednesday through Saturday evenings, and on Sunday evenings in summer, for $10 per lesson. 1834 Columbia Rd. NW (at Mintwood St.). www.habanavillage.com. ☎ **202/462-6310.** Cover $6 Fri–Sat after 9pm (no cover for women and no cover if you've paid for dinner or dance classes). Metro: U St./Cardozo or Woodley Park–Zoo, then catch the D.C. Circulator.

Howard Theatre A $29-million renovation of this historic arts landmark theater, built in 1910, has helped restore not just the building but also a piece of history. The Howard Theatre of old was the Black Broadway showcase for the likes of Duke Ellington and Ella Fitzgerald, and later hosted performances by Marvin Gaye and the Supremes. The theater reopened in April 2012, with a lineup of stars, from the Roots to Mos Def. With its 1,200 seats arranged at tables, the venue is both supper club and concert venue. Cuisine is American with a soul influence, naturally, and food and drink are served throughout the show. A gospel brunch takes place every Sunday. 620 T St. NW (at 7th St.). www.thehowardtheatre.com or www.howardtheatre.org. ☎ **202/588-5595.** Tickets $15–$95 (most $25–$55). Metro: Shaw/Howard University (7th and S sts. exit.)

The Hamilton Kind of amazing, this place is. Brought to you by the Clyde's Group (see **Old Ebbitt Grill,** p. 193; **1789,** p. 214; **Clyde's,** p. 254; and **The Tombs,** above), the Hamilton is a two-level establishment holding 850 people in all. Upstairs is the American restaurant, where you choose from a menu that covers every meal, breakfast burrito to late-night lobster roll, because get this: The Hamilton is open 24/7. The subterranean level is the live music venue, with blues, rock, jazz, R&B, and folk performances staged nightly. You sit at communal tables and dine from the upstairs menus. Located in the heart of the Penn Quarter, the Hamilton debuted December 2011, and everybody's still talking about it. 600 14th St. (at F St.). www.thehamiltondc.com. ☎ **202/787-1000.** Live music acts $$15–$50; most main courses under $20. Metro: Metro Center (13th St. exit).

HR-57 This cool club in the Atlas District is named for the House Resolution passed in 1987 that designated jazz "a rare and valuable national American treasure." More than a club, HR-57 is also the Center for the Preservation of Jazz and Blues. Step inside Wednesday through Saturday evenings for a jazz jam session or perhaps a star performance. Newly transplanted from the U Street Corridor neighborhood (darn it—it really belongs there rather than here, because of U St.'s jazz roots), HR-57 seems to be settling in just fine. 816 H St. NE (at 9th St.). www.hr57.org. ☎ **202/253-0044.** Cover $8 Wed–Thurs; $15 Fri–Sat. Drive or take a taxi.

Madam's Organ Restaurant and Bar 🍴 This beloved Adams Morgan hangout fulfills owner Bill Duggan's definition of a good bar: great sounds and sweaty people. There's live music nightly: a funk/jazz/blues group on Sunday and Monday, R&B on Tuesday, bluegrass with Bob Perilla & the Big Hillbilly Bluegrass

Live music at Madam's Organ Restaurant and Bar.

Band on Wednesday, and the salsa sounds of Patrick Alban on Thursday, which is also Ladies' Night. On Friday and Saturday nights, regional blues groups pack the place; hope for Bobby Parker or Cathy Ponton King. The club includes a wide-open bar decorated eclectically with an antique gilded mirror, stuffed fish and animal heads, and paintings of nudes. The second-floor bar is called Big Daddy's Love Lounge & Pick-Up Joint, which tells you everything you need to know. Keep climbing the stairs to the rooftop deck, which is now open all year; you can't hear the music up there, but you'll discover an awesome view. You can play darts here, and redheads pay half price for Rolling Rock beer. Food is served, but I'd eat elsewhere. 2461 18th St. NW (at Columbia Rd.). www.madamsorgan.com. (C) **202/667-5370.** Cover $3–$7. Metro: U St./Cardozo or Woodley Park–Zoo, then catch the D.C. Circulator.

Twins Jazz   This intimate, crowded, second-floor jazz club offers live music every night but Monday. You're likely to hear local artists weeknights and bigger-name, out-of-town acts, such as Bobby Watson and Gil Scott-Heron, on week-ends. The menu features American, Ethiopian, and Caribbean dishes. The age group of the crowd varies. 1344 U St. NW (at 14th St.). www.twinsjazz.com. (C) **202/234-0072.** Cover $10–$30, with a $10 per-person minimum on food/drink/merchandise. Metro: U St./Cardozo (13th St. exit).

U-topia   Unlike most music bars, the arty New York/SoHo–style U-topia is serious about its restaurant operation. A moderately priced international menu ($12–$21 for entrees) features dishes such as vegetable couscous curry and shrimp jambalaya. There's an interesting wine list and a large selection of beers and single-malt Scotches. The setting is cozy and candlelit, with walls used for a changing art gallery show. The eclectic crowd here varies with the music, ranging from early 20s to about 35, including many expats and international visitors. There's live music Wednesday through Sunday, with Thursday always featuring live Brazilian jazz. 1418 U St. NW (at 14th St.). www.utopiaindc.com. (C) **202/483-7669.** No cover, but $15 per-person minimum for drink or food. Metro: U St./Cardozo (13th St. exit).

Zoo Bar ✒ This establishment is located across the street from—you guessed it—the zoo. During the day, it caters to hungry families, but Thursday through Saturday nights after 10pm, it's a blues joint. Expect a divey setting and a crowd that skews older. The quality of the music varies: Sometimes you'll stop in and find a serious bluesman from New Orleans, the next night it'll be a local boomer band fronted by a 20-something singer who can really belt it out. If you're looking for a hot club scene, this ain't it. But if you're a blues lover, the Zoo Bar's worth checking out. Plus it's cheap—no cover—and conveniently located, right on Connecticut Avenue, a short walk from the Woodley Park–Zoo Metro stop on the Red Line. 3000 Connecticut Ave. NW (above Cathedral Ave. NW). www.zoobardc.com. ✆ **202/232-4225.** Metro: Woodley Park–Zoo (Woodley and Connecticut Ave. exit).

ROCK, HIP-HOP & DJS

This category focuses on live-music clubs but also includes a sprinkling of night-clubs known for their DJs and dance floors.

Black Cat This comfortable, low-key alternative rock club opened in 1993 and seems likely to keep on kicking for all eternity. Every rocker who's anyone has played here over the years, from Morphine in the early days to the Decemberists and Black Lips more recently. The Black Cat has two stages: its main concert hall, which holds more than 600 people and hosts national, international, and local indie and alternative groups; and Backstage, where soloists, smaller bands, and DJs hold court, and where film screenings and poetry readings also take place. The Red Room Bar, a funky, red-walled lounge with booths, tables, pinball machines, a pool table, and a jukebox stocked with an eclectic collection, offers quieter entertainment. A college crowd collects on weekends, but you can count on seeing a 20- to 30-something bunch here most nights, including members of various bands who stop in for a drink. Say hello to affable owner Dante Ferrando while you're here. Concerts take place almost nightly, sometimes twice in a single night, on different stages. 1811 14th St. NW (btw. S and T sts.). www.blackcatdc.com. ✆ **202/667-4490.** Cover $5–$25 for concerts; no cover in the Red Room Bar. Metro: U St./ Cardozo (13th and U sts. exit).

Eighteenth Street Lounge This place maintains its "hot" status. First you have to find it, and then you have to convince the bouncer to let you in. So here's what you need to know: Look for the mattress shop south of Dupont Circle, then

look up: "ESL" (as those in the know call it) sits above the shop. Wear something exotic and sexy, anything but preppy or jock-ish. If you pass inspection, you may be surprised to find yourself in a restored, century-old mansion (Teddy Roosevelt once lived here) with fire-places, high ceilings, and a deck out back. You're here to flirt and dance; the lounge stages both live music and DJ-spun tunes most nights, a range of acid jazz, hip-hop, reggae, Latin jazz, soul, and party sounds. Get out there on the hardwood floors and bust a move. It's open Tuesday through Friday from 5:30pm, Saturday and Sunday from

Eighteenth Street Lounge in Dupont Circle.

Spirit Animal performs at Red Palace.

9:30pm. 1212 18th St. NW (at Jefferson Place and Connecticut Ave.). www.eighteenthstreet lounge.com. ✆ **202/466-3922.** No cover Tues–Thurs and Sun; cover $5–$15 after 10pm Wed and Fri–Sat. Metro: Dupont Circle (South/19th St. exit) or Farragut North (L St. exit).

9:30 Club   Housed in a converted warehouse, this major live-music venue hosts frequent record-company parties and features a wide range of top perform-ers. This is where Adele performed not very long ago, but those days are gone. But you might catch Snow Patrol, Drive-By Truckers, the Clarks, Jakob Dylan, Wale, Neko Case, Jamie Lidell, or even Tony Bennett. It's open only when there's a show on, which is almost every night (but call ahead), and, obviously, the crowd (as many as 1,200) varies with the performer. Best to buy tickets ($10–$50) in advance, whether at the box office or online. The sound system is state-of-the-art, and the sightlines are excellent. There are four bars: two on the main dance-floor level, one in the upstairs VIP room (anyone is welcome here unless the room is being used for a private party), and another in the distressed-looking cellar. The 9:30 Club is a stand-up place, literally—there are few seats. 815 V St. NW (at 9th St.). www.930.com. ✆ **202/265-0930.** Metro: U St./Cardozo (10th St. exit).

Red Palace   Located along D.C.'s edgiest nightlife avenue, H Street NE, this club aims to offer an intimate setting for singer-songwriter acts, although louder local and touring indie-rock bands frequently appear. In late 2010, owners com-bined the formerly separate but neighboring properties, the Red & the Black and the Palace of Wonders, to create this larger venue with a bigger stage and an extra bar, but the emphasis is still on presenting a club rather than concert-hall experi-ence. The two-story club features a New Orleans–style bar on its first level, with a tin ceiling and red-velvet drape decor, jambalaya on the menu, and Abitas listed among the beers. Bands take the stage nightly upstairs. 1212 H St. NE. (at 12th St.) www.redpalacedc.com. ✆ **202/399-3201.** Cover $5–$8. Drive or take a taxi.

Rock and Roll Hotel   On the same street as the Red Palace, the Rock and Roll Hotel opened first, attracting devoted music lovers and night crawlers to come shoot pool in its second-floor pool hall, listen to live bands in its 400-person concert hall, or toss back shots in its bar. Washingtonians are loving the punk-rock decor of vintage furniture and flying guitars, but most especially the nightly acts, which range from local garage bands to national groups on tour. *FYI:* "Hotel" is just part of the name—no sleeping here! 1353 H St. NE (at 14th St.). www.rockandroll hoteldc.com. ✆ **202/388-7625.** Cover $8–$15. Drive here or take a taxi.

Comedy Clubs

In addition to these three comedy venues, the **Warner Theatre** (see "Headliner Concert Venues," above) and **Harmon Hall** at the Shakespeare Theatre (see above) also occasionally feature big-name comedians or troupes.

The Capitol Steps  This musical political satire troupe is made up of former congressional staffers, equal-opportunity spoofers all, who poke endless fun through song and skits at politicians on both sides of the aisle and at government goings-on in general. Washingtonians have been fans since the Steps got started in 1981. Since then the troupe has performed thousands of shows and released more than 30 albums, including the latest, *Liberal Shop of Horrors* and *Barackin' Around the Christmas Tree*. Shows take place in the amphitheater on the concourse level of the Ronald Reagan Building and International Trade Center, at 7:30pm Friday and Saturday. Order tickets from Ticketmaster (www.ticketmaster. com; ℘ **202/397-7328**). In the Ronald Reagan Building, 1300 Pennsylvania Ave. NW (at 13th St.). www.capsteps.com. ℘ **202/312-1555**. Tickets $40.25. Metro: Federal Triangle.

The Improv The Improv features top performers on the national comedy-club circuit as well as comic plays and one-person shows. *Saturday Night Live* performers David Spade, Chris Rock, and Adam Sandler have all performed here, as have comedy bigs Ellen DeGeneres, Jerry Seinfeld, and Robin Williams. Shows are about 1½ hours long and include three comics (an emcee, a feature act, and a headliner). Showtimes are 8pm Tuesday through Sunday, with a second show at 10:30pm on Friday and Saturday. To snag a good seat, have dinner here (make reservations); this allows you to enter the club as early as 6:30pm for the early show. Only drinks and appetizers are served at the Friday and Saturday 10:30pm show. Dinner entrees include sandwiches and Tex-Mex fare (nothing more than $11). You must be 18 to enter. 1140 Connecticut Ave. NW (btw. L and M sts.). www.dc improv.com. ℘ **202/296-7008**. Tickets $15–$35, plus a 2-item minimum per person. Metro: Farragut North (L St. exit).

The Capitol Steps, a political satire troupe that pokes fun at government goings-on.

LATE-NIGHT bites

If your stomach is grumbling after the show is over, the dancing has ended, or the bar has closed, you can always get a meal at one of these veteran late-night or all-night eateries.

In Georgetown, the **Bistro Francais,** 3124 M St. NW (✆ **202/338-3830**), has been feeding night owls for years; it even draws some of the area's top chefs after their own establishments close. Open until 4am Friday and Saturday, until 3am every other night, Bistro is thoroughly French, serving steak frites, omelets, and pâtés.

On U Street, **Ben's Chili Bowl** (p. 204), 1213 U St. NW (✆ **202/667-0909**), serves up chili dogs, turkey subs, and cheese fries until 4am on Friday and Saturday nights.

In Adams Morgan, one all-night dining option is the **Diner,** 2453 18th St. NW (✆ **202/232-8800**), which serves some typical (eggs and coffee, grilled cheese) and not-so-typical (a grilled fresh salmon club sandwich) diner grub.

Finally, in Dupont Circle, stop in at **Kramerbooks & Afterwords Café,** 1517 Connecticut Ave. NW (✆ **202/387-1400**), for big servings of everything from quesadillas to french fries to French toast. The bookstore stays open all night on weekends, and so does its kitchen.

Riot Act   This Penn Quarter newcomer on the comedy circuit follows the usual formula of nightly acts, two on weekends. But the club is much larger (400-person capacity) than the Improv and its comics more nationally known. Look for the likes of Judy Gold, Dylan Ratigan (I know—I didn't realize he was a comic, either), and Dick Gregory. Sunday through Thursday, the Club offers an 8:30 show; Friday and Saturday there are two acts, at 8:30pm and 10:30pm. Dinner is available for the 8:30 show, but a two-item minimum policy is in effect for both shows (you can apply the minimum to drinks and light-fare purchases). 801 E St. NW (at 8th St.). www.riotactcomedy.com. ✆ **202/697-4900.** Tickets $15–$25, plus a 2-item minimum per person. Metro: Gallery Place (9th St. exit).

THE GAY & LESBIAN SCENE

Dupont Circle is the gay and lesbian hub of Washington, D.C., with at least 10 gay or lesbian bars within easy walking distance of one another. Here are two from that neighborhood, plus another with two locations, the original on Capitol Hill and the second—you guessed it—in Dupont Circle. (Also refer to Destination D.C.'s *GLBT Traveler's Guide,* available on the Destination D.C. website, www.washington.org; see p. 356 for more information.)

Cobalt   Cobalt has collected a lot of accolades over its 10-plus years: The *Washington Post* names it one of D.C.'s best gay nightspots, saying it's a "no-frills dance club with great house and retro DJs, cabaret acts, and shirtless bartenders." The local gay-oriented newspaper, *Washington Blade,* recommends Cobalt as a "Best Place to Meet Guys." The club lies on the third level of a handsome Dupont Circle building that houses a restaurant on its first floor and the lounge 30 Degrees on its second floor. Nightly themed events include Martini Mondays

Jell-O wrestling at Phase One.

and a Best Package Contest every Thursday. 1639 R St. NW (at 17th St.). www.cobaltdc. com. ℰ 202/232-4416. Cover $6–$10, usually Fri–Sat only. Metro: Dupont Circle (Q St. exit).

J.R.'s Bar and Grill   This casual and intimate all-male Dupont Circle club draws a crowd that is friendly, upscale, and very attractive. The interior—not that you'll be able to see much of it, because J.R.'s is always sardine-packed—has a 20-foot-high pressed-tin ceiling and exposed-brick walls hung with neon beer signs. The big screen over the bar area is used to air music videos, showbiz sing-alongs, and TV shows. Every night offers a special deal, like the Sunday all-night $2 Skyy Highball or Thursday's "Retro Night" with free shots at midnight. The balcony, with pool tables, is a little more laid-back. Food is served daily until 7pm (5pm on Sun). 1519 17th St. NW (btw. P and Q sts.). www.jrsbardc.com. ℰ **202/328-0090.** Metro: Dupont Circle (Q St. exit).

Phase One   Open since 1970, Phase One is the oldest continuously operating lesbian bar in the country. Part of its secret must be the no-pressure vibe here. During the week, you might see a mix of persuasions in this neighborly joint; come the weekends, the place is packed with women. A pool table, a tiny dance floor, and televisions are mere distractions. Phase One now has Phase One at Dupont ("the East Coast's largest lesbian bar"), at 1415 22nd St. NW (at P St.). 525 8th St. SE (at G St.). www.phase1dc.com. ℰ **202/544-6831.** Metro: Eastern Market.

ALTERNATIVE ENTERTAINMENT

It may not be the first place you'd think of, but Washington's museums offer some of the best nightlife entertainment around. From the Phillips Collection's Phillips After Five evenings combining live music, cash bar, modern art, and lectures every first Thursday of the month, to the International Spy Museum's second-Friday-of-the-month Spy at Night adventures in which participants sip cocktails while they tour the exhibits and take on spy skill challenges, D.C.'s main attractions can be even more fun to visit after hours. (See individual listings

After Hours party at the Hirshhorn Museum.

in chapter 4 for further suggestions.) Well, and then there's karaoke, and bowling, and poetry slams. Consider the following.

Busboys and Poets Salon, bookstore, restaurant, performance space, lounge, bar, political activist hangout: Busboys and Poets is all these things. The name pays tribute to poet Langston Hughes, who worked as a busboy at the Wardman Park Hotel in the 1920s, writing poems on the side. Busboys has been popular right from the start, and a diverse crowd collects here day and night to peck on their laptops, plan the revolution, and listen to spoken-word performances, pausing only to take a sip of a preferred beverage, whether a Corona or champagne. Busboys' success has led owner Andy Shallal to open locations in the Mount Vernon Square neighborhood (1025 5th St. NW; ✆ **202/789-2227**), and in Arlington, Virginia (4251 Campbell Ave.; ✆ **703/379-9756**). 2021 14th St. NW (at V St.). www.busboysandpoets.com. ✆ **202/387-7638.** Metro: U St./Cardozo (13th St. exit).

H Street Country Club This playground for hipsters opened in June 2009, and not a moment too soon—the wait appears to have been excruciating for local gadabouts, judging from blog comments. Located in the Atlas District, the two-level club invites one and all to come play Skee-ball, shuffleboard, pool, and the jukebox downstairs, or to head upstairs to play nine holes at D.C.'s only indoor miniature golf course. Libations abound, naturally; it is first and foremost a bar, after all. But if you're hungry, the club serves up some fine Mexican food, as well. 1335 H St. NE (at 13th St.). www.hstreetcountryclub.com. ✆ **202/399-4722.** Metro: Union Station, then take a cab.

Hill Country Barbecue Everybody knows to go to this Penn Quarter restaurant for awesome barbecue, strong drinks, and, downstairs, live music nearly nightly. The music tends toward outlaw country and honkytonk. But one of the most popular acts in town is one that patrons themselves deliver here every Wednesday night (usually after tossing back a couple of tequilas). The Hari-Karaoke Band provides live backup as a singer takes the microphone and "rocks 'n twangs" her heart out. 410 7th St. NW (at D St.). www.hillcountrywdc.com. ✆ **202/556-2050.** Metro: Gallery Place/Chinatown (7th and F sts. exit) or Archives–Navy Memorial.

The Best of D.C.'s International Scene

Washington is home to more than 180 embassies and international culture centers, which greatly contribute to the city's cosmopolitan flavor. There are a number of ways to soak up this international scene. First go to the website **www.embassy.org**, mouse over "Embassies," and click on "Embassy Row Tour" for a detailed tour that leads you past embassies along Massachusetts and New Hampshire avenues NW and includes information about the neighborhoods, the embassies, and all that you see along the way.

The website contains specialized information about individual embassies. Lots of embassies host events that are open to the public—sometimes for free, sometimes at minimal cost. In my opinion, the **French Embassy's Maison Française** (www.la-maison-francaise.org) and the Swedish Embassy's **House of Sweden** (www.houseofsweden.com) offer the most interesting events. A highlight is

Nordic Jazz Week, cosponsored by the embassies of Sweden, Denmark, Norway, Finland, and Iceland every June, with the best performances staged on the roof of the House of Sweden building on the Georgetown waterfront overlooking the Potomac River. The cost is usually $25 per person per concert; the experience is priceless.

Finally, you can buy tickets for **Embassy Series** (www.embassyseries. com; ☏ **202/625-2361**) program events. These are world-class, mostly classical-music performances hosted by individual embassies, held at the embassy or at the ambassador's residence. Admission tends to be pricier for these events than for those staged separately by the embassy. For instance, on June 1, 2012, the Embassy of Armenia hosted a concert performed by a clarinetist and pianist; a ticket cost $80 per person, which also covered a buffet of Armenian food. Totally worth it!

Rep. Chris Van Hollen (D-MD) and author Sanford Gottlieb discuss politics at Busboys and Poets.

Bowling at Lucky Strike Lanes.

Lucky Strike Lanes   Drink up and bowl the night away at this bowling alley/ lounge in the heart of the Penn Quarter, on the same block as the Verizon Center. Here you'll find a rambunctious crowd cheering, drinking, and giving the game their best shot, as a DJ plays loud hip-hop and R&B tunes. If you have to wait for a lane (likely, if you haven't called ahead to reserve one), you can lounge on a sofa, play pool, have a drink or a bite to eat at the 50-foot bar, or watch sports on one of the 10 projection screens. Ages 21 and older after 8pm. 701 7th St. NW (at G St). www.bowlluckystrike.com. (*) **202/347-1021.** Metro: Gallery Place/Verizon Center (7th and H sts. exit).

SPECTATOR SPORTS

Washington, D.C. has professional football, basketball, baseball, ice hockey, and soccer teams, and of those five, it's the Capitals, the ice hockey team, whose fans are the most passionate. And visible: In season you'll see the red-jersey'd devotees swarming the downtown before and after the match at the Verizon Center. Tickets to the Caps games are attainable but not cheap. It's the tickets to the Redskins football matches that remain most elusive, thanks to a loyal subscription base. Here's all you need to know about the major spectator sports events and venues in the city.

Annual Sporting Events

Marine Corps Marathon   Thirty thousand runners compete in this 26.2-mile race (the fifth-largest marathon in the United States), which begins at the Marine Corps Memorial (the Iwo Jima statue) and passes major memorials. The race takes place the last Sunday in October; 2013 marks its 38th year. www.marinemarathon.com. (*) **800/786-8762.**

Marine Corps Marathon.

Legg Mason Tennis Classic This U.S. Open series event attracts more than 72,000 people to watch tennis pros compete for big bucks. The classic benefits a good cause: the Washington Tennis and Education Foundation. The tournament takes place for about 9 days, from late July into early August, at the Fitzgerald Tennis Center in Rock Creek Park. www.leggmasontennisclassic.com. ℂ 202/721-9500.

General Spectator Sports

Baseball Washington, D.C.'s Major League Baseball team, the **Nationals,** play at the finely designed **Nationals Ballpark** (www.nationals.com; ℂ **202/ 675-6287**), which opened on March 30, 2008. Located in southeast Washington, the 41,000-seat stadium is helping to spark development in this old neighborhood, which now goes by the name "Capitol Riverfront," a reference to its location on the water and near the Capitol. The closest Metro stop is Navy Yard off of the Green Line (Navy Yard West exit).

Basketball The 20,600-seat **Verizon Center,** 601 F St. NW, where it meets 7th Street (www.verizoncenter.com; ℂ **202/628-3200**), in the center of downtown, is Washington's premier indoor sports arena, where the **Wizards** (NBA), the **Mystics** (WNBA), and the **Georgetown University Hoyas** basketball teams play. The stretch of F Street NW between 6th and 7th streets has been renamed "Abe Pollin Way" to honor the philanthropist and entrepreneur who developed the Verizon Center—and in doing so revitalized this downtown area. (He died in 2009.) For tickets to any of these games, go to the Verizon Center's website and click on "Event Schedule."

Football The **Redskins** National Football League team plays at the 85,000-seat stadium **FedEx Field,** outside of Washington, in Landover, Maryland. Obtaining tickets is difficult thanks to season ticket holders, but if you want to try, visit www.redskins. com/fedexfield.

Ice Hockey The **Capitals** of the National Hockey League are beloved in this city. The team rink is inside the 20,600-seat **Verizon Center,** 601 F St. NW (www.verizoncenter.com; ℂ **202/628-3200**), in the center of downtown. Purchase tickets online through the Verizon Center website.

Soccer D.C.'s men's soccer team, **D.C. United** (www.dcunited.com), has been around since 1994 but continues to play its matches at the creaky 55,000-seat **Robert F. Kennedy Memorial Stadium,** 2400 E. Capitol St. SE (ℂ **202/547-9077**).

A Washington Wizards game.

WHERE TO STAY

9

W hether you come to D.C. for business or pleasure, on your own or as part of a crowd, one of Washington, D.C.'s 130 hotels surely will suit you. As varied as the clienteles they cater to, the city's hotels include hefty, thousand-room-size properties like the Washington Hilton (p. 291), recommended for big groups; luxury hotels such as the Four Seasons (p. 303), beloved by VIPs; trendy establishments like Donovan House (p. 284) that draw hipsters; and all-suites hotels, like the Embassy Suites (p. 284 and 297), especially appealing to families. Washington's compact size and the fact that most of its hotels are located on or near major avenues mean that no matter where you stay, you're never far from some attraction or other. The challenge for most travelers comes down to budget: how to afford an overnight stay in the nation's capital, where hoteliers can count on a steady stream of tourists, conventioneers, and government-business–related visitors, and set their rates accordingly.

BEST HOTEL BETS

- **Best Historic Hotel:** The **Willard InterContinental** celebrated its 100th anniversary in 2006 as the "new" 12-story Willard, replacing the original, smaller "City Hotel" that existed here between 1816 and 1906. Whether known as the City or the Willard, the hotel has hosted nearly every U.S. president since Franklin Pierce in 1853. President Ulysses S. Grant liked to unwind with

Price categories	
Very Expensive	$400 and up
Expensive	$300–$400
Moderate	$200–$300
Inexpensive	Under $200

cigar and brandy in the Willard lobby after a hard day in the Oval Office, and such literary luminaries as Mark Twain and Charles Dickens used to hang out in the Round Robin bar. See p. 283.

- **Best Location:** Two contenders win in this category: For a true heart-of-the-city experience, the **Monaco Washington, D.C., a Kimpton Hotel** (p. 281) can't be beat. The hotel lies halfway between the White House and Capitol Hill, a short walk from the Mall, across the street from the Verizon Center (also a Metro stop, FYI) and two Smithsonian museums, and in the middle of a neighborhood known for its many restaurants, shops, and clubs. Closer to the White House but also within easy reach of the

The prices given in this chapter and the price categories given above are rack rates, the maximum that a hotel might charge for a "double" room. **Note:** The word "double" refers to the number of people in the room, not to the size of the bed. Most hotels charge one rate, regardless of whether one or two people occupy the room. In a few cases, a hotel specifies separate rates for "single" and "double" occupancy, and I provide that information.

At most hotels, you probably won't pay the very highest rate unless you visit in the spring—especially during cherry blossom season in late March and early April—and during inauguration Januarys, every four years (heads up: 2013 is one such year). These categories are intended as a general guideline only, since rates can rise and fall dramatically, depending on how busy the hotel is. In this chapter, I've tried to show a more realistic picture, providing peak and off-peak rates, sometimes presented as a range, for each hotel.

Discounts are often available on the hotels' own websites, or by booking through the agencies listed on p. 308, or through websites such as Hotels.com or Expedia (see "Getting the Best Deal," later in this chapter, for more tips). When the timing's right, it's not impossible to obtain a room at an expensive property for the same rate as a more moderate one. If you're the gambling type, you can bid for a room on Priceline. And if you're persistent, you can try besting the hotel's own discount by searching for a better price on the websites of the major discounters, then calling the hotel and quoting the discovered cheaper rate—it's usually hotel policy to match the lower price.

Note: Quoted discount rates almost never include breakfast or hotel tax.

Mall is the **W Washington, D.C.** (p. 282), whose canopied rooftop bar overlooks the Executive Mansion, as well as the Washington Monument, less than a half-mile away.

o **Best for a Romantic Getaway:** Posh **Ritz-Carlton Georgetown** (p. 304) lies in the heart of Georgetown but just enough off the beaten path to make you feel like you've really escaped; its small size, only 86 rooms, adds an air of intimacy. While the Ritz's spa, sexy bar and bistro, sumptuous rooms, and solicitous service may tempt you to stay put, it would be a shame to pass up the chance to stroll hand-in-hand along Georgetown's quaint streets to dine close by at one of the city's most romantic restaurants—1789 (p. 214) and La Chaumiere (p. 216) among them. Every bit as romantic is the **Jefferson** (p. 293), which also captures top honors for "Best Splurge Hotel" (see below).

o **Best for Business Travelers:** Though many hotels might qualify in this category, the **Sofitel Washington, D.C. Lafayette Square** (p.287) is the one mentioned most as a favorite by business travelers, who appreciate its prime location (near the White House, administration offices, and K St.'s powerhouse law and lobbyist offices) and its righteous combination of personal and professional amenities, including comfy bedding and expansive desks in the spacious guest rooms, an on-site fitness center, a restaurant serving "French comfort food," a popular bar, a business center, Wi-Fi, and a multilingual staff. Those desiring proximity to Capitol Hill should consider the **George, a Kimpton Hotel** (p. 280), which lies a short walk from the Capitol and offers free Wi-Fi and an excellent in-house power dining spot, **Bistro Bis** (p. 180), among other business-friendly amenities.

- **Best Bang for Your Buck:** Its great Georgetown location, spacious studio and one-bedroom suites with kitchens, free Wi-Fi, and rates that range from a low of $115 to a high of $255 recommend **Georgetown Suites** (p. 304) as one of the best values in town. The hotel's website is especially helpful since it posts a month-by-month calendar showing daily availability and lowest rates. Dupont Circle's **Tabard Inn** (p. 208), beloved by locals for its charming quirks and excellent restaurant, is often mentioned as a wallet-friendly choice (rooms with shared bathrooms start as low as $125), but one of the best things about the rates is that they're consistent and don't fluctuate as wildly as those at other hotels. A multitude of restaurants, bars, art galleries, and shops lie within walkable reach of both the Georgetown Suites and the Tabard Inn.

- **Best Service:** The **Four Seasons** (p. 303) staff pampers you relentlessly and greets you by name. The hotel also offers an "I Need It Now" program that delivers any of some 100 left-at-home essentials (tweezers, batteries, cuff links, electric hair curlers, and so on) to you in 3 minutes, at no cost. And then there's the **Mandarin Oriental, Washington, D.C.** (p. 277), where gracious staff speak in hushed tones. Its hotel spa features something called an amethyst steam room, and the very design of the hotel follows the principles of feng shui, the better to attract good fortune.

- **Best Splurge:** The **Jefferson** (p. 293) wins one over with its friendly, professional service and 99 exquisitely decorated guest rooms, several with stunning views of the White House and the Washington Monument. You need never leave the hotel, since it offers a chance for sipping epicurean libations in its hotspot bar, **Quill,** either in the main room or in one of its nearby pull-the-curtain niches, perfect for private canoodling; a Spa Suite, which combines a guest bedroom and adjoining spa treatment room; the intimate, fine-dining restaurant **Plume** (p. 207); and a cozy Book Room, where a fire crackles in the hearth. In case you haven't guessed already, the Jefferson is also a stellar choice for a romantic stay. The **Four Seasons** (p. 303) is another superb splurge option.

- **Best Views:** The **Hay-Adams** (p. 287) has such a great, unobstructed view of the White House that the Secret Service comes over regularly to do security sweeps of the place. Ask for a room on the H Street side of the hotel, on floors six through eight. For a coveted overlook of Washington's famous cherry blossoms in spring or of the Tidal Basin and Jefferson Memorial year-round, stay at the **Mandarin Oriental, Washington, D.C.** (p. 277), specifying a room offering that particular view. The **W Washington, D.C.** (p. 282) is the White House's next-door neighbor to the east and offers unparalleled views of both the White House and the Washington Monument, from its rooftop bar and some guest rooms.

STAYING green IN D.C.

D.C. hotels are taking the green cause to heart, though with varying degrees of fervor. The following list, though not comprehensive, is a good starting point for assessing the level of ecological commitment at some D.C. hotels.

- **Four Seasons** (p. 303) has a behind-the-scenes program that directs various departments toward practices that conserve energy and reduce, reuse, and recycle whenever possible. The hotel's "Supporting Sustainability" program allows guests the option of keeping the same bed linens and towels during their stay. In addition, the hotel's **Bourbon Steak** restaurant (p. 213) cultivates its own herb garden on the property. The hotel uses saltwater rather than chemicals to maintain sanitary conditions in its lap pool.

- All **Kimpton hotels** in D.C. participate in the chain's EarthCare program, which uses low-flow toilets, sinks, and showerheads; nontoxic cleaning agents; in-room recycle bins; and a service that allows guests to keep the same linens and towels during their stay, saving on water and energy use. Individual properties go a bit further; for instance, the Madera provides free parking to guests with hybrid cars. All of D.C.'s Kimptons have received a four- or five-star rating by the Green Key Eco-Rating Program, a science-based environmental standards organization.

- The **Willard InterContinental** (p. 283) buys all of its electricity from such renewable energy sources as wind power. A hybrid car is available for guest transport. All of the hotel's light bulbs are now low-impact fluorescents. The hotel invests in local environmental and social justice causes, such as the cleanup and maintenance of Pershing Park, across the street from the Willard, and supporting Children of Mine, which helps local children in need.

- **Phoenix Park Hotel** (p. 281) has a green procurement program, "Going Green," which includes recycling goods and purchasing recycled goods as much as possible; using energy-efficient light bulbs and sensors, timers, and nontoxic cleaning supplies; and installing low-flow showerheads, sinks, and toilets. The hotel also offers guests the option of keeping the same linens and towels during their stay to conserve water and energy, and to reduce the use of detergents.

- All **Marriott properties,** in D.C. and elsewhere, have low-flow toilets and showerheads, fluorescent lighting in place of standard light bulbs, and linen reuse programs. Marriott partners with several environmental groups, including Conservation International and the National Audubon Society, to determine ways to reduce its carbon footprint. The company in 2010 rolled out a "green hotel" prototype, whose design will reduce a hotel's energy and water consumption by 25%; Marriott intends to use the prototype as it develops new hotels, starting with its Courtyard by Marriott brand.

○ **Best for Families:** The **Omni Shoreham Hotel** (p. 305) is adjacent to Rock Creek Park and within walking distance of the National Zoo and the Metro, and it has a large outdoor pool and kiddie pool. The neighborhood has plenty of kid-friendly eateries, including fast-food choices like McDonald's and local favorites like **Lebanese Taverna** (p. 221). Children receive a backpack upon check-in, and the concierge can provide board games and books (at no charge; just remember to return them). Parents appreciate receiving the first aid/safety kit holding outlet covers, nightlights, and a list of emergency numbers. Also see "Family-Friendly Hotels," later in this chapter.

○ **Best Bed-and-Breakfast:** D.C. has its share of inns, but none so lovely as **Swann House** (p. 295). Owner Mary Ross has individually decorated each of the 12 guest rooms with warm colors and fine furnishings, and manager Rick is gracious and attentive. This is an 1883 mansion, whose architectural features (such as a turret and working fireplaces) and sophisticated decor enchant romancing couples, girlfriends on a getaway, and business travelers.

NEAR CAPITOL HILL & THE NATIONAL MALL

A handful of hotels forms a cluster just north of the Capitol, adjacent to Union Station; southwest of the Capitol, near the National Mall, three or four stand-alone hotels are scattered over several blocks.

Best for: Travelers who have business at the Capitol and tourists who want to be as close as possible to the National Mall, Smithsonian museums, and the Capitol.

Drawbacks: Lively during the day, these neighborhoods grow quiet at night. This is most true for the southwest pocket, where you'll need to take the Metro or a taxi to find nighttime entertainment.

Very Expensive

Mandarin Oriental, Washington, D.C. ★★★   This fabulously luxurious hotel is just a short walk from the National Mall and Smithsonian museums, a quick cab ride to the Capitol, and a Metro stop away from other parts of town. By day the locale is ultraconvenient; at night, not so much.

Never mind. Once you're ensconced inside the Mandarin, you may have no inclination to leave. The hotel's landscaped terraces overlook the Tidal Basin, marina, and Jefferson Memorial; a footbridge crosses to the lip of the Tidal Basin, within steps of the Jefferson—and, in spring, the famous blossoming cherry trees. The hotel's **CityZen** restaurant (p. 179) is among the city's best.

Guest-room decor combines Asian and American traditions, each room's layout following the principles of feng shui. Corner guest rooms overlook both the city and the water; all rooms are capacious, measuring upward of 400 square

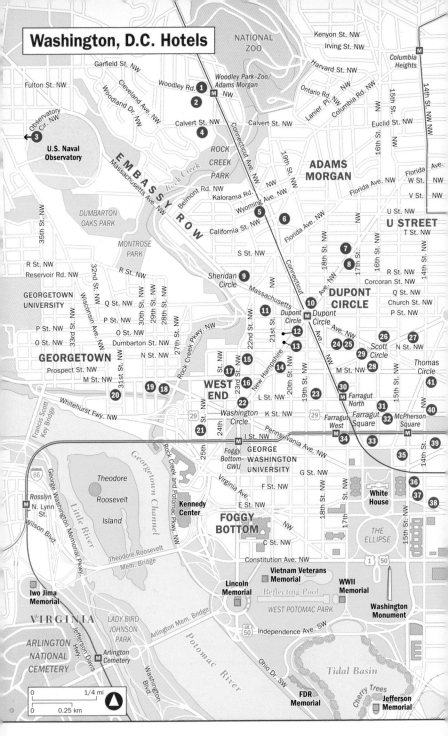

Washington, D.C. Hotels

NATIONAL ZOO

Kenyon St. NW

Irving St. NW

Columbia Heights

Garfield St. NW

Fulton St. NW

Woodley Rd. NW ❶

Woodley Park-Zoo/ Adams Morgan ❷

Harvard St. NW

Ontario Rd. NW

Lanier Pl. NW

Columbia Rd. NW

14th St. NW

Cleveland Ave. NW

Woodland Dr. NW

Calvert St. NW ❹

Calvert St. NW

Euclid St. NW

Observatory Cir. NW ❸

U.S. Naval Observatory

ROCK CREEK PARK

ADAMS MORGAN

16th St.

15th St.

Florida Ave. W St. NW

V St. NW

Belmont Rd. NW

Kalorama Rd.

Wyoming Ave. NW

Florida Ave. NW

19th St. NW

18th St. NW

U St. NW

U STREET

T St. NW

DUMBARTON OAKS PARK

California St. NW

S St. NW

Florida Ave. NW

17th St.

16th St.

R St. NW

Corcoran St. NW

14th St. NW

MONTROSE PARK

R St. NW

Reservoir Rd. NW

R St. NW

Sheridan Circle ❾

Massachusetts Ave. NW

❼

❽

Q St. NW

Church St. NW

P St. NW

GEORGETOWN UNIVERSITY

Q St. NW

P St. NW

O St. NW

Dumbarton St. NW

N St. NW

❶❶

Dupont Circle

Dupont Circle ❶❶

Connecticut Ave. NW

❶❷

❶❸

❷❹ ❷❺

❷❾

❷❽

DUPONT CIRCLE

❷❻

❷❼

Scott Circle

N St. NW

Thomas Circle

❹❶

GEORGETOWN

Prospect St. NW

M St. NW

❶❾ ❶❽

❷❶

❶❺

❶❼

❶❻

WEST END

❷❷

Washington Circle

❶❹

New Hampshire Ave. NW

L St. NW

K St. NW

❷❸

M St. NW

❸❷

❸❶

Farragut North ❸❶

Farragut Square ❸❷

McPherson Square

❹❶

❹❶

Rock Creek Pkwy. NW

❷❹th St.

Pennsylvania Ave. NW

Farragut West ❸❹

❸❸

❸❾

❸❺

Whitehurst Fwy. NW

Francis Scott Key Bridge

❷❹ ❷❹

GEORGE WASHINGTON UNIVERSITY

G St. NW

F St. NW

E St. NW

14th St. NW

❸❻

❸❼

❸❽

Georgetown Channel

Theodore Roosevelt Island

Rosslyn
N. Lynn St.

George Washington Memorial Pkwy.

66

Little River

Kennedy Center

FOGGY BOTTOM

C St. NW

Foggy Bottom-GWU

Virginia Ave. NW

18th St. NW

17th

White House

THE ELLIPSE

Wilson Blvd.

Rock Creek and Potomac Pkwy. NW

Theodore Roosevelt Mem. Bridge

Constitution Ave. NW

Vietnam Veterans Memorial

Lincoln Memorial

Reflecting Pool

WEST POTOMAC PARK

WWII Memorial

Washington Monument

1 50

VIRGINIA

Iwo Jima Memorial

LADY BIRD JOHNSON PARK

Jefferson Davis Hwy.

Arlington Mem. Bridge

Independence Ave. SW

alt 50

ARLINGTON NATIONAL CEMETERY

Arlington Cemetery

Washington Blvd.

Potomac River

Ohio Dr. SW

Tidal Basin

Cherry Trees

FDR Memorial

Jefferson Memorial

0   1/4 mi

0   0.25 km

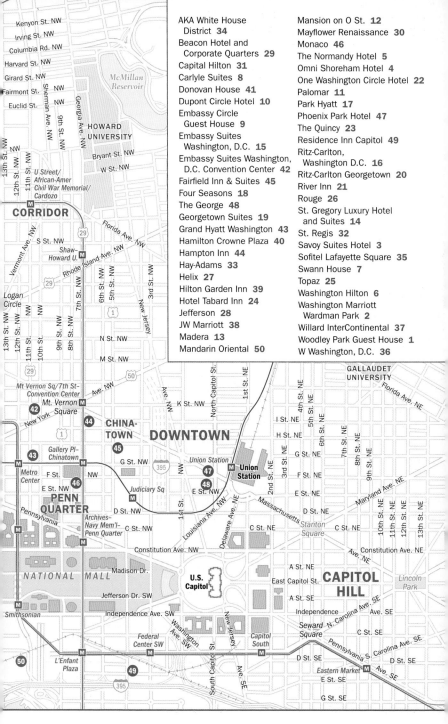

AKA White House
  District **34**

Beacon Hotel and
  Corporate Quarters **29**

Capital Hilton **31**

Carlyle Suites **8**

Donovan House **41**

Dupont Circle Hotel **10**

Embassy Circle
  Guest House **9**

Embassy Suites
  Washington, D.C. **15**

Embassy Suites Washington,
  D.C. Convention Center **42**

Fairfield Inn & Suites **45**

Four Seasons **18**

The George **48**

Georgetown Suites **19**

Grand Hyatt Washington **43**

Hamilton Crowne Plaza **40**

Hampton Inn **44**

Hay-Adams **33**

Helix **27**

Hilton Garden Inn **39**

Hotel Tabard Inn **24**

Jefferson **28**

JW Marriott **38**

Madera **13**

Mandarin Oriental **50**

Mansion on O St. **12**

Mayflower Renaissance **30**

Monaco **46**

The Normandy Hotel **5**

Omni Shoreham Hotel **4**

One Washington Circle Hotel **22**

Palomar **11**

Park Hyatt **17**

Phoenix Park Hotel **47**

The Quincy **23**

Residence Inn Capitol **49**

Ritz-Carlton,
  Washington D.C. **16**

Ritz-Carlton Georgetown **20**

River Inn **21**

Rouge **26**

St. Gregory Luxury Hotel
  and Suites **14**

St. Regis **32**

Savoy Suites Hotel **3**

Sofitel Lafayette Square **35**

Swann House **7**

Topaz **25**

Washington Hilton **6**

Washington Marriott
  Wardman Park **2**

Willard InterContinental **37**

Woodley Park Guest House **1**

W Washington, D.C. **36**

feet. Ecofriendly efforts include triple-paned windows and a recycling program.

1330 Maryland Ave. SW (at 12th St.), Washington, DC 20024. www.mandarinoriental.com/washington. © **888/888-1778** or 202/554-8588. Fax 202/787-6161. 400 units. $495–$695 double; $1,150–$8,000 suite. Children 12 and under stay free in parent's room. For information about special packages, call the hotel directly or check the website. AE, DC, DISC, MC, V. Parking $38. Metro: Smithsonian (Independence Ave./12th St. exit). Pets under 40 lb. accepted, with certain restrictions. **Amenities:** 2 restaurants; 2 bars; babysitting; children's programs; concierge; concierge-level rooms; world-class health club and full-service spa, w/heated indoor pool, sauna, and Jacuzzi; room service; complimentary Wi-Fi in public spaces. *In room:* A/C, TV/DVD, CD player, hair dryer, minibar, MP3 docking station, Wi-Fi ($15/day).

Expensive

The George, a Kimpton Hotel ★★   Behind a facade of stainless steel, limestone, and glass is one of Washington's hippest places to stay, and it's within easy reach of both the Capitol and Union Station. Clientele leans toward powerbrokers and celebrities, who often meet in the hotel's **Bistro Bis** restaurant (p. 180). Decor in the nicely sized guest rooms (around 260 sq. ft.) is minimalist, all creamy white and modern, with fluffy vanilla-colored comforters resting on over-large beds. The smoke-free hotel has two one-bedroom suites. The George adheres to the Kimpton hotels' EarthCare program (see "Staying Green in D.C.," above).

15 E St. NW (at N. Capitol St.), Washington, DC 20001. www.hotelgeorge.com. © **800/546-7866** or 202/347-4200. Fax 202/347-4213. 139 units. Weekdays $289–$489 double; weekends $139–$299 double; $750–$1,050 suite. Children 17 and under stay free in parent's room. Rates include hosted evening wine hour. Ask about seasonal and corporate rates, and the "Hot Dates, Great Rates" deal. Extra person $25. AE, DC, DISC, MC, V. Parking $40. Metro: Union Station (Massachusetts Ave. exit). Pets accepted. **Amenities:** Restaurant; bar; children's amenity program; concierge; small exercise room w/steam rooms; room service. *In room:* A/C, TV, CD/DVD player, hair dryer, minibar, MP3 docking station, Wi-Fi (free).

Residence Inn Capitol   Three Native American tribes are 49% owners of this hotel, which makes it the first multitribal partnership with nontribal partners on land off a reservation. Nearby are the National Museum of the American Indian, the National Mall, and Capitol Hill—an easy walk by day but not recommended at night, when the route between hotel and Independence Avenue is dark and unpopulated.

This is an all-suite hotel whose rooms are twice the size of standard hotel rooms. All units have fully equipped kitchens. A recently completed $4.5-million renovation added and/or replaced carpeting, granite counters, furniture, and artwork; redesigned the common areas; and enlarged the business center. The hotel's many ecofriendly practices include generating 50% of its electricity from wind power and using fluorescent lighting throughout the hotel. The entire property is nonsmoking.

333 E St. SW (at 4th St.), Washington, DC 20024. www.marriott.com/wascp. © **800/331-3131** or 202/484-8280. Fax 202/484-7340. 233 units. Peak $399 studio, $419 1-bedroom suite, $459 2-bedroom suite; off-peak $159 studio, $169 1-bedroom suite, $299 2-bedroom suite. Call about seasonal and long-term rates. Rates include hot breakfast daily, light dinner Mon–Wed, and grocery delivery service. AE, DC, DISC, MC, V. Parking $30 plus tax. Metro: Federal

Center SW or L'Enfant Plaza. Pets accepted for a fee. **Amenities:** Concierge; health club w/ fitness center, indoor pool, whirlpool, and sun deck. *In room:* A/C, TV, hair dryer, full kitchen, Wi-Fi (free).

Moderate

Phoenix Park Hotel ★   The Phoenix Park's location, across from Union Station and 2 blocks from the Capitol, makes it a favorite of business folks in town to meet with government officials. Its popular and authentic Irish pub, the **Dubliner** (p. 255), helps set the tone of Irish hospitality for the entire property. Guest-room features include pillow-topped mattresses and high-definition flatscreen TVs, along with Irish decorative accents, from linens and artwork to soaps. The standard-size rooms are of different configurations; best are those on the top floors overlooking Massachusetts Avenue, the National Postal Museum, and a smidgen of Union Station. Six suites are available, in one- or two-story units, with kitchenette, working fireplace, and spiral staircase. The Phoenix also gets points for its sustainability efforts; see "Staying Green in D.C.," earlier in this chapter.

520 N. Capitol St. NW (at Massachusetts Ave.), Washington, DC 20001. www.phoenixparkhotel. com. ✆ **800/824-5419** or 202/638-6900. Fax 202/393-3236. 149 units. Peak $149–$489 double; off-peak $99–$299 double; from $699 suite. Extra person $30. Children 16 and under stay free in parent's room. AE, DC, DISC, MC, V. Parking $40. Metro: Union Station (Massachusetts Ave. NW exit). **Amenities:** Irish pub; small exercise room; room service. *In room:* A/C, TV, hair dryer, Wi-Fi (free).

PENN QUARTER

At the center of the city is this hot locale, jammed with restaurants, bars, museums, theaters, and the Verizon Center sports/concert arena. The plentiful hotels include modern venues catering to convention crowds and historic properties switched up for luxury-loving funseekers.

Best for: Those who love being in the thick of it all. Business travelers are within easy reach of downtown offices, the convention center, and Capitol Hill. Likewise, the Penn Quarter is prime home base for exploring tourists.

Drawbacks: Crowded sidewalks and noisy traffic can be annoying—even overwhelming.

Very Expensive

Monaco Washington, D.C., a Kimpton Hotel ★★   When you stay at the Monaco, you're not just downtown, you're part of the scene. Museumlike in appearance, the Monaco occupies a four-story, all-marble, mid-19th-century building. Spacious guest rooms measure about 400 square feet and feature vaulted ceilings, long windows, and eclectic furnishings. Interior rooms overlook the courtyard and the restaurant, **Poste** (p. 189); exterior rooms view city sights, the higher up the better. The interior rooms on the first floor are somewhat subterranean (a window close to the ceiling lets in some light). The best rooms are the 32 Monte Carlos, which are nearly twice the standard size but cost an extra $50; located on the second, third, and fourth floors, these rooms have huge windows. The entire property is nonsmoking.

700 F St. NW (at 7th St.), Washington, DC 20004. www.monaco-dc.com. ✆ **800/649-1202** or 202/628-7177. Fax 202/628-7277. 184 units. Weekdays $299–$499 double, $509–$1,200 suite; weekends $169–$319 double, $269–$800 suite. Extra person $20. Children 17 and under stay free in parent's room. Rates include complimentary organic coffee in morning and a hosted evening wine hour. AE, DC, DISC, MC, V. Parking $40. Metro: Gallery Place (7th and F sts. exit). Pets welcome—they get VIP treatment, with their own registration cards at check-in, maps of neighborhood fire hydrants and parks, and gourmet puppy and kitty treats. **Amenities:** Restaurant; bar; children's amenity program; concierge; spacious fitness center w/ flatscreen TVs; room service. *In room:* A/C, TV w/pay movies, CD player, hair dryer, minibar, Wi-Fi (free).

JW Marriott Washington, D.C. ★

This 28-year-old property pursues a thoroughly modern appeal with its leather-wrapped columns and flatscreen-TV-covered media walls in the atrium lobby, and a plug-in technology panel in each guest room that allows guests to split the TV screen and simultaneously watch TV and check e-mail.

The hotel is primely located on Pennsylvania Avenue near theaters, the White House, the National Mall, and restaurants. Ask for a room on floors 3 through 15 facing Pennsylvania Avenue for views of the avenue and of the Washington Monument beyond. Floors 7 and 12 on the Pennsylvania Avenue side have balconies; floors 14 and 15 are the concierge level. Politicos and corporate types fill the hotel on weekdays, families take over on weekends. Like all Marriott properties, this one participates in ecofriendly practices by offering guests carbon offset options, among other things (see "Staying Green in D.C.," earlier in this chapter). The entire hotel is nonsmoking.

1331 Pennsylvania Ave. NW (at E St.), Washington, DC 20004. www.marriott.com/wasjw. ✆ **800/393-2503** or 202/393-2000. Fax 202/626-6991. 772 units. Peak (Feb 23 to Jun 27) $399–$489, off-peak (Jun 28 to Feb 22) $279–$489 double; year-round from $650 suites. Extra person free. AE, DC, DISC, MC, V. Valet parking $39. Metro: Metro Center (13th St. NW exit). **Amenities:** 2 restaurants; Starbucks; concierge; executive-level rooms; extensive health club w/full fitness center, indoor swimming pool, whirlpool, and sauna; room service. *In room:* A/C, TV, hair dryer, Internet ($13/day), minibar.

W Washington, D.C. ★★

The W wants to blow you away, and it doesn't mess around. **P.O.V.** (p. 256), its posh, year-round rooftop lounge and terrace, is unique in serving unbeatable views of the White House and the Washington Monument. Its SWEAT fitness center offers similar landmark sights. The hotel claims the capital's only Bliss Spa, known for over-the-top treatments such as "peeling groovy" and "hangover herbie" facials. **J&G Wine Bar** opens to a sidewalk terrace on Pennsylvania Avenue. Renowned Jean-Georges Vongerichten is the chef behind the hotel's sublime **J&G Steakhouse** (p. 189).

Guest rooms of varying configurations cross ultramodern, ice-white furnishings with antique accents. Best are those that wrap around the corner of the hotel, where 15th Street meets Pennsylvania Avenue. The grand arches in the "Living Room" (lobby) reach two stories high toward the ornate cornices, a splendid reminder that this structure used to be the historic Hotel Washington. *FYI:* The Living Room doubles as a DJ and cocktail lounge, much favored by boisterous urbanistas. The W is entirely nonsmoking.

Also consider my pick for "Best Hotel for Families," the **Omni Shoreham Hotel** (p. 305).

Embassy Suites Washington, D.C. (p. 297)   Close to both a Red Line and a Blue Line Metro station (the zoo is on the Red Line; the Smithsonian museums are on the Blue Line) and within walking distance of Georgetown, this hotel lets your kids sleep on the pullout sofa in the separate living room. Rooms have some kitchen facilities, but the complimentary breakfast in the atrium is unbelievable. There are also an indoor pool and a free game room. Also consider the Embassy Suites Hotel D.C. Convention Center (p. 284), within walking distance of Penn Quarter attractions.

Four Seasons (p. 303)   Spare the parents and spoil the child at this luxurious hotel, whose amenities include age-appropriate snacks and amusements, from fuzzy duckies and coloring books to *Teen Vogue.* The hotel's Georgetown location makes it a good choice for teens, especially if they like to shop; its

location on the C&O Canal recommends it for family hikes along the towpath. (The Four Seasons does have its own pool, but it's a lap pool and not particularly kid-friendly.)

Monaco Washington, D.C., a Kimpton Hotel (p. 281)   You're in the heart of the city, literally surrounded by attractions (International Spy Museum, two Smithsonian museums, the National Crime and Punishment Museum, and the Verizon Center), with the National Mall just a few blocks away. The Red Line Metro stop is across the street. Meanwhile the hotel's KimptonKids program offers welcome gifts, a list of kid-friendly activities, and the loan of high chairs, cribs, and other equipment. The hotel's excellent restaurant, **Poste** (p. 189), offers a fun and tasty kid's menu. And as with all Kimptons, you get a goldfish delivered to your room if you or your little one so desires.

515 15th St. NW (at Pennsylvania Ave.), Washington, DC 20004. www.wwashingtondc.com. ⓒ **877/WHOTELS** (946-8357) or 202/661-2400. Fax 202/661-2405. 317 units. From $369 double; from $1,000 suites. Base rate allows up to 4 people in room. Book online for best offers and rates. AE, DC, DISC, MC, V. Parking $50. Metro: Metro Center (13th St. exit). Dogs and cats under 40 lb. and service dogs welcome; $25 charge plus nonrefundable $100 cleaning fee. **Amenities:** Restaurant; 4 bars; concierge; state-of-the-art, fully equipped fitness center; room service; over-the-top spa with retail store; Wi-Fi (free, in lobby). *In room:* A/C, TV/DVD, CD player, hair dryer, minibar, MP3 docking station, Wi-Fi ($15/day).

Willard InterContinental ★★★   This is one of D.C.'s finest hotels and certainly its most historic, having served as temporary home to two presidents (Lincoln in 1861, Coolidge in 1923) and as the setting for many historic events (this is where Dr. Martin Luther King, Jr. completed his "I Have a Dream" speech).

Standard-size guest rooms have been recently renovated and present a handsome decor, contemporary in style but with a nod to Federal and Edwardian roots. Best are the oval suites overlooking Pennsylvania Avenue to the

Capitol and the rooms fronting Pennsylvania Avenue. Courtyard-facing rooms are the quietest.

Stop at the **Round Robin Bar** for a mint julep (introduced to Washington here by Senator Henry Clay), and listen to barman Jim Hewes spin tales about previous guests, from Mark Twain to Bill Clinton. The **Scotch Bar** features a vast selection of single-malt whiskeys.

Heads of state, corporate execs, and getaway travelers are among the overnight clientele, but locals are always passing through, whether to sip a cocktail in the Round Robin or to applaud the caroling performances staged at Christmas time in the ornate lobby. Any excuse'll do.

See "Staying Green in D.C.," earlier in this chapter, for info about the Willard's award-winning sustainability program. The Willard is entirely nonsmoking.

1401 Pennsylvania Ave. NW (at 14th St.), Washington, DC 20004. www.washington.intercontinental. com. ℂ **866/487-2537** or 202/628-9100. Fax 202/637-7326. 335 units. Peak (Mar 1 to Jun 30 and Sept 13 to Dec 31) weekdays from $459, weekends from $319 double; off-peak (Jan 1 to Feb 28 and Jul 1 to Sept 12) weekdays from $359, weekends from $259 double. Suites from $434 off-peak to $634 peak. Ask about special promotions and packages. AE, DC, DISC, MC, V. Parking $42. Metro: Metro Center (13th St. exit). Small pets accepted. **Amenities:** Cafe w/seasonal terrace; 2 bars; seasonal afternoon tea in Peacock Alley; babysitting; children's programs; concierge; thoroughly equipped and luxurious Red Door health club and spa w/steam room, Jacuzzi, and sauna; room service. In room: A/C, TV, CD player, fridge, hair dryer, minibar, MP3 docking station, Wi-Fi ($10.95/ day, $44/week).

Expensive

Embassy Suites Washington, D.C.—Convention Center ★ ☺

Thanks to its location a short walk from both the convention center and Penn Quarter attractions, this hotel often sells out—with families during school breaks, with conventioneers at other times. Suites average 550 square feet in size, each with the living room and bedroom separated by the bathroom. The upbeat decor employs light woods, earth tones, and glass accents. Each living room has a pull-out sofa. The hotel's attractive common areas include the glass- and wood-paneled, six-story-high atrium and the restaurant's sunroom, where a stunning complimentary breakfast is served daily. The hotel hosts a nightly, complimentary cocktail reception in the two-level bar. The second floor's window-fronted exercise room and pool overlook D.C.'s downtown. Embassy Suites recycles bottles and paper as part of its sustainability program.

900 10th St. NW (btw. New York Ave. and K St.), Washington, DC 20001. www.washington conventioncenter.embassysuites.com. ℂ **800/EMBASSY** (362-2779) or 202/739-2001. Fax 202/739-2099. 384 units. Peak weekdays $269–$389, weekends $189–$279 double; off-peak weekdays $229–$329, weekends $149–$209 double. Extra person $25. Children 18 and under stay free in parent's room. Book online for best rates. AE, DC, DISC, MC, V. Valet parking $35. Metro: Metro Center (11th St. NW exit). **Amenities:** Restaurant; bar; concierge; fitness center w/cardio equipment, free weights, indoor pool, and whirlpool; Wi-Fi (free, in business center, lobby, and restaurant). In room: A/C, TV w/pay movies, fridge, hair dryer, Internet ($9.95/day), microwave, MP3 docking station.

Fairfield Inn & Suites, Washington, D.C./Downtown ★

Atypical of Marriott's Fairfield Inn properties, which target budget-oriented business people, this Fairfield switches up the experience—and the rates. No one's complaining. The hotel positively hums with activity and good vibes, beginning with the welcome you receive from the concierge and the reception clerks as soon as you enter the bustling lobby. Many of the staff have been here a while, having survived the property's changeover from Comfort Inn to Red Roof Inn to the current ownership in March 2011. The Asian-themed decor reflects the hotel's excellent location in Chinatown, with splashes of Chinese red and references to the five elements of nature (water, wind, metal, wood, and fire) found in the carpeting and fabrics. Elevators require key access to operate, a nice safety feature is this part of town. Rooms are of decent size and newly outfitted with reinforced windows, granite-topped vanities, and a "jackpack," for plugging in all of your electronic devices, laptops to iPods. Best rooms are the "deluxe kings," which have a full-size pullout sofa, and the corner suites that end in "25," which are a bit larger than other rooms. The hotel is nonsmoking.

500 H St. NW (at 5th St.), Washington, DC 20001. www.marriott.com/wasfc. ℂ **202/289-5959.** Fax 202/682-9152. 198 units. Peak (Mar–June and Sept to mid-Nov) weekdays $259–$349 double, weekends $149–$199 double; off-peak (Jan–Feb, July–Aug, and mid-Nov to Dec) weekdays $199–$309 double, weekends $109–$189 double. Add $10 for a deluxe king room and $20 for a suite. Children 17 and under stay free in parent's room. Rates include continental breakfast. AE, DC, DISC, MC, V. Parking $33 (no oversize vehicles). Metro: Gallery Place–Chinatown (7th and H sts. exit). **Amenities:** Restaurant; bar; 24-hr. fitness center; room service. In room: A/C, TV, hair dryer, Wi-Fi (free).

Grand Hyatt Washington ★   With its room count of 888, the Grand Hyatt is the largest hotel near the convention center, which is 3 blocks away. (For now, anyway: The 1,175-room Marriott Marquis opens next to the convention center in 2014!)

Guest rooms are average size, measuring 325 square feet, and feature a contemporary look of dark hardwood furniture and hues of brown and gold. A recent upgrade added a 42-inch flatscreen TV and an iHome stereo with iPod docking station to every room. Rooms with interior views overlook the hotel atrium; otherwise rooms offer city views. The fitness club is state-of-the-art, offering cardio and weight equipment; spa treatment rooms; Pilates, yoga, and aerobics classes; and massages. The hotel participates in a recycling program and offers guests the option of reusing linens and towels during stays of more than a day.

1000 H St. NW (at 10th St.), Washington, DC 20001. www.grandhyattwashington.com. ℂ **800/233-1234** or 202/582-1234. Fax 202/637-4781. 888 units. Weekdays $199–$429 double; weekends $129–$239 double; $450–$2,500 suite. Extra person $25. Children 17 and under stay free in parent's room. Ask about special promotions and packages. AE, DC, DISC, MC, V. Valet parking $40/24 hr.; self-parking $30/24 hr. Metro: Metro Center (11th St. exit). **Amenities:** 4 restaurants; 2 bars; Starbucks; concierge; executive-level rooms; health club w/ lap pool, steam and sauna rooms, aerobics, and spa (hotel guests pay $10 per room per day for club use); room service. In room: A/C, TV w/pay movies, hair dryer, minibar, MP3 docking station, Wi-Fi ($10.99/day).

Moderate

Hampton Inn Washington-Downtown–Convention Center ★   This 13-story hotel, which opened in 2005, is 2 blocks from the convention center, within walking distance of Penn Quarter restaurants and attractions. (Though not technically "in" the Penn Quarter, the hotel lies close enough to be included.) From its fitness center with swimming pool and whirlpool, to guest rooms that feature a charcoal and chocolate-brown color scheme, fluffy duvets, ergonomic chairs, 32-inch LCD/HD flatscreen TVs, and lapboard bed trays, this Hampton Inn is a cut above the standard for this particular Hilton brand. Ask for a corner room on the Massachusetts Avenue side, high up, for best city views. The hotel is entirely nonsmoking.

901 6th St. NW (at Massachusetts Ave.), Washington, DC 20001. www.washingtondc.hampton inn.com. © **800/HAMPTON** (426-7866) or 202/842-2500. Fax 202/842-4100. 228 units. Weekdays $201–$349 double; weekends $129–$199 double; $249–$329 suite. Rates can vary widely, so always call to confirm. Extra person $10. Children 17 and under stay free in parent's room. Rates include "Hot Breakfast Buffet." AE, DC, DISC, MC, V. Parking $34. Metro: Gallery Place–Chinatown (7th and H sts. exit) or Mt. Vernon Sq./Convention Center. **Amenities:** Concierge; cardio fitness center w/indoor pool and spa. In room: A/C, TV w/pay movies, fridge, hair dryer, microwave, Wi-Fi (free).

Hilton Garden Inn, Washington, D.C. Downtown This hotel is conveniently located across the street from the Metro's Blue and Orange lines' McPherson Square station, within a short walk of the White House. Rooms are spacious, with either king-size or double beds; a dial on the side of each mattress allows guests to adjust its firmness. Other room features include a cushiony chair with an ottoman and a large desk with an ergonomic chair and adjustable lighting. Guests can enjoy HD content on the room's flatscreen LCD TV. Best for space and views are rooms facing 14th Street, at the front of the hotel. The hotel's 24-hour pantry sells essentials; the 24-hour business center allows free use of a computer, faxing, and copying services. A limited number of rooms on the 14th floor are reserved for guests who smoke; otherwise the hotel's guest rooms are smoke free. Each of the hotel's 20 suites holds a small pullout sofa in the living room. A renovation completed in February 2012 updated all guest rooms, following on the heels of a renovation of the fitness center that added Precor fitness equipment, free weights, and a weight center.

815 14th St. NW (btw. H and I sts.), Washington, DC 20005. www.washingtondcdowntown. stayhgi.com. © **877/782-9444** or 202/783-7800. Fax 202/783-7801. 300 units. Weekdays $209–$349 double, $409 suite; weekends $109–$149 double, $179 suite. Extra person $10. No more than 4 people per room. Children 17 and under stay free in parent's room. AE, DC, DISC, MC, V. Parking $30. Metro: McPherson Sq. (Franklin Sq./14th St. exit). **Amenities:** Restaurant; bar; 24-hr. fitness center w/indoor pool; room service. In room: A/C, TV w/pay movies, fridge, hair dryer, microwave, Wi-Fi (free).

MIDTOWN

Think of the White House as center stage, with an array of hotels, law and lobbyist office buildings, and restaurants at its feet. Several stunningly renovated historic hotels, as well as less sophisticated, more affordable, contemporary properties, are among the options.

Best for: Travelers interested in a central location that's less raucous than the Penn Quarter at night. Also those on business with the executive branch or at one of the law, lobbying, or association offices that line K Street.

Drawbacks: Budget accommodations are lacking in this part of town.

Very Expensive

Hay-Adams ★★★   In its 85-year history, the Hay-Adams has welcomed the world's most illustrious, from Amelia Earhart in 1928 to a certain family named Obama in January 2009. The hotel lies just across Lafayette Square from the White House. In fact, the hotel's first-floor dining room and H Street–side guest rooms floors six through eight overlook Lafayette Square, the White House, and the Washington Monument. Beyond its superb location and views, the classic Hay is boutique in size and comfortably sophisticated, with ornate plaster moldings, ornamental fireplaces, a walnut-paneled lobby, and high ceilings. Guest rooms average 385 square feet in size and feature custom European linens, marble bathrooms, and, following a 2010–11 renovation, laptop-accommodating in-room safes. Also new is the Top of the Hay, an enclosed rooftop event space, proffering that unparalleled sight of the White House. Stop downstairs for a drink in the Off the Record bar, a favorite place for media and administration types.

The hotel secures 100% of its electricity through renewable sources, uses ecofriendly cleaning products, and implements a recycling program.

1 Lafayette Sq. (at 16th and H sts.), Washington, DC 20006. www.hayadams.com. Ⓒ **800/853-6807** or 202/638-6600. Fax 202/638-2716. 145 units. Weekdays $425–$1,250 double; weekends $329–$929 double; from $829 junior suite; from $1,299 1-bedroom suite. Two-bedroom suites available. 3rd person $30. Children 17 and under stay free in parent's room. AE, DC, DISC, MC, V. Valet parking $35. Metro: Farragut West (17th St. exit). Pets under 25 lb. accepted. **Amenities:** Restaurant; bar; concierge; state-of-the-art fitness facility; room service. *In room:* A/C, TV w/pay movies, Bose CD player w/CD library and MP3 connector, hair dryer, minibar, Wi-Fi (free).

Sofitel Washington, D.C. Lafayette Square ★★   The Sofitel borders Lafayette Square and is just minutes from the White House. This early-20th-century building's distinctive facade includes decorative bronze corner panels

The historic Hay-Adams offers spectacular views of downtown D.C.

and bas-relief sculptural panels at ground-floor level. Inside hotel staff dressed in designer uniforms greet you with *"Bonjour!"*—a hint that the French company Accor Hotels manages the Sofitel.

Because of the corner location and exceptionally large windows, guest rooms are bright with natural light, and second- and third-floor rooms facing 15th or H streets boast windows that extend nearly from floor to ceiling. Rooms average 350 square feet in size, each furnished with a long desk, a plasma-screen TV, a creamy duvet on a king-size bed (17 have two double beds), a marbled bathroom, and original artwork. The hotel's ICI Urban Bistro restaurant and Le Bar lounge are popular gathering spots, especially in pleasant weather, when urbanistas jam ICI's and Le Bar's terrace tables. Recycling and water conservation programs are among the Sofitel's ecofriendly practices. The Sofitel is a nonsmoking property.

806 15th St. NW (at H St.), Washington, DC 20005. www.sofitel.com/gb/hotel-3293-sofitel-washington-dc-lafayette-square/index.shtml. © **800/763-4835** or 202/730-8800. Fax 202/730-8500. 237 units. Peak weekdays $305–$500 double, weekends $169–$400 double, $495–$1,600 suite; off-peak $175–$225 double. For lowest rates at any time, call directly to the hotel and ask about specials or packages; also check out the website. Extra person $25. Children 12 and under stay free in parent's room. AE, DC, DISC, MC, V. Parking $40. Metro: McPherson Sq. (Vermont Ave./White House exit). Pets accepted with prior approval. **Amenities:** Restaurant; bar; concierge; state-of-the-art fitness center; library w/books about D.C. and Paris; room service. *In room:* A/C, TV w/pay movies, CD player, hair dryer, minibar, MP3 docking station, Wi-Fi ($9.95/day).

The St. Regis Washington, D.C. ★★ A glance to the right as you enter or to the left as you exit the St. Regis confirms that you can only be in Washington, D.C.: That's the White House, all right, staring back at you from the end of 16th Street. A major renovation completed in 2008 thoroughly redesigned the hotel's interior, making already-elegant guest rooms more so, with the addition of built-in, handcrafted armoires hiding the TV, minibar, wine fridge, drawers, and closets. Rooms are larger, too, measuring 350 to 1,100 square feet. Add plumped-up beds and sofas, and antiqued desks and tables, and you've got an especially lovely place to stay the night. Don't miss ultracool amenities, like the television embedded in the bathroom mirror—the picture appears within the glass. The hotel's 25 suites offer individually designed, ultradeluxe rooms, one-bedrooms, and junior suites. The cherry on top is the fabulous restaurant, Alain Ducasse's **Adour** (p. 196).

926 16th St. NW (at K. St), Washington, DC 20006. www.stregis.com/washington. © **866/716-8116** or 202/638-2626. Fax 202/638-4231. 182 units. High season $980 double; junior suite $1,580; 1-bedroom suite $1,580–$3,300; specialty suite from $3,500. Check the website for best available rates, which can be much lower at holiday and off-peak times. 3rd person $75. Children 12 and under stay free in parent's room. AE, DC, DISC, MC, V. Valet parking $49. Metro: Farragut West (17th St. exit) or Farragut North (K St. exit). Pets under 25 lb. allowed for $100 nonrefundable fee plus $25 per day. **Amenities:** Restaurant; bar; babysitting; signature butler service (suite guests only); children's programs; concierge; exercise room; room service. *In room:* A/C, TV w/pay movies, CD/DVD player, fridge, hair dryer, minibar, MP3 docking station, Wi-Fi ($15/day).

Expensive

Capital Hilton ★ Located just 2 blocks from the White House, this hotel has hosted 13 presidents since it opened in 1943. Though the hotel's historic stature once translated into "old in appearance," a major renovation completed in 2012 spruced up its traditional look while introducing modern features. Best change of all is the sophisticated, fresh redo of guest rooms, which include handsome new mahogany finishes, Williamsburg- and Federal-style color palettes, and black-and-white photographs of D.C. landmarks. Corner rooms on the 16th Street side are the most spacious and offer the best city sights; a handful present a partial view of the White House. A number of suites are available, including three with outdoor patios. Also new: MINT DC, a state-of-the-art health club and spa. Free Wi-Fi is available in the lobby and bar.

Capital Hilton is committed to the Hilton chain's goal of reducing energy consumption by 10% to 20% by 2014 and employs many other ecofriendly practices.

1001 16th St. NW (btw. K and L sts.), Washington, DC 20036. www.thecapitalhilton.com. ⓒ **800/ HILTONS** (445-8667) or 202/393-1000. Fax 202/639-5784. 544 units. Peak $299–$519 double; off-peak $139–$399 double (add $50–$60 for executive units); $219–$459 minisuite. Extra person $25. Children 18 and under stay free in parent's room. Weekend packages and other discounts available. For deals follow @CapitalHilton on Twitter, "Like" Capital Hilton on Facebook, or call the toll-free reservations number. AE, DC, DISC, MC, V. Parking $42. Metro: Farragut North (K St. exit) or McPherson Sq. (Vermont Ave./White House exit). **Amenities:** Restaurant; bar; concierge; concierge-level rooms; all-new health club and spa; room service. *In room:* A/C, TV w/pay movies, hair dryer, MP3 docking station, Wi-Fi ($13.95/day).

Donovan House, a Kimpton Hotel ★★ Donovan House gets high marks for hipness, starting with the lobby: An arty chandelier/sculpture, a buzzing bar scene, Italian leather chairs, and a banquette nook set in the wall endow a nightclub vibe. Ditto the guest rooms; a brown leather strip acts as a headboard for the bed and extends up to and across the ceiling. The pristine bathroom features a snail-shell-like shower stall, whose cylindrical shape protrudes into the guest room—its opaque walls ensure the shower-er is not on show. "People are art" is the theme, so mirrors take the place of artwork. Floor-to-ceiling windows overlook Thomas Circle, nearby landmark churches, and cityscapes. The best spot for great views, though, is the seasonal rooftop pool and bar, **ADC** ("Above DC"); come summer evenings, ADC turns into a major

Extended Stays in the Heart of the City

Travelers to Washington, D.C. who plan to visit for a week or longer should know about the centrally located **AKA White House District** apartments/hotel, 1710 H St. NW (www.stayaka.com; ⓒ **202/904-2500**). The D.C. location is one of nine AKA properties (others are in NYC, Beverly Hills, Philadelphia, London, and Arlington, VA), all of which offer luxuriously furnished one- and two-bedroom apartments, sometimes for short stays but mostly for extended stays. Federal employees will be happy to learn that AKA accepts the government's per-diem rate. Check out the website to see for yourself some of the property's fine appointments and amenities, including fully equipped kitchens, stylish decor, free Wi-Fi, an on-site fitness center, a washer/dryer in each apartment, and complimentary continental breakfast. K Street law offices, the White House, the Smithsonian's Renwick Gallery, and excellent restaurants, like **BLT Steak** (p. 196), are just some of the property's notable neighbors.

party scene. Seventeen one-bedroom suites are available. Back at street level is **Zentan,** the hotel's excellent Asian restaurant.

1155 14th St. NW (at Thomas Circle), Washington, DC 20005. www.donovanhousehotel.com. ✆ **800/383-6900** or 202/737-1200. Fax 202/521-1410. 193 units. Weekdays $249–$499 double; weekends $179–$459 double; from $449 suite. 3rd person $30. Children 17 and under stay free in parent's room. AE, DISC, MC, V. Valet parking $42. Metro: McPherson Sq. (Franklin Sq./14th St. exit). **Amenities:** Restaurant; 2 bars; concierge; state-of-the-art fitness center; rooftop pool; room service. *In room:* A/C, TV w/pay movies, hair dryer, minibar, MP3 docking station, Wi-Fi ($15/day).

Hamilton Crowne Plaza ★   This well-placed hotel is 1 block from the McPherson Square Metro station, 4 blocks from the White House, and within walking distance of the vibrant Penn Quarter neighborhood and the National Mall, too, a ¾-mile hike away. The Historic Hotels of America lists the Hamilton Crowne Plaza in its collection, thanks to the Beaux Arts building's 1920s architecture (check out the lobby's vaulted ceiling and arched stained-glass window) and its hosting of famous events and personages (FDR staged an inaugural ball here). Newly renovated guest rooms evince a residential air with dark-wood furnishings and comfortable seven-layer beds whose headboards offer reading lights. Average room size is 325 square feet. K Street–side rooms overlook Franklin Park, and those on the concierge floors (12 and 14) offer views of the city skyline. Locals like the hotel's restaurant patio (open year-round) for people-watching and its bar for happy hour. The entire hotel is nonsmoking.

1001 14th St. NW (at K St.), Washington, DC 20005. www.hamiltonhoteldc.com. ✆ **800/263-9802** or 202/682-0111. Fax 202/682-3801. 318 units. Weekdays $169–$429 double, $450–$900 suite; look for lower rates on weekends. Extra person $20. Children 17 and under stay free in parent's room. AE, DC, DISC, MC, V. Parking $38. Metro: McPherson Sq. (Franklin Sq./14th St. exit). Pets accepted. **Amenities:** Restaurant; bar; Starbucks; concierge; executive-level rooms; fully equipped fitness center; room service. *In room:* A/C, TV w/pay movies, CD player, hair dryer, Wi-Fi ($12.95/day).

The Mayflower Renaisssance ★   The Mayflower's illustrious history began at its opening in 1925, when it served as the site of Calvin Coolidge's inaugural ball. President-elect FDR and family lived in room 776 while waiting to move into the White House; this is where he penned the words, "The only thing we have to fear is fear itself."

Guest rooms feature pure-white duvets atop Marriott's signature "Revive" pillowtop mattresses, embroidered drapes, silk wall coverings, and plush armchairs. Many guest rooms have their own marble foyers; all have a high ceiling and Italian marble bathroom. The Mayflower has a club level on the eighth floor, as well as 74 one-bedroom suites.

A 2011 renovation redesigned the lobby, closing down the beloved Town & Country Lounge and moving the **Thomas Pink** store into that space. (The plan is to turn the space originally occupied by Thomas Pink into the hotel's new restaurant and bar area.) The hotel's lovely **Café Promenade** remains a popular power-breakfast and -lunch spot.

The Mayflower is a nonsmoking property.

1127 Connecticut Ave. NW (btw. L and M sts.), Washington, DC 20036. www.renaissancemayflower. com. ✆ **800/228-7697** or 202/347-3000. Fax 202/776-9182. 657 units. Weekdays $299–$519 double, $499–$599 suites; weekends $179–$299 double, $499–$599 suites. No charge for extra person in room. AE, DC, DISC, MC, V. Parking $45. Metro: Farragut North (L St. exit). Pets under 100 lb.

9

Midtown

WHERE TO STAY

allowed for flat $100 fee. **Amenities:** Restaurant; lobby cafe/lounge; bar; concierge; concierge-level rooms; fitness center; room service. *In room:* A/C, TV w/pay movies, hair dryer, Internet ($12.95/day), minibar.

Moderate

The Quincy ★ ✔   The Quincy remains a more affordable option in this expensive part of town. Its "conservative contemporary" decor goes for a bright, very 21st-century feel. Suites are large and comfortable; about 28 are equipped with full kitchens, while the rest have wet bars (minifridge, microwave, and cof-feemaker). All guest rooms are furnished with pillowtop mattresses, sectional sofas, flatscreen TVs, complimentary high-speed Internet access, and double-paned windows. The Quincy has direct access to Mackey's, an Irish pub right next door, and to Recessions, a lounge on the lower level serving American/Mediterranean cuisine.

Tourists and corporate travelers offer repeat business for the Quincy and are often rewarded for it with goodies in the room or complimentary room upgrades.

The Quincy is a nonsmoking property.

1823 L St. NW (btw. 18th and 19th sts.), Washington, DC 20036. www.thequincy.com. ⓒ **800/424-2970** or 202/223-4320. Fax 202/293-4977. 99 units. Year-round weekdays $189–$289; weekends $99–$149. Children 17 and under stay free in parent's room. AE, DC, DISC, MC, V. Parking $30 (in adjoining garage). Metro: Farragut North (L St. exit). Pets under 25 lb. accepted for $150 nonrefundable deposit. **Amenities:** Restaurant; bar; concierge; free passes to nearby full-service Results Gym; room service. *In room:* A/C, TV w/pay movies, fridge, hair dryer, micro-wave, Wi-Fi (free).

ADAMS MORGAN

The hotels listed here are situated just north of Dupont Circle, at the mouth of Adams Morgan rather than within its actual boundaries. The handful that perch along this Connecticut Avenue slope represent a vast range in hotel size, from one of the city's largest to one of its smallest.

Best for: Those seeking rooms with a city skyline view and travelers who want to stay "in" the city but out of the fray.

Drawbacks: The closest Metro stop (Dupont Circle) is several blocks away.

Expensive

Washington Hilton ★ ☺   This sprawling hotel, built in 1965, occupies 5½ acres. A $140-million renovation completed in 2010 thoroughly refurbished guest rooms and a large outdoor courtyard with fire pits and a dining area.

The hotel's vast conference facilities make it a sure pick for big tour and business groups. Its ballroom is one of the largest on the East Coast, accommo-dating more than 4,000. The hotel's position halfway up a hill overlooking the city means that if you stay in a south-side guest room on the fifth floor or higher, you'll have panoramic views of the capital. Restaurants and bars are all close by.

Those with families in tow should know about the Hilton's family-friendly amenities, which include the seasonal outdoor pool and children's wading pool; its location not too far from the National Zoo; and its status as a stop on the Open Top sightseeing tour bus (tickets are sold at the hotel's tour desk). A Hertz rental-car service and FedEx Office business center are on-site.

1919 Connecticut Ave. NW (at T St.), Washington, DC 20009. www.washington.hilton.com. *(C)* **800/HILTONS** (445-8667) or 202/483-3000. Fax 202/232-0438. 1,070 units. $119–$369 double; $50 more for executive rooms. Look for deals on the website or by calling the toll-free reservations number; you can also follow @HiltonWash on Twitter or "Like" Washington Hilton on Facebook. Extra person $20. Children 18 and under stay free in parent's room. AE, DC, DISC, MC, V. Valet parking $37; self-parking $32. Metro: Dupont Circle (North/Q St. exit). Pets under 75 lb. allowed for a flat $75 fee. **Amenities:** Restaurant; gourmet coffee outlet (the California-based Coffee Bean & Tea Leaf) and grab-n-go; 2 bars; concierge; concierge-level rooms; extensive health club; seasonal outdoor pool; room service; Wi-Fi (free, in lobby, bar, and the Coffee Bean & Tea Leaf). *In room:* A/C, TV w/pay movies, hair dryer, MP3 docking station, Wi-Fi ($13.95/day).

Moderate

The Normandy Hotel ★ 🎁   This small gem of a hotel lies on a quiet street surrounded by handsome residences; the embassies of Afghanistan, Syria, and Senegal; and the Alliance Française. Nearby are great restaurants, bars, clubs, shops, galleries, and the Dupont Circle Metro station. A 2009 renovation transformed the six-story property. Guest-room decor serves up chic, individual versions of fashionable, such as charcoal and ivory toile wall coverings and drapes; all rooms come with raspberry velvet-cushioned slipper chairs, boxy lamps, and variegated marble-walled bathrooms. Rooms are small, with the best ones overlooking tree-lined Wyoming Avenue. The Normandy's public spaces are also improved, with the newly plush lounge offering a comfortable spot to sit by the fire in winter or enjoy a good breakfast in the morning. Because of its location, the hotel hosts many embassy-bound guests; you may discover this for yourself during the evening, when guests gather in the lounge, conservatory, and garden patio for complimentary hors d'oeuvres and spirits. The hotel is entirely nonsmoking.

2118 Wyoming Ave. NW (at Connecticut Ave.), Washington, DC 20008. www.doylecollection. com/normandy. *(C)* **866/534-6835** or 202/483-1350. Fax 202/387-8241. 75 units. $129–$349 double,. Call or go online for best deals, which can fall well below the rack rate. Extra person $20. Children 12 and under stay free in parent's room. AE, DC, DISC, MC, V. Limited parking $28. Metro: Dupont Circle (North/Q St. exit). Dogs 20 lb. or under allowed. **Amenities:** Access to the neighboring Dupont Circle Courtyard's pool and exercise room. *In room:* A/C, TV/DVD, fridge, hair dryer, Wi-Fi (free).

DUPONT CIRCLE

This neighborhood of quaint town houses and beautiful embassies, bistro restaurants, art galleries, and bars is home to more hotels than any other neighborhood in the city. Boutique hotels reign supreme, though a few chains have outposts here, too.

Best for: Travelers who love a city scene minus the office buildings. Also for gay and lesbian visitors, since Dupont Circle is LGBT Central.

Drawbacks: If you have business on Capitol Hill or in the Penn Quarter, this might not be your first choice, since there are plenty of closer options.

Very Expensive

The Jefferson ★★★   Following a 2-year renovation, the Jefferson reopened in August 2009 and less than 6 months later was awarded an esteemed Relais & Châteaux designation, the only D.C. lodging to be recognized by the 59-year-old organization. The hotel's exquisitely decorated rooms are done in a variety of pleasing palates, and Jefferson's life and times in Washington, Virginia, and Paris come to life in the decorative details: Precious original artworks recall Jefferson's varied interests; bedcover toile designs depict scenes of Monticello; and soap fragrances are inspired by herbs and botanicals native to Charlottesville. Corner rooms at the front of the house reveal the Washington Monument about a mile away; some rooms look straight down 16th Street to the White House. Ramble around the first floor in the morning and you may stumble upon the pastry chef emerging from the kitchen with a sheet pan of shortbread, or the bartender setting up for business in the quiet-for-now **Quill** bar and lounge (p. 257); breakfast still under way in the sky-lit, marble-floored **Greenhouse;** or staff preparing tables for dinner in the jewel box of a dining room, **Plume** (p. 207). The hotel is tranquil during the day but quite lively in the evening, when Quill fills with flirting singles and Plume's tables are all taken with fine-dining lovers.

The Jefferson's ecofriendly practices include use of a water filtration system and reusable glass bottles. The hotel has five ADA-approved rooms, including one suite. The Jefferson is nonsmoking.

1200 16th St. NW (at M St.), Washington, DC 20036. www.jeffersondc.com. ✆ **202/448-2300.** Fax 202/448-2301. 99 units. $350–$600 double; $650–$11,000 suite. Extra person $30. Children 12 and under stay free in parent's room. AE, DC, DISC, MC, V. Parking $45. Metro: Farragut North (L St. and Connecticut Ave. exit). Dogs welcome, with guest required to sign a form at check-in guaranteeing payment for any damages. **Amenities:** 2 restaurants; bar/lounge; children's amenities; concierge; 24-hr. on-site fitness center; spa w/hair salon, massages, and facials; room service. In room: A/C, TV w/pay movies, hair dryer, minibar, Bose radio w/MP3 docking station, Wi-Fi (free).

The Mansion on O Street ★ 🏠   A legend in her own time, H. H. Leonards Spero operates this Victorian property, made up of five interconnecting four- and five-story town houses. It's a museum, an event space, a private club, and a hotel.

Most breathtaking of the guest rooms is the two-level Log Cabin loft suite, with Remington sculptures, a bed whose headboard encases an aquarium, and an ecofriendly bathroom with sauna. The Art Deco–style penthouse takes up an entire floor, with a large living room, two bathrooms, a bedroom, and a kitchen; it has its own security cameras and elevator. The newest creation is the Lighthouse Suite, which includes an old-fashioned wooden soaking tub. The mansion also has conference spaces, 32 far-out bathrooms, 18 fireplaces, and art, antiques, and books everywhere (all of it for sale). Be sure to look for the guitars displayed throughout the mansion, each signed by a famous musician, including Bob Dylan, Bruce Springsteen, and Sean Ono Lennon. It's possible to rent the entire mansion or a portion of it. Full business services are available. It also hosts Sunday brunches, live music concerts, and a drag show the last Monday of every month.

2020 O St. NW (btw. 20th and 21st sts.), Washington, DC 20036. www.omansion.com. ℂ **202/496-2000.** 23 units, all with private bathroom. $350–$850 double; $550–$2,000 suites. Nonprofit, group, government, and long-term rates available. Rates include continental breakfast. AE, DC, DISC, MC, V. Parking $25 by reservation. Metro: Dupont Circle (South/19th St. exit). **Amenities:** Babysitting; children's programs; concierge; free passes to Sports Club/LA health club at the nearby Ritz-Carlton; Jacuzzi; room service; sauna. *In room:* A/C, TV, MP3 docking station, Wi-Fi (free).

Expensive

Beacon Hotel and Corporate Quarters ★   Opened in 2005, the Beacon attracts a lively local gathering in its bar and grill, right off the lobby, which adds to the overall genial ambience of the hotel. All rooms are furnished with flatscreen TVs and contemporary touches, like down-filled duvets and large leathery-looking headboards. The best rooms are the one-bedroom suites, one per floor, that perch in the "turret" in the corner of the building. But the New York–style junior suites offer a great deal: Each suite's compact kitchen includes a dishwasher, fridge, stovetop, microwave, and cabinets. Add the roomy living room with a sleep sofa and you've got a good home base—for both corporate folks on business and families on holiday. The hotel's seasonal Sky Bar is open Tuesday to Saturday and offers views of the Dupont Circle neighborhood, the boulevards of the city, and—come the Fourth of July—the fireworks on the Mall.

1615 Rhode Island Ave. NW (at 17th St.), Washington, DC 20036. www.beaconhotelwdc.com. ℂ **800/821-4367** or 202/296-2100. Fax 202/331-0227. 199 units. Peak weekdays $329–$529, weekends $129–$309; off-peak weekdays $199–$289, weekends $109–$189. Ask for AAA or AARP discounts, or check the website for best rates; always ask for promotional rates. Extra person $20. 3-adult maximum per room. Children 13 and under stay free in parent's room. AE, DC, DISC, MC, V. Parking $33 weekdays, $29 weekends; no oversize SUVs, buses, or conversion vans. Metro: Dupont Circle (South/19th St. exit). **Amenities:** Restaurant; 2 bars (1 is seasonal rooftop bar); in-house cardio fitness center, plus free access to nearby fully equipped YMCA w/indoor pool; room service. *In room:* A/C, TV w/pay movies, fridge, hair dryer, Wi-Fi ($12/day).

Palomar Washington D.C., a Kimpton Hotel ★★   If you prefer a hotel to be more than simply a place to sleep, you'll love the Palomar. This Kimpton hotel lies in the heart of the fun Dupont Circle neighborhood, and it regularly invites local artists to pop in for the evening wine hour. The Palomar fancies itself a kind of art gallery, from its displays of handcrafted decorative arts in the lobby to the splashes of mulberry and magenta, zebrawood, and faux-leather finishes in the guest rooms. These are spacious rooms, averaging 520 square feet (!), and they are comfortably appointed, some with a maneuverable, oversize elliptical desk and an ergonomic mesh chair, and some with an undulating chaise lounge. The bathrooms hold granite-topped vanities and Aveda bath products. Specialty rooms include 18 "Tall" rooms (the beds are 90-in. kings) and eight "Motion" rooms (each comes with in-room exercise equipment). Ask for an executive king room with floor-to-ceiling windows overlooking P Street for the best in-the-neighborhood experience. This is a nonsmoking property.

2121 P St. NW (at 21st St.), Washington, DC 20037. www.hotelpalomar-dc.com. ℂ **877/866-3070** or 202/448-1800. Fax 202/448-1801. 335 units. Sun–Thurs $299–$499 double; Fri–Sat

$179–$399 double; from $500 suite. Book online for best rates. Extra person $20. Children 17 and under stay free in parent's room. Rates include complimentary morning coffee and hosted evening wine reception (in lobby). AE, DC, DISC, MC, V. Parking $38. Metro: Dupont Circle (South/19th St. exit). Pets welcome. **Amenities:** Restaurant; bar/lounge; children's amenity program; concierge; fitness center; outdoor (seasonal) lap pool w/sun deck and private cabanas; room service. *In room:* A/C, TV w/pay movies, CD/DVD players, hair dryer, minibar, MP3 docking station, Wi-Fi (free).

St. Gregory Luxury Hotel and Suites ★   The St. Gregory is an affordable luxury property, whose most recent renovation pushed decor toward a softly sophisticated but sexy look. Wingback chairs, soft benches in place of coffee tables, high-backed sofas, flat-panel TVs, and multilayered mattresses are just some of the fresh appointments. Most units are one-bedroom suites with separate living room and bedroom. For privacy and views, choose one of the 16 "sky" rooms on the top floor, each with a terrace overlooking the city. Of the 101 suites, 85 have pantry kitchens, including microwaves, ovens, and full-size refrigerators.

The St. Gregory's clientele is mostly corporate but also includes a steady flow of performing artists in town for an engagement; government guests, who are eligible for special rates; and families during spring and summer. Check the website for stellar offerings. The St. Gregory is entirely nonsmoking.

2033 M St. NW (at 21st St.), Washington, DC 20036. www.stgregoryhotelwdc.com. ✆ **800/829-5034** or 202/530-3600. Fax 202/466-6770. 155 units. Weekdays $285–$435 double or suite; weekends $139–$309 double or suite. Extra person $30. Children 13 and under stay free in parent's room. Ask about discounts, long-term stays, AAA and AARP rates, and packages. AE, DC, DISC, MC, V. Parking $33 weekdays, $29 on weekends (garage has maximum 6-ft. clearance). Metro: Dupont Circle (South/19th St. exit). **Amenities:** Restaurant; coffee bar; bar/lounge; babysitting; concierge; concierge-level rooms; state-of-the-art fitness center, as well as access to the nearby fully equipped YMCA w/indoor pool; room service. *In room:* A/C, TV w/pay movies, fridge, hair dryer, Wi-Fi ($12/day).

Swann House ★★ 🏠   Among D.C.'s stable of wonderful B&Bs, Swann House stands out. The stunning architecture of the 1883 mansion, with its turrets, balcony, and arches, catches the attention of passersby. Inside the handiwork of owner Mary Ross takes over. Applying her fine eye for interior design and her love of textiles, Ross has decorated each of the 12 guest rooms (four are suites) and the public areas in individually beguiling ways, painting walls in rich, warm colors and constantly changing out furnishings, from antique beds to pedestal sinks. Manager Rick adds his graciously capable touch, sparking interesting conversations as he sees to guests' needs. Hard to say which room is prettiest: the Blue Sky Suite, with walls painted blue-gray, its original rose-tiled working fireplace, a queen-size bed, and a sitting room? Il Duomo, with its Gothic windows, cathedral ceiling, and angel-muraled walls within the turreted bathroom? The main floor is just as lovely. Check the inn's website for rate specials. This is a nonsmoking property.

1808 New Hampshire Ave. NW (btw. S and Swann sts.), Washington, DC 20009. www.swannhouse.com. ✆ **202/265-4414.** Fax 202/265-6755. 12 units, all with private bathroom (4 with whirlpool). $175–$395, depending on unit and season. General policy 2-night minimum weekends, 3-night minimum holiday weekends, but always ask. Extended-stay and government rates available. Extra person $35. Rates include expanded continental breakfast. AE, DISC, MC, V. Limited off-street parking $16. Metro: Dupont Circle (North/Q St. exit). No children 12 and under. **Amenities:** Outdoor pool. *In room:* A/C, TV, CD player, hair dryer, MP3 docking station, Wi-Fi (free).

Moderate

Carlyle Suites ★★ ✦   Spacious accommodations with small but nearly complete kitchens (with stovetops, but no ovens) and dining nooks make Carlyle Suites a good choice for families and for long-term guests. (**FYI:** A Safeway is a short walk away.) State Department visitors and other international travelers are frequent guests. The eight-story property occupies a converted Art Deco landmark building on a fairly quiet residential street near Dupont Circle. Art Deco flourishes turn up in the stylized chrome room numbers on guest room doors and in cleverly designed moldings and lighting fixtures in hallways. All suites are studios, but some include a sleeper sofa; the largest, the corner suites whose numbers end in "33" or "37" on every floor, are spacious enough that the sofa can be placed in a little niche of its own. In addition to its restaurant/bar, the Carlyle has a separate cafe open for breakfast and Sunday jazz brunch. On the lower level is a laundry room with coin-op washer/dryers and vending machines. The hotel's location is ideal for exploring Dupont Circle attractions. The Carlyle is nonsmoking.

1731 New Hampshire Ave. NW (betw. R and S sts.), Washington, DC 20009. www.carlylesuites. com. ☎ **800/964-5377** or 202/234-3200. Fax 202/387-0085. 170 units. From $129 classic studio suite off season to $349 grand studio suite with sleep sofa in high season. Extra person $20. Children 18 and under stay free in parent's room. AE, MC, V. Free parking (25 spaces available). Metro: Dupont Circle. Pets welcome (no fee). **Amenities:** Restaurant; bar; concierge; complimentary access to nearby state-of-the-art fitness center; room service. *In room:* A/C, TV w/pay movies, fridge, hair dryer, microwave, Wi-Fi (free).

The Dupont Circle Hotel ★ ✦   This hotel gets high marks for convenience (it's right on Dupont Circle), service, and comfort. A 2009–10 renovation added a ninth floor ("Level Nine") and a duplex Presidential Suite (the only such in the city), and put an urban-chic spin on guest-room decor and amenities. Striped carpeting, leather headboards, and dark woods and fabrics lend rooms an overall handsome and streamlined look—a look, actually, that applies throughout the hotel, including in the bar, the restaurant, and the lobby. Bathrooms have heated marble floors; most have showers only. Despite its prime location in a sometimes-raucous neighborhood, the hotel is designed to guard against rude intrusions, its guest rooms insulated from the noise. But if you want to see what's going on out there, ask for a room overlooking Dupont Circle; streets lined with cafes, bookstores, galleries, bars, and boutiques surround the hotel. The Dupont is nonsmoking.

1500 New Hampshire Ave. NW (across from Dupont Circle), Washington, DC 20036. www.doyle collection.com/dupont. ☎ **866/534-6835** or 202/483-6000. Fax 202/328-3265. 327 units. From $239 double; from $650 suite. Extra person $20. Children 17 and under stay free in parent's room. AE, DC, DISC, MC, V. Parking $32. Metro: Dupont Circle (either exit). Dogs 20 lb. or under allowed, with flat $150 nonrefundable fee. **Amenities:** Restaurant; bar; babysitting; children's programs; concierge; concierge-level rooms; state-of-the-art fitness center w/cardio and weight machines; room service. *In room:* A/C, TV, hair dryer, minibar, MP3 docking station, Wi-Fi (free).

Embassy Suites Washington, D.C. ★ ☺   This well-placed hotel offers great value within walking distance of Georgetown and Dupont Circle. A tropical eight-story atrium is the setting for an ample complimentary breakfast, as well as complimentary cocktails and light snacks every evening.

Every unit is a two-room suite. The living room holds a full-size sofa bed, 32-inch plasma TV, easy chair, and table and chairs. The bedroom lies at the back of the suite, overlooking a quiet courtyard or the street; a king-size bed or two queen-size beds, a TV, an armchair, and a bureau furnish this space. Between the living room and the bedroom are the bathroom, a small closet, and a microwave and minifridge. Request a room on the eighth or ninth floor for views of Georgetown and beyond; request an "executive corner suite" for a slightly larger unit. Another plus: Free Internet is available at nine mobile kiosks throughout the public area and at three business center computers.

1250 22nd St. NW (btw. M and N sts.), Washington, DC 20037. www.washingtondc.embassy suites.com. 🕾 **800/EMBASSY** (362-2779) or 202/857-3388. Fax 202/293-3173. 318 suites. Peak $269–$369 double; off-peak $169–$259 double. Rates include full breakfast and evening reception. Ask for AAA discounts or check the website for best rates. Extra person $20 weekdays, $25 weekends. Children 18 and under stay free in parent's room. AE, DC, DISC, MC, V. Parking $34.35. Metro: Dupont Circle (19th St. exit) or Foggy Bottom. **Amenities:** Restaurant; bar; concierge; state-of-the-art fitness center w/indoor pool and whirlpool; mobile and free Internet kiosks in public area and business center; room service. *In room:* A/C, TV w/pay movies, fridge, hair dryer, microwave, Wi-Fi ($13/day).

Helix, a Kimpton Hotel ★   A recent sprucing-up refreshed this hotel's decor of eye-popping patterns and bright colors. Guest rooms have a minimalist feel; the platform bed is placed behind sheer drapes in an alcove (in the king deluxe rooms), leaving the two-person settee, a triangular desk, and the flatscreen TV out in the open. Roomiest are the 18 suites, each with a separate bedroom and slate-blue sectional sofas in the living room. Specialty rooms include "Eats" rooms, which have Italian cafe tables, bar stools, and a fully equipped kitchenette; and kid-friendly "Bunk" rooms that have a separate bunk bed area with a TV/DVD player combo. The Helix Lounge is popular with locals, especially from May to October, when its outdoor patio is open. The Helix is nonsmoking.

1430 Rhode Island Ave. NW (btw. 14th and 15th sts.), Washington, DC 20005. www.hotelhelix.com. 🕾 **800/706-1202** or 202/462-9001. Fax 202/521-2714. 178 units. $149–$329 double. Add $30 for specialty rooms, $100 for suites. Best rates usually Fri–Sun. Extra person $20. Children 17 and under stay free in parent's room. Rates include hosted evening "bubbly hour" (champagne). AE, DC, DISC, MC, V. Parking $36. Metro: McPherson Sq. (Vermont St./White House exit). Pets welcome. **Amenities:** Bar/cafe; babysitting; exercise room; room service. *In room:* A/C, TV/DVD, CD player, fridge, hair dryer, minibar, Wi-Fi (free).

Madera, a Kimpton Hotel ★   The Madera fancies itself a kind of ecoconscious *pied-à-terre* for travelers. Guest rooms are large, with those on the New Hampshire Avenue side offering balconies and city views. If you have trouble sleeping, ask for a higher-up room on this side, because you're directly over the entrance to the restaurant, **Firefly.** Or ask for a back-of-the-house room on floors 6 through 10, from which Rock Creek Park and the Washington National Cathedral can be seen. All rooms are comfortable and furnished with beds whose headboards are giant dark-wood panels inset with a patch of vibrant blue padded mohair. Other distinct touches: pillows covered in animal print or satiny fabrics, grass-cloth-like wall coverings, and black granite with chrome bathroom vanities. This Kimpton hotel's specialty rooms include "Snack" rooms (studio with kitchenette and grocery shopping service), "Tranquility" rooms (with personal massage chair), and "Cardio" rooms (with treadmill, exercise bike, or elliptical steps). Madera is nonsmoking.

1310 New Hampshire Ave. NW (btw. N and O sts.), Washington, DC 20036. www.hotel madera.com. (©) **800/430-1202** or 202/296-7600. Fax 202/293-2476. 82 units. $149–$439 double. Add $40 for a specialty room. For best rates, call direct to the hotel or go to its website. Extra person $20. Children 17 and under stay free in parent's room. Rates include complimentary morning coffee (6–9am) and hosted evening wine hour. AE, DC, DISC, MC, V. Parking $38. Metro: Dupont Circle (South/19th St. exit). Pets welcome. **Amenities:** Restaurant/ bar; babysitting; bikes; children's amenity program; concierge; complimentary access to the nearby Gold's Gym; room service. *In room:* A/C, TV w/pay movies, hair dryer, minibar, MP3 docking station, Wi-Fi (free).

Rouge, a Kimpton Hotel ★

An extensive renovation in 2011 traded out the Rouge's retro feel and replaced it with a more chic look, but don't worry—the place is more rouge than ever, from the red terrazzo tile floor in the lobby to the guests rooms' red faux-leather headboards and bed frames covered with red-piping-bordered white duvets. As before the dressing room holds an Orange Crush–colored dresser, whose contents include a built-in minibar and its scarlet goodies, such as red wax lips. Rooms are spacious enough to easily accommodate Italian-style lounge chairs, pedestal nightstands modeled after Grecian

A chic guest room at the Rouge in Dupont Circle.

columns, a huge mirror positioned to reflect the living-room-like space, and a 10-foot-long mahogany desk. Ask about the specialty rooms, my favorite of which is the Bunk Room; the space includes an area for Mom and Dad and a cozy little nest of a bunkbed for the kids, with drapes to pull closed for privacy and secrets, and a tiny fridge that one can stock with kiddie treats. Rouge is nonsmoking.

1315 16th St. NW (at Massachusetts Ave. and Scott Circle), Washington, DC 20036. www.rouge hotel.com. © **800/738-1202** or 202/232-8000. Fax 202/667-9827. 137 units. $149–$359 double. Add $40 for a specialty room. Best rates available on the website or by calling the toll-free reservations number and asking for promotional price. Extra person $20. Rates include complimentary bloody marys and cold pizza weekend mornings 10–11am and hosted evening wine hour weeknights 5–6pm. Children 17 and under stay free in parent's room. AE, DC, DISC, MC, V. Parking $36. Metro: Dupont Circle (South/19th St. exit). Pets welcome and pampered. **Amenities:** Restaurant/bar; children's amenity program; modest-size fitness center; room service. *In room:* A/C, TV w/pay movies, CD/DVD player, hair dryer, minibar, Wi-Fi (free).

Topaz, a Kimpton Hotel ★ The Topaz lies on a quiet residential street whose front-of-the-house windows overlook picturesque town houses. That traditional exterior contrasts with the look you'll find inside: exotica, or at least that's what the designer has in mind. The guest rooms are "one part Moroccan Bazaar and one part Le Cirque," according to the designer's statement. So look for headboards swathed in deep blue velvet, silver accent pillows, carved wooden drapery valances, and plentiful use of royal blue, purple, and pale green colors. The guest rooms haven't changed shape—they're still unusually large, averaging 400 square feet, and half have alcoves and separate dressing rooms. Topaz is nonsmoking.

1733 N St. NW (btw. 17th and 18th sts., next to the Hotel Tabard Inn [see below]), Washington, DC 20036. www.topazhotel.com. © **800/775-1202** or 202/393-3000. Fax 202/785-9581. 99 units. $149–$369 double; $40 more for specialty rooms. It is very likely you can get a much lower rate by calling direct to the hotel or by booking a reservation online. Extra person $25. Children 17 and under stay free in parent's room. Rates include complimentary morning Power Hour serving energy potions, and hosted evening wine reception. AE, DC, DISC, MC, V. Parking $38. Metro: Dupont Circle (North/Q St. NW). Pets welcome. **Amenities:** Bar/restaurant; babysitting;

bikes; children's amenity program; concierge; access to nearby health club ($5 per guest); room service. *In room:* A/C, TV w/pay movies, CD/DVD player, hair dryer, minibar, MP3 docking station, Wi-Fi (free).

Inexpensive

Hotel Tabard Inn ★ If you favor the offbeat and personal over cookie-cutter chains, try the Tabard. Named for the hostelry in Chaucer's *Canterbury Tales*, the Tabard is one of the oldest continuously operating hotels in the city, having opened in 1922. The heart of the ground floor is the dark-paneled lounge, with worn furniture, a fireplace, and the original beamed ceiling. Washingtonians come here for drinks nightly, jazz on Sundays, and to linger before or after dining in the charming **Tabard Inn** restaurant (p. 208).

From the lounge, the inn leads you up and down stairs, along dim corridors, and through nooks and crannies to guest rooms furnished with antiques and flea-market finds. Perhaps the most eccentric room is the spacious top-floor "penthouse," which has skylights, exposed brick walls, an ample living room, and the feel of a New York City loft. Quaint as it appears, the Tabard is progressive when it comes to going green: Its roofs are planted with herb and rose gardens, and the Tabard's restaurant uses the fresh herbs in its cooking; the inn hopes soon to install solar panels to provide hot water heating. The Tabard Inn is also nonsmoking. ***Note:*** Because of stairs and narrow hallways, the inn is not easily accessible to guests with disabilities.

1739 N St. NW (btw. 17th and 18th sts.), Washington, DC 20036. www.tabardinn.com. © **202/785-1277.** Fax 202/785-6173. 38 units, 29 with private bathroom (6 with shower only). $125–$145 single with shared bathroom; $165–$250 single with private bathroom. Add $20 for 2nd person. Rates include continental breakfast. AE, DC, DISC, MC, V. Limited street parking, plus nearby public parking garages. Metro: Dupont Circle (South/19th St. exit). Small and confined pets accepted for a $20 fee. **Amenities:** Restaurant w/lounge (free live jazz Sun evenings); free computer access in lobby (fax and printing available for small fee); hair dryer and iron available at front desk; free access to nearby YMCA w/extensive facilities that include indoor pool, indoor track, and racquetball/basketball courts. *In room:* A/C, Wi-Fi (free).

FOGGY BOTTOM/WEST END

This section of town is halfway between the White House and Georgetown; Foggy Bottom lies south of Pennsylvania Avenue, and the West End north. Together the neighborhoods are home to town-house-lined streets, the George Washington University, International Monetary Fund offices, World Bank headquarters, and mostly all-suites and upscale lodging choices.

Best for: Parents visiting their kids at GW, international business travelers, and those who desire proximity to the Kennedy Center, which is also located here.

Drawbacks: There are 11,000 students who attend GW and who sometimes make their presence known throughout the Foggy Bottom neighborhood in ways you'd rather they wouldn't. On the flip side, the West End might seem too quiet if you like being where the action is.

Very Expensive

Park Hyatt Washington, D.C. ★★ This luxury hotel features spacious lodging, from the "Park Deluxe" rooms measuring 408 square feet to the

"Premier Park Deluxe" rooms that measure 618 square feet. Wood-slat blinds are on the windows, puffy down duvets cover the beds, and decorative features include comfy, creamy-yellow leather chairs and coffee-table books on American culture, like Annie Leibowitz's photo portraits of American musicians. The flatscreen television in the Premier Park Deluxe rooms pivots in the wall to present an antique chessboard on its reverse side (decorative, not functional). Bathrooms are spalike, with floor, ceiling, and walls of dark gray limestone. Everything is out in the open, from the deep soaking tub to its adjoining rain shower.

Don't miss the hotel's Tea Cellar, complete with a tea humidor for storing the cellar's collection of rare and single-estate teas, and the restaurant, the **Blue Duck Tavern** (p. 210), which serves food that's out of this world. The hotel has two guest rooms for smokers; otherwise the property is nonsmoking.

1201 24th St. NW (at M St.), Washington, DC 20037. www.parkhyattwashington.com. $\copyright$ **800/778-7477** or 202/789-1234. Fax 202/419-6795. 216 units. From $249 Park Deluxe Room double; from $299 Premier Park Deluxe double; from $750 suites. For best rates, go to the hotel's website or call the main reservation number. Children 16 and under stay free in parent's room. Families should ask about the family plan. AE, DC, DISC, MC, V. Parking $42. Metro: Foggy Bottom. Pets welcome, with $150 fee per stay. **Amenities:** Restaurant; bar/lounge; tea cellar; bikes; concierge; fitness center w/whirlpool, indoor pool, and spa; room service. *In room:* A/C, TV, hair dryer, mini-bar, Wi-Fi ($10.95/day).

The Ritz-Carlton, Washington, D.C. ★★★

The Ritz staff is always looking after you: Doormen greet you effusively when you arrive, and poised young waitresses swan around the bar, gracefully serving cocktails. Some guest rooms overlook the hotel's peaceful landscaped courtyard; rooms on the outside perimeter view the West End's cityscape. Deluxe rooms are spacious (standard guest rooms average 450 sq. ft.) and richly furnished with decorative inlaid wooden furniture, a comfy armchair and ottoman, a flatscreen TV, and pretty artwork. Large marble bathrooms offer ample counter space, a separate bathtub and shower stall, and the toilet in its own room behind a louvered door. The phone features a button for summoning the "technology butler" (a complimentary, 24/7 service for guests with computer questions). For a $15 fee, guests may use the two-level, 100,000-square-foot **Sports Club/LA,** the best hotel health club in the city (guests staying on the concierge level receive complimentary access). The hotel's **Westend Bistro by Eric Ripert** (p. 212) is one of the hottest restaurants in town. The Ritz is nonsmoking.

1150 22nd St. NW (at M St.), Washington, DC 20037. www.ritzcarlton.com/hotels/washington_dc. $\copyright$ **800/241-3333** or 202/835-0500. Fax 202/835-1588. 300 units. Weekdays from $599 double, from $699 suite; weekends from $329 double, from $459 suite. Ask about discount packages. AE, DC, DISC, MC, V. Valet parking $45. Metro: Foggy Bottom. Pets accepted and pampered (no fee). **Amenities:** Restaurant; bar/lounge; concierge; concierge-level rooms; health club and spa; room service. *In room:* A/C, TV w/pay movies, fridge, hair dryer, minibar, MP3 docking station, Wi-Fi ($9.95/day).

Moderate

One Washington Circle Hotel This hotel attracts corporate guests and families alike, thanks to its outdoor pool; its rave-worthy in-house restaurant (**Circle Bistro**); its prime location near Georgetown, downtown, and the Metro;

and each suite's full kitchen with oven, microwave, and refrigerator (about 10% of rooms have kitchenettes). Five types of suites are available, ranging in size from 390 to 710 square feet. The one-bedroom suites have a sofa bed and dining area; all rooms are spacious, evince a contemporary look, and have walkout balconies, some overlooking the Circle and its statue of George Washington. Guest rooms have double-paned windows, which help keep the sounds of the city at bay; for the quietest rooms of all, ask to stay on the L Street side. Call the hotel directly for best rates; mention a GWU affiliation if you have one and you may receive a discount. The hotel is nonsmoking.

1 Washington Circle NW (btw. 22nd and 23rd sts. NW), Washington, DC 20037. www.the circlehotel.com. © **800/424-9671** or 202/872-1680. Fax 202/887-4989. 151 units. Weekdays $159–$299 smallest suites, $199–$339 largest suites; weekends $109–$199 smallest suites, $159–$239 largest suites. Call hotel or look on the website to get best rates. Extra person $20. Children 12 and under stay free in parent's room. AE, DC, MC, V. Parking $30. Metro: Foggy Bottom. **Amenities:** Restaurant; bar; fitness center; outdoor pool; room service. *In room:* A/C, TV w/pay movies, iHome docking station, hair dryer, free Internet, kitchen (in most suites; w/ oven, fridge, microwave).

The River Inn ★ 🏨   The River Inn is a sweet little secret that lies on a quiet residential street of town houses near both the Kennedy Center and Georgetown. Guest rooms feature pillowtop mattresses on beds, comfortable armchairs with soft leather footstools, ebony armoires, and a cool chaise longue that unfolds into a sofa bed. Suites include a dressing room and a separate, well-equipped kitchen. All but 31 suites combine the bedroom and living-room areas, and include an oversize desk that doubles as a workspace and dining table in a corner off the kitchen. Those 31 suites are roomy one-bedrooms, with an expansive living room (with sleep sofa) and a separate bedroom that holds a king-size bed and a second TV. Best are the suites on the upper floors, offering views of the Potomac River and, from some (no. 804, for example), the Washington Monument. The River Inn is nonsmoking.

924 25th St. NW (btw. K and I sts.), Washington, DC 20037. www.theriverinn.com. © **888/874-0100** or 202/337-7600. Fax 202/337-6520. 125 units. Peak weekdays $299–$354 double, weekends $149–$199 double; off-peak weekdays $159–$255 double, weekends $99–$149 double. Add $35 for 1-bedroom suite. Extra person $20. Children 17 and under stay free in parent's room. AE, DC, DISC, MC, V. Parking $34 plus 18% tax. Metro: Foggy Bottom. Pets under 40 lb. welcome for nonrefundable $150 fee. **Amenities:** Restaurant; bar; bikes; concierge; small fitness center; room service. *In room:* A/C, TV w/pay movies, fridge, hair dryer, microwave, MP3 docking station, Wi-Fi (free).

GEORGETOWN

Bustling day and night with shoppers and tourists, Georgetown has surprisingly few hotels. The city's most sublime accommodations, as well as one that I believe to be the best value in town, are among your options.

Best for: Shopaholics, and parents and academics visiting Georgetown University.

Drawbacks: Crowds throng sidewalks; cars snarl traffic daily. College kids and 20-somethings party hearty here nightly, but especially on weekends.

Very Expensive

Four Seasons ★★★ ☺   The Four Seasons tops my list for "best hotel in Washington." (It shares that billing with the **Jefferson,** p. 293.) The kind of service you receive from staff is unparalleled; the hotel keeps track of repeat guests' preferences and trains staff to recognize guests and greet them by name. The concierge team knows its stuff. Clientele draws from the world's wealthiest and most distinguished, from Hollywood actors to Middle Eastern statesmen. Located at the mouth of Georgetown, the hotel's original (east) wing holds spacious guest rooms, with custom-crafted furniture. Most rooms have sleeper sofas. Choose the west wing for an ultraprivate feel and larger rooms (625 to 4,000 square feet); choose the east wing if you like being closer to the action—the original part of the hotel is where you'll find Michael Mina's immensely popular **Bourbon Steak** (p. 213) restaurant and the bar, as well as the newly renovated and reopened Seasons, known especially as a power-breakfast and -lunch spot. The hotel's fabulous spa is also located in the main building.

2800 Pennsylvania Ave. NW (which becomes M St. a block farther along), Washington, DC 20007. www.fourseasons.com/washington. (✆ **800/332-3442** or 202/342-0444. Fax 202/944-2076. 222 units. Weekdays $595–$895 double; $950–$15,000 suite; weekends from $395 double, from $625 suite. Extra person $50. Children 18 and under stay free in parent's room. AE, DC, DISC, MC, V.

 Inside & Outside the Beltway: Beyond-D.C. Hotel Options

Normally, I don't like to recommend hotel options outside the capital, since I believe that to get a real sense of a place, you need to wake up in it. Circumstances sometimes dictate otherwise, however. If you have an early flight to catch and want to be close to the airport, or if you're having a hard time finding available and/ or affordable rooms at D.C. hotels, look to the following options.

In northern Virginia, Rte. 1, also known as Jefferson Davis Highway within Crystal City limits, is lined with hotels for every budget. Crystal City and its Northern Virginia neighbors are also prime locations if you want to stay near Ronald Reagan Washington National Airport, which is less than a mile away. (National Airport, by the way, is only 4 miles from downtown Washington.) Whether you're looking for vacancies or affordable lodging, or simply want to guarantee a free shuttle and a quick trip between your hotel and National Airport, go to the Metropolitan Washington Airports Authority website (**www.mwaa.com**), click on "Travel Tips," and then click on "Local Hotels," in the Local Tourism section on that page, to discover a long listing of hotels. One of the closest to the airport is the **Crystal City Marriott,** 1999 Jefferson Davis Hwy. (✆ **703/413-5500**).

Likewise, if you want to stay as close as possible to Washington Dulles International Airport, refer to the same website, but click on the "Travel Tips" line in the Dulles box, then the "Local Hotels" line within Local Tourism. Of the hotels listed, one is actually located on airport property: the **Washington Dulles Marriott,** 45020 Aviation Dr. (✆ **703/471-9500**).

Finally, the Baltimore–Washington International Thurgood Marshall Airport's website, www.bwiairport.com, currently lists only one hotel, the **Four Points by Sheraton,** 7032 Elm Rd. (✆ **410/859-3300**), which is the sole hotel located on BWI Airport property.

Parking $50. Metro: Foggy Bottom. Pets accepted up to 15 lb. **Amenities:** 2 restaurants; bar; bikes; boutique; children's amenities program; concierge; extensive state-of-the-art fitness club and spa w/personal trainers, lap pool (indoor), facials, and synchronized massage; room service. *In room:* A/C, TV w/pay movies, CD/DVD player, hair dryer, minibar, MP3 docking station, Wi-Fi ($10–$15/day).

The Ritz-Carlton Georgetown, Washington, D.C. ★★★   This Ritz is

exclusively small, designed like a sophisticated refuge in the middle of wild and woolly Georgetown. Privacy-seeking celebrities and romancing couples love it. Look for the 130-foot-high smokestack to guide you to the hotel, which is built on the site of a historic incinerator and incorporates the smokestack into its design. The lobby's front brick wall is original to the incinerator, the restaurant is called Fahrenheit, the bar Degrees, and the signature drink the "Fahrenheit 5 Martini." Guest rooms lie one level below the lobby, accessible by an elevator that requires a key card to operate, so anyone visiting you must either be escorted by you or a staff person. Large guest rooms average 450 square feet and feature lots of dark-wood furniture and accents. Bathrooms, likewise, are spacious and deluxe, with a marble vanity, a separate tub and shower, and fancy wood shelving. More than a third of the rooms are one-bedroom suites. The Ritz is nonsmoking.

3100 South St. NW (at 31st St., btw. K and M sts.), Washington, DC 20007. www.ritzcarlton.com/hotels/georgetown. ℂ **800/241-3333** or 202/912-4100. Fax 202/912-4199. 86 units. Weekdays from $699 double, from $799 suite; weekends from $459 double, from $599 suite. Check the website or call the toll-free reservations number for weekend packages and specials. AE, DC, DISC, MC, V. Valet parking $39. Metro: Foggy Bottom. Pets under 30 lb. accepted (no fee). **Amenities:** Restaurant; bar; concierge; state-of-the-art fitness center and spa; room service. *In room:* A/C, TV w/pay movies, CD/DVD player, hair dryer, minibar, Wi-Fi ($9.95/day).

Moderate

Georgetown Suites ★ 🖋   This hotel offers great value for its location and rates: friendly service; clean, bright, and spacious lodging; and up-to-date amenities. It has two sites within a block of each other. The main building is on quiet, residential 30th Street, steps away from Georgetown's action. The Harbor Building, on 29th Street, is situated next to Whitehurst Freeway and across from the Washington Harbor complex, so it's a bit noisier.

Accommodations at both sites have living rooms, dining areas, and fully equipped kitchens; bedding with fluffy duvets; and high-definition flatscreen televisions. Half are studios (550 sq. ft.), half are one-bedroom suites (800 sq. ft.). Renovations in 2011 upgraded bathrooms and replaced furniture, and in 2012 renovated kitchens. The biggest and best suites are the three two-level, two-bedroom town houses attached to the main building. Also recommended are two penthouse suites with their own terraces overlooking Georgetown rooftops.

1111 30th St. NW (just below M St.) and 1000 29th St. NW (at K St.), Washington, DC 20007. www.georgetownsuites.com. ℂ **800/348-7203** or 202/298-7800. Fax 202/600-2802. 220 units. Weekdays $185 studio, $215 1-bedroom suite; weekends $155 studio, $185 1-bedroom suite; penthouse suites from $350; town houses from $425. Rollaway or sleeper sofa $10 extra. Rates include continental breakfast. AE, DC, DISC, MC, V. Limited parking $20. Metro: Foggy Bottom. **Amenities:** Executive-level rooms; small exercise room. *In room:* A/C, TV, CD player, hair dryer, kitchen (w/fridge, microwave, and dishwasher), Wi-Fi (free).

WOODLEY PARK

This Connecticut Avenue–centered upper northwest enclave is a residential neighborhood of little stores and restaurants, the National Zoo, and Washington's biggest hotel.

Best for: Families who like a tamer experience than found downtown and proximity to Rock Creek Park and the zoo. Business travelers attending a meeting in one of Woodley Park's big hotels.

Drawbacks: This area may be a little too quiet for some, especially at night.

Expensive

Omni Shoreham Hotel ★ ☺ Though its size (11 acres, 836 rooms) and ample meeting space make this hotel popular among conferencegoers and other groups, the Shoreham is also a favorite for families, who love its access to beautiful Rock Creek Park, its proximity to the National Zoo, its seasonal outdoor pools, and its children's gifts at check-in. Back-of-the-house guest rooms overlook the park and beyond—you can spot the Washington Monument from some rooms. The Shoreham rightfully boasts its status as the city's largest AAA four-diamond hotel, as well as its membership in Historic Hotels of America. Built in 1930, it has been the scene of inaugural balls for every president since FDR. Do you believe in ghosts? Ask about room no. 870, the haunted suite (available for $3,000 a night).

2500 Calvert St. NW (near Connecticut Ave.), Washington, DC 20008. www.omnishoreham hotel.com. © **800/843-6664** or 202/234-0700. Fax 202/265-7972. 836 units. $199–$359 double; from $350 suite. Call the hotel directly for best rates. Extra person $30. Children 17 and under stay free in parent's room. AE, DC, DISC, MC, V. Valet parking $30. Metro: Woodley Park–Zoo. Pets under 25 lb. allowed; $50 cleaning fee. **Amenities:** Restaurant; bar/lounge; children's amenities program; concierge; fitness center w/heated outdoor pool, separate kids' pool, whirlpool, and spa services by appointment; room service. *In room:* A/C, TV w/pay movies, hair dryer, Wi-Fi (free).

Washington Marriott Wardman Park ★ This is Washington's biggest hotel, resting on 16 acres just down the street from the National Zoo and several good restaurants. Its size and location (the Woodley Park–Zoo Metro station is literally at its doorstep) make it a good choice for conventions, tour groups, and individual travelers. The hotel's oldest section, built in 1918, houses about 100 rooms, each with high ceilings, ornate crown moldings, and an assortment of antique French and English furnishings. The main building completed a major renovation of all guest rooms in 2008, updating their look and furnishings by adding multilayered, Marriott-brand bedding; flatscreen TVs; and long desks with high-backed chairs. The overhaul also installed new state-of-the-art equipment in the fitness center and vastly improved the in-house restaurant, now called the Stone's Throw. Harry's Bar, meanwhile, serves well as a comfortable place to have a drink after your meeting. The entire hotel is nonsmoking.

2660 Woodley Rd. NW (at Connecticut Ave.), Washington, DC 20008. www.marriott.com/ wasdt. © **800/228-9290** or 202/328-2000. Fax 202/234-0015. 1,314 units. Weekdays $309 double; weekends $119–$289 double; $350–$2,500 suite. Children 17 and under stay free in parent's room. AE, DC, DISC, MC, V. Valet parking $37; self-parking $32. Metro: Woodley Park–Zoo. Pets under 20 lb. accepted, but charges may apply; call for details. **Amenities:** Restaurant;

2 bars; babysitting; concierge; concierge-level rooms; well-equipped fitness center w/outdoor heated pool and sun deck; room service. *In room:* A/C, TV w/pay movies, hair dryer, Internet ($13/day).

Inexpensive

Woodley Park Guest House   This charming, 15-room B&B offers cozy lodging, low rates, a super location, and a personable staff. Guests hail from around the globe, a fact that inspired the owners to add a globe to the breakfast room, around which guests often gather to point out exactly where they live: Brazil, Seattle, the Arctic Circle. Special features of the guesthouse include a wicker-furnished, tree-shaded front porch; exposed, century-old brick walls; beautiful antiques; and original art. (The innkeepers buy works only from artists who have stayed at the guesthouse.) Rooms have either one or two twins, one double, or one queen-size bed. The guesthouse benefits from its across-the-street proximity to the **Washington Marriott Wardman Park** (see above), where airport shuttles and taxis are on hand. The Woodley Park–Zoo Metro stop, good restaurants, Rock Creek Park, and the National Zoo are all a short walk away. If you're interested in staying closer to the heart of the city, consider the owners' other excellent B&B, the **Embassy Circle Guest House** (www. dcinns.com), which is located in the Dupont Circle/Embassy Row neighborhood. Both guesthouses are nonsmoking.

2647 Woodley Rd. NW (at Connecticut Ave.), Washington, DC 20008. www.dcinns.com. ℂ **866/ 667-0218** or 202/667-0218. Fax 202/667-1080. 15 units, 11 with private bathroom (shower only), 4 singles with shared bathroom. Peak $145 room with shared bath to $250 room with a queen bed and private bath; off-peak $135 room with shared bath to $175 room with queen bed and private bath. Rates include continental breakfast. AE, MC, V. Seasonal discounts may be available in winter and mid-July/Aug. Limited on-site parking $20. Metro: Woodley Park–Zoo. Well-behaved children 12 and over accepted. *In room:* A/C, Wi-Fi (free).

GLOVER PARK

North of Georgetown, south of the Washington National Cathedral, Glover Park is a residential neighborhood of family homes and group houses for Georgetown and American University students, all of whom gather at the bars and low-priced eateries that line the main drag, Wisconsin Avenue NW. The couple of hotels located here are informal and moderately priced.

Best for: Visiting professors and parents of college-age children at nearby American, George Washington, and Georgetown universities; those on business at area embassies; and families on vacation.

Drawbacks: Glover Park has public bus transportation but no Metro stop.

Moderate

Savoy Suites Hotel ★ ✦   Situated on a hill above Georgetown, the Savoy's elevated location means its back rooms on the top floors offer a sweeping vista of distant Washington landmarks, from the Washington Monument to the Capitol dome. That view is the best feature of guest rooms. So decor is short on charm, maybe, but the Savoy does deliver certain remarkable perks, among them free parking (!), a free shuttle to and from the Woodley Park–Zoo Metro station (Glover Park has buses but no subway service), complimentary access to the nearby Washington Sports Club, Tempur-pedic bedding in all guest rooms, kitchens (cooktop, microwave, refrigerator) in 21 suites, and Jacuzzis in 23 suites. In 2011 the Savoy gutted bathrooms, replacing everything, from tubs to vanities. The Savoy's "Going Green" program uses ecofriendly cleaning agents in housekeeping and a comprehensive recycling practice. The Savoy is nonsmoking.

2505 Wisconsin Ave. NW (at Calvert St.), Washington, DC 20007. www.savoysuites.com. ✆ **800/944-7477** or 202/337-9700. Fax 202/448-2301. 150 units. $109–$359 double. Best rates most likely Thurs–Fri and Sun; check the website for primo deals. Extra person $20. Children 18 and under stay free in parent's room. AE, DC, MC, V. Free parking. Metro: Free shuttle runs throughout day between hotel and Woodley Park–Zoo station. **Amenities:** Restaurant; bar/lounge; complimentary passes to nearby full-service fitness center; room service. *In room:* A/C, TV w/pay movies, fridge, hair dryer, Wi-Fi (free).

PRACTICAL MATTERS: THE HOTEL SCENE

The Big Picture

"You can't really be a hotel chain in America without Washington," said Richard Branson, owner of Virgin Hotels (and founder of the Virgin Group of airlines and other businesses). Quoted in a January 31, 2011, *Washington Post* Business section article about Washington's lusty lodging market, Branson's remark points up a basic fact about the city's hotel possibilities: If you have a favorite brand of hotel chain, you're likely to find it represented here, from the big boys like Marriott (19!), Hilton, and Sheraton, to international chains like Ireland's gracious Doyle and France's chic Sofitel. Kimpton Group Hotels, the un-chainlike chain, now counts 11 hotels in the D.C. area and continues to up the ante on whimsically chic lodging. Hipster brands include Kimpton's Donovan House and W Hotels' W Washington, D.C.

Will Branson's new Virgin Hotels chain of upscale, sophisticated properties soon have a location in the capital? Perhaps, and if it does, it will be joining a crowded market.

Luxury lodging is big business in D.C. Again, the high-end chains are here, including the Four Seasons, two Ritz-Carltons, and the Mandarin Oriental, all vying with each other—and with four exquisite, historic establishments in the Hay-Adams, the St. Regis, the Jefferson, and the Willard InterContinental—for the patronage of the wealthy. Now enter real estate impressario Donald Trump. Trump is creating a grand hotel out of the Old Post Office Pavilion, a historic 1899 structure on Pennsylvania Avenue best known for its clock tower, rising 315 feet skyward. The National Park Service, which operates and maintains the tourable tower, has stated that the tower is absolutely not included in the hotel deal.

Washington also has a number of vital homegrown accommodations, from the romantic Swann House in the Dupont Circle neighborhood to the Georgetown Suites, always a remarkable deal given its buzzing locale.

Inexpensive and moderately priced hotels are always in short supply. In fact, the cheapest rates are found more readily outside the District, in suburban Virginia and Maryland motels and hotels—that's where school groups usually stay.

WHEN all else FAILS

If your luck and time are running out and you still haven't found a place to stay, these ideas are worth a try:

○ **Call one of the free reservations services** listed above. Talk to someone "on location" who can work with you to find a place.

○ **Check out the Vacation Rentals by Owner website.** Go to www.vrbo. com and click on the "DC" option on the map to read about furnished apartments for rent around the city.

○ **Consider house swapping.** Try **HomeLink International** (www. homelink.org), the largest and oldest home-swapping organization, founded in 1953, with more than 13,000 listings worldwide ($119 for a yearly membership).

○ **Call Washington's tourism bureau, Destination D.C.** (℡ **202/789-7000**), and ask the tourist rep for the names and numbers of any **new or**

about-to-open hotels. If the rep isn't sure, ask her to check with the marketing director. Up-and-coming hotels may have available rooms, for the simple reason that few people know about them. Four hotels scheduled to open in D.C. in 2013 included the **Capella Georgetown Hotel,** in Georgetown; **Half Street Hotel,** near Nationals Park, in the Capitol Riverfront neighborhood; an international boutique hotel called **ME Hotel, The Arts at 5th and I,** in the Mount Vernon Triangle neighborhood; and an Ian Schrager/Marriott boutique collaboration, **Edition,** in Adams Morgan.

○ **Consider staying outside the city.** See "Inside & Outside the Beltway: Beyond-D.C. Hotel Options," earlier in this chapter.

Getting the Best Deal

Want the secret for getting the best hotel deal ever in Washington? Easy: Come to Washington when Congress is out, when cherry blossom season is over, or during the blazing hot days of July or August or the icy-cold days of a noninauguration-year January or February. Not possible? Okay, let's put it this way: Don't try to negotiate a good deal for late March or early April (cherry blossom season); hotel reservationists will laugh at you. I've heard them.

Consider these tips, too:

○ Visit on a weekend if you can. Hotels looking to fill rooms vacated by weekday business travelers lower their rates and might be willing to negotiate even further for weekend arrivals.

○ Ask about special rates or other discounts and whether a room less expensive than the first one quoted is available. You may qualify for substantial corporate, government, student, military, senior, or other discounts. Mention membership in AAA, AARP, frequent-flier programs, or trade unions, which may entitle you to special deals as well.

○ Book online. Many hotels offer Internet-only discounts or supply rooms to Priceline, Travelocity, or Expedia at rates lower than the ones you can get through the hotel itself.

- Look into group or long-stay discounts. If you come as part of a large group, you should be able to negotiate a bargain rate because the hotel can then guarantee occupancy in a number of rooms. Likewise, if you're planning a long stay (at least 5 days), you might qualify for a discount. As a general rule, expect 1 night free after a 7-night stay.

- Consider enrolling in hotel "frequent-stay" programs, which aim to win the loyalty of repeat customers. Frequent guests can accumulate points or credits to earn free hotel nights, airline miles, in-room amenities, merchandise, tickets to concerts and events, and discounts on sporting facilities. Perks are awarded not only by many chain hotels and motels (Hilton Honors and Marriott Rewards, to name two), but also by individual inns and B&Bs.

- Finally, whether or not you've gotten the best deal possible on your room rate, you can still save money on incidental costs. D.C. hotels charge unbelievable rates for overnight parking—up to $50 a night at some hotels, plus tax—so if you can avoid driving, you can save yourself quite a bit of money. Avoid dialing direct from hotel phones, which usually have exorbitant rates—as do the room's minibar offerings.

Keep in mind that D.C. hotel sales tax is a whopping 14.5%, merchandise sales tax is 6%, and food and beverage tax is 10%, all of which can rapidly increase the cost of a room.

Reservations Services

If you suffer from information overload and would rather someone else do the research and bargaining, you can always turn to one of these two reputable—and free!—local reservations services:

- **WDCAHotels.com** (www.wdcahotels.com; © **800/554-2220** or 202/289-2220): Formerly known as Washington, D.C. Accommodations, this company has been in business for 28 years and, in addition to finding lodgings, can advise you about transportation and general tourist information, and even work out itineraries.

- **BedandBreakfastDC.com** (www.bedandbreakfastdc.com; © **877/893-3233**): In business since 1978, this organization works with a large selection of private homes, inns, guesthouses, and unhosted furnished apartments to find lodging for visitors.

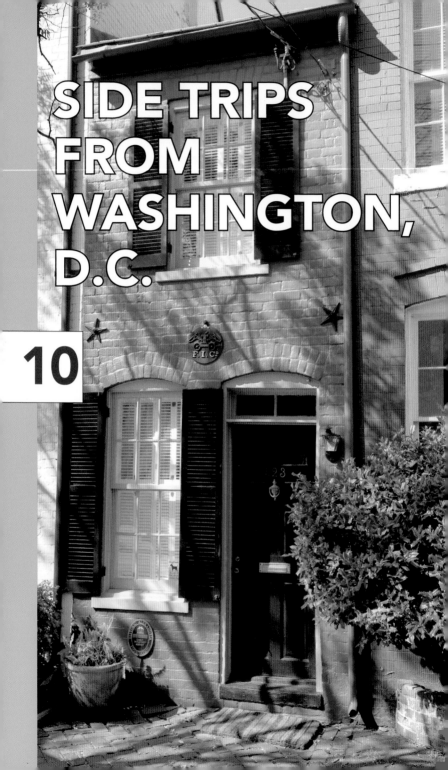

SIDE TRIPS FROM WASHINGTON, D.C.

10

Y ou've come as far as Washington, D.C.—why not travel just a bit farther to visit the home of the man for whom the capital is named? "Washington slept here" is a claim bandied about by many a town. "Washington lived here for 45 years" is a claim only Mount Vernon can make. Located 16 miles south of Washington, D.C., the estate was George Washington's home from 1754 until his death in 1799 (as much as the American Revolution and Washington's stints as the new republic's first president would allow). And where did Washington go to kick up his heels or to worship? In nearby Old Town Alexandria, whose cobblestone streets and historic churches and houses still stand, surrounded now by of-the-moment eateries and chic boutiques. Make time, if you can, for visits to both Old Town and Mount Vernon.

MOUNT VERNON

Only 16 miles south of the capital, George Washington's Southern plantation dates from a 1674 land grant to the president's great-grandfather.

Essentials

GETTING THERE If you're going by car, take any of the bridges over the Potomac River into Virginia and follow the signs pointing the way to National Airport/ Mount Vernon/George Washington Memorial Parkway. Travel south on the George Washington Memorial Parkway, the river always to your left, and pass by National Airport on your right. Continue through Old Town Alexandria, where the parkway is renamed "Washington Street," and head 8 miles farther, until you reach the large circle that fronts Mount Vernon.

You might also take a bus or boat to Mount Vernon. These are narrated bus and boat tours, and their prices **include the price of admission to Mount Vernon.**

Gray Line Buses (www.grayline dc.com; ☎ **800/862-1400,** 301/386-8300, or 202/289-1995 for Union Station) offers three tours daily to Mount Vernon (except on Christmas, Thanksgiving, and New Year's Day). The two 4-hour tours travel past Old Town Alexandria to Mount Vernon; the 9-hour tour travels to Mount Vernon and includes stops in Old Town

ABOVE: **Mount Vernon's 14-room mansion.**
PREVIOUS PAGE: **Historic Alexandria.**

The George Washington Memorial Parkway

Though few people realize it, the George Washington Memorial Parkway is actually a national park. The first section was completed in 1932 to honor the bicentennial of George Washington's birth. The parkway follows the Potomac River, running from Mount Vernon, past Old Town and the nation's capital, and ending at Great Falls, Virginia. Today the parkway is a major commuter route leading into and out of the city. Even the most impatient driver, however, can't help but notice the beautiful scenery and views of the Jefferson and Lincoln memorials and the Washington Monument that you pass along the way.

Alexandria and at Arlington National Cemetery on your return. All tours depart from the bus terminal at Union Station. The 4-hour tours depart at 8am and 1pm and return by 12:30 and 5:30pm, respectively; the longer tour leaves at 8am, returning by 5pm. The ticket kiosk is on the first level of the parking garage. The cost is $65 per adult (ages 12 and older), $20 per child (3-11) for the 9-hour tour, and $55 per adult and $20 per child for the 4-hour tour. The tour is free for children 2 and under. (AAA members receive a 10% discount when they purchase tickets at the Union Station kiosk and show their membership card.) Gray Line offers several other tours, so call for further information or see "Guided Tours," in chapter 11.

The **Spirit of Washington Cruises'** (www.spiritcruises.com; ✆ **866/ 302-2469** or 202/554-8000) *Spirit of Mount Vernon* is a seasonal operation, cruising to Mount Vernon March through October (call or check online for daily schedules, which can vary). The vessel leaves from Pier 4 (6th and Water sts. SW; 3 blocks from the Green Line Metro's Waterfront station) at 8:15am, returning by 3pm. The cost is approximately $48 per adult, $42 per child (ages 6–11; free for younger children), including taxes and surcharges.

Miss Christin, run by the **Potomac Riverboat Company** (www. potomacriverboatco.com; ✆ **877/511-2628** or 703/684-0580), operates Tuesday through Sunday April through August, Friday to Sunday September to mid-October, and Saturday and Sunday mid-October until November 1. It departs at 10:30am for Mount Vernon from the pier adjacent to the Torpedo Factory, where Union and Cameron streets intersect, at Old Town Alexandria's waterfront. The rate is $40 per adult, $20 per child (ages 6–11; free for children 5 and under). Arrive 30 minutes ahead of time at the pier to secure a place on the boat. The narrated trip takes 90 minutes each way, stopping at Gaylord's National Harbor to pick up and discharge passengers. The boat departs Mount Vernon at 4pm to return to Old Town by 5:30pm, via Gaylord's.

And here's a clever way to travel to and from Mount Vernon: The Potomac Riverboat Company and **Bike & Roll** (p. 155) have teamed up to offer **Bike & Boat,** which includes bike rental from Bike & Roll's Old Town Alexandria location at the waterfront, admission to Mount Vernon, and a narrated return trip back to Old Town aboard the *Miss Christin.* You pedal your own way along the Mount Vernon Trail (p. 322) to reach the estate. The package costs $58 for ages 13 and older, $38 ages 6 to 12, and $20 ages 2 to 5.

If you're up for it, you can rent a bike and pedal the 18-mile round-trip distance at your own pace any time of year. See p. 155 for bike rental information.

Finally, it is possible to take **public transportation** to Mount Vernon by riding the Metro to the Yellow Line's Huntington station and proceeding to the lower level, where you catch the Fairfax Connector bus (no. 101) to Mount Vernon. The connector bus departs hourly on weekends, every 30 minutes weekdays; it's a 25-minute ride and costs $1.70. Call ✆ **703/339-7200** or check www.fairfaxconnector.com for schedule information.

Touring the Estate

Mount Vernon Estate and Gardens ★★   If it's beautiful out and you have the time, you could easily spend half a day or more soaking in the life and times of George Washington at Mount Vernon. The centerpiece of a visit to this 500-acre estate is a tour through 14 rooms of the mansion, whose oldest part dates from the 1740s. The plantation was passed down from Washington's great-grandfather, who acquired the land in 1674, to George's half-brother, and eventually to George himself in 1754. Washington proceeded over the next 45 years to expand and fashion the home to his liking, though the American Revolution and his years as president kept Washington away from his beloved estate much of the time.

Start your tour by visiting the estate's modern **Ford Orientation Center** and the **Donald W. Reynolds Museum and Education Center,** located just inside the main gate. Much of the complex is built underground so as not to take away from the estate's pastoral setting. A 15-minute film in the orientation center fills you in on the life and character of George Washington. The education center's 25 galleries and theater presentations, and display of 500 original artifacts, inform you further about Washington's military and presidential careers,

Visitors touring the outbuildings at Mount Vernon.

Mount Vernon's lush gardens.

rounding out the whole story of this heroic, larger-than-life man. It's especially helpful to absorb this information and gain some context for the life and times of Washington before setting off for the mansion, where tours are self-guided. Attendants stationed throughout the house and grounds do provide brief orientations and answer questions; when there's no line, a walk-through takes about 20 minutes. What you see today is a remarkable restoration of the mansion, displaying many original furnishings and objects used by the Washington family. The rooms have been repainted in the original colors favored by George and Martha.

After leaving the house, you can tour the outbuildings: the kitchen, slave quarters, storeroom, smokehouse, overseer's quarters, coach house, and stables. A 4-acre exhibit area called George Washington, Pioneer Farmer includes a replica of Washington's 16-sided barn and fields of crops that he grew (corn, wheat, oats, and so forth). Docents in period costumes demonstrate 18th-century farming methods. At its peak, Mount Vernon was an 8,000-acre working farm, which reminds us that Washington considered himself first and foremost a farmer.

You'll want to walk around the grounds (especially in nice weather) and see the wharf (and take a 40-min. narrated excursion on the Potomac, offered several times a day May–Aug and weekends only in Apr and Sept; $10 per adult, $6 per child 2–11), the slave burial ground, the greenhouse, the lawns and gardens, and the tomb containing George and Martha Washington's sarcophagi (24 other family members are also interred here). In spring 2007, Mount Vernon opened the restored distillery, located 3 miles south of the estate, next to the gristmill.

Special Activities at Mount Vernon

Events at Mount Vernon, especially in the summer, include tours on 18th-century gardens, slave life, Colonial crafts, or archaeology, and, for children, hands-on history programs and treasure hunts. Call or check the website for schedule details.

Costumed staff members demonstrate 18th-century techniques as they operate the gristmill and distillery, which is open April through October. Admission is $4 per adult and $2 per child, or, when combined with your Mount Vernon admission, $2 per adult and $1.50 per child 6 to 11; kids 5 and under enter free. You'll have to get to the gristmill on your own or take the Fairfax Connector bus no. 152 (www.fairfaxconnector.com; ✆ **703/339-7200**).

Celebrations are held at the estate every year on the third Monday in February, the date commemorating Washington's birthday; admission is free.

Mount Vernon belongs to the Mount Vernon Ladies' Association, which purchased the estate for $200,000 in 1858 from John Augustine Washington, great-grandnephew of the first president. Without the group's purchase, the estate might have crumbled and disappeared, for neither the federal government nor the Commonwealth of Virginia wanted to buy the property when it was earlier offered for sale.

Today more than a million people tour the property annually. The best time to visit is off season; during the heavy tourist months (especially in spring, when schoolchildren descend in droves), it's best to arrive in the afternoon, whether on a weekday or weekend, since student groups will have departed by then.

3200 Mount Vernon Memorial Hwy. (mailing address: P.O. Box 110, Mount Vernon, VA 22121). www.mountvernon.org. ✆ **703/780-2000.** Admission $15 adults, $14 seniors, $7 children 6–11, free for children 5 and under. Apr–Aug daily 8am–5pm; Mar and Sept–Oct daily 9am–5pm; Nov–Feb daily 9am–4pm.

Dining & Shopping

Mount Vernon's comprehensive **gift shop** offers a wide range of books, children's toys, holiday items, Mount Vernon private-label food and wine, and Mount Vernon licensed furnishings. A **food court** features indoor and outdoor seating and a menu of baked goods, deli sandwiches, coffee, grilled items, pizza, and cookies. Although you can't **picnic** on the grounds of Mount Vernon, you can drive a mile north on the parkway to Riverside Park, where there are tables and a lawn overlooking the Potomac. However, I recommend the Mount Vernon Inn restaurant.

Demonstrating colonial crafts at Mount Vernon.

A costumed Martha Washington greets guests at Mount Vernon.

Mount Vernon Inn AMERICAN TRADITIONAL Lunch or dinner at the inn is an intrinsic part of the Mount Vernon experience. It's a quaint and charming Colonial-style restaurant, complete with period furnishings and three working fireplaces. The waiters are all in 18th-century costumes. Lunch entrees range from Colonial turkey "pye" (a sort of early American stew served in a crock with garden vegetables and a puffed pastry top) to a pulled-pork barbecue sandwich. There's a full bar, and premium wines are offered by the glass. At dinner tablecloths and candlelight make this a more elegant setting. Choose from soups, perhaps the homemade peanut and chestnut; entrees such as roasted duck served with George Washington's favorite apricot sauce, or roast venison with peppercorn sauce; and dessert, such as whiskey cake or English trifle.

Near the entrance to Mount Vernon Estate and Gardens. www.mountvernon.org. © **703/780-0011.** Reservations recommended for dinner. Main courses lunch $9.25–$12.50, dinner $16–$25. AE, DISC, MC, V. Daily 11am–3:30pm (11:30am–2:30pm weekdays in winter); Mon–Thurs 5–8:30pm; Fri–Sat 5–9pm.

ALEXANDRIA

Old Town Alexandria is about 8 miles S of Washington.

The city of Washington may be named for our first president, but he never lived there. No, he called this other side of the Potomac home from the age of 11, when he joined his half-brother Lawrence, who owned Mount Vernon. Washington came to Alexandria often, helping to survey its 60 acres when he was a lad of 17, training his militia in Market Square, worshiping at Christ Church, and dining and dancing at Gadsby's Tavern.

The town of Alexandria is actually named after John Alexander, the Scot who purchased the land of the present-day town from an English ship captain for "six thousand pounds of Tobacco and Cask." Incorporated in 1749, the town

Alexandria's Market Square.

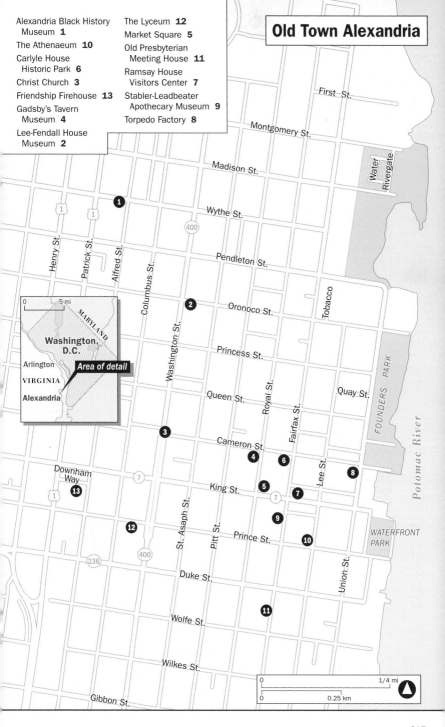

Old Town Alexandria

Alexandria Black History Museum **1**

The Athenaeum **10**

Carlyle House Historic Park **6**

Christ Church **3**

Friendship Firehouse **13**

Gadsby's Tavern Museum **4**

Lee-Fendall House Museum **2**

The Lyceum **12**

Market Square **5**

Old Presbyterian Meeting House **11**

Ramsay House Visitors Center **7**

Stabler-Leadbeater Apothecary Museum **9**

Torpedo Factory **8**

First St.

Montgomery St.

Madison St.

Wythe St.

Henry St.

Patrick St.

Alfred St.

Columbus St.

Pendleton St.

Oronoco St.

Washington St.

Princess St.

Tobacco

Queen St.

Royal St.

Fairfax St.

Quay St.

Cameron St.

Lee St.

King St.

Downham Way

St. Asaph St.

Pitt St.

Prince St.

Duke St.

Union St.

Wolfe St.

Wilkes St.

Gibbon St.

FOUNDERS PARK

Potomac River

WATERFRONT PARK

Water Rivergate

0   5 mi

MARYLAND

Washington, D.C.

Arlington

VIRGINIA

Alexandria

Area of detail

0   1/4 mi

0   0.25 km

soon grew into a major trading center and port, known for its handsome houses.

Today many of those handsome houses and the places frequented by George Washington stand at the heart of Old Town, a multimillion-dollar urban-renewal historic district. Market Square is the site of the oldest continuously operating farmers' market in the country. (Catch it on Sat btw. 7am and noon, and you'll be participating in a 260-year-old tradition.) Christ Church and Gadsby's Tavern are still open and operating. Many Alexandria streets still bear their original Colonial names

Historic houses in Old Town.

(King, Queen, Prince, Princess, Royal), while others, like Jefferson, Franklin, Lee, Patrick, and Henry, are obviously post-Revolutionary.

Twenty-first-century America thrives in Old Town's many shops, boutiques, art galleries, bars, and restaurants. But it's still easy to imagine yourself in Colonial times as you listen for the rumbling of horse-drawn vehicles over cobblestone (portions of Prince and Oronoco sts. are still paved with cobblestone), dine on Sally Lunn bread and other 18th-century grub in the centuries-old Gadsby's Tavern, and learn about the lives of the nation's forefathers during walking tours that take you in and out of their houses.

Essentials

GETTING THERE   If you're driving from the District, take the Arlington Memorial Bridge or the 14th Street Bridge to the George Washington Memorial Parkway south, which becomes Washington Street in Old Town Alexandria. Washington Street intersects with King Street, Alexandria's main thoroughfare. Turn left from Washington Street onto one of the streets before or after King Street (southbound left turns are not permitted from Washington St. onto King St.), and you'll be heading toward the waterfront and the heart of Old Town. If you turn right from Washington Street onto King Street, you'll still be in Old Town, with King Street's long avenue of shops and restaurants awaiting you. You can obtain a free parking permit from the visitor center (see "Visitor Information," below), or park at meters or in garages. The town is compact, so you won't need a car.

The easiest way to make the trip is by Metro; Yellow and Blue Line trains travel to the King Street station. From the station, you can catch the free King Street Trolley, which operates daily 11:30am to 10pm, making frequent stops between the Metro station and the Potomac River. The eastbound AT2, AT5, or AT7 blue-and-gold DASH bus (www.dashbus.com; ✆ 703/370-3274) marked OLD TOWN or BRADDOCK METRO will also take you up King Street. Ask to be dropped at the corner of Fairfax and King streets, across the street from Ramsay House Visitors Center. The fare is $1.50. Or you can walk, although it's about 1½ miles from the station into the center of Old Town.

VISITOR INFORMATION The **Alexandria Convention and Visitors Association's** Ramsay House Visitors Center, 221 King St., at Fairfax Street (www.visitalexandriava.com; ✆ **800/388-9119** or 703/746-3301), is open daily April through December from 10am to 8pm (closed Thanksgiving, Dec 25, and Jan 1), and 10am to 5pm January through March. Here you can obtain a map/self-guided walking tour and brochures about the area, learn about special events that might be scheduled during your visit and get tickets for them, and receive answers to any questions you might have about accommodations, restaurants, sights, or shopping. The center supplies materials in five languages. You can also call ahead or go on the website to order a visitors guide and other information.

If you come by car, get a free 1-day parking permit here for any 2-hour meter for up to 24 hours. Make sure you put money in the meter to cover parking until you get back outside with your permit, then head into the visitor center and provide your license plate number to obtain your permit. The permit can be renewed for a second day.

ORGANIZED TOURS Though it's easy to see Alexandria on your own and with the help of the Colonial-attired guides at individual attractions, you might consider taking a comprehensive walking tour of the town. Architecture and history tours leave from the visitor center garden April through mid-November, at least once a day, weather permitting. Tours depart at 10:30am Monday through Saturday and at 2pm on Sunday, with additional tours during busy seasons. These walk-up tours (no reservations needed) take 1½ hours and cost $15 per person (free for ages 6 and under). You pay the guide when you arrive.

Alexandria Colonial Tours (www.alexcolonialtours.com; ✆ **703/519-1749**) conducts a number of different tours. Its **Ghosts and Graveyard Tour** is offered March through November (weather permitting) at various

Trolley bus on King Street.

Alexandria waterfront.

times and days—best to call for exact schedule. This 1-hour tour departs from Ramsay House and costs $12 for adults, $6 for children ages 7 to 17; it's free for children 6 and under. Reservations are recommended, though not required, for these tours; you can purchase tickets from the guide, who will be dressed in Colonial attire and standing in front of the visitor center.

CITY LAYOUT Old Town is very small and laid out in an easy grid. At the center is the intersection of Washington Street and King Street. Streets change from north to south when they cross King Street; for example, North Alfred Street is the part of Alfred north of King Street (closest to Washington, in other words). Guess where South Alfred Street is.

Alexandria Calendar of Events

The **Alexandria Convention and Visitors Association** (www.visitalexandriava.com; ☏ **800/388-9119** or 703/746-3300) posts its calendar of events online and in its visitors guide, which you can order by phone or on its website. Event highlights include:

FEBRUARY

George Washington's Birthday is celebrated over the course of several days, including Presidents' Weekend, which precedes the federal holiday (the third Mon in Feb). Festivities typically include a Colonial-costume or black-tie banquet, followed by a ball at Gadsby's Tavern, a 10km race, special tours, a Revolutionary War encampment at Fort Ward Park (complete with uniformed troops engaging in skirmishes), the nation's largest George Washington Birthday Parade (50,000–75,000 people attend every year), and 18th-century comic opera performances. Most events, such as the parade and historical reenactments, are free. The Birthnight Ball at Gadsby's Tavern requires tickets for both the banquet and the ball.

MARCH

St. Patrick's Day Parade takes place on King Street on the first Saturday in March.

Historic Garden Week in Virginia is celebrated with tours of privately owned local historic homes and gardens the third Saturday of the month. Call the visitor center ((℃) **703/746-3301**) in early 2013 for more information about tickets and admission prices for the tour.

Alexandria's birthday (its 264th in 2013) is celebrated with a concert performance by the Alexandria Symphony Orchestra, fireworks, birthday cake, and other festivities. The Saturday following the Fourth of July. All events are free.

Alexandria Festival of the Arts features the ceramics, sculpture, photography, and other works of more than 200 juried artists. On a Saturday and Sunday in early September. Free.

The 72nd Annual Tour of Historic Alexandria Homes takes you to some of the city's most beautifully restored and decorated private homes. Third Saturday in September. Tickets and information at the visitor center.

Ghost tours take place year-round but pick up around **Halloween.** A lantern-carrying guide in 18th-century costume describes Alexandria's ghosts, graveyards, legends, myths, and folklore as you tour the town and graveyards. Call the visitor center for information.

Christmas Tree Lighting is in Market Square, usually the Saturday after Thanksgiving. The ceremony, which includes choir singing, puppet shows, dance performances, and an appearance by Santa and his elves, begins at 7pm. The night the tree is lit, thousands of tiny lights adorning King Street trees also go on.

The Annual Scottish Christmas Walk takes place on the first Saturday in December. Activities include kilted bagpipers, Highland dancers, a parade of Scottish clans (with horses and dogs), caroling, fashion shows, storytelling, booths (selling crafts, antiques, food, hot mulled punch, heather, fresh wreaths, and holly), and children's games. Admission is charged for some events. Call the Alexandria Convention and Visitors Association at (℃) **800/388-9119** for details.

The Historic Alexandria Candlelight Tour, the second week in December, visits seasonally decorated historic Alexandria homes and an 18th-century tavern. Colonial dancing, string quartets, madrigal and opera singers, and refreshments are part of the celebration. Purchase tickets at the Ramsay House Visitors Center.

There are so many **holiday-season activities** that the Visitors Association issues a special brochure about them every year. Pick up one to learn about decorations, workshops, walking tours, tree lightings, concerts, bazaars, bake sales, craft fairs, and much more.

10

SIDE TRIPS FROM WASHINGTON, D.C. | Alexandria

What to See & Do

Colonial and post-Revolutionary buildings are Old Town Alexandria's main attractions. My favorites are the Carlyle House and Gadsby's Tavern Museum, but they're all worth a visit.

These sites are most easily accessible via the King Street Metro station, combined with a ride on the free King Street Trolley to the center of Old Town. The exceptions are the Alexandria Black History and Resource Center, whose closest Metro stop is the Braddock Street station, and Fort Ward, to which you should drive or take a taxi.

biking **TO OLD TOWN ALEXANDRIA & MOUNT VERNON**

One of the nicest ways to view the Washington skyline is from across the river while biking in Virginia. You'll have a breathtaking view of the Potomac and of Washington's grand landmarks: the Kennedy Center, Washington Monument, Lincoln Memorial, Jefferson Memorial, and National Cathedral off in one direction, and the Capitol off in the other. Rent a bike at one of Bike & Roll's locations or at Thompson Boat Center, across from the Kennedy Center and right on the bike path (p. 155). Hop on the pathway that runs along the Potomac River and head toward the monuments and the Arlington Memorial Bridge. In Washington this is the Rock Creek Park Trail; when you cross Memorial Bridge (near the Lincoln Memorial) into Virginia, the name changes to the Mount Vernon Trail, which leads, not surprisingly, straight to Mount Vernon.

Of course, this mode of transportation is also a great way to see Old Town Alexandria and Mount Vernon. The trail carries you past Reagan National Airport via two pedestrian bridges that take you safely through the airport's roadway system. Continue on to Old Town, where you should lock up your bike, walk around, tour some of the historic properties listed in this chapter, and take in some refreshment from one of the many excellent restaurants before you proceed to Mount Vernon. The section from Memorial Bridge to Mount Vernon is about 19 miles in all.

Old Town is also known for its fine shopping opportunities. Brand-name stores, charming boutiques, antiques shops, art galleries, and gift shops sell everything you might desire. The visitor center offers brochures for specific stores as well as a general guide to shopping. Notable local favorite shops include Bellacara, 1000 King St. (http://bellacara.com; ✆ **703/299-9652**) for fragrant soaps and more than 50 brands of luxe skin- and haircare products; Society Fair, 277 S. Washington St. (www.societyfair.net; ✆ **703/683-3247**), Cathal Armstrong's (of Restaurant Eve; p. 329) latest venture, part bakery/market/butchery/wine bar/demo kitchen; An American in Paris, 1225 King St., Ste. 1 (www.anamericaninparisoldtown.com; ✆ **703/519-8234**), where one must knock on the door to enter and sort through the beautiful, one-of-a-kind cocktail dresses and evening gowns for sale; and Why Not?, 200 King St. (✆ **703/548-4420**), around for nearly 50 years selling children's clothes, books, and toys. Also see chapter 7 for a description of the **Old Town Farmers Market** (p. 227).

Alexandria Black History Resource Museum In 1940, African Americans in Alexandria staged a sit-in to protest the segregation of blacks from Alexandria's main library. The black community built its own public library, and it is this 1940s building that now serves as the Black History Resource Museum. The center exhibits historical objects, photographs, documents, and memorabilia relating to black citizens of Alexandria from the 18th century forward. In addition to the permanent collection, the museum presents rotating exhibits and other activities. If you're interested in further studies, check out the center's Watson Reading Room. A half-hour may be enough time to spend at the center.

The museum is actually on the outskirts of Old Town. Once you've explored the museum, it makes sense to walk into Old Town, rather than taking the Metro or even a taxi. Have a staff person point you in the direction of Washington Street, east of the center; if you choose, you can turn right (or south) at Washington Street and walk 2 blocks or so to the **Lee-Fendall House** (p. 326) at Oronoco and Washington streets.

902 Wythe St. (at N. Alfred St.). www.alexblackhistory.org. ☎ **703/746-4356.** Admission $2. Tues–Sat 10am–4pm. Metro: Braddock Road; from the station, walk across the parking lot and bear right until you reach the corner of West and Wythe sts., where you'll proceed 5 blocks east along Wythe until you reach the center.

The Athenaeum This grand building, with its Greek Revival architectural style, stands out among the narrow Old Town houses on the cobblestone street. Built in 1851, the Athenaeum has been many things: the Bank of the Old Dominion, where Robert E. Lee kept his money prior to the Civil War; a commissary for the Union Army during the Civil War; a church; a triage center where wounded Union soldiers were treated; and a medicine warehouse. Now the hall serves as an art gallery and performance space for the Northern Virginia Fine Arts Association. Pop by to admire the Athenaeum's imposing exterior, including the four soaring Doric columns and its interior hall: 24-foot-high ceilings, enormous windows, and whatever contemporary art is on display. This won't take you more than 20 minutes.

201 Prince St. (at S. Lee St.). www.nvfaa.org. ☎ **703/548-0035.** Free admission (donations accepted). Thurs–Fri and Sun noon–4pm; Sat 1–4pm. Closed major holidays.

Carlyle House Historic Park One of Virginia's most architecturally impressive 18th-century homes, Carlyle House also figured prominently in American history. In 1753, Scottish merchant John Carlyle completed the mansion for his bride, Sarah Fairfax of Belvoir, a daughter of one of Virginia's most prominent families. It was designed in the style of a Scottish/English manor house and is lavishly furnished;

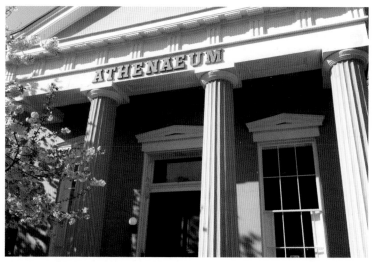

The Athenaeum's Doric columns.

Carlyle, a successful merchant, had the means to import the best furnishings and appointments available abroad for his new Alexandria home.

When it was built, Carlyle House was a waterfront property with its own wharf. A social and political center, the house was visited by the great men of the day, including George Washington. But its most important moment in history occurred in April 1755, when Major General Edward Braddock, commander-in-chief of His Majesty's forces in North America, met with five Colonial governors here and asked them to tax colonists to finance a campaign against the French and Indians. Colonial legislatures refused to comply, one of the first instances of serious friction between America and Britain. Tours are given on the hour and half-hour and take about 45 minutes; allow another 10 or 15 minutes if you plan to tour the tiered garden of brick walks and boxed parterres. Two of the original rooms, the large parlor and the dining room, have survived intact; the former, where Braddock met the governors, still retains its original fine woodwork, paneling, and pediments. The house is furnished in period pieces; however, only a few of Carlyle's possessions remain. In an upstairs room, an architecture exhibit depicts 18th-century construction methods.

> **Planning Note**
>
> Many Alexandria attractions are closed on Mondays.

10

121 N. Fairfax St. (btw. Cameron and King sts.). www.carlylehouse.org. ☏ **703/549-2997.** Admission $5 adults, $3 children 5–12, free for children 4 and under. Tues–Sat 10am–4pm; Sun noon–4pm.

Christ Church   This sturdy red-brick Georgian-style church would be an important national landmark even if its two most distinguished members had not been Washington and Lee. It has been in continuous use since 1773; the town of Alexandria grew up around this building that was once known as the "Church in the Woods." Over the years, the church has undergone many changes, adding the bell tower, church bell, galleries, and organ by the early 1800s, and the "wine-glass" pulpit in 1891. For the most part, the original structure remains, including the handblown glass in the windows.

Christ Church has had its historic moments. Washington and other early church members fomented revolution in the churchyard, and Robert E. Lee met here with Richmond representatives to discuss Lee's taking command of Virginia's military forces at the beginning of the Civil War. You can sit in the pew where George and Martha sat with her two Custis grandchildren, or in the Lee family pew. You might also want to walk through the graveyard and note how old the tombstones are, including the oldest stone, dated March 20, 1791.

World dignitaries and U.S. presidents have visited the church over the years. One of the most memorable of these visits took place shortly after Pearl Harbor, when Franklin Delano Roosevelt attended services with Winston Churchill on the World Day of Prayer for Peace, January 1, 1942.

Of course, you're invited to attend a service (Sun at 8, 9, and 11:15am and 5pm; Wed at 7:15am and 12:05pm). There's no admission charge, but donations are appreciated. A guide gives brief lectures to visitors. A gift shop is open Tuesday through Saturday 10am to 4pm, and Sunday 8:45am to 1pm. Twenty minutes should do it here. Be sure to check out the website before you visit, since it offers a wealth of information about the history of the church and town.

118 N. Washington St. (at Cameron St.). www.historicchristchurch.org. © **703/549-1450.** Donations appreciated. Mon–Sat 9am–4pm; Sun 2–4pm. Closed all federal holidays.

Fort Ward Museum & Historic Site ☺   A short drive from Old Town is a
45-acre museum and park that transports you to Alexandria during the Civil War. The
action here centers, as it did in the early 1860s, on an actual Union fort that Lincoln
ordered erected. It was part of a system of Civil War forts called the "Defenses of
Washington." About 90% of the fort's earthwork walls are preserved, and the Northwest Bastion has been restored with six mounted guns (originally there were 36). A
model of 19th-century military engineering, the fort was never attacked by Confederate forces. Self-guided tours begin at the Fort Ward ceremonial gate.

Visitors can explore the fort and replicas of the ceremonial entrance gate
and an officer's hut. A museum of Civil War artifacts on the premises features
changing exhibits that focus on subjects such as Union arms and equipment,
medical care of the wounded, and local war history.

There are picnic areas with barbecue grills in the park surrounding the fort.
Living-history presentations take place throughout the year. This is a good stop if
you have young children, in which case you could spend an hour or two here
(especially if you bring a picnic).

4301 W. Braddock Rd. (btw. Rte. 7 and N. Van Dorn St.). www.fortward.org. © **703/746-4848.**
Free admission (donations welcome). Park daily 9am–sunset. Museum Tues–Sat 10am–5pm; Sun
noon–5pm. Call for information regarding special holiday closings. From Old Town, follow King
St. west, go right on Kenwood Ave., then left on W. Braddock Rd.; continue for a mile to the
entrance on the right.

Friendship Firehouse   Alexandria's first firefighting organization, the Friendship Fire Company, was established in 1774. In the early days, the company met in
taverns and kept its firefighting equipment in a member's barn. Its present Itali-
anate-style brick building dates from 1855; it was erected after an earlier building
was, ironically, destroyed by fire. Local tradition holds that George Washington was
involved with the firehouse as a founding member, active firefighter, and purchaser
of its first fire engine, although research does not confirm these stories. The
museum displays an 1851 fire engine, old hoses, buckets, and other firefighting
apparatus. This is a tiny place that you can easily visit in 20 minutes.

107 S. Alfred St. (btw. King and Prince sts.). www.alexandriava.gov/friendshipfirehouse. © **703/
746-3891.** Admission $2. Sat–Sun 1–4pm.

Gadsby's Tavern Museum ★   Alexandria was once at the crossroads of 18th-
century America. Its social center was Gadsby's Tavern, which consisted of two
buildings—one Georgian, one Federal, dating from around 1785 and 1792, respectively. Innkeeper John Gadsby combined them to create "a gentleman's tavern,"
which he operated from 1796 to 1808; it was considered one of the finest in the
country. George Washington was a frequent dinner guest; he and Martha danced
in the second-floor ballroom, and it was here that Washington celebrated his last
birthday. The tavern also welcomed Thomas Jefferson, James Madison, and the
Marquis de Lafayette (the French soldier and statesman who served in the American army under Washington during the Revolutionary War and remained close to
Washington). It was the setting of lavish parties, theatrical performances, small
circuses, government meetings, and concerts. Itinerant merchants used the tavern
to display their wares, and traveling doctors treated a hapless clientele (these were
rudimentary professions in the 18th c.) on the premises.

Inside Gadsby's Tavern Museum.

The rooms have been restored to their 18th-century appearance. On the 30-minute tour, you'll get a good look at the Tap Room, a small dining room; the Assembly Room, the ballroom; typical bedrooms; and the underground icehouse, which was filled each winter from the icy river. Tours depart 15 minutes before and after the hour. Cap off the experience with a meal right next door, at the restored Colonial-style restaurant, **Gadsby's Tavern,** 138 N. Royal St., at Cameron Street (© 703/548-1288; www.gadsbystavernrestaurant.com).

134 N. Royal St. (at Cameron St.). www.gadsbystavern.org. © **703/746-4242.** Admission $5 adults, $3 children 5–12, free for children 4 and under. Tours Apr–Oct Tues–Sat 10am–5pm, Sun–Mon 1–5pm; Nov–Mar Wed–Sat 11am–4pm, Sun 1–4pm. Closed most federal holidays.

Lee-Fendall House Museum This handsome Greek Revival–style house is a veritable Lee family museum of furniture, heirlooms, and documents. "Light Horse Harry" Lee never actually lived here, though he was a frequent visitor, as was his good friend George Washington. He did own the original lot but sold it to Philip Richard Fendall (himself a Lee on his mother's side), who built the house in 1785. Thirty-seven Lees occupied the house over a period of 118 years (1785–1903), and it was in this house that Harry wrote Alexandria's farewell address to George Washington, delivered when he passed through town on his way to assume the presidency. (Harry also wrote and delivered the famous funeral oration to Washington that contained the words, "First in war, first in peace, and first in the hearts of his countrymen.") During the Civil War, the house was seized and used as a Union hospital.

Thirty-minute guided tours interpret the 1850s era of the home and provide insight into Victorian family life. You'll also see the Colonial garden, with its magnolia and chestnut trees, roses, and boxwood-lined paths. Much of the interior woodwork and glass is original.

614 Oronoco St. (at Washington St.). www.leefendallhouse.org. © **703/548-1789.** Admission $5 adults, $3 children 11–17, free for children 10 and under. Wed–Sat 10am–3pm; Sun 1–3pm.

Call ahead to make sure the museum is open, since it often closes for special events. Tours on the hour 10am–3pm. Closed Jan and Thanksgiving.

The Lyceum   This Greek Revival building houses a museum depicting Alexandria's history from the 17th to the 20th century. It features changing exhibits and an ongoing series of lectures, concerts, and educational programs. You can obtain maps and brochures about Virginia state attractions, especially Alexandria attractions. The knowledgeable staff will be happy to answer questions.

The striking brick-and-stucco Lyceum also merits a visit. Built in 1839, it was designed in the Doric temple style to serve as a lecture, meeting, and concert hall. It was an important center of Alexandria's cultural life until the Civil War, when Union forces appropriated it for use as a hospital. After the war it became a private residence, and still later it was subdivided for office space. In 1969, however, the city council's use of eminent domain prevented the Lyceum from being demolished in favor of a parking lot. Allow about 20 minutes here.

201 S. Washington St. (off Prince St.). www.alexandriahistory.org. (✆ **703/746-4994.** Admission $2. Mon–Sat 10am–5pm; Sun 1–5pm. Closed Jan 1, Thanksgiving, and Dec 25.

Old Presbyterian Meeting House   Presbyterian congregations have worshiped in Virginia since the Rev. Alexander Whittaker converted Pocahontas in Jamestown in 1614. This brick church was built by Scottish pioneers in 1775. Although it wasn't George Washington's church, the Meeting House bell tolled continuously for 4 days after his death in December 1799, and memorial services were preached from the pulpit here by Presbyterian, Episcopal, and Methodist ministers. According to the Alexandria paper of the day, "The walking being bad to the Episcopal church the funeral sermon of George Washington will be preached at the Presbyterian Meeting House." Two months later, on Washington's birthday, Alexandria citizens marched from Market Square to the church to pay their respects.

Many famous Alexandrians are buried in the church graveyard, including John and Sarah Carlyle; Dr. James Craik (the surgeon who treated—some say killed—Washington, dressed Lafayette's wounds at Brandywine, and ministered to the dying Braddock at Monongahela); and William Hunter, Jr., founder of the St. Andrew's Society of Scottish descendants, to whom bagpipers pay homage on the first Saturday of December. It is also the site of a Tomb of an Unknown Revolutionary War Soldier. Dr. James Muir, minister between 1789 and 1820, lies beneath the sanctuary in his gown and bands.

The original Meeting House was gutted by a lightning fire in 1835, but parishioners restored it in the style of the day a few years later. The present bell, said to be recast from the metal of the old one, was hung in a newly constructed belfry in 1843, and a new organ was installed in 1849. The Meeting House closed its doors in 1889 and for 60 years was used sporadically. But in 1949 it was reborn as a living Presbyterian U.S.A. church, and today the Old Meeting House looks much as it did following its first restoration. The original parsonage, or manse, is still intact. There's no guided tour. Allow 20 minutes to look around.

321 S. Fairfax St. (btw. Duke and Wolfe sts.). www.opmh.org. (✆ **703/549-6670.** Free admission, but you must obtain a key from the office to tour the church. Sun services 8:30 and 11am (only 10am in summer).

Stabler-Leadbeater Apothecary Museum   When its doors closed in 1933, this landmark drugstore was the second oldest in continuous operation in America. Run for five generations by the same Quaker family (beginning in

Antique, handblown glass bottles at the Stabler-Leadbeater Apothecary Museum.

1792), the store counted Robert E. Lee (who purchased the paint for Arlington House here), George Mason, Henry Clay, John C. Calhoun, and George Washington among its famous patrons. Gothic Revival decorative elements and Victorian-style doors were added in the 1840s. Today the apothecary looks much as it did in Colonial times, its shelves lined with original handblown gold-leaf-labeled bottles (the most valuable collection of antique medicinal bottles in the country), old scales stamped with the royal crown, patent medicines, and equipment for bloodletting. The clock on the rear wall, the porcelain-handled mahogany drawers, and two mortars and pestles all date from about 1790. Among the shop's documentary records is this 1802 order from Mount Vernon: "Mrs. Washington desires Mr. Stabler to send by the bearer a quart bottle of his best Castor Oil and the bill for it." The museum is open for guided tours only, which take place 15 minutes before and after the hour, and last 30 minutes.

105–107 S. Fairfax St. (near King St.). www.apothecarymuseum.org. ✆ **703/746-3852.** Admission $5 adults, $3 children 5–12, free for children 4 and under. Apr–Oct Tues–Sat 10am–5pm, Sun–Mon 1–5pm; Nov–Mar Wed–Sat 11am–4pm, Sun 1–4pm. Closed major holidays.

Torpedo Factory This block-long, three-story building was built in 1918 as a torpedo shell-case factory but now accommodates some 82 artists' studios, where 165 professional artists and craftspeople create and sell their own works. Here you can see artists at work in their studios: from potters to painters, as well as those who create stained-glass windows and fiber art.

On permanent display are exhibits on Alexandria history provided by Alexandria Archaeology (✆ **703/746-4399;** www.alexandriaarchaeology.org), which is headquartered here and engages in extensive city research. A volunteer or staff member is on hand to answer questions. Art lovers may end up browsing for an hour or two.

105 N. Union St. (btw. King and Cameron sts., on the waterfront). www.torpedofactory.org. ✆ **703/838-4565.** Free admission. Daily 10am–6pm (Thurs until 9pm). Archaeology exhibit

area Tues–Fri 10am–3pm; Sat 10am–5pm; Sun 1–5pm. Closed Jan 1, Easter, July 4, Thanksgiving, and Dec 25.

Where to Eat

There are a number of Alexandria restaurants that are so well liked that Washingtonians often drive over just to dine here. The following are among the best to suit assorted budgets, tastes, and styles; all are easily accessible via the King Street Metro station, combined with a ride on the free King Street Trolley to the center of Old Town.

EXPENSIVE

Restaurant Eve ★★★ NEW AMERICAN Named for the first child of owners Cathal (the chef) and Meshelle Armstrong, Eve is nationally recognized and locally beloved, which means it can be hard—really hard—to score a reservation, so call way ahead. Dine in the casual bistro or in the elegant tasting room, where five-course ($120 per person), seven-course ($135 per person), and nine-course ($150 per person) menus are offered. Bistro entrees might include bouillabaisse and sirloin of veal; tasting-menu items range from butter-poached lobster with heirloom carrots to gnocchi with spring garlic and golden beets. Chef Armstrong has long been committed to seasonal cooking, using the fresh produce of local farmers. Don't miss Eve's best dessert: an old-fashioned "birthday cake," which is a mouthwatering slice of white cake layered and iced with pink frosting and sprinkles. And be sure to read over the wine and cocktails list, since sommelier and "liquid savant" Todd Thrasher has gained such renown for his inventive concoctions—"Millions of

"Millions of Peaches" at Restaurant Eve.

Peaches" (peach vodka, champagne-vinegar-pickled peaches, and poached peaches), "Jose's Yin and Tonic" (made with house-made tonic)—that he's opened a nearby speakeasy lounge, **PX,** located just above **Eamonn's A Dublin Chipper** (see below), where he dispenses more fun drinks and good times.

110 S. Pitt St. (near King St.). www.restaurant eve.com. *✆* **703/706-0450.** Reservations recommended. Jacket advised for men in bistro; jacket and tie advised for men in tasting room. Bistro lunch items $18–$25; dinner main courses $28–$41; tasting room fixed-price 5-course dinner $110, 7-course $130, 9-course $150; bistro fixed-price 3-course dinner Fri–Sat $65; lunch menu (served at the bar weekdays 11:30am–4pm) $15 for any two items. AE, DC, DISC, MC, V. Bistro Mon–Fri 11:30am–2:30pm; Mon–Sat 5:30–10pm. Tasting room Mon–Sat 5:30–9:30pm.

MODERATE

Majestic Café ★ SOUTHERN A lively bar fronts the narrow restaurant, making a dining experience here a little noisy; that can be either annoying or festive, depending on your mood. I promise, though, that you'll enjoy the grilled calamari salad, soft-shell crabs, artichoke and fontina cheese tart, spoon bread, hush puppies, and, for dessert, German chocolate cake. The Majestic offers a bar lunch special Monday through Friday from 11:30am to 2:30pm—any lunch entree for $12—and a Sunday dinner special: $22 per person and a set menu.

911 King St. (near Alfred St.). www.majesticcafe.com. ✆ **703/837-9117.** Reservations recommended. Main courses lunch $11–$24, dinner $19–$27. AE, DC, DISC, MC, V. Mon–Sat 11:30am–2:30pm; Mon–Thurs 5:30–10pm; Fri–Sat 5:30–10:30pm; Sun 1–9pm.

INEXPENSIVE

Eamonn's A Dublin Chipper ★ FISH & CHIPS   Fish and chips and a few sides (onion rings, coleslaw)—that's what we're talking here. But it's charming. Upstairs is **PX,** an exclusive lounge, where mixologist Todd Thrasher may be on hand to shake the drinks he's created. This is another in the priceless strand of rare restaurant experiences that Cathal and Meshelle Armstrong are perpetrating on this side of the Potomac. The Chipper is named after their son Eamonn, **Restaurant Eve** (see above) for their firstborn daughter. The Armstrongs have a following, so expect a crowd.

728 King St. www.eamonnsdublinchipper.com. ✆ **703/299-8384.** Reservations not accepted. Main courses $5–$9. AE, DC, DISC, MC, V. Mon–Wed 11:30am–10pm; Thurs 11:30am–11pm; Fri 11:30am–midnight; Sat noon–midnight; Sun noon–closing.

La Madeleine ☺ FRENCH CAFE   It may be part of a self-service chain, but this place has its charms. Its French-country interior has a beamed ceiling, oak floors, a wood-burning stove, and maple hutches displaying crockery and pewter mugs. The range of affordable menu items here makes this a good choice for families with finicky eaters in tow.

La Madeleine opens early—at 6:30am every day—so come for breakfast to feast on fresh-baked croissants, Danish, scones, muffins, and brioches, or a heartier bacon-and-eggs plate. Throughout the day, there are salads, sandwiches (including a traditional croque-monsieur), and hot dishes ranging from quiche and pizza to rotisserie chicken with a Caesar salad. After 5pm additional choices include pastas and specials such as beef tenders *en merlot* or herb-crusted pork tenderloin, both served with garlic mashed potatoes and green beans amandine. Conclude with a fruit tart, or chocolate, vanilla, and praline triple-layer cheesecake with graham-cracker crust. Wine and beer are served.

500 King St. (at S. Pitt St.). www.lamadeleine.com. ✆ **703/739-2854.** Reservations not accepted. Main courses breakfast $4.50–$9, lunch and dinner $5–$13. AE, DISC, MC, V. Sun–Thurs 6:30am–10pm; Fri–Sat 6:30am–11pm.

Nightlife

Old Town Alexandria's nightlife options center on the bar scene, which is nearly as varied as the one across the Potomac in the District. In fact, a number of popular, in-town restaurant-bars have outposts here, including **Pizzeria Paradiso** (p. 208), at 124 King St. (www.eatyourpizza.com; ✆ **703/837-1245**), whose cozy bar is situated behind a large glass fireplace and serves 14 drafts, one cask ale, American microbrews and Belgian beers. Among the notable only-in–Old Town establishments is the brick-fronted and decades-old **Tiffany Tavern,** 1116 King St. (www.tiffanytavern.com; ✆ **703/836-8844**), known for its live bluegrass music, burgers, and open mike events. If you're in the mood for raucous singalongs, make your way to **Murphy's Pub,** 713 King St. (www.murphyspub. com; ℂ **703/548-1717**), where live Irish music plays nightly. And for sophisticated ambience, check out **Vermilion,** 1120 King St. (www.vermilionrestaurant. com; ℂ **703/684-9669**), which is both a fine restaurant and upscale cocktail lounge, complete with cushioned benches, specialty drinks, and all the other trappings of a hipster scene. Come here Tuesday or Wednesday nights at 9:30pm and you'll enjoy live performances by established local musicians.

Where to Stay

With a total of 4,200 hotel guest rooms, Alexandria will have no trouble accommodating you should you decide to stay overnight. Hotels run the budget gamut, from **Comfort Inns** (www.comfortinn.com) at the low end to the posh new **Lorien Hotel and Spa,** 1600 King St. (www.lorienhotelandspa.com; ℂ **703/894-3434**) at the luxe end. Two properties lie especially close to the heart of historic Old Town. The **Hotel Monaco Alexandria,** at 480 King St. (www.monaco-alexandria.com; ℂ **800/368-5047** or 703/549-6080), is a former Holiday Inn, recently converted by boutique hotel group Kimpton Hotels into a luxury property with 241 stylish rooms, a pool, a health club, and a chef-driven restaurant. Rates vary by season and date, but expect to pay from $170 to $300 on the weekends, $229 to $370 weekdays, for a standard double room.

Another Kimpton property, **Morrison House,** 116 S. Alfred St. (www.morrison house.com; ℂ **866/834-6628** or 703/838-8000), is also a standout, often chosen by *Condé Nast Traveler* for its Gold List and by TripAdvisor travelers as a winner for best service. Its 45 rooms are appointed with canopied four-poster beds, mahogany armoires, decorative fireplaces, and the like. Rates can start at $129 for the smallest room off season on the weekend and at $289 for a standard room on a weekday in season. Morrison House is known for its restaurant, the **Grille,** which presents award-winning contemporary American cuisine.

For other recommendations, check the **Alexandria Convention and Visitors Association** website, **www.visitalexandriava.com**, where you can book an online reservation and also read about various promotions that hotels are offering.

PLANNING YOUR TRIP TO WASHINGTON, D.C.

s with any trip, a little preparation is essential before you travel to Washington, D.C. This chapter provides a variety of planning tools, including information on getting to D.C., tips on transportation within the city, and additional on-the-ground resources.

GETTING THERE
By Plane

Three airports serve the Washington, D.C. area. General information follows that should help you determine which airport is your best bet. See the appendix at the back of this book for the full listing of airlines that travel to Washington, D.C. and their toll-free numbers and websites.

A note for **international visitors:** Some large airlines offer transatlantic or transpacific passengers special discount tickets under the name **Visit USA,** which allows mostly one-way travel from one U.S. destination to another at very low prices. Unavailable in the U.S., these discount tickets must be purchased abroad in conjunction with your international fare. If Washington, D.C. is just one of the places you're visiting in the United States, you might want to check out the Visit USA program, which might prove the easiest, fastest, and cheapest way for you to see the country.

Ronald Reagan Washington National Airport (DCA) lies 4 miles south of D.C., across the Potomac River in Virginia, about a 10-minute trip by car in non-rush-hour traffic, and 15 to 20 minutes by Metro anytime. Its proximity to the District and its direct access to the Metro rail system are reasons why you might want to fly into National.

Approximately 12 airlines serve this airport, which has nonstop flights to 78 U.S. cities, plus Nassau, Bermuda, Halifax, Montreal, Ottawa, and Toronto. Nearly all nonstop flights are to and from cities located within 1,250 miles from Washington; the exceptions are flights between National and Phoenix, Denver, Las Vegas, Seattle, Los Angeles, and Salt Lake City. Among the airlines serving National Airport are **Air Canada, Alaska Airlines, American, Continental, Delta, United,** and **US Airways,** and discount airlines **JetBlue, Frontier, Spirit,** and **AirTran.** Delta and US Airways together offer hourly or nearly hourly flights weekdays between National and Boston's Logan Airport, and National and New York's LaGuardia Airport, and frequent weekend service between these cities.

National Airport's traveler-friendly services include ticket counters that provide charging stations for laptops and phones; more than 40 eateries (notably, T.G.I. Friday's and hometown favorite Five Guys for burgers and fries), 40 shops (look for America! and the Smithsonian Museum Store for last-minute gifts), complimentary Wi-Fi service throughout the airport, currency-exchange stations, commissioned artwork displayed throughout the terminals (go on a tour if your flight's been delayed), and climate-controlled pedestrian bridges that connect the terminal directly to the Metro station, whose Blue and Yellow lines stop here. The Metropolitan Washington Airports Authority oversees both National and Dulles airports, so the website is the same for the two facilities: **www.mwaa. com**. Check there for airport information, or call ✆ **703/417-8000.** For Metro information, go online at **www.wmata.com** or call ✆ **202/637-7000.**

Washington Dulles International Airport (IAD) is 26 miles outside the capital, in Chantilly, Virginia, a 35- to 45-minute ride to downtown in non-rush-hour traffic. Of the three airports, Dulles handles more daily flights, with more than 32 airlines flying nonstop to 132 destinations, including 49 foreign cities. The airport serves as a hub for United Airlines. The airport is not as convenient to the heart of Washington as National, but it's more convenient than BWI, thanks to an uncongested airport access road that travels half the distance toward Washington.

A decades-long expansion project at Dulles is nearly complete. Improvements include new security screening areas on the mezzanine level of the airport; AeroTrain, the airport's underground train system and station that debuted January 2010, replacing most, but not all, of the cumbersome mobile lounges as a way of transporting travelers between the main and midfield terminals; a moving walkway for pedestrians between the main terminal and concourse B; the addition of a fourth runway; and a much larger and more streamlined international arrivals facility. Eventually the airport will add a fifth runway, which is expected to more than triple its annual passenger traffic to 55 million.

Among Dulles's major domestic airlines are **American, Delta, United,** and **US Airways,** and discount airlines **AirTran, JetBlue, Southwest,** and **Virgin America.** The airport's major international airlines include **Aeroflot, British Airways, Air France, Lufthansa, Virgin Atlantic, ANA Airways,** and **Saudi Arabian Airlines.**

Dulles's many eateries and shops include **Gordon Biersch Brewery and Restaurant, Five Guys** for burgers and fries, **Brooks Brothers** clothiers, and the **Smithsonian Museum Store.** Like National, Dulles has complimentary Wi-Fi service throughout the airport and several currency-exchange stations and ATMs.

The airport's website is **www.mwaa.com** and its information line is ✆ **703/ 572-2700.**

Last but not least is **Baltimore–Washington International Thurgood Marshall Airport (BWI),** which is located about 45 minutes from downtown, a few miles outside of Baltimore. A vast expansion has added 11 gates to a newly improved concourse and skywalks from parking garages to terminals, and the number of parking spaces has tripled. One factor especially accounts for this tremendous growth, the same that recommends BWI to travelers: the major presence of **Southwest Airlines,** whose bargain fares and flights to about 50 cities seem to offer something for everyone. (Southwest also serves Dulles Airport, but in a much smaller capacity.)

In all about 11 airlines serve BWI, flying nonstop to at least 74 destinations, including seven foreign cities. Major domestic airlines include **American, Delta, United,** and **US Airways** and discount airlines **AirTran, Southwest,** and **JetBlue.** Major international airlines include **British Airways** and **Air Canada.**

Among BWI's on-site attractions are plenty of eateries, like Baltimore favorite **Obrycki's Restaurant**; some shops, like **America!** and **Godiva Chocolatier**; currency-exchange stations; ATMs; and Wi-Fi service, which is available throughout the airport if you access **Boingo Wireless** (www.boingo.com) and pay for a daily or monthly plan.

Call ℂ **800/435-9294** for airport information, or point your browser to **www.bwiairport.com**.

GETTING INTO TOWN FROM THE AIRPORT

Each of the three airports offers similar options for getting into the city. Follow the signs to "ground transportation" and look for the banners or a staff representative of the service you desire. All three airports could really use better signage, especially because their ground transportation desks always seem to be located quite a distance from the gate at which you arrive. Keep trudging, and follow baggage claim signs, too, since ground transportation operations are always situated near baggage carousels.

TAXI SERVICE For a trip to downtown D.C., you can expect a taxi to cost close to $15 for the 10- to 20-minute ride from National Airport, $57 to $64 for the 30- to 45-minute ride from Dulles Airport, and about $90 for the 45-minute ride from BWI.

SUPERSHUTTLE These vans offer shared-ride, door-to-door service between the airport and your destination, whether in the District or in a suburban location. You make a reservation by phone or online (www.supershuttle.com; ℂ **800/258-3826**) and then proceed to the SuperShuttle desk in your airport to check in. The only drawback to this service is the roundabout way the driver must follow, as he or she drops off or picks up other passengers en route. If you arrive after the SuperShuttle desk has closed, you can summon a van by calling customer service at ℂ **800/258-3826.** The 24-hour service bases its fares on zip code, so to reach downtown, expect to pay about $14, plus $10 for each additional person, from National; $29, plus $10 per additional person, from Dulles; and $37 plus $12 per additional person, from BWI. SuperShuttle also tacks on a $2 fuel charge to every trip. If you're calling the SuperShuttle for a ride from a D.C.-area location to one of the airports, you must reserve a spot at least 24 hours in advance.

LIMOUSINES Limousine service is the most costly of all options, with prices starting at about $40 at National, $75 at Dulles, and $90 at BWI for private car transportation to downtown D.C. One service to recommend is **Red Top Executive Sedan** (www.redtopsedan.com; ℂ **800/296-3300** or 202/882-3300). Or choose a limousine service from the list posted on Destination D.C.'s website, www.washington.org, in its downloadable Visitors Guide. (From the homepage, go to the bottom of the page and click on "Visitors Guide," then look within the list of downloadable sections to find the category that includes transportation and tours options. Click on that category and scroll through the pages until you find information about additional transportation services.)

Free hotel/motel shuttles operate from all three airports to certain nearby properties. Inquire about such transportation when you book a room at your hotel.

Transportation Options by Airport

FROM RONALD REAGAN WASHINGTON NATIONAL AIRPORT   If you are not too encumbered with luggage, you should take **Metrorail** into the city. Metro's Yellow and Blue lines stop at the airport and connect via an enclosed walkway to level two, the concourse level, of the main terminal, adjacent to terminals B and C. If yours is one of the airlines that still uses the "old" terminal A (Spirit, AirTran, JetBlue, Air Canada, Frontier), you will have a longer walk to reach the Metro station. Signs pointing the way can be confusing, so ask an airport employee if you're headed in the right direction; or, better yet, head out to the curb and hop a shuttle bus to the station, but be sure to ask the driver to let you know when you've reached the enclosed bridge that leads to the Metro (it may not be obvious, and drivers don't always announce the stops). **Metrobuses** also serve the area, should you be going somewhere off the Metro route. But Metrorail is fastest, a 15- to 20-minute non-rush-hour ride to downtown. It is safe, convenient, and cheap; the base fare is $1.70 and goes up from there depending on when (fares increase during rush hours) and where you're going.

If you're renting a car from an on-site **car rental agency—Alamo** (☎ 888/215-0010), **Avis** (☎ 703/419-5815), **Budget** (☎ 703/419-1021), **Enterprise** (☎ 703/553-7744), **Hertz** (☎ 703/419-6300), **National** (☎ 888/215-0010), or **Thrifty** (☎ 877/283-0898)—go to level two, the concourse level, follow the pedestrian walkway to the parking garage, find garage A, and descend one flight. You can also take the complimentary Airport Shuttle (look for the sign posted at the curb outside the terminal) to parking garage A. If you've rented from off-premises agencies **Dollar** (☎ 800/800-4000) or **Thrifty** (☎ 800/367-2277), head outside the baggage claim area of your terminal, and catch the Dollar or Thrifty shuttle bus.

To get downtown by car, follow the signs out of the airport for the George Washington Parkway, headed north toward Washington. Stay on the parkway until you see signs for I-395 north to Washington. Take the I-395 north exit, which takes you across the 14th Street Bridge. Stay in the left lane crossing the bridge and follow the signs for Route 1, which will put you on 14th Street NW. (You'll see the Washington Monument off to your left.) Ask your hotel for directions from 14th Street and Constitution Avenue NW. Or take the more scenic route, always staying to the left on the GW Parkway as you follow the signs for Memorial Bridge. You'll be driving alongside the Potomac River, with the monuments in view across the river; then, as you cross over Memorial Bridge, you're greeted by the Lincoln Memorial. Stay left coming over the bridge, swoop around to the left of the Memorial, take a left on 23rd Street NW, a right on Constitution Avenue, and then, if you want to be in the heart of downtown, left again on 15th Street NW (the Washington Monument will be to your right).

FROM WASHINGTON DULLES INTERNATIONAL AIRPORT   The **Washington Flyer Express Bus** (www.washfly.com; ☎ 888/927-4359) runs between Dulles and Metro's Orange Line station at West Falls Church, where you can purchase a Metro farecard to board an Orange Line train bound for New Carrollton, which heads into D.C. In the airport, look for signs for the dulles airport shuttle, which leaves from Door 4 on the Arrivals level (follow the ramp up to the ticket counter). Buses to the West Falls Church

Metro station run daily, every 30 minutes, and cost $10 one-way. (By the way, **"Washington Flyer"** is also the name under which the taxi service operates at Dulles.)

More convenient is the **Metrobus** service (no. 5A) that runs between Dulles (buses depart from curb 2E, outside the Ground Transportation area) and the L'Enfant Plaza Metro station, located across from the National Mall and the Smithsonian museums, and downhill from nearby Capitol Hill. The bus departs every 30 to 40 minutes weekdays, hourly on weekends. It costs $6 and takes 45 minutes to an hour.

If you are renting a car at Dulles, head down the ramp near your baggage claim area and walk outside to the curb to look for your rental car's shuttle-bus stop. The buses come by every 5 minutes or so en route to nearby rental lots. These include **Alamo** (✆ 703/661-3200), **Avis** (✆ 703/661-3505), **Budget** (✆ 703/437-9373), **Dollar** (✆ 866/434-2226), **Enterprise** (✆ 703/661-8800), **Hertz** (✆ 703/471-6020), **National** (✆ 703/661-3200), and **Thrifty** (✆ 877/283-0898).

To reach downtown Washington from Dulles by car, exit the airport and stay on the Dulles Access Road, which leads right into I-66 east. Follow I-66 east, which takes you across the Theodore Roosevelt Memorial Bridge; be sure to stay in the center lane as you cross the bridge, and this will put you on Constitution Avenue (Rte. 29). Ask your hotel for directions from this point.

FROM BALTIMORE–WASHINGTON INTERNATIONAL AIRPORT Washington's Metro service runs an Express Metro Bus ("B30") between its Metrorail Green Line Greenbelt station and BWI Airport. In the airport, head to the lower level and look for public transit signs to find the bus, which operates daily, departs every 40 minutes, takes about 30 minutes to reach the station, and costs $6. At the Greenbelt Metro station, you purchase a Metro farecard and board a Metro train bound for Branch Avenue, which will take you into the city. Depending on where you want to go, you can either stay on the Green Line train to your designated stop or get off at the Fort Totten station to transfer to a Red Line train, whose stops include Union Station (near Capitol Hill) and various downtown locations. Transfers can be tricky, so you may want to ask a fellow passenger or a Metro attendant to make sure you're headed in the right direction.

You also have the choice of taking either an **Amtrak** (www.amtrak. com; ✆ 800/872-7245) or the Penn line of the **Maryland Rural Commuter** train, or MARC (http://mta.maryland.gov/marc-train; ✆ 800/325-7245), into the city. Both trains travel between the BWI Railway Station (✆ 410/672-6169) and Washington's Union Station (✆ 202/906-3104), about a 30-minute ride. Amtrak's service is daily ($14–$42 per person, one-way, depending on time and train type), while MARC's is weekdays only ($6 per person, one-way). A courtesy shuttle runs every 10 minutes or so between the airport and the train station; stop at the desk near the baggage-claim area to check for the next departure time of both the shuttle bus and the train. Trains depart about once per hour.

BWI operates a large off-site car rental facility. From the ground transportation area, you board a shuttle bus that transports you to the lot. Rental agencies include **Alamo** (✆ 410/859-8092), **Avis** (✆ 410/859-1680), **Budget**

(📞 410/691-2913), **Dollar** (📞 800/800-4000), **Enterprise** (📞 800/325-8007), **Hertz** (📞 410/850-7400), **National** (📞 410/859-8860), and **Thrifty** (📞 410/850-7112).

Here's how you reach Washington: Look for signs for I-195 and follow the highway west until you see signs for Washington and the Baltimore–Washington Parkway (I-295); head south on I-295. Get off when you see the signs for Rte. 50/New York Avenue, which leads into the District, via New York Avenue NE. Ask your hotel for specific directions from New York Avenue NE.

By Car

More than one-third of visitors to Washington arrive by plane, and if that's you, don't worry about renting a car. In fact, it's better if you don't, since the traffic in the city and throughout the region is absolutely abysmal, parking spaces are hard to find, garage and lot charges are exorbitant, and hotel overnight rates are even worse. Furthermore, Washington is amazingly easy to traverse on foot—so easy, in fact, that assorted sources, from *Prevention* magazine to the Brookings Institution, name D.C. among the best walkable cities in the country. Our public transportation and taxi systems are accessible and comprehensive, as well.

But if you are like most visitors, you're planning on driving here, traveling on one of the following major highways: I-70 and I-270, I-95, and I-295 from the north; I-95 and I-395, Rte. 1, and Rte. 4 from the south; Rte. 50/301 and Rte. 450 from the east; and Rte. 7, Rte. 50, I-66, and Rte. 29/211 from the west.

No matter which road you take, there's a good chance you will have to navigate some portion of the **Capital Beltway** (I-495 and I-95) to gain entry to D.C. The Beltway girds the city, its approximately 66-mile route passing through Maryland and Virginia, with some 56 interchanges or exits leading off from it. The Beltway is nearly always congested, but especially during weekday morning and evening rush hours (roughly 5:30–9:30am and 3–7pm). Drivers can get a little crazy, weaving in and out of traffic.

Get yourself a good map before you do anything else, and you can start with the foldout map found at the back of this book. **Destination D.C.'s** website, **www.washington.org**, posts printable maps that are quite helpful. Another great source is the **American Automobile Association** (AAA; www.aaa.com; 📞 **800/763-9900** for emergency road service and for connection to the mid-Atlantic office), which provides its members with maps and detailed Trip-Tiks that give precise directions to a destination, including up-to-date information about areas of construction.

If you are driving to a hotel in D.C. or its suburbs, contact the establishment to find out the best route to the hotel's address and other crucial details concerning parking availability and rates.

The District is 240 miles from New York City, 40 miles from Baltimore, 700 miles from Chicago, 500 miles from Boston, and about 630 miles from Atlanta.

By Train

Amtrak (www.amtrak.com; 📞 **800/USA-RAIL** [872-7245]) offers daily service to Washington from New York, Boston, and Chicago. Amtrak also travels daily between Washington and points south, including Raleigh, Charlotte, Atlanta, cities in Florida, and New Orleans. Amtrak's **Acela Express** trains offer the quickest service along the "Northeast Corridor," linking Boston, New York, Philadelphia, and Washington. The trains travel as fast as 150 mph, making the trip between New York and Washington in times that range from less than 3 hours to 3 hours and 45 minutes, depending on the number of stops in the schedule. Likewise, Acela Express's Boston-Washington trip takes anywhere from 6½ hours to more than 8 hours, depending on station stops.

Amtrak runs fewer Acela trains on weekends, and honors passenger discounts, such as those for seniors and AAA members, only on weekend Acela travel, not on weekdays.

Amtrak offers a smorgasbord of good-deal rail passes and discounted fares; although not all are based on advance purchase, you may have more discount options by reserving early. The bargain fares can be used only on certain days and hours of the day; be sure to find out exactly what restrictions apply. Tickets for children ages 2 to 15 cost half the price of a regular coach fare when the children are accompanied by a fare-paying adult. For more information, go to **www.amtrak.com** and click on the website's "Deals" section, where you'll find assorted discount possibilities. *Note:* Most Amtrak travel requires a reservation, which means that every traveler is guaranteed, but not assigned, a seat.

Both American and international visitors who plan to travel to other places in the country can buy a **USA Rail Pass,** good for 15, 30, or 45 days of unlimited travel on **Amtrak** (www.amtrak.com; ✆ **800/USA-RAIL** [872-7245]). The pass is available online or through many overseas travel agents. See Amtrak's website for the cost of travel throughout the United States. The passes are not the same as tickets, which you buy separately using your pass. Reservations are generally required and should be made as early as possible. Other rail passes are also available.

Amtrak trains arrive at historic **Union Station,** 50 Massachusetts Ave. NE (www.unionstationdc.com; ✆ **202/371-9441**), a short walk from the Capitol, across the circle from several hotels, and a short cab or Metro ride from downtown. Union Station is a turn-of-the-20th-century Beaux Arts masterpiece that was magnificently restored in the late 1980s. Offering a three-level marketplace of shops and restaurants, this stunning depot is conveniently located and connects with Metro service. Taxis are almost always available. (For more on Union Station, see chapters 4 and 7.)

By Bus

Bus travel is now in vogue, thanks as much to the economy as to the rise of fabulously priced, comfortable, clean, and fast bus services. Quite a number of buses travel between Washington, D.C. and New York City, and a growing number travel between D.C. and cities scattered up and down the East Coast.

Check out one of these fleets: **BoltBus** (www.boltbus.com; ✆ **877/265-8287**) travels multiple times a day between D.C.'s Union Station and NYC for $1 to $25 each way. **Megabus** (www.megabus.com; ✆ **877/462-6342**) travels between Washington, D.C.'s Union Station and NYC (also many times a day), as well as 17 other locations, including Boston, Toronto, and Knoxville, Tennessee, for as little as $1 and as much as $43, one-way, depending on distance and other factors; most fares run in the $13 to $25 range.

Vamoose Bus (www.vamoosebus.com; ✆ **877/393-2828**) travels between Rosslyn, Virginia's stop near the Rosslyn Metro station and Bethesda, Maryland's stop near the Bethesda Metro station, and NYC's Penn Station, for $30 each way, with a coupon given at the end of each trip: Collect four and ride one-way for free.

Greyhound (www.greyhound.com; © **800/231-2222**) is actually the company behind BoltBus, whose service it launched in 2008. In the meantime, Greyhound continues to offer its traditional and, oddly, often more expensive service between D.C. and some of the same destinations served by BoltBus, as well as to many other cities nationwide, and in Mexico and Canada. The D.C. Greyhound bus depot, at 1005 1st St. NE, is a pretty unsavory place to begin or end a journey. Certain advantages remain, including the Greyhound North American Discovery Pass. The pass, which offers unlimited travel and stopovers in the U.S. and Canada, can be obtained from foreign travel agents or through **www.discoverypass.com**.

GETTING AROUND

Washington is one of the easiest U.S. cities to navigate, thanks to its comprehensive public transportation system of trains and buses. Ours is the second-largest rail transit network and the fifth-largest bus network in the country. But because Washington is of manageable size and marvelous beauty, you may find yourself shunning transportation and choosing to walk. A very good source for considering your transportation options is the website **www.godcgo.com**, an initiative of the D.C. government's Department of Transportation, which continually updates the information.

City Layout

Washington's appearance today pays homage to the 1791 vision of French engineer Pierre Charles L'Enfant, who created the capital's grand design of sweeping avenues intersected by spacious circles, directed that the Capitol and the White House be placed on prominent hilltops at either end of a wide stretch of avenue, and superimposed this overall plan upon a traditional street grid. The city's quadrants, grand avenues named after states, alphabetically ordered streets crossed by numerically ordered streets, and parks integrated with urban features are all ideas that started with L'Enfant. President George Washington, who had hired L'Enfant, was forced to dismiss the temperamental genius after L'Enfant apparently offended quite a number of people. But Washington recognized the brilliance of the city plan and hired surveyors Benjamin Banneker and Andrew Ellicott, who had worked with L'Enfant, to continue to implement L'Enfant's design. (For further background, see chapter 2.)

The U.S. Capitol marks the center of the city, which is divided into **northwest (NW), northeast (NE), southwest (SW),** and **southeast (SE) quadrants.** Most, but not all, areas of interest to tourists are in the northwest. The boundary demarcations are often seamless; for instance, you are in the northwest quadrant when you visit the National Museum of Natural History, but by crossing the National Mall to the other side to visit the Freer Gallery, you put yourself in the southwest quadrant. Pay attention to the quadrant's geographic suffix; as you'll notice when you look on a map, some addresses appear in multiple quadrants (for instance, the corner of G and 7th sts. appears in all four).

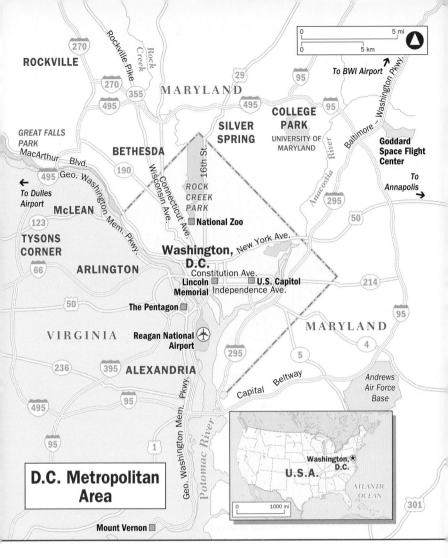

MAIN ARTERIES & STREETS   From the Capitol, North Capitol Street and South Capitol Street run north and south, respectively. East Capitol Street divides the city north and south. The area west of the Capitol is not a street at all, but the National Mall, which is bounded on the north by Constitution Avenue and on the south by Independence Avenue.

The primary artery of Washington is **Pennsylvania Avenue,** which is the scene of parades, inaugurations, and other splashy events. Pennsylvania runs northwest in a direct line between the Capitol and the White House—if it weren't for the Treasury Building, the president would have a clear view of the Capitol—before continuing on a northwest angle to Georgetown, where it becomes M Street.

Pennsylvania Avenue in front of the White House—between 15th and 17th streets NW—remains closed to cars for security reasons but has been remade into an attractive pedestrian plaza, lined with 88 Princeton American Elm trees.

Constitution Avenue, paralleled to the south most of the way by Independence Avenue, runs east-west, flanking the Capitol and the Mall. If you hear Washingtonians talk about the "House" side of the Hill, they're referring to the southern half of the Capitol, the side closest to Independence Avenue and home to Congressional House offices and the House Chamber. Conversely, the Senate side is the northern half of the Capitol, where Senate offices and the Senate Chamber are found, closer to Constitution Avenue.

Washington's longest avenue, **Massachusetts Avenue,** runs parallel to Pennsylvania (a few avenues north). Along the way, you'll find Union Station and then Dupont Circle, which is central to the area known as Embassy Row. Farther out are the Naval Observatory (the vice president's residence is on the premises), Washington National Cathedral, American University, and, eventually, Maryland.

Connecticut Avenue, which runs more directly north (the other avenues run southeast to northwest), starts at Lafayette Square, intersects Dupont Circle, and eventually takes you to the National Zoo, on to the charming residential neighborhood known as Cleveland Park, and into Chevy Chase, Maryland, where you can pick up the Beltway to head out of town. Connecticut Avenue, with its chic-to-funky array of shops and clusters of top-dollar to good-value restaurants, is an interesting street to stroll.

Wisconsin Avenue originates in Georgetown; its intersection with M Street forms Georgetown's hub. Antiques shops, trendy boutiques, nightclubs, restaurants, and pubs all vie for attention. Wisconsin Avenue basically parallels Connecticut Avenue; one of the few irritating things about the city's transportation system is that the Metro does not connect these two major arteries in the heart of the city. (Buses do, and, of course, you can always walk or take a taxi from one avenue to the other; read about the supplemental bus system, the D.C. Circulator, below.) Metrorail's first stop on Wisconsin Avenue is in Tenleytown, a residential area. Follow the avenue north and you land in the affluent Maryland cities of Chevy Chase and Bethesda.

FINDING AN ADDRESS If you understand the city's layout, it's easy to find your way around. As you read this, have a map handy.

Each of the four corners of the District of Columbia is exactly the same distance from the Capitol dome. The White House and most government buildings and important monuments are west of the Capitol (in the northwest and southwest quadrants), as are major hotels and tourist facilities.

Numbered streets run north-south, beginning on either side of the Capitol with 1st Street. Lettered streets run east-west and are named alphabetically, beginning with A Street. (Don't look for J, X, Y, or Z streets, however—they

Transit Tip

If you plan to use D.C.'s Metrorail and bus service a lot while you're here, you might want to do what most Washington commuters do: purchase a **SmarTrip** card, which is a permanent, rechargeable farecard that's way faster to use than a regular farecard—you just touch it to the target on a faregate inside a Metro station or farebox inside a Metrobus. The SmarTrip card also replaces the now obsolete paper transfers; when you transfer from Metrobus to Metrorail, you simply flash your SmarTrip card, which discounts your fare by 50¢; when you transfer from Metrorail to Metrobus using your SmarTrip card, you're discounted 20¢. SmarTrip cards are also usable on other area transit systems, including D.C. Circulator buses and DASH buses in Old Town Alexandria. You can purchase SmarTrip cards online at www.wmata.com; at vending machines in certain Metro stations; and at WMATA headquarters (weekdays only), 600 5th St. NW; its sales office at Metro Center (weekdays only), 12th and F streets NW; or at one of many retail stores, like Giant or Safeway grocery stores. You can add value as needed at the passes/farecard vending machines in every Metro station, or even on a Metrobus, using the farebox. For more information, contact Metro (www.wmata.com; © **888/762-7874**).

don't exist.) After W Street, street names of two syllables continue in alphabetical order, followed by street names of three syllables; the more syllables in a name, the farther the street is from the Capitol.

Avenues, named for U.S. states, run at angles across the grid pattern and often intersect at traffic circles. For example, New Hampshire, Connecticut, and Massachusetts avenues intersect at Dupont Circle.

With this in mind, you can easily find an address. On lettered streets, the address tells you exactly where to go. For instance, 1776 K St. NW is between 17th and 18th streets (the first two digits of 1776 tell you that) in the northwest quadrant (NW). *Note:* I Street is often written as "Eye" Street to prevent confusion with 1st Street.

To find an address on numbered streets, you'll probably have to use your fingers. For instance, 623 8th St. SE is between F and G streets (the sixth and seventh letters of the alphabet; the first digit of 623 tells you that) in the southeast quadrant (SE). One thing to remember: You count B as the second letter of the alphabet even though B Street North and B Street South are now Constitution and Independence aves., respectively, but because there's no J Street, K becomes the 10th letter, L the 11th, and so on. To be honest, I don't know anyone who actually uses this method for figuring out an exact location.

By Public Transportation
METRORAIL

The **Metrorail** system continues to be the best way to get around the city, in spite of the fact that it's showing its age: 37 years old. In fact, a $177-million rehabilitation project is underway now and will continue for many years on the Metro system.

You should expect delays on the Red Line, especially throughout the long period of repair and maintenance, as trains travel at reduced speeds and schedules are disrupted to allow for service. As a tourist, you may not notice or be as affected as regular commuters are by these changes. For more information, contact **Washington Metropolitan Area Transit Authority** (**WMATA;** www. wmata.com; *©* **202/637-7000**). If you have concerns, you can always ride the buses (see information below), which will always be slower than the train system, but will get you wherever you want to go.

If you do ride Metrorail, try to avoid traveling during rush hour (Mon–Fri 5–9:30am and 3–7pm), since delays can be frequent, lines at farecard machines long, trains overcrowded, and Washingtonians at their rudest. You can expect to get a seat during off-peak hours (basically weekdays 10am–3pm, weeknights after 7pm, and all day weekends). All cars are air-conditioned and fitted with comfortable upholstered seats.

Metrorail's system of 86 stations and 106 miles of track includes locations at or near almost every sightseeing attraction; it also extends to suburban Maryland and northern Virginia. There are five lines in operation—Red, Blue, Orange, Yellow, and Green. The lines connect at several central points, making transfers relatively easy. All but Yellow and Green line trains stop at Metro Center; all except Red Line trains stop at L'Enfant Plaza; all but Blue and Orange line trains stop at Gallery Place–Chinatown. See the color map inside the back cover of this book.

Metro stations are indicated by discreet brown columns bearing the station's name and topped by the letter M. Below the M is a colored stripe or stripes indicating the line or lines that stop there. When entering a Metro station for the first time, go to the kiosk and ask the station manager for free, helpful brochures, including the *Metro System Pocket Guide.* It contains a map of the system, explains how it works, and lists the closest Metro stops to points of interest. The station manager can answer questions about routing or purchase of farecards. You can download a copy of the pocket guide and loads of information, including schedules, from Metro's website (www.wmata.com). The pocket guide is available in 10 languages besides English: Arabic, Italian, French, Chinese, Japanese, Spanish, Korean, Portuguese, Vietnamese, and German.

To enter or exit a Metro station, you need a computerized **farecard,** available at vending machines near the entrance. The machines take nickels, dimes, quarters, and bills from $1 to $20; they can return up to $4.95 in change (coins only). The vending machines labeled passes/farecards accept both cash and credit cards. Depending on how far you're traveling, Metrorail fares range between a minimum of $1.70 and a maximum of $3.50 during non-peak hours (Mon–Fri 9:30am–3pm and 7pm–midnight; all day Saturday until midnight; and all day Sunday) and between $2.10

 Metro Etiquette 101

To avoid risking the ire of commuters, be sure to follow these guidelines: Stand to the right on the escalator so that people in a hurry can get past you on the left. And when you reach the train level, don't puddle at the bottom of the escalator, blocking the path of those coming behind you; move down the platform. Eating, drinking, and smoking are strictly prohibited on the Metro and in stations.

Getting to Georgetown

Metrorail doesn't go to Georgetown, and though Metro buses do (nos. 31, 32, 36, 38B, D1, D2, D3, D5, D6, and G2), the public transportation I'd recommend is that provided by the **D.C. Circulator** (p. 347), which travels two Georgetown routes: one that runs between the Rosslyn, Virginia and Dupont Circle Metro stations, stopping at designated points in Georgetown along the way, and a second one that runs between Georgetown and Union Station. The buses come by every 10 minutes from 7am to midnight Sunday through Thursday, 7am to 2am Friday and Saturday. One-way fares cost $1, or 50¢ with a SmarTrip card.

and $5.75 during peak hours (Mon–Fri 5–9:30am and 3–7pm; Fri and Sat midnight–3am).

Metro has eight transfer hubs, and probably the busiest hub is at Metro Center, where tracks crisscross on upper and lower levels and passengers can switch to a Red, Blue, or Orange line train; read and follow the signs carefully, or ask someone for help, to make sure you get to the right track.

If you plan to take several Metrorail trips during your stay, put more value on the farecard to avoid having to purchase a new card each time you ride. For stays of more than a few days, your best value would be the **7-Day Fast Pass,** for $47 per person, which allows you unlimited travel; **1-Day Rail Passes** are available for $14 per person. You can buy these passes online or at the Passes/Farecards machines in the stations. You can also purchase them at WMATA headquarters (weekdays only), 600 5th St. NW (www.wmata.com; ☎ **202/637-7000**); its sales office at Metro Center (weekdays only), 12th and F streets NW; or one of the retail stores, like Giant or Safeway grocery stores, where farecards are sold.

Up to two children ages 4 and under can ride free with a paying passenger. Seniors (65 and older) and people with disabilities (with valid proof) ride Metrorail and Metrobus for a reduced fare.

When you insert your card in the entrance gate, the time and location are recorded on its magnetic tape, and your card is returned. Don't forget to snatch it up and keep it handy; *you have to reinsert your farecard in the exit gate at your destination,* where the fare will automatically be deducted. The card will be returned if there's any value left on it. If you arrive at a destination and your farecard doesn't have enough value, add what's necessary at the Exitfare machines near the exit gate.

Most Metro stations have more than one exit. To save yourself time and confusion, try to figure out ahead of time which exit gets you closer to where you're going. In this book, I include the specific exit you should use for every venue mentioned, including hotels, restaurants, and attractions. For instance, if you ride the Blue and Orange lines to the Smithsonian stop, you'll want to exit at the Mall to visit the museums, but exit at 12th Street and Independence Avenue SW if you're headed to the Mandarin Oriental Hotel.

Metrorail opens at 5am weekdays and 7am Saturday and Sunday, operating until midnight Sunday through Thursday, and until 3am Friday and Saturday. *Note:* Call ☎ **202/637-7000** or visit www.wmata.com for holiday hours and for information on Metro routes.

Know Before You Go

Metro information for both bus and subway travel is available by phone Monday through Friday 6am to 8:30pm, Saturday and Sunday 7am to 8:30pm; call ☎ 202/637-7000 and request a free map and time schedule, and find out any other details you need. It's usually faster and easier to obtain information and purchase farecards online, at **www.wmata.com**.

METROBUS

The Transit Authority is in the process of improving its bus system, a comprehensive operation that encompasses 1,500 buses traveling 319 routes, making 12,227 stops, operating within a 1,500-square-mile area that includes major arteries in D.C. and the Virginia and Maryland suburbs. The system is gradually phasing in the new, sleekly designed, red and silver buses that run on a combination of diesel and electric hybrid fuel, as the older red-white-and-blue buses succumb to maintenance problems and are put out to pasture. Both the old and the new buses post the bus's destination above the windshield and on the boarding side of the vehicle.

The Transit Authority is also working to improve design elements and placement of bus stop signs. For now look for red, white, and blue signs that tell you which buses stop at that location. Eventually, signage should tell you the routes and schedules for the buses that stop there. In the meantime, the Transit Authority has inaugurated a cool new alert system that allows riders to use cellphones or PDAs to find out when the next bus is due to arrive. You simply use a cellphone to call Metro's main number, ☎ **202/637-7000,** then type in the seven-digit bus stop identifier that's posted on the bus stop sign to find out when the next bus is expected to arrive.

Base fare in the District is $1.70, or $3.85 for the faster express buses, which make fewer stops. There may be additional charges for travel into the Maryland and Virginia suburbs. Bus drivers are not equipped to make change, so if you have not purchased a SmarTrip card (see box) or a pass (see below), be sure to carry exact change.

If you'll be in Washington for a while and plan to use the buses a lot, consider buying a 1-week pass ($15), which must be loaded onto a SmartCard (see above) and is available online and also at the Metro Center station and other outlets. See also "Transit Tip," above.

Most buses operate daily around-the-clock. Service is quite frequent on weekdays, especially during peak hours, and less frequent on weekends and late at night.

Up to two children 4 and under ride free with a paying passenger on Metrobus, and there are reduced fares for seniors (☎ **202/637-7000**) and people with disabilities (☎ **202/962-1245** or 962-1100; see "Disabled Travelers," later in this chapter, for transit information). If you leave something on a bus, on a train, or in a station, call Lost and Found Tuesday through Friday 11am to 5pm at ☎ **202/962-1195.**

By Car

If you're traveling to Washington as a tourist (rather than on business), you're probably planning to drive here. Most vacationing visitors do. But when you arrive, my advice is to park your car and get around on foot or by Metro or the D.C. Circulator.

📎 D.C. Circulator

D.C. offers a fantastic supplemental bus system that is efficient, inexpensive, and convenient. The D.C. Circulator's fleet of air-conditioned red-and-gray buses travel five circumscribed routes in the city: the Southeast D.C. route between the Potomac Metro Station and points in Anacostia (weekdays 6am–7pm Oct–Mar, weekdays 6am–9pm and Sat 7am–9pm Apr–Sept); the east-west route between upper Georgetown and Union Station (7am–9pm daily, with a special service added between upper Georgetown and the intersection of 14th and K sts. NW, from 9pm–midnight Sun–Thurs, 9pm–2am Fri–Sat); a second Georgetown route that travels between the Rosslyn Metro station in Virginia and the Dupont Circle Metro station in the District, via Georgetown (Sun–Thurs 7am–midnight, Fri–Sat 7am–2am); the Union Station–to–Washington Navy Yard track (located near Nationals Park, the service operates 6am–7pm weekdays Oct–March, 6am–9pm weekdays and 7am–9pm Sat Apr–Sept, with extended hours on Nationals game days); and the route that travels between the Woodley Park–Zoo Metro station and the McPherson Square Metro station (7am–midnight Sun–Thurs; 7am–3:30am Fri–Sat). Buses stop at designated points on their routes (look for the distinctive red-and-gold sign, often topping a regular Metro bus stop sign) every 10 minutes. The fare at all times is $1, and you can order passes online at www.commuterdirect.com, or pay upon boarding with the exact fare or the use of a SmarTrip Metro card, or with a D.C. Circulator pass purchased at a street meter near the bus stop. For easy and fast transportation in the busiest parts of town, you can't beat it. Call ✆ **202/962-1423** or go to www.dccirculator.com.

If you must drive, be aware that traffic is always thick during the week, parking spaces are hard to find, and parking lots are ruinously expensive. You can expect to pay overnight rates of $25 to $50 at hotels, hourly rates starting at $8 at downtown parking lots and garages, and flat rates starting at $20 in the most popular parts of town, like Georgetown and in the Penn Quarter when there is an event at the Verizon Center. If you're hoping to snag a parking space on the street, you may or may not be happy to know that the D.C. government makes it as easy as possible for you to pay for that spot: Although the city still has many traditional parking meters that take coins, most downtown meters now accept cellphone remote "call it in" service, which allows you to call the phone number marked on the meter, provide your location and license plate number, and charge your parking expense using a credit or debit card, adding more time remotely if you're not able to return to your car before the allotted time is up. Alternatively, parking kiosks are increasingly prevalent on city streets: When you park on the street and don't see a meter, you'll notice a kiosk on the block instead; you use cash or a credit card at the kiosk to pay for parking time, print a receipt, then place the receipt against the windshield inside your car, so that it's visible to the officer checking on expired parking coverage.

Gasoline, as you're well aware, is expensive everywhere. At press time, in the Washington region, the cost of gasoline (also known as gas, but never petrol), is more than $4 a gallon. Taxes are already included in the printed price. One U.S. gallon equals 3.8 liters or .85 imperial gallons.

Fill-up locations are known as gas or service stations. In the District, I can tell you of one centrally located service station that offers some of the best rates: the Sunoco White House, at 1442 U St. NW (at 15th St. NW). You'll know you've found it when you see the number of cabbies pulling up to the pumps—always a good sign that the gas price is probably a better deal than elsewhere. For a listing of other D.C. stations selling the cheapest gas, access the local AAA website, www.aaamidatlantic.com, and go to the Fuel Price Finder function.

Watch out for **traffic circles.** The law states that traffic already in the circle has the right of way. No one pays any attention to this rule, however, which can be frightening (cars zoom into the circle without a glance at the cars already there). The other thing you'll notice is that while some circles are easy to figure out (Dupont Circle), others are nerve-rackingly confusing (Thomas Circle, where 14th St. NW, Vermont Ave. NW, M St. NW, and Massachusetts Ave. NW come together, is to be avoided at all costs). Changing lanes while in the belly of the circle is especially treacherous.

Sections of certain streets in Washington become **one-way** during rush hour: Rock Creek Parkway, Canal Road, and 17th Street NW are three examples. Other streets change the direction of some of their traffic lanes during rush hour. Connecticut Avenue NW is the main one: In the morning, traffic in four of its six lanes travels south to downtown, and in late afternoon/early evening, downtown traffic in four of its six lanes heads north; between the hours of 9am and 3:30pm, traffic in both directions keeps to the normally correct side of the yellow line. Lit-up traffic signs alert you to what's going on, but pay attention. Unless a sign is posted prohibiting it, a right-on-red law is in effect. The speed limit within city boundaries is usually 25 mph, up to 30 mph on some streets.

To keep up with street closings and construction information, go online to the *Washington Post's* home page, www.washingtonpost.com, and click on "Local," then "Traffic" to learn about current traffic and routing problems in the District and suburban Maryland and Virginia. As mentioned earlier, another helpful source is the website **www.godcgo.com**, which covers daily transportation options, from parking to Metro service alerts.

CAR RENTALS

If you need to rent a car while you're here, you have several options.

Residents and tourists alike seem to be turning to car rental clubs that allow you more flexible car-use arrangements, whether you need a car for an hour or for a month, with parking and other services included. One such company in Washington is **Zipcar** (www.zipcar.com; ℂ **866/494-7227**), which has a downtown office at 403 8th St. NW, entrance on 8th Street (ℂ **202/737-4900**), and pickup locations all over town.

Here's how it works: You apply and pay an application fee plus either an annual or monthly membership fee ahead of time online, order the car online or by phone using a credit card, and establish exactly when and where you need a car. You receive a special card in the mail, which you use to activate the specific car you've reserved at the specific location, time, and day you've prearranged. The idea is that this special card unlocks the reserved car and you climb inside to retrieve the keys, following instructions you're given ahead of time. Zipcar's rates vary depending on the plan you sign up for; once you've joined, the lowest starting rate is $6.98 an hour, and this fee covers gas and insurance.

Or you can go the usual route and rent a car from one of the major car rental companies. The major rental agencies are located throughout the city, including at Union Station (p. 72), where Alamo, Avis, Budget, and Hertz operate. Also see "Getting Into Town from the Airport," earlier in this chapter, for airport car rental locations.

Car rental rates can vary even more than airfares. Check out **BreezeNet. com**, which offers domestic car-rental discounts with some of the most competitive rates around. Also worth visiting are Orbitz, Hotwire, Travelocity, and Priceline, all of which offer competitive online car rental rates.

If you're visiting from abroad and plan to rent a car in the United States, keep in mind that foreign driver's licenses are usually recognized in the U.S., but you should get an international one if your home license is not in English. International visitors should also note that insurance and taxes are almost never included in quoted rental-car rates in the U.S. Be sure to ask your rental agency about additional fees for these; they can add a significant cost to your car rental. One U.S. gallon equals 3.8 liters or .85 imperial gallons.

It helps to do your homework: Take the time to shop around and ask a few key questions, and you might save hundreds of dollars:

○ Are weekend rates lower than weekday rates? Ask if the rate is the same for pickup Friday morning, for instance, as it is for Thursday night.

○ Is the weekly rate cheaper than the daily rate? Even if you need the car for only 4 days, it may be cheaper to keep it for 5.

○ Does the agency assess a drop-off charge if you don't return the car to the same location where you picked it up? Is it cheaper to pick up the car at the airport or at a downtown location?

○ Are special promotional rates available? If you see an advertised price in your local newspaper, be sure to ask for that specific rate; otherwise you may be charged the standard cost. Terms change constantly.

○ Are discounts available for members of AARP, AAA, frequent-flier programs, or trade unions?

○ How much tax will be added to the rental bill? In the District, you'll pay a 10% sales tax, plus possible surcharges.

○ What is the cost of adding an additional driver's name to the contract?

○ How many free miles are included in the price? Free mileage is often negotiable, depending on the length of your rental.

○ Are there extra charges if you're under 25? *Note:* All car rental agencies require drivers be at least 21.

Some companies offer "refueling packages," in which you pay for an entire tank of gas upfront. The price is usually fairly competitive with local gas prices, but you don't get credit for any gas remaining in the tank. If a stop at a gas station on the way to the airport will make you miss your plane, then by all means take advantage of the fuel purchase option. Otherwise, skip it.

For information on insurance, review your own car insurance policy and contact the **American Automobile Association** (**AAA;** © **800/763-9900**) for advice and helpful information.

By Taxi

The D.C. taxicab system charges passengers according to time- and distance-based meters. Fares may increase, but at press time, fares began at $3, plus $2.16 per each additional mile, $1 per additional passenger, and 50¢ per piece of luggage that the driver places in the trunk. Other charges might apply (for instance, if you telephone for a cab, rather than hail one in the street). **Note:** Generally speaking, taxis accept only cash for payment, not credit cards.

Try **Diamond Cab Company** (© **202/387-4011**) or **Yellow Cab** (© **202/546-7900**).

For more information, call © **202/645-6018** or check out the D.C. Taxicab Commission's website, www.dctaxi.dc.gov. Also refer to **www.godcgo.com** for a full listing of D.C. cab companies.

By Bike

Thanks to a robust bike-share program, Washington, D.C. is increasingly a city where locals themselves get around by bike. The flat terrain of the National Mall and many neighborhoods, including the Penn Quarter, Capitol Hill, Dupont Circle, the U Street Corridor, and lower Georgetown make these areas conducive to biking. Fifty miles of bike lanes throughout D.C., and bike paths through Rock Creek Park, the C&O Canal in Georgetown, and around the National Mall encourage the practice, too. Interested? Check out the **Capital BikeShare** website, www.capitalbikeshare.com, for more information about bike rental memberships and bike station locations, which are all over, including at the National Mall and in Georgetown. The Capital BikeShare program is a better option economically for members who use the bikes for short commutes; see p. 155 for traditional bike rental companies, which are also plentiful.

GUIDED TOURS

One of the best ways to orient yourself to the city is to take a guided tour. D.C. offers a slew of them, from themed jaunts that take you to sites at which famous scandals occurred to Segway tours of Capitol Hill. Before you start getting yourself from place to place, consider signing up for one of these treks around town. Also go to the **Cultural Tourism D.C.** website, **www.culturaltourismdc.org**, and click on "Things to Do and See" to find information about self-guided neighborhood heritage walking trails and for a few other guided tour options than those provided here (click on "Tours and Trails").

On Foot

A Tour de Force (www.atourdeforce.com; © **703/525-2948**) is historian and raconteur Jeanne Fogel's 29-year-old company. She offers various modes of transport, from walking to bus, SUV, and limo tours. Fogel custom-designs the route around the city per your request and the size of your group, from a romantic tour for a couple to a traditional sightseeing excursion for a convention crowd. Fogel (or her stand-in) peppers her narration with little-known anecdotes and facts about neighborhoods, historic figures, and the most visited sites. Call for rates.

Spies of Washington Walking Tours (www.spiesofwashingtontour.com; © **703/569-1875**) offers four walking tours that focus on espionage-related sites in Georgetown and around the White House, Pennsylvania Avenue, Capitol Hill, and the Russian Embassy areas. Carol Bessette, a retired Air Force intelligence officer, conducts the tours, which cost $12 per person. Private tours and bus tours are also available.

Anecdotal History Tours of Washington, D.C. ★ (www.dcsightseeing. com; ✆ **301/294-9514**) offers private and occasional public tours that take you on walks through the streets of Georgetown, Adams Morgan, and other locations guided by author/historian Anthony S. Pitch. Inquire about rates.

Segway Tours (www.citysegwaytours.com/Washington; ✆ **877/734-8687**) offers a 3-hour tour year-round daily at 10am and 2pm, with an additional tour at 6pm March to December, as well as a 2-hour version available daily March through December at 11am and 3pm. Though technically they aren't "on foot," Segways are self-propelling scooters that operate based on "dynamic stabilization" technology, which uses your body movements. The 2-hour tours cost $65 per person; the 3-hour tours cost $75 per person. The cost includes training. Ages 16 and up.

Washington Walks (www.washingtonwalks.com; ✆ **202/484-1565**) offers an amazing and fun assortment of walking tours, from the Columbia Heights Historical Drinkabout to a narrated meander around the exterior of the Capitol. The cost is $15 per person, the 2-hour tours take place rain or shine, and you just show up, no reservations required. Bus, group, and private tours are also available.

By Bus

Martz Gray Line of Washington, D.C. (www.graylinedc.com; ✆ **800/862-1400** or 301/386-8300) operates quite a number of good sightseeing tours, among them an After Dark tour, a 2-hour Taste of D.C., D.C. in a Day, D.C. in 2 Days, and tours aboard a double-decker bus (the red Open Top sightseeing buses you'll see everywhere). Schedules vary by tour, and rates range from $8.50 for the Arlington Cemetery tour to $99 for the 2-day Washington, D.C. Grand Tour. In early 2012, the National Park Service awarded Gray Line the contract to provide interpretive tours of Arlington Cemetery (p. 123), a narrated bus tour of the sites in National Mall and Memorial Parks, and an un-narrated express shuttle service between Arlington Cemetery and Union Station, with a few stops en route. These are the only tour and shuttle services sanctioned by the National Park Service to operate on this parkland. See "Getting Around the National Mall and Memorial Parks by Bus," p. 89.

Old Town Trolley tours (www.trolleytours.com; ✆ **888/910-8687** or 202/832-9800) offer fixed-price, on-off service as you travel in three loops around the city, with a transfer point at the Lincoln Memorial stop to go on to Arlington Cemetery, and a second transfer point near Ford's Theatre to get to Georgetown and to Washington National Cathedral. Many hotels sell tickets; otherwise you can purchase tickets online or at the Old Town Trolley Tour booths at Union Station and Georgetown Park, and many other places around town. Buses operate daily from 9am to 5:30pm. The cost is $35 for adults, $18 for children 4 to 12, free for children 3 and under. You can buy tickets online in advance and at a discount, and use those e-tickets to board at any of the stops on the route. The full tour, which is narrated, takes 2 hours (if you don't get off and tour the sites, obviously), and trolleys come by every 30 minutes or so.

By Boat

Since Washington is a river city, why not see it by boat? Potomac cruises allow sweeping vistas of the monuments and memorials, Georgetown, the Kennedy Center, and other Washington sights. Read the information below carefully, since not all boat cruises offer guided tours. Some of the following boats leave from the Washington waterfront and some from Old Town Alexandria.

Spirit of Washington Cruises, Pier 4 at 6th and Water streets SW (www. spiritofwashington.com; **☎ 866/302-2469;** Metro: Waterfront), offers a variety of trips daily, including evening dinner, lunch, brunch, and moonlight dance cruises, as well as a half-day excursion to Mount Vernon and back. Lunch and dinner cruises include a 40-minute musical revue.

The *Spirit of Washington* is a luxury climate-controlled harbor cruise ship with carpeted decks and huge panoramic windows designed for sightseeing. There are three well-stocked bars onboard.

Dandy Restaurant Cruises (www.dandydinnerboat.com; **☎ 703/683-6076**) operates *Nina's Dandy,* a climate-controlled, all-weather, glassed-in floating restaurant that runs year-round. You board the vessel in Old Town Alexandria, at the Prince Street pier, between Duke and King streets. Trips range from a 2½-hour weekday lunch cruise to a 3-hour Saturday dinner cruise.

Odyssey (www.odysseycruises.com; **☎ 866/306-2469**) was designed specifically to glide under the bridges that cross the Potomac. The boat looks like a glass bullet, with its snub-nosed port and its streamlined 240-foot-long glass body. The wraparound see-through walls and ceiling allow for great views. You board the *Odyssey* at the Gangplank Marina, on Washington's waterfront at 6th and Water streets SW (Metro: Waterfront). Cruises available include lunch, Sunday brunch, and dinner excursions, with live entertainment provided during each cruise.

From April through October, the **Potomac Riverboat Company ★** (www. potomacriverboatco.com; **☎ 877/511-2628** or 703/684-0580) offers several 90-minute round-trip, narrated tours aboard sightseeing vessels that take you past Washington landmarks or along Old Town Alexandria's waterfront; certain cruises also travel to Mount Vernon, where you hop off and re-board after you've toured the estate. You board the boats at the pier behind the Torpedo Factory in Old Town Alexandria at the foot of King Street, or, for the Washington monuments and memorials tour, at Georgetown's Washington Harbour. A concession stand selling light refreshments and beverages is open during the cruises.

The **Capitol River Cruise's** *Nightingales* (www.capitolrivercruises.com; **☎ 800/405-5511** or 301/460-7447) are historic 65-foot steel riverboats that can accommodate 90 people. The *Nightingales'* narrated jaunts depart Georgetown's Washington Harbour every hour on the hour, from noon to 9pm, April through October (the 9pm outing is offered in summer months only). The 45-minute narrated tour travels past the monuments and memorials to National Airport and back. A snack bar onboard sells light refreshments, beer, wine, and sodas; you're welcome to bring your own picnic aboard. To get here, take the Metro to Foggy Bottom and then walk into Georgetown, following Pennsylvania Avenue, which becomes M Street. Turn left on 31st Street NW and follow to the Washington Harbour complex on the water.

Old Town Trolley also operates **DC Ducks** (www.dcducks.com; **☎ 202/832-9800**), which feature unique land and water tours of Washington aboard the *DUKW,* an amphibious army vehicle (boat with wheels) from World War II that accommodates 30 passengers. Ninety-minute guided tours aboard the open-air canopied craft include a land portion taking in major sights—the Capitol, Lincoln Memorial, Washington Monument, White House, and Smithsonian museums—and a 30-minute Potomac cruise. Purchase tickets online or inside Union Station at the information desk; board the vehicle just outside the main entrance to Union Station. Hours vary, but departures usually follow a daily schedule mid-March through October: 10am to 4pm, every hour on the hour.

By Bike

Bike and Roll/Bike the Sites, Inc. ★ (www.bikethesites.com; © **202/842-2453**) offers a more active way to see Washington, from March to December. The company has designed several different biking tours of the city, including the popular Capital Sites Ride, which takes you past museums, memorials, the White House, the Capitol, and the Supreme Court. The ride takes 3 hours, covers 7 to 8 miles, and costs $40 per adult, $30 per child 12 and under. Bike the Sites provides you with a comfortable mountain bicycle fitted to your size, a bike helmet, a water bottle, a light snack, and two guides to lead the ride. Tours depart from three locations: the rear plaza (12th St. NW side) of the Old Post Office Pavilion, which is located at 1100 Pennsylvania Ave. NW (Metro: Federal Triangle, on the Blue and Orange line); Union Station (© **202/962-0206**); or Old Town Alexandria (© **703/548-7655**). Guides impart historical and anecdotal information as you go. The company rents bikes to those who want to go their own, unnarrated way; rates vary depending on the bike you choose but always include helmet, bike, lock, and pump; there's a 2-hour minimum. Another option: customized guided bike rides to suit your tour specifications.

[FastFACTS] WASHINGTON, D.C.

Area Codes Within the District of Columbia, the area code is 202. In Northern Virginia it's 703, and in D.C.'s Maryland suburbs, the area code is 301. If you are calling a 202 number from a 202 number, you don't need to dial the area code. Otherwise you must use the area code when dialing a phone number, whether it's a local 202, 703, or 301 phone number.

Business Hours Most museums are open daily 10:30am to 5:30pm; some, including several of the Smithsonians, stay open later in spring and summer. Most banks are open from 9am to 3pm Monday through Thursday, with some staying open until 5pm on Friday and some open for business on Saturday mornings. Stores typically open between 9 and 10am and close between 5 and 6pm from Monday to Saturday. See chapter 7 for more specific information about store hours.

Car Rental See "Getting Into Town from the Airport" and the car rental information in "Getting Around," both earlier in this chapter.

Cellphones See "Mobile Phones," below.

Crime See "Safety," below.

Customs

For customs information, consult your nearest U.S. embassy or consulate, or the U.S. Customs website, www.cbp.gov. In Washington, D.C. the U.S. Customs and Border Protection agency has an office at 1300 Pennsylvania Ave. NW, Washington, DC 20229 (www.cbp.gov; ✆ **877/227-5511**).

Disabled Travelers

Although Washington, D.C. is one of the most accessible cities in the world for travelers with disabilities, it is not perfect—especially when it comes to historic buildings, as well as some restaurants and shops. Theaters, museums, and government buildings are generally well equipped. Still, rule of thumb for least hassle is to call ahead to places you hope to visit to find out specific accessibility features. In the case of restaurants and bars, I'm afraid you'll have to work to pin them down—no one wants to discourage a potential customer. Several sources might help: The local nonprofit organization **Access Information's** website, www.disabilityguide.org, offers helpful information, including restaurant reviews, accessible tours, transportation options, and much more. The **Washington Metropolitan Transit Authority** publishes accessibility information on its website, www.wmata.com, or you can call ✆ **202/962-1100** (TTY 202/962-2033).

Doctors

Before you leave, talk to your local physician and ask for a referral in the D.C. area, should you need one. If your doctor isn't able to help, talk to the concierge or general manager at your hotel. Most hotels are prepared for just such medical emergencies and work with local doctors who are able to see ill or injured hotel guests. Also see "Hospitals," below.

Drinking Laws

The legal age for purchase and consumption of alcoholic beverages is 21; proof of age is required and often requested at bars, nightclubs, and restaurants, so it's always a good idea to bring ID when you go out. Do not carry open containers of alcohol in your car or any public area that isn't zoned for alcohol consumption. The police can fine you on the spot. Don't even think about driving while intoxicated.

Liquor stores are closed on Sunday. District gourmet grocery stores, mom-and-pop grocery stores, and 7-Eleven convenience stores often sell beer and wine, even on Sunday. Bars and nightclubs serve liquor until 2am Sunday through Thursday and until 3am Friday and Saturday.

Driving Rules

See "Getting Around," earlier in this chapter.

Electricity

Like Canada, the United States uses 110–120 volts AC (60 cycles), compared to 220–240 volts AC (50 cycles) in most of Europe, Australia, and New Zealand. Downward converters that change 220–240 volts to 110–120 volts are difficult to find in the United States, so bring one with you.

Embassies & Consulates

All embassies are located here in the nation's capital. If your country isn't listed below, call for directory information in Washington, D.C. (✆ 202/555-1212) or check www.embassy.org/embassies.

The embassy of **Australia** is at 1601 Massachusetts Ave. NW, Washington, DC 20036 (www.usa.embassy.gov.au; ✆ 202/797-3000). Consulates are in Honolulu, Houston, Los Angeles, New York, and San Francisco.

The embassy of **Canada** is at 501 Pennsylvania Ave. NW, Washington, DC 20001 (www.canadainternational.gc.ca/Washington; ✆ 202/682-1740). Other Canadian consulates are in Buffalo, New York; Detroit; Los Angeles; New York; and Seattle.

The embassy of **Ireland** is at 2234 Massachusetts Ave. NW, Washington, DC 20008 (www.embassyofireland.org; ✆ 202/462-3939). Irish consulates are in Boston, Chicago, New York, San Francisco, and other cities. See website for complete listing.

The Embassy of **New Zealand** is at 37 Observatory Circle NW, Washington, DC 20008 (www.nzembassy.com; ☎ 202/328-4800). New Zealand consulates are in Los Angeles, Salt Lake City, San Francisco, and Seattle.

The embassy of the **United Kingdom** is at 3100 Massachusetts Ave. NW, Washington, DC 20008 (www.ukinusa.fco.gov.uk; ☎ 202/588-6500). Other British consulates are in Atlanta, Boston, Chicago, Cleveland, Houston, Los Angeles, New York, San Francisco, and Seattle.

Emergencies   Call ☎ **911** for police, fire, and medical emergencies. This is a toll-free call. (No coins are required at public telephones.)

If you encounter serious problems, contact the **Travelers Aid Society International** (www.travelersaid.org; ☎ **202/546-1127**), a nationwide, nonprofit, social-service organization geared to helping travelers in difficult straits, from reuniting families separated while traveling, to providing food and/or shelter to people stranded without cash, to emotional counseling. Travelers Aid operates help desks at Washington Dulles International Airport (☎ **703/572-8296**), Ronald Reagan Washington National Airport (☎ **703/417-3975**), and Union Station (☎ **202/371-1937**). At Baltimore–Washington International Thurgood Marshall Airport, a volunteer agency called **Pathfinders** (☎ **410/859-7826**) mans the customer service desks throughout the airport.

Family Travel   Field trips during the school year and family vacations during the summer keep Washington, D.C. crawling with kids all year long. More than any other city, perhaps, Washington is crammed with historic buildings, arts and science museums, parks, and recreational sites to interest young and old alike. The fact that so many attractions are free is a boon to the family budget.

Check out *Frommer's Washington, D.C. with Kids,* which makes an excellent companion piece to this book, providing in-depth coverage of sightseeing with children in Washington.

To locate accommodations, restaurants, and attractions that are particularly kid-friendly, look for the "Kids" icon throughout this guide.

Gasoline   See "By Car," under "Getting Around," earlier in this chapter.

Hospitals   If you don't require immediate ambulance transportation but still need emergency-room treatment, call one of the following hospitals (and be sure to get directions): Children's Hospital National Medical Center, 111 Michigan Ave. NW (☎ **202/476-5000**); George Washington University Hospital, 900 23rd St. NW, at Washington Circle (☎ **202/715-4000**); Georgetown University Medical Center, 3800 Reservoir Rd. NW (☎ **202/444-2000**); or Howard University Hospital, 2041 Georgia Ave. NW (☎ **202/865-6100**).

Insurance   For information on traveler's insurance, trip cancellation insurance, and medical insurance while traveling, visit www.frommers.com/tips.

Internet & Wi-Fi   More and more hotels, resorts, airports, cafes, and retailers are going Wi-Fi (wireless fidelity), becoming "hotspots" that offer free Wi-Fi access or charge a small fee for usage. Most laptops sold today have built-in wireless capability. To find public Wi-Fi hotspots in Washington, go to **www.jiwire.com**; its Hotspot Finder holds the world's largest directory of public wireless hotspots (402 within the city of Washington, last time I checked). Or you could just head to your corner Starbucks, which has offered Wi-Fi service with its lattes for quite some time.

Likewise, all three D.C. airports offer Wi-Fi; both National and Dulles offer complimentary service, but BWI does not.

All of the D.C. hotels listed in chapter 9 offer Internet access; in each hotel description, I indicate whether the service is wired, wireless, or both, and whether the hotel charges a daily fee or provides the service for free.

If your laptop does not have wireless capability and/or the hotel where you're staying is one of the few that does not offer wireless service, bring a **connection kit** of the right power and phone adapters, a spare phone cord, and a spare Ethernet network cable—or find out whether your hotel supplies them to guests.

Hotels increasingly provide guests computer and Internet access in their hotel business centers, often as a complimentary service. Both of D.C.'s **Embassy Suites Hotels,** the **Downtown** location and the **Convention Center** property (p. 297 and 284) are examples. Washington, D.C. is lacking in Internet cafes, probably because everyone here carries a Blackberry, laptop, iPhone, or some other form of PDA. I know of only one public Internet cafe: in Dupont Circle's **Kramerbooks & Afterwords** bookstore, 1517 Connecticut Ave. NW (✆ **202/387-1400**), which has one computer available for free Internet access, with a 15-minute time limit.

Legal Aid   While driving, if you are pulled over for a minor infraction (such as speeding), never attempt to pay the fine directly to a police officer; this could be construed as attempted bribery, a much more serious crime. Pay fines by mail or directly into the hands of the clerk of the court. If accused of a more serious offense, say and do nothing before consulting a lawyer. In the U.S., the burden is on the state to prove a person's guilt beyond a reasonable doubt, and everyone has the right to remain silent, whether he or she is suspected of a crime or is actually arrested. Once arrested, a person can make one telephone call to a party of his or her choice. The international visitor should call his or her embassy or consulate.

LGBT Travelers   The nation's capital is most welcoming to the gay and lesbian community. In fact, as of March 9, 2010, same-sex couples can now legally marry each other in the nation's capital. How does that grab you? If you're interested in coming here to get hitched, the tourism bureau's Destination D.C. website, www.washington.org, tells you everything you need to know, from names of local officiates happy to perform the ceremony, to florist and venue recommendations, to a complete Q&A list that leads you through procedural details. That information appears on the LGBT home page for Destination D.C. From www.washington.org, click on "Experience DC," then scroll down to find the "For LGBT" link.

Even if you're not planning to get married here, you should visit this website for generally helpful information about Washington, D.C.'s large and vibrant gay and lesbian community. This special section covers the history of the gay rights movement in the capital; a calendar of noteworthy events, like the annual, weeklong Capital Pride Celebration held in June, complete with a street fair and a parade; and favorite-place recommendations made by local gays and lesbians. Better yet is Destination D.C.'s *LGBT Traveler's Guide,* which covers just about every aspect of the not-straight life in D.C. You can order the 65-page guide by calling Destination D.C.'s main number, ✆ **202/789-7000,** or download it from the website.

Dupont Circle is the unofficial headquarters for gay life, site of the annual 17th Street High Heel Drag race on the Tuesday preceding Halloween, and home to long-established gay bars and dance clubs (see chapter 8 for some suggestions), but the whole city is pretty much LGBT-friendly.

Mail   At press time, domestic postage rates were 32¢ for a postcard and 45¢ for a letter. For international mail, a first-class letter of up to 1 ounce costs $1.05 (85¢ to Canada or

Mexico); a first-class postcard costs the same as a letter. For more information, go to **www.usps.com**.

If you aren't sure what your address will be, mail can be sent to you, in your name, c/o General Delivery, at the main post office of the city or region where you expect to be. (Call 📞 **800/275-8777** for information on the nearest post office.) The addressee must pick up mail in person and must produce proof of identity (driver's license, passport, etc.). Most post offices will hold mail for up to 1 month, and are open Monday to Friday from 8am to 5pm, with some open on Saturday from 8am to noon.

Always include zip codes when mailing items in the U.S. If you don't know your zip code, visit www.usps.com/zip4.

Medical Requirements Unless you're arriving from an area known to be suffering from an epidemic (particularly cholera or yellow fever), inoculations or vaccinations are not required for entry into the United States.

Mobile Phones If you are American and own a **cellphone,** bring your phone with you to D.C., making sure first, of course, that your cellphone service does not charge excessively—or at all—for long-distance calls. In fact, if you are from outside the country and own an international cellphone with service that covers the Washington area, bring that phone along. The point is that hotels often charge outrageous fees for each long-distance or local call you make using the phone in your hotel room.

AT&T, Verizon, Sprint Nextel, and T-Mobile are among the cellphone networks operating in Washington, D.C., so there's a good chance you'll have full coverage anywhere in the city—except possibly on the subway. Verizon has long been the sole provider of Metrorail's wireless service, but now the system is in the process of expanding cellphone and wireless services to include those provided by AT&T, Sprint Nextel, and T-Mobile; coverage infrastructure should be in place by 2013. You can expect reception to be generally excellent throughout the city.

International visitors should check their **GSM (Global System for Mobile Communications) wireless network** to see where GSM phones and text messaging work in the U.S.; go to the website www.t-mobile.com/coverage.

In any case, take a look at your wireless company's coverage map on its website before heading out. If you know your phone won't work here, or if you don't have a cellphone, you have several options:

You can **rent** a phone before you leave home from **InTouch USA** (www.intouchusa.us; 📞 **800/872-7626** in the U.S., or 703/222-7161 outside the U.S.).

You can **buy** a phone once you arrive. All three Washington-area airports sell cellphones and SIM cards. Look for the **Airport Wireless** shops at Dulles International Airport (📞 **703/661-0411**), at National Airport (📞 **703/417-3983**), and at BWI Airport (📞 **410/691-0262**).

You can purchase a pay-as-you-go phone from all sorts of places, from Amazon.com to any Verizon store. In D.C., Verizon has a store at Union Station (📞 **202/682-9475**) and another at 1314 F St. NW (📞 **202/624-0072**), to name just two convenient locations.

If you have Web access while traveling, consider a broadband-based telephone service (in technical terms, **Voice over Internet Protocol,** or **VoIP**) such as Skype (www.skype.com) or Vonage (www.vonage.com), which allow you to make free international calls from your laptop or in a cybercafe. Neither service requires the people you're calling to also have that service (though there are fees if they do not). Also look into Google's phone-calling option, www.google.com/voice, which allows free calls in the U.S. and charges varying rates for calls to destinations outside the U.S. Check the websites for details.

Money & Costs   Frommer's lists exact prices in the local currency. The currency conversions quoted below were correct at press time. However, rates fluctuate, so before departing consult a currency exchange website such as **www.oanda.com/currency/converter** to check up-to-the-minute rates.

THE VALUE OF THE U.S. DOLLAR VS. OTHER POPULAR CURRENCIES

US$	Aus$	Can$	Euro€	NZ$	UK£
1	.97	.99	.76	1.23	.62

WHAT THINGS COST IN WASHINGTON, D.C.

	US$
Taxi from National Airport to downtown	18.00
Double room, moderate	250.00
Double room, inexpensive	150.00
Three-course dinner for one without wine, moderate	50.00
Glass of wine	8.00
Cup of coffee	2.00
1 gallon regular unleaded gas	4.10
Admission to most museums	Free
1-day Metrorail pass	14.00

Anyone who travels to the nation's capital expecting bargains is in for a rude awakening, especially when it comes to lodging. Less expensive than New York and London, Washington, D.C.'s daily hotel rate nevertheless reflects the city's popularity as a top destination among U.S. travelers, averaging $204 (according to most recent statistics). D.C.'s restaurant scene is rather more egalitarian: heavy on the fine, top-dollar establishments, where you can easily spend $100 per person, but with plenty of excellent bistros and small restaurants offering great eats at lower prices. When it comes to attractions, though, the nation's capital has the rest of the world beat, since most of its museums and tourist sites offer free admission.

In Washington, D.C., ATMs are ubiquitous, in locations ranging from the National Gallery of Art's gift shop, to Union Station, to grocery stores. **MasterCard's** (www.mastercard.com; ✆ **800/424-7787**) Maestro and Cirrus, and **Visa's** (www.visa.com; ✆ **800/336-3386**) PLUS networks operate in D.C., as they do across the country. Go to your bank card's website or call one of your branches to find ATM locations in Washington. Be sure you know your personal identification number (PIN) and daily withdrawal limit before you depart. If your PIN is five or six digits, you should obtain a four-digit PIN from your local bank before you leave home, since four-digit PINs are what most ATMs in Washington accept.

Note: Many banks impose a fee every time you use a card at another bank's ATM, and that fee is often higher for international transactions (up to $5 or more) than for domestic ones (where they're rarely more than $2).

Credit cards are the most widely used form of payment in the United States: **Visa** (Barclaycard in Britain), **MasterCard** (Eurocard in Europe, Access in Britain, Chargex in Canada), **American Express, Diners Club,** and **Discover.** Beware of hidden credit card fees while traveling. Check with your credit or debit card issuer to see what fees, if any, will be charged for overseas transactions. Recent reform legislation in the U.S., for example, has curbed some exploitative lending practices. But many banks have responded by increasing fees in other areas, including fees for customers who use credit and debit cards while out of the country—even if those charges were made in U.S. dollars. Fees can amount to 3% or more of the purchase price. Check with your bank before departing to avoid any surprise charges on your statement.

ATM cards with major credit card backing, known as **"debit cards,"** are now a commonly acceptable form of payment in most stores and restaurants. Debit cards draw money directly from your checking account. Many stores, such as grocery stores, enable you to receive cash back on your debit card purchases as well. The same is true at most U.S. post offices.

For help with currency conversions, tip calculations, and more, download Frommer's convenient Travel Tools app for your mobile device. Go to www.frommers.com/go/mobile and click on the Travel Tools icon.

Newspapers & Magazines   Washington's preeminent newspaper is the *Washington Post,* available online and sold in bookstores, train and subway stations, drugstores, and sidewalk kiosks all over town. These are also the places to buy other newspapers, like the *New York Times,* and *Washingtonian* magazine, the city's popular monthly full of penetrating features, restaurant reviews, and nightlife calendars. The websites of these publications are: www.washingtonpost.com, www.nytimes.com, and www.washingtonian.com.

Also be sure to pick up a copy of *Washington Flyer* magazine, available free at the airport or online at www.washingtonflyer.com, to find out about airport and airline news and interesting Washington happenings.

Passports   Virtually every air traveler entering the U.S. is required to show a passport. All persons, including U.S. citizens, traveling by air between the United States and Canada, Mexico, Central and South America, the Caribbean, and Bermuda are required to present a valid passport. *Note:* U.S. and Canadian citizens entering the U. S. at land and sea ports of entry from within the Western Hemisphere must now also present a passport or other documents compliant with the Western Hemisphere Travel Initiative (WHTI; see www.getyouhome.gov for details). Children 15 and under may continue entering with only a U.S. birth certificate, or other proof of U.S. citizenship.

Australia   Australian Passport Information Service (www.passports.gov.au; ℭ 131-232).

Canada   Passport Office, Department of Foreign Affairs and International Trade, Ottawa, ON K1A 0G3 (www.ppt.gc.ca; ℭ 800/567-6868).

Ireland   Passport Office, Setanta Centre, Molesworth Street, Dublin 2 (www.foreign affairs.gov.ie; ℭ 01/671-1633).

New Zealand   Passports Office, Department of Internal Affairs, 109 Featherston St., Wellington, 6140 (www.passports.govt.nz; ℭ 0800/225-050 in New Zealand or 04/473-9360).

United Kingdom   Visit your nearest passport office, major post office, or travel agency, or contact the Identity and Passport Service (IPS), 89 Eccleston Sq., London, SW1V 1PN (www.ips.gov.uk; ℭ 0300/222-0000).

United States   To find your regional passport office, check the U.S. State Department website (www.travel.state.gov/passport) or call the National Passport Information Center (📞 877/487-2778) for automated information.

Petrol   See "By Car," under "Getting Around," earlier in this chapter.

Police   The number of different police agencies in Washington is quite staggering. They include the city's own Metropolitan Police Department, the National Park Service police, the U.S. Capitol police, the Secret Service, the FBI, and the Metro Transit police. The only thing you need to know is: In an emergency, dial 📞 **911.**

Safety   In the years following the September 11, 2001, terrorist attack on the Pentagon, the federal and D.C. governments, along with agencies such as the National Park Service, have continued to work together to increase security, not just at airports, but also around the city, including at government buildings and tourist attractions, and in the subway. The most noticeable and, honestly, most irksome aspect of increased security at tourist attractions can be summed up in three little words: **waiting in line.** Although visitors have always had to queue to enter the Capitol, the Supreme Court, and other federal buildings, now it can take more time to get through because of more intense scrutiny when you finally reach the door.

Besides lines, you will notice the intense amount of security in place around the White House and the Capitol, as well as a profusion of vehicle barriers. A tightly secured underground visitor center at the Capitol, which opened in late 2008, was built in great part to safeguard members of Congress as well as all who work for them (see chapter 4, "Exploring Washington, D.C.," for more information about the center). Greater numbers of police and security officers are on duty around and inside government buildings, the monuments, and the Metro.

Just because so many police are around, you shouldn't let your guard down. Washington, like any urban area, has a criminal element, so it's important to stay alert and take normal safety precautions.

Ask your hotel front-desk staff or the city's tourist office if you're in doubt about which neighborhoods are safe. See "The Neighborhoods in Brief," in chapter 3, to get a better idea of where you might feel most comfortable.

Avoid deserted areas, especially at night, and don't go into public parks at night unless there's a concert or a similar occasion that will attract a crowd.

Avoid carrying valuables with you on the street, and don't display expensive cameras or electronic equipment. If you're using a map, consult it inconspicuously—or better yet, try to study it before you leave your room. In general the more you look like a tourist, the more likely someone will try to take advantage of you. If you're walking, pay attention to who is near you as you walk. If you're attending a convention or event where you wear a name tag, remove it before venturing outside. Hold on to your purse, and place your wallet in an inside pocket. In theaters, restaurants, and other public places, keep your possessions in sight. Also remember that hotels are open to the public, and in a large hotel, security may not be able to screen everyone entering. Always lock your room door.

Senior Travel   Members of **AARP,** 601 E St. NW, Washington, DC 20049 (www.aarp. org; 📞 **888/687-2277**), get discounts on hotels, airfares, and car rentals. AARP offers members a wide range of benefits, including *AARP The Magazine* and a monthly newsletter. Anyone over 50 can join.

With or without AARP membership, seniors often find that discounts are available to them at hotels, especially chain hotels such as the Hilton, so be sure to inquire when you book your reservation.

Venues in Washington that grant discounts to seniors include the Metro; certain theaters, such as the Shakespeare Theatre; and those few museums, like the Phillips Collection, that charge for entry. Each place has its own eligibility rules, including designated "senior" ages: The Shakespeare Theatre's is 60 and over, the Phillips Collection's is 62 and over, and the Metro discounts seniors 65 and over.

Frommers.com offers more information and resources on travel for seniors.

Smoking   The District is smoke free, meaning that the city bans smoking in restaurants, bars, and other public buildings. Smoking is permitted outdoors, unless otherwise noted.

Taxes   The United States has no value-added tax (VAT) or other indirect tax at the national level. Every state, county, and city may levy its own local tax on all purchases, including hotel and restaurant checks, and airline tickets. These taxes will not appear on price tags. The sales tax on merchandise is 6% in the District, 6% in Maryland, and 5% in Virginia. Restaurant tax is 10% in the District, 6% in Maryland, and varied in Virginia, depending on the city and county. Hotel tax is 14.5% in the District, from 5% to 8% in Maryland, and an average of 9.75% in Virginia.

Telephones   Many convenience groceries and packaging services sell **prepaid calling cards** in denominations up to $50. Many public pay phones at airports now accept American Express, MasterCard, and Visa. You can use a **public pay telephone,** although these are increasingly hard to find. Many public pay phones at airports now accept American Express, MasterCard, and Visa credit cards.

Local calls made from most pay phones in the District cost 50¢. Most long-distance and international calls can be dialed directly from any phone. **To make calls within the United States and to Canada,** dial 1 followed by the area code and the seven-digit number. **For other international calls,** dial 011 followed by the country code, the city code, and the number you are calling.

Calls to area codes **800, 888, 877,** and **866** are toll free. However, calls to area codes **700** and **900** (chat lines, bulletin boards, "dating" services, and so on) can be expensive— charges of 95¢ to $3 or more per minute. Some numbers have minimum charges that can run $15 or more.

For **reversed-charge or collect calls,** and for person-to-person calls, dial the number 0 then the area code and number; an operator will come on the line, and you should specify whether you are calling collect, person-to-person, or both. If your operator-assisted call is international, ask for the overseas operator.

For **directory assistance** ("Information"), dial 411 for local numbers and national numbers in the U.S. and Canada. For dedicated long-distance information, dial 1 then the appropriate area code, plus 555-1212.

Time   The continental United States is divided into **four time zones:** Eastern Standard Time (EST)—this is Washington, D.C.'s time zone—Central Standard Time (CST), Mountain Standard Time (MST), and Pacific Standard Time (PST). Alaska and Hawaii have their own zones. For example, when it's 9am in Los Angeles (PST), it's 7am in Honolulu (HST),10am in Denver (MST), 11am in Chicago (CST), noon in New York City (EST), 5pm in London (GMT), and 2am the next day in Sydney.

Daylight saving time (summer time) is in effect from 1am on the second Sunday in March to 1am on the first Sunday in November, except in Arizona, Hawaii, the U.S. Virgin Islands, and Puerto Rico. Daylight saving time moves the clock 1 hour ahead of standard time.

For help with time translations and more, download the Frommer's Travel Tools app. Go to www.frommers.com/go/mobile and click on the Travel Tools icon.

Tipping   In hotels tip **bellhops** at least $1 per bag ($2–$3 if you have a lot of luggage) and tip the **chamber staff** $1 to $2 per day (more if you've left a big mess for him or her to clean up). Tip the **doorman** or **concierge** only if he or she has provided you with some specific service (for example, calling a cab for you or obtaining difficult-to-get theater tickets). Tip the **valet-parking attendant** $1 every time you get your car.

In restaurants, bars, and nightclubs, tip **service staff** and **bartenders** 15% to 20% of the check, tip **checkroom attendants** $1 per garment, and tip **valet-parking attendants** $1 per vehicle.

As for other service personnel, tip **cab drivers** 15% of the fare; tip **skycaps** at airports at least $1 per bag ($2–$3 if you have a lot of luggage); and tip **hairdressers** and **barbers** 15% to 20%.

For help with tip calculations, currency conversions, and more, download our convenient Travel Tools app for your mobile device. Go to www.frommers.com/go/mobile and click on the Travel Tools icon.

Toilets   You won't find public toilets or "restrooms" on the streets of D.C., but they can be found in hotel lobbies, bars, restaurants, museums, and service stations, and at many sightseeing attractions. Starbucks and fast-food restaurants abound in D.C., and these might be your most reliable option. Restaurants and bars in resorts or heavily visited areas may reserve their restrooms for patrons.

VAT   See "Taxes," above.

Visas   The U.S. State Department has a Visa Waiver Program (VWP) allowing citizens of the following countries to enter the United States without a visa for stays of up to 90 days: Andorra, Australia, Austria, Belgium, Brunei, Czech Republic, Denmark, Estonia, Finland, France, Germany, Greece, Hungary, Iceland, Ireland, Italy, Japan, Latvia, Liechtenstein, Lithuania, Luxembourg, Malta, Monaco, the Netherlands, New Zealand, Norway, Portugal, San Marino, Singapore, Slovakia, Slovenia, South Korea, Spain, Sweden, Switzerland, and the United Kingdom. (**Note:** This list was accurate at press time; for the most up-to-date list of countries in the VWP, consult www.travel.state.gov/visa.) Even though a visa isn't necessary, in an effort to help U.S. officials check travelers against terror watch lists before they arrive at U.S. borders, visitors from VWP countries must register online through the Electronic System for Travel Authorization (ESTA) before boarding a plane or a boat to the U.S. Travelers must complete an electronic application providing basic personal and travel eligibility information. The Department of Homeland Security recommends filling out the form at least 3 days before traveling. Authorizations will be valid for up to 2 years or until the traveler's passport expires, whichever comes first. Currently, there is one $14 fee for the online application. Existing ESTA registrations remain valid through their expiration dates. **Note:** Any passport issued on or after October 26, 2006, by a VWP country must be an e-Passport for VWP travelers to be eligible to enter the U.S. without a visa. Citizens of these nations also need to present a round-trip air or cruise ticket upon arrival. E-Passports contain computer chips capable of storing biometric information, such as the required digital photograph of the holder. If your passport doesn't have this feature, you can still travel without a visa if the valid passport was issued before October 26, 2005, and includes a machine-readable zone; or if the valid passport was issued between October 26, 2005, and October 25, 2006, and includes a digital photograph. For more information, go to www.travel.state.gov/visa. Canadian citizens may enter the United States without visas but will need to show passports and proof of residence.

Citizens of all other countries must have (1) a valid passport that expires at least 6 months later than the scheduled end of their visit to the U.S. and (2) a tourist visa.

For information about U.S. visas, go to **www.travel.state.gov** and click on "Visas." Or go to one of the following websites:

Australian citizens can obtain up-to-date visa information from the **U.S. Embassy Canberra,** Moonah Place, Yarralumla, ACT 2600 (𝄐 **02/6214-5600**) or by checking the U.S. Diplomatic Mission's website at **http://canberra.usembassy.gov/visas.html**.

British subjects can obtain up-to-date visa information by calling the **U.S. Embassy Visa Information Line** (𝄐 **09042-450-100** from within the U.K. at £1.23 per minute, or 𝄐 866-382-3589 from within the U.S. at a flat rate of $16 and payable by credit card only) or by visiting the "Visas to the U.S." section of the American Embassy London's website, **http://london.usembassy.gov/visas.html**.

Irish citizens can obtain up-to-date visa information through the **U.S. Embassy Dublin,** 42 Elgin Rd., Ballsbridge, Dublin 4 (http://dublin.usembassy.gov; 𝄐 **1580-47-VISA** [8472] from within the Republic of Ireland, at €2.40 per minute).

Citizens of **New Zealand** can obtain up-to-date visa information by contacting the **U.S. Embassy New Zealand,** 29 Fitzherbert Terrace, Thorndon, Wellington (http://new zealand.usembassy.gov; 𝄐 **644/462-6000**).

Visitor Information **Destination D.C.** is the official tourism and convention corporation for Washington, D.C., 901 7th St. NW, 4th Floor, Washington, DC 20001-3719 (www. washington.org; 𝄐 **800/422-8644** or 202/789-7000). Before you leave home, order (or download) a free copy of the bureau's *Washington, D.C. Visitors Guide,* which covers hotels, restaurants, attractions, shops, and more and is updated twice yearly. Call 𝄐 **202/789-7000** to speak directly to a staff "visitor services specialist" and get answers to your specific questions about the city.

Besides using Destination D.C.'s website to obtain a copy of the visitors guide, you can read about the latest travel information, including upcoming exhibits at the museums and anticipated closings of tourist attractions. The website is also a source for maps, which you can download and print from the site or order for delivery by mail.

Once you've arrived, stop by Destination D.C.'s offices on 7th Street NW (Metro: Gallery Place–Chinatown, H St. exit), to pick up the visitors guide and maps, and to talk to visitors services specialists. Office hours are Monday to Friday 8:30am to 5pm.

If you're arriving by plane or train, you can think of your airport or the train station as visitor information centers; all three Washington-area airports and Union Station offer all sorts of visitor services. See "Getting There," earlier in this chapter.

Also look for business improvement district (BID) offices and their patrolling "ambassadors," who dispense information, directions, and other assistance in their individual neighborhoods. Among the most established are: the **Downtown D.C. Business Improvement District (Downtown D.C. BID),** 1250 H St. NW (www.downtowndc. org; 𝄐 **202/638-3232**); the **Golden Triangle Business Improvement District (Golden Triangle BID),** 1120 Connecticut Ave. NW (𝄐 **202/463-3400;** www.goldentriangledc. com); the **Capitol Hill Business Improvement District (Capitol Hill BID),** 30 Massachusetts Ave. NE, inside Union Station's garage (www.capitolhillbid.org; 𝄐 **202/842-3333**); and the **Georgetown Business Improvement District (Georgetown BID),** 1000 Potomac St. NW (www.georgetowndc.com; 𝄐 **202/298-9222**).

National Park Service information kiosks are located inside or near the Jefferson, Lincoln, FDR, Vietnam Veterans, Korean War, and World War II memorials, and at the Washington Monument (www.nps.gov/state/dc for all national parklands in D.C. or www. nps.gov/nama for National Mall and Memorial Parks sites; 𝄐 **202/426-6841** or 619-7222).

The **White House Visitor Center,** on the first floor of the Herbert Hoover Building, Department of Commerce, 1450 Pennsylvania Ave. NW (btw. 14th and 15th sts.;

☏ **202/208-1631,** or 202/456-7041 for recorded information), is open daily (except for New Year's Day, Christmas Day, and Thanksgiving) from 7:30am to 4pm.

The **Smithsonian Information Center,** in the Castle, 1000 Jefferson Dr. SW (www. si.edu; ☏ **202/633-1000,** or TTY [text telephone] 633-5285), is open every day but Christmas from 8:30am to 5:30pm; knowledgeable staff answer questions and dispense maps and brochures.

Visit the D.C. government's website, **www.dc.gov**, and that of the nonprofit organization Cultural Tourism D.C., **www.culturaltourismdc.org**, for more information about the city. The latter site in particular provides helpful and interesting background knowledge of D.C.'s historic and cultural landmarks, especially in neighborhoods or parts of neighborhoods not usually visited by tourists.

Check out **www.washingtonpost.com, www.washingtonian.com, www.dcist.com,** and one of my favorite websites, **www.welovedc.com,** for the latest commentary and information about Washington happenings.

Also consider buying the Frommer's D.C. travel app at www.frommers.com/go/mobile.

Wi-Fi   See "Internet & Wi-Fi," earlier in this chapter.

Index

PHOTO CREDITS